POLITICAL

GEOGRAPHY

McGRAW-HILL SERIES IN GEOGRAPHY

John C. Weaver, Consulting Editor

Bennett　Soil Conservation

Cressey　Asia's Lands and Peoples

Cressey　Land of the 500 Million: A Geography of China

Finch, Trewartha, Robinson, and Hammond　Elements of Geography: Physical and Cultural

Finch, Trewartha, Robinson, and Hammond　Physical Elements of Geography (A republication of Part I of the above)

Pounds　Europe and the Mediterranean

Pounds　Political Geography

Raisz　General Cartography

Raisz　Principles of Cartography

Thoman　The Geography of Economic Activity

Trewartha　An Introduction to Climate

Trewartha, Robinson, and Hammond　Fundamentals of Physical Geography

Van Riper　Man's Physical World

Vernor C. Finch was Consulting Editor of this series from its inception in 1934 to 1951.

POLITICAL GEOGRAPHY

NORMAN J. G. POUNDS

PROFESSOR OF GEOGRAPHY, INDIANA UNIVERSITY

McGRAW–HILL BOOK COMPANY, INC.

NEW YORK   SAN FRANCISCO   TORONTO   LONDON

PREFACE

THIS BOOK HAS GROWN OVER A PERIOD OF YEARS FROM MATERIALS prepared for class use, and each chapter, representing about a week's work, has been studied and criticized by many semesters of students. The approach to the subject is systematic, and it is assumed that any regional study of political geography must be predicated upon an understanding of the concepts outlined here. Hartshorne's definition of political geography has been accepted; it is "the study of the variation of political phenomena from place to place in interconnection with variations in other features of the earth as the home of man. Included in these political phenomena are features produced by political forces and the political ideas which generate those forces."[1] The state is the dominant political phenomenon in the modern world. It has, in the words of Douglas Jackson, "been accepted by geographers generally as the formal or central subject matter of political geography."[2] If this book has any theme running through it, it is the geographical nature, the policy, and the power of the state. The state exists to fulfill a function which is most often construed as the desire of a nation for a political identification with the area of land which it inhabits. The state has its policy, most simply expressed as self-preservation and welfare, which it implements by means of its power. Colonies, bases, allies, and trade are relevant to the study of the political geography of a state because they are among the external determinants of its power, just as location, population resources, and industry are among the internal determinants.

The author wishes to thank those who have in various ways helped and advised him. Among them are his friends and colleagues at Indiana University: Professors Thomas F. Barton, Donald C. Bennett, J. Fraser Hart, G. H. T. Kimble, Robert C. Kingsbury, and Otis P. Starkey of the Department of Geography; Professors

---

[1] Richard Hartshorne, "Political Geography in the Modern World," *Journal of Conflict Resolution,* vol. 4, p. 52, 1960.

[2] W. A. Douglas Jackson, "Whither Political Geography," *A.A.A.G.,* vol. 48, p. 178, 1958.

Vaclac L. Benes, Edward H. Buehrig, and Joseph L. Sutton of the
Department of Government; C. Leonard Lundin, of the Depart-
ment of History; Austin V. Clifford, of the School of Law. He is
indebted also to friends in other schools and institutions: Colonel
Ottis M. Plant, of the General Command Staff College, Fort
Leavenworth; Colonel Robert G. Taylor, of the Air Force Academy,
Colorado Springs; Professor Harry H. Caldwell, of the University
of Idaho; Professor Walter M. Kollmorgen, of the University of
Kansas. He is greatly indebted to Professor Robert C. Kingsbury
for his help in drafting the maps and to Theodore C. Myers and
Mrs. Sue Simons Ball for their painstaking and unstinted help with
the text. He wishes to thank the agencies which made photographs
or other materials available; their help is acknowledged at the
appropriate places in the text.

Norman J. G. Pounds

CONTENTS

The following abbreviations have been used for periodicals in footnotes in the text and in items in the bibliographies:

A.A.A.G.   Annals of the Association of American Geographers
E.G.   Economic Geography
G.J.   Geographical Journal
G.R.   Geographical Review
J.ofG.   Journal of Geography
P.G.   Professional Geographer
S.G.M.   Scottish Geographical Magazine

The Government Printing Office *Style Manual* has been used as the authority for the spelling of geographic locations.

1 THE STATE AND THE NATION

The spirit of nationality is a sour ferment of the new wine of democracy in the old bottles of tribalism.   A. J. TOYNBEE, A STUDY OF HISTORY

. . . a multitude of rational creatures associated in a common agreement as to the things which it loves.   ST. AUGUSTINE, DE CIVITATE DEI

POLITICAL GEOGRAPHY IS CONCERNED WITH POLITICALLY ORGANIZED areas, their resources and extent, and the reasons for the particular geographical forms which they assume. In particular, it is concerned with that most significant of all such areas, the state. There are in the world today about 120 states (Exhibits 1 to 4; Appendix I, page 20). Their number has fluctuated and is now tending to increase. The essence of the state is sovereignty. Each is independent, each is self-governing, and each owes to other states and outside organizations only such obligations as it voluntarily assumes.

But approximately a sixth of the land surface of the earth, though organized politically, is not made up of independent and fully self-governing states. It has some kind of dependent status. This status has changed over the years, and the general trend has been in the direction of independence. There nevertheless remain today many different degrees of dependence on some "imperial" power or other, in most instances European or Soviet. Dependent territories fall within the province of political geography in the same way as states themselves.

States [1] are part of a hierarchy of politically organized areas,

[1] The term *state* is used here, not in the sense of one of the fifty United States, but as an autonomous political unit, such as France, Mexico, or the United States. When one of the fifty States of the United States is indicated, the word is capitalized as *State*.

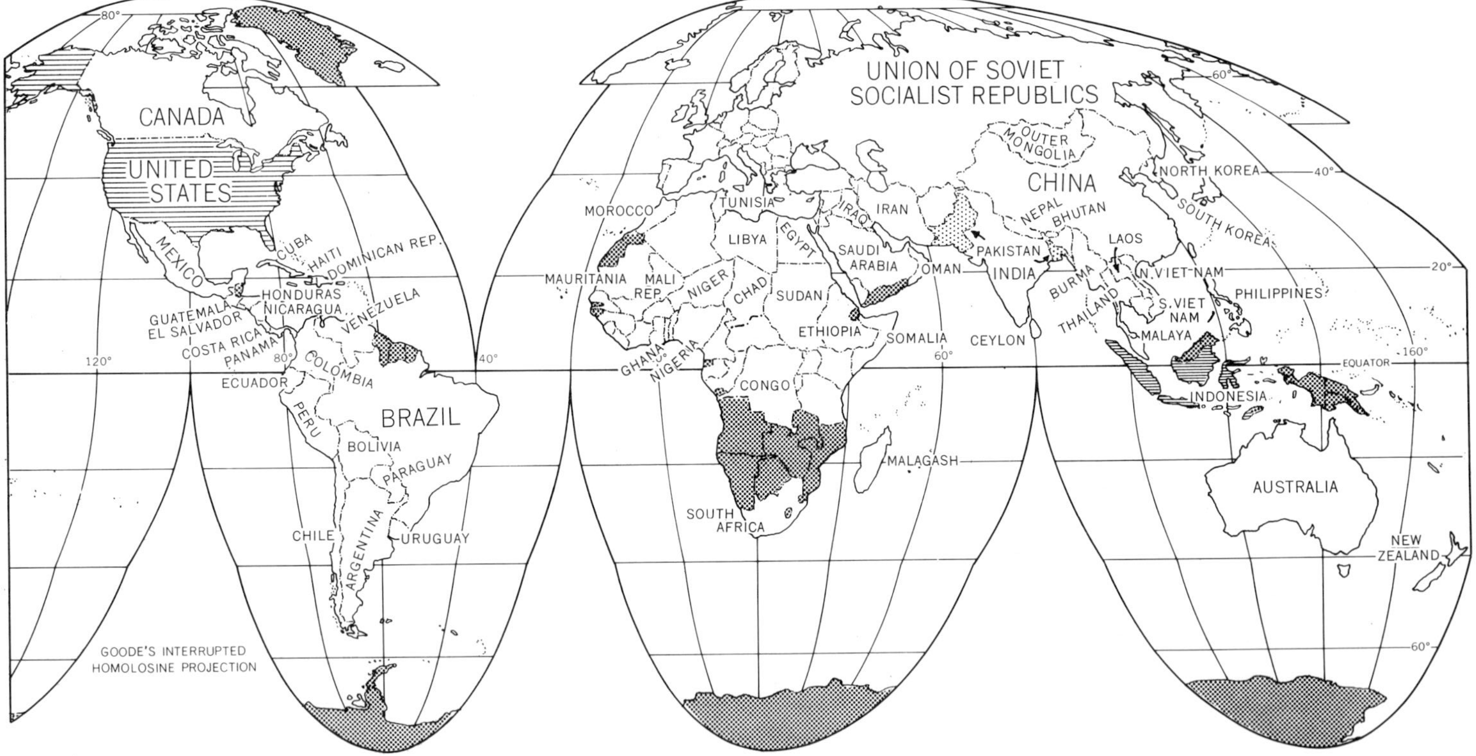

Exhibit 1 *Political map of the world.*

though unquestionably the most important level in this hierarchy. Above them are international organizations, in which states may accept membership, generally on a voluntary basis. Such supranational organizations include politically oriented bodies such as the North Atlantic Treaty Organization (NATO), the South-East Asia Treaty Organization (SEATO) and the United Nations (UN) itself, and economically oriented bodies such as the European Free Trade Association (EFTA) and the Colombo Plan. These are, as the title of one of them suggests, organizations to facilitate the pursuit by their members of certain political and economic ends which are defined in their treaties of association. In general these organizations do not represent the surrender by the member states of any significant part of their sovereignty. The states themselves remain completely independent, merely accepting the obligation to obey certain rules which they have helped to formulate.

A second group of suprastate organizations consists of those in which the contractual obligations go deeper and involve to some extent a surrender of part of their national sovereignty. When in 1952 the European Coal and Steel Community (ECSC), now absorbed into the Common Market, was established, the six member nations [2] accepted the jurisdiction of an international court of law over certain of their internal affairs. Its jurisdiction was limited, it is true, to matters pertaining to the coal, iron, and steel industries, but it nevertheless represented an encroachment upon the autonomy of the member states, which have not always found the judgments of the court entirely to the liking of each and all of them.

The Communist bloc may perhaps be said to be an involuntary organization of sovereign states. The Communist countries of eastern Europe are certainly not free agents, as their policies are shaped in some degree by decisions made in the Soviet Union. The mutual relationships of members of this bloc do not rest entirely, however, upon any published treaty or contract, and it can be argued, too, that the dependent status of these countries was not assumed voluntarily.

Below the level of the state is the whole structure of local government areas. In most parts of the world these form a hierarchy. The hierarchy for the United States of America may be cited because it is a relatively simple one; other and similar administrative hierarchies are examined in Chapter 8.

[2] Belgium, France, West Germany, Italy, Luxembourg, and the Netherlands.

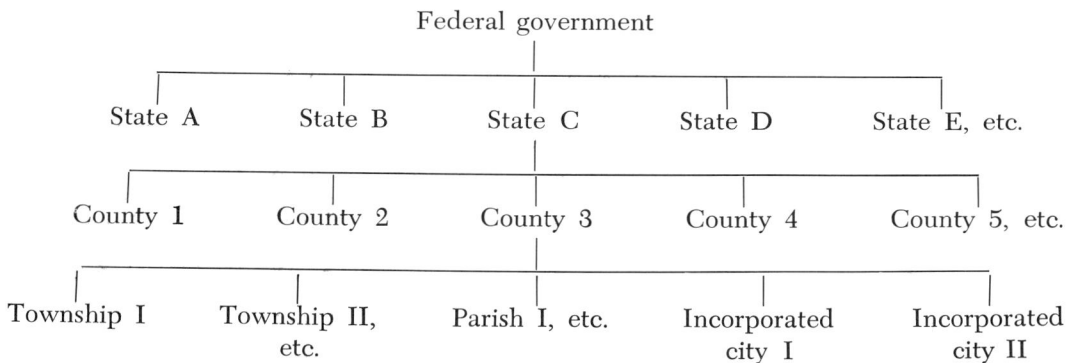

Federal government

State A	State B	State C	State D	State E, etc.

County 1	County 2	County 3	County 4	County 5, etc.

Township I	Township II, etc.	Parish I, etc.	Incorporated city I	Incorporated city II

The table shows one level in the administrative hierarchy that is not found in most such tables, because the government of the United States is a federal one. The governmental functions are found to be, in general, of diminishing significance as the base of the pyramid is approached, and the township serves, in fact, as little more than a territorial unit for the purpose of electing representatives to serve in the decision-making body which stands next above it in the hierarchy.

But in each case the political area in the geographical sense is clearly defined. In the developed areas of the world, its boundaries are known and are marked on maps even if they are not in all cases demarcated on the ground. It is possible to measure the area and population and to estimate its resources. In each case, the area was defined as a result of a human decision or of a sequence of such decisions. For each it is permissible to ask why the unit area has the geographical form which it does have, though it is not always possible to arrive at an answer to this question.

Thus we have a complex pyramid of political authority, ranging from township or parish at the base to international organizations at the summit.

Most politically organized areas can be fitted into the scheme that has here been outlined, but not all. In all countries, except the least developed, some areas are marked off for specific purposes. Unit areas, such as the American precincts, are units for voting purposes only and are not administrative areas in any wider sense than this. Others serve as administrative areas for river and flood control, for irrigation projects, for the receipt of government assistance or subsidy, for the location of factories or the preservation of land under cultivation. Such special-purpose areas may cut across the more general administrative areas with, in some instances, significant conflicts of interest between the special and the general administrative areas. The area subject to the administrative jurisdiction of the Tennessee Valley Authority (TVA), for example, cuts across state and local government divisions in seven States of the Union. In the early years of the Authority, the conflict between it and other types of jurisdiction in the area which it served was particularly bitter and frustrating.

This, then, is the primary purpose of political geography: to examine the geographical form assumed by political units at whatever level in the political hierarchy

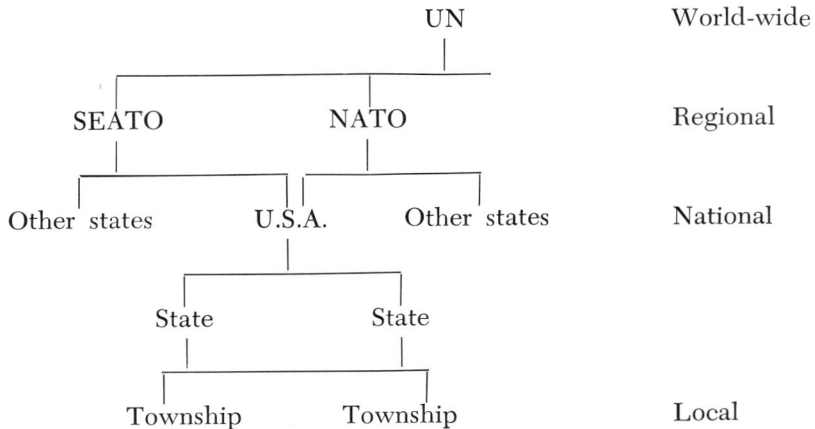

```
                        UN              World-wide
                         |
          |--------------|--------------|
        SEATO          NATO              Regional
          |              |
       |-----|        |-----|
    Other states   U.S.A.   Other states  National
                      |
                 |---------|
               State      State
                 |          |
              Township   Township          Local
```

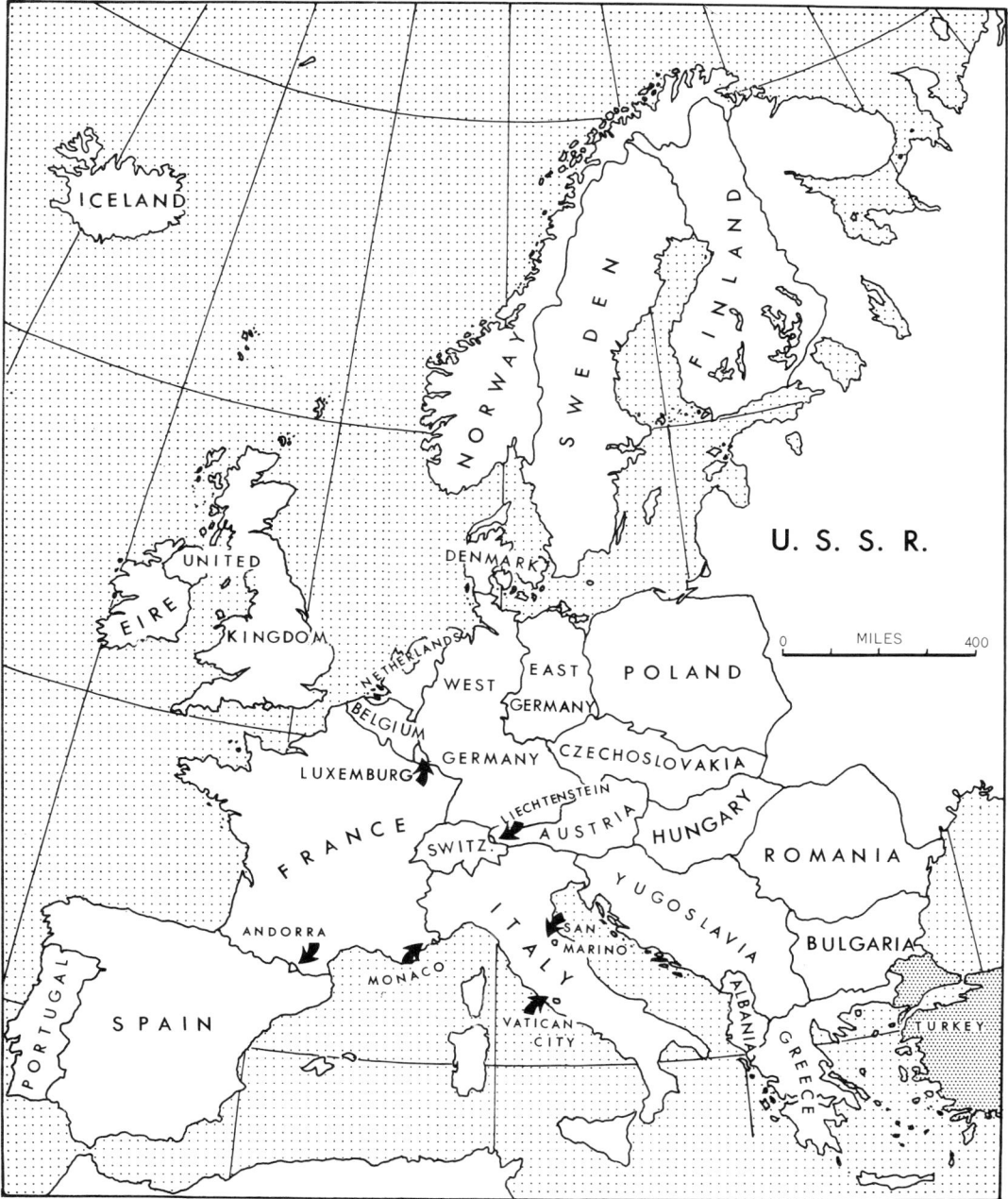

Exhibit 2 Political map of Europe.

they occur. But since the decisions which most closely touch our welfare are made at the state level, and since the state commands a higher degree of loyalty and obedience from us than political units at other levels, most of our attention must be given to the political geography of the state.

THE STATE

So far we have not defined the state beyond saying that it is a politically organized area. Indeed it is impossible to conceive of a state as existing, or existing for long, without a territorial base. In wartime there may be a "government in exile" while its country is temporarily occupied by another power. But that is probably the only exception that can be admitted. It is implicit that the state has people, and since decisions are made for, and on behalf of, the people, there must be a decision-making authority or government. Furthermore, if the decisions are to lead to action, the government must be in effective control of the area within which it claims to operate. A definition of the state may therefore be formulated: an area organized politically in an effective manner by an indigenous people with a government in effective control of the area.

We tend, in ordinary conversation and journalistic writing, to personify the state. We say that France did this and that Germany did that. Of course, if we stop to think, we realize that these were acts of the governments of these countries. Each state must have a person or group of persons whose function it is to formulate policy and make the decisions by which that policy is to be implemented. In a democratic country this decision-making authority is ultimately responsible to public opinion and owes its position to some form of the election process. In states with more authoritarian governments, the decision

maker achieves his (or the group) position by other means and is not in the same way responsible to public opinion. But, however the position is established, we can trace the mechanical process by which the decision-making body achieves this position, formulates policy, and implements it by whatever means it chooses to use from those at its command. Its decisions, furthermore, are made by individuals who share the prejudices and the preconceived ideas of their social group, as well as having their own vested interests. All these *may* influence their judgment of a situation and the resulting decision. H. H. and M. Sprout have demonstrated [3] that, while the actions of people in the mass may perhaps be predicted on the basis of probability, those of small groups are less amenable to rational prediction and those of individuals least of all.

This discussion has been introduced here to demonstrate one point only, that the state implies a mechanism of government through which individuals, the decision makers, operate and that it is "not an organism capable of consciously purposeful behavior." [4] A state per se cannot have a policy capable of being implemented by the making of decisions; least of all can it have a policy directed to the same end over a period of centuries, except in so far as the individual decision makers during this period of time arrive at similar conclusions and make similar decisions. Nor does a state grow or decay, rise or fall, except in so far as its decision makers make wise and intelligent or unwise and foolish decisions. If states are not organisms, analogous to natural organisms, they are, therefore, not subject to the

[3] H. H. Sprout and M. Sprout, *Man-Milieu Relationship Hypotheses in the Context of International Politics,* Center of International Studies, Princeton University, Princeton, N.J., 1956, p. 56.
[4] *Ibid.,* p. 9.

competition for space and resources which characterizes natural organisms. The theory of natural selection, propounded by Darwin over a century ago, applies only to the natural organisms to which Darwin himself restricted it. To extend the application of Darwin's theory to the interrelation of states is illogical. It is also dangerous, because it assumes a condition of intense competition, merging into hostility, as a normal condition in the relations of states to one another.

THE NATION

A state is made up of area, people, and an effective mechanism of government. But in most states of the modern world the people themselves have some bond of union, holding them together and distinguishing them from the people of other states, over and above the land area and the governmental mechanism which they share. Two examples may serve to emphasize this. We think of the people of France as being French. Their "Frenchness" is demonstrated primarily by their speaking the French language, though this is spoken also by a significant part of the population of both Belgium and Switzerland. But within the whole body of French speakers, the French themselves are distinguished by a complex of social ideas and attitudes. These have in turn been shaped through centuries and are known to us as French tradition or French culture. This is the cement which binds the people together and makes them cohere into a nation. As Bertrand Russell has expressed it, "A creed or sentiment of some kind is essential to social cohesion, but if it is to be a source of strength it must be genuinely and deeply felt by the great majority of the population. . . ." [5]

[5] Bertrand Russell, *Power: A New Social Analysis,* George Allen & Unwin, Ltd., London, 1938, pp. 158–159.

If the French may be said to constitute a good example of national solidarity and coherence, the population of India may be said to furnish a poor example. The Indian nation of some 403 million is marked by extreme diversity. An Indian geographer has characterized the situation in the following words: "Through centuries of conquest and infiltration India has become a veritable maze of races, languages, creeds, and customs. . . . The pattern of language in this country is extremely complex, crossing racial, religious, and political boundaries. Politico-geographically speaking, the diversity in religion and language creates a serious national problem." [6] Nevertheless, the writer goes on to say, "There is a degree of unity underlying the diversity of Indian culture. Centuries of living together and intermingling have given the various races and religious groups a community of interest that is characteristically Indian. A common historical background and common interest are the cement that bind the Indian population together."

There are even states in which two or more nations or communities live in circumstances of virtual hostility. In Cyprus, for example, a "system of virtual *apartheid* [rigid separation] between the Turkish and Greek communities seems almost as tight as ever," and "the outward trappings of nationhood evoke no popular enthusiasm; one hardly ever sees a Cyprus flag except on official buildings, and no one seems at all interested in a national anthem." [7]

Evidently the cement of French unity is stronger than that of Indian, but there are countries in which it is even weaker than in India. In Cyprus, as in the Repub-

[6] P. P. Karan, "Geopolitical Structure of India," *Proceedings of the Eighth General Assembly, Seventeenth Congress of the International Geographical Union,* Washington, 1952, pp. 524–527.

[7] *Economist,* Nov. 19, 1960.

lic of the Congo and perhaps also in Indonesia and perhaps in Nigeria there is scarcely any cement at all. It is important, as we shall show later in this chapter, for the population of a state to demonstrate as high a degree of social cohesion as possible, for this greatly influences the *power* of a state. Ideally the state should be paralleled by the nation; it should be "an entity formed by a particular population group which for a variety of reasons is conscious of itself as a political community. . . ." [8]

The quotation from Bertrand Russell's study of power suggests that the intense feeling of belonging to a nation and of sharing deeply in its traditions may not characterize *all* the people who inhabit the territory of a state. There are often minority groups of some kind or other. Some of these may have found themselves caught within the territorial limits of the state when it was being established. Others may represent strongly marked "regionalisms." Regionalisms, such as those represented in the American South and in Scotland and Wales, are the cultural ghosts that survive from an earlier period when they were politically active and even politically independent. On the other hand, regionalisms may intensify, until they reach upward from the level of cultural consciousness to that of political activity. Demands for "home rule" in the Spanish Basque provinces and in Catluña and "national" movements among some peoples of Central Europe during the nineteenth century and of the Middle East more recently each began as cultural movements. Their leaders collected folk songs before they started to collect votes.

Nationalism, the desire of cultural, linguistic, and religious groups to achieve a political status that would give them a

limited measure of self-government, sufficient at least to allow them to protect and deepen their cultural individuality, is a fairly recent social phenomenon. Many of the states of the present day had achieved approximately their present limits before nationalism became a significant force in the formation of states. France, Switzerland, Denmark, Sweden, and the United Kingdom are among these. In these instances the nation, becoming self-conscious *after* the state was already in existence, tended to fill out the boundaries of the latter. The process can be demonstrated in detail in many of them. For example, Cornwall, previously remote from the centers of English political life, with its own language and folk culture, began in the sixteenth century to be slowly absorbed into the stream of English life, not, however, without opposition and a lingering, backward glance at its long history of Celtic detachment. An English writer of about 1600 wrote that the Cornish "seem yet to retain a kind of concealed envy against the English, whom they yet affect with a kind of desire for revenge for their fathers' sakes. . . ." [9] The absorption of Scotland and Wales into English life was resisted more vigorously and violently, and Ireland was never drawn in. On the other hand, the Swiss Confederation had assumed more or less its present shape by the sixteenth century, and a cohesive bond was forged between its differing linguistic and religious groups that, apart from the attempt of the Catholic cantons to split the Confederation on the basis of religious affiliation in the War of the Sonderbund, 1847, has stood the test of the last four hundred years.

Of what, then, is the cement of the nation made? It is difficult to enumerate and impossible to measure the intangibles that make a nation. "Nationalities come into

---

[8] R. Hartshorne, "The Politico-geographic Pattern of the World," *Annals of the American Academy of Political and Social Science*, vol. 218, pp. 45–57, 1941.

[9] John Norden, *Description of Cornwall*, written 1584 but published 1728, p. 28.

existence only when certain objective bonds delimit a social group. A nationality generally has several of these attributes; very few have all of them. The most usual of them are common descent, language, territory, political entity, customs and traditions, and religion." [10] Reinhold Niebuhr has thus defined "the forces of cohesion for the integral community," or nation:

. . . common language and a sense of ethnic kinship, geographic unity and contiguity, a common historical experience and frame of political thought, a common area of economic mutuality, and sometimes, the fear of a common foe. Any of these forces may be defective, but they cannot all be defective if the unity of the nation is to be preserved. A common religion was usually regarded as an equally important prerequisite until modern religiously pluralistic nations . . . refuted the theory. It is worth noting, however, that only solid communities, bound by other ties of mutuality, can afford the luxury of religious pluralism.[11]

Belief in a common biological descent may have some cohesive force among tribal societies, but among the more developed nations it is dismissed for what it is, a myth. Similarly, the claim that a nation belongs en masse to a biological race, as the Nazis claimed that the Germans were members of a hypothetical Aryan race, though less extreme, is nevertheless nonsense.

A common language is the most frequent and obvious sign of social cohesion. Nevertheless some Frenchmen speak German, and some Italians, French; Switzerland has four official languages, and Belgium, Canada, and South Africa each has two. Separate nations, the Danes and Norwegians, the Dutch and the Belgian Flemings, the British and the Americans, have, in effect, the same languages.

[10] Hans Kohn, *The Idea of Nationalism,* New York, 1945, p. 13.
[11] Reinhold Niebuhr, *The Structure of Nations and Empires,* Charles Scribner's Sons, New York, 1959, p. 149.

Figure 1 *Scotland and Wales are now part of the United Kingdom, but local pride and tradition demand that ancient boundaries be recognized.*
PHOTOGRAPH BY N. J. G. POUNDS

Customs and traditions, folkways, feasts and festivals, costume and decorations can all be evidence of national cohesion. They can also be evidence of regionalisms powerful enough to threaten the integrity of the state. Some of the national movements in nineteenth-century Europe began with the assiduous cultivation of everything pertaining to the customs and folklore of the national groups of which it was comprised.

Religion has ceased to be an important factor in national unity over much of the world. The more developed states have neither a state church nor a state religion. Even in Great Britain, with its "established" church, there is a *de facto* equality for all faiths and creeds. But in some states, religion still provides either a cohesive or a dividing force. In Yugoslavia the division between Orthodox and Catholic is, in effect, a national division. India split along religious lines into Hindu India and Mouslim Pakistan when British rule was withdrawn. It cannot be doubted that religion is a powerful political force in the Arab world, nor that the Catholic Church constitutes a significant part of the cement of the Polish and Irish nations.

Perhaps the most significant outward

Figure 2 The Voortrekker Monument, near Pretoria, South Africa. It is intended to represent and commemorate the migration and struggles of the Boers to create a Boer state. Notice the frieze of ox-wagons, intended to symbolize their journey into the interior of Africa. COURTESY: SOUTH AFRICAN GOVERNMENT INFORMATION OFFICE

factor in the formation of nationalities is a common territory. There is a presumption that those peoples who, through the accident of birth, inhabit a single state area will acquire the marks of the corresponding nation. "Political frontiers tend to establish nationalities." [12] The pressures brought to bear on such peoples by the society amid which they find themselves are so strong that it requires a conscious and purposeful effort to resist them. Minority and dissident groups tend, in general, to be absorbed or assimilated ultimately by their enveloping societies. Thus the Bretons have, on the whole, been absorbed by the French nation; the Welsh by the British; the Slavic Lusatians by the Germans. This process of absorption or assimilation of minority groups, or *subnations*, by the dominant so-

[12] Kohn, *op. cit.*, p. 15.

ciety amid which they live may be either hastened or resisted. Modern history records innumerable instances of the state attempting to suppress the individuality of such groups within its borders: the Prussian campaign against the Poles in the nineteenth century; the Polish campaign against the Ukrainians after 1919; the Hungarian against the Slovak, Rumanian, and other minorities before 1914; the Spanish against the Catalans; the Russian against the Baltic peoples and numerous other groups, and the current Turkish measures to suppress all non-Turkish elements in the state. Such efforts may occasionally be successful; usually they leave a legacy of lasting hate.

But such groups may resist the slow, quiet assertion of its superiority by the dominant group. Such resistance is rarely violent and rarely successful. It gives rise to a romantic antiquarianism, to the treasuring of ancient symbols, which constitute an acceptable alternative to a political, separatist movement. On the other hand, if a dominant group is active in forcing its culture upon a reluctant subnation and the latter is vigorous in resisting such pressure, the scene is set for a struggle for national preservation and independence. Such struggles acquire heroic proportions; they are the raw material of legend and a source of inspiration to later generations. They may provide the cement which welds a nation together, and if successful, they may create a state to match the nation. The Polish struggle against the Russians in the nineteenth century; that of the Czechs against the Austrians, of the Latin-American republics against Spain, of the Serbs, Bulgars, and Greeks against the Turks; perhaps also the struggle of the Tibetans against the Chinese and of the Algerian Berbers against the French—these are examples of the strivings of national groups to resist absorption into a larger and more powerful group.

Such experiences normally intensify the feeling of cohesion, of belonging to the group. The most articulate nations today have in some measure been molded by pressures. The pressure may not always be an attempt by an outside power to thwart or destroy the nation. It may be merely an experience through which its members have passed. For example, in the mid-sixteenth century, the territory which now forms the Netherlands was made up of several small, separate, and quarrelsome states. Yet:

The Dutch nation was born, coherent, and distinct from other national units. It was born because, during the second half of the sixteenth century, a state came into existence, within whose territory men lived and strove together, and shared experiences so crowded and so intense that they found themselves

Figure 3   The Old Town Square (Stary Rynek) in Warsaw, capital of Poland, as it was rebuilt after the Second World War. The rebuilding, which followed closely the Renaissance pattern, was intended as a memorial both to those who died resisting the Germans and to the former greatness of Poland. PHOTOGRAPH BY N. J. G. POUNDS

overnight where it had taken the people of other national states centuries to arrive.[13]

The birth of other nations can rarely be dated with such precision, but many have passed through an intense emotional experience which has matured them quickly.

Thus the French nationality was born of the enthusiastic manifestation of will in 1789. A French nation, the population of the French kingdom, existed before, as did some of the objective conditions necessary for the foundation of a nationality. But only the newly aroused consciousness and will made these elements active and effective, fused them into a source of immense centripetal power, and gave them a new importance and meaning.[14]

The English nation took shape under Queen Elizabeth I in the second half of the sixteenth century. Shakespeare expressed the feelings of newly found nationhood in many passages, but nowhere bet-

[13] G. J. Rennier, The Dutch Nation: An Historical Study, George Allen and Unwin, Ltd., London, 1944, p. 10.
[14] Kohn, op. cit., p. 15.

ter than in the speech of John of Gaunt, in *King Richard II:*

> This fortress built by Nature for herself
> Against infection and the hand of war,
> This happy breed of men, this little world,
> This precious stone set in the silver sea,
> Which serves it in the office of a wall,
> Or as a moat defensive to a house,
> Against the envy of less happier lands,
> This blessed plot, this earth, this realm, this
> England. . . .

The German poet and dramatist, Friedrich Schiller, in his *Wilhelm Tell,* saw the birth of the Swiss nation in the legendary oath sworn by the Swiss on the Rutli, *Wir wollen sein ein einig Volk von Brudern.*

This mythical declaration, "We wish to be one single nation of brothers," was uttered at the birth of every nationality, whether this birth happened, after a long pregnancy, in the enthusiasm of a revolutionary period, or whether the awakening of the masses required many years of ceaseless propaganda.[15]

In most instances a body of heroic legend has gathered around the history of the origin of a nation. The deeds of historical persons are enlarged and distorted, and sometimes purely mythical personages are introduced. Tales of William Tell, Francis Drake, and Paul Revere are part of this necessary body of heroic legend. Every nation has its peculiar symbols, customs, and practices, which Jean Gottmann has called its iconography.[16] The feeling of being a nation is compounded of any or all of these elements, and no two nations feel the same way for the same reasons.

THE NATION-STATE

A state is likely to show the greatest stability and permanence when it corre-

sponds closely with a nation. In such instances the state is the political expression of the nation, the mechanism through which the welfare of the nation is safeguarded and its identity preserved. The purpose which the state fulfills is, in these cases, obvious. But the nation-state is very much a phenomenon of our own times, and not all states have become nation-states; some are multinational, such as the old Hapsburg empire; some, like Canada and Czechoslovakia, even today have two distinct nations. In South Africa there are three, the English, the Boers, and the underprivileged African majority. In extreme cases there may be several groups, differing in varying degrees from one another in each of the aspects outlined above, perhaps even struggling with one another for political power. At some stage in their history Yugoslavia, Syria, and Spain have each illustrated such an extreme lack of social cohesion. What purpose does such a state serve?

Raison d'Etre: Professor Hartshorne sees in his study of the purpose which the state serves the central task of political geography. His analysis has become widely accepted, and it provides us with a unified and coherent view of the nature of political geography as a discreet branch of geographical study. Hartshorne sees "the central problems of political geography in terms of the functions of state-areas."[17] He further defines his argument:

Any state, to become well established, must present to the populations of its areal parts a distinct *raison d'être,* its justification for existence as an areal unit separate from the neighboring state-areas. This *raison d'être* must be based upon desires or values of first importance to the populations of the regions included in the state. . . . These include, notably: reli-

---

[15] *Ibid.,* p. 16.
[16] Jean Gottmann, *La Politique des états et leur géographie,* Hachette, Paris, 1952, pp. 157–159.

[17] Richard Hartshorne, "The Functional Approach in Political Geography," *A.A.A.G.,* vol. 40, pp. 95–130, 1950.

gion, language and literature, historic memories, and the form of government. . . . Since few state areas are homogeneous in all these respects, the problem is to construct a *raison d'être* that will enlist the loyalty of regional groups having different associations and ideals.[18]

Centrifugal Forces: In every state there are forces tending to reduce its cohesion. In extreme cases they may break the state into two or more parts, as Czechoslovakia was broken up early in 1939 and British India in 1947. In others, it may serve merely to make administration more difficult and to weaken the political *power* of the state. Such centrifugal tendencies may result from the simple geographical factors of size, shape, and difficulty of communication and transportation within a state. Several railroads have been built for political, rather than economic, reasons, to strengthen the internal ties within a politically organized area. The division of a state area into two or more parts by the territory of another, as Pakistan is divided today, is a matter of serious importance. Australia, split by the uninhabited waste of its central desert; Ecuador, divided into the coastal lowlands and the Andean Plateau, contrasted regions with contrasted outlooks; the north and the south of Italy, with a similar though less extreme contrast —all are examples of division induced by *physical* features.

More actively felt is the division of the state's population into contrasting cultural, religious, and linguistic communities. Few states in the world are without minority groups, and in some, the friction generated by their conflict threatens the stability or even the existence of the state. In the extreme case, that of British India,

Figure 4 *In Belgium, Walloons and Flemings are not always on speaking terms.* COURTESY: LEE EBNER, LOUISVILLE COURIER-JOURNAL

a political unit was divided in a fashion that did violence to every other geographical consideration in order to separate Hindu from Muslim. Yugoslavia, Czechoslovakia, Rumania, Finland, Canada, and Belgium are merely a few of the countries whose integrity either has once been or perhaps still is threatened by such "communal" differences.

In many other countries such differences are politically significant, without, however, actually threatening the existence of the state. Political and social attitudes differ from one end of a country to another. As Hartshorne has remarked:

> We need a map, a series of maps, portraying different kinds and degrees of Jim Crowism in the United States. These I would rate as a first requirement for an understanding of the internal political geography of the United States, for in no other factor do we find such marked regional cleavages, such disruption to the national unity of our state.[19]

"Jim Crowism" is not likely to disrupt this nation, but it certainly weakens its social cohesion.

Centripetal Forces: All forces which tend toward the weakening or disruption

[18] Richard Hartshorne, "The Concepts of 'Raison d'Être' and 'Maturity' of States; Illustrated from the Mid-Danube Area," *A.A.A.G.*, vol. 30, pp. 59–60, 1940.

[19] Richard Hartshorne, "The Functional Approach in Political Geography," *op. cit.*, quoted from p. 108.

Figure 5 *The Parliament Building and statue of Field Marshal Mannerheim,
who for all Finns typifies their struggle for independence against the Russians.*
PHOTOGRAPH BY N. J. G. POUNDS

of the state are classed as *centrifugal* forces.
Those which tend in the opposite direction,
that is, toward strengthening and unifying
the state, are *centripetal* forces. Unless the
latter predominate over the former, a state
is not likely to last for long.

The fact that a country has a name and a
government, that an international treaty recognized its existence as a state and defines its
territorial limits—all that does not produce a
state. To accomplish that, it is necessary to
establish centripetal forces that will bind together the regions of that state, in spite of
centrifugal forces that are always present.[20]

The basic centripetal force is, as Hartshorne has demonstrated, "some concept or
idea justifying the existence of [the] particular state."[21] At the lowest level, this

[20] *Ibid.,* p. 110.
[21] *Ibid.,* p. 110.

basic idea consists merely in loyalty to or
belief in an individual, a chief, a king, or an
emperor. On a higher plane, it consists in
the acceptance of a system of values which
the state may be said to represent and to
safeguard. The limited or constitutional
monarch of today survives only when he
has shed his absolute powers and comes to
embody those values which the state represents. Along with the values themselves,
there usually goes an interest in the ways
in which those values were acquired and
developed. The distortion of historical fact,
at least in the popular understanding of
it, in the course of building up a corpus
of heroic legend is to be regarded as normal
among all the more successful nations.

Any examination of the state system of
the world today reveals a number of states
in which the centrifugal forces appear to

Figure 6 *The grave of Mannerheim in Finland has become almost a national shrine.* PHOTOGRAPH BY N. J. G. POUNDS

outweigh the centripetal. How, one may ask, did such states come into being, and why do they survive? Clearly, if the internal forces of the state tend on balance toward disruption, the state must be held together by some external force.

The central African territory of the Cameroun has been administered by France under United Nations trusteeship. It is, at the same time, acquiring independence and lapsing into anarchy. "Cameroon's trouble springs from the fact that she has no ethnic, religious or geographic unity." [22] The territory had been held together by French rule, which had been superimposed upon it. Of course, if this rule had been of longer duration and more successful, it might have developed a sense of unity among the diverse peoples of the Cameroun.

[22] *New York Times,* Jan. 3, 1960.

On the whole, this is what the British succeeded in doing on the Gold Coast (Ghana) and, perhaps less successfully, in Nigeria. It is what the Belgians conspicuously failed to do in the Congo, the British

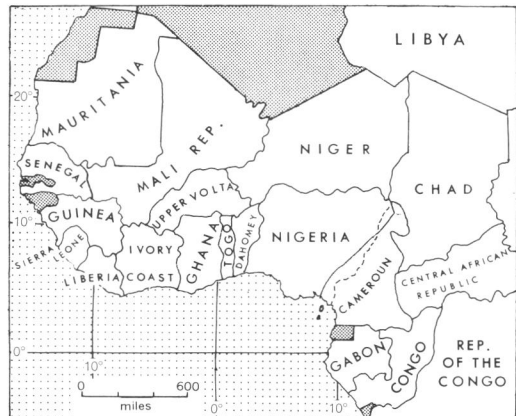

Exhibit 3 *Political map of West Africa.*

in Cyprus and India, and the Austrians in the old Hapsburg empire.

Often an independent or sovereign state is created with such pronounced centrifugal forces at the start that its very existence is threatened. Yugoslavia and Syria are examples. These states represent initial attempts on the part of the groups within the countries to sink their differences, because independence was likely to be achieved and preserved against external forces only by union. To some extent, they represent territorial units that were built too big, because their friends and allies, for their own political reasons, wished to see them strong. It does not follow that a large and diverse state is stronger than a smaller and more homogeneous state, but, as will be discussed later, sheer size has often carried with it an illusion of power. Occasionally a state, unfit for statehood by reason of its own internal lack of cohesion, has attained statehood because the greater powers could not agree on what else to do with it: Albania in 1913; Libya in 1951; Laos in 1954. Numerous examples could be taken from central and eastern Europe and from the Middle East of states whose *raison d'être* does not lie wholly or even partially in the will to statehood of a nation. In the Iberian peninsula, centrifugal tendencies are strong. Except for a period in the sixteenth and seventeenth centuries, Portugal has retained its independence, and Cataluña, geographically and socially different from the Meseta region of central Spain, has periodically attempted to free itself from close control by authorities in Madrid. Under the short-lived Spanish Republic, Cataluña, along with the Basque province of Vizcaya, achieved a measure of autonomy. They have since become reunited politically with Spain, not because that was the wish of the Catalan and Basque peoples, but because Franco, with the aid of Italian troops and German equipment, won the Spanish Civil War (1936–1939). How many more states are there that would fly apart if the application or the threat of force were withdrawn? Let it suffice to observe here that several states owe at least their origin, not to the volition of their

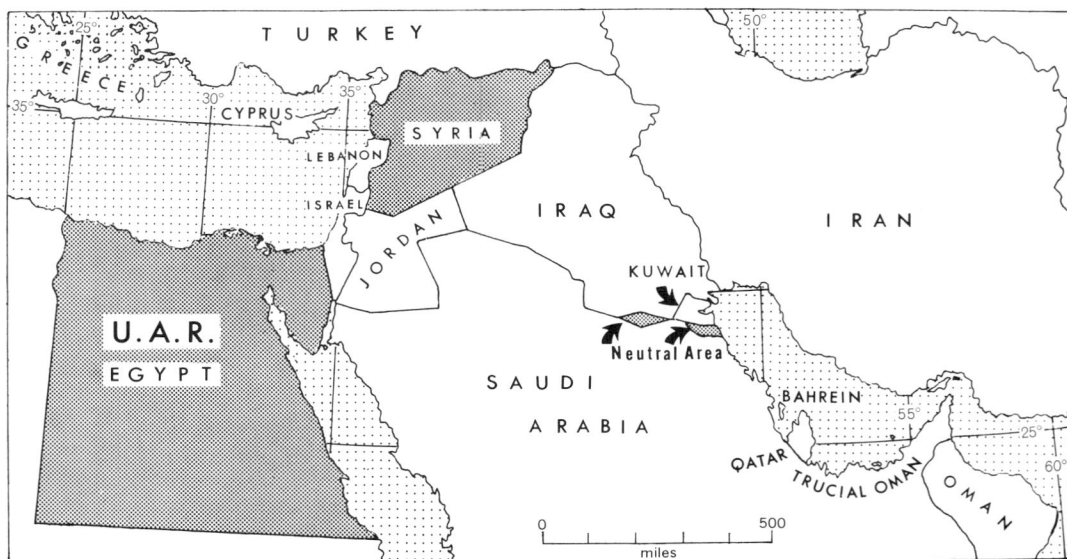

Exhibit 4 *Political map of the Middle East.*

citizens, but to the power balance between a few great states.

POWER

The decision makers in any given state must possess power. If they did not, they would not be able to occupy and to retain their decision-making role in the state, for power is "that which permits participation in the making of decision." [23] Political power is of two kinds. It consists first in the ability to make and enforce decisions inside the boundaries of the state. Power in this sense depends upon the support of or control over public opinion and the organs, such as radio and the press, which shape it; it depends in part also on influence over the attitudes of the police, the military, the legislature, and the judiciary. Second, power consists in the ability to make decisions and implement them in fields which either lie geographically outside the boundaries of the state or impinge on the interests of other states. It is easy to think of states in which the decision makers exercise great power in the former context but negligible power in the latter.

Power of the former kind is dependent on the political structure of the state. It has nothing to do with the state's intrinsic wealth or resources. Though it may sometimes be supported by regional feeling within the state, it is essentially nongeographical in its nature. Power to participate effectively in "the system of actions, reactions and interactions between and among . . . states" [24] has no essential connection with internal power, though it must be admitted that a government that is secure, respected, and likely to endure for a period of years is likely to find its authority to

conduct foreign policy increased thereby. But it remains true that in international politics power is basically related to the area, population, resources, and industrial potential of the state, as modified by geographical location and level of technology. The basis of political power in this context is fundamentally *geographical*.

It may be postulated that the primary objective of the decision maker in any state is to achieve the well-being and prosperity of the state itself. "Because territory is an inherent part of a state, self-preservation means defending its control over territory; . . . the basic objective of the foreign policy of all states is the preservation of territorial integrity and political independence." [25] A further objective may be the retention of the reins of power in the hands of the decision maker, but this is likely to be rather a matter of internal politics. The security of the state is the dominant objective of policy vis-à-vis other states, whatever may be the political strategy employed to attain it, and power is necessary for its pursuit.

Political power in the international sphere has been classified as: [26]

1. Military power
2. Economic power
3. Power over opinion

Military power is the ultimate basis of power, and in the last resort, the sanction whereby a state enforces its decisions is war or threat of war. As E. H. Carr has put it, "War lurks in the background of international politics just as revolution lurks in the background of domestic politics." [27]

Power to wage war is dependent upon

[23] Stephen B. Jones, "The Power Inventory and National Strategy," *World Politics*, vol. 6, p. 422, 1954.

[24] Sprout and Sprout, *op. cit.*, p. 6.

[25] N. J. Spykman, *America's Strategy in World Politics*, Harcourt, Brace and Company, Inc., New York, 1942, p. 17.

[26] E. H. Carr, *The Twenty Years Crisis, 1919–1939*, Macmillan & Co., London, 1939, pp. 138–185.

[27] *Ibid.*, p. 140.

the geographical factors—location and area, population, resources, and industry—which have already been mentioned. The relative value of each of these factors has changed and is still changing. Napoleon was able to march all over Europe at a time when France's population was greater by far than that of any of her rivals, except perhaps Czarist Russia. The rise of German military power coincided with the development of modern industry, for which Germany was geographically better suited than France. As Keynes observed, "The German Empire has been built more truly on coal and iron than on blood and iron." [28] The heavy industries today may be losing something of their significance for military power, and their place may be taken by the lighter industries on which electronics are based. Perhaps the future great power will be built more truly on uranium and the light metals than on coal and iron.

Military power is related to economic power. The supply of military equipment is likely to be difficult, unless there already exists a capacity to produce civilian equipment. Ability to purchase scarce commodities from abroad; to stock-pile materials; to exist for a period on an autarchic, or self-sufficing, basis; to deny essential materials to a potential enemy, as the United States in 1938 limited the export of steel scrap; or to make goods available to allies, as they did under the policy of Lend-Lease—all these are examples of economic power used by a state to attain its chosen political goals.

Power over opinion is less tangible. E. H. Carr has observed that "the organized use of power over opinion as a regular instrument of foreign policy is a modern development." [29] It springs in part from the realization that in any state there are

segments of the population not completely dedicated to the ends pursued by the majority and that these centrifugal groups can be used to weaken both the internal and the external power of the decision maker in the state.

The cohesion of the population is thus a very significant factor in the power of a state. Dissident groups within it are not likely to cooperate enthusiastically with the policy adopted by the decision maker, and in extreme cases they may be centers of disloyalty, ready and waiting for an enemy to use. The German use of the Irish, the Belgian Flemings, and the Ukrainians during the First World War are examples of such exploitation of minority groups.

In its appeal to public opinion, both at home and abroad, the agents of government usually couch their arguments in universal terms. They are fighting for *liberté, égalité, fraternité,* or the "forgotten man," or to "make the world safe for democracy." The ideals of the French Revolutionaries and of the Russian Communists have certainly had great weight outside their countries of origin. Is this only because of their universality, or is it partly because each was backed by military power? It appears unhappily to be true that the power of ideas varies directly with the number of bayonets that support it. Mussolini's remark "I offer you peace with a hundred thousand bayonets" was unfortunately too true a statement of political realities at that time.

WHAT IS POLITICAL GEOGRAPHY?

Political geography is, as we have seen, concerned with the state. The state exists to perform a particular function, and in most instances this function is to protect, foster, and give political expression to that

[28] J. M. Keynes, *The Economic Consequences of the Peace,* Macmillan & Co., London, 1919, p. 75.
[29] Carr, *op. cit.*

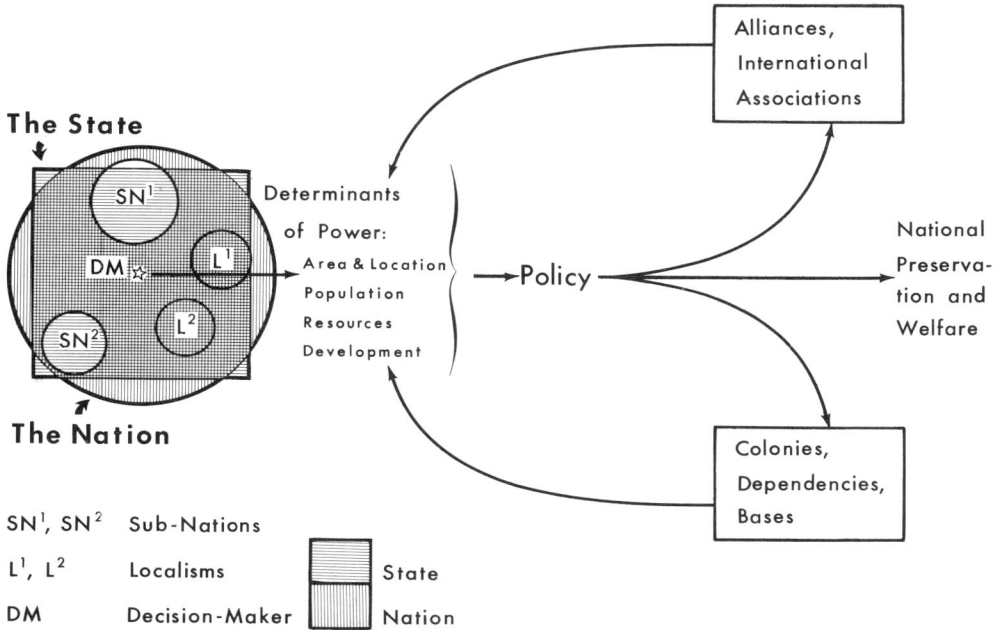

Exhibit 5 Diagram showing the relationship of state, nation, policy, and power.

body of ideas and ideals which characterizes the nation. Occasionally the state has come into being for some other reason, and in these instances its existence is dependent upon the balance of outside pressures. But for the nation-states, which constitute the great majority of states, we may say that the objective of the state is the welfare and integrity of the nation or nations of which it is the political expression.

The scope of political geography may be expressed as:

1. The geographical coincidence of state and nation. This raises the question of political boundaries and claims to territory, of dissident groups within and of related groups without the limits of the state.

2. The resources which the state can command in the pursuit of its objective, the well-being and integrity of its people. These resources consist of the location, size, and shape of the state, which influence its strategy and defense and, through communications and transportation, its cohesion; second, the population, its structure, competence, and skills; and, lastly, naturally occurring resources, their utilization, and the degree of industrial and technical development.

3. The social cohesion of the population. Since this is in all respects an important factor in national power, the focus of loyalties within the state and the division of the state for administrative purposes acquire in some instances a political importance In some respects the social cohesion within a state is reflected in the geographical patterns of voting habits, which thus become an important element in the study of political geography.

4. The state does not rely wholly on its own internal resources. It is likely to have allies and dependencies which in varying degrees support it in the pursuit of its pri

mary objective. The geographical pattern of its alliances, the distribution of colonies, dependencies, and bases, and the division or joint use of resources are all factors in the power of a state.

5. Every state carries on trade, however limited in scope this may be in some instances. Trade may be a source of strength, or excessive dependence upon certain goods and markets may spell weak-

ness. Trade can be, and sometimes has been, used as an instrument of policy, and an evaluation is necessary of the significance of trade in the power potential of the state.

These factors and relationships may be expressed in a formula or a schematic diagram (Exhibit 5). This book is in large measure a study of the application and implications of this schema for the states of the world.

APPENDIX I

Sovereign States, Their Areas and Population, 1963

	Area, sq km	Population, thousands	Density per sq km
Africa:			
Algeria	2,381,741	10,930	5
Cameroun	432,500	3,225	7
Central African Republic	617,000	1,185	2
Chad	1,284,000	2,600	2
Congo (Brazzaville)	342,000	795	2
Congo (Léopoldville)	2,344,932	13,821	6
Dahomey	115,762	1,581 [1]	15
Ethiopia	1,184,320	21,800	18
Gabon	267,000	420	2
Ghana	237,873	6,691	28
Guinea	245,857	2,727	11
Ivory Coast	322,463	2,390 [1]	10
Liberia	111,370	1,250	11
Libya	1,759,540	1,172	1
Madagascar	590,000	5,239	9
Mali	1,204,021	4,300	4
Mauritania	1,085,805	730	1
Morocco	443,680	10,550	24
Niger	1,188,794	2,555	2
Nigeria	878,447	33,663	38
Senegal	197,161	2,102 [1]	12
Sierra Leone	72,326	2,400	33
Somalia	637,661	1,990	3
South Africa	1,223,409	14,673	12
Sudan	2,505,823	11,459	5
Tanganyika	937,061	8,788	10
Togo	57,000	1,041	19
Tunisia	125,180	3,935	31
Upper Volta	274,122	3,537	13
United Arab Republic (Egypt)	1,000,000	25,365	25

Sovereign States (Continued)

	Area, sq km	Population, thousands	Density per sq km
North America:			
Canada	9,976,177	17,442	2
Costa Rica	50,700	1,126	22
Cuba	114,524	6,599	58
Dominican Republic	48,734	2,894	59
El Salvador	21,146	2,520	119
Guatemala	108,889	3,652	34
Haiti	27,750	3,464	125
Honduras	112,088	1,887	17
Jamaica	11,425	1,614	142
Mexico	1,969,367	33,304	17
Nicaragua	148,000	1,424	10
Panama	74,470	1,024	14
Trinidad and Tobago	5,128	828	165
United States	9,363,387	177,700	19
South America:			
Argentina	2,778,412	20,614	7
Bolivia	1,098,581	3,416	3
Brazil	8,513,844	64,216	8
Chile	741,767	7,465	10
Colombia	1,138,338	13,824	12
Ecuador	270,670	4,169	15
Paraguay	406,752	1,718	4
Peru	1,285,215	10,524	8
Uruguay	186,926	2,535 [1]	14
Venezuela	912,050	6,512	7
Asia:			
Afghanistan	650,000	13,150	20
Bahrain	598	143	259
Bhutan	50,000	660	13
Burma	678,033	20,457	30
Cambodia	172,511	4,845	28
Ceylon	65,610	9,612	147
China (mainland)	9,561,000	669,000	70
China (Taiwan)	35,961	10,232	285
Cyprus	9,251	558	60
Federation of Malaya	131,313	6,698	51
India	3,263,373	402,600	123
Indonesia	1,491,562	90,300	61
Iran	1,648,000	20,149	12
Iraq	444,442	6,952	16
Israel	20,700	2,061	100
Japan	369,661	92,740	251
Jordan	96,610	1,636	17
Korea, North	123,962	8,100	65
Korea, Republic of	96,929	23,848	246
Kuwait	15,540	219	14

Sovereign States (Continued)

	Area, sq km	Population, thousands	Density per sq km
Laos	236,800	1,760	7
Lebanon	10,400	1,353 [1]	149
Maldive Islands	298	89	299
Mongolian People's Republic	1,531,000	1,057	1
Muscat and Oman	212,380	550	3
Nepal	140,798	9,044	64
Pakistan	944,824	86,823	92
Philippines	299,681	24,718	82
Qatar	22,014	40	2
Saudi Arabia	1,600,000	6,036	4
Sikkim	7,107	150	21
Syria	184,479	4,539	25
Thailand	514,000	21,881	43
Trucial Oman	83,600	86	1
Turkey	780,576	26,881	34
Vietnam, North	155,228	15,170	98
Vietnam, South, Republic of	170,806	13,790	81
Yemen	195,000	4,500 [1]	23
Oceania:			
Australia	7,704,159	10,061	1
New Zealand	268,676	2,331	9
Western Samoa	2,927	104	36
Europe:			
Albania	28,748	1,556	54
Andorra	453	7	16
Austria	83,850	7,049	84
Belgium	30,507	9,104	298
Bulgaria	110,669	7,798	70
Czechoslovakia	127,859	13,559	106
Denmark	43,042	4,547	106
Finland	337,009	4,416	13
France	551,208	45,097	82
Germany, Eastern	107,431	16,213	151
Germany, Federal Republic	247,960	52,785	213
Greece	132,562	8,258	62
Holy See	0	1	2,273
Hungary	93,030	9,953	107
Iceland	103,000	172	2
Ireland	70,283	2,846	40
Italy	301,226	49,052	163
Liechtenstein	157	16	101
Luxembourg	2,586	324	125
Monaco	2	23	15,000
Netherlands	32,450	11,346	350
Norway	323,917	3,556	11
Poland	311,730	29,257	94

Sovereign States (Continued)

	Area, sq km	Population, thousands	Density per sq km
Portugal	92,200	9,052	98
Rumania	237,500	18,256	77
San Marino	61	13	246
Spain	503,486	29,894	59
Sweden	449,682	7,454	17
Switzerland	41,288	5,240	127
United Kingdom	244,016	52,157	214
Yugoslavia	255,804	18,448	72
Union of Soviet Socialist Republics	22,403,000	210,500	9
Including:			
Byelorussian S.S.R.	207,600	8,112	39
Ukrainian S.S.R.	576,600	41,869	73

Of the states listed here, the United States government does not (as of September, 1961) formally recognize:

The Chinese People's Republic
The Soviet Zone of Germany
North Korea
North Vietnam

The following states are defined by the Department of State as "semi-independent":

Aden Protectorate	Sikkim [2]
Bahrain [2]	Singapore
Brunei	Tonga
Maldive Islands [2]	Trucial States [2]
Qatar [2]	Zanzibar

[1] Population estimate of 1953.
[2] Listed above and by the UN as sovereign and independent.

BIBLIOGRAPHY

American Geography: Inventory and Prospect, Preston E. James and Clarence F. Jones (eds.), Syracuse University Press, 1954.

Boggs, S. Whittemore: "Geographic and Other Scientific Techniques for Political Science," American Political Science Review, pp. 223–238, vol. 42, 1948.

Carr, E. H.: "The Forms of Political Power," in H. H. Sprout and M. Sprout (eds.), Foundations of National Power, Princeton University Press, Princeton, N.J., 1945, pp. 31–38.

Deutsch, Karl W.: "The Growth of Nations: Some Recurrent Patterns of Political and Social Integration," World Politics, vol. 5, pp. 168–195, 1952–1953.

———: Nationalism and Social Communication, Technology Press of Massachusetts Institute of Technology and John Wiley & Sons, Inc., New York, 1953.

East, W. G.: "The Nature of Political Geography," *Politica,* vol. 2, pp. 259–286, 1936–1937.

Gottmann, Jean: "Geography and International Relations," *World Politics,* vol. 3, pp. 153–173, 1950–1951.

Hartshorne, Richard: "Recent Developments in Political Geography," *American Political Science Review,* vol. 29, pp. 784–804, 943–966, 1935.

———: "The Concepts of 'Raison d'Être' and 'Maturity' of States; Illustrated from the Mid-Danube Area," *A.A.A.G.,* vol. 30, pp. 59–60, 1940.

———: "The Politico-geographic Pattern of the World," *Annals of the American Academy of Political and Social Science,* vol. 218, pp. 45–57, 1941.

———: "The Functional Approach in Political Geography," *A.A.A.G.,* vol. 40, pp. 95–130, 1950.

———: "Political Geography in the Modern World," *Journal of Conflict Resolution,* vol. 4, pp. 52–66, 1960.

Hertz, Frederick: *Nationality in History and Politics,* Kegan Paul, Trench, Trubner & Co., London, 1944.

Jackson, W. A. Douglas: "Whither Political Geography?" *A.A.A.G.,* vol. 48, pp. 178–183, 1958.

Janowsky, Oscar I.: *Nationalities and National Minorities,* The Macmillan Company, New York, 1945.

Jones, Stephen B.: "A Unified Field Theory of Political Geography," *A.A.A.G.,* vol. 44, pp. 111–123, 1954.

Jones, Stephen B.: "The Power Inventory and National Strategy," *World Politics,* vol. 6, pp. 421–452, 1954.

Kohn, Hans: *The Idea of Nationalism,* The Macmillan Company, New York, 1945.

Mackinder, H. J.: "The Physical Basis of Political Geography," *S.G.M.,* vol. 6, pp. 78–84, 1890.

Murdock, G. P., *Africa: Its Peoples and Their Culture History,* McGraw-Hill Book Company, Inc., New York, 1959.

Niebuhr, Reinhold: *The Structure of Nations and Empires,* Charles Scribner's Sons, New York, 1959.

Pye, Lucian W.: *Politics, Personality and Nation Building—Burma's Search for Identity,* Yale University Press, 1962.

Ratzel, Friedrich: "Die Gesetze des räumlichen Wachstums der Staaten," *Petermanns Mitteilungen,* vol. 42, pp. 97–107, 1896.

Russell, Bertrand: *Power: A New Social Analysis,* George Allen & Unwin, Ltd., London, 1938.

Sprout, H. H., and M. Sprout: *Man-Milieu Relationship Hypotheses in the Context of International Politics,* Center of International Studies, Princeton University, Princeton, N.J., 1956.

——— and ———: "Geography and International Politics in an Era of Revolutionary Change," *Journal of Conflict Resolution,* vol. 4, pp. 145–161, 1960.

Spykman, N. J.: *America's Strategy in World Politics,* Harcourt, Brace and Company, Inc., New York, 1942.

2 AREA AND LOCATION OF

THE STATE

In the study of geography we inquire not merely into the shapes and dimensions of countries, but also . . . into their positions with reference to each other.   STRABO

The fact that certain people live . . . on an island has in itself no effect on their history; what has an effect is the way they conceive that insular position; whether for example they regard the sea as a barrier or as a highway to traffic.   R. G. COLLINGWOOD, THE IDEA OF HISTORY

IT IS ONLY THROUGH HIS CONTROL OVER THE ELEMENTS OF POWER that the decision maker is able to implement his policy. Whatever overtones it may acquire, this policy must remain focused upon a double objective: internally, the stability and welfare of the state; externally, its security and integrity. The ultimate sanction which the decision maker can use is force or war, though he can usually achieve his objective by the use or threat of sanctions less drastic than this. But whatever the sanction employed, it remains ineffective unless backed by power.

The chief elements of power were mentioned in the previous chapter. It is necessary now to systematize these elements and to examine them more critically. The location of the state in relation to other states is one of the most significant factors in its power. It may be vulnerable, or it may be in a position to threaten other states. Its shape lends itself to easy defense or allows it to serve as a springboard for attack. It may exist in more than one territorial unit, and these units may be separated by a potentially hostile state. The power value of location is changing with changes in the technology of communication, transportation, and weapons. Both the United Kingdom and the United States have been obliged in turn to abandon their positions of "splendid isolation" as technological developments made such positions untenable.

Area is no less significant, though its importance may be more difficult to evaluate. There is normally a direct, though not necessarily simple, relationship between area and resources, and the territorially large state can usually be expected to satisfy more of its needs from within its own borders than the small. The large state also gains advantages from the scale of its industrial, transportation, and social operations, and these may be reflected in the political power which it may use to support its policies.

Closely related to location and area is the question of boundaries. The fierce struggles between states for small fragments of territory suggest that the precise alignment of a boundary is of very great importance to them. The political boundaries between sovereign states are the most significant discontinuities on the surface of the earth, excepting only the meeting of land and sea. It is clearly important to know how these discontinuities originated and function, even if their relationship to the power potential of a state is not always close.

Population as an essential factor in power needs no comment here, except to note that the importance of the quality of the population rather than its crude size is gaining. Last among the physical elements of power are naturally occurring resources, such as soil, water supply, fuel, minerals, and their degree of utilization in agriculture and industry. The technical level of both agriculture and industry, together with the related problems of transportation, is an essential element in the calculus of power. At the present time, it is the possession of a single item of technology, the hydrogen bomb, that distinguishes the really powerful states from those which are less powerful.

THE AREA OF STATES

The UN now has 110 (October, 1962) member states. These are separate and self-governing; they do not, however, exhaust the list of sovereign states in the world today. Switzerland, for example, in accordance with its policy of neutrality, has not sought membership in the UN, although it was a member of the League of Nations. The People's Republic of China, commonly known as Communist, or "Red," China, has been excluded from membership. Neither the Federal German Republic (West Germany) nor the Democratic German Republic (East Germany) is a member because their status and relationship to one another still await definition, nor is Mauritania in Africa, nor Mongolia in Asia. Further, a number of very small states—Andorra, Liechtenstein, Monaco, San Marino, and the Vatican City—are not member states, though some of them do participate in the work of some of the Specialized Agencies of the UN.[1] Altogether there are today about 120 sovereign states, and this list is likely to be increased as territories with a colonial status at present acquire independence. A list of sovereign states is given on pages 20 to 23.

These 120 states range in size from the Vatican City State, with an area of less than $\frac{1}{4}$ square mile,[2] to the Soviet Union, with 8,647,560 square miles;[3] the Chinese

---

[1] On membership of the Specialized Agencies, see *The Statesman's Yearbook,* "United Nations."

[2] Its area is actually 44 hectares (108.7 acres).

[3] This figure includes the Ukrainian S.S.R. (231,986 square miles) and the Byelorussian S.S.R. (80,134 square miles), which are represented separately in the UN.

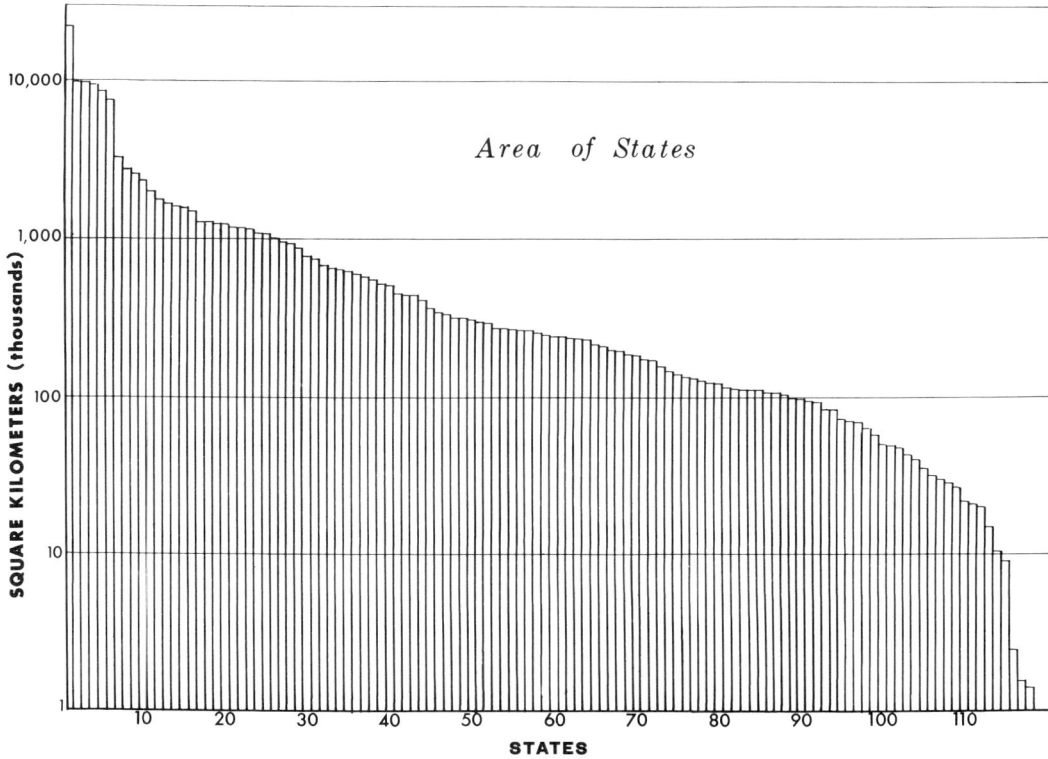

Exhibit 6 **Graph showing the area of states.** *The vertical numbering is according to a logarithmic scale.*

TABLE 1 *Area of States*

	Area, sq km	Number	Approximate total area, sq km
Giant states........	Over 6,000,000	6	67,000,000
Outsize states.......	2,500,000–6,000,000	3	8,565,000
Very large states....	1,250,000–2,500,000	10	16,400,000
Large states........	650,000–1,250,000	16	15,700,000
Medium states......	250,000–650,000	24	10,540,000
Small states.........	125,000–250,000	20	4,400,000
Very small states....	25,000–125,000	30	2,400,000
Microstates.........	Under 25,000	18	150,000
Total............		127	125,155,000

People's Republic, with 3,032,663 square miles; and Brazil, with 3,288,240 square miles (Exhibit 6). Table 1 shows the size distribution and the total area of states within each of the chosen size categories.

The largest state is about two million times as large as the smallest.[4] The average size is about 1,040,000 square kilometers, or about 390,000 square miles—about the size of Bolivia, Colombia, or Egypt—and nearly half come within the range of 25,000 to 250,000 square kilometers. Even so, one cannot deduce from this any optimum size for a state.

The Growth of a State: Many of the states have achieved their present size by a period of growth. They have been able to annex fragments of the territory of adjoining states and to incorporate them within their own boundaries. France, for example, has extended its territory to the east over a period of several centuries. Rumania grew to its present size from the two relatively small principalities of Walachia and Moldavia; Yugoslavia, from the earlier kingdom of Serbia; and the United States, from the original thirteen Colonies.

Territorial growth of a state appears to be so normal that it has been postulated as a fundamental law governing the behavior of states. The German geographer, Friedrich Ratzel, whose very great importance we shall notice again in the last chapter, argued that the boundaries of a state should never be regarded as fixed nor the state area as something definite.[5] The people of a state press against the boundaries of the state area, trying to force them wider. "The area of a state expands as its culture develops. . . . The lower the cultural level, the smaller will be the territory of the state,

so that the size of a state becomes a measure of its culture. No primitive people has ever created a large state, nor even one equivalent in area to an intermediate German state [*von der Grosse eines deutschen Mittelstaates*]."[6]

If one were to accept this view of Ratzel's which was also held by many other German geographers, the growth of culture would be indissolubly linked with expansion of territory. Such German writers pointed, in support of their argument, to the expansion of the British Empire in the eighteenth and nineteenth centuries, to the westward spread of the United States in the nineteenth century, and to the rise of the German Reich itself in the late nineteenth century: small states, they claimed, were "on the way out" and would sooner or later be absorbed by larger ones. In the end there would be a few great states of truly continental dimensions. This argument was predicated upon the assumption, touched upon briefly in Chapter 1, that the state is an organism[7] and that growth is normal and necessary in an organism.

We have already rejected this postulate, and we may dismiss also the arguments which Ratzel and others have erected on this basis. If states expand territorially, it is because the decision makers choose this as *their* policy for the state and have the power to carry this policy into effect; if states contract, it is because they lack the power to retain the territory which they formerly held.

It is better—and more accurate—to regard states as fundamentally stable. Despite a number of well-known examples of

---

[4] Excluding the Vatican City State.

[5] Friedrich Ratzel gives a short and succinct statement of his views in "Die Gesetze des räumlichen Wachstums der Staaten," *Petermanns Mitteilungen*, vol. 42, pp. 97–107, 1896.

[6] *Ibid.*, pp. 98–99; the translation is rather free.

[7] F. Ratzel wrote: ". . . dass wir es im Staate mit einem organischen Wesen zu thun haben. Der Natur des Organischen widerspricht aber nichts mehr als die starre Umgrenzung. . . ." *Ibid.*, p. 97.

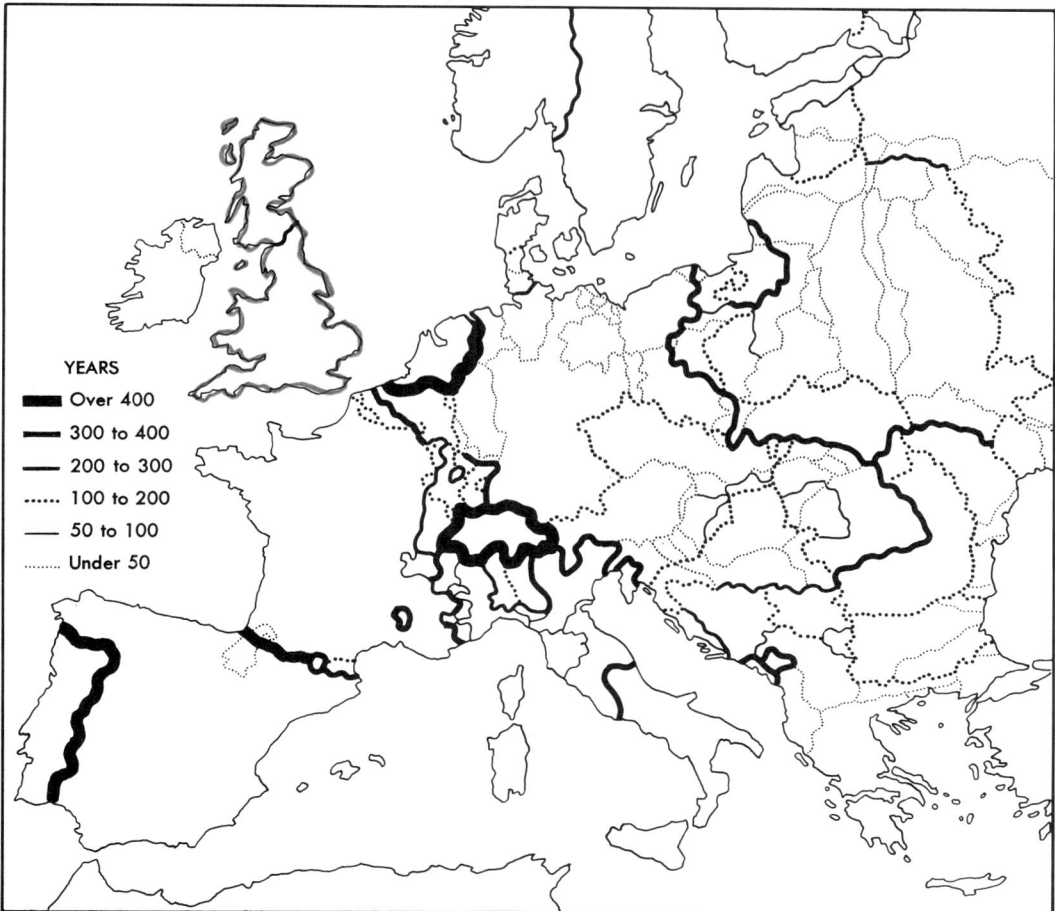

Exhibit 7 *Map showing the permanence of European boundaries.* BASED ON A MAP BY S. COLUMB GILFILLAN

territorial expansion and of unstable boundaries, the total length of boundary that has *not* changed is very many times the length of that which has. A map (Exhibit 7) showing the durability of boundaries in Europe during the last 450 years gives a rather surprising picture of the general stability of states.[8]

The Golden Mean: Clearly, then, the present size of states has nothing to do with

[8] S. Columb Gilfillan, "European Political Boundaries," *Political Science Quarterly*, vol. 39, pp. 458–484, 1924.

an alleged urge to expand. Is there a more rational approach to this question than that provided by Ratzel? In his *Contrat social*, first published in 1762, Jean-Jacques Rousseau wrote:

A body politic [i.e., a state] may be viewed in two ways—according to the extent of its territory, or according to the size of its population, and the proper size of any state depends upon a ratio between these two. It is men who make a state, but it is land that provides them with their food and sustenance. The ideal is achieved when the land can sup-

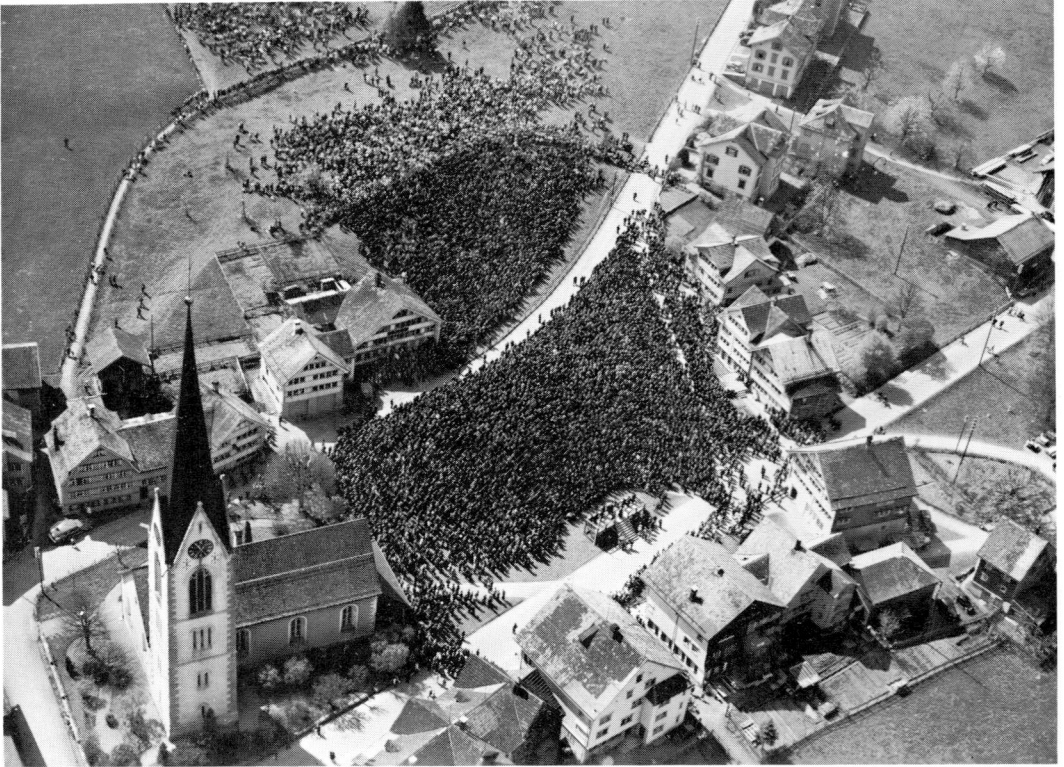

Figure 7   The classical ideal of a state so small that all its citizens could be gathered together in a single "town meeting" continues to be represented in the Swiss canton of Appenzell.   COURTESY: AEROFILMS

port its population, and when the population is of a size to absorb all the products of the land. Only where these two demands are met can a given number of inhabitants be said to have attained its maximum strength. For when a land is too large for its population, its defense becomes a burden; the fields are inadequately farmed, and there is too large a margin of natural products. Such conditions are the immediate causes of defensive wars. Where, on the other hand, a country is too small to maintain its population, it is at the mercy of its neighbors from whom alone it can obtain the commodities it lacks, and this produces aggression. Every country which, because of its situation, is forced to choose between trade and war, is essentially weak. . . . Its existence is bound to be precarious and short. Either it

conquers, and thereby changes its situation, or it is conquered and ceases to exist.[9]

So much for the ratio of area to population; land should not be annexed unless there are people to occupy it. But the availability of population is not the only consideration. Rousseau examined the question from the administrative angle:

Just as nature has set limits to the growth of a well-formed man, beyond which it produces only giants or imbeciles, so, too, there are limits of extent outside which a state cannot have the best possible constitution. It must

[9] *The Social Contract,* book 11, chap. 10. The edition of Sir Ernest Barker, Oxford University Press, London, 1946, is used here.

be neither too large to make good government impossible, nor too small to defend itself unaided.[10]

Rousseau argued that, the larger a state became, "the more the social bond is stretched" and, as a result, the less do the people think of themselves as a group with objectives and ideals in common. Almost two centuries after Rousseau wrote his *Contrat social,* a distinguished modern economist, Simon Kuznets, remarked that the challenge to small nations is "how to use the stronger sense of community, the closer coherence of the population, the greater elasticity of social institutions, to overcome the disadvantage of small size." [11] Furthermore, in Rousseau's words, "administration becomes increasingly difficult over long distances" and thus less and less efficient. Rousseau had in mind the technical and administrative apparatus of the eighteenth century. But even today, with the automobile and the aircraft, the telephone and the radio, distance interposes administrative difficulties and creates regionalisms. Lastly, the larger the state, the greater is likely to be the variety both of peoples and of physical environment. "It is impossible that the same laws should be suitable to so many different provinces, each with its own customs, its own climatic conditions, and its own ideas about the type of government it would like." Rousseau is somewhat naïve in his consideration of the problems presented by geographical variety, but he nevertheless presents clearly and succinctly the basic problems of the size of states.

These principles, which Rousseau laid down, were actually used in 1792, when the French National Convention had to decide whether or not to include Savoy within its boundaries. Would its incorporation make France unreasonably large or difficult to rule? It was concluded, as might have been expected, that Savoy was just what France needed to round out her territories.[12]

Rousseau looked for "a condition of equilibrium" between states, none too large to be administered easily, nor too small to be secure, with stability guaranteed by the fact that all had the optimum conditions for self-defense. The political map, however, is not cast on this model. Its relative stability exists in spite of the gross disparity in the sizes of states. In 1942, Professor G. T. Renner sought to produce a new political map, in which the political units would be conceived more logically. Small, "indefensible" states were to be eliminated, and a rough equality of area and resource was to be achieved, and with it peace and stability. The map (Exhibit 8) shows the brave new world of G. T. Renner.

Of course the proposal was stillborn. It sacrificed nationalism, the most powerful political force in the modern world, on the altar of areal equality between states. It was ignored by statesmen and forgotten by the public. If the jungle law of Friedrich Ratzel has no validity and the principle of equality and stability enunciated by Rousseau has little applicability, what principle, if any, can we apply as a measuring rod in discussing the size of states?

The Area of the State Idea: In Chapter 1 we examined the idea that the state is the political expression of the nation. The size of the state should then express the areal distribution of the nation. There

[10] *Contrat social,* in C. E. Vaughan (ed.), *The Political Writings of Rousseau,* Cambridge University Press, Cambridge, 1915, book 11, chap. 9.

[11] S. Kuznets, "Economic Growth of Small Nations," in E. A. G. Robinson (ed.), *Economic Consequences of the Size of Nations,* Macmillan & Co., Ltd., London, 1960, p. 31.

[12] Norman J. G. Pounds, "France and 'Les Limites Naturelles' from the Seventeenth to the Twentieth Centuries," *A.A.A.G.,* vol. 44, pp. 51–62, 1954.

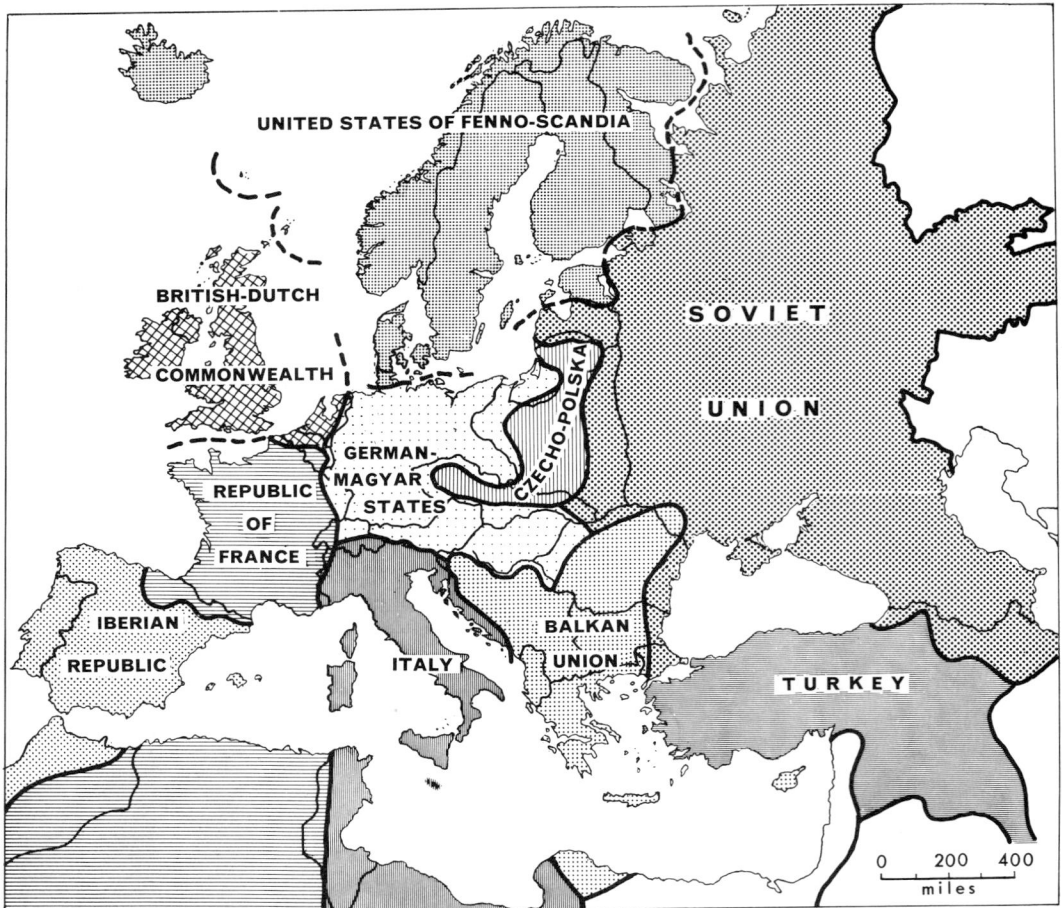

Exhibit 8 *The "brave new world" proposed in 1942 by George T. Renner.*
BASED ON A MAP PUBLISHED IN COLLIER'S

should be doubt or dispute regarding the limits of the state only where the national allegiance of subnations or groups is in question. Such a principle is widely applicable, but it does not explain the existence of the very small states: the Monegasques, for example, are to all outward appearances French; the Liechtensteiners are German-speaking Swiss; and the citizens of San Marino are Italians. And there are states in which several groups, or parts of groups, are gathered together; the Middle Eastern states, Rumania, and Yugoslavia are examples. There is no *logical*

reason why fragments of some of these should not be broken off and incorporated into the territory of their neighbors. Boundary changes during the last 100 years have been proposed and justified on the grounds that such a change is in the best interests of the people in the border region, who are said to belong naturally to the adjoining nation and state.[13] Beginning with the Ger-

---

[13] Richard Hartshorne, "A Survey of the Boundary Problems of Europe," in Charles C. Colby (ed.), *Geographical Aspects of International Relations,* University of Chicago Press, Chicago, 1938, pp. 165–166.

man annexation of Alsace-Lorraine in 1871, boundary changes have sought to achieve a closer correspondence between state and nation. It need be mentioned here only that their success has been partial, partly because there are other factors besides nationalism in claims to territory (see Chapter 9).

We may describe as *anomalous* those states whose function it is to express some other purpose than the will to statehood of a nation. The *raison d'être,* in these instances, lies outside the state. It was in the interests of outside powers that they were created: perhaps to form a buffer, as with Belgium or Jordan; perhaps to prevent the outside states themselves from fighting for possession of the area, as was the case with Albania; perhaps because the outside states could agree on no other course, as with Libya. The size of such states was usually the smallest that would satisfy the desires and the needs of the others.

Two hundred years ago the political map, at least of Europe, was dotted with minute states. Only a handful of these have survived. Even their survival is unrealistic, in so far as the financial costs of administering such small territories is high, and their citizens do not differ culturally from their neighbors. But in each case, there is a *raison d'être* strong enough to prevent such a state from being merged completely with its neighbor. As these small states do not maintain an army or conduct a foreign policy, their citizens enjoy a certain tax immunity. It is in such advantages as these, coupled with the financial advantages of being "quaint" or "old-fashioned," that their *raisons d'être* probably lie.

FEDERALISM

Thus, if any principle governing the size of states emerges, it is that they are—or try to be—at least as large as the nations which form them. If a state falls short, and part of its nation lies beyond its borders, it is likely to have an irredentist policy.[14] Since the primary objective of a state is to preserve its own culture and traditions, such aims, pursued with whatever means the state has at its command, must be regarded as normal. In the last resort, the reasons for the size of states must be sought in the fields of anthropology and linguistics; they are culture areas.

The Large State and Federalism: The argument of Rousseau that, the larger a state becomes, the greater will be both its internal variety and the problems of its administration has weight, despite modern developments in the field of communication. The federal principle is a governmental device whereby outward unity is maintained, while allowing a degree of autonomy in some fields of government to the constituent regions of the state. "Portions of mankind," wrote J. S. Mill more than a century ago, "who are not fitted or disposed to live under the same internal government, may often with advantage be federally united as to their relations with foreigners both to prevent wars among themselves, and for the sake of more effectual protection against the aggression of powerful states." [15] All large states, except China, have a federal constitution at the present time, though it could, of course, be argued that the federal constitution of some, the Soviet Union, for example, is in fact only a façade covering a unitary system. Several small states, in which there is strong regional feeling, have also adopted this practice of having a federation.

The study of federalism thus belongs to the field of political geography, because it is one of the devices by which the state

[14] So called from *Italia irredenta,* an area of northern Italy, inhabited by Italians, which lay beyond the limits of the Italian state for a period after its unification.
[15] J. S. Mill, *Considerations on Representative Government,* Oxford edition, 1948, p. 389.

is adjusted to the nation, and vice versa. A federation has been called "the most geographically expressive of all political systems." [16]

The modern federal practice began in the United States, where, after the revolt of the American Colonies, thirteen States found themselves with a common language; a material culture that did not differ greatly between them; a geographical distribution over a narrow strip of land almost 1,200 miles long; deep, local vested interests; and a distrust, born of British rule, of strong centralized government. The constitutional debates and the papers published as the *Federalist* put the whole case for and against federation: the advantages of a single foreign and commercial policy against the fear of the domination by a New York or a Philadelphia over the rest; the broad view of the coastal cities against the sectionalism of those who lived back in the Piedmont and the mountains.

The distribution of power, as between the central or federal government and the government of the States or Provinces, may reflect geographical conditions and the strength of local feeling. By the terms of the United States Constitution all governmental rights and obligations not specifically reserved to the Federal government, known as the *reserve of powers*, devolve upon the governments of the States. States' rights were thought to be well protected. It was even argued that a State could, in the last resort, secede from the Union, until a ruinous war (1861–1865) put an end to this assumption. The trend has been toward the enlargement of the sphere of the Federal government, both at the expense of the States and also by the assumption of roles which had not previously been considered as falling within the sphere of government.

[16] K. W. Robinson, "Sixty Years of Federation in Australia," *G.R.*, vol. 51, p. 1, 1961.

The Canadian experiment is, in point of time, second only to that of the United States. In the mid-nineteenth century the basic problem, apart from the great area of Canada itself, was the existence of English-speaking communities in Ontario and the Maritime Provinces separated by Quebec, distinguished by its French language, law, and institutions and its Roman Catholic faith. Lord Durham, appointed in 1838 to examine the mechanism of government in Canada and to recommend changes, at first favored a federal union of British North America but set aside this view because, in his words, he "could not doubt that any independent powers within the federation which French Canada might possess would be used against the policy and the very existence of any form of British Government." [17] In other words, he doubted that in Canada social cohesion was sufficient to provide a *raison d'être* even for a federal state. The unitary system of government that was set up to force unity upon a reluctant Canada did not prove to be successful, and in 1867 the federal constitution was adopted which, with modifications, has lasted until today.

The Canadian constitution differs sharply from the Constitution of the United States. The desire for unity among the several groups in Canada was so weak that it was feared that they might fly apart, as the Southern States had tried to do only a year or two before. On the other hand, the divergences were so great that there was no question of maintaining a unitary state. The constitution gave certain powers to the Provinces [18] but left the reserve of powers with the central organs of administration.

[17] Quoted in *The Cambridge History of the British Empire*, vol. 6, *Canada and Newfoundland*, Cambridge University Press, Cambridge, 1930, p. 303.

[18] This term, regularly used in Canada, is weaker in its meaning than the term States as used in the United States.

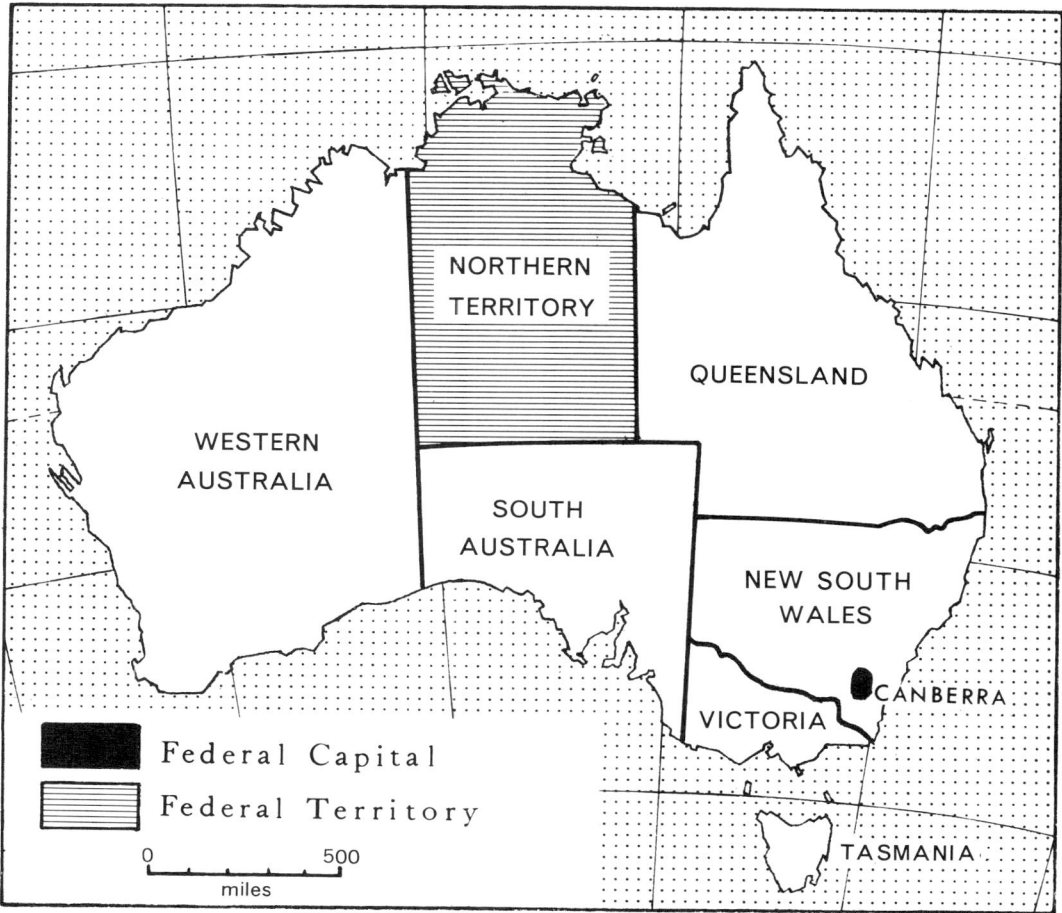

Exhibit 9 *Australia: federal divisions.*

Australia reverted to the American practice. The six States, all established as British Colonies, with populations that were predominantly English-speaking and English in culture, existed as separate political units from the date of their foundation until 1900. In that year, they came together into a federation somewhat reluctantly (Exhibit 9) and probably would not have done so then but for "the dread of danger from imperialising powers in the Pacific." [19] In consequence the federation was a weak one; the reserve of powers rested with the States, which were individually so strong that each maintained its own government agencies in London and elsewhere.

The *Union of South Africa* in 1910 formed a federation so nearly unitary in its structure that political scientists hesitate to regard it as federal at all (Exhibit 10). Only its name is suggestive of a federal structure. The reason stems, like the Canadian constitution, from the extreme complexity of the ethnic structure of the new state. There were two peoples of European origin, roughly equal in numbers and at war

[19] C. F. Strong, *Modern Political Constitutions*, Sidgwick & Jackson, Ltd., London, 1939, p. 110.

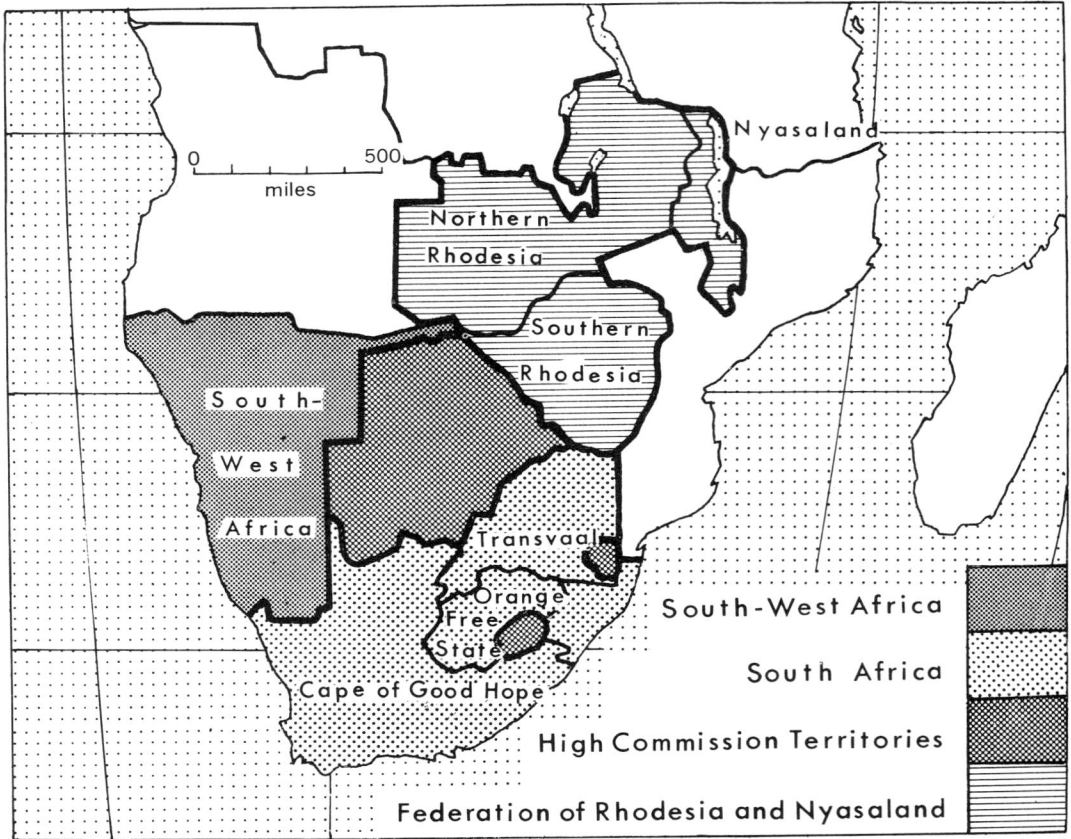

Exhibit 10 Republic of South Africa and the Federation of Rhodesia and Nyasaland.

with one another only a few years earlier, the Boers and the English; there were immigrant groups such as the Indians; and there was the African majority, itself by no means homogeneous and regarded as a standing threat to white supremacy. Some unity of policy at most levels seemed necessary, and "a true federal constitution with inalienable provincial rights was recognized to be unsuitable for South Africa." [20] The powers of the four provincial governments were listed, so that the reserve of powers

[20] J. A. Williamson, A Short History of British Expansion, Macmillan & Co., Ltd., London, 1947, vol. 2, p. 261.

rested with the central government, and the rights of the Provinces were further restricted by the constitutional enactment that "any ordinance made by a provincial council shall have effect in and for the province as long and as far only as it is not repugnant to any Act of Parliament" of the Union. The Union itself thus came to have a power of veto over the individual acts of the Provinces.

It is paradoxical that, in the four federal or quasi-federal territories considered so far, the two with the most diverse social structures, Canada and South Africa, have political systems that are the most unitary, while culturally homogeneous Aus-

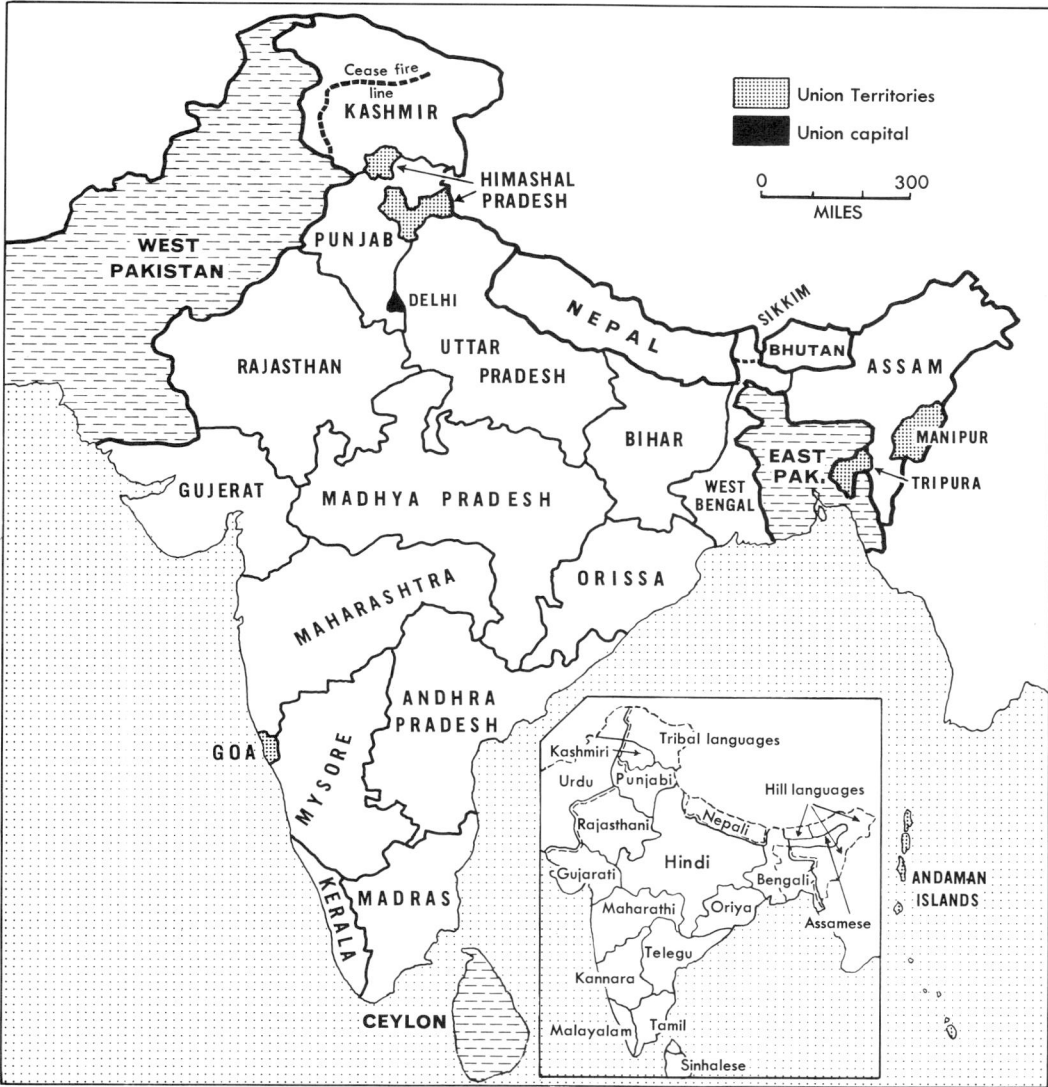

Exhibit 11   *India and Pakistan: federal divisions.*

tralia stands most firmly for "States' rights." This merely demonstrates that there is no simple equation of size and diversity with degree of federalism.

Six other states, each of a great deal more than average size, also have a federal constitution: India, Malaya, the U.S.S.R., Argentina, Brazil, and Mexico.

India is a union of fourteen States,[21] together with a number of Territories, whose nature and status are discussed below (Exhibit 11). This territorial organization derives from the highly complex structure of British India. The basis of this division into

[21] Following the reorganization of 1956; previously the Republic of India had 27 States.

Exhibit 12   Federation of Malaya.

States is substantially cultural and linguistic but is, in fact, no measure of the extreme diversity of India. It is a compromise, and most of the fourteen States have their own ethnic minorities. There is still a degree of instability in the geography of the present federation, and the State of Bombay has recently split into Gujerati-speaking and Marathi-speaking areas, and the Sikhs have demanded that the Punjab be reshaped to accord with their own pattern of distribution. The constitution reserves certain fields of government to the States but permits the central government to invade the sphere of state administration if a matter assumes a national importance or creates a national emergency. It is thus more distinctly federal than the South African constitution, but its high degree of centralization is related rather to the difficulties of administration than to the variety of cultures involved.

The *Federation of Malaya* (Exhibit 12) is made up of a number of petty states, which preserve their traditional modes of government. The presence of two compet-

ing ethnic groups, Malay and Chinese, is not reflected in the Federal Constitution (see page 43). It seems likely that Singapore will accede to the Federation, which may even be broadened to include the British possessions in Borneo.

The *Union of Soviet Socialist Republics* was established in 1922, and the member Republics were admitted during the ensuing years. There have been numerous changes in the number and the boundaries of the Republics and of the subordinate regions, which stand lower in political status. At present (1960), there are 15 Republics and 10 National Areas, but within the Republics themselves there are 28 more autonomous areas (Exhibit 13).[22] The Republics and autonomous areas were planned to accord geographically with the ethnic groups of the Soviet Union; the autonomous areas, most of which are within the Russian S.S.R., are, in fact, the sparsely peopled areas of numerous small ethnic groups. The constitution of 1936 lists the fields of governmental activity which belong to the central government, so that theoretically the reserve of powers resides in the member Republics. But there is undoubtedly a wide gap between the theory and the practice of the constitution, and the amount of real power that has been left to most of the autonomous areas, despite recent moves to "decentralize," is probably small. The Union Republics, nevertheless, appear to have a considerable administrative power.

The constitution of the Soviet Union provides for two elected bodies for the federation as a whole. The Soviet of the Union consists of one deputy for each 300,000 of the population; the Soviet of Nationalities is made up of delegations from each of the autonomous areas and regions of the Soviet Union. The general resemblance to the

[22] These are made up of 19 autonomous Republics and 9 autonomous regions.

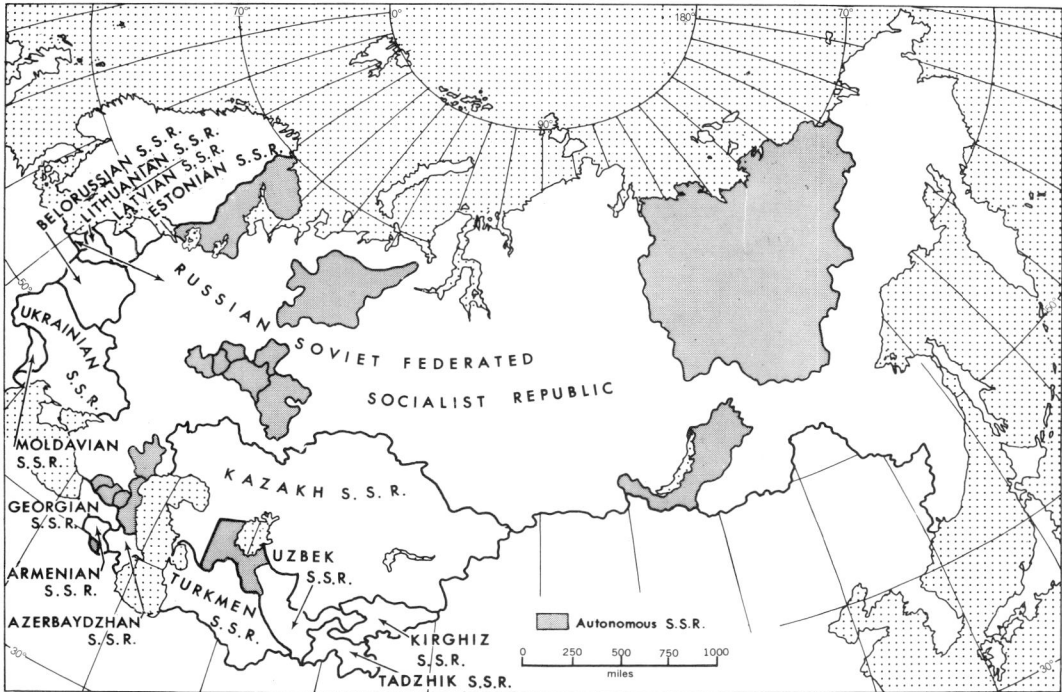

Exhibit 13 *The Soviet Union.*

two-house structure in many other federations is apparent, though it can be argued that the representation of the nationalities of the Soviet Union has in fact little meaning or significance.

The largest of the Union Republics, the Russian, has itself a federal constitution within that of the Soviet Union as a whole and is made up of a large number of units, consisting of (1) six territories, (2) forty-nine regions, (3) fifteen autonomous Soviet Socialist Republics, (4) six autonomous regions, and (5) ten national areas. Each, in this array of minor political units, has certain political privileges and functions, but probably here, even more than in the U.S.S.R. itself, something more than a reserve of powers resides at the center.

Three republics of Latin America, *Argentina, Brazil* (Exhibit 14), and *Mexico*, also have federal constitutions, all in some degree based on the Constitution of the United States. In all, except Mexico, the reserve of powers rests with the Provinces, but in none has the constitution ever functioned smoothly, and dictators have gen-

Exhibit 14 *The United States of Brazil.*

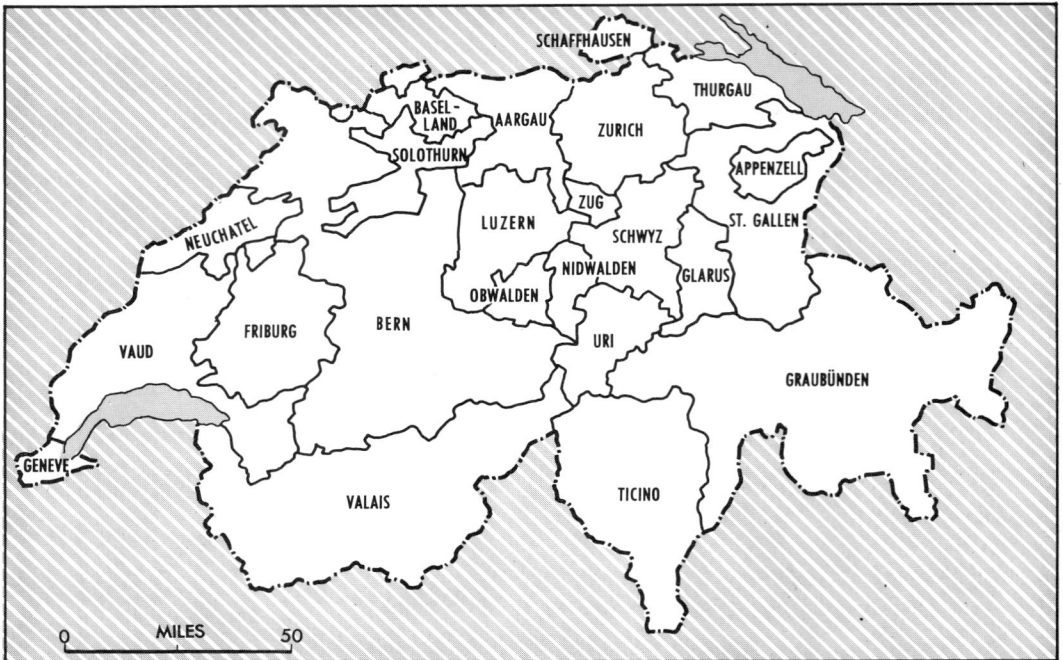

Exhibit 15   *The Swiss Confederation.*

erally gathered at the center greater power than the constitution had provided.

Three very much smaller countries also have federal constitutions: Switzerland, West Germany, and Yugoslavia. In each, the present constitution can be understood only in terms of the country's history. The *Swiss Confederation* (Exhibit 15) grew out of a loose alliance of cantons which originated in 1291 with the union of the four "Forest Cantons" in self-defense.[23] The *raison d'être* of the Confederation was, from the start, the profit derived by its members from the lucrative trans-Alpine trade. The Confederation, a term reserved for federal organizations of a very loose order, grew, reaching approximately its present limits by the mid-sixteenth century. Switzerland, in origin the loosest possible form of federation, gradually acquired a

[23] These were Uri, Schwyz, and Ob- and Nidwalden.

tighter organization. This was made necessary by the tensions and pressures of the modern world. The attempt of some of the cantons to secede led in 1848 to the acceptance of a federal constitution in place of the earlier Confederation. Nevertheless, the old cantonal organization of the state remains dominant. Such an organization of small, self-governing valley communities, separated from one another by spurs of the Alpine range, was a normal one for the Middle Ages. It was the cantons which fought for and achieved political independence, and around their struggles is woven the body of Swiss heroic legend. Swiss democracy is closely bound up with the cantonal system, which lies too deep in Swiss political experience to be lightly abandoned, even if, in modern political practice, it has ceased to be essential.

The *Federal Republic of Germany* (Exhibit 16) also derives from a loose ag-

glomeration of States, the German Confederation of the nineteenth century. A
federal structure was retained by its successors, the German Empire (1871–1918)
and the Weimar Republic (1919–1933). A
unitary system was established by Hitler,
but in 1949 West Germany regained both
its federal constitution and, a few years
later, its sovereignty. The federal government has prescribed rights and duties, and
the reserve of powers resides in the 10
Länder. The constitution provides for the
inclusion of Berlin as an eleventh *Land*,
but this clause is at present inoperative.
This federal organization is capable of being extended to embrace the territory of
the German Democratic Republic, or East
Germany.

In Germany, as in Switzerland, the federal structure of government is explained
by historical tradition rather than geographical diversity. Regional feeling is
quite strongly marked, but probably no
more so than in many unitary states such
as France and Great Britain.

The *Federal People's Republic of Yugoslavia* (Exhibit 17), to give it its official
name, was created after the Second World
War. The Yugoslav state was established
in 1919 as a unitary state comprising a
variety of related peoples—Serbs, Croats,
Slovenes—together with smaller communities of Germans, Bulgarians, Albanians,

Exhibit 16   *The Federal German Republic.*

and others. The first constitution played
down the social variety and, after it had
failed conspicuously to cope with the diverse ethnic groups, was superseded in
1939 by a federal constitution, which did
much to satisfy the national claims of at
least the Croats. The constitution of 1953
modified the geographical arrangements of
its predecessor and created six Republics,
each corresponding with one of the major
cultural groups, and two autonomous areas,
the Vojvodina and Kosovo-Metohija, in
each of which there was considerable cultural diversity. It claimed considerable autonomy for the six Republics but failed to
define clearly the fields in which this au-

Exhibit 17   *The Federal People's Republic of Yugoslavia.*

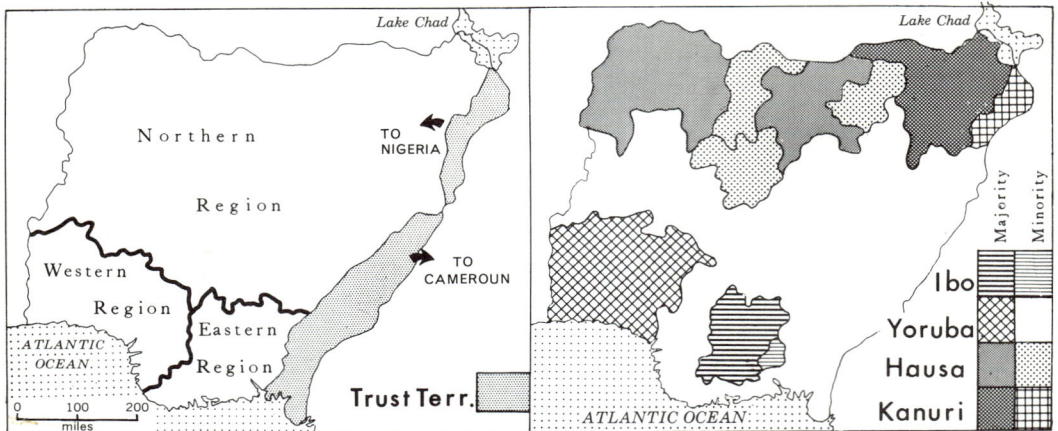

Exhibit 18   *The Federation of Nigeria.*

tonomy might operate. It appears that Yugoslav federalism, which is in keeping with the geographical diversity of the country, is nevertheless little more than the façade for a highly unitary Communist state. It should be added, too, that the experience of Yugoslavia during the Second World War has done much to create a Yugoslav feeling.

The *Federation of Nigeria* (Exhibit 18) is the most recent of sovereign federations. It has four federated regions, together with a federal capital in Lagos. The divisions are adjusted to the considerable ethnic and cultural diversities of Nigeria.

To this list should be added several territories, which do not yet enjoy complete political independence and are thus not states by our definition. The first is the Federation of Rhodesia and Nyasaland, established by the union in 1953 of three separate colonies.[24] The Federation is a loose one. Certain powers are vested in the federal government, but a large reserve of powers remains with the three territories. The second is the Federation of the West Indies, formed in 1958 by the union of ten

[24] Southern Rhodesia and the Protectorates of Northern Rhodesia and Nyasaland.

islands or island groups, but internal rivalries and fears—particularly the jealousies of the two largest units, Jamaica and Trinidad—appear to have postponed indefinitely the realization of a sovereign, federal state. In 1953 the East Africa High Commission was constituted for Kenya, Tanganyika, and Uganda. The Commission is charged with administering certain services which are common to the three, but a federation of the three is not contemplated, and Tanganyika has (December, 1961) gained independence.

A feature of many federal states is the presence within their borders of areas either economically backward or inhabited by ethnic groups unsuited to that degree of autonomy accorded to the States of any particular Union. In the United States there is the status of Territory, in which a politically organized area serves apprenticeship before being admitted to the Union. Australia has its Northern Territory and Canada its Yukon Territory and Northwest Territories, all of them sparsely populated and underdeveloped. India has its Union Territories, mainly backward and mountainous areas along its Himalayan frontier. Brazil has a number of federal territories and one federal district, and Argentina a single federal district. The Soviet Union has a hierarchy of autonomous territories and regions, each supposedly adjusted to the cultural and political level of its inhabitants. Lastly, Yugoslavia has similar areas in the Vojvodina and Kosovo-Metohija, each inhabited by a population with little social cohesion.

Federal states, unless they border on the unitary system, have a geographical problem in the location of their federal capital. Jealousies between the federated units, in many instances, prevent it from being located *on* the territory of one of them, though this has had to be done in every case until a federal capital district could be created by some kind of compromise. The establishment of Washington, D.C., is typical of the process. The District of Columbia, purchased from the State of Maryland, is federally owned and belongs to no single state. As a further guarantee of its lack of political bias, its citizens were placed outside the political mechanism of the States themselves and enjoy no direct political representation.

This model was followed by Australia, which in 1911 acquired from the State of New South Wales the territory of Canberra, on which, since 1923, a federal capital has been built. The capital of the United States of Brazil has hitherto been in Rio de Janeiro, which constitutes a federal district detached from the State of Rio de Janeiro. In 1956 it was decided to create a new federal capital, to be called Brasilia, on a tract of land acquired by the federal government for this purpose far in the interior of the State.

New Delhi had been established by the British as the capital of the politically and geographically complex Dominion of India. It was retained as the federal capital of the Republic of India and in 1956 was created a Union Territory outside the jurisdiction of the State of Uttar Pradesh, in which it lies.

In other instances, the federal constitution provides for a federal capital distinct from the State capitals—the Canadian at Ottawa; the Pakistan first at Karachi and now at Islamabad, to the northeast of Rawalpindi; the South African fragmented between Capetown, Pretoria, and Bloemfontein—but does not provide for its political separation from the State in which it lies. Generally speaking, the federal capital is located *outside* the States in those cases where the constitution leaves the greatest political power in the hands of the States themselves.

Table 2 lists the federal states existing at present, together with the number of constituent units and territories, generally underdeveloped or ethnically very complex, which are in some degree controlled by the federation as a whole.

Local Autonomy: What other ways are there of adjusting the state area to the varying cultural and other groups which make up its population? Federalism on the Australian model stops only a little short of the re-creation of six unitary states. The four South African Provinces are so unitary as to cease to be a federation. The establishment within a unitary state of provinces, within each of which the administration is adjusted to the local social or geographical conditions, does not constitute a federation. The central administration of the state creates these local immunities and is free to change them (Exhibit 19). The People's Republic of China, which is by far the largest unitary state in the world, adopted such a practice rather than resort to federalism on the Soviet model. The constitution of 1954 declared that:

1. All the nationalities are equal . . . and have freedom to use and develop their

spoken and written languages, and to preserve or reform their habits and customs.

2. Regional autonomy shall be applied in areas compactly inhabited by national minorities. National autonomous areas are inalienable parts of the People's Republic of China.

The decision to create such an autonomous area for, let us say, Tibet or Inner Mongolia is entirely a matter for the central government in Peking. The Spanish Republic, during its brief career from 1931 to 1939, granted home rule to Cataluña (1931) and the Basque area (1932) in order to satisfy the strongly expressed desires for autonomy in these Provinces. With the triumph of Franco's rebellion and the imposition of his dictatorship, a strongly unitary system was restored, and the privileges of the Basques and the Catalans were terminated.

TABLE 2   *Federal States*

State	Area, sq miles	Population, 1959	Reserve of powers	Federal territory Units [1]	Federal territory Area	Federal capital Name	Federal capital In federal territory
Argentina	1,079,965	20,614,000	States	. . .	. . . .	Buenos Aires	No
Australia	2,974,581	10,061,235	States	1	523,620	Canberra	Yes
Brazil	3,288,240	64,216,000	States	5	294,735	Rio de Janeiro	No
						Brasilia	Yes
Canada	3,887,878	17,442,000	Federal	2	1,458,784	Ottawa	No
Congo	905,144	13,821,000	[4]	. . .	. . . .	Léopoldville	No
Ethiopia	395,000	21,800,000	States	. . .	. . . .	Addis Ababa	No
Germany, West	95,735	52,785,000	States	. . .	. . . .	Bonn	No
India	1,220,000	402,600,000	[2]	5	27,162	New Delhi	Yes
Malaya	50,690	6,698,000	. . . .	. . .	. . . .	Kuala Bumpur	No
Mexico	760,375	33,304,000	States	2	47,397	Mexico City	Yes
Nigeria	373,250	33,663,000	States	. . .	. . . .	Lagos	Yes
Pakistan	361,007	86,823,000	. . . .	. . .	. . . .	Karachi-Islamabad	Yes
Switzerland	15,944	5,240,000	. . . .	. . .	. . . .	Bern	No
U.S.A.	3,554,634	177,700,000	. . . .	5	4,196	Washington	Yes
U.S.S.R.	8,708,070	210,500,000	. . . .	[3]	. . . .	Moscow	No
Yugoslavia	99,000	18,448,000	. . . .	2	12,534	Beograd	No

[1] Excluding federal capitals.

[2] The constitution is so complex that it is impossible to say in simple terms where the reserve of powers is.

[3] Such units are parts of the federated Republics.

Indonesia was a federal state from 1949 to 1950, and Venezuela until 1953. Federations which are not at present wholly self-governing are Rhodesia and Nyasaland and the Federation of South Arabia. Yemen was for a time in a very loose federation with the United Arab Republic.

The Federation of the West Indies broke up when Jamaica and Trinidad and Tobago refused to remain in it after independence.

[4] The political situation in the Congo is at present too chaotic for such precision to be possible.

Italy, faced with similar problems, has also adopted the expedient of limited home rule in certain provinces. The Valle d'Aosta, with its French-speaking population; the Trentino–Alto Adige (South Tyrol), with its German-speaking population; Friuli–Venezia Giulia, with its mixed Italian-Slovene population; and Sicily and Sardinia, where the problems are constituted not so much by linguistic minorities as by distance from the capital, backwardness, and a regional outlook—each has been granted a degree of independence by the central government (Exhibit 20).

Other states which have similarly accorded some degree of autonomy, however modest, to a distinctive part of their territory include the *United Kingdom*, which has conferred extensive home-rule privileges on the six counties of Northern Ireland. In several ways Scotland is politically distinct from England, and its interests are represented in the Cabinet by a Minister of State for Scottish Affairs. Public law and the system of education are distinctive, but Scotland has no system that could possibly be called "home rule."

The *Aaland Islands*, which were awarded to Finland by the Permanent Court of International Justice after a dispute with Sweden, have been constituted an autonomous county by Finland. In Burma, the Shan, Kachin, Karen, and Kayah States, together with the Chin area, have a high degree of local autonomy. Their area covers a large proportion of the mountainous north and northeast of Burma and is inhabited mainly by tribes which are culturally distinct from the Burmese. The Iranian Provinces of Kurdistan and Baluchistan (not to be confused with the Pakistan Province of the same name) have limited degrees of self-government.

Related to this question of home rule is that of extraterritoriality, the principle by which certain persons and places are

Exhibit 19   *The autonomous areas of China.*
AFTER GEORGE B. CRESSEY

conceived of as being outside the territory of the state in which they live. The most important group enjoying extraterritorial rights today is made up of ambassadors, consuls, and their staffs, that is, those who possess diplomatic immunity. The precise distribution of their territorial immunities cannot be claimed to have geographical

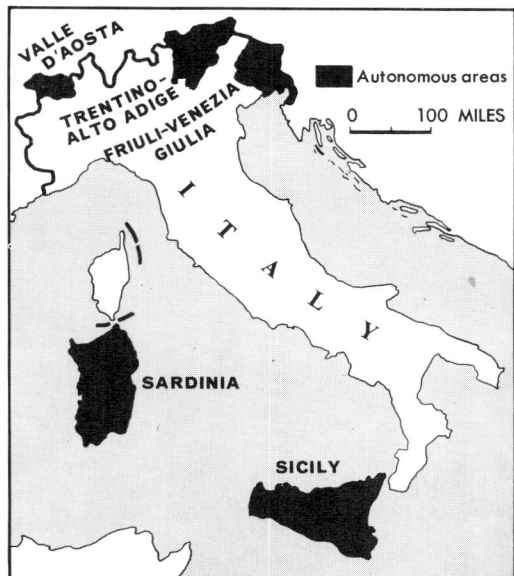

Exhibit 20   *The autonomous areas of Italy.*

significance, and its examination is omitted. On the other hand, the extraterritorial rights of certain national groups were formerly geographically important. Several countries obtained for their nationals extraterritorial rights in China, and similar rights were once common in other Asiatic and in some African territories.[25] All such rights have now been rescinded, but they were formerly important geographically, because certain European states acquired *power* through the activities of such privileged persons within the territory of another state but outside the scope of its laws.

THE SHAPE OF THE STATE AREA

The geometrical shape of a state presents problems only a degree less acute than those raised by its geographical extent. Ideally, it has been claimed, a state should be circular in plan, though no state is or could be of so regular a geometrical form. One can only say that states are compact or the reverse, and the only possible measure of this is the length of the boundary in relation to the area. Such a calculation presents difficulties and has not been made for more than a few states. Table 3 gives some examples, which may be taken to represent the extremes.

Lack of compactness is politically significant only in so far as it increases the variety of social groups and physical environments, adds to the difficulties of travel and communications, and increases the length of boundary to be guarded. It is not difficult to think of countries whose unusual shape has added to their political and administrative problems. Chile and Norway are cases in point. Neither has a railroad which runs the whole length of its

[25] L. Oppenheim, *International Law*, H. Lauterpacht (ed.), Longmans, Green and Co., London, 1937, vol. 1, pp. 542–545.

TABLE 3. *Index of Compactness of States*

State	*Length of boundary as percentage of the minimum boundary* [1]
Uruguay	105
Rumania	137
Hungary	146
Switzerland	164
Belgium	167
Mexico	258
Chile	310

[1] Calculated by taking the length of boundary as a percentage of the shortest boundary (i.e., a circle) which could enclose the area of the state.

territory. Norway has an all-weather road, but not Chile. Both have to rely heavily on a somewhat uncertain coastal shipping, and Chile has been obliged to relax its tariff regulations for its most northerly Province and its three most southerly. The great west-to-east extension of Czechoslovakia, coupled with the existence of mountain barriers, has hindered communications and contributed to the separatist feelings of Slovakia. The most westerly and most isolated Province of Austria, Vorarlberg, once tried to secede and join the Swiss Confederation.

It is easy to enumerate examples of oddly shaped territories, "peninsulas" of one state intruding into the territory of another. Most of these have no political significance. The narrow extension of South-West Africa up to the Zambezi River, Caprivi's Finger (Exhibit 21) as it is often called, is now merely a curious cartographic relic of Germany's imperial ambitions of 1890. The Alaska Panhandle derives from Russian imperialist claims of the first half of the nineteenth century and cuts some Canadians off from direct access to the Pacific Ocean. Shape probably has today a diminishing importance as the means of overcoming distance and physical barriers become available. Four problems related to the shape and the physical geog-

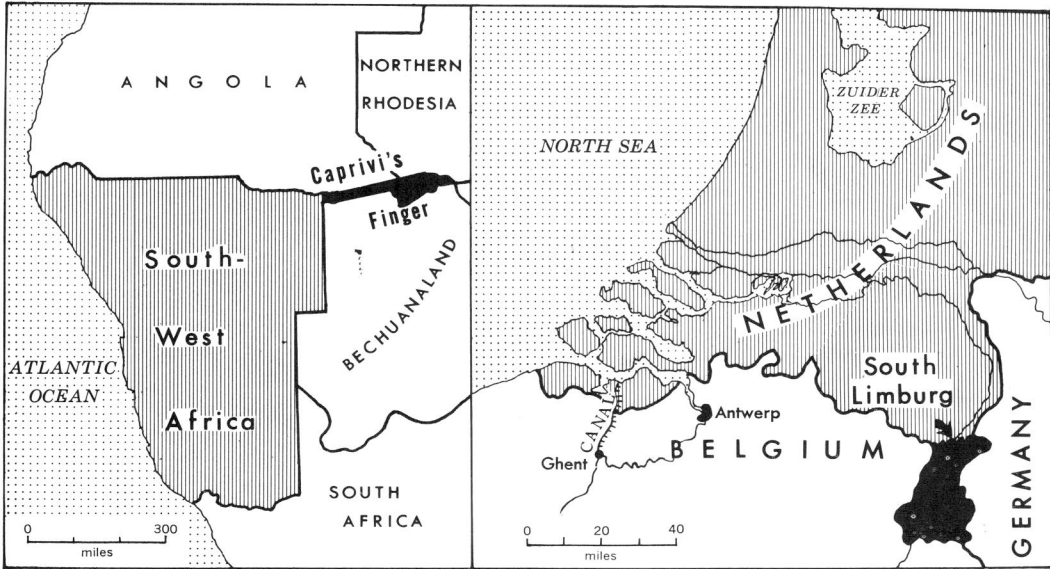

Exhibit 21 *The Limburg Appendix and Caprivi's Finger.*

raphy of a state deserve a fuller discussion. They are:

The Divided State: "The possession of an uninterrupted territory is one of the principal requisites for the smooth functioning of a political entity." [26] Yet a number of states are divided in some way. The extreme case is the division of Pakistan into West and East Pakistan, which are, at their nearest points, separated by nearly 900 miles of Indian territory. The two are accessible to one another by ship, but the distance by sea between the ports of Karachi and Chittagong is about 3,000 miles. This fact alone has necessitated a federal constitution; it has increased immeasurably the defense problems and weakened seriously the homogeneity of the state, because the journey from one part to the other necessitates expensive foreign travel. Furthermore, the northern boundary of East Pakistan approaches so close to the Hima-

[26] G. W. S. Robinson, "West Berlin: The Geography of an Exclave," *G.R.*, vol. 43, p. 540, 1953.

layan State of Nepal that the Indian State of Assam is joined to the rest of India only by a very narrow corridor, some 15 miles wide, across very difficult terrain. Assam has, in fact, to be approached from the rest of India *across* East Pakistan, though India is now constructing improved transportation facilities through this "gap."

From 1919 to 1939, the Province of East Prussia had been separated from Germany by the so-called Polish "Corridor." Though every consideration was, in this case, given to German transit traffic, the separation of East Prussia from the rest of Germany was greatly resented by some Germans. It cannot be said, however, that it significantly weakened administration, and, through the propaganda use that was made of it, it may actually have served to intensify national feeling in Germany.

Alaska is separated from the continental United States by Canada, though it must be added that most of the traffic between them would go by sea in any case. Panama is divided into two approximately

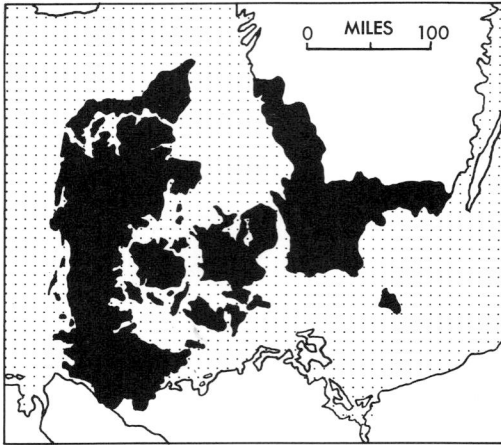

Exhibit 22   The medieval Danish sea state.

equal parts by the Canal Zone. There are a few instances of very unequal division of state territory. In Europe, there are four minute outliers—exclaves, as they are called—of Spain, Italy, Belgium, and Germany, respectively. Each is under ten square miles in area, and none has a popu- of over fifteen hundred.[27] They "are not important phenomena in political geography," and it has been their lack of significance that has permitted them to continue to exist. None of the four countries concerned functions with appreciably less efficiency because a minute fraction of its territory lies detached and embedded in the territory of another. Such problems as they present are important chiefly for their local population, and these may gain more than they lose as the result of the immunity conferred by distance.

The few examples that have been cited of territorially divided states are all that remain of the much greater number that formerly existed. The territories of the West European countries, in particular, formerly interpenetrated one another to a formidable degree, but most of these irregularities have been eliminated.

[27] Ibid.

The Sea State: Another kind of territorial division remains very important, that effected by arms and gulfs of the sea. No less than twenty of the sovereign states of the world are made up of either islands or a stretch of the continental mainland with a fringe of offshore islands.[28] The latter are sometimes close inshore, as with Chile and Norway; sometimes they lie at considerable distances from the mainland, as with Italy, Greece, and, of course, the United States. The significance of such "sea states" was formerly much greater than it is today.[29] A glance at a historical atlas will show that the city-states of classical Greece formed an alliance which lay *around* the coasts of the Aegean Sea. The early medieval kingdom of Denmark (Exhibit 22) was partly in England, partly in Denmark, and later Denmark covered not only the Danish peninsula and islands but also southern Sweden. The Anglo-Norman kingdom covered southern England and northern France, and medieval Aragon embraced many of the islands of the western Mediterranean and, temporarily at least, the island of Sicily.

The rise of these sea states is not hard to understand. They developed at a time when movement, especially of merchandise, was difficult by land but relatively easy by sea. Their economy was based on seaborne trade; their political expansion was by sea; and their civilization was carried by their ships. The sea, so often regarded as a highly desirable frontier, became a bond of union. More recently, Sweden came to dominate the Baltic Sea, and during the present century the island state of Japan has expanded in the same way, controlling the opposite coasts of Korea and China and turning the interven-

[28] This, of course, excludes colonial dependencies.
[29] H. C. Darby, "The Medieval Sea-state," *S.G.M.*, vol. 47, pp. 136–149, 1932.

ing sea into a Japanese lake. But the sea state has long been in decline in Europe. The French drove the English from their foothold in northern France; Germans and Russians drove the Swedes from their many bases on the southern and eastern shores of the Baltic Sea; and, most recently of all, Japan has lost all her possessions on the Asiatic mainland and is again restricted to the Japanese islands. Such sea states as appear on the map today are relics, like exclaves, of an earlier and more widespread phenomenon. Today, states which spread over an island group—Denmark, Philippines, Indonesia, Japan, even the United Kingdom—are under a considerable handicap. Ferries, sometimes costly to operate and always liable to interruption, are not generally sufficient to overcome the social barrier created by a few miles of sea.

Physical Barriers within the State: Within any state, the degree of unity and ease of administration are influenced by the terrain and the resulting difficulty or ease of travel. On the political map, Ecuador appears as a compact state of medium size. In reality, it is divided into three almost equal physical regions, the plain along the Pacific Coast, the ranges and high plateaus of the Andes, and the plains which slope down in the east toward the Amazon. The three have never been integrated. The last is difficult of access and sparsely peopled. The Pacific coastal plain and the Andes differ markedly in climate and resources and are inhabited, by and large, by two different racial groups, the Mestizo and the Indian. "Communications over the high passes of the Andes are extremely difficult, and in the forested lowlands only the rivers provide routes of travel." [30] In consequence, the states of Colombia and Peru have been able to annex fragments of Ecuadorian territory in recent years.

Ecuador is an extreme case of the dis-

[30] Preston E. James, *Latin America*, London, Cassell and Co., 1942, p. 134.

ruptive influence of physical geography within even a small state. The other Andean states differ only in the degree to which relief and climate hinder the formation of unified states. In Europe, the relief, no less than the shape, of Norway has hindered the development of internal communications and necessitated a strong local government structure. The federal constitution of Switzerland is a concession to the strongly marked relief and its influence on social groupings. The barrier of hill and mountain which encloses the central tableland (meseta) of Spain, while it does not impose any great limitations on travel, does, nevertheless, create areas of sparse population and, thus, weakens social intercourse between the coastal regions and the interior. The strongly marked centrifugal tendencies in the Iberian peninsula have already been noted.

Relief influences the ease and economy of railroad building and, thus, the facility of communications. In Great Britain it is almost impossible to travel by train from the south of Wales to the north. The rail-

Figure 8 A consequence of the division of Denmark by arms of the sea is the need for an elaborate system of ferries. Here a car ferry, which crosses the Great Belt, is seen backing into the dock at Nyborg, on the island of Fyn. PHOTOGRAPH BY N. J. G. POUNDS

roads have an approximately east-to-west orientation, following the valleys, and when Welshmen have to meet, they often find it most convenient for all to gather in England. In every country, it is easy to show how political union would have been helped if man could have changed the alignment of mountains or the direction of flow of rivers. Even plain states, such as Hungary and Poland, have their physical barriers to communication and movement, for the scale of such obstacles is entirely relative.

The State as a Natural Unit: Political theorists of the eighteenth century argued that there was a right and proper limit to the size of states. This argument was combined with the teleological view which held that, since the habitable earth was conceived and created as the home of man, all elements in its surface relief must combine for his good. Man is, as the ancient Greeks believed and political thinkers have since generally agreed, a political animal who finds his fullest expression through the state. Therefore, a framework for the establishment and territorial extent of states should be implicit in the relief and drainage patterns and in other aspects of the physical landscape. As an American Congressman [*] declared early in the nineteenth century, "The Father of the Universe, in his peculiar providence, had given natural boundaries to every continent and kingdom —permanent, physical imperishable barriers, to every nation, to shield it from invasion. . . ." The French political writers of the early eighteenth century argued that each state has its "natural limits," which it should strive to attain but never to exceed.[31] In the words of Rousseau, "The lie of the mountains, seas and rivers which

serve as frontiers for the various nations who people it [i.e., Europe], seems to have fixed forever their number and their size. We may fairly say that the political order of the continent is, in some sense, the work of nature."[32] In the debate in the French National Convention regarding the incorporation of Savoy (see page 31), the question was apparently settled by reference to this principle. A speaker in the debate declared that "Before considering whether you should . . . incorporate it [i.e., Savoy] in the French Republic, you should consult the Law of Nature and see what it permits and requires in this respect. . . ." The Law of Nature, needless to say, permitted France to incorporate Savoy: "Ceaselessly the Alps have been forcing it into the realm of France, and the natural order would be violated if France and Savoy were not united."[33]

Not dissimilar arguments were used in the United States where the idea of "manifest destiny" was an expression of the dogma "that America's incorporation of all adjacent lands was the virtually inevitable fulfilment of a moral mission delegated to the nation by Providence itself."[34] The continued British occupation of Canada led Samuel Adams to claim for the United States "what Nature designs we should have," that is, Canada itself,[35] and Senator Jackson, who also seems to have had inside knowledge, asserted that "God and nature have destined New Orleans and the Floridas to belong to this great and rising empire."[36] Again, Congressman Trimble declared to the Sixteenth Congress in even more sweeping terms that "The great Engineer of the Universe has fixed the natural

[*] Albert K. Weinberg (see Bibliography).

[31] Baron de Montesquieu, *L'Esprit des lois,* book X, chap. 9. A similar argument appears in John Locke, *An Essay Concerning the True Original Extent and End of Civil Government,* 1690, chap. 16.

[32] C. E. Vaughan (ed.), *The Political Writings of Rousseau,* Cambrige University Press, Cambridge, 1915, vol. 1, pp. 365–387.

[33] *Moniteur,* vol. 14, p. 587, 1792.

[34] Albert K. Weinberg, *Manifest Destiny,* The Johns Hopkins Press, Baltimore, 1935, pp. 1–2.

[35] Quoted by Weinberg, *ibid.,* p. 22.

[36] *Ibid.,* p. 47.

limits of our country, and man cannot change them. . . ." [37] Congressman Trimble, unhappily, was wrong, and the political geographical system is not so simple. The earth's surface is not made up of cells or compartments into each of which a state could, and should, be fitted. Nevertheless, we have heard this claim made often enough. The government of the Irish Republic denounces the partition of the "natural" unit, the island of Ireland. Franco has been known to claim that the Iberian peninsula was created to be a political unit. Nehru denounced the creation of the state of Pakistan, separate from India, because the huge area enclosed between the Kirthar, Sulaiman, and Himalayan ranges and the sea was a natural unit.

River basins were in several cases regarded as such natural units. On many occasions, it seemed proper to locate boundaries along the high ground which separates such basins. Thus, the boundary of the United States was defined in 1783 as following the "divide" betwen the streams which flow to the Atlantic and those which flow to the St. Lawrence. Similarly, when the Louisiana Territory was purchased in 1803, a claim was made to much of what is now Texas, because "that possession is understood as extending into the interior country, to the sources of the rivers . . . to all their branches, and the country they covered." [38]

It is interesting to note how some of the people who, thus, proposed a doctrine of what has been called "geographical predestination" were equally insistent on the rights of peoples to have governments of their own choice. The geographical pattern of nations does not and probably never has agreed with that of "natural" units. The assertion of J. G. Herder in the late eighteenth century, that nature had "separated nationalities by woods, mountains, seas and

deserts," [39] is wholly contrary to the facts. As we have already seen, the tendency for at least a century has been to make the state accord with the nation, not with some arbitrarily chosen framework in physical geography.

LOCATION

The geographical location of a state, as distinct from its shape and size, is significant in two ways. The first is its *absolute* location in relation to the terrestrial globe, which influences in particular its climate. The second is its location *relative* to other states. Early writers on politics often laid particular stress on the former. Plato wrote in the *Laws* that "we must not fail to notice that some districts are naturally superior to others for the breeding of men of a good or bad type." [40] "Soft countries," wrote Herodotus, "invariably breed soft men. . . . The Persians elected to live as an imperial people in a rough country rather than to cultivate the lowlands as some other nation's slaves." [41] The early Greek medical writer, Hippocrates, was even more precise when he wrote: "The deficiency of spirit and courage observable in the human inhabitants of Asia has for its principal cause the low margin of seasonal variability in temperature of that continent, which is approximately stable through the year. . . ." [42]

Such views were firmly held by the ancient writers [43] and continued to be accepted by most medieval and many modern writers. Jean Bodin, writing toward the

[37] 16th Cong., 1st Sess., pp. 1762, 1768.
[38] Quoted by Weinberg, *op. cit.*, p. 51.

[39] J. G. Herder, *Sämtliche Werke,* Herder Weidmann, Berlin, vol. 13, p. 341.
[40] Plato, *Collected Works,* Oxford University Press, vol. 5, p. 747.
[41] Herodotus, *History,* Book IX, chap. 122.
[42] Hippocrates, *Influences of Atmosphere, Water, and Situation,* chap. 16.
[43] Arnold J. Toynbee, *Greek Historical Thought from Homer to the Age of Heraclitus,* J. M. Dent & Sons, Ltd., London, 1924.

end of the sixteenth century, remarked that "northern peoples excel in bodily physical strength, southern peoples in craft and genius. Climate being most favorable between these extremes, the middle peoples are best adapted to control politics. . . ." Montesquieu wrote similarly in the eighteenth century: "One should not be astonished that the weakness of the inhabitants of warm climates should make them slaves, and the courage of those in cold climates should keep them free. This is a result of natural conditions." [44] Political power is by this argument clearly related to climate and, through climate, to geographical location. In case one should regard such views as belonging entirely to a past age, it should be pointed out that they have continued to find expression, despite their manifest extravagances, by such writers as Ellsworth Huntington [45] and S. F. Markham. [46]

Those who have tried to explain the rise of civilization and the location of power in terms of climate have had to face the fact that civilizations, however defined, have developed at some time or other in most climatic zones and that neither political wisdom nor political power has ever been a monopoly of the Temperate Zone. Huntington has tried to resolve this problem by assuming that the climate has changed; Markham, by asserting that man's accumulating technical skills have allowed him to cope with climates more and more adverse. Neither succeeds, and the basic hypotheses of all the climatic determinists can be proved to be unfounded. This is not to claim, however, that climate has no

[44] Baron de Montesquieu, *L'Esprit des lois,* book XVII, chap. 2.

[45] Ellsworth Huntington in his *Civilization and Climate,* Yale University Press, New Haven, Conn., 1924, gives the best expression of his views.

[46] S. F. Markham, *Climate and the Energies of Nations,* Oxford University Press, New York, 1942.

influence—merely to suggest that its influence is neither regular nor predictable.

Relative Location: This is a vastly more significant factor in the power of states. The study of the political map shows their immensely complicated and interlocking shapes. We have already looked, from the inside, at some of the problems raised by these shapes. It is necessary, now, to examine their influence on the relations between states. A prolongation of territory, or "panhandle," of state A may separate state B from state C, or it may cut state D off from the sea or from access to a navigable river or to a source of some much needed raw material. When the boundaries of a state are determined or altered, the primary consideration, at least during the present century, has been nationalism, the political aspirations of its peoples. But in almost every instance, there has had to be some compromise with the factor of relative location. The locational disadvantages of a boundary, based entirely on ethnic or linguistic considerations, have been compensated for by establishing "corridors," free zones, transit rights, etc. Only too often these do some violence to the national hopes of neighboring peoples. The claim of an inland state to an outlet to the sea, regardless of the cost to neighboring states, is an example that will be discussed in Chaper 9.

It must suffice here to examine a few examples of the ways in which some states, by virtue of their geographical location, block the legitimate aspirations of others. The map shows the Province of Limburg, a southward extension of the territory of the Netherlands. Before 1815, the Netherlands included a number of exclaves in this area, but in 1815 these were joined to the main area of the Netherlands by the cession of the intervening areas of Belgian (then Austrian) territory. The Province of Limburg, thus created, reached from the plains of the Netherlands into the hills which make up southern Belgium. Belgium is not completely separated from Germany, but it was impossible to cut a low-level canal from central Belgium to the river Rhine in Germany without crossing the Dutch territory of Limburg (Exhibit 21). By the Treaty of Versailles (1919), Germany was obliged to facilitate the construction of such a canal if the Belgian government desired it. For technical reasons, it could not be constructed *around* the southern end of Limburg, and the Dutch government refused to allow it to be cut *across* Limburg.

This is a simple example of the effects of the location of one country on the relations between two others. It was, in a sense, accidental that Limburg intervened between Belgium and Germany. A number of states have, on the other hand, been deliberately created or maintained for the purpose of separating two other countries. These are often known as *buffer* states, and they have played an important role in modern political geography.

Buffer States: Such states have been defined as "small political units located between large nations. They survive because they separate states that would otherwise be powerful neighbors and because the attempt to conquer them would be met, not by the relatively weak resistance of the buffer, but by the much stronger opposition of the other neighbor." [47] Thus, the Netherlands, Belgium, and Luxembourg have served as a buffer between France and Germany; Poland, Czechoslovakia, and Rumania, as buffers between Central Europe and the Soviet Union. This is not to suggest that these states existed only by virtue of their role as buffers, but the fact that some powers wanted them to serve as such

[47] N. J. Spykman, "Frontiers, Security and International Organization," *G.R.*, vol. 32, pp. 436–447, 1942.

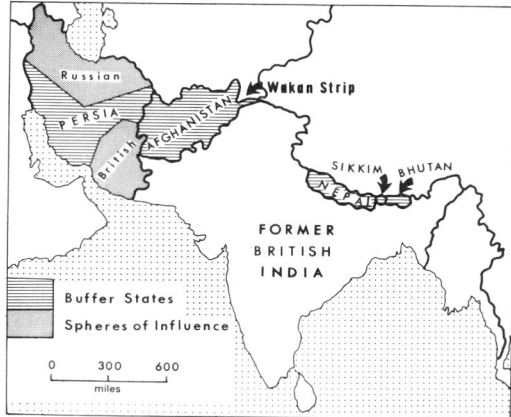

Exhibit 23   The tier of buffer states lying to the north of India and Pakistan.

enhanced their importance and allowed them to acquire more territory than they might otherwise have done.

During the nineteenth century, the British in India feared most the growing power of Czarist Russia to the north. For this reason, they created or maintained the buffer states of Iran (Persia) and Afghanistan between British territory and Russia (Exhibit 23). A long, narrow extension of Afghan territory, the Wakhan Province, stretches eastward to join up with Chinese Sinkiang. Though British-occupied territory lay within 15 miles of the Russian border, the two were never contiguous. The Himalayan States of Nepal, Sikkim, and Bhutan can be regarded as an eastward continuation of this protecting belt of buffer states.

Strategic Location: The importance of location varies with the political situation. States, or parts of states, may, under certain circumstances, acquire a strategic importance. This means that they are bases from which the sea, land, or air could be patrolled, routes protected, or an attack launched. The possession of strategic bases may protect a state or threaten its enemies. In either case, it adds to the state's power.

The value of strategic location varies with the balance of political forces and also with changes in technology. In the eighteenth century, Great Britain got possession of the Falkland Islands in the South Atlantic. They were then of strategic importance, because they dominated the sea route around the southern tip of South America, and they played an important part in the destruction of the German fleet of Von Spee in 1914. But the opening of the Panama Canal in that year quickly reduced the importance of the Cape Horn route, and now the strategic importance of the Falkland Islands is negligible.

While the importance of the Falkland Islands is diminishing, that of Iceland has been growing. As long as movement across the Atlantic was primarily by ship, Iceland lay too far north and its seas were too dangerous to be much used by transatlantic shipping. But aircraft, flying on the great-circle routes from West European to North American cities, pass close to Iceland and now regularly use its airports.

The Arctic Ocean, formerly so remote and inaccessible, is now crossed by commercial airlines. And the outer line of American defense, formerly in western Europe, the Caribbean, or the islands of the Pacific Ocean, is now along the Dew Line in the arctic wastes of northern Canada and Greenland.

BIBLIOGRAPHY

Barnett, Harold J.: "The Changing Relation of Natural Resources to National Security," *E.G.*, vol. 34, pp. 189–201, 1958.

Darby, H. C.: "The Medieval Sea-state," *S.G.M.*, vol. 47, pp. 136–149, 1932.

Geographic Reports, Office of the Geographer, Department of State, no. 2, *Major Political Entities of the World*, 1961.

Gilfillan, S. Columb: "European Political Boundaries," *Political Science Quarterly*, vol. 39, pp. 458–484, 1924.

Goblet, Y. M.: *Political Geography and the World Map*, Frederick A. Praeger, New York, 1935.

Golay, J. F.: *The Founding of the Federal Republic of Germany*, University of Chicago Press, Chicago, 1958.

Hartshorne, R.: "The Politico-geographic Pattern of the World," *Annals of the American Academy of Political and Social Science*, vol. 218, pp. 45–57, 1941.

Johnson, Robert B.: "Political Salients and Transportation Solutions," *A.A.A.G.*, vol. 39, pp. 71–72, 1949.

Morrison, John A.: "Russia and Warm Water," *United States Naval Institute Proceedings*, vol. 78, pp. 1169–1179, 1952.

Political and Strategic Interests of the United Kingdom, Royal Institute of International Affairs, Oxford University Press, Oxford, 1939.

Pounds, N. J. G.: "France and 'Les Limites Naturelles' from the Seventeenth to the Twentieth Centuries," *A.A.A.G.*, vol. 44, pp. 51–62, 1954.

Ratzel, F.: "Die Gesetze des räumlichen Wachstums der Staaten," *Petermanns Mitteilungen*, vol. 42, pp. 97–107, 1896.

Renner, George T.: "Maps for a New World," *Collier's*, vol. 109, pp. 14–16, June 6, 1942.

Robinson, E. A. G. (ed.): *Economic Consequences of the Size of Nations*, Macmillan & Co., Ltd., London, 1960.

Robinson, G. W. S.: "West Berlin: The Geography of an Exclave," *G.R.*, vol. 43, pp. 540–557, 1953.

———: "Ceuta and Melilla: Spain's Plazas de Saberaniá," *Geography*, vol. 43, pp. 266–269, 1958.

———: "Exclaves, *A.A.A.G.*, vol. 40, pp. 283–295, 1959.

Robinson, K. W.: "Sixty Years of Federation in Australia," *G.R.*, vol. 51, pp. 1–20, 1961.

Rousseau, J.-J.: *Contrat social*, in C. E. Vaughan (ed.), *The Political Writings of Rousseau*, Cambridge University Press, Cambridge, 1915.

Spykman, N. J.: "Geography and Foreign Policy," *American Political Science Review*, vol. 32, pp. 28–50, 213–236, 1938.

———: "Frontiers, Security and International

Organization," *G.R.*, vol. 32, pp. 436–447, 1942.

Strausz-Hupé, R., and Stefan T. Possony: *International Relations*, McGraw-Hill Book Company, Inc., New York, 1954.

Strong, C. F.: *Modern Political Constitutions*, Sidgwick & Jackson, Ltd., London, 1939.

Toynbee, A. J.: *Greek Historical Thought from Homer to the Age of Heraclitus*, J. M. Dent & Sons, Ltd., London, 1924; also a Mentor Book, The New American Library, New York, 1952.

Weigert, Hans, and others: *Principles of Political Geography*, Appleton-Century-Crofts, Inc., New York, 1957, part 1.

Weinberg, A. K.: *Manifest Destiny*, The Johns Hopkins Press, Baltimore, 1935.

Whittlesey, D.: *The Earth and the State*, Henry Holt and Company, New York, 1944.

3 FRONTIERS AND BOUNDARIES

Frontiers are indeed the razor's edge on which hang suspended the modern issues of war or peace, or life or death to nations.
LORD CURZON OF KEDLESTON

I need not again insist that boundaries are not set up in this world of human ambitions and land hunger for the purpose of assimilating the peoples on either side, or of providing them with suitable accommodation for meeting one another. SIR THOMAS H. HOLDICH

BOUNDARIES SEPARATE THE SOVEREIGNTY OF ONE STATE FROM THAT OF its neighbors. No state has rights of tax collecting, of conscription, of law enforcement, or of military occupation outside its boundaries, except in those few instances where such a right is conferred by international treaty or guaranteed by international law. A state may not allow its aircraft to fly over the territory of neighboring states, unless some agreement on this has been reached with its neighbors, though no agreement has been reached to restrict the flight of satellites. Nor do its citizens have the right—though they often enough have the privilege—of crossing the boundaries and traveling at will over the area of their neighbors. In the past century or more, the sovereignty of the state over everything that exists or happens within its boundaries has been the state's foremost characteristic. Sovereignty has been jealously guarded and every encroachment on it strenuously resisted. A welcome feature of these middle years of the twentieth century has been the voluntary limitation of sovereignty by some states, especially of their right to control commerce and fix the level of tariffs regardless of their neighbors (see Chapter 10). But in most respects, the sovereignty of states is unrestricted, and the sharpness of boundaries which separate them is diminished only to a slight extent.

Boundaries at sea or through water bodies such as bays and estuaries present different problems from those raised by land boundaries, and their examination is postponed to the next chapter. Here we are concerned only with the land boundaries of the state.

CHANGING CONCEPTS OF BOUNDARIES

The nature of boundaries has changed through historical time because their function, the separation of sovereignties, has also changed. As the population of the world becomes greater and its settlements thicken on the land, and as the rights and obligations of the state increase, so must boundaries be drawn and marked with greater precision. The modern boundary is a finite line along which two sovereignties meet. The last inch of soil is claimed on each side, and taxes are levied by both right up to the boundary line. Gone are the days, in most of the world at least, when the effective sovereignty of one state was separated from that of its neighbor by a a wide belt of anomalous territory in which its sovereignty gradually faded out as the state relinquished, one by one, its rights and obligations over land.

"Ideas about boundaries are related," as Stephen Jones has expressed it, "to their geographical and historical milieu." [1] Primitive peoples in general have simple ideas and concepts. A no man's land separates the territory that is inhabited and used by one tribe from that occupied by the next. This is a frontier in the strict sense; a border zone, unclaimed, unsettled, and unused, into which peoples from each side may at times intrude, but over which neither side claims or exercises an exclusive control.

This is a primitive concept of a boundary, a zone rather than a line; but it is still held and applied today in some remote and thinly peopled areas of the world. But even among primitive peoples, it was by no means universal. There are many examples, some of them enumerated by Jones, of boundaries between tribes which had achieved a high degree of precision. [2] Even when the tribes were separated from one another by wide, uninhabited tracts, their mutual boundary was generally clear, though in fact it set limits to nothing more than rights to hunt game or to fish.

The great empires of the past, such as the Roman and the Chinese, commonly had distinct boundaries around at least part of their area, though these did not separate states of equal rights and significance. They served, at least in the minds of those who drew them, to cut civilization off from outer barbarism. The Romans established their boundary in Europe along the line of two rivers, the Rhine and Danube, supplementing it with walls and banks in northern England, in South Germany, and near the Danube mouth. These works were certainly not very efficacious militarily, but they served to say to the barbarians beyond, "Come this far if you wish, but intrusion within these lines means war." Similarly in China, though the Great Wall was militarily far more effective than the walls which the Romans built in Europe, it seems to have been valued chiefly because it gave precision to the contrast between what was Chinese and what was not. "The idea of a stable and exact Frontier—a Great Wall Frontier—was inherent in the structure of China as a whole. What could not be included must be excluded," [3] And again, "A line of cleavage existed, somewhere, be-

[1] Stephen B. Jones, "Boundary Concepts in the Setting of Place and Time," *A.A.A.G.*, vol. XLIX, pp. 241–255, 1959.

[2] *Ibid.*, pp. 242–243.

[3] Owen Lattimore, *Inner Asian Frontiers of China*, American Geographical Society of New York, 1951, pp. 482–483.

Figure 9   *The Great Wall of China, which stretches for over fifteen hundred miles across the north of China, embodies the desire for a "stable and exact" boundary.*   COURTESY: PAUL POPPER

tween the territories and peoples that could advantageously be included in the Chinese empire and those that could not. This was the line that the Great Wall was intended to define." [4]

The Romans and the Chinese were not the only wall builders. The early Anglo-Saxons built walls, and archaeology as well as the study of air photographs occasionally turns up the evidence of other linear walls, banks, and ditches. It is inconceivable, in many instances, that there could have been enough people to defend these walls and banks, though they often did take every advantage of natural slope. At most, they could have deterred a band of raiders; they could not have restrained an invasion.

Roman and Chinese concepts of sov-

[4] Owen Lattimore, "Origins of the Great Wall of China," *G.R.*, vol. 27, pp. 529–549, 1937.

ereignty were not unlike our own. Sovereignty in the feudal society of medieval Europe was quite different. Whereas modern sovereignty is territorial, feudal sovereignty was personal. The modern state has authority over land and all within its limits; the medieval king or emperor had jurisdiction over people, wherever they might be. To some extent, these personal relations of feudalism reflected the breakdown of the institutions and mechanism of government at the beginning of the Middle Ages. A man's safety came to depend, not on the government's efficiency in law enforcement, but on his personal relations to a particular strong man. He became the latter's "man," promising him loyalty and service in return for protection. This kind of "gang" society became institutionalized in the feudal system. Territorial sovereignty

Figure 10 *Hadrian's Wall, built across the north of England by the Emperor Hadrian in the second century A.D., was shorter and less ambitious than the Great Wall of China but embodied the same ideal.* COURTESY: BRITISH IN-FORMATION SERVICES

was inconceivable, or at least ineffective, when the central governmental institutions by which the will of the central authority might be enforced at the local level had broken down. Local authority was exercised by the local baron, subject only to his personal relationship to a remote superior. The latter was similarly restricted only by his personal obligations to another person yet higher in the feudal hierarchy. Kings were not concerned with boundary problems as we understand them. They were interested chiefly in retaining their authority over individuals.

Taxation is closely bound up with boundaries. The feudal state had no general, uniform system of taxation. Only classes of people were taxed. The clergy and the merchants, for example, paid taxes which were related to their professions.

The knights contributed so many days each year of personal service in the army of their suzerain or a money payment in lieu of such service. Few taxes devolved upon the land itself,[5] and if the kings did not tax the land as such over which they ruled, there was little need to be unduly precise in defining its limits. It was mainly through the administration of justice that precision became desirable. If an offense had been committed or if there was a lawsuit, it was necessary to know in whose court the case ought to be heard. The hearing of cases was a source of profit to the barons, who had the right to hold the courts, and they sometimes disputed with one another the geographical limits of their respective jurisdictions in order to get the right to hear

[5] The Danegeld of Anglo-Saxon England and later "hearth taxes" are exceptions.

a particular case. The result of such disputes has, in some instances, shaped the course of a political boundary for centuries. There are a number of instances of the fixing of short stretches of the boundary between France and Germany in order to settle a purely legal question, the right to hear a case.[6]

The ruler of the medieval or feudal state did not know precisely how his state was made up; its boundaries were clearly defined only here and there, where for some reason or other there had arisen a need for precision. It is a strange reversal of our present state of affairs to find that medieval rulers did not know the extent of the lands they ruled and, when they were in doubt, consulted the local people. An incident which happened in 1546 illustrates this. The Emperor Charles V was passing along the eastern, or imperial, bank of the Meuse when he noticed the newly built French fortress town of Villefranche near Mouzon on the opposite side. The chronicler Du Bellay [7] recorded that "When he had reached this place the Emperor complained to the ambassador of the French king, who happened to be with him, that the town had been built upon imperial territory. The records of the district covering two centuries were brought and examined, and it was shown that the inhabitants of the new town were subjects of the French king."[8]

A feature of the political geography of feudalism was its "patchwork political map. Discontinuous holdings were common, and were tolerable because of the decentralized nature of feudal rule and warfare." [9] One of the tasks of subsequent

centuries has been to smooth and straighten boundaries and to clear up the confused pattern of sovereignty in Europe. This task has not yet been completed.

Boundaries of the Nation-State: The transition from medieval to modern concepts of boundaries is bound up with the rise of the nation-state. The medieval state was personal. It was put together by its ruler or his forebears. He could divide it between his children; he could sell or even pawn part of it. The feudal state did not reflect—or reflected only very imperfectly —the desire of a human group to live together under one common ruler. When the German poet Schiller, in 1804, put into the mouth of one of the founding fathers of the Swiss Confederation the desire "to be one single nation of brothers" (see page 12), he was guilty of a gross anachronism, as also was Shakespeare when he put into the mouth of John of Gaunt and Henry V the national and political aspirations that belonged to his own day and age.

National consciousness was a fruit that matured slowly. But the nation-state, once it had emerged, had to modify early concepts of boundaries. Ordinary people ceased to be pawns, pushed around from one feudal ruler to another; they became— or were, at least, thought of as—people with a culture that inclined them toward one nation-state or another. As national consciousness ripened, it demanded that boundaries should be drawn with ever-increasing attention to the aspirations of peoples, until we have now some boundaries that are based exclusively upon the expressed will of the people who lived near them.

The history of boundaries in most long-settled areas is one of increasing definition and precision and also of increasing adjustment to the facts of cultural geography. The former process is completed when the boundary is reduced to a line; the latter

---

[6] Norman J. G. Pounds, "The Origin of the Idea of Natural Frontiers in France," *A.A.A.G.*, vol. 41, pp. 146–157, 1951.

[7] Martin and Guillaume du Bellay were French chroniclers of the sixteenth century.

[8] Pounds, *op. cit.*, pp. 148–149.

[9] Jones, *op. cit.*, p. 247.

is never completed. The boundary should ideally separate different cultures; at the same time, it should not create difficulties by splitting up functional units such as coal basins and irrigation systems. Furthermore, if the boundary has any value as a line of military defense, it is commonly regarded as doubly successful. Let it be stated now that no land boundary anywhere in the world combines all these qualities. Each is in some degree a compromise, the result of conflicting pressures brought to bear not only by the states directly concerned but also by their allies and their enemies.

The increasing precision of boundaries does not preclude the possibility of change. Most boundaries, with the exception of some of those in the colonial world (see Chapter 13), are national boundaries. But the national affiliations of the border people are sometimes a matter of political and even academic dispute. The boundary between cultural national groups is very rarely sharp. Groups live intermixed with one another over the belt of territory which separates their main areas of settlement. Thus variation in tracing a national or ethnic boundary between them is possible, and the line that is drawn is likely to reflect the balance of political power on each side of that line. It will not necessarily represent what is right and proper in any absolute sense, and it is subject to change with each change in the relative power of the states concerned. This is well illustrated by some of the "ethnic" boundaries established in Europe at the end of the First World War. Undoubtedly, the scales of justice were tipped at this time against Hungary and Bulgaria and in favor of Poland, Czechoslovakia, Rumania, and Yugoslovia, and this provided the excuse for further boundary changes before and during the Second World War. The ultimate objectives of policy—the preservation

of the state and the welfare of its citizens—translated into boundary terms, became the attainment of a defensible boundary and the inclusion within it of all those who identify themselves, or are identified with, the nation-state.

Arbitrary and Geometrical Boundaries: There is another type of boundary which reflects only the relative strength of the states concerned, paying no attention to local conditions and the desires of indigenous peoples. These are the lines drawn by European powers around their colonial dependencies. Take, for instance, those of South-West Africa, formerly a German colony. This area of 317,887 square miles has about 2,100 miles of land boundary, of which 725 miles follow the windings of the Orange, Kunene, Okovanggo, and Zambezi Rivers. The rest is made up of straight lines drawn arbitrarily across a map by persons who in all probability had never been to Africa, were ignorant of the geography of the lands which they partitioned, and took no regard for the welfare of the sparse, indigenous population. The same happened in most other parts of Africa. Boundaries were drawn as straight lines from one known point to another or were made to follow physical features prominent enough to be shown on early maps of Africa. In each case they divided tribes, brought hostile tribes together, and separated tribes from their grazing areas and water holes.

Such boundaries, imposed arbitrarily from without, proved satisfactory in some instances. The boundaries, for example, in Australia and the Sahara Desert partitioned areas that were uninhabited and unexplored. These boundaries were antecedent to human settlement and development, and the settlers who came later adjusted themselves without difficulty to the pre-existing boundaries. But where the new boundaries were superimposed upon existing societies and cultures, as in West Africa, very serious problems have arisen. Over a long enough period of time, it might perhaps be assumed that these societies would adjust themselves to the boundaries, gradually severing cultural ties with peoples outside and intensifying those with peoples lying within. It is by no means certain that this would in fact have happened. In reality, the arbitrary segments of African territory which the European powers erected into colonies have existed for too short a period of time for this to be tested. It might be noted that the much longer British rule in India failed conspicuously to reconcile the two main communal groups and to create a sense of all-Indian unity. Now that the strong hand of European rule is releasing its grip on colonial Africa, the harm wrought by these ill-considered boundaries is becoming increasingly apparent. One may perhaps look forward to a period during which boundaries will become adjusted rather more closely to African societies (see Chapter 14), though whether this can be done without war is perhaps doubtful.

A CLASSIFICATION OF BOUNDARIES

So far we have been concerned in this chapter primarily with the question of the adjustment of political boundaries to the realities of social, communal, or ethnic groupings. Unquestionably, these are the factors which today exercise the most profound influence on the alignment of boundaries. Yet many boundaries, and highly successful ones at that, have survived into the present from a period which antedates the rise of nationalism in their particular areas. The boundaries of Switzerland, for example, separate French-speaking peoples from France, German-speaking from Germany,

and Italian-speaking from Italy. Yet these segments of three distinct peoples, cut off from the great mass of their cultural groups by the accident of history, have unquestionably developed a cohesion and a sense of belonging to one another.

There is, thus, every degree of gradation, from boundaries that were established before significant human settlement occurred in an area, to those established long after human societies and cultures had been fully formed. A classification of boundaries has been established on the basis of this spectrum; its nomenclature is derived from physical geography, though the analogy with the mechanics of river development is imperfect.[10]

1. *Antecedent boundaries* are those "that preceded the development of most of the features of the cultural landscape." As societies developed, they adjusted themselves to the boundary, which thus acquired a historical and pragmatic sanction. The boundary between Canada and the United States, established and modified by treaty agreements between 1782 and 1846, belongs to this category. There were, of course, a few settlers and a more numerous body of nomadic trappers and Indians along the line of this boundary during the period when it was delimited. It was not, therefore, totally antecedent. On the other hand the boundary between Canada and Alaska at the time when it was agreed upon (Anglo-Russian Treaties of 1825 and 1827) ran through entirely unsettled and undeveloped territory. Such a boundary is totally antecedent, or *pioneer.*

2. *Subsequent boundaries* were established after the cultural pattern had been formed, and, as a general rule, they con-

[10] This most valuable model has been devised by Richard Hartshorne; see his "Suggestions on the Terminology of Political Boundaries," *A.A.A.G.,* vol. 26, pp. 56–57, 1936.

Figure 11 *An obviously antecedent boundary runs across the Atacama Desert between Chile and Peru.* COURTESY: PAUL POPPER

form with the borders between "major or minor divisions of natural and cultural regions." As has already been pointed out, there has been a tendency for boundaries, especially those in Europe, to approximate more and more closely the cultural divisions created by the differences of language. The boundary of India and Pakistan is in approximate conformity with a cultural division. All recent transfers of territory (see Chapter 2) and exchanges of population (see Chapter 5) have been designed to bring political boundaries and cultural divisions into closer harmony with one another.

3. *Superimposed boundaries* were established, like *subsequent* boundaries, after the territory to be divided had been settled and developed, but, unlike the latter, they ignore completely the cultural and ethnic characteristics of the area divided. The boundaries of the Hapsburg empire before 1918 belong to this type. They cut off Rumanians from Rumania, Poles from Poland, Serbs from Serbia, and Italians from Italy. They were vigorously opposed by these minority peoples and did not survive the breakup of the Hapsburg empire in 1918. Many of the colonial boundaries in Africa also belong to this group, especially those of Ghana, Togo, Dahomey, Nigeria, and Cameroun. Each of these bisects one or more tribal territories.

Figure 12   *One boundary between France and the principality of Monaco runs through built-up areas and is clearly superimposed. In fact, it runs* through *the filling station, and there has been a fierce dispute as to whether the proprietor should pay French taxes on his sales or not.* COURTESY: PAUL POPPER

To the category of superimposed boundaries may also be allocated those which derive from truce lines, established at the conclusion of hostilities and never significantly modified by a subsequent treaty. The boundary between the Netherlands and Belgium derives from such a truce line. Today the boundaries between North and South Korea and North and South Vietnam are substantially truce lines. The boundary around the Gaza Strip (Figure 14) and that enclosing the western extension of Jordan were established when fighting ceased between Israel and her neighbors in 1949 and have been neither modified nor confirmed by international agreement.

4. *Relict boundaries* are boundary lines which have been abandoned for political purposes, but which, nevertheless, remain discernible in the cultural landscape. Hartshorne has described the way in which one may trace the former Russo-German border through the industrial region of Upper Silesia by studying the styles of architecture of homes and public buildings, which differed from one another in the two empires. Today there is a change in the pattern of fields as one crosses the former boundary of Poland and Germany. Evidences of Turkish architectural styles in the Balkans and of Spanish in the American Southwest also serve to show that these

areas formerly lay on the other side of an important political boundary and derived aspects of their culture from a different source from the culture which predominates today.

Such relict boundaries are seldom more than curiosities in the landscape. They are of political importance only when the former political area of which they are evidence has left a residue of political feeling. The relict boundary in Upper Silesia has today no political importance; Russian styles of architecture on the one side do not give rise to any feelings of attachment to the Soviet Union. It would not be true, on the other hand, to say that German sur-

vivals in the landscape of western Poland are without political significance. There continue to live in this area people whose attachment to Germany is none the less real even if unexpressed.

Delimitation and Demarcation: A boundary change is made, or a new boundary established, by an agreement or treaty between the states primarily concerned. Such an agreement may not be wholly voluntary on the part of one of them, but nevertheless it is held to be binding. Germany, for example, accepted and signed the Treaty of Versailles in 1919, with the boundary changes which it prescribed, under protest, but this did not prevent the newly

Figure 13 *On the Franco-Belgian boundary, near Armentières, the line marked by the bar literally runs through the back yard of some French cottages.* PHOTOGRAPH BY N. J. G. POUNDS

established boundaries from becoming the legal boundaries until they were changed by a fresh agreement.

A boundary treaty is generally prepared by persons having no firsthand knowledge of the area to be divided. Their knowledge of it is usually derived from maps and reports, and the more general or less accurate these are, the more faulty is the ensuing treaty likely to be. The treaty is, however, usually couched in highly general terms: the boundary shall run from A to B; it shall separate an area predominantly French from one predominantly German; it shall keep so many miles from point X or from river Y; it shall follow river C or the crest of the chain of hills from D to E.

The treaty then provides for the transfer of this verbal description (helped out occasionally by a small-scale map) to the landscape itself. This is normally done by a boundary commission, consisting usually of a small, mixed group. The commission is likely to contain delegates from the governments of the states which are to be separated by the boundary. It will contain surveyors, and it may have a small military force for its own protection. The actual definition of the boundary in treaty or other

Figure 14 *Some boundaries arise from the accidents of military campaigning and follow "truce lines."* The photograph illustrates the marked truce line, guarded by UN forces, in the Gaza Strip, on the·Egyptian-Israeli border.
COURTESY: UNITED NATIONS

Figure 15 *Precision is necessary in the demarcation of the boundary between West and East Berlin. This photograph was taken shortly before the building of the wall which now runs in front of the Brandenburg Gate.* PHOTOGRAPH BY N. J. G. POUNDS

agreement is known as *delimitation;* the process of interpreting on the ground the intentions of the treaty makers is the *demarcation* of the boundary. These two terms were introduced by Sir Henry McMahon, who himself was responsible for the delimitation of the boundary between India and Tibet. In an article on boundaries he wrote: " 'Delimitation' I have taken to comprise the determination of a boundary line by treaty or otherwise, and its definition in written, verbal terms; 'Demarcation' to comprise the actual laying down of a boundary line on the ground, and its definition by boundary pillars or other similar physical means." [11]

[11] Sir Henry McMahon, "International Boundaries," *Journal of the Royal Society of Arts* (*London*), vol. 84, pp. 2–16, 1935.

A considerable discretionary power normally is vested in the boundary commission, which tries, so far as is consistent with its terms of reference, not to separate a village from its fields, a city from its source of water supply, and, in one unique case, a cemetery from the country to which the dead belonged.[12]

BOUNDARIES OF THE UNITED STATES

The principles that have been outlined so far in this chapter can mostly be illustrated from the boundaries of the United States. The boundaries of the United States

[12] The Treaty of Frankfurt, 1871, gave Germany possession of certain of its own war graves.

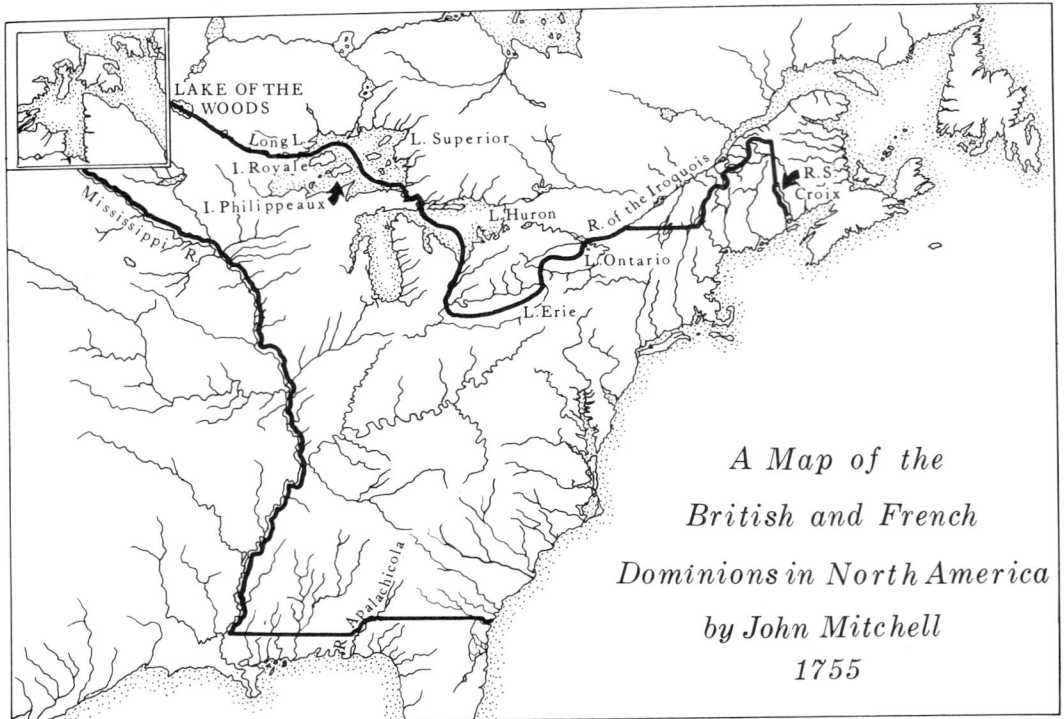

A Map of the
British and French
Dominions in North America
by John Mitchell
1755

Exhibit 24   John Mitchell's map of the English Colonies of 1755, and the boundary line of 1782–1783.

as a whole were first defined by the Treaty of Paris in 1783. This treaty was drawn up in Paris, by persons having no direct knowledge of the boundary areas to be delimited. They relied almost exclusively on John Mitchell's map of North America, published twenty-seven years earlier. It was in many respects a good map, but it was not based upon an accurate survey, and for parts of the area shown, its compiler was indebted to the hearsay evidence of traders and trappers. A copy of the relevant parts of the Mitchell map is given in Exhibit 24 (compare Exhibit 25). The text of article II, the boundary clause, of the Treaty of Paris follows·

Article II. From the northwest angle of Nova Scotia, viz., that angle which is formed by a line drawn due north from the source of the St. Croix River to the highlands; along

the highlands which divide those rivers that empty themselves into the river St. Lawrence, from those which fall into the Atlantic Ocean, to the northwesternmost head of Connecticut River; thence down along the middle of that river to the 45th. degree of north latitude; from thence, by a line due west on said latitude until it strikes the river Iroquois or Cataraquy [St. Lawrence]; thence along middle of said river into Lake Ontario, through the middle of said lake until it strikes the communication by water between that lake and Lake Erie; thence along the middle of said communication into Lake Erie, through the middle of said lake until it arrives at the water communication between that lake and Lake Huron; thence along the middle of said water communication into the Lake Huron; thence through the middle of said lake into the water communication between that lake and Lake Superior; thence through Lake Superior northward of the Isles Royal and Phe-lippeaux, to the Long Lake; thence through the middle of said Long Lake, and water communication between it and the Lake of the Woods, to the said Lake of the Woods; thence through the said lake to the most north-western point thereof, and from thence on a due west course to the river Mississippi; thence by a line to be drawn along the mid-dle of the said river Mississippi until it shall intersect the northernmost part of the 31st. degree of north latitude. South, by a line to be drawn due east from the determination of the line last mentioned, in the latitude of 31

Figure 16 *The Canadian government welcomes the traveler who crosses by the Rainbow Bridge at Niagara, with impressive style.* COURTESY: EWING GALLOWAY

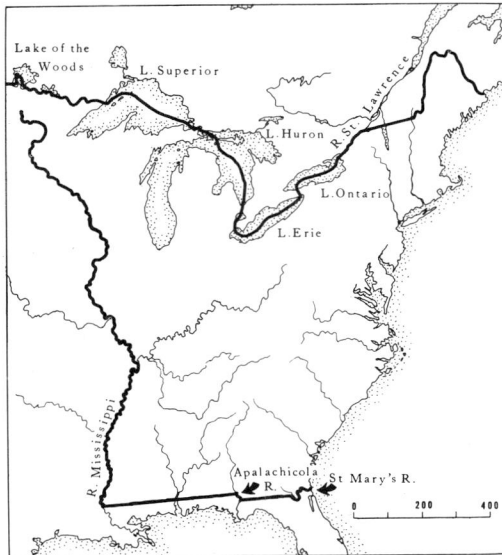

Exhibit 25   *The boundary of 1782–1783 on a modern map.*

shown on the map. As it was made to run through areas almost, if not entirely, uninhabited, it could, therefore, be related only to the major physical features—lakes, rivers, and mountain ranges—or to the invisible but nevertheless discoverable lines of latitude and longitude. The total land boundary of the United States (including that through the Great Lakes) was at this time made up approximately as shown in the following table:

	Miles	Percentage of total distance
Rivers and lakes.........	3,582	75
Hill and mountain ranges.	362	8
Parallels and meridians...	827	17

degrees north of the equator, to the middle of the river Apalachicola or Catahouche; thence along the middle thereof to its junction with the Flint River; thence straight to the head of St. Mary's River to the Atlantic Ocean. East, by a line to be drawn along the middle of the river St. Croix, from its mouth in the bay of Fundy to its source, and from its source directly north to the aforesaid highlands which divide the rivers that fall into the Atlantic Ocean from those which fall into the river St. Lawrence; comprehending all islands within twenty leagues of any part of the shores of the United States, and lying between lines to be drawn due east from the points where the aforesaid boundaries between Nova Scotia on the one part and East Florida on the other, shall respectively touch the Bay of Fundy and the Atlantic Ocean; excepting such islands as are now, or heretofore have been, within the limits of the said province of Nova Scotia. . . .

This treaty is notable in two respects: the ways in which it delimited the boundary, and the errors which it made in doing so. The boundary had to be related to something which existed on the ground and was

Unquestionably, waterways were preferred by the authors of the Treaty of 1782. It is superfluous to argue whether these made good or bad boundaries, whether they were defensible or not. They were chosen because they were obvious and because it was assumed that there could be no dispute about their location.

The complex nature of hill and mountain ranges does not appear to have been fully apparent to statesmen in the eighteenth century or, indeed, to those of succeeding ages. The statesmen themselves were not altogether to blame. The practice of representing hills as "hairy caterpillars" was widespread, and this encouraged the belief that a line of hills would have a single, simple crest line, from which rivers would discharge in each direction. To adopt a line of hills as a boundary would, therefore, seem as obvious as to select a river.

Unfortunately, such simplicities do not exist in nature, and, if they did, they probably would have been wrongly represented on John Mitchell's map. The boundary, as delimited in the treaty, could not be demarcated, because some of the geographical conditions postulated were contrary to fact. In 1794, the Treaty of London between the United States and Great Britain contained the following: "Whereas it is uncertain whether the river Mississippi extends so far to the northward as to be intersected by a line to be drawn due west from the Lake of the Woods. . . ."

And again: "Whereas doubts have arisen what river was truly intended under the name of the river St. Croix, mentioned in the said treaty of peace [i.e., of 1783]. . . ." Numerous conventions, commissions, and treaties were necessary before all the irregularities, ambiguities, and inaccuracies in the Paris Treaty were remedied. One of the results of the initial mistakes is seen in the present boundary in the neighborhood of the Lake of the Woods (Exhibit 26), where a fragment of Minnesota now lies detached and accessible by land from the rest of the state only through Canadian territory.[13] Another area where the interpretation of the treaty presented serious difficulties was in Passamaquoddy Bay, which constitutes the mouth of the St. Croix River. This waterway is so studded with islands that it is difficult to determine which channel continues the course of the river. It was not until 1910 that, by an agreement between the United States and the United Kingdom (for Canada), this matter was finally settled.

Another and equally difficult problem was that posed by the phrase in the Treaty of 1782 which defined the northern boundary of Maine as running "along the high-

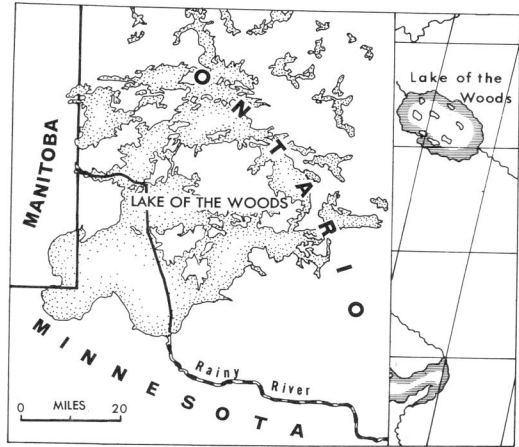

Exhibit 26 *The boundary in the region of the Lake of the Woods. Right, lake on Mitchell's map.*

lands which divide those rivers which empty themselves into the river St. Lawrence, from those which fall into the Atlantic Ocean. . ." (Exhibit 27). There is no topographical feature that could be said to correspond with the "highlands" of the treaty, and the divide between the two drainage basins is too complex to be really suitable as a boundary. A compromise agreement was reached between the United States and United Kingdom and was given legal validity in the Webster-Ashburton Treaty of 1842.[14]

The purchase of the Louisiana Territory in 1803 necessitated the extension westward of the boundary between the United States and Canada beyond the longitude of the Lake of the Woods and the Mississippi River. There was considerable doubt about the extent of the territory thus acquired. Its original definition (1712) as "all the countries, territories, lakes in the land, and the rivers emptying directly or indirectly into . . . the river St. Louis [i.e., the Mississippi]" appeared to limit it to the

[13] This is reviewed in *Boundaries, Areas, Geographic Centers, and Altitudes of the United States and the Several States,* Geological Survey Bulletin 817, U.S. Department of the Interior, 1932, pp. 9–27, and S. Whittemore Boggs, *International Boundaries,* Columbia University Press, New York, 1940, pp. 33–54.

[14] See *Boundaries, Areas, Geographic Centers, and Altitudes of the United States and the Several States, op. cit.,* pp. 16–20.

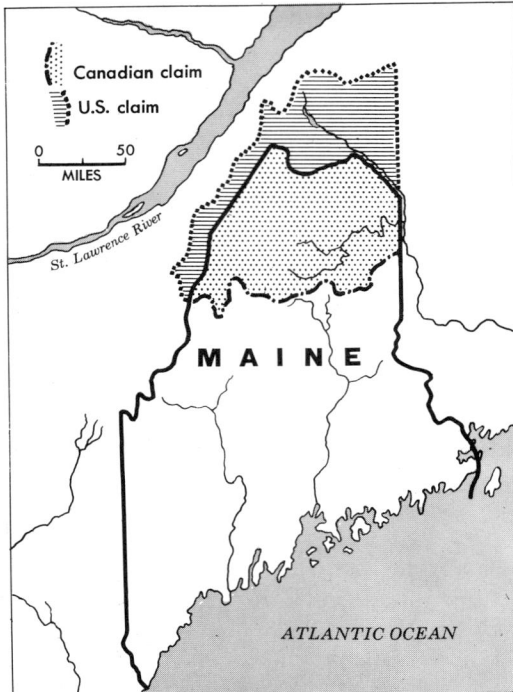

Exhibit 27 The United States–Canada boundary in northern Maine.

Mountains, the western limit, as it was then supposed, of the Mississippi Basin. Sovereignty over the territory that lay between the Rocky Mountains and the Pacific Ocean was undetermined. Spanish sovereignty was held to extend as far north as the 42d parallel in California; Russian, as far south as the parallels of 54°40′ in Alaska. The vast territory bounded by these two lines of latitude and by the Rocky Mountains was to remain "free and open to the nationals of both the United States and Canada." [15] It was only after prolonged and acrimonious discussion that this territory was partitioned by the Anglo-American Treaty of 1846. Article I of the treaty ran as follows:

From the point in the forty-ninth parallel of north latitude, where the boundary laid down in existing treaties and conventions between the United States and Great Britain terminates, the line of boundary between the territories of the United States and those of Her Britannic Majesty [i.e., Queen Victoria] shall be continued westward along the forty-ninth parallel of north latitude to the middle of the channel which separates the continent from Vancouver's Island; and thence southerly through the middle of the said channel, and of Fuca's Straits, to the Pacific Ocean. . . .

Thus was the northern boundary delimited from ocean to ocean. Its demarcation was not without its difficulties. It was necessary to trace the boundary between the islands of the St. Lawrence River. The Treaty of 1783 had delimited it along the "middle" of the several rivers and lakes which separated the two countries. Such a line, at least in the river St. Lawrence, proved to be indeterminable. The Treaty of Ghent (1814) provided for the appointment of commissioners who would be charged with the task of delimiting more precisely the course of the boundary. Their

drainage basin of the Mississippi River. Such a definition would have excluded the Red River Valley of Minnesota and the Dakotas. This clearly was not the understanding of the Americans who bought the territory, and they probably thought of the Mississippi River, as the authors of the Treaty of 1782 had done, as originating at least as far north as the Lake of the Woods. This would have extended the Louisiana Territory also this far to the north.

The matter was settled by the Anglo-American Treaty of 1818, by which the 49th parallel, from the Lake of the Woods westward to the Rocky Mountains, was held to be the boundary between the United States and the British colony of Canada. The Louisiana Purchase was held to have given the United States sovereignty as far west as approximately the Rocky

---

[15] J. B. Brebner, *North Atlantic Triangle*, Yale University Press, New Haven, Conn., 1945, p. 95.

role was, in effect, that of arbitrators; their solution was to allocate each islet in the river to one side or the other.[16] But even that was not altogether the end of the matter; the "middle" of the waterway between two islands, or between an island and the river's bank, is itself susceptible of more than one interpretation. This term, used also of the course of the boundary through the Great Lakes and through the Juan de Fuca Strait, needed further definition (see page 88).

Problems relating to the more precise delimitation and the demarcation of the boundary between the New England States on the one hand and Quebec and the Maritime Provinces on the other, and also of the boundary in the vicinity of the Lake of the Woods, have already been discussed. It might be supposed that the delimitation along the 49th parallel would present no problems. This was, it is true, a precise and ascertainable line. But it was chosen with little knowledge of the terrain over which it was to be traced. It cut across some of the northern tributaries of the Missouri River, as well as the Columbia River and several of its more important tributaries. This has given rise to problems of water supply and water use which will be taken up in Chapter 11.

The survey and demarcation of the boundary itself were begun in 1872 and were not completed until the present century. The survey, at least in its earlier stages, was not wholly accurate, and the resulting boundary does not trace precisely the 49th parallel but lies alternately to the north and south of it. Its "site is inconvenient to the

verge of freakishness," yet its success has been complete, largely because, in Jones's words, "with insignificant exceptions . . . [it] totally antedates settlement (other than Indian) in the border zone. It has therefore been an environmental factor persisting through all modern stages of occupation." [17]

The boundary between the United States and Canada illustrates admirably certain kinds of difficulties that are of widespread occurrence in the delimitation and demarcation of boundaries: delimitation by reference to erroneous maps and other incorrect data; the tracing of water boundaries; errors in surveying; and the vagueness and ambiguity of many descriptions embodied in treaties. The remaining boundaries of the United States provide further examples of these and also raise other problems.

The Boundary with Mexico: The boundary between the United States and Mexico was first defined by the Republic of Texas in 1836, when it claimed as its southwestern and western boundary "the mouth of the Rio Grande, thence up the principal stream of said river to its source, thence due north to the forty-second degree of north latitude. . . ." [18]

After the Spanish-American War, the Treaty of Guadalupe Hidalgo (1848) extended the territorial limits of the United States and delimited as its boundary:

The boundary line between the two Republics [i.e., The United States and Mexico] shall commence in the Gulf of Mexico, three

[16] The text of their decision is printed in part in *Boundaries, Areas, Geographic Centers, and Altitudes of the United States and the Several States, op. cit.,* pp. 10–13; fully in W. M. Malloy, *Treaties, Conventions, etc., between the United States and Other Powers, 1776–1909,* Government Printing Office, 1913.

[17] Stephen B. Jones, "The Forty-ninth Parallel in the Great Plains: the Historical Geography of a Boundary," *J. of G.,* vol. 31, pp. 357–368, 1932; "The Cordilleran Section of the Canada–United States Borderland," *G.J.,* vol. 89, pp. 439–450, 1937.

[18] Quoted in *Boundaries, Areas, Geographic Centers, and Altitudes of the United States and the Several States, op. cit.,* p. 37.

leagues from land, opposite the mouth of the Rio Grande . . . or opposite the mouth of its deepest branch, if it should have more than one branch emptying directly into the sea; from thence up the middle of that river, following the deepest channel where it has more than one, to the point where it strikes the southern boundary of New Mexico; thence, westwardly, along the whole southern boundary of New Mexico . . . to its western termination; thence, northward, along the western line of New Mexico, until it intersects the first branch of the river Gila; (or if it should not intersect any branch of that river, then to the point on the said line nearest to such branch, and thence in a direct line to the same;) thence down the middle of the said branch and of the said river, until it empties into the Rio Colorado; thence across the Rio Colorado, following the division line between Upper and Lower California, to the Pacific Ocean.

Treaty draftsmen had learned much since they drew up the Treaty of 1782, and in this Treaty of 1848 they made provision for the inaccuracies and inadequacies of the maps available. Five years later, a tract of land known as the *Gadsden Purchase*, lying to the south of the Gila River, was purchased from Mexico. The boundary was redefined in the following terms:

. . . up the middle of that river [Rio Grande] to the point where the parallel of 31 degrees 47′ north latitude crosses the same; thence due west one hundred miles; thence south to the parallel of 31 degrees 20′ north latitude; thence along the said parallel of 31 degrees 20′ to the 111th. meridian of longitude west of Greenwich; thence in a straight line to a point on the Colorado River twenty English miles below the junction of the Gila and Colorado Rivers; thence up the middle of the said river Colorado until it intersects the present line between the United States and Mexico.

Most of this boundary, as delimited in the treaty and demarcated on the ground, ran through barren, uninhabited country.

In general, it presented few problems, and these of only small importance. It does, however, introduce into our discussion a boundary problem of a kind not encountered to any important degree along the Canadian border. Mexico and the United States share two important rivers, the Rio Grande and the Colorado, the one serving as a boundary for about 1,321 miles, the other flowing from the United States across Mexican territory to the sea. Most of the boundary between the United States and Canada runs through humid country where water resources, though valuable, are not the scarce commodity that they become along the Mexican border. The northern rivers are regular and dependable compared with those on the Mexican border. The latter are dry for long periods, then break into violent flood as the irregular storms sweep the desert. The resulting political problems are of two kinds: those arising from the changes in the course of the boundary river during the floods, and those presented by the competition for use of the river's water.

The Rio Grande, in particular, is an unstable river. Not only does its swift current erode its outer bank as it swings in broad curves and adds deposits to its inner bank, thus gradually shifting its bed; but it may also, in time of flood, desert its old channel and create a new one. At all stages of the river except flood, the river flows, not like most northern rivers in a single broad stream, but in a series of interlacing channels, an effect known as a *braided stream*, among which it is extremely difficult to define the principal channel. Such a river would, at best, afford a very unstable boundary. This came to be realized, and in conventions between the governments of the United States and Mexico in 1884 and 1905, the probability of changes in the river bed was taken into consideration. The 1884 convention ruled that:

Figure 17   ***The Rio Grande at Laredo, Texas.*** *The American-Mexican bound-ary follows the middle of the river. Nuevo Laredo (Mexico) is seen in the distance.*   COURTESY: EWING GALLOWAY

The dividing line shall . . . follow the center of the normal channel of the rivers named, not withstanding any alterations . . . effected by natural causes through the slow and gradual erosion . . . and not by the abandonment of an existing bed and the open-ing of the new one.

Any other change wrought by the force of the current . . . shall produce no change in the dividing line as fixed by the surveys . . . but the line then fixed shall contine to follow the middle of the original channel bed, even though this should be wholly dry.

The principle thus established, that gradual change in the course of a river through erosion of one bank and *accretion* of the other brings about an equally grad-ual shift of boundary, while the avulsion, or sudden shift of the stream, does not, has come to be widely accepted.[19] It is applied not only to rivers which separate sovereign

[19] See discussion of this by Stephen B. Jones in *Boundary Making,* Carnegie Endowment for International Peace, Division of Cultural Law, Washington, D.C., 1945, pp. 119–123.

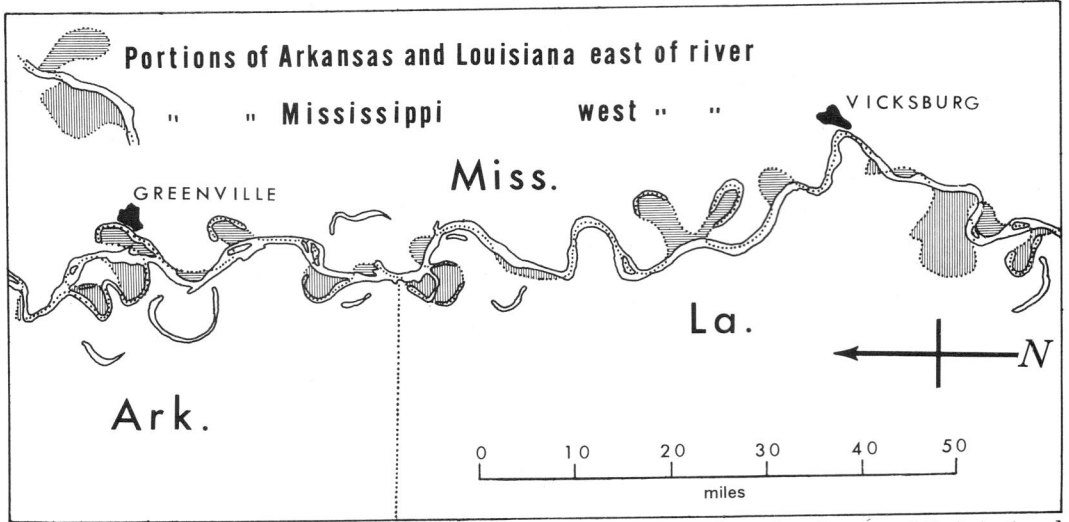

Exhibit 28 **Cutoffs on the Mississippi River boundary between Mississippi and** Arkansas.

states but also to those between the units of a federal state. A legal opinion of 1897 on the boundary between Texas and Oklahoma, where this follows the Red River, was to the effect that it "is the line of the middle of the main channel of Red River as it existed when Texas was annexed to the United States, and subsequent sudden changes in the current or main channel of said river will not in any way affect the location or position of said boundary line as it lay upon the earth's surface when established." [20] A glance, even at an oil-company road map of the States which border the Mississippi River, shows how numerous are the fragments of territory which now lie, as a result of sudden changes in the course of the river, separated by its broad stream from the States to which they belong (Exhibit 28).

These detached areas of American States are a source of minor administrative

[20] Quoted in *Boundaries, Areas, Geographic Centers, and Altitudes of the United States and the Several States, op. cit.,* p. 172.

inconvenience, but the situation along the Rio Grande was even more complex. The Mexican Treaty of 1905 explained, with detail more commonly found in a textbook of physical geography, that when the "said river abandons its old channel . . . there are separated from it small portions of land known as *bancos* bounded by the said old bed. . . . Whereas the said *bancos* are left at a distance from the new river bed, and by reason of successive deposits of alluvium, the old channel is becoming effaced, the land of said *bancos* becomes confused with the land of the *bancos* contiguous thereto, thus giving rise to difficulties and controversies." The preamble went on to show that the application to the *bancos* of the principle established in the convention of 1884 raised more problems than it solved. It was agreed that sovereignty by either state over *bancos* lying on the other side of the river should be eliminated, except in cases where the *banco* covered more than 250 hectares (0.97 square mile) or was inhabited by over 200 persons. More recently, part of the Rio Grande has been regulated and straightened, and by agreement the boundary between the two countries has been made to conform with the middle of the newly established river course.

The second problem presented by the international rivers on the United States–Mexican boundary has been the use of the limited volume of water brought down from the Cordilleran region of the United States. During the present century, the intensive development of irrigated argiculture along the subtropical valleys of the lower Colorado and Rio Grande has greatly increased the demand for water on both sides of the international boundary. To this has been added the growing requirements of cities more remote from the rivers, for example, Los Angeles. The supply of water for all these purposes is limited to that which comes down from the mountains. This volume can, it is true, be increased somewhat by greater control of run-off and the prevention of evaporation. Even so, the maximum discharge of the rivers is known, and it does not suffice for all the demands that are likely to be made. Thus, a dispute arose between the United States and Mexican governments regarding the distribution of that very water which was earlier supposed, in the case of the Rio Grande, to set a permanent and incontrovertible barrier between the two states. The case of the Rio Grande (the Colorado is a boundary river for only 19 miles) provides clear evidence of the functional unity which characterizes many river basins and demonstrates the basic weakness of using a river as a boundary.

The Boundaries of Alaska: Alaska was purchased by the United States government from the Russians in 1867. Its boundaries had been defined by a treaty negotiated between the United Kingdom and Russia in 1825. This earlier delimitation was repeated in the terms of the agreement of 1867 between the United States and Russia. The boundary ran:

. . . from the southernmost point of the island called Prince of Wales Island, which point lies in the parallel of 54 degrees 40 minutes north latitude, and between the 131st and 133rd degree of west longitude . . . the said line shall ascend to the north along the channel called Portland channel, as far as the point of the continent where it strikes the 56th. degree of north latitude; from this last-mentioned point the line of demarcation shall follow the summit of the mountains situated parallel to the coast as far as the point of intersection of the 141st degree of west longitude . . . ; and finally, from the said point of intersection, the said meridian line of the 141st degree, in its prolongation as far as the Frozen [i.e., the Arctic] ocean.

The mountains which bordered the Pacific Ocean were in 1825 little known and quite unsurveyed. The negotiators had good reason to doubt whether their delimitation was applicable, and so they added the reservation that:

Whenever the summit of the mountains . . . shall prove to be at the distance of more than ten marine leagues [i.e., 30 miles] from the ocean, the limit [i.e., boundary] . . . shall be formed by a line parallel to the winding of the coast, and which shall never exceed the distance of ten marine leagues therefrom.

For many years the boundary remained undemarcated, because there seemed to be no good reason to go to the expense of this extraordinarily difficult task. It was only when Canada desired to gain access to the developing gold fields of the Yukon Territory *across* the Alaskan Panhandle that the geographical problems presented by the Treaty of 1825, and the repetition of its territorial clauses in the Treaty of 1867, were brought to the fore. The geographical

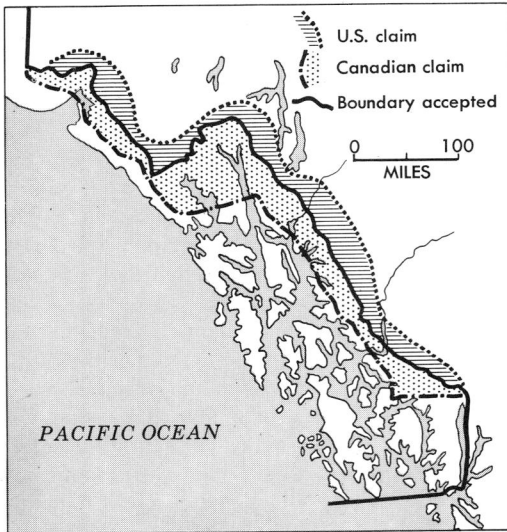

Exhibit 29 *The boundary between Canada and Alaska.*

fact is that the coastal range is broken into a series of short segments by fiords which extend inland, in places, as much as 140 miles from the outermost islands. If the boundary could be understood to follow, as the Canadians now claimed, this interrupted range (Exhibit 29), Canada would, thus, acquire the upper parts of many of the fiords and, along with it, the privilege of constructing ports. The United States naturally denied this claim and argued that it was the intention of the treaty to specify the most westerly *continuous* range which ran behind the heads of the fiords.

The matter was settled by a mixed tribunal of United States and Canadian representatives, who, between 1903 and 1906, agreed on a boundary line which conformed approximately with the American contention. It ran from peak to peak without, at any point, extending farther inland than 30 miles (10 marine leagues) from the heads of the fiords. This line was subsequently demarcated by a boundary commission throughout its whole length.

The foregoing account has reviewed the nature of, and the problems raised by, the landward boundaries of the United States. These boundaries may be said to have been, in most instances, *antecedent* to human settlement. In many, they may be described as *pioneer* (see page 62). This is, of course, one of the reasons why they have been relatively successful. Most of the problems raised are due more to the vagueness and inaccuracies of the original delimitation than to any rights and privileges that they may have violated. Most boundaries in the New World, as well as in Australia and in some parts of Africa, are similar in antedating human settlement and development. In most other parts of the world, boundaries are later in date than human settlement. In such cases, either the boundaries have been gradually adjusted to the ethnic and cultural features, or they violate them. It does not really matter how *antecedent* boundaries are defined, provided that the definition is unambiguous. How *subsequent* and *superimposed* boundaries are defined, on the other hand, may make a great deal of difference to the relations of the states that are separated by them.

A MORPHOLOGICAL CLASSIFICATION

On pages 62 to 65, we presented a genetic classification of boundaries in which their origin was related to the development of the societies which they separate. More often, however, boundaries are classified according to their relationship to conspicuous features of the landscape. Such so-called "natural" boundaries have been grouped according to the degree of success with which they separate political societies. It is the primary purpose of boundaries to separate jurisdictions, and they may be judged successful when they do this with a minimum of dispute and friction.

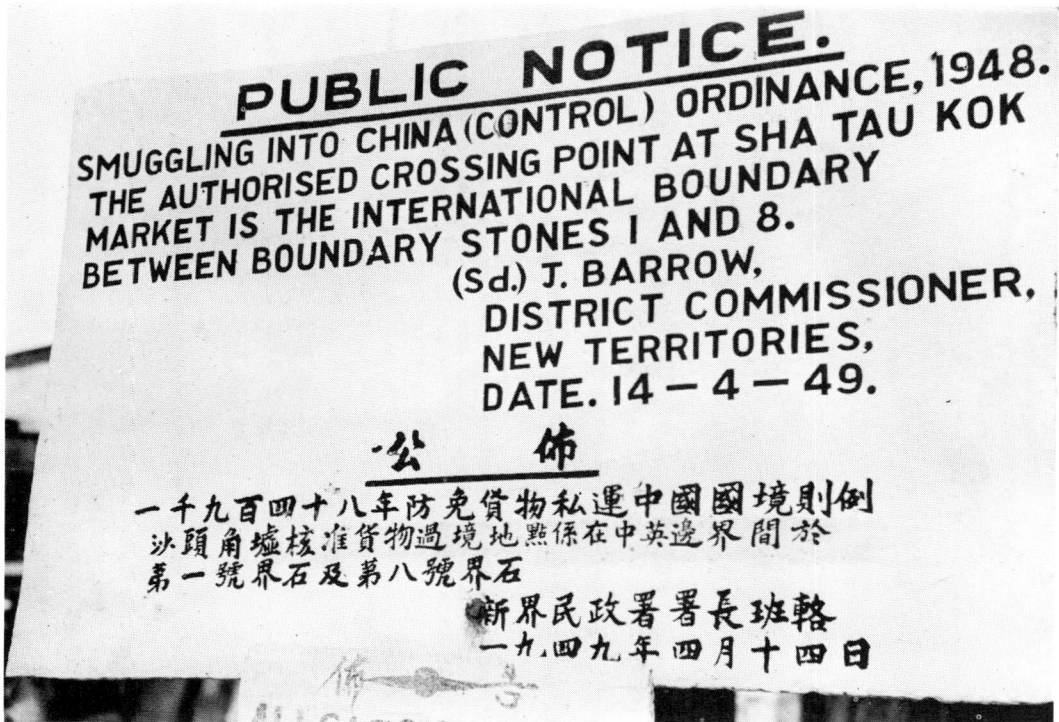

Figure 18 *One of the purposes of a boundary is to prevent smuggling. On the boundary between the leased territories of Hong Kong and Mainland China, the permitted crossing points are carefully defined and clearly marked.*
COURTESY: SHELL PHOTOGRAPHIC UNIT

The preceding pages have shown that in the drawing up of treaties there has been a conspicuous tendency to make boundaries conform with some natural feature that is marked on maps, a river or a line of hills or mountains. That these were sometimes less conspicuous in the landscape than on the map did not always seem to be recognized. At the same time, in those areas where boundaries were slowly crystallizing from a wide barrier tract between political societies, they also tended to conform with something visible and tangible in the landscape. However inconspicuous a river might be, it could, nonetheless, serve to define a political boundary. Thus, over much of the world, the limits of states came to be "natu-

rally marked boundaries." [21] There is, in general, nothing inevitable about such boundaries; they are not natural boundaries, or lines that in the nature of things must be boundaries. The idea that nature had prescribed limits to human societies and had expressed these limits in features of the natural landscape is an old one, and it dies hard. In no context are the words of L. Febvre more applicable than in the study of boundaries: "There are no necessities but everywhere possibilities and man, as master of the possibilities is judge of their use." And again, "What finally matters is the idea adopted by the people—the po-

[21] The term is Hartshorne's, *loc. cit.*

Figure 19   **A closed boundary.** *The road from Goslar* (*West Germany*) *to Wernigerode* (*East Germany*) *is closed and overgrown.* PHOTOGRAPH BY N. J. G. POUNDS

litical group—with regard to their geographical position, of its characteristics and advantages or inconveniences, though this idea may be quite wrong or have no basis in reality." [22] All boundaries are artificial in that they originate in human decision. The widely used term natural boundary, with its overtones of compulsion or necessity, is best avoided.

The function of a boundary is to separate political jurisdictions; does it also make intercourse and communication difficult? This has often been assumed to be the case. In extreme cases, the boundary has become a physical barrier, a bank and ditch, a wall, or a thicket of barbed wire, the purpose of

[22] Lucien Febvre, *A Geographical Introduction to History*, Kegan Paul, London, 1932, *passim*.

which is to limit movement across the boundary. In cases where such obstacles as these have not been created, there is, nevertheless, a limited number of crossing points at which officials are present to check documents and inspect merchandise. There are few boundaries where it is not possible for any athletic person to slip across, but such actions are punishable by one or the other of the states and are severely discouraged. Even the "unguarded boundary" between the United States and Canada has a limited number of crossing points (see Figure 16, p. 69), and the good will that exists on both sides has never been sufficient to permit unlimited and unrestricted passage across their mutual boundary. The idea that a boundary is "a place

Figure 20 *A degree of confusion seems to reign where the railroad from Hong Kong crosses the Bamboo Curtain on its route to Canton in Mainland China. Trains do not now run through, and passengers have to walk along the track, where it crosses the boundary, to a waiting train on the other side.*
COURTESY: SHELL PHOTOGRAPHIC UNIT

of intercourse with the foreigner" [23] and should be chosen so as to facilitate such meeting and mixing is a strange perversion of reality.

Naturally marked boundaries have been subjected to almost endless classification. The relative merits of different natural features for the purpose have often been

[23] C. B. Fawcett, *Frontiers: A Study in Political Geography,* Oxford University Press, Oxford, 1918, p. 30.

examined and one kind of boundary preferred to another. Such discussion, however, has little point, because when such boundaries were adopted, their advantage lay chiefly in the fact that they were obvious and unambiguous. In the first instance, they were not chosen because they were difficult to cross or because they presented a military barrier to invasion. It is only in recent times that the actual course of a political boundary has come to be a

Figure 21 *The Norwegian check point on the Swedish boundary between Skulerud and Arvika.* PHOTOGRAPH BY N. J. G. POUNDS

matter of military significance to the state that is enclosed by it.

The boundary lines themselves are of only two kinds: those made to conform with conspicuous features of the natural landscape, and those defined in geometrical terms, such as parallels, meridians, arcs of circles, and straight lines drawn between turning points. The principle on which a particular line is chosen, whether to separate ethnic or cultural groups, or to provide access for a state to resources or facilities, has nothing to do with the way in which it is made to conform, or not to conform, with landscape features. The latter is a morphological classification; the former, a functional.

From the morphological point of view, boundaries may, for convenience, be grouped into those which have been made (1) to follow the course of a mountain or hill range, (2) to follow the line of rivers, canals, and lakes, (3) to run through a desert, a forest, or a swamp, or (4) to conform with some other feature that may once have been conspicuous in the landscape.

Mountains and Hills: "Of all these natural features," wrote Sir Thomas Holdich, "a definite line of watershed carried by a conspicuous mountain ridge, or range, is undoubtedly the most lasting, the most unmistakable and the most efficient as a barrier." [24] Generally, though not always, mountain ranges separate cultural groups, by virtue of the relative difficulty in crossing them. For the same reason, they have always been thought of as good strategic or military boundaries. At least the more

[24] Sir Thomas H. Holdich, *Political Frontiers and Boundary Making,* Macmillan & Co., Ltd., London, 1916, pp. 146–147.

conspicuous ranges have been shown with varying degrees of error on the earliest maps, and it is not surprising that in boundary delimitation they have frequently been chosen as the line of a political boundary. Yet they are not the simple features of the landscape that the nongeographer often regards them as being. They are complex; they have width; only in the rarest instances is there a clearly defined crest line, and never does a crest line continue far without being interrupted by a transverse valley. Usually they are made up of a number of subparallel ranges, separated by interconnected valleys. A coincidence between the crest and the natural divide between rivers flowing in one direction and those in the other cannot be assumed and, in fact, is likely to be rare. Both sides of the highest and most continuous mountain range in the world, the Himalayas, are drained ultimately to the same river system.

A conspicuous mountain range has breadth as well as length, and in its valleys dwell human societies, which share the mountain environment and have adjusted their economies to it. Most of the more formidable mountain ranges constitute cultural regions, not cultural divides. Any boundary chosen tc follow a chain of mountains must, unless the area is totally uninhabited, break up human societies to some degree.

Boundaries drawn along mountains and hills, which seemed so unambiguous when first delimited, have proved to be the source of bitter controversy. Examples from

Figure 22   The crest of the Brenner Pass, shown here, was adopted in 1919 as the Austro-Italian boundary. Its only advantage was the strategic protection which it gave to Italy. PHOTOGRAPH BY N. J. G. POUNDS

Figure 23 **The solution of the Chile-Argentina boundary dispute was cemented in 1891 by the erection of the Christ of the Andes on the crest of the Uspallata Pass, which here constitutes the boundary.** COURTESY: EWING GALLOWAY

the United States—the boundary between the New England States and Canada and that between Alaska and Canada—demonstrate the difficulties in the way of reconciling simple geographical description with the complexities of a mountain range. Another, and equally interesting, case study is that of the Andean boundary between Chile and Argentina. The dispute over this boundary "raged for half a century with a vigor which was all the more intense in that the actual basis of it was always obscure—either buried in the universal ignorance which prevailed as to the physical conditions of the districts concerned, or enveloped in a cloud of conjecture when those districts were but half explored." [25] A boundary treaty of 1881 between the two countries "failed, in as much as it admitted of diverse interpretations when the terms of it were applied to the existing physical features of the Patagonian Andes." [26] This should cause no surprise, for, as Holdich observed, "Politicians, lawyers and even geographers, to a certain extent, lost sight of the fact that there is hardly a geographical term expressing a natural feature that will always and under all conditions, bear one unalterable interpretation." [27] That the interpretations of the Treaty of 1881 were diverse is clear from the map (Exhibit 30).

There was no crest line in the Andes; the water parting did not conform with the higher ranges, and the two countries, having failed to reach a compromise on their own, agreed to accept the arbitration of King Edward VII. Holdich's book set out to describe the field-work, preparatory to this arbitration. The final award, made in 1902, was commemorated by the huge

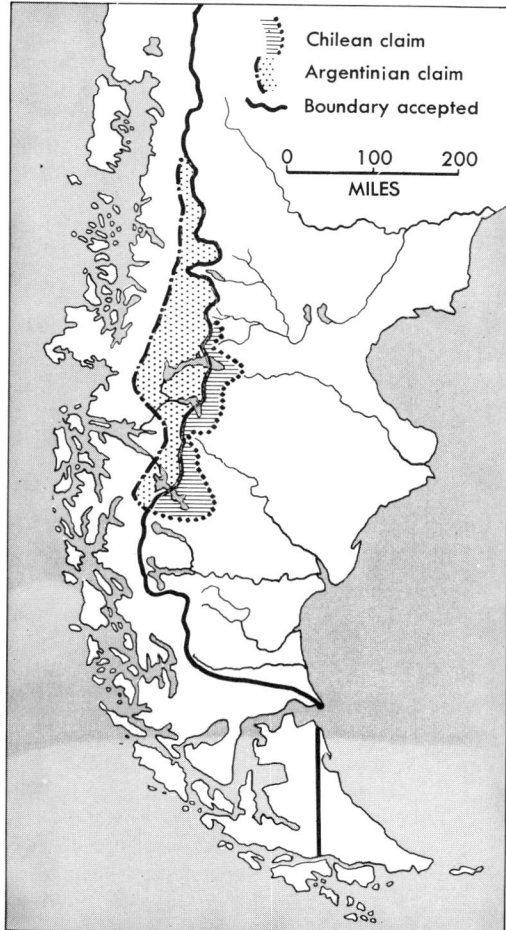

Exhibit 30   *The boundary between Chile and Argentina in the southern Andes.*

statue, the Christ of the Andes, erected where the boundary crossed the summit of the Uspallata Pass. The line adopted was, of course, a compromise between the conflicting claims of Chile and Argentina.

The current dispute between India and China regarding their mutual boundary in Tibet is in some ways analogous to the Andean dispute. The boundary, known as the *McMahon Line*, was delimited in 1914 in general terms by a treaty signed by Great Britain (for India), Tibet, and

[25] Sir Thomas H. Holdich, *The Countries of the King's Award,* Macmillan & Co., Ltd., London, 1904, p. 2.

[26] *Ibid.*, p. 2.

[27] *Ibid.*, p. 3.

Figure 24 The river Olsa forms part of the boundary between Poland and Czechoslovakia. It divides the city of Cieszyn (Polish, in the foreground) from that of Česky Těšín (Czechoslovak, in the background). The actual boundary is along the middle of the river, and the barriers are at the ends of the bridge. PHOTOGRAPH BY N. J. G. POUNDS

China,[28] but has never been—and probably could never be—demarcated. The boundary was designed to follow the line of the Himalaya and other ranges. The maps used may very well have left room for error, and there are places along the boundary where a slightly different alignment would be equally consistent with the Treaty of 1914. This, however, does not excuse the brusque

demands of China. Indeed, one might say that the acceptance of the McMahon Line for some forty years without protest from either side has given it almost a legal validity.

Rivers and Lakes: Rivers and lakes have the advantage of being more clearly marked on maps and more narrowly defined on the land than mountains and hills. For this reason, they have often been adopted in boundary delimitation. They seemed to require no further emphasis in the form of markers; in themselves they constituted a barrier to movement and, furthermore, were at one time thought of as

[28] P. P. Karan, "The India-China Boundary Dispute," *J. of G.*, vol. 59, pp. 16–21, 1960. The treaty was never ratified by China. See also Sir Olaf Caroe, "The Geography and Ethnics of India's Northern Frontiers," *G.J.*, vol. 125, pp. 298–309, 1960.

having some military value. Against the use of rivers as boundaries, it has often been argued that they do not usually coincide with the divisions between human societies. "A valley is a natural unit; and as the land becomes fully occupied the river tends to become the axial line of an area of dense population, and so a place of frequent intercourse in trade and social life, so that the peoples of its banks become more or less assimilated to one another." [29] Furthermore, as Jones has pointed out, "The unifying effects of rivers are increasing," [30] as their waters come to be used to an increasing degree for navigation, irrigation, and power generation, and as, at the same time, the need for water control over the entire basin as a whole comes to be realized (see Chapter 11).

Irrespective of such considerations, however, the decision to locate a boundary along a watercourse itself raises problems. These are of two kinds: the position of the boundary, which is a line, in relation to the river itself, which has width; and, second, the natural changes which occur in the bed of the river. It is quite inadequate to specify in the delimitation clauses of a treaty that the boundary shall follow a river. This has to be made more precise: the boundary may follow the median or middle line of the stream; it may follow the windings of the navigable channel; it may be traced along one bank or the other; or it may join up turning points in the stream itself.[31] All these expedients have been used. The Paris Treaties of 1919–1920 adopted the common principle that, when a boundary followed a river, it should be the median line of non-

navigable rivers and the middle of the "principal channel" (the *thalweg*) in the case of navigable rivers. This clumsy distinction was made all the more difficult to interpret by the fact that it is almost impossible to distinguish between rivers that are navigable and those which are not, without detailed reference to the season of the year, the level of water, and the size of craft involved. Such detail as this has never been specified in treaties, and there must be many a river wherein the precise position of the international boundary would be a matter of dispute if only the nations on each side showed any disposition to dispute it.

The practice described above (page 76), regarding the treatment of changes in the course of the Rio Grande and of other American rivers, has come to be the accepted international practice.[32] Avulsion does not change the course of the boundary, though accretion may bring about a gradual change in it. The formation of outliers of a state's territory beyond the main stream of the river itself, and frequently not accessible by a bridge, creates minor administrative problems. In the case of the United States–Mexican boundary along the Rio Grande, as has already been seen, these minor outliers of territory have been eliminated by the International Boundary Commission that was established to supervise the boundary as a whole, but they are all too numerous between the States occupying the drainage basin of the Mississippi.

In other parts of the world, there are boundary rivers where changes of course and the frequency of islands may raise the the same kind of difficulty. The Mekong and Salween in Asia, the Congo, Volta, and Zambezi in Africa, the Paraguay, Orinoco,

[29] Fawcett, *op. cit.,* p. 54.

[30] Stephen B. Jones, *Boundary Making,* Carnegie Endowment for International Peace, Division of Cultural Law, Washington, D.C., 1945, p. 110.

[31] Turning points are fixed points, between which the boundary is formed by straight-line sections.

[32] L. Oppenheim, *International Law,* 8th ed., Longmans, Green & Co., Ltd., London, 1955, vol. 1, p. 533.

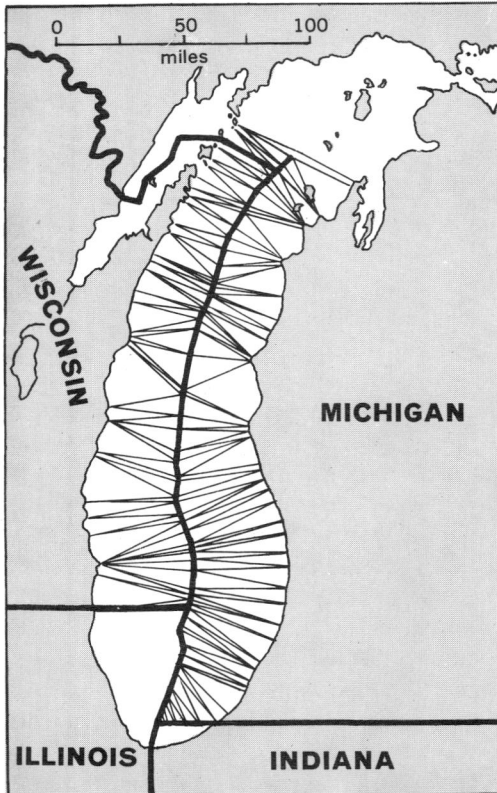

Exhibit 31   *The median line in Lake Michigan.*
AFTER S. WHITTEMORE BOGGS

and Uruguay in South America, not to mention a host of lesser rivers, could all become politically important.

The boundary through lakes is commonly made to follow the median, or middle, line. There obviously can be no question of demarcating such a boundary, but its precise delimitation is, nevertheless, a matter of importance. Jurisdiction over accidents and incidents that may occur to ships and control over fisheries are both dependent upon the alignment of the boundary. The term median line, or middle line, is itself susceptible of more than one interpretation. Does it, for instance, divide the lake into two equal parts, is it a line at all points equally distant from

either shore, or is it a line drawn through the middle points of a number of lines drawn from shore to shore across the lake? This question was settled for Lake Erie by the International Waterways Commission. A line was traced on the map of Lake Erie so that, at every point along it, it was equidistant from each shore.

Nowhere else has the course of an international boundary through a lake been studied in such detail as in the Great Lakes (Exhibit 31), and the principles established here have been made applicable to the rest of the Great Lakes system, including Lake Michigan, through which runs the state boundary between Wisconsin and Michigan. It also applies to boundaries in the African lakes Tanganyika, Mweru, and Nyasa.

On the other hand, straight lines, following meridians or parallels, have sometimes been used to delimit boundaries in lakes. This practice has, for example, been adopted in Lake Victoria in Africa.

Forests, Swamps, and Deserts: These features of the earth's surface have in common only their irregular extent and their scanty population. They have frequently served as frontiers between communities. The relative difficulty of traversing them has held communities apart, thus intensifying their differences from one another. Forest, swamp, and desert have tended at many times and in many different parts of the world to form a wide no man's land, into which settlements have sometimes penetrated slowly from each side. The Sahara Desert has, throughout most of human history, separated the distinctive cultures of the African savanna from those of the Mediterranean Basin. The forests of northeastern Europe have similarly constituted cultural barriers, separating Finn from Russian, Russian from Lithuanian, and Lithuanian from Pole. Swamps are, in general, less extensive than either desert or forest and thus less effective as a cultural barrier. Nevertheless, the marshes along the lower Rhine and Meuse Valleys are not unrelated, through their influence on military campaigns, to the subsequent political boundary between Belgium and the Netherlands. The Pripet Marshes in eastern Poland are today traversed by the boundary between Poland and the Soviet Union. The projected Curzon Line ran through the marshes, and at several periods they have formed part of Poland's eastern frontier. It is rare, however, for one of these barrier areas to be deliberately chosen for the alignment of a boundary. Where the latter shows an apparent conformity with forest, desert, or swamp, it is usually because it is adjusted to an ethnic divide which coincides with one of these.

Geometrical Boundaries: In the absence of clearly determined physical features, boundaries have frequently been delimited in geometrical terms. One of the earliest uses of this method was in the Papal Bull of 1481, when the Pope divided the still undiscovered parts of the world between Spain and Portugal. The Pope's line was subsequently amended by another Papal Bull in 1493 and accepted by the two parties in the Treaty of Tordesillas (1494). This time it was defined as the meridian running 370 leagues west of the Cape Verde Islands. An early use of a parallel of latitude was in the delimitation of the northern boundary of Florida in 1795 by treaty between the United States and Spain. In 1818, the 49th degree of latitude was accepted as the northern boundary of the United States westward from the Lake of the Woods. Most of the boundaries between the States west of the Mississippi are defined in geometrical terms (Exhibit 32); almost all the boundaries within Australia, and a large part of those in Africa, are similarly geometrical.

Geometrical boundaries are, first and foremost, lines of latitude (parallels) and longitude (meridians). These are easy to define on paper, and their demarcation in the field, with modern methods of survey-

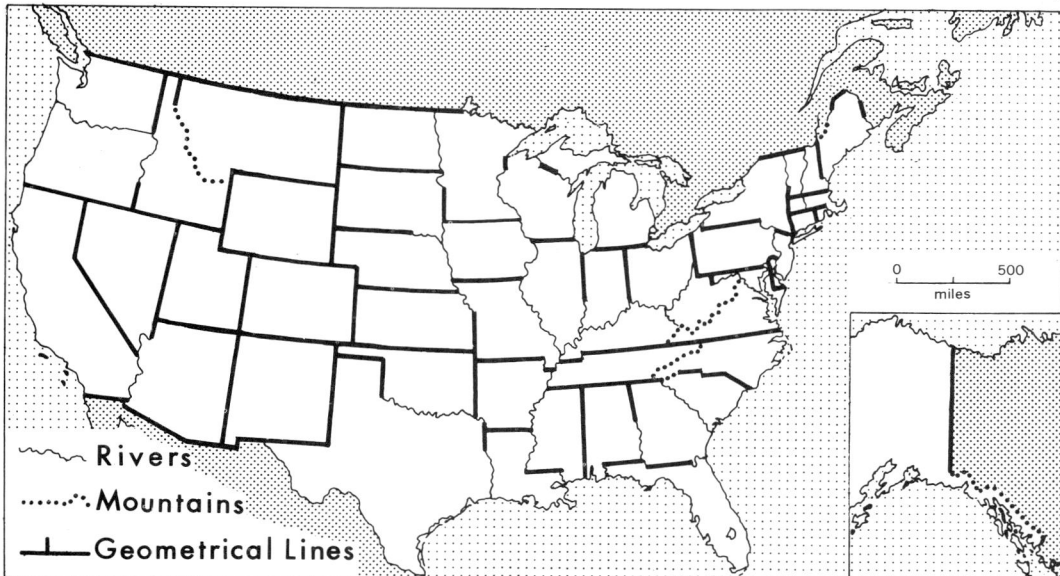

Exhibit 32 *Boundaries within the continental United States.*

ing, presents no problems. There is a super-ficial similarity between meridians and par-allels and other straight lines drawn be-tween points, known as turning points, whose location is already known with pre-cision. A number of boundaries are actually made up of a series of short, straight, oblique (i.e., neither north-south nor east-west) segments, traced between turning points. The boundary of the Gadsden Pur-chase was defined by the Treaty of 1853 as "a straight line" from the point 31°20′ N latitude, 111° W longitude, to "a point on the Colorado River twenty English miles below the junction of the Gila and Colorado rivers." This line is oblique. If the turning points are close together, there can be little difficulty in demarcating the connecting lines. If, on the other hand, they are far apart, the problem becomes immensely complicated. A straight line drawn on a map may not, according to the projection of the map, be the shortest distance on the ground. A line of constant compass bearing between two points will appear as a straight line on only one commonly used map projection [33] and will not be a straight line on the ground. Straight-line boundaries, provided that they are neither parallels nor meridians, can all be interpreted in dif-ferent ways on the ground. The fact that they have not occasioned dispute is in large measure attributable to the fact that the territory in question has hitherto not been worth disputing.

Many boundaries in Africa are oblique, as are also a few interstate boundaries in the United States, including the southwest-ern boundary of Nevada, a part of that be-tween Arkansas and Oklahoma, and several short lengths of boundary between the Eastern States, as well as some boundaries in the Middle East, the Soviet Union, and Australia.

[33] This is, of course, Mercator's projection.

The use of geometrical lines implies, in general, an ignorance of the nature of the terrain. Their use shows a total lack of concern for such people as may live in the area to be divided, and in some instances they have, in fact, cut across tribal terri-tories. Such boundaries are politically suc-cessful only when they are antecedent to settlement, if not also entirely pioneer. For this reason, it has not been important that there were errors in demarcation, provided that demarcation took place before settle-ment.

On the other hand, a geometrical boundary may be accepted at the confer-ence table because it affords the only pos-sible compromise between two states or groups of states. The 38th parallel in Ko-rea was established in 1945 as the boundary between North and South Korea by nego-tiation between the great powers (princi-pally the United States and the Soviet Union) without reference to the country which they so arbitrarily cut in two. Simi-larly, a line which corresponds roughly with the 17th parallel was accepted as the bound-ary between North and South Vietnam and reflected the balance of forces between the Chinese and the French, supported by their allies, when the Indo-Chinese war ended in 1954. In both these instances the boundary was both *geometrical* and *super-imposed*.

A final category of geometrical bound-aries consist of arcs of circles, drawn with prescribed centers and radii. Thus, part of the boundary of the State of Delaware is, according to an agreement of 1760 between Pennsylvania and Delaware, the arc of a circle of 12 English statute miles in radius, drawn from the center of the city of New Castle, Delaware. An arc of a circle was also used to define a part of the Franco-German boundary of 1871 near Belfort. The boundary of the British colony of Gambia, defined by treaty as running parallel to the river Gambia, has become, owing to the meanders of the river, a series of arcs of circles, with their centers on the stream itself. Examples of such boundaries are few and relatively unimportant.

The Complexity of Modern Boundaries: In a long-settled continent, such as Europe, and even in Latin America and much of Asia, comparatively few of the boundaries conform with any of the features of the landscape described in the previous pages. Most of them are superimposed. They have been delimited and demarcated long after human settlement began, in many instances long after the land had been brought under cultivation and settlement and industries had developed. As a general rule, boundaries in such areas have gradually hardened or crystallized as need arose. They may for short distances follow the line of small streams, but as a general rule, it can be said only that they separate field from field and house from house. Recent boundary changes have aimed to include specific communities or specific resources or services within a particular country. Boundary commissions have generally tried not to break up villages, farms, or field systems, in so far as this was consistent with the general purpose of the boundary delimitation.

What Boundary Is Best? This at once raises the question: What is the most desirable form that a boundary can take? An immense literature has been devoted to this subject, much of it based upon the assumption that a good boundary must be a strategic one—one likely to discourage attack and to facilitate defense. This military factor in boundaries was on several occasions important during the nineteenth century. The boundary established between Germany and France by the Treaty of Frankfurt of 1871 was in part at least based upon what the Germans considered militarily defensible. "The dominant positive fac-

tor," in the words of Richard Hartshorne, "was the strategic concern to secure the fortress of Metz and the control of the Moselle route. . . ." [34] This route was overlooked on its western side by the steep escarpment of the Côtes de Moselle. "The new boundary . . . was located throughout its extent, save for one minor exception apparently overlooked at the time, a few miles back of the edge of the escarpment." [35]

A similar example of the deliberate placing of a boundary in order to secure the maximum military advantage from it comes from the Treaty of Berlin (1878–1879), regulating the boundary between Turkey and Bulgaria. The boundary was made to conform with the "military crest," which was defined in this region of rounded hills as "the line connecting the points where the slope, being generally rather gentle at the summit along the crest, is accentuated and becomes steeper to form the side of a valley, river or ravine." The boundary thus "follows the lower and exterior margin of the hills or the saddles; so that the whole relatively level surface of the passes or of the saddles themselves remains in the sole possession of one state," [36] namely, Bulgaria.

Somewhat similar was the claim of the Soviet Union in 1939 to part of the Finnish Province of Karelia. The reason given was that the Finnish boundary lay only about seventeen miles from Leningrad— within easy artillery range—and that this constituted a threat to the security of the city. When Finland rejected the Soviet demand, the Soviet Union declared war (the "Winter War") and by the Treaty of Mos-

[34] Richard Hartshorne, "The Franco-German Boundary of 1871," *World Politics*, vol. 2, p. 221, 1949–1950.

[35] *Ibid.*, p. 247.

[36] C. V. Adami, *National Frontiers in Relation to International Law*, T. T. Behrens (trans.), Oxford University Press, Oxford, 1927, p. 10.

cow in 1940 advanced her boundary in Karelia to at least ninety miles from the threatened city. Similar, too, was the case of the French city of Belfort. In 1871, the Germans conceded that their boundary should not lie within artillery range of the city, which remained in France.

Less specific was Czechoslovakia's claim to the "historic boundaries" of Bohemia, which run through the Šumava, Krušné Hory, and Krkonoše Hory. The line here was chosen only in part to secure a tactical advantage for Czechoslovakia, though Czechoslovakia failed to gain all the territory claimed for strategic reasons. Locally, Czechoslovak territory was dominated by the higher ground lying inside Germany, but for much of its length, the boundary ran through hills or mountainous country, which, it was supposed, would have made aggression against Czechoslovakia difficult. At the same time, some sections of French public opinion called for the establishment of Germany's western boundary along the river Rhine, which, it was claimed, would have added to France's military security. The Western Allies did, however, garrison the left bank of the Rhine for a number of years.

When Great Britain delimited her boundary in India with Afghanistan and Tibet, its course was strongly influenced by military considerations. Along the especially disturbed Afghan border, a narrow belt of territory was left between the legal boundary—the Durand Line—and the administrative boundary. This buffer strip (now part of Pakistan) insulated the territory of India proper from the tribes within Afghanistan. The boundary between India and Tibet was defined as following the crest of the Himalayan mountains (the McMahon Line). On the boundary of French Indo-China (now Vietnam) and Thailand, a buffer strip, similar to that on the Indian northwest frontier, was left

along two sections of the river Mekong. One could catalogue many such examples of the alignment of a political boundary along some feature of tactical importance and, alternatively, the establishment of a waste zone over which sovereignty was claimed but not exercised. In the context of nineteenth- and early twentieth-century warfare, such boundaries had military significance. Today they have very little. There may still be some military significance in the physical nature of a boundary separating peoples not equipped with modern weapons, but as between the greater powers of the modern world, there is no such thing as a strategic or scientific boundary.

Boundaries, Ethnic and Economic: The nation-states aim, as we have seen, to establish boundaries that include, within the territory of each, all people of the corresponding nation and, conversely, to exclude all others. The treaties negotiated at Paris in 1919–1920 aimed at establishing ethnic boundaries, the purpose of which was to separate nations from each other. Their success was somewhat less than complete. The new states of India, Pakistan, and Burma were established on bases that may loosely be called "ethnic." Among the newly emerging states of Africa, there is the possibility that boundaries may be changed to make them accord with tribal divisions, and a danger that this may not be achieved peacefully. "At the Paris Conference" (1918–1920), wrote Eric Fischer, "language was regarded as the best criterion for drawing boundaries. . . . Shift of emphasis from physical features to cultural characteristics . . . reflected the popular swing toward self-determination." [37] This ideal was written into the peace treaties. The numerous plebiscites of the postwar years were aimed only at securing a greater correlation of the social or ethnic bound-

[37] Eric Fischer, "On Boundaries," *World Politics*, vol. 1, p. 196, 1948–1949.

ary with the political, and the Minorities Treaties were designed to secure the rights of ethnic groups that could not possibly be satisfied politically.

The author just quoted detects a change of emphasis by the end of the Second World War. Those who negotiated the settlements of 1945 and subsequent years "were primarily and openly concerned with the economic effects of their decisions. This shift in stress within a short time from one factor to another reflects the transient character of some criteria of boundary-making." [38] Economic considerations were far from neglected at the Paris Conference. The care taken to assure commercial outlets for the trade of Poland, Czechoslovakia, and Yugoslavia, to satisfy France's need for coal, to observe an Open Door policy (see Chapter 10) in the former colonial territories, to include the cities of the margin of the Hungarian Plain with the mountain areas which they served is evidence of this. But, in general, ethnic considerations prevailed, even to the extent of partitioning the coal-basin and industrial area of Upper Silesia on linguistic lines between Germany and Poland and of separating the city of Danzig politically from the country whose needs it served.

Most of the territorial changes that have taken place since the Second World War have been made in spite of—rather than as a result of—ethnic distributions. Poland's westward movement to the Oder-Neisse (Odra-Nysa) line, though not without historical justification, was made chiefly to compensate for territories lost in the east. Minor changes along the boundary of Germany with the Netherlands and Belgium were mainly technical and economic in nature. In Poland and Czechoslovakia, and to a lesser extent also in Yugoslavia and the Balkans, ethnic boundaries have

been adjusted to economic by the forced migration of minority groups. Rather than risk losing valuable industrial and other resources through a change of boundary, governments have expelled the minority peoples from their territory (see Chapter 5). It is premature, however, to suggest that technical and economic considerations are now of foremost importance in boundary delimitation. The partition of the Punjab (see page 294) in 1947 was made according to communal (that is, religious) differences, and despite the grave objection to the division of the irrigation system based on the Indus Rivers. The boundaries between Israel and Jordan, established in 1948 in the heat of a communal war, could not possibly have been more poorly conceived from the technical and economic aspects of irrigation. The two countries have successfully prevented each other from making proper use of the water of the river Jordan (see Chapter 11).

How Important Are Boundary Questions? More than half a century ago, Lord Curzon wrote that "frontiers [i.e., boundaries] are indeed the razor's edge on which hang suspended the modern issues of war or peace, of life or death for nations." [39] A few years later, that veteran member of boundary commissions, Sir Thomas H. Holdich, could write that "in the recent history of the world most of the important wars, and of international quarrels to which war seemed to be the inevitable sequel, have arisen over disputed boundaries." [40] As important a work as Isaiah Bowman's *The New World* [41] devotes, what might seem to us forty years later, unnecessary

[38] *Ibid.*

[39] Lord Curzon of Kedleston, *Frontiers*, Oxford University Press, Oxford, 1908, p. 7.

[40] Sir Thomas H. Holdich, *Political Frontiers and Boundary Making*, Macmillan & Co., Ltd., London, 1916, p. 1.

[41] The first edition of *The New World* appeared in 1921 (see Bibliography).

space to boundary problems. The political boundaries of the world have not greatly changed since he wrote; yet they seem to us much less important. Has this change in attitude and emphasis come about because boundaries are really less important than they were? To some extent this is the case. International organizations, some of them calling for complete freedom of trade between their members, others requiring greater liberty of movement of both people and goods, have deprived boundaries of some of their function. Then, too, the brashness has worn off from some of the new-found nationalism, and with this some of the intolerance and distrust toward other peoples and communities. To some degree, too, boundary problems have been suppressed by problems that seem more urgent. They remain important but are blanketed by a greater conflict. It would be highly unbecoming to raise minor boundary questions between the NATO powers when they are trying to present a united front. Austria, with her neutral status, cannot be provoked into raising, at least officially, the question of the Austro-Italian boundary of the South Tyrol. And between members of the Communist camp, boundary claims and counterclaims cannot be raised, because the Kremlin, too, does not allow the monolithic unity of its alliances to show any crack. The farther a country is removed—both geographically and ideologically—from the present East-West tensions, the more likely are boundary questions and conflicts to assert themselves. Hungary does not raise her voice against Czechoslovakia or Rumania, but Ecuador still presses her claims to territory near the headwaters of the Amazon, and claims and counterclaims in tropical Africa as well as in Central America are likely to continue.

There is one important exception to the statement that boundary problems are sig-

nificant only in areas remote from the cold-war issues. Along the Curtain—whether Iron, Bamboo or some other material—where the two worlds are in direct juxtaposition, boundary questions are brought to the fore. West German claims, so far unofficial, for a revision of the western boundaries of Poland and Czechoslovakia, Bulgarian claims on Macedonia, Albanian on Yugoslavia, occasional Yugoslav mutterings about Trieste, Soviet desires for a change in her boundary with Turkey, Chinese claims against India, and North Vietnam's against Laos—all fit into the general pattern of conflict along the boundary between the Communist and the free worlds.

The traveler in Europe before the Second World War, or even a few years ago, was obliged to face customs and immigration officials each time he crossed a political boundary. Now the traveler in western Europe has little of this. Customs examinations are perfunctory, if indeed they are conducted at all. Travel between the Scandinavian countries does not even require a passport. Here boundaries may be described as weak. A broadly similar condition prevails within the Commonwealth and between the United States and Canada. In contrast with this is the strength of the boundary separating Communist and non-Communist countries. Crossing points are few, and illicit crossing is prevented by all the obstacles that barbed wire and electrified fences can offer. Permission to cross for the citizens of both sides is difficult to obtain. The weakening of boundaries within each of the Great Power blocs, as well as the strengthening of the boundaries between them, is perhaps the most significant contemporary trend in the function of boundaries.

In 1945, before the East-West conflict had emerged into the open, Stephen Jones wrote that "the major sources of serious boundary friction lie in the general situation rather than in the line itself. Hence it is too much to expect that any shift in boundary sites can guarantee peace. A fallacy of many schemes for territorial redistribution lies in this fact." [42] In other words, if every boundary question that is supposed to disturb or threaten the peace of nations were settled or removed, the over-all conflict would remain. This is a far cry from the convictions of Curzon. A boundary dispute today is likely to be merely a symptom of a dispute far more profound and far less tractable. Boundaries have ceased to be the razor's edge.

The Ideological Boundary: Boundaries are of diminishing importance, both in people's daily lives and also as a source of conflict. Yet conflict continues, and international tensions today are perhaps greater than at any time in the recent past. Formerly tensions were between nation-states, and wars began along their boundaries. The "loyalty to the nation and the nation-state" [43] became the overriding loyalty. In retrospect, the period of nation-states and national wars was one of delightful simplicity, with the issues in every conflict, both geographical and ideological, apparently simple and clear-cut. But, as Ladis Kristof has put it:

New ideas sprang up and generated new values and new loyalties. Today, not only is the old consensus undermined, but the very concept of territorial law is challenged. "Proletarians have no fatherland" and "proletarians of all countries unite" are the best known but not by any means the only ideas which try to transgress on the territorially organized socio-political order. In the resulting confusion friends are sought in enemy territory, and

enemies discovered among fellow citizens of the homeland. [44]

The conflict is transferred from the boundaries of territorially organized states to the minds of men. In all states, whether Communist or non-Communist, there are individuals who have not accepted the ideology of the state in which they live and who retain a loyalty to the ideas and ideals of the other camp. There are, further, the large numbers who are not committed to either side, sometimes opportunists waiting for a crucial turn in events, sometimes political agnostics not yet convinced by either side.

The boundary between the followers of the two dominant ideologies of the present age, together with the location of the uncommitted "frontier" people who lie in between, is not a geographical phenomenon. It occurs everywhere where there are people. It penetrates every state like the lines which separate political parties. The relevance of this new form of boundary to national power is too obvious to need demonstration. It is an essentially political matter, which the methods of geographical analysis can do little to illuminate.

But each ideology has a geographical focus, and it is possible to describe in geographical terms the areas which are officially committed to one ideology or the other. The degree of control which the Soviet Union exercises over its allies may be difficult in all instances to assess, but there can be no doubt about the limits of the Communist bloc. The status and importance of the boundaries between members of the bloc are weak; those of the boundary around the bloc as a whole are immensely strong. As Kristof has pointed out, "The importance and 'strength' of a boundary—the degree to which it restricts

[42] Stephen B. Jones, *Boundary Making*, Carnegie Endowment for International Peace, Division of Cultural Law, Washington, D.C., 1945, p. 13.

[43] Ladis K. D. Kristof, "The Nature of Frontiers and Boundaries," *A.A.A.G.*, vol. 49, p. 278, 1959.

[44] *Ibid.*

and 'impinges on life'—today depends largely on whether or not it coincides with the limits of an ideological ecumene." [45]

The free world is less easy to define in geographical terms. Certain groups of countries belong unreservedly to it, but it also has its false friends and doubtful allies, countries that may lapse into neutralism or even adhere to the opposite camp. Between lies the "gray" area, the "uncommitted third," some parts of it open to receive the blandishments of either side, some rigidly neutral. This last region of the world has been called the "international frontier." "With the division of the earth into two power blocs," wrote Duncan Hall, "the international frontier has suddenly become more sharply defined and more menacing." [46] The same author wrote that, thanks to the Monroe Doctrine, "No part of the Western Hemisphere—unless it is the Polar Regions—can be said to fall within any of the zones of the international frontier." [47] But the international frontier is fluid. One can no longer say with any degree of assurance that the New World belongs wholly to the non-Communist world; for there is more than one area in which loyalties to the "Western" ideology are more than suspect.

In Europe, the international frontier embraces the formally neutral countries of Switzerland and Austria, and also those whose present policy tends toward neutrality: Sweden, Finland, and Yugoslavia. Most of the Middle East, India, Burma, and Indonesia, as well as most of independent Africa, belong also to the international frontier. It is within this frontier that most of the problems of the international frontier occur at the present time. Here the rival ideologies are struggling, not to annex a few square miles of land in the name of a nation, but to control men's economic organization and social thought.

BIBLIOGRAPHY

Adami, C. V.: *National Frontiers in Relation to International Law,* T. T. Behrens (trans.), Oxford University Press, Oxford, 1927.

Alexander, Lewis M.: "Recent Changes in the Benelux-German Boundary," *G.R.,* vol. 43, pp. 69–76, 1953.

Bloomfield, L. M., and Gerald F. Fitzgerald: *Boundary Waters Problems of Canada and the United States,* The Carswell Company Limited, Toronto, Canada, 1958.

Boggs, S. Whittemore: *International Boundaries,* Columbia University Press, New York, 1940.

Boundaries, Areas, Geographic Centers, and Altitudes of the Several States, Geological Survey Bulletin 817, U. S. Department of the Interior, 1932.

Bowman, Isaiah: *The New World,* World Book Company, Yonkers, N.Y., 1921–1928.

Brebner, J. B.: *North Atlantic Triangle,* Yale University Press, New Haven, Conn., 1945.

Curzon of Kedleston, Lord: *Frontiers,* Oxford University Press, Oxford, 1908.

Fawcett, C. B.: *Frontiers: A Study in Political Geography,* Oxford University Press, Oxford, 1918.

Fischer, Eric: "On Boundaries," *World Politics,* vol. 1, pp. 196–222, 1948–1949.

Geographic Reports, Office of the Geographer, Department of State, no. 1, *Boundary Concepts and Definitions,* 1961.

Gilfillan, S. Columb: "European Political Boundaries," *Political Science Quarterly,* vol. 39, pp. 458–484, 1924.

Hall, H. Duncan: "Zones of the International Frontier," *G.R.,* vol. 38, pp. 615–625, 1948.

Hartshorne, Richard: "Suggestions on the Terminology of Political Boundaries," *A.A.A.G.,* vol. 26, pp. 56–57, 1936.

———: "A Survey of the Boundary Problems of Europe," in Charles C. Colby (ed.),

[45] *Ibid.,* p. 281.

[46] H. Duncan Hall, "Zones of the International Frontier," *G.R.,* vol. 38, p. 615, 1948.

[47] *Ibid.,* p. 617.

Geographic Aspects of International Relations, University of Chicago Press, Chicago, 1938, pp. 161–213.

Hartshorne, Richard: "The Franco-German Boundary of 1871," *World Politics,* vol. 2, pp. 209–250, 1949–1950.

Holdich, Sir Thomas H.: *The Countries of the King's Award,* Macmillan & Co., Ltd., London, 1904.

———: *Political Frontiers and Boundary Making,* Macmillan & Co., Ltd., London, 1916.

House, J. W.: "The Franco-Italian Boundary in the Alpes Maritimes," *Institute of British Geographers: Transactions and Papers,* 1959, pp. 107–131.

International Boundary Studies, Office of the Geographer, Department of State, no. 1, *Algeria-Libya Boundary,* 1961; no. 2, *Libya-Niger Boundary,* 1961; no. 3, *Chad-Libya Boundary,* 1961; no. 4, *France-Italy Boundary,* 1961; no. 5, *Dominican Republic–Haiti Boundary,* 1961; no. 6, *Afghanistan-Iran Boundary,* 1961; no. 7, *Belgium-Germany Boundary,* 1961.

Jackson, W. A. Douglas: *The Russo-Chinese Borderlands,* D. Van Nostrand Co., Inc., Princeton, N.J., 1962.

Jones, Stephen B.: "The Forty-ninth Parallel in the Great Plains: the Historical Geography of a Boundary," *J. of G.,* vol. 21, pp. 357–367, 1932.

———: "The Cordilleran Section of the Canada–United States Borderland," *G.J.,* vol. 89, pp. 439–450, 1937.

———: *Boundary Making,* Carnegie Endowment for International Peace, Division of Cultural Law, Washington, D.C., 1945.

———: "Boundary Concepts in the Setting of Place and Time," *A.A.A.G.,* vol. IL, pp. 241–255, 1959.

Karan, P. P.: "The Indo-Chinese Boundary Dispute," *J. of G.,* vol. 59, pp. 16–21, 1960.

Kristof, Ladis K. D.: "The Nature of Frontiers and Boundaries," *A.A.A.G.,* vol. IL, pp. 269–282, 1959.

Lattimore, Owen: "Origins of the Great Wall of China," *G.R.,* vol. 27, pp. 529–549, 1927.

———: *Inner Asian Frontiers of China,* American Geographical Society of New York, 1951; paperback edition, Beacon Press, Boston, 1962.

Mayo, Lawrence S.: "The Forty-fifth Parallel: A Detail of the Unguarded Boundary," *G.R.,* vol. 13, pp. 255–265, 1923.

McCune, Shannon: "The Thirty-eighth Parallel in Korea," *World Politics,* vol. 1, pp. 223–232, 1948–1949.

McMahon, Sir Henry: "International Boundaries," *Journal of the Royal Society of Arts (London),* vol. 84, pp. 2–16, 1935.

Oppenheim, L.: *International Law,* 8th ed., Longmans, Green & Co., Ltd., London, 1955, vol. 1.

Pounds, N. J. G.: "The Origin of the Idea of Natural Frontiers in France," *A.A.A.G.,* vol. 41, pp. 146–157, 1951.

———: "France and 'Les Limites Naturelles' from the Seventeenth to the Twentieth Centuries," *A.A.A.G.,* vol. 44, pp. 51–62, 1954.

Spain, James W.: "Pakistan's North-west Frontier," *Middle East Journal,* vol. 8, pp. 27–40, 1954.

Timm, Charles A.: "Some Observations on the Nature and Work of the International Boundary Commission, United States and Mexico," *Southwestern Social Science Quarterly,* vol. 15, pp. 271–297, 1934–1935.

4 THE TERRITORIAL SEA

Man marks the earth with ruin—his control stops with the shore. . . . BYRON

The rightful jurisdiction of Her Majesty, her heirs and successors, extends and has always extended over the open seas adjacent to the coasts of the United Kingdom and of all other parts of Her Majesty's dominions to such a distance as is necessary for the defence and security of such dominions. . . . UNITED KINGDOM, TERRITORIAL WATERS JURISDICTION ACT, 1878

ONLY TWENTY STATES IN THE MODERN WORLD ARE COMPLETELY SURrounded by the territory of their neighbors. All others have some frontage on the sea. A few, such as Japan, New Zealand, and the Malagash Republic, are entirely surrounded by the sea (Exhibit 33). Others, such as Iraq and Jordan, have a coast line of only a few miles. But however short their coast may be, these states all share the problem of setting some seaward limit to the extent of their sovereignty.

Sovereignty over the sea differs in many respects from that over the land. The sea has no permanent, settled inhabitants. Its resources —other than the minerals that may occur beneath the ocean floor— are in its fisheries. Sovereignty over the sea can consist only in denying to others the right to fish, to extract minerals, to navigate, or even to fly over that portion of the sea which is said to be sovereign. Many claims have been made at various times to sovereignty over the sea. In the sixteenth century, Spain and Portugal claimed sovereignty over much of the ocean surface of the globe and, in so far as they were able, excluded the ships of other states. Early in the seventeenth century the famous Dutch lawyer, Hugo Grotius, in his *Mare liberum*, put forward the idea that no state could con-

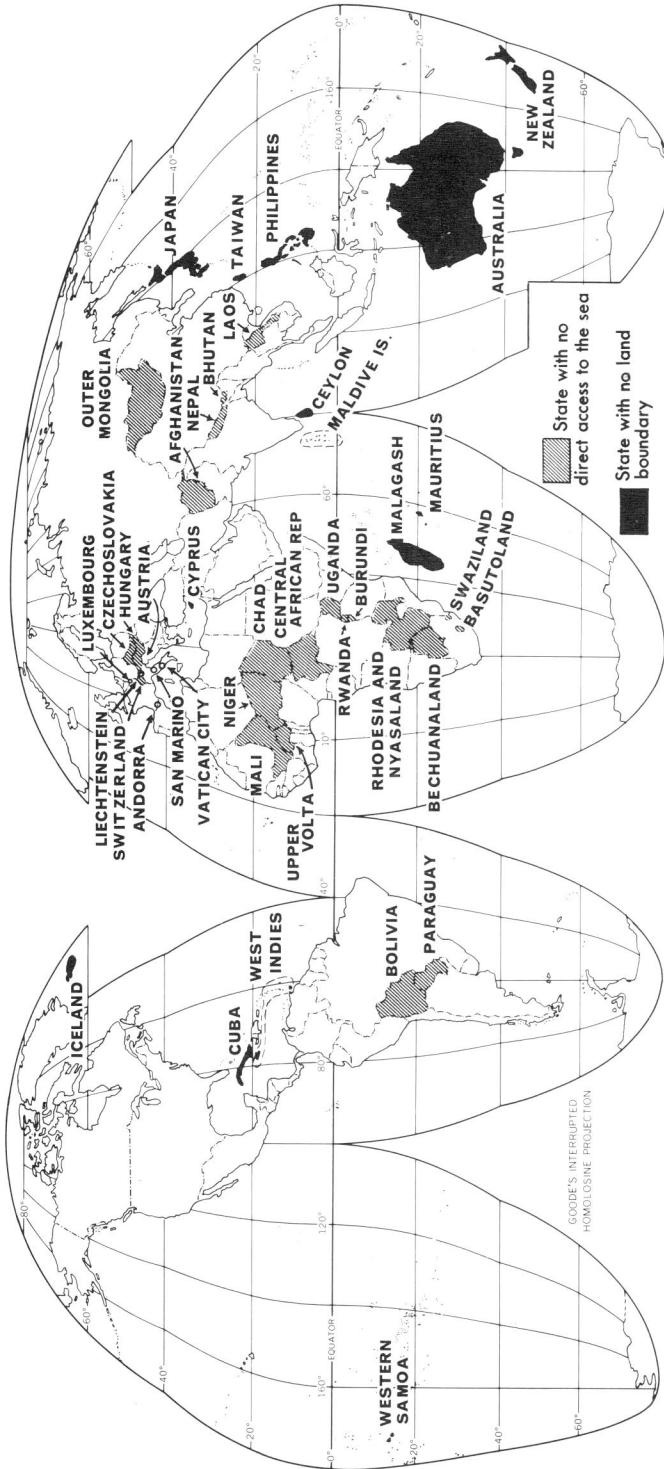

Exhibit 33 *Map of states and other politically organized areas.* (*a*) Those having no coast line; (*b*) those having no land boundaries.

Map labels:

ICELAND
WEST INDIES
CUBA
BOLIVIA
PARAGUAY
WESTERN SAMOA

GOODE'S INTERRUPTED
HOMOLOSINE PROJECTION

LIECHTENSTEIN
SWITZERLAND
ANDORRA
SAN MARINO
VATICAN CITY
UPPER VOLTA
MALI
NIGER
CHAD
CENTRAL AFRICAN REP
RHODESIA AND NYASALAND
BECHUANALAND
RWANDA
UGANDA
BURUNDI
MALAGASH
MAURITIUS
SWAZILAND
BASUTOLAND
LUXEMBOURG
CZECHOSLOVAKIA
HUNGARY
AUSTRIA
CYPRUS
OUTER MONGOLIA
AFGHANISTAN
NEPAL
BHUTAN
LAOS
JAPAN
TAIWAN
PHILIPPINES
CEYLON
MALDIVE IS.
AUSTRALIA
NEW ZEALAND

State with no direct access to the sea

State with no land boundary

trol and rule the open sea. The English jurist, John Selden, replied,[1] claiming that England "owned" the seas which surrounded the British Isles and separated them from Europe. But the basis of modern practice in this regard was set forth by another Dutch jurist, Cornelius van Bynkershoek, who, in 1702, published his views in *De Dominio maris*. In this treatise he outlined "a conception of sea sovereignty much more modern than anything that had been suggested in the previous century."[2] He argued that, while the sea was common to all, "dominion of the adjacent seas, as far as a cannon could throw a shot, was reasonable, and could be conceded to those who owned the shore."[3]

We find a steady progress towards the principle of the absolute freedom of the sea. By the nineteenth century this freedom had become axiomatic. . . . The high sea . . . is free to all. Even though a state were powerful enough to possess it, the claim to exercise rights of sovereignty over it would not now be recognized as just, not so much by reason of the difficulty of effective possession, as because no good reason for its possession could be put forward."[4]

The proposal of Van Bynkershoek, that a coastal state should exercise sovereignty over that part of the surrounding sea which it could command by means of guns mounted upon the shore, came to be generally accepted.[5] This was, of course, an extremely variable distance, dependent upon the size of the gun and its charge, and upon whether it was mounted on a cliff

top or near the water's edge. These finer points were never worked out. Later in the century it was suggested—erroneously as it happened—that 3 miles represented the maximum range of artillery,[6] and it came to be accepted that a line 3 nautical miles[7] from the shore represented the limit of the sovereignty of the coastal state. Outside it lay the high seas.

The "cannon-shot" rule still holds. Most countries claim sovereignty up to a distance of 3 miles from their shores; a few have moved the distance up to 4, 6, 10, or even 12 miles. Only the States of Louisiana and Texas have tried to "catch up with" technology by estimating the range of modern artillery and moving their territorial limits outward accordingly. In 1938, the State of Louisiana proclaimed that "Whereas, since the said three-mile limit was so established as the seaward boundary . . . modern cannon have been improved to such an extent that . . . a state can now make its authority effective at least 27 marine miles out to sea from low-water mark, . . . the gulfward boundary" of the State should be moved "24 marine miles further out in the Gulf of Mexico than the said three-mile limit."[8] Three years later the State of Texas moved its boundary to the limit of the continental shelf.

Advances in the science of ballistics have outdated even the advanced claims of Louisiana. The coming of the intercontinental missile has made any claim to sovereignty, based on the power to command the sea from the land, seem ridiculous. Clearly, the condition specified in the

---

[1] John Selden, *Mare clausum, seu de dominio maris, libri duo,* London, 1635.

[2] William McFee, *The Law of the Sea,* J. B. Lippincott Company, Philadelphia, 1950, p. 139.

[3] *Ibid.,* p. 140.

[4] Green H. Hackworth, *Digest of International Law,* Government Printing Office, 1941, vol. 2, p. 654.

[5] Van Bynkershoek's maxim was: Imperium terrae finiri ubi finitur armorum potestas.

[6] The claim was made by Galiani in 1782 and was widely repeated. No guns at this time could fire so great a distance. See M. W. Mouton, *The Continental Shelf,* M. Nihjoff, The Hague, 1952, pp. 195–198.

[7] The nautical mile, or minute of arc, is longer than the statute, or land, mile. It is 6,080 feet, or 1.114 land miles.

[8] Quoted in Mouton, *op. cit.,* p. 208.

Louisiana statute of 1938, that "sufficient security must exist for the lives and property of the State," can no longer be fulfilled even by the widest of territorial seas.

THE FUNCTION OF THE TERRITORIAL SEA

Defense has always been the most important function of the territorial sea. A sneak attack could, of course, be made through the territorial waters of a state as easily as across the high seas, but a state nevertheless has the right to exclude or to search suspicious vessels within its limits, to erect defensive works in the sea, and to lay mines. These formerly conferred some small degree of protection. But if defense were the only reason for maintaining the institution of the territorial sea, it might now just as well be abandoned. There are, however, other good reasons for it.

Protection against Smuggling: Smuggling is an ancient and almost honorable practice. It has existed as long as there have been laws regulating trade. For a long period governments fought a losing battle against the smuggler. Some of the most expansive claims to jurisdiction over the sea that have ever been made were aimed at checking the practice of smuggling. The British Parliament, for example, stated that vessels of the government might intercept and search any vessel found "hovering" within 2 leagues (6 nautical miles) of the shore. The distance within which such arrests might be made was gradually stepped up to 3, then 4 leagues, until ultimately the government arrogated to itself the right to search vessels up to 100 leagues from the shore. Such a claim seems both ridiculous and superfluous; yet Great Britain's right was not disputed by other states, which may perhaps have exercised a similar right on occasion. A member of the government claimed in 1739 that Great Britain was merely exercising "the liberty which every nation enjoys, of searching, on suspicion of unlawful trade, the ships of foreigners that approach near to their coast without any necessity." [9]

We are thus obliged to think of a number of overlapping spheres, within each of which a particular state was claiming and exercising the right of search. Nevertheless, it was claimed that these laws permitted the activities of the smugglers to be reduced to small proportions. As far as Great Britain was concerned, the resulting legal confusion was ended in 1876, when the right of search for the purpose of preventing smuggling was limited to 9 nautical miles. By an act of 1790, the United States claimed the same right up to a distance of 4 leagues (12 nautical miles) from the coast. Spain in 1874–1875 claimed a zone of 6 nautical miles "for general maritime jurisdiction" and drew a distinction between what its spokesman called "military jurisdiction" (i.e., complete sovereignty) and "fiscal jurisdiction," or the right to protect the revenue by suppressing smuggling.

These attempts to extend a limited political control over a wide belt of the ocean acquire a particular interest in virtue of the problems faced by the United States after the Eighteenth Amendment (1919) had introduced prohibition. The law of 1790 was used as a legal justification for apprehending rumrunners outside the territorial sea. Great Britain, grown suddenly virtuous, protested against the use of such authority more than 3 miles from the shore. Judge Morton stated in his judgment in the case of a British vessel that had been arrested while unloading liquor outside the 3-mile limit: "The line between territorial waters and the high seas is not like the

[9] The Earl of Illay, in the House of Lords, as quoted in William E. Masterson, *Jurisdiction in Marginal Seas*, The Macmillan Company, New York, 1929, p. 29.

boundary between us and a foreign power. There must be . . . a certain width of debatable waters adjacent to our coasts. How far our authority shall be extended into them for the seizure of foreign vessels which have broken our laws is a matter for the political departments of the government to determine."[10] The Tariff Act of 1922 reenacted the relevant clauses of the 1790 law and stated that Coast Guard officers "may at any time go on board any vessel or vehicle at any place in the United States or within four leagues of the coast . . . to examine the manifest, and to inspect, search, and examine the vessel or vehicle." A treaty between the United States and Great Britain declared the intention of both countries to abide by the traditional 3-mile limit of the territorial sea, but the British government, out of deference to the wishes of the American, agreed "not to object to the boarding and searching of vessels" outside these limits, but (a very curious qualification) "not at a greater distance from the coast than can be traversed in one hour by the vessel suspected of endeavoring to commit the offense."

The effect of these acts and decisions has been to emphasize that, while general sovereignty ends at the territorial limits, a more restricted jurisdiction can be effectively claimed over a wide area of the high seas. In the words of W. E. Masterson, "Practically all the nations are prepared to agree that jurisdiction may be taken beyond these waters for the purpose of securing the fiscal interests of the state, as well as certain other interests."[11] We now turn to some of these other interests.

Fisheries Protection: The sea contains two resources of obvious importance to those who dwell on its shores: fish, and the minerals that occur in and beneath the water. As long as fishing craft remained small and incapable of making long voyages, the exercise and protection of fishing rights presented few problems. But, in recent years, increasing demands for fish as a source of food, combined with the use of ocean-going fishing vessels, have changed this situation. Although a few countries claimed for their citizens the exclusive right to catch fish in their own coastal waters during medieval and early modern times, the question of fishing rights did not become important until the past century. The principle that sovereignty extended over the territorial sea obviously conferred upon the state an exclusive right to fish within this area. This right was never disputed. Fishermen caught in the act of taking fish within the territorial sea of another state are liable to arrest and fine. Such cases are not infrequent in the courts of coastal cities of some parts of western Europe. This does not, however, prevent a state from occasionally allowing foreign fishermen to operate within its territorial sea, but such permission is usually embodied in an international treaty. Occasionally one finds a state which regularly fails to enforce its own rights in this respect. There is, for example, a considerable degree of freedom to fish in the waters around the coast of Ireland. At the opposite extreme, inshore fishing by foreign fishermen not only has been carefully organized but has served as a cover for espionage. The activities of Japanese sponge fishers along the unprotected northern coast of Australia in the years immediately preceding the Second World War are a familiar example of this operation. On the other hand, there have been agreements, such as the International North Pacific Fisheries Convention of 1953, to limit the right to take fish, even on the high seas, in the interests of conservation.

In recent years a number of claims

---

[10] Quoted in Masterson, *op. cit.*, p. 22.
[11] *Ibid.*, p. 400.

have been made by coastal states to control fisheries beyond the limits of the territorial sea. Reasons for such extensions of national control are twofold: first to protect the fishing industry of the country in question, and, second, to prevent the depletion of certain fish species. Thus, Japanese fishermen have been excluded since the end of the Second World War from the Sea of Okhotsk, which, though technically high seas, is almost enclosed by Soviet territory. Similarly, the South Koreans have claimed exclusive fishing privileges over a section of the Sea of Japan and have enforced their claims by the use of gunboats. A few countries are heavily dependent on fisheries. Iceland is the extreme case; about 14 per cent of the Gross National Product is derived from fishing (excluding the processing of fish), and fish and fish products make up over 90 per cent by value of Iceland's exports. In recent years the Icelandic government has claimed that the surrounding seas have been overfished and that the resulting diminution of the catch constitutes a serious hardship for Iceland. In 1948 the Icelandic government was empowered by the Icelandic Parliament to extend its exclusive control over fishing as far as the edge of the continental shelf. It did not, however, go as far as this. Instead, in 1952, it extended control to a distance of 4 nautical miles from a stated base line, and, 6 years later, yet farther, to a distance of 12 miles measured from the same base line. Foreign fishermen were denied the right to fish within these limits, and the rights of Icelanders themselves were somewhat restricted.

Icelandic waters had been much frequented by foreign fishing craft, especially British and German, and about 13 per cent of the total catch of northwestern Europe came from the Iceland fishing grounds. The decision of 1952 had met with protests from Great Britain. The further extension of fisheries control to 12 miles had the effect of closing off about 6,600 square miles of water to foreign fishermen and, furthermore, to exclude them almost completely from the plaice fishing and from a large part of the cod and haddock fishing. British fishing boats continued to frequent the Iceland fishing grounds during the 1958 season and fished inside the 12-mile limit under the protection of gunboats. Iceland's action was at the time probably contrary to international law. World opinion is, however, tending to accept the view that, outside the territorial sea in the established sense, a state may legitimately claim to exercise some kind of control, short of complete sovereignty, and that this control may sometimes extend to the fisheries in certain instances. Great Britain has since accepted Iceland's claim and has desisted from fishing within 12 miles of her base line, in view of the exceptional importance of the fisheries to Iceland.

There are, however, other ways of conserving, protecting, or monopolizing the fisheries. A country may, for instance, take in a wider area of sea within its territorial limits by manipulating the base line from which the width of the territorial sea is measured. This was the method used by Norway in 1935 (Exhibit 34) and ultimately sanctioned by the Permanent Court of International Justice in its settlement of the Anglo-Norwegian fisheries dispute in 1952 (see page 111). There may be treaty arrangements, as between the United Kingdom and Denmark, regulating the fisheries around the Faroes Islands and establishing closed areas and closed seasons. The United States and Canada have similarly agreed to limit the salmon fisheries in certain areas of the high seas off the coast of the Pacific Northwest. Agreements have also been occasionally made to control the size of mesh used in fishing nets and

Exhibit 34 *Base line for the measurement of the Norwegian territorial sea.*

to restrict the use of trawl nets, which drag the sea floor and are especially injurious to fish larvae.

Quarantine and Sanitation: The territorial sea is less important in regard to quarantine and sanitation. It is sometimes argued that such a zone of sea is necessary in which to examine incoming vessels for possible quarantine before they reach a port. Another, and perhaps more important, reason is to be able to prevent pollution of the sea with oil and, thus, of the neighboring coast by ships.

THE CONTINENTAL SHELF

The problems relating to the territorial sea have been intensified by modern technological developments. This is especially true with regard to those which concern the floor of the sea. Until recently the sea floor, at least below a depth of a few fathoms, was unexplored and had no value. Modern technology has put some of its resources within the reach of man and has made its possession advantageous to the state.

The land masses are surrounded by a shallow shelf, on the average about 100 miles wide, but varying in fact from 5 to over 600 miles. The angle of slope of the shelf is very gentle and is almost imperceptible. At a depth of about 100 fathoms (600 feet) the angle of slope increases, and the sea floor drops more steeply to the deep sea floor. This area of greater steepness is the continental slope. The depth at which the continental shelf gives way to the continental slope varies, and at the Geneva Convention on the Law of the Sea (February–April, 1958) it was the subject of prolonged debate, as the depth at which it is assumed to lie clearly influences the width of the shelf itself. The figure finally adopted was 200 meters, or 656.2 feet. As defined in this way, the continental shelves of the world cover 10,617,780 square miles, or about 7.6 per cent of the total area of the oceans. The shelf is geologically a part of the continent; it is composed of the same kinds of rocks and is likely to contain the same minerals as those of the continent itself. Minerals have occasionally been extracted from below the sea floor by means of deep shafts and drifts sunk from the land. This was done in some of the tin mines of Cornwall and also in the coal mines of Cape Breton Island. But only a small fraction of the underwater resources is accessible in this way. A more direct method of reaching them is to sink a shaft directly *through* the overlying water from moored vessels or platforms erected in the sea. At present, only fluid resources, such as oil and natural gas, that can be pumped to the surface have been extracted in this way. There is no technical reason why sulfur and rock salt could not also be obtained by a similar process.

Figure 25 *Oil drilling, seven miles off the coast of the United States, in the Gulf of Mexico, in an area which is recognized as the high seas.* COURTESY: STANDARD OIL COMPANY OF NEW JERSEY

The very gentle slope of the continental shelf makes it clear that the technical ability to drill for oil is not restricted to the territorial sea and might eventually extend over the whole area of the shelf. The area of the shelf, outside territorial limits, had been regarded as high seas, an area over which no state might claim sovereignty. It was not difficult to envisage the consequences of unrestricted drilling for oil outside the 3-mile limit of the United States. Accordingly, on September 28, 1945, President Truman proclaimed that:

It is the view of the government of the United States that the exercise of jurisdiction over the natural resources of the sub-soil and sea-bed of the continental shelf by the contiguous nation is reasonable and just, since the effectiveness of measures to utilize or conserve these resources would be contingent upon cooperation and protection from the shore, since the continental shelf may be regarded as an extension of the land mass of the coastal nation and thus naturally appurtenant to it, since these resources frequently form a seaward extension of a pool or deposit lying within the territory, and since self-protection compels the coastal nation to keep close watch over activities off its shores which are of the nature necessary for utilization of these resources. . . . [therefore] the government of the United States regards the natural resources of the sub-soil and sea-bed of the continental shelf beneath the high seas but contiguous to the coasts of the United States as appertaining to the United States and subject to its jurisdiction and control.

This proclamation was followed by similar declarations by twenty other powers, most of whom had reason to believe that their offshore areas contained oil. Truman's proclamation attempted to separate sovereignty from control. Sovereignty extended up to the territorial limit. The sea beyond this line remained the high seas. The contiguous state (i.e., the United States) claimed the right to use the mineral resources in the sea floor; it claimed no rights over other resources, such as fish, nor control over shipping in the sea itself. Not all the states that followed Truman's example were as modest in their pretensions. A month later Mexico claimed "the whole continental shelf adjacent to its coasts and all and every one of the natural riches . . . which are found in it. . . ." [12] And Argentina a year later blatantly asserted that "The Argentine Epicontinental Sea and Continental Shelf are subject to the sovereign powers of the nation." Chile, Peru, and Ecuador claimed sovereignty over the continental shelf for a distance of 200 miles, though, as is well known, the shelf along most of the west coast of South America does not extend for much of this distance more than about 40 miles.

Not all the Latin-American states

which made such extravagant claims had reason to suppose that their offshore areas contained oil. Some were eager only to assert a monopolistic control over the sea fisheries or to embrace disputed islands within their territorial limits. The Middle Eastern states, however, were motivated largely by their desire to extend their oil holdings. Here Saudi Arabia, the United Arab Republic, and all states bordering the Persian Gulf claimed sovereignty over the adjacent area of the continental shelf. In the case of the latter, however, the shelf in the strict sense does not exist, as there is neither continental slope nor deep-sea floor. The boundaries between their respective claims in the shallow floor of the Persian Gulf were left to be decided between them.

Problems that might arise from conflicting claims to the continental shelf were foreseen by the Geneva Conference (1958) on the Law of the Sea. In the absence of any agreement, the boundary would be assumed to follow the median line (see page 109).

Many problems remain unresolved. Few geologists would be satisfied with the definition of the continental shelf. At no point has the question been raised of the deep channels or canyons, in the surface of the shelf, which have often been carved to depths of many hundreds of feet below it.

CLAIMS TO THE TERRITORIAL SEA

"Never have national claims in adjacent seas," wrote S. Whittemore Boggs, "been so numerous, so varied, or so inconsistent." [13] The 3-mile limit, strenuously asserted by the United States, the United Kingdom, and a number of other leading maritime powers, was never universally

[12] Quoted in Mouton, *op. cit.*, pp. 73–74.

[13] S. Whittemore Boggs, "National Claims in Adjacent Seas," *G.R.*, vol. 41, pp. 185–209, 1951.

adopted, but departures from this practice had been few and generally unimportant. In recent years more extensive claims to sovereignty over the adjacent seas have been made by a number of states. Many of these claims, as we have already seen, are limited in their scope and relate to fisheries control or the exploitation of minerals. Others are outright claims to sovereignty.

International law is imprecise in this respect. A 3-mile limit has become a common practice, but there is no prohibition against making larger claims. The question is entirely one of whether other states will recognize such claims. Some states have never formally made any claim and, in answer to questions, state that they abide by the provisions of international law; in other words, they accept the 3-mile limit. The countries listed in Table 4 have formally laid claim to sovereignty over a wider belt of sea than the traditional 3 miles. It should be noted that this table relates to sovereignty, not to some limited form of control. Several of the countries listed claim the right to control fisheries or to exploit oil over an even wider belt of sea.

This pattern of claims to the territorial sea is confusing, but it has at least this degree of rationale. The leading maritime powers maintain modest claims for themselves and object to wide claims on behalf of other states. For example, about 80 per cent of the world's merchant shipping is owned in the countries which claim only a 3-mile limit and a further 9.7 per cent by the Scandinavian countries, which claim 4.[14] It has always been the great commercial nations, at first the Dutch and more recently the British and American, who supported most strenuously the freedom of the seas over as large a part of the water

TABLE 4   *Width of the Territorial Sea*

4 miles	Norway, Sweden, Finland
5 miles	Cambodia
6 miles	Spain, Italy, Yugoslavia, Greece, Uruguay, Lebanon, Colombia, Iran, Rio de Oro, Haiti, Ceylon, India, Israel, Portugal, Thailand
6.48 miles	Honduras
9 miles	Mexico
10 miles	Albania
12 miles	U.S.S.R., Guatemala, China, Bulgaria, Ethiopia, Indonesia, Libya, Rumania, Saudi Arabia, United Arab Republic, Venezuela
50 km	Chile

surface of the earth as possible. The extension of the territorial sea from 3 to, let us say, 12 miles over the earth as a whole would seriously reduce the area of the high seas. The territorial sea of the continental United States (excluding Alaska) has an area of 17,320.8 square miles.[15] The extension of the territorial limits to 12 miles would increase this area to about 70,000 square miles. The case of Hawaii is even more interesting. Here the length of coast line is very great in relation to the area of the islands, none of which lie closer to one another than 7 miles, and which are thus separated by areas of the high seas. At present the Hawaiian Islands, with an area of 6,423 square miles, are surrounded by 3,069 nautical square miles of the territorial sea. The increase of the limits to 6 miles would increase the sea area to about four times this figure, or twice as large as the area of the islands themselves.

More serious, probably, than any restriction of the total area of the high seas would be the closure of a number of straits of international importance (see Chapter 10). In time of peace all vessels enjoy the right of innocent passage through the territorial waters of another state, but in time

[14] Figures compiled by S. Whittemore Boggs and published in *G.R.*, vol. 41, p. 204, 1952. It is unlikely that they have changed substantially.

[15] That is, nautical square miles, equal to about 1⅓ square miles.

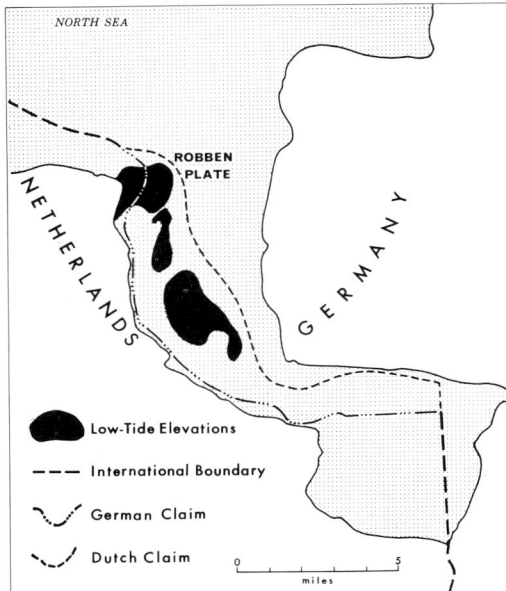

Exhibit 35 Seaward extension of the boundary between the Netherlands and the Federal German Republic.

of war this right is restricted. A state may choose to exclude ships of particular powers in order to safeguard its neutrality. It may remove aids to navigation, such as buoys, lighthouses, and markers, and it may even set mines. Straits more than 6 miles wide have, in general, a belt of high seas running through their midst within which it is clearly contrary to international law for any state controlling the coast line to obstruct or impede navigation. An extension of territorial limits to 6 miles would, in this sense, close the Straits of Gibraltar, of Malacca, and of Bab-al-Mandeb to the completely free passage of shipping. A 12-mile limit would close the Straits of Dover, the entrances to the Gulfs of Bothnia and of Finland and to the Aegean Sea, the sea passage between Italy and the island of Corsica, and the Straits of Hormuz, at the entrance to the Persian Gulf. The interest of the maritime powers in keeping territorial limits to a minimum is obvious.

Let us turn now to some of the local problems raised by the claims of coastal states to control part of the neighboring sea. At no less than about 150 points on the coast line, international boundaries reach the coast. In some instances they follow the course of a river and continue through its estuary to the sea. Usually, such a boundary is made to follow the *thalweg*, or deep channel, of the estuary, or the median line is used. The alignment of the boundary is, in general, governed by agreement between the states which it divides. The boundary of the Netherlands and the German Federal Republic is a case in point. It follows the lower course of the river Ems and the navigable channel through the Dollart, or estuary of the Ems, to the sea. The Dollart happens to have two navigable channels, separated by a low-tide elevation. Both Germany and the Netherlands claim that the boundary follows the channel farthest from its own shore (Exhibit 35). In most instances boundaries reach the coast, where there are no such interruptions, and are continued, in theory at least, across the territorial sea and continental shelf. The seaward extension of the boundary may not seem to be a matter of great importance. Nevertheless, a principle has been established at the 1958 Geneva Conference whereby it can be defined whenever this should be necessary. On a straight coast the boundary would presumably continue into the sea at right angles to the line of the coast. But the coast rarely is straight for more than a very short distance. The boundary is therefore extended as if it were a median line, any point on the boundary line being equidistant from the coast on either side of it. Exhibit 36 shows the seaward extension of a boundary drawn according to the principle accepted at Geneva.

The existence of offshore islands can complicate immeasurably the problem of

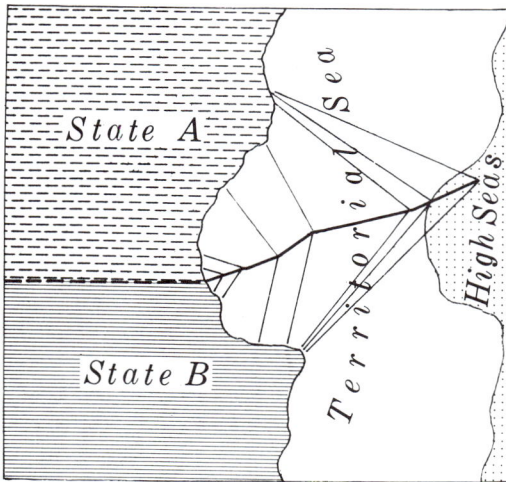

Exhibit 36 *Seaward extension of a boundary.*

drawing boundaries through the sea. The islands first have to be allocated to one side or the other, and only then can a median line be drawn to separate them. Locations where this problem has arisen are where the boundary between the United States and Canada reaches the Pacific Ocean, on the shores of Puget Sound, and the Atlantic Ocean, at the mouth of the St. Croix River, in Passamaquoddy Bay.

The boundary of Norway and the Soviet Union reaches the Arctic Ocean on the south shore of the irregularly shaped Varanger Fiord. The problem of defining the offshore boundary between the two states was increased by conflicting claims to territorial seas, Norway claiming 4 miles and the Soviet Union 12. Norway also claims to measure her territorial sea from a closing line drawn across the entrance to the Varanger Fiord. The agreement of 1957 between Norway and the Soviet Union is illustrated in Exhibit 37.

Another obstinate and still unsettled problem is that of the seaward continuation of the boundary between Belgium and the Netherlands. The difficulty here arises from the fact that the navigable channel of

the river Scheldt, known as the Wielingen Channel, keeps very close to the coast after reaching the sea. For approximately 15 miles it lies parallel to the Belgian coast line and inside the line that would normally be regarded as the limit of Belgium's territorial sea (Exhibit 38). The Netherlands claims sovereignty over the whole of the Wielingen Channel on historical grounds, as this is the principal outlet of the river Scheldt.

Measurement of the Territorial Sea: It has come to be accepted that the territorial sea should be measured from the low-tide mark. But this is itself subject to variations with the weather and the state of the tides. The datum line has been variously defined in different countries as low-water mark of mean tides, low-water mark of spring tides, and low-water mark of equinoctial spring tides. On most coasts the difference between them amounts to only a few feet, but in some areas, parts of the British coast, for example, the difference is considerable.

On a simple, straight coast, without islands or shoals, the delimitation of the territorial sea presents no problem. But most

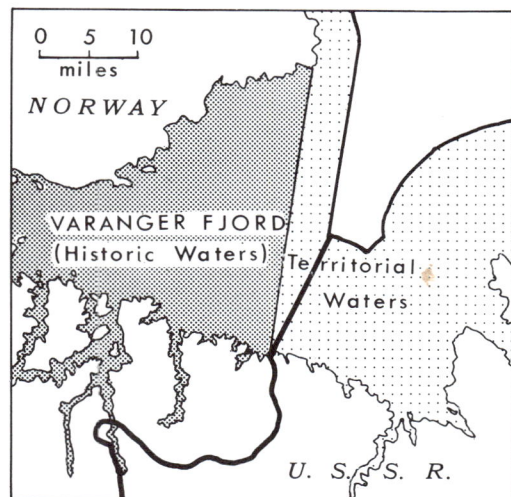

Exhibit 37 *Seaward extension of the Norwegian-Soviet boundary.*

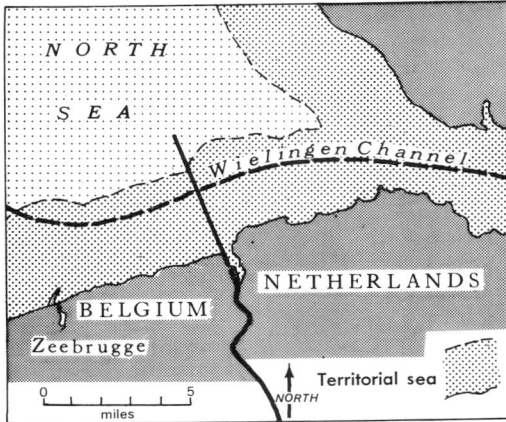

Exhibit 38   *Seaward extension of the boundary between the Netherlands and Belgium.*

coasts are neither simple nor straight. They may be irregular in the extreme, with off-shore islands and submerged rocks. The latter may be submerged only at high tide (drying rocks) or so low that waves break over them at all stages of the tide (awash). There may be sandbanks exposed at low tide (low-tide elevations), slowly but continuously changing their shape and position. How is the base- or datum line to be delimited on such a coast?

It has long been assumed that an island capable of being settled, however small it may be, has a territorial sea of its own. If the island is at a sufficient distance, there may be an area of the high seas between it and the mainland. If the island lies within the normal territorial sea, this would have the effect of extending it farther from the coast (Exhibit 39).

Bays and estuaries present a more complex situation. If either is less than 6 miles across, assuming that the territorial seas have a width of 3 miles, then the whole is part of the territorial sea. In fact, a closing line drawn across the entrance to the bay or estuary would be taken as the base line for the measurement of the territorial sea. Bays and estuaries are, however, often much wider than this. Some such openings in the coast are claimed as territorial waters on historic grounds, the state having always asserted its sovereignty over these waters. The Varanger Fiord on the Norwegian coast (Exhibit 37) is an example of a historic claim that was accepted by the Soviet Union in the delimitation proceedings of 1957. Many of the wider bays and estuaries on the coast of the British Isles have also been claimed as historic waters, for example, the Wash, the Moray Firth, and Sligo (Donegal) Bay. But some historic claims are very slender, and for other claims there may be no basis in history at all. The Geneva Conference ac-

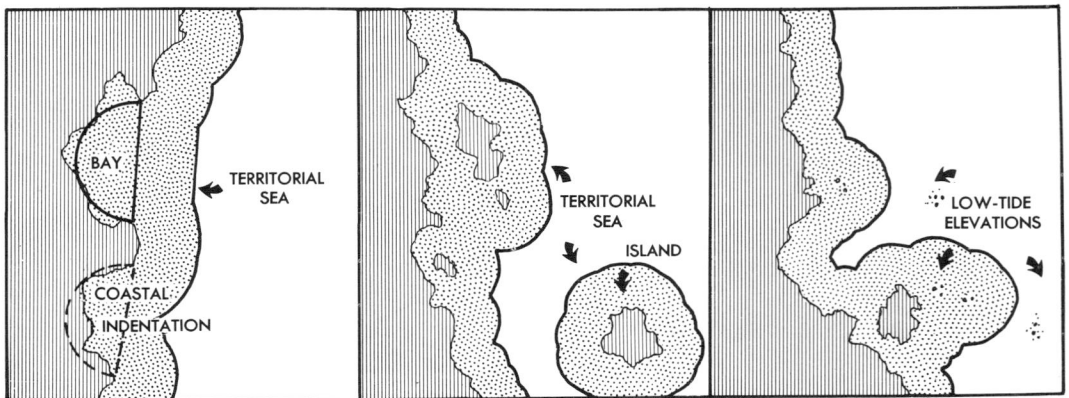

Exhibit 39   *How the territorial sea is measured.*

cepted a rule whereby the base line across bays and estuaries might be established. "In event that the distance between the natural entrance points of a bay exceeds that distance [i.e., 6 miles], a straight baseline of [not more than] 24 miles is drawn within the bay in such a way as to enclose the maximum water area that is possible with a line of that length" (Exhibit 39).[16]

It now becomes necessary to distinguish between a bay and a mere coastal indentation. For this the semicircle rule is applied. A straight line is drawn between the natural entrance points of the indentation. "The water thus closed off forms a bay if its area is as large as, or larger than, that of a semicircle the diameter of which is equal in length to the closing line."[17] If smaller, it is regarded merely as a coastal indentation, and the limit of the territorial sea is drawn parallel to the curvature of the coast.

Low-tide elevations—areas of the sea floor exposed at low tide—and small, uninhabitable rocks, which so frequently lie offshore, also present a difficult problem. It had been widely assumed that such features might not be used in drawing a base line up to the time when the whole question was reviewed by the Permanent Court of International Justice in its settlement of the Anglo-Norwegian fisheries case. In 1935 the Norwegian government officially defined the base line from which it measured its territorial sea. The immediate reason was the need to delimit the area of the sea from which foreign fishermen might be excluded. A series of straight base lines was drawn between forty-eight points, some of them on the mainland, others on offshore islands, islets, and drying rocks (Exhibit 39). Base lines were drawn across the en-

trances to a number of shallow bays, many of which exceeded 24 miles in width. The largest of these—Lopphavet—was no less than 44 miles across its entrance. The British government, whose fishermen regularly worked the Norwegian seas, protested against this alleged encroachment on the area of the high seas and ordered its fishermen not to observe the Norwegian decree. It pointed out that the change in the Norwegian base line had the effect of reducing the area of the high seas by 2,388 square miles. The British government brought the case before the Permanent Court of International Justice, which in 1952 gave judgment in favor of Norway. The British had claimed, among other things, that the base line should follow the low-water mark on *permanently* dry land, that some of the closing lines chosen by the Norwegians were too long, and that others were drawn across coastal indentations, such as Lopphavet, that were too shallow to be regarded as bays. The Court's decision was surprising, and in conflict with legal opinions that had previously been widely held. This decision strongly influenced the discussions at the Geneva Conference.

It is now the established rule that low-tide elevations and drying rocks are to be taken as measuring points for the territorial sea, provided that they occur within what would be considered the normal territorial limits of the coast. If they occur outside the normal limit of the territorial sea, they are to be ignored. The map (Exhibit 39) of a section should make the application of this rule clear.

The coast line is continually changing under the influence of both natural processes and human effort. Low-tide elevations, such, for example, as the sandbanks lying off the Gulf Coast or the coast of Virginia and North Carolina, change with the deposition of fresh silt and sand. Such changes bring with them changes in the base

[16] G. Etzel Pearcy, "Measurement of the U.S. Territorial Sea," *Department of State Bulletin,* June 29, 1959, p. 965.

[17] *Ibid.,* pp. 964–965.

line from which the territorial sea is measured. If the coast line itself builds forward (progrades) or retreats under the impact of the waves, the same happens: the territorial limits advance or retreat. It makes no difference that such changes are effected by man. A man-made island, a jetty or pier projecting into the sea, or the reclamation of coastal lands—all have the effect of advancing the territorial limits farther into the ocean.

The Geneva Conference has not delimited the territorial seas. It has merely provided a body of rules which may serve as a guide for their delimitation when need arises. No one claims that disputes regarding the territorial seas are of major importance in world politics, nor that a country's security is threatened by an adverse decision regarding them. In a few instances, however, Iceland and Norway in particular, control of fisheries can reasonably be held to be a significant factor in the welfare of the state. In some others the receipt of oil royalties is contingent upon control over submarine resources. But national pride is a peculiarly sensitive thing, and it can be

roused by a dispute of intrinsically small importance. The Icelandic fisheries dispute aroused deep feelings in Iceland, and emotions only a degree less deep—though much less warranted—in Great Britain. It is by such little matters as this that public opinion is shaped, and public opinion in turn helps to shape public policy. Such petty disputes may not be the "razor's edge," but they are not unimportant in determining the attitudes of states.

ZONES OF THE TERRITORIAL SEA

The sovereignty of a state ends at the limit of its territorial sea, but some measure of control extends, as we have seen, farther into the ocean. Indeed, there is no clearcut outer limit to such control. On the shoreward side of the territorial sea are waters, enclosed by the base line, which are regarded, not even as part of the territorial sea, but as internal waters of the state. Five zones of jurisdiction can thus be distinguished (Exhibit 40), not all of them present on any particular stretch of the

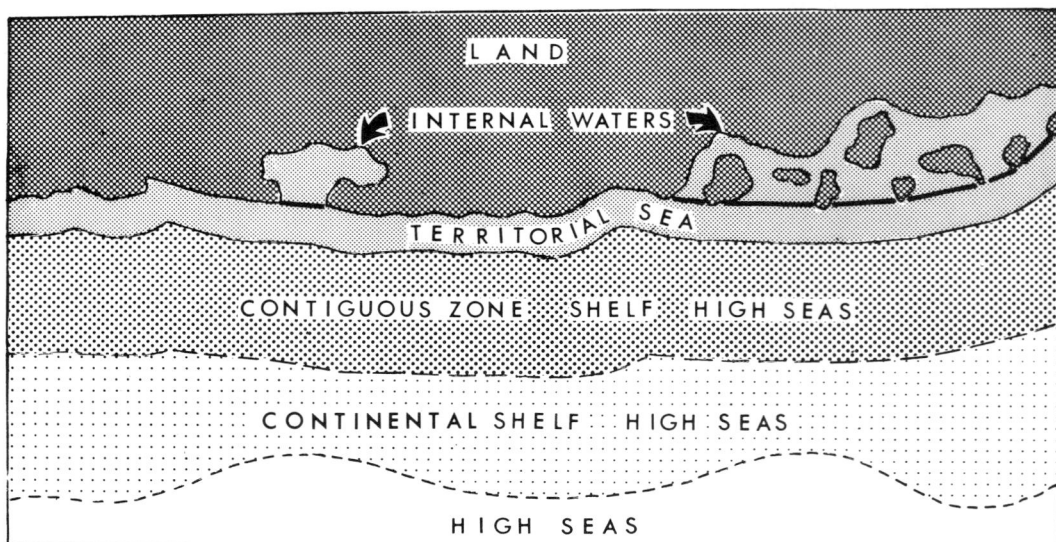

Exhibit 40 *Zones of the territorial sea.*

coast, but all of them likely to be represented:

1. Internal waters. These are the estuaries, bays, and lagoons which lie *inside* the base line from which the territorial seas are measured.

2. Territorial sea. This extends from the base line, whether construed as low-water mark or as a base line drawn arbitrarily between fixed points, for a prescribed distance into the ocean or sea. Within this zone the sovereignty of the state is absolute.

3. Contiguous zone. This is a belt, of varying width from one state to another, within which the state claims to exercise some form of control. This may be the right to intercept and search vessels suspected of smuggling; it may extend to fisheries control or to the control of the exploitation of minerals in the sea bed.

4. Continental shelf. It is difficult to distinguish between the contiguous zone and the continental shelf. Rights which in some states are claimed for a contiguous zone of specified width are in others appropriated for the continental shelf, whatever its extent. In most instances, rights claimed over the continental shelf extend only to those of exploiting minerals, in a few also to the control of fisheries. An exclusive right to fisheries, it might be added, over so vast an area of the sea is almost impossible to enforce. Occasional claims have been made to the control of the wealth of the sea, "whatever its depth." [18] But at the present time any attempt to develop mineral resources from depths greater than those of the continental shelf cannot be regarded as practicable. The reality of any claims beyond the continental shelf is entirely academic.

5. High seas. This is the zone, making up the greater part of the oceans, in which there is neither sovereignty nor control by any state. Here the freedom to navigate is

[18] Declaration by the government of Peru, August, 1947.

axiomatic. This freedom of the seas extends also to the right to lay cables on the sea floor and to fly aircraft above it. The high seas are the only part of the earth's surface not subject to the political jurisdiction of a state.

It is interesting to note that, in many of the proclamations claiming political rights beyond the territorial limits, these rights were specifically limited to the sea floor and its subsoil. Any attempt to infringe upon the freedom of the seas was specifically denied. Thus, the boundary of the state's sovereignty may be thought of as a vertical plane at the limit of the territorial sea. This plane is carried downward to the sea floor, which it follows outward to the edge of the continental shelf, the 200-meter isobath, or whatever limit has been legally determined. Here the plane becomes vertical again and extends downward indefinitely toward the center of the earth.

FREEDOM OF THE SKIES

A consideration of the freedom of the seas leads naturally to a discussion of the freedom of the skies. The sovereignty of a state extends vertically downward for an indefinite distance beneath its surface. Can its sovereignty be said to extend also vertically upwards indefinitely into space? There have been opinions on this but no accepted body of rules. The principle of Roman law was that there was no upward limit to sovereignty. On the other hand, it has been suggested that sovereignty terminates at a specific height, such as 10 miles or the boundary of the stratosphere. There have been many attempts to formulate a law of outer space, similar in all points to the law of the sea. The lower atmosphere would thus correspond with the territorial sea; outer space, with the high seas. A physical boundary, such as the tropopause or ionized layers, it has been suggested, may correspond with the continental slope. But no government has hitherto committed itself to a specific boundary between "territorial air" and outer space. The matter is, however, becoming urgent. There is a lot of "hardware" circulating in space. Some may fall to earth and do considerable damage; some may even be mistaken on the radar screen for a more lethal weapon from another continent.

Only one reason can be given for claiming sovereignty in the higher atmosphere—the military security of the state lying beneath. If, at any height within the range of aircraft, there is a freedom of the skies, a state can be intimidated by bomb-carrying airplanes and its surface features and activities can be observed. Earlier attempts, therefore, to limit sovereignty to some specific zone of the lower atmosphere appear to have been abandoned. An earlier Russian declaration of 1958 in this respect that "No state has the right to subject parts of cosmic space to its own legislation, administration and jurisdiction" [19] has since been reversed, and another Soviet spokesman has declared more recently that "It is scarcely to be expected that governments should be indifferent to acts of foreign intelligence directed against them solely because they are conducted not in the air but in cosmic space." [20] Earth satellites, moving through space at heights ranging from fifty to several hundreds of miles, must in time violate the air space of every state. Yet there has been no diplomatic protest, not even when such a satellite is able to record pictures of cloud formations in the upper atmosphere and transmit them back to the earth.

The legal situation regarding the higher atmosphere is very unclear. There can,

[19] A. Galina, quoted in the *New York Times,* June 1, 1960.
[20] E. A. Korovin, quoted in the *New York Times,* June 1, 1960.

however, be no doubt of the situation regarding the lower atmosphere, within the range of manned aircraft. Sovereignty over air space in this sense would be claimed by every state. It would claim also that the aircraft of foreign states—even of friendly states—have no absolute right to fly across its territory and that they may do so only with permission and under specified conditions. Those conditions include almost certainly a requirement that the aircraft keep to certain "lanes" and fly at prescribed heights. They may also be prohibited from flying at certain hours of the day or night. This exercise of sovereignty obviously extends outward to the territorial limits of the state. Thus, any extension of the territorial sea automatically extends also the area over which the movements of aircraft are restricted. Such restrictions are in part justified by the need to control the course and height of aircraft in the interest of safety. But their chief justification is the threat to national security presented by the flights of foreign aircraft.

BIBLIOGRAPHY

Alexander, Lewis M.: "The Expanding Territorial Sea," *P.G.*, vol. 11, pp. 6–8, 1959.
———: *A Comparative Study of Offshore Claims in Northwestern Europe,* Office of Naval Research, 1960.
Boggs, S. Whittemore: "Delimitation of the Territorial Sea," *American Journal of International Law,* vol. 24, pp. 541–555, 1930.
———: "Problems of Water-boundary Definition," *G.R.*, vol. 27, pp. 445–456, 1937.
———: "National Claims in Adjacent Seas," *G.R.*, vol. 41, pp. 185–209, 1951.
Colombos, C. John: *The International Law of the Sea,* Longmans, London, 1959.
Garcia Amador, F. V.: *The Exploitation and Conservation of the Resources of the Sea,* A. W. Sythoff, Leyden, 1959.
Laws and Regulations on the Regime of the

Territorial Sea, United Nations Legislative Series, ST/LEG/SER. B/6, New York, 1957.

McFee, William: *The Law of the Sea*, J. B. Lippincott Company, Philadelphia, 1950.

Masterson, William E.: *Jurisdiction in Marginal Seas*, The Macmillan Company, New York, 1929.

Minghi, Julian V.: "The Conflict of Salmon Fishing Policies in the North Pacific," *Pacific Viewpoint*, vol. 2, pp. 59–86, 1961.

Moodie, A. E.: "The Continental Shelf: Some Territorial Problems Associated with the Continental Shelf," *Advancement of Science*, vol. 11, pp. 42–48, 1954–1955.

Moodie, A. E.: "Maritime Boundaries," in W. Gordon East and A. E. Moodie (eds.), *The Changing World*, George G. Harrat and Co., Ltd., London, 1956, pp. 942–959.

Mouton, M. W.: *The Continental Shelf*, M. Nijhoff, The Hague, 1952.

Pearcy, G. Etzel: "Hawaii's Territorial Sea," *P.G.*, vol. 11, no. 6, pp. 2–6, 1959.

———: "Measurement of the U.S. Territorial Sea," *Department of State Bulletin*, June 29, 1959, pp. 963–971.

Survey of Space Law: Staff Report of the Select Committee on Astronautics and Space Exploration, House Document 89, 86th Cong. 1st Sess., 1959.

5 POPULATION

A body politic may be viewed in two ways—according to the extent of its territory, or according to the size of its population, and the proper size of any state depends upon a ratio between these two.   JEAN-JACQUES ROUSSEAU

I was ever of the opinion that the honest man who married and brought up a large family, did more service than he who continued single and only talked of population.   OLIVER GOLDSMITH

THE ESSENTIAL ELEMENTS OF THE STATE ARE LAND AND PEOPLE. THE state is, as Ratzel said, *ein Stück Boden, ein Stück Menschen,* "a bit of land and some people." Without population it can have neither policy nor the power with which to carry policy into effect. The Antarctic continent, without permanent residents, cannot be considered a state, and it is doubtful whether, in such sparsely populated areas as the Sahara Desert or the deserts and plateaus of Central Asia, the scanty local population could be said to be in effective control of the whole area. The size and density of population are thus basic to the study of national power.

THE CENSUS

"Counting the heads of the people" seems to be such a necessary and regular function of government that it is difficult to conceive of areas where it is technically impossible and of times when it was considered morally wrong. Historians derive estimates of early population totals from such evidence as tax rolls, but early attempts to *count* the population were usually limited to certain categories of people and were usually made for special purposes. The accuracy of such totals is always suspect, as many individuals, with good reason, tried not to be listed.

The first attempt to discover the total number of the population, without any ulterior motive being attached, was probably made in Canada toward the end of the seventeenth century. During the eighteenth century several countries, including Denmark, Sweden, and some of the Italian States, organized censuses. The United States and Great Britain held their first censuses in 1800 and 1801, respectively. The errors and inaccuracies in the data derived from the faulty mechanism for collecting them, not from the limitation of the census to certain categories of persons. During the nineteenth century most European countries not only instituted censuses but extended them to their colonial dependencies. Before the end of the century Czarist Russia held its first census. There is now no part of the world where governmental agencies have not attempted to assess the number of the population, though the accuracy diminishes in the less-developed areas.

The length of series of population figures and also their accuracy vary greatly from country to country. In some they may be projected back for several centuries, but this can be done only with the aid of non-census data, and the reliability of such early estimates is low. For example, the estimated population of England, or of the greater part of it, in the closing years of the eleventh century, is based upon Domesday Book, which lists only those persons—presumably they were heads of households—who owed labor services on the fields of their lords. By what constant should one multiply the number of persons enumerated in order to arrive at a total population?

Estimates vary from 3 to 5, and the resulting population totals vary to the same degree.

Nevertheless, long "runs" are valuable because they help us to assess the trend, that is, the direction of growth or decline, and the rate at which change is taking place. Past trends provide clues for estimating future numbers, and the size of the future population is almost as important as that of the present in evaluating the contribution of population to national power.

Population Growth: It is probable that the population of the world has been continuously growing since the earliest periods of human history. It is certain, however, that growth has been regular neither through time nor even in spatial distribution. Estimates, based, it must be admitted, on data that are not wholly satisfactory, show a more than fivefold increase in world population during the last three centuries:

1650	465,000,000
1750	660,000,000
1800	836,000,000
1850	1,098,000,000
1900	1,551,000,000
1929	1,820,000,000
1959	2,905,000,000

The geographical pattern of population has changed sharply during this period, with a decline of Africa's share in the total and an increase in that of North and South America (see Table 5). The most remarkable features of this table are, first, the continued rise in Europe's percentage of the total, at least until 1929, despite the large migration to the Americas and Australia, and, second, the fairly constant ratio of Asia's population to the world total. The fact is that, over the last three hundred years, the large relative increase of population has been among the peoples of European, not among those of Asiatic, origin.

TABLE 5   *Percentage Distribution of Population, 1650–1959*

	1650	1750	1800	1850	1900	1929	1959
Europe	21.5	21.5	22.4	24.2	25.9	26.3 [1]	21.6 [1]
North America	0.2	0.2	0.7	2.4	5.2	7.3	6.7
Central and South America	2.6	1.7	2.2	3.0	4.0	5.8	6.9
Australasia	0.4	0.3	0.2	0.2	0.4	0.5	0.5
Africa	21.5	15.1	12.0	9.1	9.1	7.7	8.1
Asia	53.8	61.5	62.5	61.1	55.4	52.4	56.2

[1] Includes U.S.S.R.
SOURCE: A. M. Carr-Saunders, *World Population,* Oxford University Press, New York, 1936, p. 30; *Demographic Yearbook, 1958,* United Nations, 1958; *Statistical Yearbook,* United Nations, 1960.

During the last generation only has the rate of Europe's population growth fallen off, relative to that of the rest of the world.

Most of the world's population, no less than about 99 per cent of it, is made up of citizens of independent, self-governing states. The range of population in the 121 states that were used in the analysis already given is almost as great as the range of areas (Exhibit 41). In Table 6 states are grouped according to the size of their population, rather than of their area.

The extent to which there is a correlation between large areal extent and large

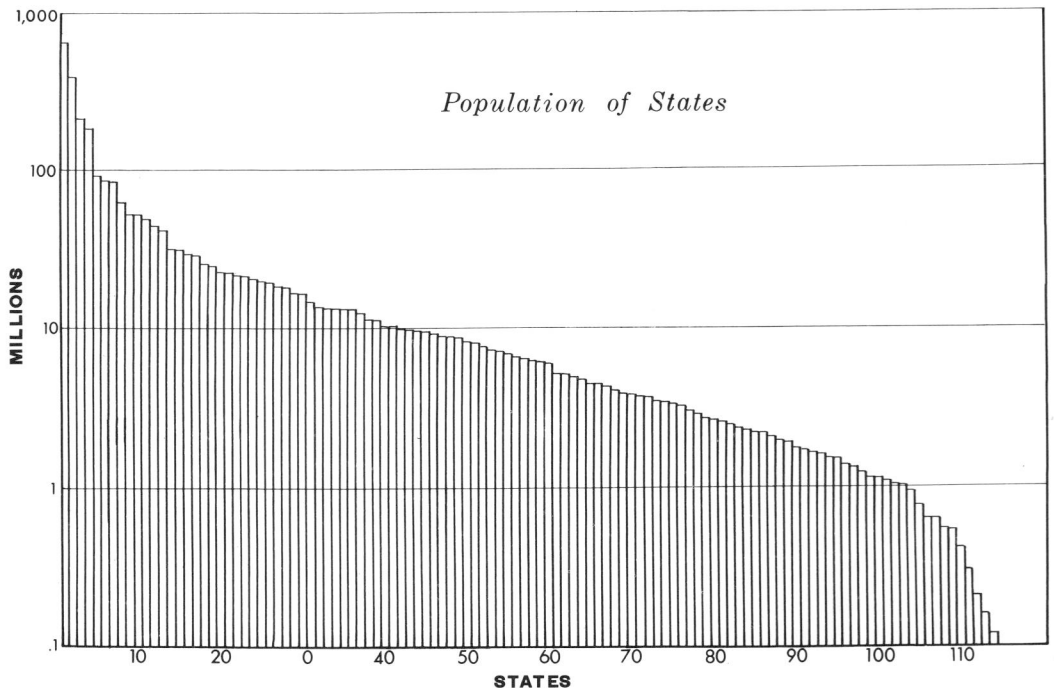

Exhibit 41 *Graph showing the population of states; the vertical numbering is according to a logarithmic scale.*

TABLE 6 *Population of States*

Millions

Over 250	2	(China, India.)
100 to 250	2	(U.S.S.R., U.S.A.)
50 to 100	6	(Japan, Indonesia, Pakistan,
25 to 50	8	Brazil, United Kingdom,
10 to 25	26	West Germany)
5 to 10	21	
1 to 5	42	
Under 1	20	
Total	127	

population is discussed in a later section. At the moment it is more important to examine to what extent crude population figures are a measure of power.

In the late eighteenth and early nineteenth centuries the dominant political power in Europe was France. French armies under Napoleon fought from Spain to Moscow. The triumph of French arms is not wholly explicable in terms either of the political weakness and internal divisions of France's enemies or of the enthusiasm which the French soldiers derived from the new social order created by the French Revolution. In large part it was a victory of numbers. The population of France at this time was about 24 million. The second largest population was that of Russia, about 19 million. Austria, Great Britain, Prussia, Sweden, and Spain were very far behind. Great Britain, according to her first census of 1801, had only 10,943,000 people. That the French victory was in reality one of "big battalions" was, in effect, recognized by Napoleon himself, who tried in his codification of French law to establish an economic incentive for large families.

In this he failed. The rate of increase of the French population in the nineteenth century was one of the lowest in Europe. Germany overtook France about 1870, and Great Britain also overtook her thirty years later. It would be far too naïve to explain the rise of German power in the second half of the nineteenth century and the German defeat and displacement of France from her position of preeminence in the war of 1870–1871 merely in terms of a changed balance of population. But the efficiency of the German Army as a fighting machine was not unrelated to its size, and, without the changed population ratio, the success of Germany might not have been so clear-cut as in fact it was. The events of the First World War demonstrated even more clearly the significance of population as a factor in power. Trench warfare, such as was conducted by both sides along the Western Front, was extravagant of men. When, in 1916, the German High Command began what is hoped would be its final offensive in the West, the Chief of Staff, General von Falkenhayn, "selected as his scene of the offensive perhaps the strongest point in the French front. The rugged, hilly, fortified salient, steel-tipped by the fortress of Verdun, was to be his battle-ground." [1] Churchill pointed out that the capture of Verdun would confer little strategic advantage and, in itself, would not end the war but explained Von Falkenhayn's plan in these words:

[Falkenhayn] had a plan of striking originality. . . . It was founded upon [his] appreciation of French psychology and German artillery. He believed that the French regarded Verdun with sentiments which had no relation to material facts. . . . To preserve Verdun the French would as Falkenhayn judged, make exertions which would exhaust their strength. Verdun would become the anvil upon which the remaining force of the French army would be pulverized in successive relays by the German heavy howitzers.

Germany could afford to lose soldiers before Verdun, and France could not. In the event, France did lose 400,000 men in the defense of Verdun, but, for the rest, Von Falkenhayn misjudged France.

In the years between the First and the Second World Wars, the disparity of pop-

[1] Winston S. Churchill, *The World Crisis: The Eastern Front*, Thornton Butterworth, Ltd., London, 1931, pp. 329–330.

ulation between France and Germany was a major consideration of French policy. "The fact of a diminishing and ageing population, the memory of the blood-letting of 1914–18, and the failure of the 1918 settlement to give France security, combined to produce in her a 'Maginot mentality.' Entrenched behind her fortifications, she hoped to avoid any further war losses and to build up her population."[2] De Gaulle's call for "12 million babies in the next ten years" not only repeated what French politicians had been saying for the previous thirty years but pointed to one of the main continuing sources of France's power weakness.

France counted on technology, the static defenses of the Maginot Line, to offset her demographic inferiority—and lost. Today we similarly rely on a technical superiority to outweigh the vast numerical superiority of the Soviet Union and the Chinese People's Republic. But vis-à-vis Korea, Vietnam, or even India, the Chinese superiority is overwhelming. In struggles between the less developed countries, the sheer weight of numbers is still an important, perhaps the most important, factor. Even among the more developed states it has significance. The Soviet Union's numerical superiority was certainly a factor in the defeat of the Germans at Stalingrad and elsewhere and in the rolling back of the German armies. It was not very long ago that Mussolini declared, ". . . The fact which . . . conditions the political, and hence the economic and moral power of nations is their demographic power. . . . What are 40,000,000 Italians against 90,000,000 Germans and 200,000,000 Slavs? . . . Italy, if she wants to count for anything, must have at least 60,000,000 inhabitants by the beginning of the second half

of this century."[3] As long as there is at least the possibility that the hydrogen bomb will not be used in any future war, weight of numbers must remain one of the more important considerations in assessing the power potential of a state.

The numerical size of the population is important in other respects besides a military sense. On the extent of the domestic population and on its purchasing power depends the size of the domestic market. Small states find it difficult and costly to establish certain types of industry:

There are certain industries or groups of industries which are ordinarily found in larger countries and not found in smaller countries. Larger countries normally possess an automobile industry, an aircraft industry, locomotive building, heavy machinery building, both mechanical and electrical. Smaller countries rarely possess any of these industries. The dividing line seems ordinarily to come between 10 and 15 million of population, though it is not difficult to find exceptions—Australia, for example.[4]

In other words, the small state is likely to have difficulty in supporting those industries which are strategically desirable. Furthermore, only a country of considerable population could operate some of the larger-scale industrial undertakings economically and effectively. "It is not going too far, perhaps, to say that . . . most of the major industrial economies of scale could be achieved by a relatively high-income nation of 50 million; that nations of 10–15 million [are] probably too small to get all the technical economies available."[5]

---

[2] Katharine Munro, *France Yesterday and Today*, Royal Institute of International Affairs, London, 1945, p. 12.

[3] Quoted by R. R. Kuczynski, *Living-space and Population Problems*, Oxford University Press, New York, 1939, p. 10.

[4] E. A. G. Robinson (ed.), *The Economic Consequences of the Size of Nations*, Macmillan and Co., Ltd., London, 1960, p. xvii.

[5] *Ibid.*, p. xviii.

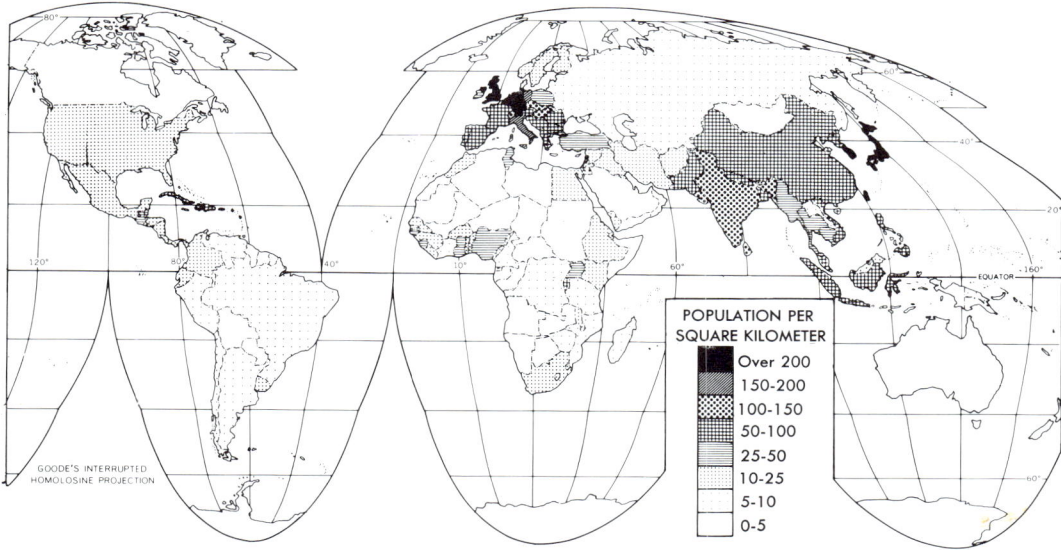

Exhibit 42 *World map of population density, by states.*

How then do we explain the obvious success, both political and economic, of some small states, the Scandinavian countries and Switzerland, for example? These states are necessarily less diversified than larger states; they have a smaller variety of resources and industries, and most are predominantly agricultural. "Despite intense nationalism and strong security feelings that are perhaps warranted, there are compelling economic factors that make it impossible for a small nation to have even a single basic plant for a number of industries that are feasible for a larger country at the same level of economic development." [6]

Yet smallness has its compensations. The population of small states, like Switzerland and the Scandinavian countries, is usually more homogeneous, and owing to "closer internal ties, [the state] may find it easier to make the social adjustments needed to take advantage of the potentialities of modern technology and economic

[6] S. Kuznets, "Economic Growth of Small Nations," in *ibid.*, p. 17.

growth." In the more successful of small states:

There exists a strong feeling of community and solidarity, a product of a long-shared historical past, and . . . in these states social decisions, necessary for the adjustment to the potentials of economic growth, may be far easier to reach than elsewhere. Among the larger nations this task is far more difficult, since the ties among the various sectors of their populations are looser, and regional and other cleavages can more readily develop. [7]

Population Density: The only way of relating population to area is by calculating the density of population per square mile. The enormous range in population density, from Saudi Arabia, with less than 1 per square mile, to the Netherlands, with about 780 (Exhibit 42), merely shows how little correlation there is between the tables already given of population and area. The graph (Exhibit 43) shows population plotted against area except for the smallest sovereign states. The spread of the ratios is

[7] *Ibid.*, p. 29.

considerable, though it is perhaps less than might have been expected. If, for example, the ratios for a single continent, or for a group of countries having similar economies, are examined, they show a certain degree of correlation. Population density varies with geographical factors, such as resources for agriculture and industry, with the birth rate and migration, and also with the

level of technological achievement. There is no ideal or optimum population density. The poor, semidesert grazing lands of northeastern Arabia may be capable of supporting only a handful of nomadic herdsmen and their animals per 100 square miles, but many times as many petroleum geologists and technicians are able to earn a living here. It requires little imagination to

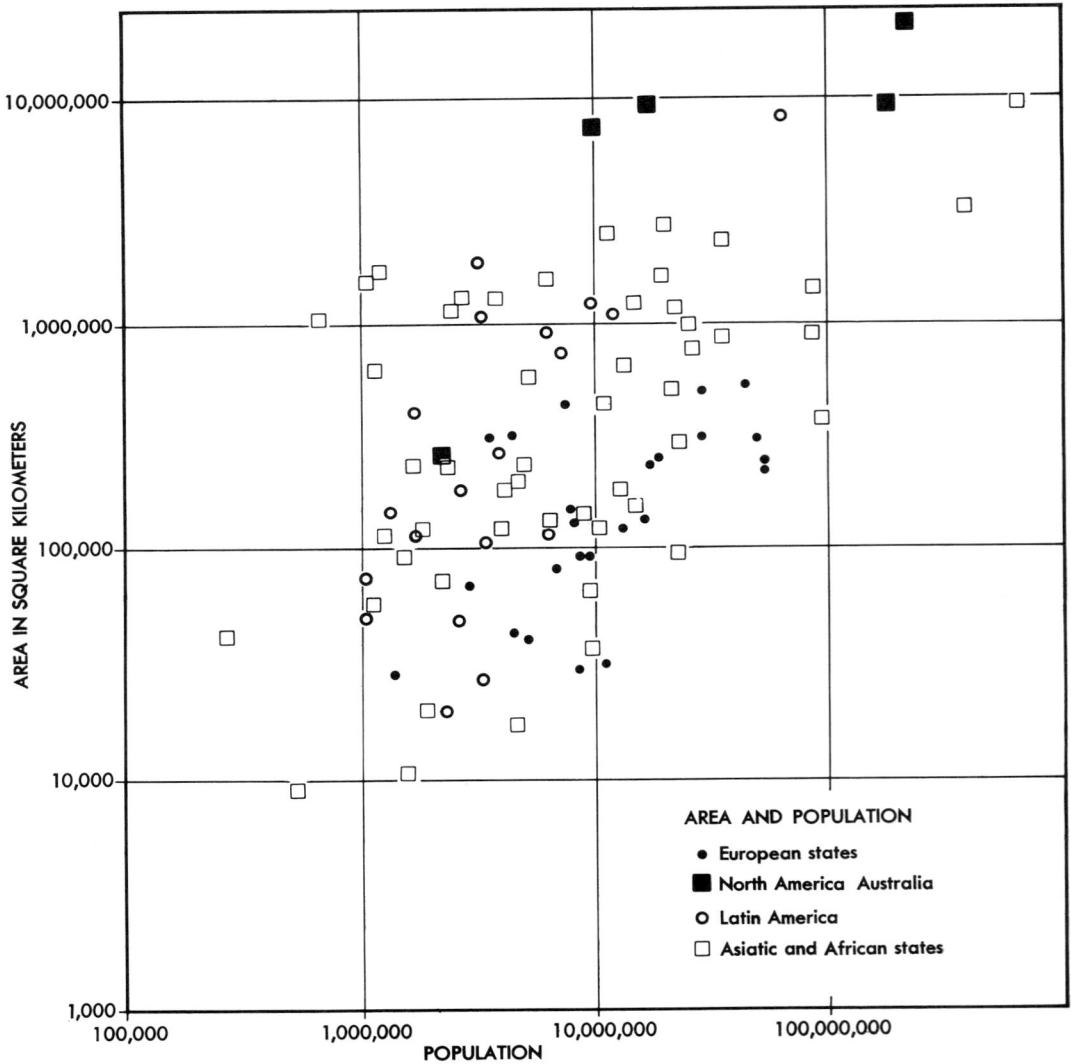

Exhibit 43 *Graph showing the relationship between area and population of states.*

suggest conditions under which many scantily peopled areas might attract a large population, though, in each instance, only as a result of technological developments.

One or two nomadic pastoralists per square mile in the Middle East may produce soil erosion by overgrazing. The area may, thus, be said to be overpopulated. But the 400 persons per square mile in an industrial country could possibly be increased with profit. Since there is no ideal population density, it cannot be said that density, per se, is a factor in national power. Population density is important only when it is high or low in relation both to local resources and to the technological stage of their development and utilization. We must consider the political implications of overpopulation and underpopulation rather than the density of population itself.

Overpopulation: As part of the propaganda before the Second World War, the German government made use of a table of population densities of the more important countries in the world. The total area of each country combined with that of all its dependent territories was used. With France was included most of Saharan Africa; with Great Britain, the Commonwealth; and with Belgium and the Netherlands, their tropical empires. The result was the following table:

	Persons per sq km
Germany	135
Poland	89.3
Japan	69.1
China	42.2
Netherlands	36.2
Brazil	5.0
Saudi Arabia	4.7
Argentina	4.6
Venezuela	3.4
Bolivia	2.4

SOURCE: R. R. Kuczynski, *Living-space and Population Problems*, Oxford University Press, New York, 1939, p. 8.

Only the top and the bottom of the table have been printed, but this is enough to show how meaningless it is. Both the United States and the British Empire (its constituent parts, including the United Kingdom, not being separately listed) were reported as having 15 per square kilometer. The density for the "British Empire" was obtained by taking not only the area and population of the United Kingdom itself but also that of Australia, Canada, South Africa, and all the other parts of the Commonwealth. Similarly the figure for the United States relates not only to densely peopled New Jersey and Connecticut but also to relatively empty Nevada, Arizona, and Alaska.

The table, then, was of very little importance as a basis for assessing national power. But it did have a political and propaganada value, and this the Germans used to the full. Hitler, in a letter to President Roosevelt, declared, "According to all common sense, logic and all principles of a general human and of a higher justice . . . all nations ought to have an equal share in the goods of this world. It should thus not happen that one nation claims so much living-space that [has] . . . not even 15 inhabitants to the square kilometer, while other nations are forced to maintain 140, 150, or even 200 in the same area. . . ." This crude presentation was not without influence both inside Germany and without. Many became convinced of the justice of Germany's claim to more territory, irrespective of where it might be obtained. The claim for "living space" had an immense emotional appeal, but even if it were technically possible to satisfy this claim, it was not really possible to show that Germany was overpopulated.

At the present time the government of Australia is advertising for settlers and is even offering to help them to meet the expense of migrating to Australia. The government of India, however, is openly expressing its fears of the consequences of the continued growth of population. In these instances the governments have admitted that their respective countries are either underpopulated or overpopulated. The terms over- and underpopulation are difficult to define. Germany claimed to be overpopulated, and this was not the case. Mussolini demanded more living space and somewhat illogically called for an increased birth rate at the same time.

The mere statement of population density, we have seen, is nothing more than a statement of an arithmetical ratio. It carries with it no connotation of too many or too few people. The capacity of land to support people varies with the resources of the land and with the technical capacity of the people to develop and use those resources, either for direct consumption or as a medium of exchange.

Let us assume that in a particular land and at a given level of technological development there is a desirable or optimum density of population. This density is the one at which the resources are fully utilized. If more people are added, the increase of productivity will not be commensurate with the size of the additional population. Similarly, if population is withdrawn, the balance of those remaining will be upset, resulting in something less than full employment. This will reduce the total production to a degree that is disproportionate to the diminution of the population itself. Of course, this ideal population density is only hypothetical. We cannot calculate precisely what it is for any state, and thus we cannot state the extent to which the population density exceeds or falls short of what is desirable in most states. Only in a few is it so obviously too great or too small, under existing conditions of technology, that such a statement is warranted.

The economic conditions of the modern world are not stable enough for any attempt to estimate the ideal density of population to be realistic. The level of technology is changing all the time. Business cycles and seasonal fluctuations give alternating periods of high and low employment, and in an industrial society there is always a body of labor that is temporarily unemployed because it is between jobs. There are, thus, an alternating shortage and abundance of labor.

A predominantly agricultural society, such as that of India or China, which is dependent to only a small degree on fluctuations in the world market, is more easily susceptible to such an analysis. Its unemployment or underemployment is structural rather than cyclical. One may take a village community and estimate without too great a margin of error whether the work of cultivating its fields or tending its herds could, in fact, be done at a smaller expenditure of labor than is presently used: ". . . it is the superfluity [of labor] with reference to a given system which is essential. In the words of a Bulgarian economist: 'If I see five sheep with three dogs and two men, I call that overpopulation.' Understood in this sense, it cannot be doubted that there really is overpopulation in Eastern Europe as a very widespread though localized phenomenon."[8] Such countries suffer from hidden unemployment: two men doing together the work of one. Although in time custom tends to sanctify such wasteful methods, the extra unit of manpower could migrate, given somewhere to go, without loss to the community and the cost of feeding him would be saved.

Such overpopulation influences na-

[8] Doreen Warriner, *Economics of Peasant Farming*, Oxford University Press, New York, 1939, p. 66. Some of the "featherbedding" practices of the United States suggest overpopulation, though actually their cause is quite different.

tional power by restricting the availability of capital for investment. If we assume that the total national product is consumed by 20 million persons, of whom 5 million are redundant, then clearly a quarter of this amount would be available for export or investment if the redundant population were to migrate. This is the basic reason why overcrowded states find it difficult to accumulate capital, to develop their technology, and so to reach a position where their overpopulation would weigh less heavily upon them. An overcrowded state is not likely to have, or is likely to have only to a restricted degree, the factories, the specialized agriculture, and the transportation network which contribute materially to the economic and, thus, to the political power of a state. Furthermore, the level of education and of health, nutrition, and welfare generally is likely to be low. The "big battalions" of such a state are likely to be poorly equipped and perhaps militarily ineffective.

Against these disadvantages of too great a population in the calculus of national power must perhaps be set the advantage of a vast body of labor which can be liberated from other employment without seriously impairing national output. Such labor is, however, essentially unskilled. It could, for instance, be employed to build a Burma Road across the mountains from Burma to the Szechwan Basin of western China; it could be used as "cannon fodder" against the Japanese; but only after training could it be used in the munitions factories.

The overpopulated countries par excellence are China, Egypt, and India, followed by Pakistan, Japan, Java, and restricted areas of eastern Europe, the Middle East, and Central America and the Caribbean. Two passages from well-known writers describe the conditions in two of these areas:

The population of China is too large to be supported by existing resources. While, in China as a whole, its mean density is low compared with that of most western countries, in certain areas it is appalling. Whole provinces, as large as European states, may properly be described as congested districts. The struggle of a swarm of human beings for a bare physical existence is an everpresent reality. All the phenomena of rural distress—minute holdings, tiny incomes, female infanticide, starvation—are the unavoidable result of it. . . . Famine is the economic, civil war the political, expression of the pressure of population on the means of subsistence.[9]

Of Egypt, Warriner writes:

To arrive at an estimate of how much population is actually surplus to requirements, it is necessary to estimate the actual labour requirements of cultivation in Egypt; the only estimate of this kind has been made by Professor Cleland. Basing his estimate of labour requirements on actual observation, Cleland found that, whereas the average area farmed by a peasant family was 1.6 acres, it was possible for a family to cultivate five times that area on the existing methods. This suggests that one-fifth of the present farm labour might be able to maintain the present volume of production; but Professor Cleland considers that a safer estimate of the surplus would be one-half the farm population in 1937; on this basis the number of farm workers could be cut by 2 millions and the farm population by some 5 million, without a decline in production.[10]

But overpopulation is not confined to predominantly agricultural countries. It may occur anywhere there is a shortage of land and capital:

[9] R. H. Tawney, *Land and Labour in China*, George Allen & Unwin, Ltd., London, 1932, pp. 103–104. This relates to conditions thirty years ago. Industrial growth has probably reduced the degree of overpopulation.

[10] Doreen Warriner, *Land and Poverty in the Middle East*, Royal Institute of International Affairs, London and New York, 1948, p. 33.

An attempt has been made to express the extent of underemployment in these countries by calculating how many workers could be withdrawn from the labour force without affecting national production. The figures arrived at, while of necessity approximate, are nonetheless impressive: 3 or 4 million for Italy . . . at least 2 million for Spain, and 1 million for Greece.[11]

Underpopulation: The weaknesses in terms of national power that arise from too small a population are equally significant and equally obvious. In such a state there is presumably an abundance of land, so that the diseconomies of minute holdings and hidden unemployment should be absent. On the other hand, the state as a whole may provide only a small market, so that the advantages of large-scale production cannot be realized, and some strategically important industries cannot be profitably established. It must be remembered, however, that the same is true of all small countries. The very thinness of the population is itself a source of weakness. Society approximates more nearly the conditions of a frontier; public order is more difficult to maintain, and the problem of defending a large area with a military force recruited from only a small population has always been a difficult one. The examples of Australia and New Zealand, with, respectively, 10,661,000 and 2,331,000 people and the very low over-all densities of 3 and 21 per square mile, come to mind. Despite efforts to encourage immigration and to develop industry at home, their population remains too small for their areas, and their foreign policy is marked by a certain insecurity.

Migration: Human history has been marked by migration, from densely peopled areas to sparse, from regions of low resources to regions more plentifully endowed, from persecution and oppression to supposed freedom and peace. In the past, before the system of states had crystallized, whole tribes or nations migrated; in modern times, it has been only a minority of any nation that moves. It has been estimated that in a little over a century, from 1821 to 1932, almost sixty million persons migrated. Most, perhaps about 98 per cent of the total, were of European origin and the bulk of the remainder from India and Japan. And most, about 90 per cent, we to the Americas, and the majority of these to the United States.[12] An examination of the countries from which these migrants came and of the dates of their emigration shows that the political factor was not the most important one in leading them to migrate. Most migrated because their own country seemed too crowded, and they migrated in most instances with the knowledge and consent of their own governments, which regarded such "bloodletting" as desirable or necessary. The migration from Ireland, which was largest in the 1840s, may have been helped by dislike of English rule but was basically due to the fact that Ireland had ceased to be able to support so large and continuously growing population. Toward the end of the century, the biggest stream was from Italy, and for precisely the same reasons. Migration for political reasons was important after the suppression of the European risings of 1848 but did not again become the dominant motive until the period of the Second World War.

We are concerned here with migration as a means of relieving population pressure in crowded countries and of increasing the population in the underpopulated states. Europe, taken as a whole, has ceased to be an overpopulated continent, if indeed it ever was. Ireland was overpopulated in the years preceding the potato famine, but elsewhere in Europe there have been only

---

[11] *International Migration, 1945–1957,* International Labor Office, Geneva, 1959, p. 257.

[12] Based on Kuczynski, *op. cit.,* p. 49.

pockets of overpopulation, such as southern Italy and Polish Galicia. To some extent these remain, but the present policies of the states concerned envisage in general a controlled internal migration and the economic development of the overcrowded areas by such means as land reform and reclamation and the establishment of new industries.

The same is happening to some extent outside Europe. In recent years there has been a small migration from the more crowded southern islands of Japan to the relatively sparsely peopled northern island of Hokkaido, from Java, one of the most densely peopled agricultural areas in the world, to the virgin lands of Borneo and Sumatra, from the crowded river valleys of China to the steppelike plains of Inner Mongolia, and there has been a large migration into Manchuria. But clearly internal migration cannot do more than ameliorate the severe population problem of China, India, Pakistan, and Egypt, to name only four countries in which it appears to be particularly acute.

Emigration from each of these, except Egypt, has been important in the past. There are today Indian communities in East and South Africa and Central America, and Chinese communities are widely scattered over Southeast Asia as well as elsewhere. Such migration can no longer be regarded as practicable. Migration from Communist China, one the most seriously overpopulated countries, to other parts of the Communist world is improbable for technical reasons and impossible to the free world for political reasons. There are also important social and economic obstacles to migration. In general countries with a higher standard of living do not welcome immigrants from countries with a lower one. Australia excluded people with a relatively low standard of living, in spite of its very real need for greater population. In Africa it has proved difficult for Asiatic immigrants to fit into the existing social pattern, and, furthermore, it is by no means certain that, despite the low population density over much of the continent, the absorptive capacity of the land has not yet been reached in many areas.

There remain North and South America. In both, immigration is strictly controlled. The United States uses a quota system which would permit only a handful of immigrants per year from the countries which have the most people to spare. Canada controls immigration through its consular officials, who issue visas to enter the country. Both countries make it clear that they are selective in their immigration policy and that they discourage the immigration of persons for whom they feel no immediate need. South America is the only continent which has both the space and the rather tolerant political and social attitude toward certain immigrants that makes possible a large-scale movement of people. But here, too, immigration from Africa and Asia is severely discouraged. In addition, other factors—political instability, lack of capital, and the undeveloped nature of large parts of the interior of the continent—all operate to restrict immigration.

It may be regarded as axiomatic that international migration will not afford an outlet for surplus population in the future, as, to some extent, it has done in the past, and this primarily for political and social reasons. The uneven distribution of population, which exists and is likely to continue, is a factor in the power of states. Italy and Japan have both seized, or attempted to seize, land for a part of their surplus population to settle in, Italy in North and East Africa, Japan on the mainland of Asia and in Oceania. The mere fact that some states, notably Australia, have empty lands is itself a factor of weakness because of the hostile intentions it arouses among the overpopulated peoples.

NATIONS AND SUBNATIONS

A nation, as we have seen in the first chapter, is "a group of people, occupying a particular area who feel themselves held together in terms of common acceptance of particular values that are of such prime importance to them that they demand that their area and people should be organized in a distinct state, as the political agency by which those values may be preserved and furthered."[13] The term nation is unfortunately used on several levels of meaning. In its most precise and restricted sense it means a clearly defined people, distinguished from others by language, folkways, traditions, and perhaps religion. The Poles, Czechs, and Hungarians are such groups. A second sense in which the word is used is to denote all the citizens of a state, irrespective of cultural divisions. Thus one might speak of the "Brazilian nation" or the "French nation." Lastly the term is used, in its broadest sense, to indicate a people which spreads over two or more states and has no common political goals. Thus the German nation may, in this sense, be taken to include all the German-speaking peoples, not only of Germany itself, but also of Austria, Switzerland, and northern Italy. So loose a use of the term is to be avoided, and in this book the term is used only in the narrowest and most precise of the senses listed above, namely, that of a linguistic-cultural group, endowed with a sense of its own individuality and separateness from all other such groups. Nevertheless, we continually use the terms national and nationality in a much more general sense. It is very difficult, even in

[13] Richard Hartshorne, "The Functional Approach in Political Geography," *A.A.A.G.*, vol. 40, p. 114, 1950.

this book, to avoid the use of such phrases as "Canadian nationality" or the "national interests" of South Africa when the connotation of the expression is state-wide.

The most important aspect of the nation, from the politico-geographical point of view, is that it is not necessarily the same as the body of citizens of a particular state. There is scarcely a state in the modern world in which every group completely accepts the cultural traditions (including language and religion) of the majority. This relationship of state to nation is represented diagrammatically in Exhibit 5.

The dominant nation is represented as extending over a larger geographical area than the state, so that the state is contained within the nation, while at the same time a part of the nation is left outside the territorial limits of the state. Exhibit 5 shows an approximate correspondence between the state and the dominant nation but leaves, as is almost inevitably the case, a fraction of the nation outside the limits of the state while including small elements of other nations. The same diagram shows the state encompassing the whole of the nation and also parts of neighboring nations.

It is easy to supply examples of each case:

Case A	Case B	Case C
Sweden	Denmark	Ethiopia
Hungary	Bulgaria	Burma
German Federal	Greece	Brazil
Republic	Spain	Rumania
German Democratic	Italy	
Republic	France	
	India	
	Japan	
	Mexico	
	Norway	
	Turkey	
	Finland	

There are, on the other hand, states which can be fitted into such a scheme only with difficulty, such as:

1. Multinational states, like Canada, Yugoslavia, and the Malaya, which are partnerships of two or more national groups on more or less equal terms

2. The states newly created in Africa, which reflect not the national, that is, cultural-linguistic groupings of the Africans, but a former power balance of the imperial states of Europe

3. The group of Spanish-speaking Latin-American countries in which, as far as concerns social cohesion, there is more in common between all persons of European origin than between the European and the Indian groups within, let us say, Ecuador

Our primary consideration in this book is with the social cohesion of the citizens of any particular state as a factor in the political power of the state. The term *subnations* is used here for national groups which constitute individually only a small minority within a state, such as the German-, Spanish-, and Flemish-speaking groups within France and the Spanish- and Finnish-speaking groups, to mention only two, in the United States. The various patterns of relationship between nation and subnation, or between the state and the several cultural-linguistic groups of which it is composed, may be summarized as follows:

1. The culturally unified states, in which there may be said to be complete unity and cohesion from the cultural-linguistic point of view. This does not, however, presuppose that there are no differences deriving from social class or economic position. Examples are the Netherlands, Hungary, Sweden, and New Zealand.

2. States in which subnations are drawn so intimately into the cultural life of the state that, whether they continue to use their own language and practice their own culture or not, they cease to be regarded as a disruptive element. The Ger-

man-speaking population of Alsace-Lorraine (France) is an example; indeed, this "seems to be the only instance in Europe of national feeling moving in opposition to language." [14] Inside the United Kingdom, the Welsh and Scotch form similar groups. No one seriously considers that these groups are likely to want complete political independence or that, on significant political issues, they feel differently from the English. In Canada, the French-speaking element is coming increasingly to think of itself as Canadian.

3. States in which subnations are not integrated with the dominant nation, in which they jealously preserve all aspects of their own culture, and in which they aim at autonomy within, or even at independence of, the state within which they live. At the present time the German-speaking community of the South Tyrol (Alto Adige, in northern Italy) is an example of such a community. Their political objective varies as between individuals from autonomy within Italy to political union with Austria. The Slovene minority in Austria, the Hungarian in Rumania, the Albanian in Yugoslavia, the Kurdish in both Iraq and Iran are all fundamentally similar, and the list could be greatly extended with examples from eastern Europe, the Middle East, and Southeast Asia.

The tendency in boundary development over the past half century has been toward making political boundaries conform as closely as is practicable with cultural-linguistic divisions. Complete identity of group and area is, as has been seen in Chapter 3, practically impossible, but the growing approximation of the two is reducing the geographical area of dispute. This trend of development is examined below in connection with minorities.

[14] H. Munro Chadwick, *The Nationalities of Europe*, Cambridge University Press, New York, 1945, p. 8.

4. States in which the population belongs mainly to two or more evenly balanced national groups. Numerically considered, one group at least is clearly a minority, but so strong a minority that it can establish its own conditions of co-existence in a multinational state. These conditions are sometimes embodied in a federal structure, but there are some multi-national states such as Belgium, Indonesia, Czechoslovakia, Peru, Ecuador, and several other Latin-American states that have not resorted to a federal constitution. The essential difference between these states and those of categories 1 to 3 is that the secession or political autonomy of one group in defiance of the others is not seriously contemplated. Political difficulties, especially if the constitution is unitary, can be serious, especially where they touch upon the matters of schooling, of church organization, and of state control of secular matters. Some examples of states which fall into this category are as follows:

Unitary states
Czechoslovakia: Czechs, 8,800,000; Slovaks, 3,700,000; Magyars, 404,000
Yugoslavia: Serbs, 9,500,000; Croats, 3,900,000; Slovenes, 1,500,000; Macedonians, 1,300,000
Belgium: Flemings, 4,500,000; Walloons, 3,800,000
Republic of South Africa:[1] African, 9,606,000; "colored," 1,360,000; Africaans-speaking white, 1,700,000; English-speaking white, 1,300,000
Federal states
Canada: French-speaking, about 4,500,000; others, mainly English-speaking, 11,500,000
Soviet Union: Russian, about 100,000,000; Ukrainian, 36,000,000; White Russian, 10,000,000; others, 60,000,000
India (1951 census): Hindus, 303,200,000; Muslims, 35,500,000; Sikhs, 6,200,000; others, about 10,000,000

[1] The Republic of South Africa has a unitary constitution with federal overtones. It represents a compromise reached early in the present century between the English- and Afrikaans-speaking peoples which is unlikely to stand the test of time.

5. States a part of whose territory is the subject of "irredentist" aims on the part of a neighboring state. This is an extension of the third category. The term derives from one of the most clear-cut examples. By 1861 most of Italy had been united politically, but the Austrians still held an area in the northeast. This was *Italia irredenta,* or "unredeemed Italy." More recent examples have been the German claims to the Sudetenland from Czechoslovakia, to the "Corridor" from Poland, and to Alsace-Lorraine from France. In the same category would be the Bulgarian claim to Yugoslav and Greek Macedonia. Again, many such claims could be listed, whether actively pursued at the present time, or lying dormant, waiting to be revived under more propitious political circumstances. The existence of an irredentist claim to a territory does not necessarily presume that the inhabitants of such a territory favor the claim themselves. Unquestionably the Italians of Venezia wished to be "redeemed" and incorporated into Italy. So apparently did many of the Sudeten Germans desire union with their *Vaterland,* but the German-speaking community of Alsace-Lorraine and the mixed population of the Polish Corridor gave no evidence of such desires.

6. Plural societies. This term is used to cover those state-wide groups in which cultural-linguistic divisions, sometimes of a very minor order, are reinforced by social and economic barriers. It has been implicit in the discussion so far that the subnation or minority group is substantially at the same economic level as the rest of the citizens of the state. As one passes from Walloon- to Flemish-speaking Belgium one is conscious of a change in language and in folkways but not of any significant difference in economic level. In other words, since both communities span the whole or at least most of the social spec-

trum, the range of social diversity is similar. There may be a shade of difference as between Czechs and Slovaks, in so far as the Slovaks have been less developed economically than the Czechs. But contrasts of this kind are always weak. The Germans of Alsace-Lorraine and South Tyrol are not economically distinguishable from the rest of their compatriots.

By contrast, in much of Latin America, a relatively weak cultural-linguistic division may be reinforced by a sharp economic barrier. It is unwise to generalize for a continent, but, broadly speaking, the Indian-mestizo groups have a level of education and a standard of living that are markedly different from those of the section of the population that is mainly of European descent. The two groups, very far from overlapping, are sharply separated and, relatively speaking, the one is poor, the other rich. Ecuador is sometimes cited as the extreme, but all Latin-American states have plural societies, except those, such as Uruguay and Argentina, which are predominantly European.

Other examples of plural societies are Malaya and Indonesia [15] and all those parts of Africa where Africans live side by side with European and Asiatic immigrants. The whole of this complex topic is taken up again in Chapter 14.

National Unity: What, then, is the impact of these divisions on the question of national unity, and thus of national power? National ideals, however expressed or defined, will be supported the most vigorously or, in the last resort, fought for the most readily by a group which accepts them to the full. Cromwell was right in his preference for "a russet-coated trooper who knows what he fights for, and loves what he knows" over any rich man who merely

showed a fleeting interest in the cause. At the very least, the subnation may show a certain lukewarmness in its support of the state in time of emergency; at most, it may constitute a focus of active opposition to what the majority regards as the national interest. Every gradation from complete cooperation to active disloyalty can be illustrated from the behavior of subnational groups during the present century.

To revert to the list of types already described (page 128), clearly no problem can arise with the first, nor in reality with the second, though it is not always easy to convince others that this is so.[16] It is the next two types of national division that are the most serious from the point of view of national power. There have been too many instances—some of them already cited—of the use of dissident or hostile minorities, or even of major national groups within a state,[17] by a hostile power as a political lever. It is unlikely that a state will grant autonomy to one of its provinces unless the local demand becomes so strong that it is less embarrassing to yield than to resist. No state likes to make any breach in its legal or juridical unity, because a breach in the monolithic structure of the unitary state looks much like a confession of weakness. Occasionally a government has in this way held out too long against the rising pressure of national feeling in one of its minority groups: Yugoslavia, against that of the Croats before the Second World War; the Hindus, against that of the Muslims in British India; the Austro-Hungarian Empire of the Hapsburgs, against that of all their Slavic and other subject peoples before the First World War. What happened in each of these in-

---

[15] J. S. Furnivall, *Netherlands India: A Study in Plural Economy,* The Macmillan Company, New York, 1944.

[16] The German attempt during the Second World War to stir up alleged anti-English feeling in Scotland is an example.

[17] The German use of the Flemings in Belgium is an example.

stances shows that it is a mark of the wisest statesmanship to yield to such national pressures before the breaking point is reached. Republican Spain did this with her Catalan and Basque groups (though this was reversed after the successful rebellion of Franco); the United Kingdom, somewhat belatedly, to the Irish of the Republic of Ireland.

The Minorities Problem: In the tenth of his Fourteen Points, President Woodrow Wilson declared that "The peoples of Austria-Hungary . . . should be accorded the freest opportunity of autonomous development." Throughout the nineteenth century, liberalism had meant, among other things, a belief in the right of cultural-linguistic groups to have political expression if they wished it. In 1919–1920, the new boundaries that were drawn in eastern Europe were made to accord, as closely as possible, with the liguistic divisions. But, at the same time, the peace conference had dealt kindly with the territorial claims of certain countries, especially Rumania, Czechoslovakia, and Poland, and correspondingly harshly with those of the neighboring countries of Hungary and Bulgaria. More subnations or minorities were included within the boundaries of some of these east European countries than Woodrow Wilson in fact approved. To safeguard their national interests, a number of countries, among them Czechoslovakia, Poland, Finland, Rumania, Turkey, Yugoslavia, Hungary, and the Baltic States, were obliged to accept minorities treaties, by which they undertook to protect the rights of national minorities.[18] The Polish Minorities Treaty, which was typical of the others, contained the following guarantees:

Article 2: Poland undertakes to assure full and complete protection of life and liberty to

[18] Isaiah Bowman, *The New World*, World Book Company, Yonkers, New York, 1928, pp. 27–31.

all inhabitants of Poland without distinction of birth, nationality, language, race or religion.

All inhabitants of Poland shall be entitled to the free exercise, whether public or private, of any creed, religion or belief, whose practices are not inconsistent with public order or public morals. . . .

Article 9: Poland will provide in the public educational system in towns and districts in which a considerable proportion of Polish nationals of other than Polish speech are resident adequate facilities for ensuring that in the primary schools the instruction shall be given in their own language.

The idea of protecting such minorities by an international treaty or guarantee was not new. Even in the seventeenth century treaties of peace sometimes contained an expressed guarantee to a particular religious group. The Russian Czar became by the terms of the Treaty of Kutchuk-Kainardji (1774) the guardian of Christian subjects of the Turkish Empire. During the nineteenth century such guarantees, although not infrequent, were by no means always effective. But none was so comprehensive as the system of minority treaties, negotiated in Paris in 1919–1920.

Plebiscites: In some areas nations are geographically so confused that it has become impossible to draw a simple boundary between them. Occasionally, language has even ceased to reflect their loyalties. The idea of voting on the crucial issue of which state a group of people chooses to belong to is not new. It was used during the period of the French Revolution to determine the wishes of the people of Avignon, who had previously belonged to the Pope, and of Nice and Savoy. During the nineteenth century the method of the plebiscite was employed several times in Italy, and its use was suggested elsewhere. But it was first used on a large scale after the First World War. In no less than six separate areas of Europe, the population was called upon to decide by voting between two distinct political loyalties (Exhibit 44). The object of the plebiscite was to do as little injustice as possible by ensuring that at least the majority in a given area was satisfied. It did not try to eliminate minorities; given the mixture of nations in some parts of Europe, that would have been impossible. But it was hoped that the minority treaties would give adequate protection to the groups caught on the wrong side of a new political boundary.

In Europe plebiscites were held in the following districts:

> Malmédy (Belgium)
> South Schlesvig (Denmark)
> Klagenfurt (Austria)
> Allenstein (Germany–East Prussia)
> Marienwerder (Germany–East
>   Prussia)
> Upper Silesia (Germany-Poland)
> Saar Territory (Germany, 1935)

In addition, plebiscites were provided for in treaties, but not held, in Teschen (Cieszyn, Těšin), Spiš, and Orava, all on the border of Czechoslovakia and Poland. In each case where a plebiscite took place, a boundary was drawn on the basis of the voters' decision, though that in Upper Silesia did violence to economic sense without really satisfying the majority of the inhabitants.

Exchange of Population: A remedy for the problems raised by the continued existence of pockets of national minorities lies in the migration or exchange of population. Such a proposal was first made, in 1913, by the Turkish Empire, which would have preferred to get rid of the Christian minorities in its midst rather than be obliged to sacrifice territory. A year later Turkey proposed to Greece that they should exchange their respective Greek and Turkish minorities, but little progress was made with this proposal until after the First

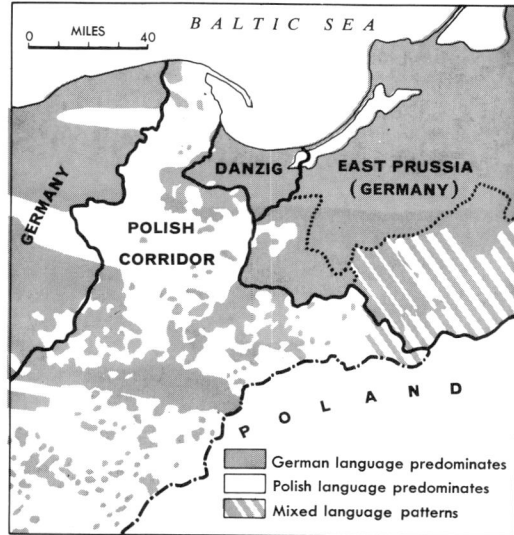

*Exhibit 44 **An example of a plebiscite area: the Allenstein-Marienwerder region of northern Poland.*** AFTER I. BOWMAN

World War. An agreement, reached in 1923, provided for "a compulsory exchange of Turkish nationals of the Greek Orthodox Religion established in Turkish territory, and of Greek nationals of the Moslem religion established in Greek territory." [19] Religion, not language, was the determining factor. According to the terms of this treaty, nearly two million people were moved. In the words of C. A. Macartney:

355,635 Moslems were transferred from Greece, most of them under fairly orderly conditions, although the later emigrants in particular suffered considerable hardships, particularly as their houses and properties were occupied by Greek refugees. The Greeks, about 1,500,000 in all, migrated under far less favorable conditions. They were often driven from their homes and kept waiting for months at the ports, without proper shelter; they were

[19] *League of Nations Treaty Series*, League of Nations, Geneva, vol. 42, pp. 76–87.

Figure 26 *Camp of Arab refugees, about sixteen miles southwest of Damascus, in Syria. There are a little under a hundred thousand Arab refugees from Israel in Syria.* COURTESY: UNITED NATIONS

unable, as a rule, to collect their debts, or to take with them more than a fraction of their movable property. . . .[20]

At about the same time a "voluntary" exchange took place between Greece and Bulgaria. It was on a much smaller scale and concerned only 101,800 Bulgars and 52,891 Greeks. It was, however, accomplished in a much more orderly way and resulted in a great deal less personal hardship.

A violent and disorderly exchange of minorities, which was certainly not foreseen by the governments concerned, was

[20] C. A. Macartney, *National States and National Minorities,* Oxford University Press, New York, 1934, pp. 445–446.

that between India and Pakistan, when, in 1947, Muslims in India and Hindus in Pakistan crowded across their mutual boundary. On this occasion an estimated seven million Hindus moved into India and about five million Muslims into Pakistan. An exchange was also planned between Czechoslovakia and Hungary, but this has not yet been fully implemented.

Exchange of population does not appear to offer a means of solving minority problems, except perhaps on a local scale. If neighboring countries are able to organize a peaceful and orderly exchange of population, they are usually civilized enough to adopt a tolerant policy that would make exchanges unnecessary.

The Refugee Question: According to a recent report on migration:

Since the end of the Second World War, migratory movements on a quite unprecedented scale have taken place throughout the world. Millions of people have been driven from their homes and the population structure of entire countries radically altered. Political upheavals involving the redrawing of frontiers, transfers of sovereignty and changes of regime have forced entire populations into exile and caused mass movements far in excess of those normally resulting from supply and demand on the world employment market.[21]

In the course of the past fifteen years, no fewer than about fifty million persons, almost 2 per cent of the world's population, have been obliged, for political or cultural reasons, to leave their homes. The Germans have two very useful words to describe these people:

1. *Vertriebenen* or *Heimatvertriebenen.* These are people who were forced to flee, usually by government action. Thus the Czechoslovak government, in 1945, forced the German-speaking population, or Sudeten Germans, to migrate to Germany. Similarly, the Poles drove the Germans out of their western Territories; the Russians drove out, or at least encouraged the departure, of both the Karelian Finns and the Poles who lived in areas of Finland and Poland, respectively, that the Soviet Union had annexed. Many other instances could be listed of minorities that were driven out of their homes in defiance both of treaty undertakings and humane considerations, merely because they were minorities.

2. *Fluechtlinge.* These are the people who fled. They might have been forcibly expelled had they remained long enough; on the other hand, they might have been subject to political and other disabilities

had they stayed. The fifty million refugees comprise large numbers who fled before the westward advance of the Russian armies or who have since fled from Communist rule in Europe or Asia. They include small groups of refugees from the petty dictatorships of Latin America or Spain, and they include the Jews who fled from Hitler or have since fled from the Communist countries where anti-Semitism has again appeared.

To some extent the refugees were able to join their own people or, at least, to become part of groups whose language and culture they shared. Thus, German-speaking refugees from eastern Europe have found a home in the Federal German Republic; Poles from the Soviet Union, in Poland; the Karelian Finns, in Finland. But this does not make their reception easy. The assimilation of refugees by a society is always difficult, and in some parts of the world impossible. For example, nearly a million Palestinian Arabs left their homes when the state of Israel was created:

About 570,000 of these refugees live in Jordan, where their presence as an unsettled, destitute multitude adds to the general state of political tensions. Lebanon has 125,000 and the Syrian section of the United Arab Republic has 105,000. About 240,000 live in the Gaza area [of Egypt], a 30-mile strip of desert where the big event is the monthly distribution of the basic ration—flour, oils, fat, sugar and rice—enough for a 1,500 calorie daily intake. . . .[22]

In other words, practically none of the Palestinian Arabs have been resettled. In Finland the refugees make up about 15 per cent of the present population. They were mainly farmers and had to be settled on land that was already cultivated as intensively as was then possible. "By 1950," to quote the International Labor Office re-

[21] *International Migration, 1945–1957,* International Labor Office, Geneva, 1959, p. 1.

[22] *New York Times,* May 21, 1959.

Figure 27   *A quasi-permanent Arab refugee camp near Saida, in Lebanon. The Republic of Lebanon at present contains about a hundred thousand Arab refugees from Israel.* COURTESY: UNITED NATIONS

port on migration, "the problem of integrating the refugees into the Finnish economy had been virtually solved, but only at the cost of heavy sacrifices on the part of the rest of the population." [23] These sacrifices included the splitting up of farms to provide land for the refugee families and the extension of farming onto marginal land.

Of the 50 million refugees who have fled their homes since the end of the Second World War, 15 million are said to be still homeless and without productive employment. About a million refugees from Communist China are in Hong Kong; about

[23] *International Migration, 1945–1957*, International Labor Office, Geneva, 1959, p. 59.

180,000 refugees from French misrule in Algeria have been living under very unsatisfactory conditions in Morocco and Tunisia. On the other hand, most of the 200,000 who fled from Hungary in 1956 have been settled, and the western European and North American economies have in general been able to absorb most other refugees from eastern Europe.

These refugees can clearly be divided into those who are *political* and those who are *national* refugees. The Arabs in Jordan are refugees because they are Arabs; their political opinions, if they have any, are irrelevant. The refugees from China and from Hungary do not differ culturally from the people whom they left behind, and they are refugees because they do not accept the dominant political creed. Their departure from their homeland does not help to resolve a minority problem but may contribute to the creation of one elsewhere. Very broadly, one may say that there have been political refugees as long as there have been political systems.

Refugees on religious grounds are more difficult to classify. Early religious refugees, such as the Huguenot refugees from France to Prussia, England, and South Africa, are best regarded as political refugees, because it was a politically imposed religious system which they were escaping. They could have conformed to it if they had wished. The Hindus who fled from Pakistan to India in 1947 were na-

tional refugees, because religion was the foremost expression of Hindu culture. One might, of course, claim that in one sense they were political refugees in that Islam became the state religion of Pakistan. Religious refugees, in the old sense, have ceased to be important, for the state has become increasingly a secular institution, not interested in religious belief as such.

In the nineteenth century the chief motive for migration—apart from the economic incentive—was political.

Refugees who may be regarded as political in so far as they were fleeing a political system left France at the time of the French Revolution (1789–1794). Refugees from the unsuccessful rising in several European countries in 1848, many of whom

Figure 28 *Derelict homes at Cheb (Eger) Czechoslovakia, from which the former German residents have either fled or been expelled.* PHOTOGRAPH BY N. J. G. POUNDS

Figure 29 *A view in the Muranów sector of Warsaw, scene of the "ghetto"*
rising of 1943. The former buildings were leveled by the Germans, and the
present apartment blocks were built upon the piles of rubble, which the Poles
lacked the means to remove. PHOTOGRAPH BY N. J. G. POUNDS

settled in the United States, were also political; so, too, were those who left Russia
when the czarist regime collapsed. The
Jews who left Germany after Hitler came
to power (1933), on the other hand, were
national; they escaped because they were
Jews, a circumstance which they could
not avoid. Since that date, Jews have provided an appreciable fraction of the world's
refugees. During the war years, with the
changes in political boundaries, there were
numerous movements—most of them relatively small—of national groups. At the
conclusion of the war, the number of national refugees increased sharply as the
German communities were driven, wholly
or in part, from Poland, Czechoslovakia,

and the Danubian countries. The million
Arabs, the seven million Hindus, and a
slightly smaller number of Indian Muslims
are also national refugees, but the Chinese,
Algerians, Hungarians, Tibetans, and those
who continue to cross from Communist
eastern Europe today are political. It cannot be assumed that there will be no further waves of refugees in the future, but
most are likely to claim to be political
refugees rather than national.

The total influence of such movements
of people on the power of states, both
those from which the refugees come and
those to which they go, is difficult to assess. Though the numbers involved appear
large, it is unlikely that most countries have

lost so many that they have suffered economically. East Germany and Czechoslovakia are, however, exceptions. The arrival of a wave of refugees can have the most varied results in different countries. On the one hand, Palestinian Arab refugees would be an insupportable burden on the Middle Eastern countries if it were not for the help given by the UN. On the other, it is difficult to believe that the Federal German Republic would have attained its present level of prosperity without the influx of skilled workers, both from the German Democratic Republic and also from Poland and Czechoslovakia. In Hong Kong, Morocco, and Tunisia, the refugees are a heavy and almost unsupportable burden on the states that have received them.

THE STRUCTURE OF THE POPULATION

So far only the total numbers and cultural divisions of the population, as elements in the power of a state, have been considered. But these are not the only criteria by which population should be judged. The age structure of the population, the balance between the sexes, the educational attainments, and the level of technical efficiency are all factors in the power potential of the state.

Age Structure: It is a common practice to represent the population of a state by means of a "population pyramid." The total population in each age group, usually for five-year periods, is represented by horizontal bars, arranged one above the other, with the youngest age groups at the bottom. Commonly the bars are divided by sex. Such a pyramid shows at a glance how the population is made up by age and sex. If it is expanding sharply, the base of the pyramid will be much larger than its superstructure, showing how age

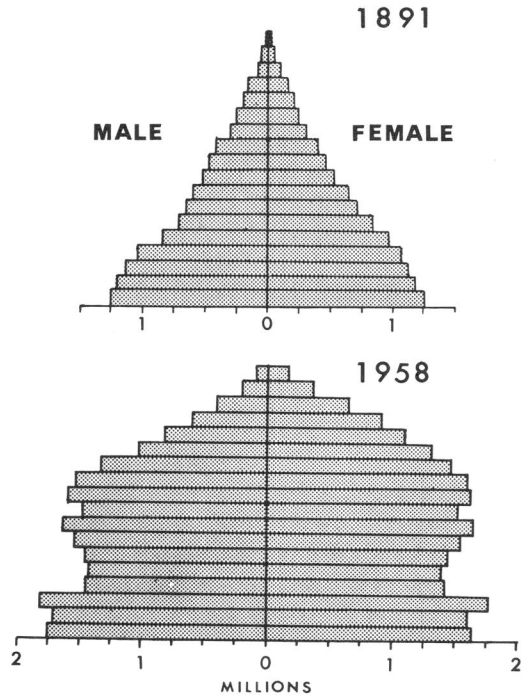

Exhibit 45 Population pyramid: United Kingdom.

groups become significantly larger as they become younger. On the other hand, a population which is declining through a diminishing birth rate will have a narrow base, because the number of children aged up to five years, may well be smaller than the number of adults between, say, twenty and twenty-five. The two pyramids shown here (Exhibit 45) are for Great Britain.[24] The first represents the population for 1891, when it was growing rapidly; the second, that for 1947, when it was showing the results of the diminished birth rate during the years of the Depression and Second World War. The pyramid for Japan (Exhibit 46) shows the consequences of the abrupt diminution of a previously very high birth rate.

[24] L. D. Stamp, *Land for Tomorrow*, Indiana University Press, Bloomington, Ind., 1952, p. 37.

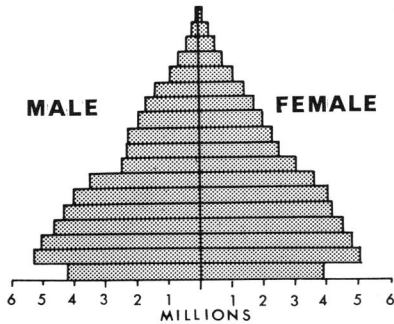

Exhibit 46   *Population pyramid: Japan.*

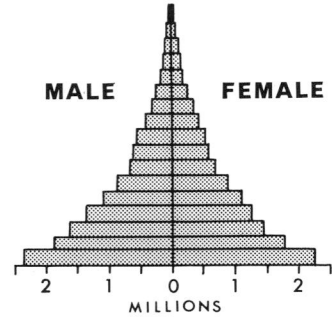

Exhibit 47   *Population pyramid: Philippines.*

The pyramid for the Philippines in 1959 (Exhibit 47) shows even more clearly the consequences of a rapidly expanding population. That for France (Exhibit 48) in 1958 is unusually complex. It shows by reduced numbers the lowered birth rates during the First and Second World Wars, respectively. It shows also, in its lack of symmetry between the sexes of those aged fifty and more, the appalling loss of life during the First World War. The effect of war on age structure is shown even more clearly for Japan in 1945. The male totals for the years twenty to thirty-nine have been drastically reduced, and those for the

years twenty-five to twenty-nine reduced almost by half.

The age pyramid is an indication of the ability of the population of a state to perform work, either at the time represented or in the foreseeable future. The length of the working life varies with the degree of economic development of a country. In the more developed it begins in the teens and goes on into the sixties and even later. In the underdeveloped countries, in which work is mainly hard manual labor in the fields or forests, it begins earlier and ends earlier. The proportion of old people in India is very much

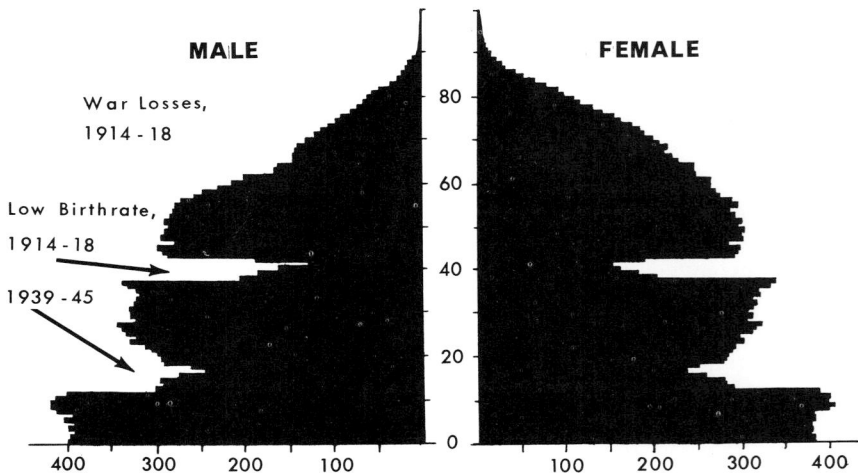

Exhibit 48   *Population pyramid: France.*

MALE   FEMALE

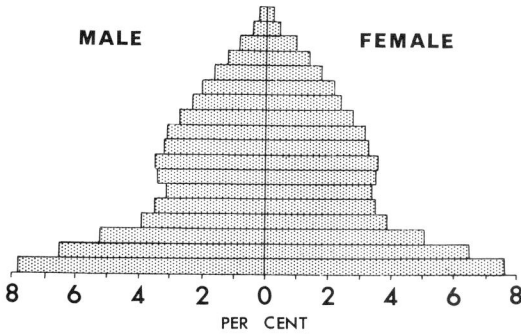

PER CENT

Exhibit 49 Population pyramid: United States.

TABLE 7 *Age Groups*

	Percentage under 15 years	*Percentage 15 to 65 years*	*Percentage 65 years and over*
Puerto Rico, 1930.........	42	55.5	2.5
India, 1931.......	40	57.8	2.2
Egypt, 1937......	39	57.4	3.6
Chile, 1940.......	36	60.5	3.5
Canada, 1931.....	31	63.5	5.5
U.S.A., 1930......	29	65.6	5.4
France, 1936......	25	60	15
United Kingdom, 1931..........	23.8	68.8	7.4
Sweden, 1945.....	21.6	68.6	9.8

Source: Compiled from statistics published in the *Demographic Yearbook, 1949–1950,* United Nations, New York, 1950.

less than in France, in part because of the incidence of disease, in part because people age more quickly and have a shorter expectation of life under such conditions.

In the more developed countries, in which the expectation of life is greater and generally is increasing, there is a relatively large proportion of the population in the higher age groups (Exhibit 49). The number of retired or industrially ineffective persons is large, and, whatever the financial mechanism whereby this is done, it has to be supported by the active and effective part of the population. Similarly the lower age groups have to be supported by the rest of the community for a period which varies with the degree of economic development. In some countries children are economically useful at ten years of age; in others, not until they are almost twice that age.

Thus, it is not the total population which is important in the estimate of power at any one time, but the total effective population, after allowance has been made for the reduced effectiveness of the young and the old. It is very difficult indeed to arrive at a figure for the effective population. Table 7 gives, for a small number of countries, the percentage of the total population that is (1) below fifteen years of age and (2) over sixty-five and thus probably

not economically useful in any large measure. [25]

It must be noted, however, that the countries with a very high proportion of the population in the younger age groups are, by and large, the underdeveloped, in which child labor is of economic importance.

Sex Structure: A second factor in estimating the effective population is the balance between the sexes. Under normal conditions, adult women outnumber men by a very minute percentage. In addition, war has always been more destructive of men than of women, as is seen in the age pyramids for France (Exhibit 48) and Japan (Exhibit 46). The much higher fraction of the total population made up of women may reduce somewhat the effective-

[25] See discussion in Frank W. Notestein and others, *The Future Population of Europe and the Soviet Union,* League of Nations, Geneva, 1944, pp. 153–163.

ness, particularly militarily, of the population in these and similar countries. But even when the balance between men and women is clearly known, we cannot be sure how many women are employed in work outside their homes. In countries in which peasant agriculture predominates, the women spend almost as long a time in the fields as the men. Even in those societies which are the most highly developed economically, many married women undertake some part- or full-time work. They may not work regularly, but in time of emergency they can always be taken into the labor force.

Thus, if any generalization is permissible, it may be said that those countries which appear near the top of the list of countries given in Table 7 have a much larger effective labor force than appears from the table, because (1) work begins at a much lower age, and (2) a larger proportion of the women work for a longer period of time. The converse is true of those countries in the lower part of the table. The average age for initiating employment may be two or three years higher, and married women may work for a smaller proportion of the time.

Education and Technical Development: Even a figure so adjusted gives us little more than the working time. It gives no index of the quantity and, perhaps, the quality of the performance. These depend upon the level both of education and of mechanical equipment. It does not require demonstration that one tractor-drawn plow, with one driver, can do as much work as half a dozen or more horse- or ox-drawn plows nor that in all fields of production machines either replace manpower or reduce greatly the need for it.

Anyone attempting to rate countries in terms of education or of mechanical skills and equipment is faced with enormous difficulties. While it is possible to count tractors and trucks, IBM machines, and self-service stores, it is not easy to equate their relative importance in terms of the manpower they save. Least of all is it easy to put any value in our power equation on education itself. We believe—and the belief is supported by experience—only that the countries which in our subjective judgment are highly mechanized are thereby able to do more than compensate for a lower rating in terms of effective labor force.

BIBLIOGRAPHY

Ackerman, Edward A.: "Population and Natural Resources," in P. M. Hauser and O. D. Duncan (eds.), *The Study of Population,* University of Chicago, Chicago, 1959, pp. 621–648.

Bowman, Isaiah: *The New World,* World Book Company, Yonkers, N.Y., 1928.

Carr-Saunders, A. M.: *World Population,* Oxford University Press, New York, 1936.

Chadwick, H. M.: *The Nationalities of Europe,* Cambridge University Press, Cambridge, 1945.

Demographic Yearbook, United Nations, New York, published annually.

Furnivall, J. S.: *Netherlands India: A Study in Plural Economy,* The Macmillan Company, New York, 1944.

———: *Colonial Policy and Practice,* New York University Press, New York, 1956.

Hauser, Philip M., and Otis Dudley Duncan (eds.), *The Study of Population,* University of Chicago Press, Chicago, 1959.

International Migration, 1945–1957, International Labor Office, Geneva, 1959.

Isaac, J.: *Economics of Migration,* Kegan Paul, Trench, Trubner & Co., London, 1947.

Kuczynski, R. R.: *Living-space and Population Problems,* Oxford University Press, New York, 1939.

Lorimer, Frank: *The Population of the Soviet Union,* League of Nations, Geneva, 1946.

Macartney, C. A.: *National States and National*

Minorities, Oxford University Press, New York, 1934.

Mead, W. R.: "The Cold Farm in Finland," *G.R.,* vol. 41, pp. 529–543, 1951.

Moore, Wilbert E.: *Economic Demography of Eastern and Southern Europe,* League of Nations, Geneva, 1945.

Notestein, Frank W., and others: *The Future Population of Europe and the Soviet Union,* League of Nations, Geneva, 1944.

Proudfoot, M. J.: *European Refugees, 1939–52: A Study of Forced Population Movement,* Northwestern University Press, Evanston, Ill., 1956.

Reddaway, W. B.: *The Economics of a Declining Population,* George Allen & Unwin, Ltd., London, 1939.

Robinson, E. A. G. (ed.): *The Economic Consequences of the Size of Nations,* Macmillan & Co., Ltd., London, 1960.

Stamp, L. D.: *Land for Tomorrow,* Indiana University Press, Bloomington, Ind., 1952.

Tawney, R. H.: *Land and Labour in China,* George Allen & Unwin, Ltd., London, 1932.

Wambaugh, S.: *The Doctrine of Self-determination,* Oxford University Press, New York, 1919.

Warriner, Doreen: *Economics of Peasant Farming,* Oxford University Press, 1939.

———: *Land and Poverty in the Middle East,* Royal Institute of International Affairs, London and New York, 1948.

Witthauer, Kurt: "Geographische Differenzierung der Bevölkerungsentwicklung 1920–1960 und Bevölkerungszahlen 1960," *Geographisches Taschenbuch, 1960–1961,* Franz Steiner Verlag GmbH., Wiesbaden, 1960, pp. 249–263.

6 RESOURCES AND POWER

Economic strength has always been an instrument of political power, if only through its association with the military.   E. H. CARR

Not only the wealth but the independence and security of a country appear to be materially connected with the prosperity of manufactures. Every nation, with a view to these great objects, ought to endeavor to possess within itself all the essentials of national supply.   ALEXANDER HAMILTON

IT IS IMPOSSIBLE TO CONSIDER THE POPULATION OF A STATE, ITS efficiency and effectiveness, without, at the same time, discussing the resources which are available for its use. People must have land on which to live and to grow their food. Almost all human food is derived directly from the soil, and its volume and quality depend directly on the extent and nature of the soil. The cultivable soil must, then, be regarded as a primary resource in the estimate of national power.

Beneath the soil are minerals. In fact the underlying rock is made up of minerals in all their variety, and some of these minerals are important for human welfare and essential in national defense. The minerals include sand, gravel, limestone, and clay, without which large modern buildings could not be constructed. They include phosphates, nitrates, salt, and sulfur, necessary in differing ways to the chemical industries, and thus to the preparation of fertilizers and more complex synthetic products. All the solid and liquid fuels occur as minerals. All the varieties of coal, ranging from hard coal or anthracite, through soft or bituminous coal, to lignite, and peat, are minerals. Petroleum is a mineral resource, though one with a less constant chemical composition than those already mentioned, and natural gas is merely petroleum in a gaseous condition.

The raw materials from which the metals are derived have a place of special importance in any discussion of national power, because modern industry cannot be carried on and modern weapons made without them. The ores of iron, of the nonferrous metals like aluminum, copper, tin, lead, zinc, and of those rarer metals such as manganese, chromium, vanadium, nickel, and molybdenum, which are used in preparing quality steel, are all of particular importance. Uranium has recently achieved an even greater political importance. A state which lacks the more important minerals or which has only small reserves may feel especially vulnerable. Examples of the influence of shortage or scarcity of such resources on national power and national policy will be examined later in this chapter.

Few resources can be used in the forms in which nature has given them to us. They need to be smelted, refined, and fabricated. Potential resources, which might be made available only after the laying down of a difficult and costly railroad and the construction of mines and smelters, all of which might take five or more years, do not greatly help. If the decision-making authority initiates a policy now, it needs the support of resources at once, not at some hypothetical date in the future. Of course, it might make plans for future action and delay the implementation of these plans until specific resources are available for immediate use. Such integration of resource planning with the state's external policy has been known. On several occasions in the past century the responsible powers in a state have been forced to admit that "we shall be in a position to risk war only if certain resources are available" and thus to delay political action until a safety margin in resources has been achieved.

So in order to be considered in the power potential of the state, the resources must be developed and available, or available after only a very short delay. This presupposes the construction of a transportation net to bring the raw resources to the factories for processing and the finished goods to those locations where their use is the most effective. The stage of industrial development of a state is of prime importance in its power potential. Not all industries, of course, add to a state's power or, in the last analysis, contribute to its ability to enforce its policy or to resist demands that might be made on it. In a rich society many goods are made in factories and used in the home which have no significance in this regard. Clearly the possession of automobiles and trucks is important in so far as they permit materials and people to be taken quickly and, on the whole, efficiently to their destinations. But it is not necessary that the automobiles should have many of the extravagant additions with which they are often decorated today. A state within which the automobiles are adorned with chrome, and the homes with gadgets, does not per se possess any greater power than one which practices greater austerity. "Conspicuous consumption" is not in itself a mark of national power. It does, however, presuppose the existence of the factory equipment necessary to fabricate these unnecessary trimmings, and the factory which makes televisions can be retooled, at some cost in time and money, to make electronic equipment—transmitters, receivers, radar—which adds significantly to the power potential. An important factor here is the length of time needed for the retooling and redeployment of industrial resources.

Professor Stephen B. Jones [1] has classified the degrees of availability of resources as follows:

[1] Stephen B. Jones, "The Power Inventory and National Strategy," *World Politics*, vol. 6, pp. 421–452, 1954.

1. Power resources available immediately. These include active mines and factories, which are already producing objects with immediate power potential, such as steel sheet and chemical fertilizer.

2. Resources available only after activation. Among such resources would be stand-by equipment and any plant not currently in production. In a sense, these resources also include the "moth-ball" fleet. The time required for activation varies from a few hours to several weeks, according to the need for "warming up." An integrated steel works might require two or three weeks before full production could be reached.

3. Resources available only after conversion. An automobile factory could turn from the production of cars to that of light trucks only after retooling which might take many months unless jigs and other equipment had been prepared in advance. Similarly, most factories producing consumer goods could convert to the manufacture of goods having power potential only after a considerable time lag.

4. Resources available only after development, such as fuel resources or ore deposits, known to exist, but awaiting the opening up of a mine or the construction of a processing plan. Such development may well take several years; it is not uncommon, for example, for the opening of a new coal mine—particularly a deep one—to cover a period of four or five years. It is unlikely, therefore, that such undeveloped resources would be taken into consideration in making political decisions. The decision to resort to war, for example, is likely to be made in the light only of resources that are already in some phase of development. On the other hand, if a war should last longer than the protagonists at first expected it to, it is likely that resources, undeveloped at the start, would

be exploited before the conclusion. The construction of such highways as the Burma Road or the Alaskan Highway are, in effect, resource developments effected during a war which were not wholly anticipated when that war was begun. Germany's development of domestic iron ores and her use of coal for making petroleum are further examples of the wartime development of resources.

5. Hypothetical resources. Coal, petroleum, ore bodies, and other resources whose existence is only presumed but not proved cannot be said to have any power value. No political authority is likely to count on them unless careful investigation has at least raised them to the level of category 4.

The same author has defined resources, within the context of political geography, as "anything a nation has, can obtain, or can conjure up to support its strategy."[2] Such a definition is certainly wide, as it should be, for "resources are as tangible as soil, as intangible as leadership, as measurable as population, as difficult to measure as patriotism. There is no common unit, and no statistical summation is possible."[3] Nevertheless, we shall attempt, later in this chapter, to present certain objective data that will be useful for evaluating national power.

There are other aspects of resources, apart from their availability, which deserve to be mentioned. A state sometimes possesses, in addition to the types of resources already enumerated, external assets, such as overseas investments or currency holdings. It is usually desirable to hold on to these, but they could be sacrificed, that is, they could be used to purchase other resources needed more immediately. Thus Great Britain sold foreign

[2] *Ibid.*, p. 423.
[3] *Ibid.*, p. 425.

investments in order to be able to purchase resources during both world wars and also traded certain Caribbean bases for a number of old destroyers, which in 1940 constituted a much more valuable resource than a few square miles of soil in the West Indies. Such expendable resources are sometimes called *fat*.

Another surplus aspect of resources is known as *slack*, the failure to make the fullest use of existing resources. This is particularly noticeable in reference to labor. A forty-hour week could be increased to forty-five or forty-eight hours; at the same time, a plant that operates on a one- or two-shift basis could be used all the time. In wartime such slack is always taken up quickly and is used to replace the services of labor that is taken into the armed forces.

The ability of an economy to permit rapid shifts from unnecessary to necessary production is a sign of its flexibility. This includes not only the possibility of retooling industrial plant but also of diverting labor from unessential to essential occupations and of the converting of grazing land, which produces relatively little food per acre, to cropland, which usually yields more.

Lastly, the quality of production under such conditions must be considered. It has been assumed that labor can be switched from one occupation to another without loss of efficiency; that a retooled industry is as efficient after as it was before the retooling process; that the length of the working day can be increased without greater weariness and carelessness on the part of the workers; that the tensions of wartime will not result in poorer workmanship. This is unfortunately not the case. The quality of the product inevitably declines during such an emergency, and this negative factor also has to be taken into consideration in the assessment of power.

FOOD RESOURCES

An adequate supply of foodstuffs is a condition of human welfare, and its assurance is necessarily a primary preoccupation of government. If a food supply is not assured in time of peace, it certainly would be precarious in wartime, when movement and transportation are usually more restricted and the labor force available to produce it reduced. A state usually needs to be able to call upon a reserve food supply in emergencies of this kind.

No great power is completely self-sufficient in respect to foodstuffs, because in no instance is the area large enough to embrace the variety of environment necessary to produce the range of food that is now thought desirable. Among more advanced states, France, the Soviet Union, and the United States perhaps come closest to being self-sufficient. But none is able to produce foodstuffs of equatorial origin without extreme difficulty. Sugar cane is not really a crop of any of these countries and is grown in two of them only with some difficulty and at a relatively high cost. It is probably true, however, that each of these three could survive without importing foodstuffs for a considerable time, if necessary, though diets might become somewhat monotonous and some form of rationing would unquestionably be necessary.

By contrast such countries as the United Kingdom, Belgium, Switzerland, West Germany, and Sweden are very much more dependent on imported foodstuffs. Under normal conditions the United Kingdom imports about half the total food consumption requirements of its population. There is a certain amount of slack in the agricultural economy, so that food production could in fact be increased for a period. But this could be done only by plowing up marginal land, which, after a few years, would have to be restored to grass.

In both the United States and the Soviet Union there is room for an extension of crop farming, and the current Soviet program of using the so-called "virgin lands" is greatly expanding food production. In most countries there is a little slack that could be taken up, if only temporarily, but the range of foods that could be produced is limited by conditions of soil and climate.

The fact that every developed country is dependent to some extent on imported foodstuffs must be counted as a negative factor in its power inventory. A successful blockade can cut off the supply of imported food, and, during recent wars, a significant object of strategy has been to do just this. In the First World War the German submarine warfare so reduced the

movement of foodstuffs into Great Britain that the possibility of starvation became very real. During the Second World War, the same strategy was less successful than during the first, largely because convoys could be protected more effectively by means of aircraft. It became a policy of the Allied Powers in both wars to cut off the supply of goods to Germany. The oldest successful use of the blockade as a strategic weapon was probably that of Athens by her Peloponnesian rivals toward the end of the fifth century B.C. Another was the successful blockade of Napoleon's Europe by the British fleet. At this time, however, Continental Europe was so nearly self-sufficient in regard to foodstuffs that the blockade had little effect on the food supply. It did, however, encourage the cultivation of sugar beets to replace the cane sugar that could no longer be imported.

The United Kingdom is the country by far the most vulnerable to a blockade,

TABLE 8   *Food Imports per Head of Population in Selected Countries*

	Gross value of food imports, millions of dollars	Net value of food imports, millions of dollars	Net import per head, dollars
United Kingdom	4,243.2	3,639.2	70
Belgium	504.2	377.1	42
West Germany	2,252.5	2,064.9	40
Sweden	308.4	214.4	29
Austria	185.8	146.6	21
Finland	129.1	92.0	21
France	1,525.6	752.4	17
Japan	726.7	516.2	5.7
Egypt	149.4	87.6	4
Greece	104.4	32.4	4
U.S.A.	3,365.8	407.8	2.4
Italy	622.7	20.8	0.4
Yugoslavia	162.7	56.9	0.3

Source: *Trade Yearbook, 1958*, Food & Agricultural Organization, United Nations, Rome.

partly because of her heavy dependence on imported food, partly also because, surrounded as she is by the sea, the danger of a naval blockade is all the greater. The Soviet Union is probably the least vulnerable, in part owing to the great range of physical environment, in part to the relatively low living standards of the mass of the people and, in consequence, the narrower range of demand. The value of imported foodstuffs per head of population is a rough guide to the vulnerability of a state to a blockade. Table 8 does not, of course, give any indication of the nature of imported foods, nor whether they are essential or not in time of war.

MINERAL RESOURCES

There are few inhabitable parts of the earth's surface that are not capable of yielding some food. No state, except some of the micro-states, produces less than about half the food intake of its population, and all could during an emergency produce more. But mineral resources are distributed much less regularly than cultivable soil. Indeed, the work of nature in scattering them through the earth's crust seems to be capricious in the extreme. Not a single developed state is self-sufficient. While iron ore is widely found, significant deposits of nickel and manganese each occur in only two countries, and tin is found only a little more widely. Under normal conditions there is, then, a large trade in minerals—both mineral fuels and the minerals from which metals are obtained.

The situation concerning mineral resources differs, however, in two major respects from that concerning food resources. In the first place, the soil, given careful management, will go on producing without significant variation. Mineral resources, on the other hand, are exhaustible, and every known deposit, if worked continuously,

will run out. This must give a certain instability to mineral resources as a factor in national power.

Second, food resources are, by and large, perishable. It is true that wheat and other grains can be stored for a period of years, but this usually necessitates a careful control of humidity and temperature, as well as protection from insects and rodents. Most minerals, on the other hand, can be stock-piled, and the majority do not deteriorate if left exposed to the weather. These two considerations greatly modify the power implications of mineral resources.

Fuel Resources: Fuel resources—coal of all kinds, as well as petroleum and natural gas—are more widely distributed than most metallic minerals. Even so, no fewer than seventy independent states, not to speak of non-self-governing territories, are without significant coal deposits, and sixty-nine produce no petroleum (Exhibit 50). Six countries only produce about 82 per cent of the world's coal, and five yield 76 per cent of the petroleum (Exhibit 51). Such an imbalance necessarily produces grave problems for the states lacking sources of mineral fuels. It may lead to the development of alternative sources of fuel, usually at a much higher cost, or to the import of fuel and thus to a high dependence on other countries for an essential raw material.

The only states with developed industries which are able to rely on domestic supplies of coal are the United States, the Soviet Union, the United Kingdom, West Germany, and Poland, and it is improbable that coal is imported into China. At the opposite extreme are the Scandinavian countries and Finland, the Republic of Ireland, the Middle East, and much of Latin America and Africa, where there are few significant coal reserves. Between the extremes are countries, such as France, which are short of specific types of coal.

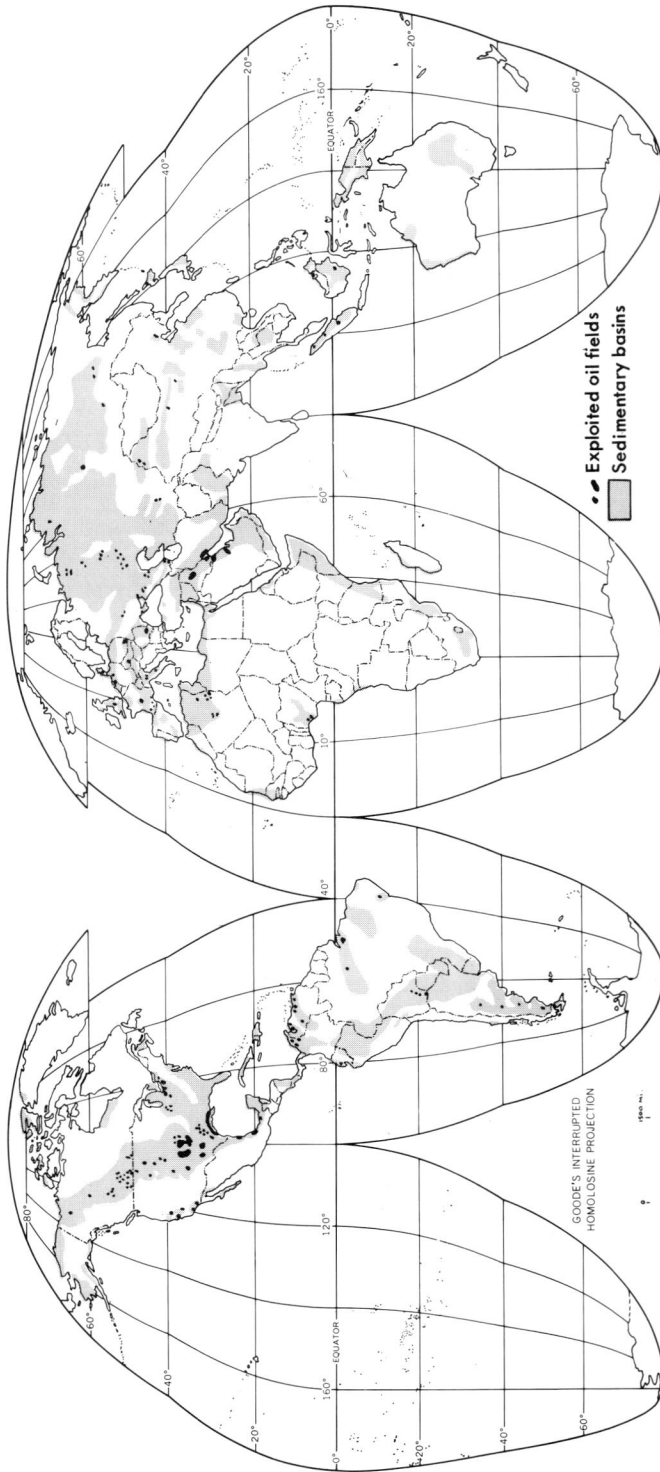

Exhibit 50 *World map: petroleum production.*

GOODE'S INTERRUPTED
HOMOLOSINE PROJECTION

Exploited oil fields
Sedimentary basins

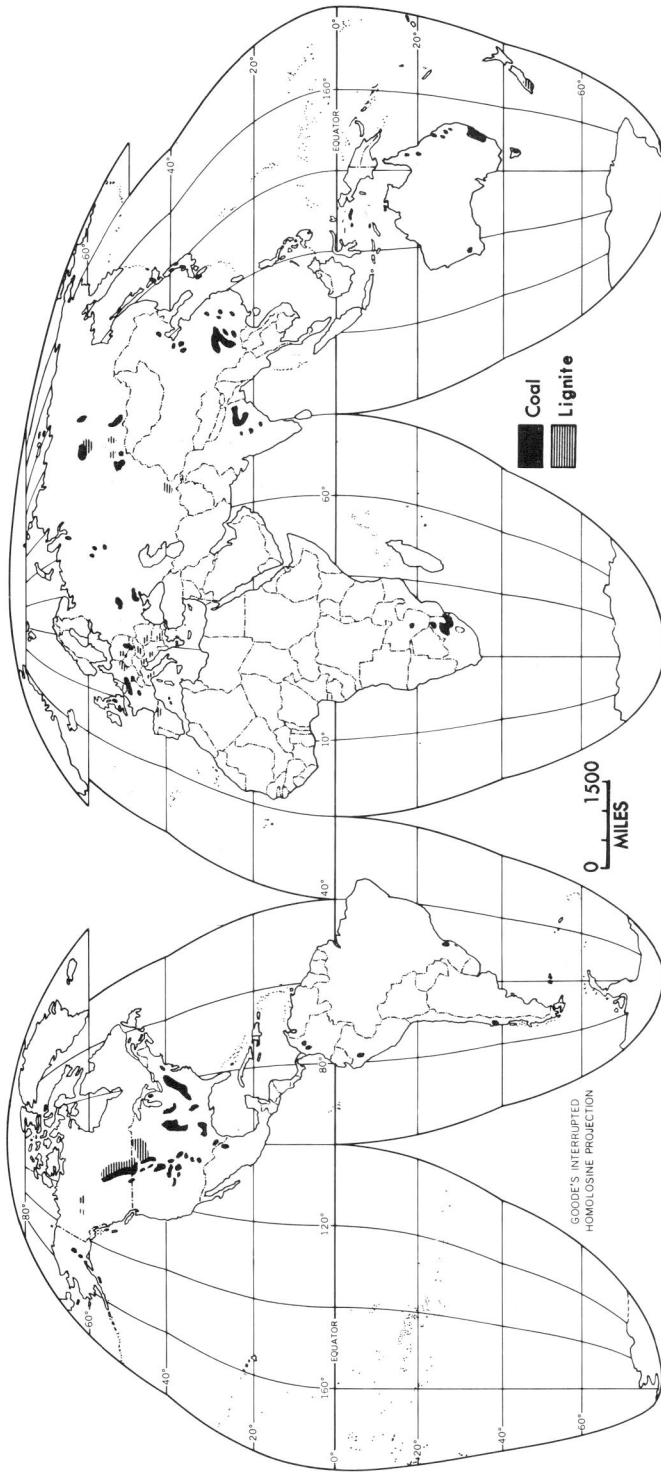

Exhibit 51 World map: coal production.

Coal

Lignite

1500

0

MILES

EQUATOR

GOODE'S INTERRUPTED
HOMOLOSINE PROJECTION

In many areas hydroelectric power is vigorously developed as an alternative to soiled fuel. Naturally, this trend is most marked in countries short of or lacking in coal: Switzerland, Austria, Italy, France, and the Scandinavian countries. In some others the development of water power is restricted merely because the incentive, the shortage of solid fuel, is absent.

Any estimate of the area and extent of petroleum reserves must continuously be subject to revision, as prospecting continues to reveal new deposits. At present it seems that a very large proportion of reserves lies close to the Andean–Rocky Mountain systems in the New World and to the Atlas, Carpathian, and Caucasus Mountains and those mountains along the southern border of Iran in the Old World. There are outlying pools near the Ural Mountains in the Soviet Union and also in Southeast Asia. Large areas of the habitable globe, including Africa south of the Sahara Desert, Australia, the eastern half of North America, and most of Brazil, are almost entirely without petroleum, and in Europe the deposits are too small to have much political weight.

International trade in petroleum and petroleum products is as important as, if not more important than, that in coal. But its pattern is simpler. The only really important exporting area is the Middle Eastern states, Iraq, Iran, Saudi Arabia, and Kuwait, together with Venezuela. The peculiar geography of the Middle East, with the Red Sea, the Persian Gulf, and the Mediterranean Sea approaching close to one another but never actually joining except by the way of the Suez Canal, gives special significance to the pipelines, to the corridors to the sea, and to the rivalries both within the Arab states and between these states and Israel. Great Britain and other west European countries are already heavily dependent on oil from the Middle East, and the United States is beginning to draw upon this source, although in the latter case to some extent this is with the object of husbanding domestic supplies. Because petroleum is necessary for industry and transportation, a steady and constant supply is a prerequisite of power. It is natural that any state would use its power to secure the continued supply of so necessary a determinant of power. This is an important reason why the countries of western Europe, especially Great Britain, have so large a stake in the Middle East. For this reason, Great Britain and France tried to maintain their grip on the Suez Canal, a main shipping route for petroleum, and this is why the Suez crisis of October, 1956, with the closing of the canal and the destruction of pipelines across the Syrian Desert, led immediately to serious repercussions as a result of fuel shortages.

Atomic power may be the industrial power of the future, but its use is at present small in scale and limited to the very few countries, including the United States and United Kingdom, which are technologically the most advanced. The west European members of the European Atomic Energy Community (Euratom) are establishing nuclear reactors as cooperative undertakings. It is too early, however, to say that the use of atomic power has done more than underline the existing power ratios among the states of the world.

Strategic Metals: Second in importance only to strategic fuels are the strategic metals. The significance of steel and of a number of nonferrous metals, especially copper, aluminum, lead, zinc, tin, manganese, nickel, and a number of other necessary metals, needs no emphasis. They are even more necessary in time of war for the manufacture of large quantities of military equipment. It has commonly been held that the loss of control over any such materials in wartime was a matter of very grave concern. The loss of the tin mines of Malaya to the Japanese, the cutting off of the Swedish iron-ore supply by the Germans, even the possession by the enemy of the mercury mines of Italy and Yugoslavia were thought to hold serious consequences to the Allied Powers during the Second World War. Similarly, a balance sheet of mineral resources as between the Western and the Soviet blocs is thought by some to be a key to the political future.[4] That it is important cannot be questioned, but the pattern of strategic needs, the capacity of expanding technology to use submarginal resources (such as the beneficiation and use of taconite), and the exhaustion of existing resources give such a balance sheet only temporary value.

Metalliferous Resources: The distribution of economic minerals is concentrated in a relatively small number of places on the earth's surface, and this gives each of these areas a certain importance. A handful of countries account for the greater part of the world's production of each of the important metallic ores, with the exception only of iron. This is due partly to the fact that most of the world's reserves are contained in a few large ore deposits, partly because modern technology makes it undersirable to work small deposits. As C. K. Leith wrote thirty years ago:

Vastly increasing mineral requirements have resulted in the intensive exploitation of the comparatively few mineral reserves capable of meeting these requirements. When the demand was small, it was often possible to secure the necessary supplies from a considerable number of scattered sources. As the mineral industries have grown, the units most favorably situated in regard to raw materials and markets have naturally outstripped the others, thereby deepening and extending the

trade channels tributary to them. In each of the principal mineral industries there now stand out a few dominating centers of supply and manufacture. . . .[5]

Table 9 lists the more important nonferrous metals, the production in 1956, and the proportion of the world total that comes from the three or four leading producers. This table represents the volume of current output, not the size of reserves. This latter is very difficult to establish because, in some instances, the preparatory geological work is incomplete; in others, there is a tendency to underestimate the total in order to minimize tax liability, and in yet others a veil of secrecy is spread over the whole question for political reasons.

Great Britain, West Germany, and Japan do not figure among the significant producers of any of these metals. The United States is a significant producer of only five and the Soviet Union of seven of the minerals. A list of strategic minerals published by President Roosevelt in 1941, and subsequently extended, ran to about a hundred.[6] Strategic materials were defined in 1944 as "those materials required for essential uses in a war emergency, the procurement of which in adequate quantities, quality, and time is sufficiently uncertain for any reason to require prior provision for the supply thereof."[7] No country can possibly be self-sufficient in this range of minerals, though the Soviet Union and the United States more nearly approach self-sufficiency than any others.

Iron ore differs from the nonferrous

[4] Demitri B. Shimkin, *Minerals: A Key to Soviet Power,* Harvard University Press, Cambridge, Mass., 1953.

[5] C. K. Leith, *World Minerals and World Politics,* Brookings Institution, Washington, D.C., 1931, pp. 6–7.

[6] John B. DeMille, *Strategic Minerals,* McGraw-Hill Book Company, Inc., New York, 1947, p. 2.

[7] As defined by the Army and Navy Munitions Board, Mar. 6, 1944.

TABLE 9   *Chief Producers of Metalliferous Minerals*

Mineral	*Percentage of world production in 1959 coming from countries listed in last column*	*Number of countries*	*Leading producers*
Aluminum (bauxite)..........	70	5 [1]	Jamaica, Surinam, France, British Guiana, U.S.A.
Antimony..................	57	3 [1]	Congo, New Caledonia, Rhodesia and Nyasaland
Chrome...................	76	4 [1]	South Africa, Philippines, Rhodesia and Nyasaland, Turkey
Cobalt....................	70	3 [1]	Congo, New Caledonia, Rhodesia and Nyasaland
Copper...................	77	5 [1]	U.S.A., Chile, Rhodesia and Nyasaland, Canada, Congo
Lead.....................	47	4 [1]	Australia, U.S.A., Mexico, Canada
Manganese................	79	5	U.S.S.R., India, Brazil, South Africa, Ghana
Molybdenum..............	89	1 [1]	U.S.A.
Nickel....................	68	3 [1]	Canada, New Caledonia, Cuba
Tin......................	83	6 [1]	Malaya, Indonesia, Bolivia, China, Congo, Thailand
Tungsten (wolfram).........	55	1	China
Vanadium.................	90	1	U.S.A.
Zinc.....................	47	4 [1]	U.S.A., Canada, Mexico, Australia

[1] No data for the Soviet Union.

SOURCE: Compiled from the *Statistical Yearbook, 1960*, United Nations, New York, and *Minerals Yearbook, 1956*, U.S. Department of the Interior.

metals already discussed by reason, in part, of the much greater demand for it, in part also of its wider distribution and its greater range of grade and quality (Exhibit 52). Iron is a common element of the earth's crust. Every state contains iron, though in most the grade, that is, the percentage of metal in the ore, is too low to have any commercial value. The effect of technological developments, however, is to increase the margin of exploitability. It had been assumed that a 30 per cent iron content within the ore was the lowest that could be smelted profitably until taconite, with a much lower metal content, began to be used. The quality, as distinct from the grade, of the ore varies greatly, but in this respect also the range of usefulness of ores is increasing as means are discovered of eliminating impurities.

At least thirty-nine of the states of the modern world have iron-smelting industries (Exhibit 53). Table 10 indicates the production of ore of the more important of these states and the extent to which, under the conditions obtaining in recent years, they are self-sufficient in this respect.

Only four of the more important iron-

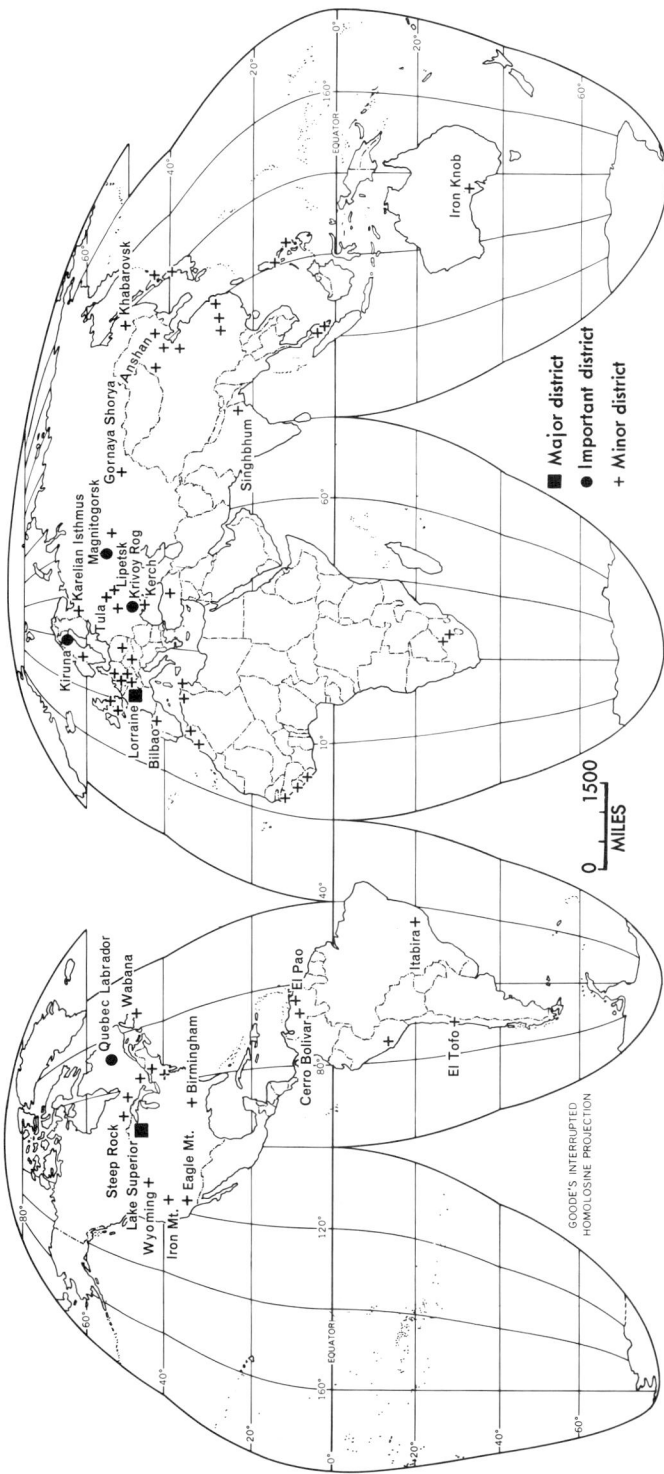

Exhibit 52 World map: iron-ore production.

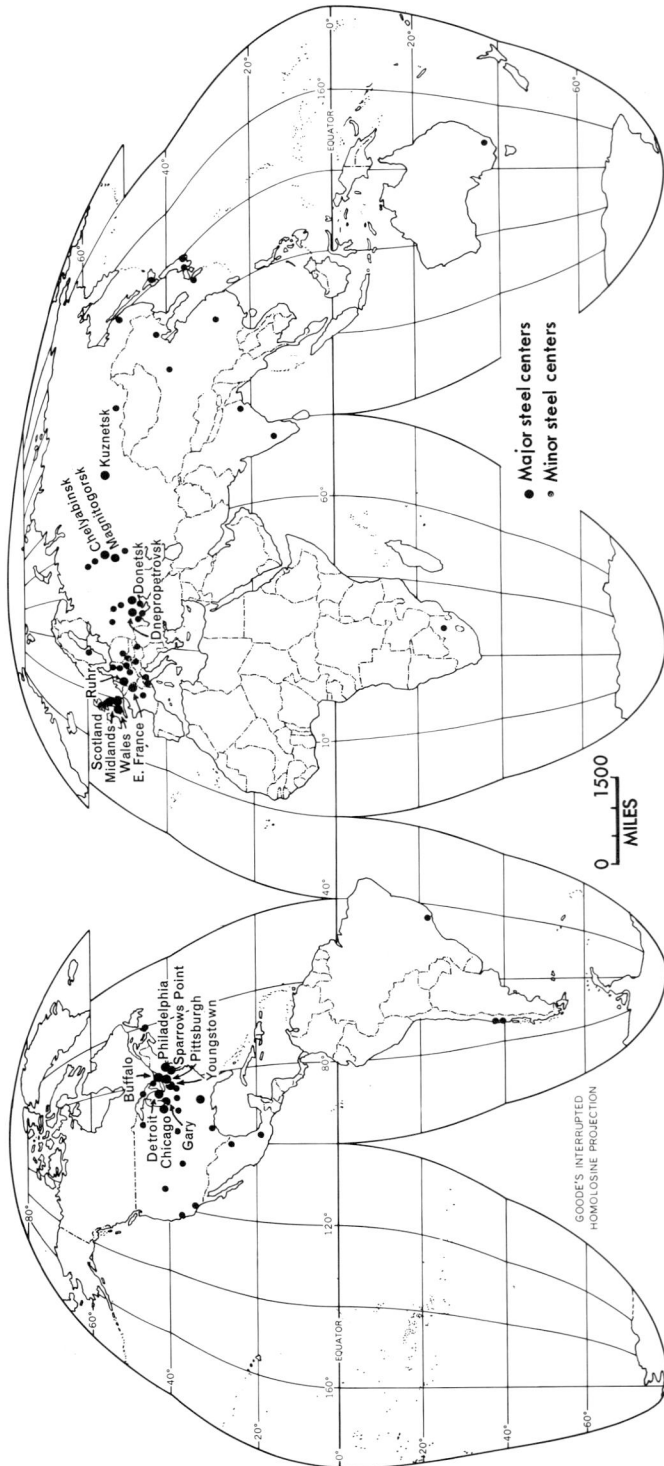

Exhibit 53 World map: iron and steel production.

Major steel centers
Minor steel centers

Scotland
Midlands
Wales
E. France
Ruhr

Chelyabinsk
Magnitogorsk
Kuznetsk
Donetsk
Dnepropetrovsk

Buffalo
Philadelphia
Sparrows Point
Pittsburgh
Youngstown
Detroit
Chicago
Gary

GOODE'S INTERRUPTED
HOMOLOSINE PROJECTION

0   1500
MILES

TABLE 10 *Iron-ore and Pig-iron Production* [1]

State	Output of pig iron, 1959, thousands of metric tons	Output of iron ore, 1959, thousands of metric tons	Estimated percentage of iron-ore needs
Benelux.	10,545	1,742	16
Canada.	3,911	12,213	100
Czechoslovakia.	4,244	897	21
France.	12,651	19,788	100
West Germany.	21,723	4,277	20
India.	3,108	4,840	100
Japan.	9,844	1,400	14
Poland.	4,380	580	13
United Kingdom.	12,785	4,231	33
United States.	56,368	32,129	57
U.S.S.R..	43,000	54,746	100

[1] Iron ore is given in tonnage of metal content.

producing countries are completely self-sufficient. Some other countries, including the United States and United Kingdom, could come appreciably nearer to self-sufficiency, though at a high cost in terms of labor and other materials and possibly with the disruption of their transportation systems.

The picture is complicated by the fact that ore is replaceable by iron and steel scrap, which can be introduced into both the blast furnace and the steel furnace. Some countries with small but significant steel industries are able to operate very largely on scrap. The Japanese industry, for example, was at one time heavily based on imported scrap metal.

As a general rule, minerals are produced because it pays to extract them from the ground. The table of production given above (Table 10) represents the normal state of affairs, in which the price mechanism controls whether a mine is worked or not. It is true that a branch of the mining industry may occasionally be kept ac-

tive, when it has ceased to pay dividends in the accepted sense, because the government sees fit to subsidize it. In this case the "public net profit" from the enterprise in terms of national security and power outweighs the lack of "private net profit." [8] In a time of emergency the rise in prices may itself bring abandoned mines back into production. The government may fix prices at a level that at other times would be quite unrealistic, or it may itself take over the operation of mines, whatever may be the cost in monetary terms. The author remembers a wolfram (tungsten-ore) mine in Cornwall which was operated by the Ministry of Supply of the British government. As a business operation it had been in the red, but the taxpayer made up the difference, involuntarily of course, in the national interest. In wartime marginal resources of all kinds may be exploited.

Such activity by the state may alter in detail the picture of dependence upon

[8] For an analysis of this see A. C. Pigou, *Economics of Welfare*, St. Martin's Press, New York, 1939.

outside sources that has been presented Another activity of the state, designed to remedy the deficiencies of nature, is stock piling. The Strategic and Critical Materials Act of July, 1946, had as its declared object "to decrease and prevent wherever possible a dangerous and costly dependence of the United States upon foreign nations . . . in times of national emergency."

Difficulties of storage are among the least serious. Good factory management requires that enough materials be kept on hand to last for a month or two, and the winter iron-ore stock piles of the various Great Lakes iron- and steelworks is larger than this. The government has to estimate the extent to which warfare is likely to interfere with its normal supply lines and to act accordingly. This may necessitate so large an entry into the raw-materials market as to send prices up. Apart from any such price rise, stock piling is likely to be a heavy drain on national revenue; it is a course that can be taken only by the wealthiest nations.[9]

A final factor which serves to modify the picture of relative scarcity among the nonferrous and ferrous metals is the reuse of old, or "scrap," metal. In peacetime it often happens that the cost of recovering, collecting, transporting, and remelting scrap is greater than that of buying new metal. In the case of iron and steel, although the scrap market has grown rapidly, the recovery rate is, nevertheless, still quite low. The recovery of tin from old tin plate and that of zinc from galvanized goods are both relatively new processes. Lead and copper, owing to their relatively high price, are recovered the most regularly of any metals except gold and silver. In an emergency the recovery rate goes up sharply.

The unrecovered scrap that lies rusting and corroding about the countryside may be regarded to a limited degree as a minor stock pile.

It is difficult to estimate the importance of the possession of metallic ores in assessing national power. This is partly because there is no formula by which the metals in question can be related to one another; nor can it be known, with any degree of certainty, what the technological level will be and what critical shortages would result if an emergency should arise or, last, what substitutes may become available in the future. It is easy to overestimate the importance of minerals in the power equation, and it is almost incorrect to claim that wars have been fought merely to gain possession of ore deposits. There is no reason whatever to suppose that Germany took part of Lorraine from France in 1871 only in order to gain possession of its iron ore,[10] or to consider Great Britain's dispute with Venezuela in 1895–1899 as being motivated entirely by a desire for minerals, or even to regard Chile's war with Bolivia as fought only for the control of the nitrate fields. On the other hand, the Suez crisis of 1956 owed much to Great Britain's anxiety to retain control of the waterway through which much of her petroleum customarily passed.

If wars are not fought for control of economic resources, this control is nevertheless an important weapon in war. The restriction, by whatever means, of the enemy's access to scarce materials is a legitimate policy of war. This may be effected by direct blockade, in which the actual flow of materials is cut off. It may also be accomplished by diplomatic or commercial means if an actual blockade is geographically impossible. The struggle to prevent

---

[9] On problems and policies in this regard see *Resources for Freedom*, 82d Cong., document 527, vol. 5, pp. 137–149.

[10] Richard Hartshorne, "The Franco-German Boundary of 1871," *World Politics*, vol. 11, pp. 209–250, 1950.

Germany and her allies from receiving an adequate supply of wolfram, the ore of tungsten, is one of many examples.

Over 95 per cent of Europe's production of wolfram came from the Iberian peninsula, and it became a central objective in Allied economic warfare to prevent Germany from obtaining this ore supply. The Allies were not dependent on wolfram from this source, but their policy "became one of pre-emption pure and simple," and "they intensified their efforts to buy wolfram away from the Germans. . . . [They] were willing to buy any and all wolfram that might be offered, at almost any price, to keep it out of German hands. And they tried consciously to raise prices both to attract any of the mineral that was not irrevocably committed to German agents, and to exhaust the latter's funds by making them pay higher for whatever they got." [11]

MANUFACTURING INDUSTRIES

A highly developed manufacturing industry is the most conspicuous determinant of power. Every "great" power of modern times has been an industrial power. No policy, however blustering and aggressive, is likely to be effective unless supported by the ability to manufacture the machines of war. The German Empire before the First World War was built, as J. M. Keynes so profoundly said,

. . . more truly on coal and iron than on blood and iron. The skilled exploitation of the great coalfields of the Ruhr, Upper Silesia, and the Saar, alone made possible the development of steel, chemical and electrical industries which established her as the first industrial nation of continental Europe. . . . In striking, therefore, at her coal supply, the

French politicians were not mistaking their target. . . .[12]

The underdeveloped countries of today, no less than the Soviet Union more than thirty years ago, realize that a key to political power is industrialization. Their mistake (see Chapter 14) is to misjudge the kind of industrialization that is best suited to their needs.

It is a truism that machines and tools, of increasing refinement and complexity, allow each worker to do an increasing amount of work. The total productivity of a state rises with its mechanization, so that gross population totals cease to be any measure of relative productive power. If in two states with approximately similar populations one has a higher level of industrial development than the other, the former is likely to have greater political power. In the optimistic words of J. G. Crowther: [13]

Some nations are much better equipped with capital than others—that is to say, they have more horse-power of machines to every pair of hands—and the productivity of each worker is therefore greater. To match 1,000 Germans in uniform, 1,000 Englishmen in uniform are needed. But to match the economic output of 1,000 Germans, only about 700 Englishmen are needed.

The logic of this is that 2,000 Englishmen may be expected always to defeat 2,000 Germans.

Manufacturing industries give two power advantages to a state. In the first place they are conducive to a higher standard of living. If man with machine accomplishes significantly more than man without, the total productivity of a highly mechanized people is, after making all

[11] David L. Gordon and Royden Dangerfield, *The Hidden Weapon,* Harper & Brothers, New York, 1947, pp. 105–106.

[12] J. M. Keynes, *The Economic Consequences of the Peace,* Macmillan & Co., London, 1924, p. 75.

[13] Geoffrey Crowther, *The Sinews of War,* Oxford University Press, New York, 1939, p. 7.

allowances for the creation and maintenance of the machines, greater than that of a people not so equipped. Much of this surplus may, of course, be abstracted by the government and used to maintain a large army or to invest in other countries or even in its own. But if neither of these happens, then the surplus will be distributed among those who help to create it. This distribution may be in the form of a shorter working week, higher incomes, insurance, pensions, welfare, or all these. But however the surplus is distributed, it creates a higher living standard. The extent to which this living standard rises above a hypothetical minimum is the slack, or fat, which can be drawn upon in an emergency.[14]

The second advantage which manufacturing industries confer is more direct. It lies in the actual possession of the plant and equipment necessary to turn out the weapons and equipment of war. A steel industry is necessary to manufacture tanks and guns; an electronics industry, to turn out radios, radar, and related equipment; and a textile industry, to make uniforms. The more varied and developed the range of industry, the less will be the degree of dependence on other countries. It is not necessary that the industry should normally be engaged in making military items, though it is probable that their manufacture on a small scale would continue, even under the most favorable international circumstances. What is important is that the industry as a whole could be converted to the manufacture of such equipment at short notice.

A manufacturing industry, especially one of the more basic and spectacular industries such as steelmaking, is thought to confer prestige. It is doubtful whether the more developed countries are greatly im-

pressed when Egypt or Indonesia or Colombia announces its industrial plans. These plans, in fact, amount to so little that they cannot add significantly to the political weight of what are essentially third-class powers. Egypt is building an uneconomically small steelworks, which is a highly expensive way of "keeping up with the Krupps." On the other hand, such an undertaking may give a powerful boost to morale. "There is" reported the *Times*, describing the building construction at Egypt's new iron- and steelworks, "a surprising sense of achievement about the busy complex of installations which has sprouted on the firm desert floor near the riverside village of El Tibin." [15] In Poland the building of the industrial complex of Nowa Huta was a minor national epic. In a developed country such an achievement passes unnoticed by the nation at large; in an underdeveloped country it may fill the people with a sense of immense achievement.

The strategic branches of industry may be said to be six in number. By general consent, the greatest importance attaches to the smelting and refining of metals. Next in importance are certainly the engineering, metal-construction, and shipbuilding industries. The production of chemicals, including high explosives, fertilizers, and cement, along with the manufacture of electrical and other instruments, would rank next. The textile and clothing industries and the food and consumers'-goods industries would probably rank last.

Most of the more advanced countries, such as the United States, United Kingdom, and West Germany, have a balance between these industries, and in some branches, the industries are larger than warranted by normal domestic, peacetime

---

[14] See A. C. Pigou, *The Political Economy of War,* Macmillan & Co., Ltd., London, 1939.

[15] Quoted in N. J. G. Pounds, *The Geography of Iron and Steel,* Macmillan & Co., Ltd., London, 1959, p. 178.

needs. These industries normally export a part of their total production, and this surplus capacity also constitutes a form of "fat" to be drawn upon in an emergency.

If it can be assumed that industrial capacity is an important measure of political power, it should be possible to arrive at some method of ranking states on this basis. Unfortunately, the only feature that all industries have in common is that they employ labor. The absolute or relative figures of the industrially employed population have little value, because the effectiveness of the labor, that is, the man-tool ratio, is not known. On the other hand, merely to tabulate the actual industrial output gives no information on whether this was achieved with a large or a small expenditure of labor. The recent Chinese production of iron in "back-yard" furnaces must represent one of the most costly, in terms of labor, of all forms of industry practiced in the modern world. Their operation is, nevertheless, practicable because of the abundance and cheapness of labor.

Table 11 gives the industrial employment in a group of countries which may perhaps be considered among the most highly developed industrially at the present time.

Does a table of industrial production

TABLE 11 *Employment in Manufacturing* [1]

State	Year	Total population, thousands	Employed in manufacturing	
			Total, thousands	Percentage
United Kingdom..	1958	51,870	7,634.1	14.7
Czechoslovakia...	1959	13,564	1,987	14.5
Belgium.........	1959	9,060	1,144.4	12.6
France..........	1958	42,951	5,349	12.5
West Germany...	1954	49,689	5,740.2	11.5
United States....	1950	151,683	17,082	11.2
Australia........	1959	9,846	1,071.2	10.9
Italy...........	1951	46,996	4,600	10.0
Poland.........	1959	29,000	2,496.8	8.6
Argentina.......	1954	18,756	1,463	7.7
Canada.........	1959	17,442	1,306	7.5
New Zealand.....	1958	2,282	168.8	7.5
Japan..........	1957	90,880	6,041.9	6.6
Venezuela.......	1953	5,440	138.1	2.6
Brazil..........	1958	62,725	1,547	2.5
Pakistan........	1957	76,959	1,431	1.8
Ecuador........	1958	4,048	28.5	0.7
Ceylon.........	1951	7,868	49.9	0.6
India..........	1957	392,440	1,813.1	0.5

[1] Data not available for the Soviet Union and China.

SOURCE: *Statistical Yearbook, 1957,* United Nations, New York; *Demographic Yearbook,* United Nations, New York, various years.

TABLE 12   *Production of Cotton Yarn, Steel, and Cement in Selected Countries*
(in thousands of metric tons)

	Cotton yarn	Rating	Crude steel	Rating	Cement	Rating
U.S.A.	1,645	1	84,773	1	59,763	1
U.S.S.R.	1,124	3	59,900	2	38,781	2
United Kingdom	275	8	20,510	4	12,793	7
West Germany	398	6	29,435	3	22,852	3
France	282	7	15,219	6	14,184	5
Japan	475	5	16,629	5	17,278	4
Italy	70	...	6,762	9	14,074	6
Benelux	176	...	11,766	8	6,231	10
India	781	4	2,473	16	6,936	9
China	1,496	2	13,350	7	12,270	8

SOURCE: *Statistical Yearbook, 1960*, United Nations, New York, 1961.

offer any better index of political power? It is difficult—if not impossible—to equate steel with textiles or chemicals with consumers' goods. How, for example, should Belgium's important iron and steel industry be weighted as against the electrical-goods industry of the Netherlands? Furthermore, within each of the main branches of industry, how should one distinguish between the producer of low-grade steel, such as France, and the producer of high-grade and alloy steels, such as Sweden; between the chemical industry which produces fertilizers and that which turns out high explosives or plastics or drugs? It is doubtful that a rating of states on any absolute basis is possible. Table 12 attempts merely to show the standing of the more important states in certain respects only. The percentage of the world production of a restricted list of commodities in each of these countries is given on the basis of production figures for 1959. The rating which thus results is only a very rough approximation, and it gives no indication whatever of the degree of self-sufficiency

in the supply of the raw materials of these industries.

Another measure of economic development of a state is the amount of power which it consumes. There is a rough correlation between power consumption and Gross National Product. In the words of J. Bronowski, "A country rich in the use of energy is also a country whose people live well and long; and a country poor by one of these measures is poor by them all." [16] It is difficult to arrive at even a reasonable approximation of the energy consumption of most countries, and very few publish careful analyses. [17] Table 13, which gives the per capita energy consumption of less than half the political units of the world, does not, however, dif-

[16] Jacob Bronowski, as quoted in *Essays on Geography and Economic Development*, N. Ginsburg (ed.), University of Chicago Press, Chicago, 1960, p. 67.

[17] Nathaniel B. Guyol, "Energy Consumption and Economic Development," in N. Ginsburg (ed.), *Essays on Geography and Economic Development*, University of Chicago Press, Chicago, 1960, pp. 65–77.

TABLE 13 *Energy Consumption (Tons of Coal Equivalent) Per Person, 1952–1954 Average*

United States	7.80	Malaya	0.37
Canada	7.17	Colombia	0.37
Norway	4.79	Lebanon	0.35
United Kingdom	4.68	Panama	0.35
Belgium-Luxembourg	3.75	Turkey	0.33
Sweden	3.74	Portugal	0.33
Australia	3.42	Brazil	0.33
Germany	2.93	Peru	0.30
New Zealand	2.67	Greece	0.28
Iceland	2.62	Egypt	0.22
Switzerland	2.46	Jamaica	0.19
France	2.29	Kenya	0.14
Denmark	2.18	Honduras	0.14
Netherlands	2.16	Ecuador	0.13
South Africa	2.07	Dominican Republic	0.12
Austria	1.85	Guatemala	0.12
Finland	1.50	Philippines	0.11
Venezuela	1.29	Ceylon	0.11
Japan	0.94	India	0.11
Israel	0.94	Korea (South)	0.10
Chile	0.90	Congo	0.09
Argentina	0.89	Pakistan	0.04
Italy	0.88	Thailand	0.04
Mexico	0.67	Burma	0.03
Cuba	0.61	Uganda	0.03
Rhodesia and Nyasaland	0.46		

SOURCE: After Nathaniel B. Guyol, "Energy Consumption and Economic Development," in N. Ginsburg (ed.), *Essays on Geography and Economic Development*, Chicago University Press, Chicago, 1960.

fer greatly in the order of the countries listed from the Table in Appendix II, page 169, which gives Gross National Product.

Despite the extraordinary difficulties of arriving at a formula expressive of national power, the attempt has recently been made by F. Clifford German.[18] Briefly it starts with the area of the state, corrected for population density and the closeness of the railroad net. It then adds a factor for population, corrected for technical efficiency, employment in industry, "morale," and the adequacy of the food supply. Allowance is made for the production of steel, solid and liquid fuels, and hydroelectric power; for the surplus or deficit in steel, petroleum, minerals, and engineering; for the size of the armed forces and its possession of what we euphemistically call the "nuclear deterrent." The formula is applied to nineteen countries and a value assigned to each. On this showing the first nineteen powers in this power calculation are shown in the table below.

It is easy to criticize this scheme. Each of the factors included requires more qualification than it receives; many significant factors are omitted, and no allowance is made for "fat" and "slack." Lastly,

[18] F. Clifford German, "A Tentative Evaluation of World Power," *Journal of Conflict Resolution*, vol. 4, pp. 138–144, 1960.

there exists no means, other than the price mechanism, of comparing one hydrogen bomb (least of all a stock pile of unknown dimensions) or 1 ton of steel with a few square miles of territory or kilowatts of

	Points
U.S.A.	6,459
U.S.S.R.	6,321
United Kingdom	1,257
China	999
West Germany	663.5
Canada	498
Japan	410.5
France	383
India	373
Poland	324.5
Australia	217
Brazil	203.5
Czechoslovakia	196
Italy	192.5
East Germany	174
Argentina	127.5
Union of South Africa	122.5
Sweden	116
Belgium	112

industrial power. And in this event, we might just as well use the figures for Gross National Product which are discussed below.

ECONOMIC SELF-SUFFICIENCY

It should be apparent from the previous pages that self-sufficiency, under conditions of modern industry and of modern life, is impossible for any state to achieve. Self-sufficiency in minerals alone would be possible only at the expense of abandoning the technical advances in metallurgy of the last century. In foodstuffs and clothing it could be achieved only by an immeasurable lowering of living standards.

This is not to say that every state could not achieve a higher degree of self-sufficiency than it at present possesses. More intensive cultivation (i.e., by a greater ex-

penditure of labor and fertilizer) would yield more food and raw materials of vegetable origin; marginal ore and fuel resources could be exploited. But in each instance the return would be likely to be too small in comparison with the increased expenditure of labor and materials. Nevertheless, governments have at times regarded some degree of self-sufficiency as desirable, because of the security which it confers. The seventeenth- and eighteenth-century economic doctrine, known as *mercantilism*, was based in part upon the assumption that to depend upon another country for any commodity is automatically to put oneself in a vulnerable position toward it politically. National self-sufficiency was then an objective of government policy, to be achieved by the protection and development of domestic agriculture and industry. The acquisition of colonies was considered desirable only if these could supply some commodity which was needed but which was otherwise unobtainable without recourse to a foreign and presumably rival state.

Such ideas gave place in the eighteenth century to those of *laissez faire;* governments did nothing, at least overtly, either to encourage or to restrict trade with other countries. The ideal of self-sufficiency was replaced by that of specialization and exchange. A return toward the ideals of self-sufficiency occurred between the First and the Second World Wars. The events of the First World War, the near success of the German submarine blockade of the British Isles, and the success of the Allied counter-blockade of Germany emphasized the need, for military reasons, of as high a degree of self-sufficiency as possible. It was a persistent, though inaccurate, opinion in Germany that the German defeat was due to the blockade and consequent starvation. The action of the League of Nations in applying economic sanctions against Italy in November, 1935—that is, cutting the country off from the supply of certain essential materials—reinforced the need for self-sufficiency. Any state which envisaged war as an instrument of policy had to ensure a supply of essential materials for at least as long a period as the war's duration.

"Guns or Butter": A higher degree of self-sufficiency is attainable only at a price. It can be achieved by using marginal resources, which require a higher labor input than those normally exploited; by developing substitute materials, which cost more to manufacture than those which they replace (otherwise the substitutes would already have displaced them); and by stockpiling scarce materials in advance of the emergency. In any case, a larger fraction of the national income must be devoted to production under such circumstances than would be necessary in the free market. Hence the alternatives which Hermann Göring offered the German people in the 1930s. Butter was derived from a dairy industry based in part on imported cattle feed. In order to be able to import, and pay for, strategic materials, it would be necessary to reduce or suspend the import of cattle feed. Thus guns were the alternative to butter in something more than a figurative sense.

All the Great Powers to some degree aim to subsidize or protect the production of strategic materials within their borders. Inducements to the farmer, in the form of price supports, lower taxation, or tariff protection, is usual. Great Britain subsidizes the sugar beet industry in order to avoid exclusive dependence on imported cane sugar. "The strenuous German efforts to expand agricultural production until it is exactly equal to the home demand, and the Italian 'Battle of Wheat,' are merely more self-conscious and far-reaching illustrations of what has been attempted in

nearly every country throughout the world."

Germany, during the years immediately preceding the Second World War, provides the extreme example of the pursuit of autarchy, or self-sufficiency, at whatever cost. Low-grade iron ores were worked; domestic production of wool was increased somewhat, and that of synthetic wool very greatly; synthetic rubber, or *Buna*, came to replace natural. In the building trades, porcelain pipes replaced metal in order to reduce the consumption of metals. A similar policy was pursued, though less intensively, in Italy. In each instance, the real cost of the synthetic or substitute material was higher than that of the material which it replaced. Its only advantage was that it could be produced from domestic resources.

Security, the ultimate objective of policy, requires that the government should give some consideration to the self-sufficiency of the state. In Germany in the 1930s this was carried to an extreme because it was considered necessary for the war which Germany was planning to wage in the near future. Such a policy could not be maintained over a long period without damaging the welfare of the state, which it should be the objective of policy to preserve. A balanced policy in this respect lies between the extremes of self-sufficiency and undue dependence upon imports. It must vary widely from state to state, depending upon local resources and industrial development, on geographical position and vulnerability, and on the government's assessment of risks and dangers. The President's Materials Policy Commission defined the major premise in these words: "The overall objective of a national materials policy for the United States should be to insure an adequate and dependable flow of materials at the lowest cost consistent with national security and with the welfare of friendly nations." [19] The Commission took five large and closely reasoned volumes to explain how this should be done.

The degree of self-sufficiency that can be attained is related to the cooperation of allies and reliance upon dependencies. The ways in which these reinforce the economic, and thus the political, power of a state are examined in later chapters.

TRANSPORTATION

The means of transporting people and equipment are a necessary element of national power. Without them, raw materials cannot be assembled for manufacture, nor, when processed, can they be distributed to a market or consumer. Defense is impossible without the facility of moving persons and equipment from one part of a country to another. The mere fact that there are "strategic roads" and "strategic railways" serves to underline their role in strengthening military power. The current construction of railroads leading to India's Himalayan boundary and the interest of the United States government in preserving enough railroad coaches for troop movements point up the same strategic need.

Two aspects of transportation deserve consideration. One is external and concerns access to foreign sources of materials; it involves the use of ships, ports, and canals, as well as the movement of goods across the land areas of other states. This aspect is examined later, in Chapter 9. The other is concerned with the internal means of transportation within a state.

A developed transport net, whether of road or rail, is generally regarded as a prerequisite to national unity. Many states have a net of both roads and railroads radiating from the capital to all parts of

[19] *Resources for Freedom*, vol. 1, p. 3.

the country, as in France, Great Britain, and the U.S.S.R. Elsewhere the completion of a line, or lines, was a prerequisite of political unity. The completion of both the Canadian and the Australian Federations was contingent upon the extension of the railroad system to the most westerly parts of the Territories. Before the Communist Revolution, a railroad was built from Moscow to the Ural Mountains and across Siberia to Vladivostok. Since then, this line has been double-tracked, supplemented by a net of branch lines, and made more effective. In China, where railroad construction had always been slight, the new and highly centralized unity under Communist rule is leading to a bigger program of railroad construction. In the United States the slow westward extension of the railroads was a kind of symbol, illustrating the growing unity of the territory of the United States. The completion, in 1869, at Promontory Point, Utah, of the first transcontinental railroad was of more than practical importance. It was a symbol that the "manifest destiny" had been achieved. Cecil Rhodes's vision of a railway "from the Cape to Cairo," never realized, and possibly never to be realized, was part of the dream of white hegemony over Africa.

The role of railroads in giving a practical and functional unity to the state is supplemented by the role of roads and waterways. Roads are more flexible than railroads; they can negotiate steeper gradients, can be constructed more quickly and cheaply, and thus tend to be adopted where the volume of traffic would not justify, or the nature of the terrain would not permit, the building of railroads. The Burma Road, the Alaskan Highway, the north-south transcontinental road of Australia are examples of road building on the grand scale. The minor roads of the mountain valleys, the bush, and the jungle typify, no less, the ability of the road and the automobile to go almost anywhere. It should be added that in most parts of the world roads not only supplement, but also parallel and duplicate, railroads and canals.

Water transport is slow, relatively cheap, and admirably adapted to the movement of bulk cargoes. It is feasible only where there are navigable rivers and canals, and this distribution is very closely controlled by the features of the terrain and by water supply. Internal waterways are not a flexible mode of transportation, and the cost of cutting a canal, especially one which has a large number of locks, is vastly in excess of that of building railroads. Canal building began in Europe in the seventeenth century and continued into the nineteenth century. At least in western Europe, most of the possible canals that were both practicable and desirable have been cut, and some of them have already been abandoned. Canals are now chiefly of importance when they supplement, extend, and interconnect the navigable river systems. The St. Lawrence Waterway, the New York State Barge Canal, the German Mittelland Canal, and some of the canals in France, the Low Countries, and Great Britain are important chiefly because each forms a part of a more extensive system of navigation. At present some waterways, especially the Rhône, Rhine, and Danube systems, are being made more easily navigable. Canals to link the Danube with the Oder and Vistula, and the Vistula, through the Pripet, to the Dnepr are planned. Both these, and also existing canals, are likely to be successful only if they are able to handle a steady and continuous movement of bulky goods such as fuel, ores, or lumber. West Germany and the Netherlands make the greatest use of water-borne transport, which in general contributes comparatively little to the transportation facilities of most countries.

For the rapid movement of large volumes of goods and numbers of people nothing can match the railroads. But at the same time they are particularly vulnerable. The wartime bombing of switchyards and railroad bridges emphasized both their immense importance and also the relative ease with which they can be destroyed.

THE BALANCE SHEET OF RESOURCES

We have been considering the material resources of the state as an element in its power potential. This power potential is both positive, that is, capable of directly influencing other states and of assisting the state in imposing its will on them, and also negative, that is, able to resist both direct and indirect attack. At times we have tried to put some kind of value on the constituent elements in this resource potential. Comparisons are clearly possible for individual elements in the power potential, but any quantitative evaluation of the complex of resources is too subjective to have much value. There are too many unknowns for the equation to be realistic. The national income of the state, defined as "the net value of all goods produced and of all services performed in it in the course of a year, the country's exports being subtracted and its imports added to give the final figure," has also been used as a measure of economic power. Professor Jones has objected to this, because the monetary terms used in expressing national income do not necessarily express the utility of an activity in this regard.[20] The national income clearly includes the value of some goods and services which have no relevance to national power. Nevertheless these *may* be convertible into goods and services which are significant;

[20] Jones, *loc. cit.*

TABLE 14 *National Income, 1956*

	In local currency, millions	In U.S. dollars, millions	National income per head, dollars
U.S.A.	361,239 (dollars)	$361,239	$2,149
Canada	23,819 (Canadian dollars)	24,772	1,545
Sweden	48,301 (kroner)	9,346	1,277
Switzerland	27,280 (Swiss francs)	6,356	1,260
New Zealand	928 (New Zealand pounds)	2,598	1,101
Australia	4,625 (Australian pounds)	10,361	1,009
Belgium	438,200 (Belgian francs)	8,764	982
United Kingdom	17,604 (pounds)	49,291	958
West Germany	160,257 (deutsche marks)	38,141	751
France	10,680,000 (French francs)	30,972	691
Italy	12,231,000 (lire)	19,570	405
Japan	8,252,000 (yen)	23,106	256
Brazil	851,900 (cruzeiros)	13,034	217
Ecuador	9,733 (sucres)	560	147
Ceylon	5,067 (rupees)	1,064	119
India	114,000 (rupees)	23,940	62
China	88,800 (yuan)	36,408	58
Pakistan	20,987 (rupees)	4,397	53

Source: National incomes in native currencies from *Yearbook of National Accounts Statistics, 1958*, United Nations, New York, converted into dollars (United States) at rates given by the Swiss Bank Corporation.

at the very least, they may constitute a form of "fat" in the economy.

Table 14 lists the national incomes and national incomes per head of a number of states for which reliable statistics are available. A fuller list is given in Appendix II at the end of this chapter. It is apparent that, in the main, this table agrees with Table 12 on industrial production, with some exceptions, however. Certain predominantly agricultural countries, New Zealand and Denmark among them, rank high in the list. This is because in these instances, to put it simply, agriculture is carried on as if it were an industry. It is a streamlined, mass-production process whereby raw materials (such as fodder) are converted into finished goods (such as

butter). Apart from these instances, however, the correlation is high. National income is a very rough indication of national power.

APPENDIX II

Comparable national income statistics are extremely difficult to obtain or to calculate. The following figures were compiled in the Office of Statistics and Reports, International Cooperation Administration, and were printed in *Foreign Aid Program, Compilation of Studies and Surveys*, document 52, 85th Cong. 1st Sess. The table bears the following note: "Precise comparisons of the levels of gross national product between the United States and other countries are not possible. The conversion into dollars has been made on the basis

Estimates of Total Gross National Product and National Product per Head, 1955

Country	Total, millions	Per head	Country	Total, millions	Per head
United States	387,200	2,343	Iraq	960	195
Canada	26,000	1,667	Mexico	5,548	187
New Zealand	2,673	1,249	Chile	1,220	180
Switzerland	6,116	1,229	Guatemala	580	179
Australia	10,920	1,215	Algeria	1,680	176
Sweden	8,460	1,165	Saudi Arabia	1,160	166
Iceland	180	1,146	Morocco	1,512	159
France	45,195	1,046	Peru	1,315	140
Belgium	9,311	1,015	Honduras	228	137
United Kingdom	61,100	998	Gold Coast (Ghana)	624	135
Norway	3,320	969	Central African		
Finland	3,984	941	Federation [1]	945	134
Denmark	4,051	913	South Vietnam	1,600	133
Germany	38,100	762	Egypt	3,065	133
Venezuela	4,400	762	Tunisia	490	131
Netherlands	7,604	708	Indonesia	10,500	127
Soviet Union	150,000	682	Ceylon	1,050	122
Uruguay	1,500	569	Syria	445	111
Israel	944	540	Paraguay	168	108
Austria	3,711	532	Liberia	155	103
Eire	1,481	509	Taiwan	1,640	102
Italy	21,220	442	Thailand	2,050	100
South Africa	5,208	381	Iran	2,110	100
Argentina	7,150	374	Sudan	885	100
Cuba	2,180	361	Congo (Belgian)	1,639	98
Panama	320	350	Jordan	135	96
Colombia	4,180	330	Libya	99	90
Costa Rica	292	307	South Korea	1,780	80
Malaya	2,170	298	Haiti	260	75
British North Borneo	310	298	India	27,400	72
Yugoslavia	5,207	297	Algeria	2,250	70
Turkey	6,463	276	Portuguese Africa	776	70
Lebanon	380	269	Bolivia	211	66
Brazil	15,315	262	Kenya-Uganda-		
Spain	7,369	254	Tanganyika	1,214	61
Nicaragua	315	254	French West Africa [2]	1,020	58
El Salvador	530	244	French Equatorial Africa [3]	270	58
Japan	21,300	240	Pakistan	4,560	56
Greece	1,996	239	China (Mainland)	35,000	56
Dominican Republic	494	205	Afghanistan	650	54
Ecuador	746	204	Ethiopia	860	54
Portugal	1,765	201	Burma	1,012	52
Philippines	4,400	201	Nepal	340	40

[1] Includes Northern and Southern Rhodesia and Nyasaland.

[2] Includes Senegal, Guinea, Ivory Coast, Togo, Dahomey, Mali, and Niger.

[3] Includes Chad, Central African Republic, Gabon, Congo Republic (Brazzaville), and Cameroun.

SOURCE: "The Role of Foreign Aid in the Development of Other Countries," Study no. 3, *Foreign Aid Program—Compilation of Studies and Surveys*, 85th Cong. 1st Sess., Document no. 52, 1955.

of the latest official exchange rates, and the purchasing power of the dollar equivalent is appreciably higher in most foreign countries than that of the dollar in the United States. Comparisons of the converted dollar figures between other countries are subject to similar limitations."

BIBLIOGRAPHY

DeMille, John B.: *Strategic Minerals*, McGraw-Hill Book Company, Inc., New York, 1947.

Eckel, E. C.: *Coal, Iron and War*, Henry Holt and Company, Inc., New York, 1920.

Emeny, B.: *The Strategy of Raw Materials*, The Macmillan Company, New York, 1934.

Fisher, A. G. B.: *Economic Self-sufficiency*, Oxford University Press, New York, 1939.

Foreign Aid Program, U.S. Senate, Special Committee to Study the Foreign Aid Program, July, 1957.

German, F. Clifford: "A Tentative Evaluation of World Power," *Journal of Conflict Resolution*, vol. 4, pp. 138–144, 1960.

Ginsburg, Norton: *Atlas of Economic Development*, University of Chicago Press, Chicago, 1961.

Gordon, David L., and Royden Dangerfield: *The Hidden Weapon*, Harper & Brothers, New York, 1947.

Jones, Stephen B.: "The Power Inventory and National Strategy," *World Politics*, vol. 6, pp. 421–452, 1954.

Leith, C. K.: *World Minerals and World Politics*, Brookings Institution, Washington, D.C., 1931.

Lincoln, George A.: *Economics of National Security*, Prentice-Hall, Inc., Englewood Cliffs, N.J., 1954.

Per Capita National Product of Fifty-five Countries 1952–1954, Statistical Papers, ser. E, no. 4, United Nations, New York, 1957.

Pigou, A. C.: *The Political Economy of War*, Macmillan & Co., Ltd., London, 1939.

Pounds, N. J. G.: *The Geography of Iron and Steel*, Macmillan & Co., Ltd., London, 1959.

——— and W. N. Parker: *Coal and Steel in Western Europe*, Indiana University Press, Bloomington, Ind., 1957.

Resources for Freedom, 82d Cong., document 527, 5 vols., 1952.

Shimkin, Demitri B.: *Minerals: A Key to Soviet Power*, Harvard University Press, Cambridge, Mass., 1953.

7 CORE AREAS AND CAPITALS

There is no little provincial state which has not had its germinal, its geographical starting-point; there is no durable political formation in whose origin we cannot discover a combination of forces, a kind of armature around which other territories could build themselves up like the soft parts round the bones of a skeleton. LUCIEN FEBVRE, A GEOGRAPHICAL INTRODUCTION TO HISTORY

THE STATES OF THE MODERN WORLD HAVE NOT, IN GENERAL, BEEN created suddenly or abruptly. In most instances they have grown slowly over a period of centuries. Sometimes, their growth was interrupted by the loss of territory. Some states, such as Hungary, Bulgaria, and perhaps Germany, look back nostalgically to a time when they covered a greater territorial area than they now do. Some have even made the recovery of a former "greater" state a dominant objective of policy, with disastrous results on their relations with neighboring states.

A minority of states have not grown; they have been created. In some instances a state so created happened to coincide with a nation and may so have reflected the political aspirations of a national group. But generally it was not for this reason that the state was created, but to suit the needs and conveniences of other states. Thus Albania appeared on the map in 1913 because it suited the Great Powers of Europe to create it, rather than to dispute with one another over the control of this strategically important territory. Similarly, Palestine, Syria, and Iraq were created primarily to satisfy the power needs of Great Britain and France. The new states of Africa—Ghana, Guinea, Nigeria, and others—reflect in their territorial limits the decisions reached around the council table in London, Paris, or elsewhere. They were never conceived as corresponding to anything in the economic life or the material or spiritual culture of the African peoples themselves.

CORE AREAS

Whatever may have been the later vicissitudes of the state area, most states have grown from a central area, where their governments and ideals first began to take shape. This is the *core area*, defined as "the area in which or about which a state originates." [1] Karl Deutsch has sought to discover what happens when a nation-state emerges; he found a recurring "pattern of integration" in the examples which he studied.[2] Foremost in this pattern was the appearance of a core area, characterized by "unusual fertility of soil, permitting a dense agricultural population and providing a food surplus to maintain additional numbers in non-agricultural pursuits; geographic features facilitating military defense of the area; and a nodal position at an intersection of major transportation routes." [3] Other features which mark the appearance of the nation-state are the shift from a self-sufficient form of agriculture to specialization and exchange of commodities, the growth of cities, with specialized industry and commerce, and the growth of a network of roads. The development of crafts and commerce brings with it living standards that are often different from, if not higher than, those of neighboring areas. This introduces the concepts of self-awareness and self-interest. The individual

who leaves the relative security and the simple folkways of an agricultural society for a wider, more amorphous, urbanized or industrialized society needs new values to which to cling. His interests, both material and intellectual, reach beyond the limits of his village and its surrounding fields. His markets, his raw materials, the routeways of his commerce, small-scale and primitive though these may be, constitute a nexus which it is beyond his power and that of his immediate kin to protect. He leans on something wider—his association with like groups beyond the range of his immediate experience. Thus the nation gradually takes shape. The concept of a nation is bound up with that of national interest, and self-interest can usually weld together the most disparate elements into a nation.

The Example of Switzerland: An example of the foregoing is the formation of the Swiss Confederation, already mentioned (page 12). The opening of the St. Gotthard Pass, early in the thirteenth century, led to the development of trade through the backward, sparsely peopled region of the central Alps. The merchants brought wealth to the primitive people whose services they used on the hard journey across the mountains. They also brought from Italy political ideas that had hitherto been quite foreign to the practice of the Swiss mountaineers. "Switzerland is the creation of the St. Gotthard Pass, just as Egypt is the gift of the Nile." [4] It was not long before the Swiss who lived near the northern approaches to the St. Gotthard Pass had got control of the trade and had combined to defend and extend their new privileges. Their political organization derived from Italian examples; the "freedom," which the original cantons combined to de-

[1] Derwent Whittlesey, *The Earth and the State,* Henry Holt and Company, Inc., New York, 1939, p. 597. The term core area is also currently used to define the area within a state that is at present economically dominant.

[2] Karl W. Deutsch, "The Growth of Nations. Some Recurrent Patterns of Political and Social Integration," *World Politics,* vol. 5, pp. 168–195, 1952–1953.

[3] *Ibid.,* p. 173.

[4] Charles Gilliard, "Les Origines de la Confédération Suisse," *Revue Belge de philologie et de l'histoire,* vol. 111, p. 111, 1924.

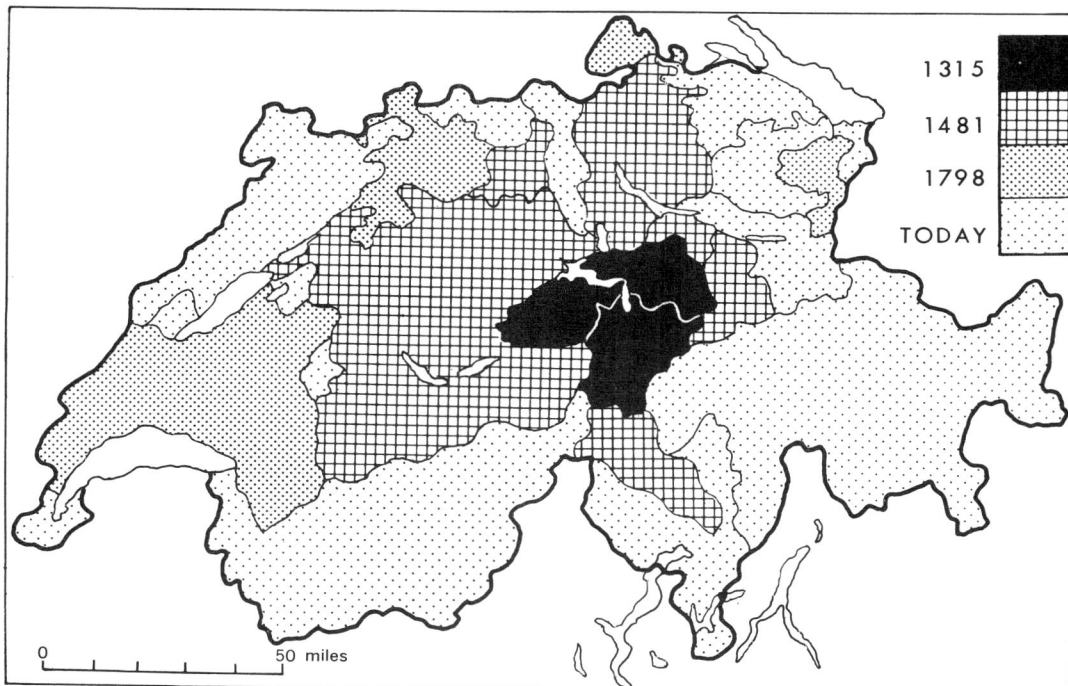

Exhibit 54   *Core area and expansion of Switzerland.*

fend, was in fact the freedom to profit to the uttermost from the trade that crossed their territory. The cement of the Swiss nation was an enlightened self-interest, which has become romanticized as the struggle of a hardy, freedom-loving people for independence from the tyrannical rule of the house of Hapsburg.

The core area of Switzerland is defined with the utmost clarity by the four Forest Cantons which bordered the steep road up to the St. Gotthard Pass, within whose tiny territory the original struggle for independence took place (Exhibit 54). Here was the locale of the Swiss heroic legend of Tell and of others among the "freedom fighters" of their age.

The rest of Switzerland has gathered around this area, as political and economic motives induced one area after another to join the original cantons. The valleys lead-

ing up to the St. Gotthard Pass are no longer the economic focus of the state; this has moved out into the Swiss "plateau," where the physical conditions are better for the building of cities, the laying down of railroads, and the construction of factories. Bern, Zürich, and Basel have replaced Schwyz, Altdorf, and Luzern as the economic centers of the Confederation; but a shift in the core area of a state is not unusual.

The Case of Poland: The state of Poland crystallized around a core area which lay between the Oder and Vistula Rivers (Exhibit 55). Unlike the core area of Switzerland, it was a region of considerable fertility. Its almost level plains had a natural protection in the marshes which lay, and to some extent continue to lie, along the valleys of the Oder, Warta, and Noteć. Within this area during the eighth and ninth centuries, a degree of military security, combined with the abundant agricultural production, resulted in a higher level of cultural development than was to be found in surrounding areas. Small cities appeared at Poznan, Gniezno, Kruszwica, and elsewhere. They were, in the main, primitive, with wood-built huts and palisades for defense. But masonry was also used. Surplus wealth was invested in stone-built churches, fragments of which have survived. At the same time, primitive crafts developed—building among them—and trade was carried on, mainly by river, northward to the Baltic coast and southward toward the Danube.

This was the core area of the earliest Polish state; its capital was at Gniezno, which also became the seat of the spiritual head, the Archbishop of the Polish Church. To this area, which is still known as Great Poland, or Wielkopolska, were subsequently added territories to the north, south, and east. During the successive changes of boundary and extent, the capital was moved first to Poznań, then to Krakow in the south, and finally to Warsaw, lying to the east of Great Poland. The former core area of Poland, like that of Switzerland, has declined in relative importance, and the focus of power has moved into Mazowsze, the neighoring province to the east.

The Case of France: France is often cited as the best example of a state with a

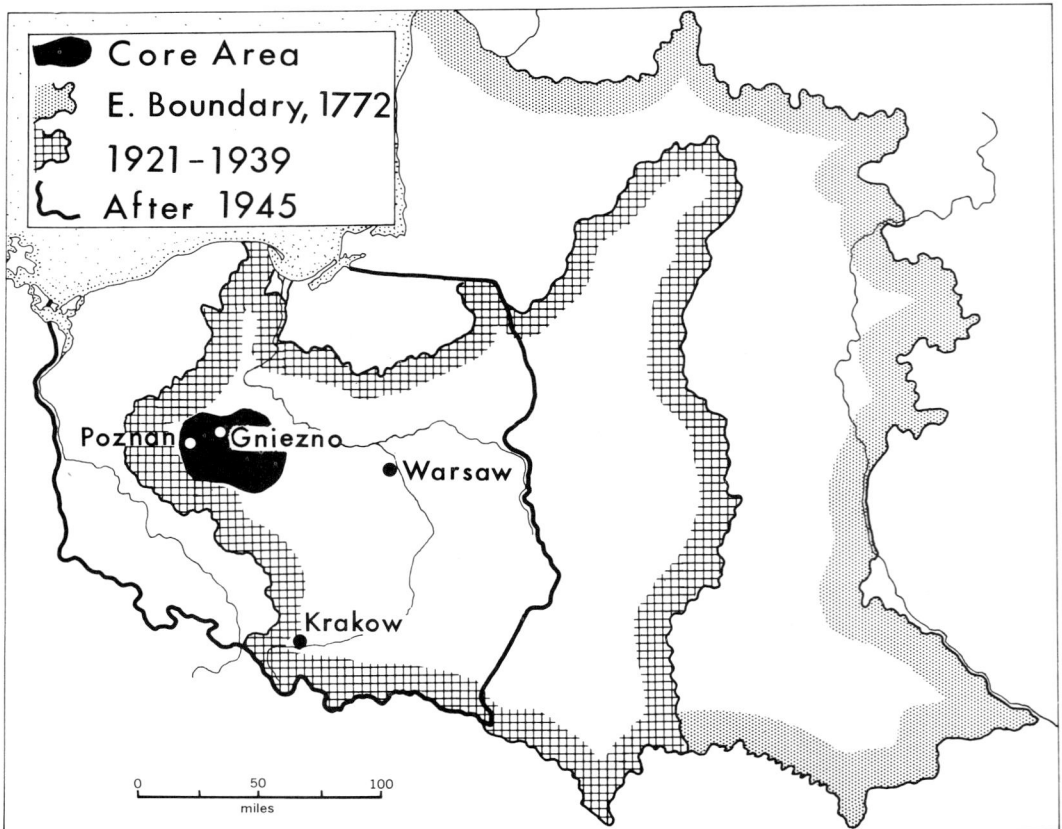

Exhibit 55   Core area and expansion of Poland.

distinct core area around which, by a process of accretion, the rest of the state area has been built up (Exhibit 56). During the first century B.C. the area of modern France was conquered by the Roman armies under Julius Caesar, and its boundaries were established along the line of the Alps and the river Rhine. The administrative capital of Roman Gaul was the city of Lugdunum, the modern Lyon, which lay in the southeast, at the junction of the Rhône and Saône Rivers, and near the western end of the alpine roads that led to Italy. From Lugdunum roads radiated over the whole of Gaul. In the fourth and fifth centuries A.D. Gaul was overrun by Germanic invaders and broke up into a number of little states. These again acquired a degree of unity under Charlemagne (771–814), who joined under his rule France, the Low Countries, and much of Italy and western Germany. His capital was Aachen, and his immediate successors regarded the northern Rhineland as the focus of their empire. But the Carolingian empire was divided in 843 into three large parts, and each of these subsequently broke up into petty states. Rule in France devolved upon the counts who ruled the many provinces, and one of these provinces, the region of Paris itself, became the core area of the French state.

Under the Romans, Paris had been merely a small provincial town, and it did not play an important role under the Carolingians. It came to the fore, along with its ruler, the count of Paris, in the late tenth century, when it resisted successfully the invasion of the Northmen. Hugh Capet, the son of the successful defender of Paris, was made king of France in 987. He exercised real authority only over the city of Paris and its immediate surroundings, and for the rest of France his authority was neither recognized nor respected. It was the task of the French kings to extend their

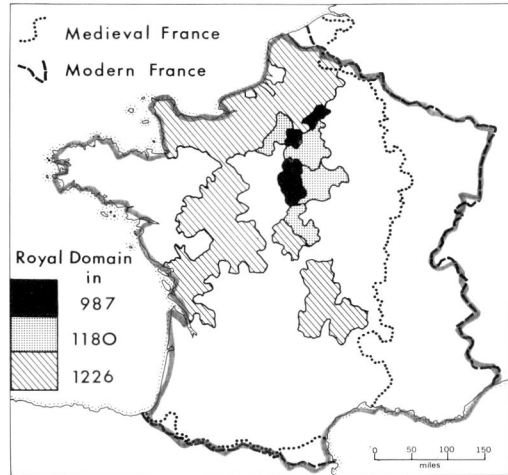

Exhibit 56 *Core area and expansion of France.*

effective control from the Paris area to the rest of France, a task which was barely achieved by the seventeenth century.

Paris lies on the river Seine, about 100 miles from the sea and near the junction of important tributaries, the Oise and Marne. The history of France, it has been said, is written in her rivers; the authority of the French kings, based on Paris, advanced, so it is claimed, up or down the rivers which converge on the city, so that the later political unity of France was, it was argued, inevitable. This is to misunderstand the creation of French unity. The rivers above Paris, in their primitive condition, were not really navigable and were scarcely used. The unification of France around the Paris region was not the result of a physical movement of people outward from the Paris area, carrying with them the weight of the king's authority, any more than Switzerland was created by the Swiss coming outward from their Forest Cantons. The unity of France was the result of successive acts of recognition by one feudal magnate after another of the *de facto* (as distinct from *de jure*) authority of the king, and the acceptance, fully or in part,

Figure 30 *Paris: this view shows the island—L' Île de la Cité—with its cathedral and public buildings, which formed the original city.* COURTESY: FRENCH EMBASSY AND INFORMATION DIVISION

of the cultural and institutional values that had come to be established in the Paris region. It resembled broadly the corresponding processes in the other states mentioned so far and differed from them only in the greater complexity of the process.

The core area of the France of the eleventh century remains the core area of France today. During the formative centuries, the provinces were made to depend so intimately on Paris that no fundamental change is now possible. France is a very highly centralized state, with the functions of government concentrated in Paris itself.

The Case of Great Britain: England provides an interesting parallel to France. The Romans, beginning in A.D. 49, con-

quered England itself but failed to make much impression on the mountainous regions of the west and north. Their core area was the valley of the Thames, widening eastward to the North Sea. Their capital was the city of Verulamium, near St. Albans, about 20 miles northwest of London, but Londinium itself was the largest city and the commercial center of Roman Britain. The boundary of the Roman province lay in effect along the Welsh and Scottish borders.

The unity of Roman Britain was destroyed by the invasions of the Anglo-Saxons and later of the Norsemen. The country broke up into a number of small, tribal kingdoms, among which Wessex gained the ascendancy. The lower Thames Valley, the core area of the Roman province, was divided by the military frontier between Wessex and the Danelaw, and its significance was temporarily reduced. The reunification of the country under the last Anglo-Saxon kings restored the importance of London. The Norman Conquest saw the complete restoration of the importance of the London area. Here was built the king's chief castle, here was the church, Westminster Abbey, in which the kings were crowned, and here the officers of state, when they gradually ceased to be peripatetic (see page 186), established their offices. A few miles to the southeast of London was Canterbury Cathedral, seat of the Archbishop and Primate of All England. Lastly, from London there still radi-

ated that network of roads constructed by the Romans, and up the Thames to the port of London came the ships of a growing commercial fleet.

Political control spread outward from the core area. At first it was slight in northern England and along the Welsh border. Gradually these areas were drawn in, first politically and then culturally. Wales was conquered in the thirteenth century, but the English system of local administration was extended here only in the sixteenth, and even today Wales is by no means fully integrated into English cultural life. The same happened with Scotland: joined to England politically in 1603, made part of Great Britain with the same governmental institutions a century later, but always standing somewhat apart cul-

Figure 31. *London: The view shows the governmental district of Westminster, with the Houses of Parliament by the river in the foreground, Westminster Abbey behind it, and Whitehall, lined by governmental departments, stretching away to the right.* COURTESY: AEROFILMS

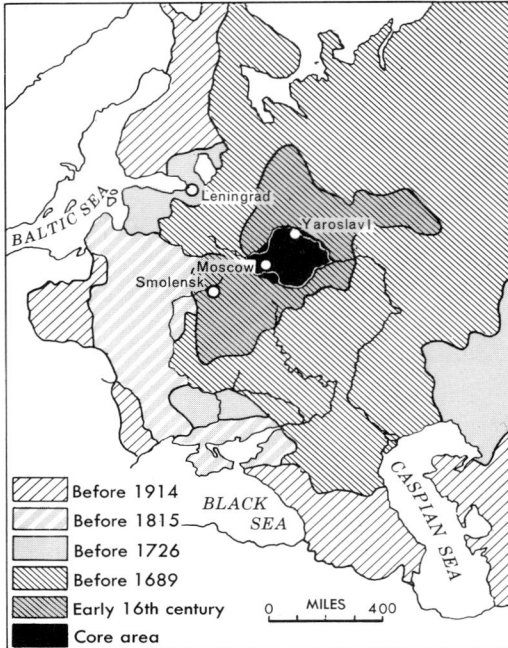

Before 1914
Before 1815
Before 1726
Before 1689
Early 16th century
Core area

BLACK SEA

0   MILES   400

Exhibit 57   *Core area and expansion of Russia.*

turally, and to some degree living with its own romantic legend and tradition.

The Case of Russia: The Moscow area embodies the traditions of Russian history, as Paris does those of France and London those of England. Across Russia, both European and Asiatic, there stretch broad belts of vegetation: in the south the steppe, north of it the forest belt, and beyond it the tundra. The first Russian state was established in the ninth century in the steppe. Its focus was the commercial city of Kiev, and it was supplied by the routeways that followed the Dnepr and other rivers between the Baltic Sea and the Black Sea. If it had not been for the invasions of Tartars from farther east in the steppe, Kiev might be today the political center of the Soviet Union. The invaders interrupted the trade and destroyed the cities. Those who could do so retreated northward into the forest belt, where the horse-riding

Tartar nomads had difficulty in following them. Here, roughly in the triangular area between the upper Volga and its tributary, the Oka, the broad-leaved trees of the south and west give place to the coniferous trees of the northern forests. Here, in the zone of mixed forest, Moscow grew up beside the Moskva River, a tributary of the Oka (Exhibit 57). It was almost seven centuries before the descendants of the founders of Moscow returned and controlled once again the steppe to the south, and by this time the tradition and character of the Russian nation were almost formed.

For several centuries the little principality of Moscow existed in relative obscurity. In the fifteenth century its territory began to expand, as settlers moved outward from the core area into the surrounding forest and even southward into the steppe. Political control even preceded the spread of settlement. This growth was interrupted by renewed Tartar attacks and also by periods of civil war within Muscovy itself but was resumed after these were over. This continued growth is something unique in history. As Professor Halecki has remarked, "What makes the Russian case absolutely unique is the practically uninterrupted continuity of an expansion on a truly tremendous scale . . . and that process has now endured for six centuries and a half. . . ." [5]

How to explain this continuity has always been a problem. "The defenders of pre-revolutionary Russia . . . claim that Russia's expansion was nothing but a quest for security, combined with a natural urge to the sea. . . ." [6] An urge to the sea has provided a plausible explanation of Russia's long record of growth and expansion, and it has been easy to visualize "a land-

[5] O. Halecki, "Imperialism in Slavic and East European History," *American Slavic and East European Review*, vol. 11, pp. 1–26, 1952.
[6] *Ibid.*, p. 3.

locked people driven by an elemental urge to break through the ring of border states which shut it off from the sea." [7] This urge has been ascribed to the Russians by no less a person than F. D. Roosevelt, and Americans, mindful of the efforts of their own Middle Western States to gain access to the sea by way of the St. Lawrence and Mississippi Rivers, have tended to sympathize.

The wide acceptance of this thesis is undoubtedly due to its beautiful simplicity. It seems to be a common human weakness to prefer broad, sweeping generalizations about nations and peoples to careful, balanced appraisals. . . . The virus of geographic determinism, more prevalent, perhaps, among historians, but not wholly absent from the writings of geographers, appears to have dulled the instinct which normally should have led them to examine carefully the historical record of Russian expansion before accepting so pat an explanation. [8]

The Russians themselves have never been conscious of this urge.

In only one instance, that of Peter the Great's seizure of part of the coast of the Baltic Sea and his foundation of St. Petersburg early in the eighteenth century, does the desire to gain access to the seacoast appear to have motivated Russian policy. The southward expansion across the steppe sprang from the need for fertile soil to cultivate and for protection from the raids of Tartars and Cossacks. Russians spread slowly eastward through the forests of Siberia, not because they smelled the Pacific Ocean ahead of them, but because they wanted furs. The same search for seal and beaver took them across to Alaska and down through the long Alaskan Panhandle

to their farthest point in the latitude of 54°40′ (See Chapter 3).

It is hard, if not impossible, to demonstrate that any state has ever pursued a coherent policy of expansion over a long period of time. The mood of government and people, the balance of international forces, the technology of transportation and of war—all change in time and make any prolonged adherence to a set policy foolish if not impossible. Each separate act of expansion or aggression can be explained only in terms of itself; it is contingent on the decision makers responsible for it. To relate it to long-term policies or trends is an unfortunate survival from a nineteenth-century, romantic, historicist view of the course of historical change.

Other European Core Areas: So far, core areas have been identified in Switzerland, France, Great Britain, and Russia (Exhibit 58). The core area of Sweden lay in the lake-studded plains to the west of Stockholm; that of Denmark, on the islands near Copenhagen; that of Greece, in the plain of Attica; that of Italy, in the plains around Rome. And so on for other countries. The map (page 181) shows by shading the approximate core areas of European states. The core area of Germany, however, presents a problem, because political union, in any unitary sense, did not come until 1871. Before that there had been a nominal unity. Representatives of the German states, which were for practical purposes sovereign, sometimes met in their "Diets." These had no regular meeting place but were held most often in the cities of the middle Rhineland: Frankfurt, Mainz, Worms, Speyer, and, farther north, Köln (Cologne). This area was, furthermore, a kind of cultural focus of early Germany. Yet when Germany came to be united, it was not around this area, but around Brandenburg-Prussia as its nucleus, and with the Hohenzollern

[7] John A. Morrison, "Russia and Warm Water," *United States Naval Institute Proceedings,* vol. 78, pp. 1169–1179, 1952.
    [8] *Ibid.,* p. 1170.

Figure 32 Stockholm, capital of Sweden. In the foreground are the islands in Lake Mälaren on which the city grew up. It has since spread over the low hills, seen in this picture, to the north of the city, as well as to the south.
PHOTOGRAPH BY N. J. G. POUNDS

dynasty as its rulers. In this sense, the core area is away to the east, in and around Berlin. There has always been a spiritual difference between the Rhinelander and the Prussian, whom the former regarded as somewhat less cultured than himself. When the Rhinelanders passed under Prussian rule, they called themselves *Musspreussen,* "Prussians against their wish." The map thus shows two core areas for Germany, the role of the one being political, that of the other, at least in recent times, more cultural and social. Today, however, with the division of the German Empire into two republics, the more westerly core area is again acquiring a political role. The political capital of West Germany is at Bonn, on its northern margin, and Frankfurt is again becoming a focus of commercial life.

The core area of Italy is clearly the city of Rome and its surrounding plain, which have been the focus of a state of some kind for some twenty-five hundred years. The modern Italian state could not be regarded as complete until it had incorporated Rome. The economic focus of the state lies, however, in the cities of the northern plain, first and foremost in Milan. Even during the Middle Ages, the industrial and commercial growth of this area had made it a rival to Rome, which has retained the role of capital largely because it embodies the longest and noblest traditions of the republic.

Belgium provides a somewhat similar example. The state itself is something of an arbitrary creation; it is the territory that was left when the Netherlands had broken away to the north and France had encroached on the southern border of the Spanish (later Austrian) Netherlands. Brussels became, and has remained, the capital in virtue of its traditions and its central location. The focus of industrial development lies along the Sambre-Meuse Valleys, from Mons to Liege, and the noblest traditions of the Belgian state belong to the cities of Flanders to the north.

Spain, despite its superficial appearance of unity, is a divided country, patched together by the accident of marriage and inheritance. It has sprung from at least three core areas, two of them (northern Leon and northern Castile) in the northern part of the high plateau of the Meseta; the third, Aragon and Barcelona, in the Ebro Valley. The first two have to some degree

coalesced, but a deep cultural rift continues to separate them from the third.

Core Areas in Asia: The states of Asia have core areas, no less than those of Europe, around which they grew, though in some instances the state was overwhelmed by invaders and reborn, as it were, during the succeeding, less troubled times. Such rebirths were sometimes in different core areas, so that the focus of a state's activities appears to wander throughout its history. This was preeminently the case with China. The cradle of Chinese civilization lay in the northwest of modern

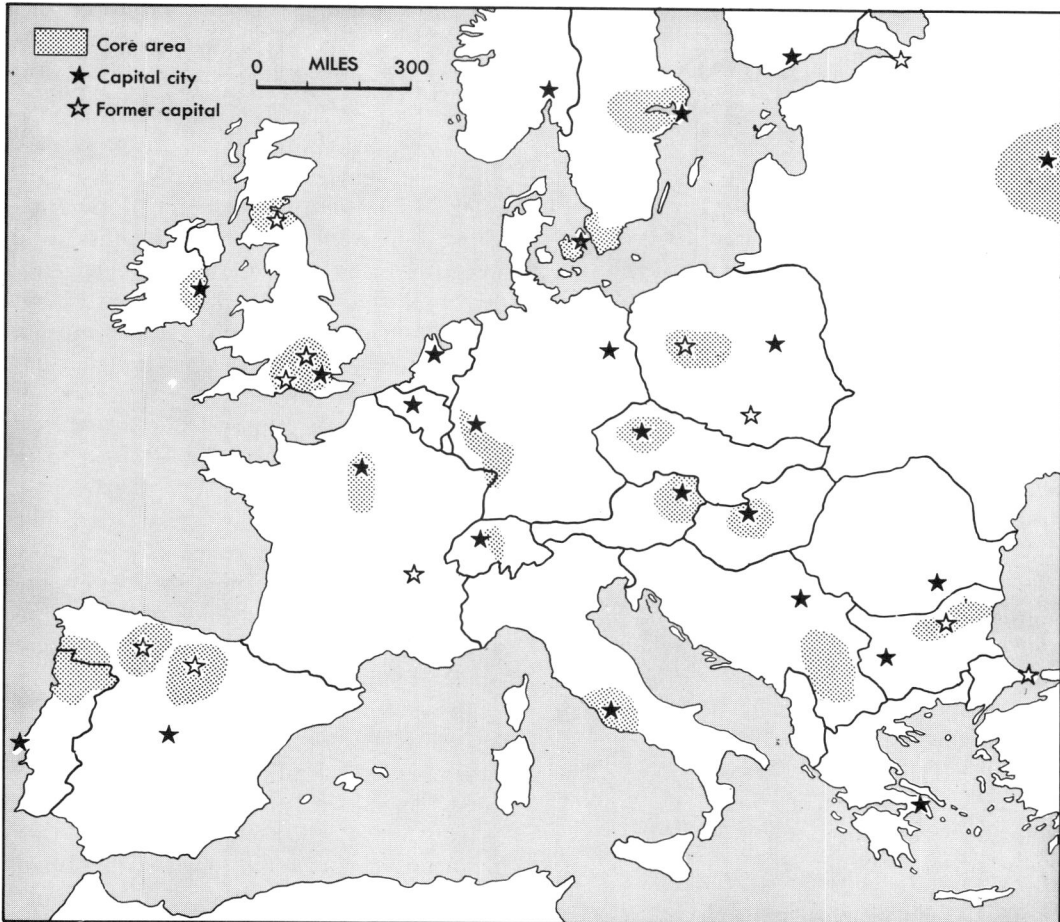

Exhibit 58 *Core areas in Europe.*

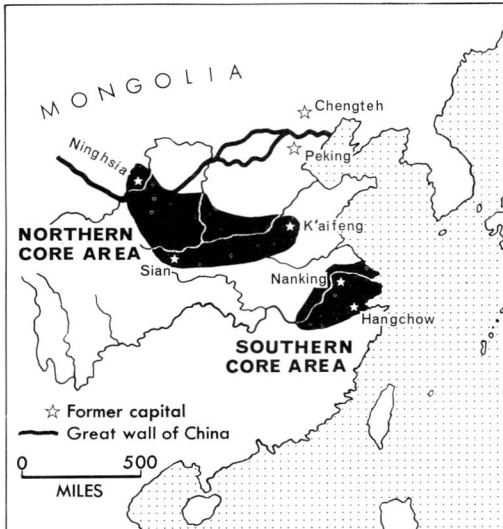

Exhibit 59   *Core areas of China*

China, in the valleys of the Hwang-ho and its tributaries (Exhibit 59). Here the loess was highly suited to primitive agriculture: "It is an unleached soil of great fertility, and both the resorting process of the wind and human agency can expose new surfaces, producing much the same effect as the renewal of the soil by the Nile floods." [9] Here were located the earliest capitals of China. As the state developed, it extended to the east and southeast. This advance brought the Chinese Empire into the Yang-tze Valley. Economic development came later here than in the valley of the Hwang-ho, but the milder climate and longer growing period allowed it to eclipse the more northerly valley as a source of food. The focus of the empire moved from the north to the center of China; and the capital was established first at Nanking, then at Hang-chow, and "Now the Yang-tze valley and the country to the south constituted one half of China in

[9] P. M. Roxby, "The Terrain of Early Chinese Civilisation," *Geography*, vol. 23, pp. 225–236, 1938.

every sense, for it was not only about equal in area to the rest, but was comparable in population and as a seat of Chinese civilization. Here the continuity of Chinese national life was preserved." [10]

But strong forces repeatedly pulled the center of Chinese political life back toward the north. Beyond the ancient centers of Chinese civilization in the valley of the Hwang-ho lay the grasslands of Mongolia, merging westward into the desert of Gobi. From these grasslands came the Mongol invaders and the Mongol dynasties they brought with them. They established their capital, not down south in the Yang-tze Valley, but close to the border of the steppe from which they had come. In the seventeenth century, the last of the dynasties, that of the Manchu, overthrew the Ming and established itself at Peking, which had become the "northern capital" under the earlier Mongol, or Yuan, dynasty. Peking remained the Chinese capital and the center of a third core area in the northeast, until the Manchu dynasty was overthrown in 1911. The capital then returned to Nanking, the "southern capital," but with a renewed growth of northern, that is, Soviet, influences upon Chinese political and social life, it has been reestablished in Peking.

Southeast Asia was never welded, like China, into a large unitary state. Many of the alluvial plains of the great rivers became the foci of states, which each covered more restricted areas: Cambodia, where the vast temple of Angkor Wat is evidence of the wealth and importance of the early city of Angkor; Thailand, where Ayutthaya, almost a hundred miles up the Chao Phrya River, was the early capital; and the middle Irrawaddy Valley, where Ava and Mandalay grew up as the early capitals of Burma.

[10] Vaughan Cornish, *The Great Capitals*, Methuen & Co., Ltd., London, 1922, p. 13.

The political unity of India was the creation of the British Raj, but various native dynasties had previously succeeded at times in controlling much of the area. Most controlled it from the Ganges Valley:

> The dominant position of the [Indo-] Gangetic Valley which makes it the core of India from every point of view is so obvious as not to require proof. . . . That Hindu opinion always viewed it as such is seen from the fact that not only is Ganges the sacred river *par excellence* of India but the area from Gaya to Mathura, from Sangam to Hardwar, is recognized by every one to be the holy land of Hinduism. Every dynasty . . . once it established its authority in its homeland dreamed of consolidating its rule by establishing itself in this area.[11]

British power came in by sea; its early bases were ports, on the coast or on navigable rivers, through which the products of India were shipped to the West. In India the flag followed trade, and political power spread outward from the trading posts. The port of Calcutta early acquired a predominant role and became the capital of British India. It was the nearest port to the Indian core area. In 1911 the British, yielding both to tradition and to expediency, shifted their capital from the coastal city of Calcutta to Delhi in the ancient core area of India.

Latin America: The states of Latin America, with the exception of Brazil, grew from the administrative divisions of the Spanish Empire. In this continent, with its small, scattered population of Indians, the Spaniards had selected the places of more than usual prosperity and promise for their own settlements. Here they established their provincial capitals and the centers of their missionary and other activities (Exhibit 60). In some parts of the continent

[11] K. M. Panikkar, *Geographical Factors in Indian History,* Bavan's Book University, Bombay, 1955, p. 25.

Exhibit 60   Core areas in South America.

their influence did not go far beyond these favored areas. The latter were in general centrally placed within the Provinces, and may fairly be regarded as the core areas of the future Latin-American republics. Those of Central America are similar, generally small basins, floored with a fertile soil and lying at a considerable elevation above the hot, humid lowlands. In only one instance, that of Mexico City, did the core area of the Spanish Province coincide with a previous center of dense population and developed culture.

North America: The two states of North America, the United States and Canada, were both developed by immigrants from Europe. In neither instance did they take over any center of native Indian population and make it a focus of their own settlement and culture. They settled the whole eastern seaboard, from Labrador to

Florida. The location of their settlements had not been carefully planned, and at least the earliest comers landed and created their homes wherever winds and currents took them. Nevertheless, during the first century of the settlement most of the desirable areas were taken, and some, which proved to be less rewarding than had been anticipated, were abandoned. Gradually five separate foci of settlement crystallized: the valley of the St. Lawrence River, the area around the Bay of Fundy, the Boston region, the coastal plain from New York south to Baltimore, and tidewater Virginia. "Communication between the North American settlements was slight and unfriendly. Intercolonial roads were almost negligible and only a few men and a few colonial newspapers fostered acquaintanceship by sea. . . . The most nearly impassable chasm between one group of North Americans and another . . . lay between the French and the British colonists." [12] In time the English-speaking Colonies coalesced, but without completely losing either their identity or the rivalry which characterized their early relations. United from 1787 by a federal constitution, they devised by means of colonizing and incorporating into the United States the whole vast area that stretched westward to the Pacific. The whole Middle West and South derived, politically and socially, from the core areas along the Atlantic seaboard. So also did the Pacific Coast settlements, especially those of California. But these, elevated to statehood long before the intervening mountain area, became a secondary core area upon which the Western States came to depend.

Development in Canada took a similar course. The core area was the St. Lawrence lowland, the strip of cultivable, if not fertile, land which stretched up river from Quebec to above Montreal. Here the settlers and their culture were predominantly French. The settlements which grew up later in Ontario derived from the English tradition, not from the French of Lower Canada, and they must be counted as a secondary core area from which the thin scatter of settlers of the Prairie and Rocky Mountain Provinces largely derived.

South Africa: In its development the Union of South Africa bears a certain resemblance to Canada. The forms of government were introduced from Europe; the earliest settlements were coastal or at least lay along navigable rivers. In both two separate core areas developed, corresponding to a cultural diversity among the immigrants. The European settlements along the coast of South Africa, foremost amongst them Capetown and Durban, were the original nuclei from which settlement spread into the interior of the continent. But the Africaans-speaking people, dissociating themselves from the other white settlers of South Africa, formed a separate and distinct core area on the High Veld of the interior, between Bloemfontein and Pretoria. Today there are two conflicting core areas, the coastal cities and the High Veld.

Most political territorial divisions in the rest of Africa are so arbitrary that one looks in vain for core areas around which they could have crystallized. Only Egypt, the Sudan, and Ethiopia may be said to have core areas in the sense of regions around which the states have coalesced and in which are embodied the traditions and ideologies of the state. In Egypt the Nile Valley upstream from Cairo has been the focus of a state since the union of the Egyptian kingdoms in the earliest historic times. Ethiopia (Abyssinia) grew around the mountain-girt basin of Addis Ababa;

[12] J. B. Brebner, *North Atlantic Triangle,* Yale University Press, New Haven, Conn., 1945, p. 32.

Sudan, around the fertile, irrigable lands along the White and Blue Niles, where they join at Khartoum. Politicogeographical development in Africa is immature, in so far as a sense of nationhood is far from inspiring all the people of each political division of the continent. Undoubtedly, incipient core areas can be detected: the northern plains of Nigeria, the Kenya Highlands, the coastal lands of Lake Victoria, the Ashanti lands of southern Ghana, the high plateau of Southern Rhodesia, the Katanga region of the Congo Republic. Whether the future state system of Africa will be built around these and other nuclei as a series of coherent units no one can tell.

Australia: Australia similarly received its people, its culture, and its governmental institutions from Europe, and here also a number of separate areas of settlement grew up around the margin of the continent. The more favored of these developed; others were abandoned or remained of slight importance. Among some half-dozen areas of coastal settlement which attained a considerable importance, two may be regarded as core areas, the regions around Sydney, in New South Wales, and Melbourne, in Victoria, with the Perth area of western Australia making up a third.

Summary: Most states in which the sense of nationhood is strongly developed have grown by a process of accretion around a nucleus, or core area. In most of these instances the core area has remained constant and usually contains today, as it did when the process of territorial expansion began, the central organs of government. A second—and smaller—group of states have grown from two or more core areas. These may be further subdivided according to whether the core areas do, or do not, represent contrasting or conflicting cultural groups. The several coastal nuclei of the United States, Brazil, Australia, and

New Zealand, in spite of a certain rivalry between them, can certainly be said to represent the same cultural tradition. Two or more core areas can also be distinguished in Japan, Indonesia, and Vietnam. On the other hand, in a number of states two or more separate core areas represent separate national groups. A list of these states would include:

State	Core areas
Yugoslavia	Zagreb (Croat), Old Serbia
Canada	Quebec, Ontario
South Africa	Capetown-Durban, Veld
Ecuador	Quito, Guayaquil
Spain	Castile, Aragon-Catalonia
Germany	Middle Rhineland, Brandenburg
Peru	Lima, high Andean plateau
Rumania	Wallachian Plain, Moldavia, Transylvania

A final group of states is made up of those which have at different periods in their history formed and re-formed around separate and distinct core areas. China, with its early focus moving between the Wei-ho Valley, the lower Yang-tze Valley, and lastly the region of Peking, is perhaps the best example. India, with the middle Ganges Valley repeatedly reasserting itself, despite the attraction of a coastal location, as the focus of Indian unity, is another. The case of Germany, with the early, abortive attempt to build a state around the cultural traditions of the middle Rhineland and the subsequent and more successful attempt to create it as an extension of the political power of Brandenburg-Prussia, is a more complex example.

Outside the category of states which have been created around core areas is the list of a dozen or more which have been created by an outside agency without adapting to the organization or consulting the desires of the local peoples. Albania was created at a conference table, at which no Albanian was present, in London in 1913. The boundaries of Ghana derive from the agreements made between the British government and the French and German governments regarding the boundaries of their colonial territories. Belgium grew from the relict area that the Spanish authorities succeeded in holding during the wars of the late sixteenth century. The extent to which a nationalism has grown to fill out the limits of the state, however arbitrary may have been the origin of the latter, varies greatly. It cannot be doubted that the Belgian consciousness of nationhood is real, though not so articulate as that of France or the Netherlands. That of Albania is being formed, and that of some of the new African republics is both immature and inarticulate, still submerged beneath tribal loyalties.

CAPITAL CITIES

The role of the political capital has changed through time. When we speak of Gniezno as capital of the early Poland or of Paris as capital of the early Capetian kingdom of France, we must not think of these cities as fulfilling a role in any way analogous to that of modern London, Rome, or Tokyo. Medieval, and earlier, administrative capacity was small, transportation undeveloped, and the field of government operation limited. The early king, whether in Europe or elsewhere, was surrounded by his officers of state and by courtiers and servants, some necessary, many of them probably not. The mechanism of taxation was rudimentary and inefficient and the market undeveloped. The king was, in the medieval English phrase, expected "to live of his own," to travel from one of his personal estates to another, consuming the foodstuffs accumulated for him. In short it was easier to take the king to his food than the food to the king. The Anglo-Saxon chronicler describes how William I of England "held his court in Winchester at Easter . . . he was by the Pentecost at

Westminster. . . . Afterward he moved about so that he came by Lammas to Sarum [i.e., Salisbury]. . . ." [13] As the king moved, so also did his ministers, with their seals of office, clerks, scribes, and wagonloads of public records. The capital was wherever the king happened to be; medieval kings, no less than modern chiefs of state, had their "winter White Houses."

But the early ruler often had one place where he liked to stay, just as the Emperor Charlemagne loved his city of Aachen. Inevitably such a place received more care; its castle and churches were enlarged and improved, and the king spent an increasing part of his time there. In time his public records ceased to go on his travels with him and were left there. In England, the Tower of London, in France, the fortified palace of Paris, situated on an island in the river Seine, were chosen. The result of such steps was cumulative; more and more governmental business was concentrated in the capital. The appearance of democratic—or at least consultative—institutions reinforced the process. In England there was no going back on London, once Parliaments had begun to meet there.

The extension in modern times of the role of government, the multiplication of its functions, and the yet more rapid increase of its functionaries have given an ever-growing importance to the capital. Service industries have been established to meet the needs of officialdom and the entertainment and marketing industries to serve both. In this way the size of capital cities has grown sharply. In most modern states the capital is also the biggest city. In the twenty-five states of Europe,[14] the political capital is the largest city in no fewer than twenty-three. The exceptions are Switzerland, where the federal capital is Bern, the fourth largest city, and West Germany,

[13] *Anglo-Saxon Chronicle,* sub. 1085.
[14] This excludes the four microstates.

where the capital was located in the relatively small city of Bonn, as a temporary expedient.

The pattern in Asia is similar. Where the capital is not also the largest city, there are exceptional reasons for this. In Turkey Istanbul, the former capital, remains the largest city, and Ankara, the present capital, is second. Tel Aviv, the present seat of the Israeli government, is larger than the Jewish-held sector of Jerusalem. Delhi, the capital of India only since 1911, is smaller than any of the great ports, Bombay, Calcutta, and Madras. In China the largest city is the port of Shanghai, with Peking, the capital, in second place. In Latin America, without exception, the capital is also the largest city.

The Role of the Capital: The capital is normally the seat of the government. It contains the official residence of the chief of state, whether this is an executive officer or a head whose functions are mainly ceremonial, the buildings which house the legislature or other representative body, and also at least the higher echelons of the executive departments of government. A close juxtaposition of these is normally necessary to secure the minimum of integration and collaboration that is achieved. In the capital also are usually to be found the heads of the judiciary, the supreme court or courts of appeal, depending upon the constitution of the particular state.

In the capital also there gather the representatives or head officers of a large number of associations, institutions, and groups which find it necesary to have frequent and speedy contact with government agencies. These would include labor and commercial organizations, educational institutions, and a great variety of bodies, official and unofficial, dedicated in some way or other to national prosperity or welfare.

In all states the functions of government have increased with the abandonment of the early nineteenth-century philosophy of *laissez faire*. The resulting concentration in the capital has been such as, in many instances, to create an undesirable pressure on space and to increase the vulnerability of the whole governmental machine. In consequence, there has been a tendency toward decentralization of at least the administrative divisions. In Great Britain, for example, the large and growing service departments are mainly housed outside London, some of them in places to which they were evacuated during the Second World War. It is unlikely that much decentralization at the executive level will take place.

The capital is also the meeting place of the representatives of the state with those of other states. The embassies and legations of friendly states are normally located there. The agents of foreign banks and commercial houses establish offices there, in part, at least, because of the facility of contacts with government.

The capital or its immediate vicinity usually contains also the household gods of the state. In European states the capital is in most instances the seat of the state church or of the dominant religious group in the state. In England, Canterbury, seat of the Primate of All England, is about fifty miles east of London. The premier see of the Catholic Church in Hungary is at Esztergom, about thirty miles northwest of the capital, Budapest. In Poland, the archiepiscopal see was moved from Gniezno, the first capital of the state, to Warsaw, its present capital. This pattern is normal in Europe. It also occurs in the areas where the Orthodox Church is dominant, with the patriarch or exarch normally residing at the seat of the lay power in the state.

In the Christian churches the boundaries of ecclesiastical jurisdictions tend generally to conform to those of civil jurisdiction, as in fact they have tended to do since the sees of the early bishops were made to conform with the limits of the Roman provinces. Changes in the boundaries of states are not followed immediately by changes in those of the episcopal sees. Indeed, the lay officials of the state have sometimes complained of the slowness of the church in giving this kind of recognition of the territorial changes effected. In general churches have been reluctant thus to recognize boundary changes unless assured that these would have some degree of permanence.

However universal the church may be, the state has usually tried to derive from it some sanction for its own existence and for the values which it represents. In no state has the nation been more completely identified with a church than in Poland and Hungary. In Yugoslavia, the difference between Serbs and Croats is, in large measure, a religious one, and the heads of their respective churches are established in the two capitals.

Location of the Capital: The normal and logical location for the capital is in the core area, where it can the most easily embody and represent the traditions and historical values of the state. In such a location the present government may derive a kind of sanction from the presence there of the evidences of centuries of continuous rule. Paris, London, Rome, Delhi, Cairo, Athens, Stockholm, Moscow, and many others are themselves monuments to the past of their respective nations.

More complex are the instances where the capital has been shifted from its ancient or original site to one better adjusted to later needs. In some instances these reflect rapidly changing requirements. A simple instance is the shift of the capitals of Burma and Thailand from the original inland locations at Mandalay and Ayutthaya to coastal locations, at Rangoon and Bangkok, respectively. In India the traditional site had lain between Patna and Delhi. Under

British influence it was moved to the port of Calcutta; now it has returned to Delhi:

. . . which was the natural site for the capital of a continental empire including the basins of both the Ganges and the Indus.

Delhi was, of course, not merely a natural site; it was also an historic one. The Mughal predecessors of the British rulers of India had governed India from Delhi since the days of Shah Jahan (imperabat A.D. 1628–59), and before Shah Jahan's day they had governed it from the neighbouring city of Agra, which was situated, like Delhi, on the banks of the Upper Jumna. The Mughals, like the British, had been aliens in the Hindu World on which they had imposed a universal state, but, unlike the British, they had never tried to govern India from a site on the threshold across which they had made their entry.[15]

In such shifts there is to be seen an interesting conflict between the desire for the capital to remain rooted in its ancestral soil and the urge to move toward a frontier, that is, in the direction of influences, commercial and cultural, from which the state hopes to profit:

Moscow was temporarily deprived of her prerogative as a result of her rulers' decision to open their doors to the West. . . . Moscow was compelled, for more than two hundred years, to see her empire governed from a capital which was not only given a new name but was planted on virgin soil on a far-distant site. . . . The transfer of the capital of the Russian Empire by Peter the Great from Moscow in the heart of Holy Russia to Saint Petersburg on the banks of the Neva, within a stone's throw of the Baltic, is comparable to Nicator's choice in its cultural and geographical aspects.[16] In this case, as in that, the seat of government of a land-locked empire was

[15] A. J. Toynbee, *A Study of History,* Oxford University Press, New York, 1954, vol. 7, p. 195.
[16] The allusion is to the choice of Seleucus Nicator of the Syrian city of Antioch, in touch with the civilization of classical Greece, rather than a completely inland site on the river Tigris.

planted in a remote corner of the empire's domain in order to provide the capital with easy access by sea to the sources of an alien civilization which the imperial government was eager to introduce into its dominions. In its political aspect, however, Peter's act was much more audacious than Nicator's; for, in seeking to supplant Moscow by Saint Petersburg, Peter was ignoring the feelings of the Orthodox Christian ruling element in Moscovy with a brusqueness reminiscent of the revolutionary acts of Julius Caesar. . . .[17]

The shift of certain Asiatic capitals to the coast are further examples of this latter movement. At the beginning of the eighteenth century the capital of Russia was moved from Moscow, the historic capital, to St. Petersburg, the newly built "window on the West," a shift symbolic of the newfound desire of the Czars for contacts with western Europe. By the time of the Communist Revolution, this westward orientation had exhausted its role; the national tradition was now to be emphasized, and the capital was restored to Moscow.

The movement in Turkey shows a more complex pattern of movement. The Ottoman Turks conquered Asia Minor in the fourteenth century and established their capital successively at sites farther and farther west until in 1326 it came to Brusa. In the fourteenth century they invaded Europe and overran the Balkan peninsula. Their capital was moved to Edirne (Adrianople), in the Maritza Valley. It remained here until it was moved to Constantinople, which fell to the Turks in 1453. Constantinople (Istanbul) was well placed to serve as capital of an empire which stretched from the Danube to the Euphrates and the Nile. When the European possessions had largely been lost and the Asiatic seriously diminished, Constantinople ceased to be as suitably placed geographically.

After 1923 Turkey became an essentially Turkish state, with very few non-Turkish peoples. The new ruler, Mustafa Kemal Attaturk, emphasized the narrowly national aspects of the state. Constantinople, whose traditions were mainly Christian and Greek, was abandoned for Ankara, a site in the midst of the plateau of Anatolia, where essentially Turkish traditions could be developed.

Brazil is in process of moving its capital from the cosmopolitan, coastal city of Rio de Janeiro to a site in the virgin bush of the interior. The new capital is being called Brasilia, a name which emphasizes the strong vein of nationalism which brought it into being.

In the previous paragraphs we have seen a peculiar contest for the state capital between an area, which may be said to represent the state's *national* aspirations, either the core area from which the nation sprang (Moscow, Delhi) or some place whose ethos is wholly national (Ankara, Brasilia), and one better placed to open up vistas of the wider world (St. Petersburg, Calcutta, Nanking, Constantinople). There is, however, yet one more element in this picture. What of the state which has come to be dominated by its own frontiersmen, or, in Toynbee's phrase, "the Capital Cities of Marchmen Empire-builders"?

Ancient Rome may serve as a simple example. It was founded on the south bank of the river Tiber, on the very northern edge of the plain of Latium. The latter was the core area of the early Roman state, and Rome itself was one of its frontier defenses. In Toynbee's words:

Rome had won her spurs by taking over from the Etruscans the wardenship of the Italian marches of the Hellenic World over against the Gauls, as Thebes had won hers by taking over from Al Kab the wardenship of the First Cataract of the Nile over against the

[17] Toynbee, *op. cit.*, vol. 7, p. 221.

barbarians of Nubia.[18] Like Thebes, again, Rome had afterwards turned her arms inwards and imposed political unity on the society of which she was a member.[19]

Two well-known European examples of the same historical process are Berlin and Vienna. Berlin grew up as the capital of a small frontier, or march, state, the Mark of Brandenburg, whose function it was to defend the eastern borders of medieval Germany. At this time the focus of German culture lay 250 miles to the west. Brandenburg stood toward it in much the same relationship as Ohio and Kentucky did to the Atlantic seaboard cities a century and a half ago. The difference was that Berlin turned and devoured what it was set to protect. It was as if our own expanding Western frontier had been more formative even than Frederick Jackson Turner had supposed and had drawn the focus of American political life, if not also of commercial, to the banks of the Missouri. Vienna was similarly founded as the capital of the *Ostmark*, or Eastern March, protecting the southeastern approaches to Germany. For a period it too turned back on and dominated politically what it was set to protect. But in the struggle which ensued between the two march states, represented by Berlin and Vienna, for control of Germany, the former won handsomely. German unity was unfortunately built around Berlin, not Vienna.

Divided Capitals: It has been assumed that the capital of a unitary state is a single city from which the functions of government are carried on. There may be some degree of dispersion of administrative offices, but the government as a whole is generally thought to be centralized. In at least two instances, however, the capital is

divided. In the Netherlands, Amsterdam is the titular capital and official residence of the monarch, but the seat of the government and the meeting place of the parliament are in The Hague. A similar division has taken place in Bolivia. Here the small town of Sucre is the legal capital, as well as the seat of the judiciary and the Archbishop, while the legislature and all governmental offices are located in the much larger city of La Paz. The Union of South Africa, which, as we have already seen, is really a unitary state, has three capitals, in each of which one essential function of government is carried on: Capetown, Bloemfontein, and Pretoria. The reason appears to be to satisfy the desires of both Africaans- and English-speaking South Africans. Capetown is the largest English-speaking city in the Union; Bloemfontein and Pretoria are the chief cities, respectively, of the Africaans-speaking Orange Free State and Transvaal.

On the island of Taiwan (Formosa) there is a somewhat similar division. Taipeh is the seat of the Nationalist government, which claims to be the legitimate government of the whole of China. To the Taipeh authorities Taiwan is only one of some twenty-five Provinces, though admittedly the only one under its authority. The provincial capital of Taiwan is Taichung,[20] and it is from this latter city that the island is itself administered. How long this pretentious and costly dichotomy can be maintained is uncertain.

Federal Capitals: Federation, as a mode of government, is generally a concession to the size or to the cultural variety of a state. However weak the central government may be in a federal state (the extreme case is Australia), a capital city is nevertheless necessary. Its location has

---

[18] The desert area of southern Egypt and northern Sudan.

[19] Toynbee, *op. cit.,* vol. 7, p. 216.

[20] In reality it is Chung-hsing-hsin-ts'un, near Taichung.

often been a matter of vigorous dispute at the time of the formulation of the constitution. The existence of local rivalries is, in a sense, implicit in the existence of a federal constitution. We have only to think for example of the rivalries that led in the United States to the choice, as a compromise, of 100 square miles in Virginia and Maryland.[21] We are all familiar with the expedients adopted to keep this District of Columbia and its city of Washington politically neutral, even to the extent of allowing its citizens no political representation.

The choice of a location for the federal capital has been difficult also in Canada, Australia, and Brazil, as in each case conflicting interests had to be balanced.

The Canadian case is particularly interesting, owing to the relatively even strength and bitter hostility of English- and French-speaking Canadians. In 1858 the practice was adopted of spending four sessions of the parliament alternately in Toronto (Province of Ontario) and in Quebec. As a permanent capital no existing city could win acceptance. A small village on the Ottawa River, near the language boundary, was suggested. "It was a reasonable geographical compromise, but it satisfied none of the more ambitious aspirants."[22] It was not until the adoption of the federal constitution, in 1867, that this same site on the Ottawa River became the city of Ottawa, the capital of the Dominion of Canada.[23]

In Australia, the rivalry was between the coastal cities of Sydney and Melbourne. The constitution of Australia provided for the establishment of a capital on territory to be acquired, like the District of Columbia, by the federal government. Fear of domination by Sydney was reflected in a clause in the constitution to the effect that "the federal capital must be in territory acquired by the Commonwealth, within the State of New South Wales, but *not less than one hundred miles from Sydney*."[24] In 1911 a site was chosen amid the Blue Mountains, and the city of Canberra was founded. It remains, like Washington and Ottawa, an essentially governmental city and has not become a significant center of industry and commerce.

The choice of a capital in other federal states in the modern world has presented less difficulty. In India, there was no good alternative to Delhi, nor, in Argentina and Mexico, to Buenos Aires and Mexico City, respectively. Brazil has, however, had greater difficulties. The number of separate and in some ways antagonistic core areas along the coast made desirable the selection of a "neutral" area as capital. The first republican constitution of 1889 required such a choice, but it was not until 1936 that the question was settled and not until 1956 that building was begun:

The delay was largely due to opposition to the whole idea of the move from Rio [de Janeiro], especially on the part of the Press, which was firmly entrenched there. Rio [de Janeiro] had become a thriving cosmopolitan city of two and a half million people, but it was essentially a commercial city, and the Government was anxious to be master in its own capital. Moreover, Rio [de Janeiro] had become overbuilt and suffered increasingly from traffic congestion. Another argument in favour

[21] As is well known, the area to the south of the Potomac River was not used and was eventually sold back to Virginia.

[22] *Cambridge History of the British Empire*, vol. 6, *Canada*, Cambridge University Press, New York, 1930, p. 346.

[23] The term *Dominion of*, adopted in 1867, has recently been removed from the state's official title.

[24] *Cambridge History of the British Empire*, vol. 7, pt. i, *Australia*, Cambridge University Press, New York, 1933, p. 511.

of the move was that the partly unexplored hinterland of Brazil was a region of enormous potential wealth, undeveloped because of the lack of centres of communication, marketing, and administration.[25]

Capitals and National Unity: The capital in most states is thought of as something more than the seat of the legislature and of the administration. It has also the role of focusing sentiment and strengthening the bonds which hold the nation together. Its monuments and its ceremonies assume a great importance. We have noted already certain instances of the shift of the capital to bring it to an area which best exemplifies the nation's concept of itself. The choice of Ankara in Turkey, the return to Moscow, the building of Brasilia, and, most recent of all, the shift of the Pakistani capital from Karachi, cosmopolitan and commercial, to Islamabad, near Rawalpindi and close to the Northwest Frontier. For the same reason the Germans would, if they could, move the seat of their government from Bonn to Berlin and the Israelis would move their capital from Tel Aviv to Jerusalem.

If one of the roles of the capital is to unify, a central location might be thought the best. Many successful capitals, notably Washington, are quite eccentric. But a central location has sometimes been chosen merely because it was central. The centrality of Ankara was in its favor, but the clearest case is the selection of Madrid, in the center of the Iberian peninsula, in the sixteenth century. The problems of disunity were great, but it is doubtful that Madrid has contributed significantly to their solution.

[25] *The Times* (London), Mar. 17, 1958.

BIBLIOGRAPHY

Bowman, I.: *The New World*, World Book Company, Yonkers, New York, 1928.

Cornish, Vaughan: *The Great Capitals*, Methuen & Co., Ltd., London, 1922.

Dickinson, R. E.: *The West European City*, Routledge and Kegan Paul, Ltd., London, 1951.

East, W. G.: *An Historical Geography of Europe*, Methuen & Co., Ltd., London, 1935.

Fryer, D. W.: "The 'Million City' in Southeast Asia," *G.R.*, vol. 43, pp. 474–494, 1953.

James, Preston E., and Speridiao Faissol: "The Problem of Brazil's Capital City," *G.R.*, vol. 46, pp. 301–317, 1956.

Jefferson, Mark: "The Law of the Primate City," *G.R.*, vol. 29, pp. 226–232, 1939.

Lowenthal, David: "The West Indies Chooses a Capital," *G.R.*, vol. 48, pp. 336–364, 1958.

Murphey, Rhoads: "New Capitals of Asia," *Economic Development and Cultural Change*, vol. 5, pp. 216–243, 1957.

Robson, Charles B., ed.: *Berlin—Pivot of German Destiny*, University of North Carolina Press, Chapel Hill, N.C., 1960.

Roxby, P. M.: "The Terrain of Early Chinese Civilisation," *Geography*, vol. 23, pp. 225–236, 1938.

Spate, O. H. K.: "Factors in the Development of Capital Cities," *G.R.*, vol. 32, pp. 622–631, 1942.

Toynbee, A. J.: *A Study of History*, especially vols. 1 and 7, Oxford University Press, New York, 1954.

Whittlesey, Derwent: *The Earth and the State*, Henry Holt and Company, Inc., New York, 1939.

8 THE GEOGRAPHY

OF ADMINISTRATIVE AREAS

We squared the country for liberty laying it off
With the post plumb on the section lines and the fences
Following due west from the creeks of Kentucky
To counties bigger than Delaware: christened for congressmen.
ARCHIBALD MACLEISH, LAND OF THE FREE

ALL STATES, WITH THE EXCEPTION ONLY OF THE VERY SMALLEST, ARE divided for purposes of internal administration into smaller unit areas. In general, these are known with precision, and in most countries they form a hierarchy with graduated functions and responsibilities. Small unit areas, each of only a few square miles, are grouped into larger areas. Sometimes the latter rank next below the state government itself; sometimes one or more additional levels of responsibility are interposed. Each unit area, however humble its status in the political hierarchy and however trifling its functions, constitutes a politically organized area and as such is susceptible of geographical study and analysis.

The study of politically organized areas can be approached from two points of view. The first and more geographical is that of the shape and size of these administrative units and the ways in which those of the lower levels of responsibility are fitted within the boundaries of those higher in the scale. The second is the division of responsibility between the several levels of local government and the state itself. These two aspects of local government areas are inseparable, though greater emphasis will in these pages be placed on the former.

THE HIERARCHY OF LOCAL GOVERNMENT AREAS

In the following pages the hierarchy of politically organized areas will be examined for the United States and for certain other countries. An attempt will be made to arrive at some correlation between the size and function of these areas and to establish empirically their desirable range of size.

United States: Let us look first at the geographical organization of local government in the States of the United States, as these may be regarded as equivalent in size to many of the world's sovereign states (Exhibit 61). All States are divided into counties. The number of counties varies from State to State. Only Alaska does not have an over-all county organization, while Rhode Island, itself little larger than many counties, is not organized on a county basis for administrative purposes. There are 3,051 counties, divided between the forty-eight States of the continental United States. Texas has 254 counties and Delaware only 3. The average area of a county is 975 square miles, but the range of size

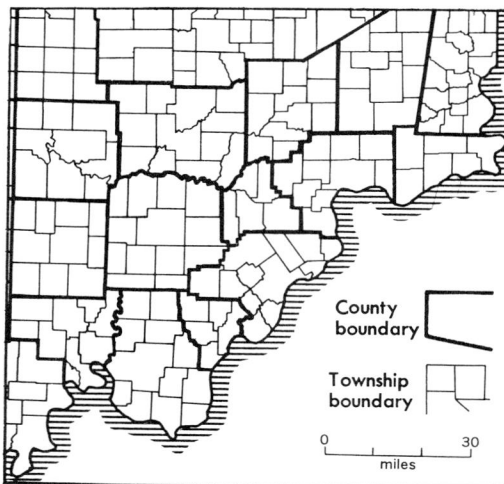

County boundary

Township boundary

0   30
miles

Exhibit 61 *County and township in the United States.*

is very great. The largest is San Bernardino County in California, with 20,131 square miles, and the smallest are a group of counties in Virginia, each with less than 100 square miles.[1] In general, the area of the counties bears a very rough relationship to the value of the land and the density of population. They are largest in the desert regions of the West; smallest in the urbanized East. But this correlation is of diminishing validity. County boundaries have changed little since they were first established, but population has grown in the meanwhile, and resources have been developed. San Bernardino County, which was once made up largely of mountains and desert, now contains such large and growing cities as Redlands and San Bernardino itself.

In almost a third of the continental United States, the counties are divided into towns or townships, the so-called minor civil divisions. In all twenty-one states are divided, wholly or in part, into these smaller units. In New England, the town was the original unit of settlement, which managed its own schools, built its own roads, and managed its other services. As settlement grew more dense, many of the original towns were divided, giving us today towns with the designations of *Upper* and *Lower, North* and *South*. The average size of the New England town has come to be about 30 square miles. In shape the towns are irregular, deriving from the needs and the activities of the original settlers. The town organization spread southward into the Middle Atlantic States, where in general it covered larger unit areas than in the more densely settled New England States.

From here the town organization spread westward across the Appalachian Mountains into the plains of the Middle

[1] They are Arlington, 24 square miles; Elizabeth City, 56; Mathews, 87; Warwick, 71.

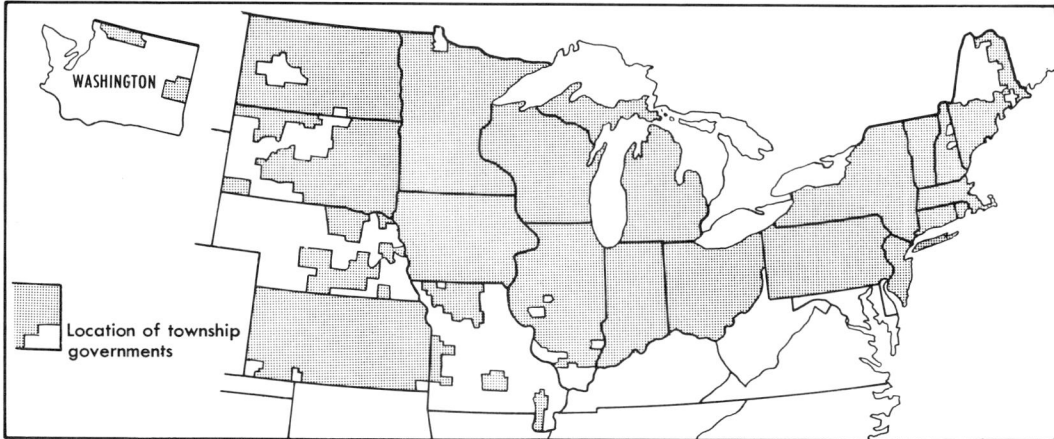

Exhibit 62   *Map of the township area in the United States.*

West (Exhibit 62). This settlement was largely preceded by the land survey. The land was divided into square units, 6 miles by 6, and subdivided into square-mile sections, each of which constituted one, two, or four farms, according to the physical conditions of the terrain. As the pattern of towns or townships is traced across New York State and Pennsylvania, it becomes more regular, until in much of the Middle West it conforms with the lines of the rectangular survey.

The congressional township of the Middle West is an area of land, 6 miles by 6, organized for the purpose of land settlement. It usually provided the framework of the civil townships, or units organized for purposes of local government. As R. G. Taylor has shown,[2] the two sometimes departed from one another. Movement and accessibility were necessary within the civil township, and its boundaries were sometimes altered from the surveyed lines of the congressional township and made to coincide with physical barriers to movement. Occasionally the civil-township lines

were drawn so as not to break up particular communities, such as religious organizations.

The township system never penetrated the South or the West, except parts of Washington. In the former the prevailing form of land occupance was originally in estates or plantations, worked by slave labor and organized on a quasi-feudal basis that left no room for the self-governing township. In the West, the sparseness of the population made the township unit unnecessary. In these areas (Exhibit 61) the county, known in Louisiana as the *parish*, is normally the lowest level of politically organized area.

The only conspicuous exception to this orderly hierarchy is the city. The American city is the creation of the State. It is normally incorporated by the action of the State legislature, which sets its limits and defines its functions. Occasionally the city may conform precisely with the limits of a county, in which case the city government absorbs the functions of the county. More often the city includes parts of counties, and its government may have an involved relationship with the county administration.

---

[2] Robert G. Taylor, *A Comparison of the Civil and Congressional Townships in Indiana*, dissertation, Indiana University, 1953.

The second aspect of the study of the hierarchy of politically organized areas is the apportionment between them of the functions of government. This is relevant here only because political geography is concerned with the function and purpose of politically organized areas. Within the United States the significance of the county organization varies greatly. The so-called "counties" of Rhode Island serve no administrative function, and in most of the Northeastern United States the sphere of action of the county is restricted by the existence of minor civil divisions. But in general, the county has considerable administrative powers, which include the maintenance of "county" roads, the control of schools, the assessment and collection of taxes, the licensing of automobiles, and sometimes a wide variety of other functions.

The role of the township, on the other hand, is of diminishing importance. It is too small an area to achieve the economies that would be possible in a larger area. The sense of community, which formerly existed within the township, is being eroded by the greater mobility of population and the increasing dependence upon distant cities for marketing and entertainment. Indeed, it is sometimes suggested that township government performs no function that could not be performed with greater administrative efficiency at the county level.

It is thus possible to represent the administrative hierarchy in the United States diagrammatically:

This is highly simplified. It is, in fact, impossible to represent fully in this way the relationship of cities and other incorporated areas to both county and State.

How do people regard these politically organized areas? Are they something more than an administrative convenience? Do they do more than provide a basis for some of the less pleasant operations of government, such as the selling of licenses and the collection of taxes? In short, do these unit areas focus the loyalties of the people who live in them? In the case of the minor civil divisions, they certainly do not; it might even be suggested that a significant part of the population does not know the name of the township in which it lives. But there are regional variations. The New England town may still attract a respect that is denied to the Middle Western township. Similarly the county is held in higher regard in the South than elsewhere. But never does the county rival the State. The State has its symbols, or iconography, its flag, seal, and motto, and such trivialities as its official flower and tree. Emotional attitudes toward the lesser territorial units have gradually been eroded, as transportation and communication have broadened peoples' mental horizons. The hierarchy of local government areas in the United States must now be compared with that in a selected group of other countries, in order to see what geographical features are common to local government in general.

Great Britain: The hierarchy of local government areas in Great Britain is somewhat more complex than that prevailing in

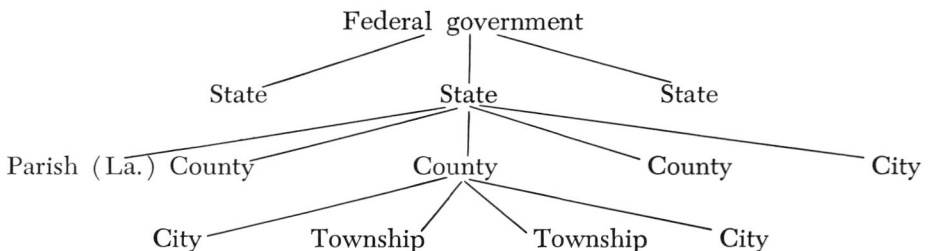

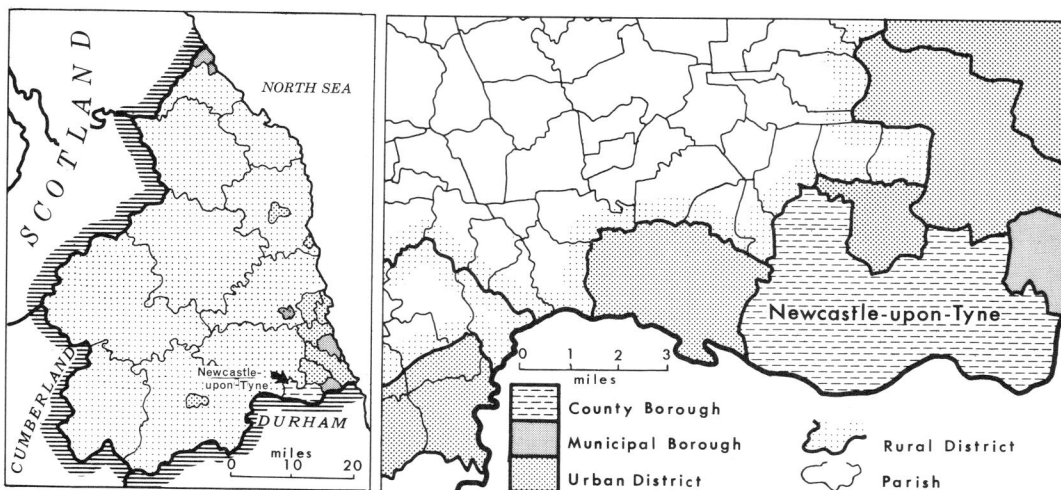

Exhibit 63   Local government units in the United Kingdom.

most of the States of the Union, largely because a heritage from a distant, and even tribal, past is present in many of them. The primary divisions are the counties (Exhibit 63).

	Number of counties	Average area, sq miles
England.............	40	1,258
Wales..............	13	617
Scotland............	33	903
Northern Ireland.....	6	874

The counties shown on the map are the historic ones (Figure 33). The oldest were tribal kingdoms during the Anglo-Saxon period. Others—the so-called "shires"—were created in the course of the reconquest of central and eastern England from the Danes in the tenth century. The thirteen counties of Wales were created after the conquest of Wales by the English during the later Middle Ages. Whatever their origin, they are by no means suited to modern administrative needs, and over the pattern of *historic* counties has come to be imposed

one of *administrative* counties. The two coincide wherever possible, but the rise of industry and the concentration of population in a few highly urbanized areas have necessitated the subdivision of many of the

Figure 33   Boundaries of local administrative divisions. In England the county boundaries are very clearly marked, and often the heraldic decoration serves to illustrate the intensity of county pride. PHOTOGRAPH BY N. J. G. POUNDS

historic counties to suit modern needs. Of the original forty counties of England seven have been split into two or more administrative counties. At the same time the larger cities—seventy-eight of them in 1960—have been administratively taken out of their counties and constituted as county boroughs, with a status equal to that of the counties.

Below the level of counties and county boroughs are the *municipal boroughs, urban districts,* and *rural districts.* The urban and rural districts, like the counties themselves, derive from a variety of Anglo-Saxon administrative divisions, such as the hundred and the wapentake, but as we know them today, they were established and their functions defined at the end of the nineteenth century. Urban districts are areas too built up and industrialized to be termed rural, but without a pronounced nucleus of population that would permit the establishment of a county or municipal borough. Besides the urban and rural districts are the municipal boroughs, with a distinct mechanism of local government but similar administrative functions.

At the base of the administrative hierarchy are the parishes. These were in origin ecclesiastical units, and they have not wholly lost this aspect of their function. They were areas large enough to require, and to be able to support, a church. This was a ready-made framework for the administration of the seventeenth-century poor law, and the parish councils subsequently were given other duties by the state, not all of them consistent with their original ecclesiastical function. In time, boundary changes were made by both church and state to bring the parish boundaries into accord with their different needs, so that now we have an organization of *civil* and another of *ecclesiastical parishes,* of which only the former has secular administrative functions. In rural areas the two often coincide. In cities, the civil parish, which still exists theoretically, has ceased to be a unit of public administration. In all, there are said to be approximately 11,800 civil parishes.

The hierarchy of administrative areas in England and Wales may be represented thus:

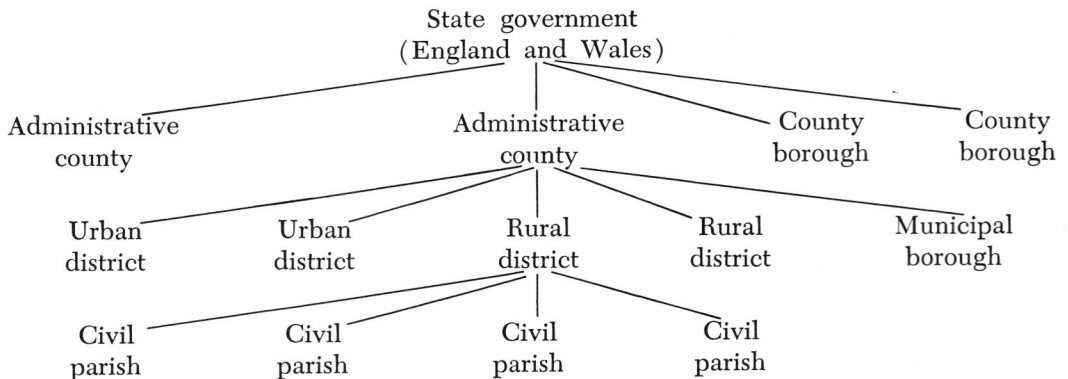

State government
(England and Wales)

| Administrative county | | Administrative county | County borough | County borough |

| Urban district | Urban district | Rural district | Rural district | Municipal borough |

| Civil parish | Civil parish | Civil parish | Civil parish |

62 administrative counties (including London)
83 county boroughs
318 municipal boroughs
564 urban districts
474 rural districts
About 11,800 civil parishes; average area, about 5 sq miles

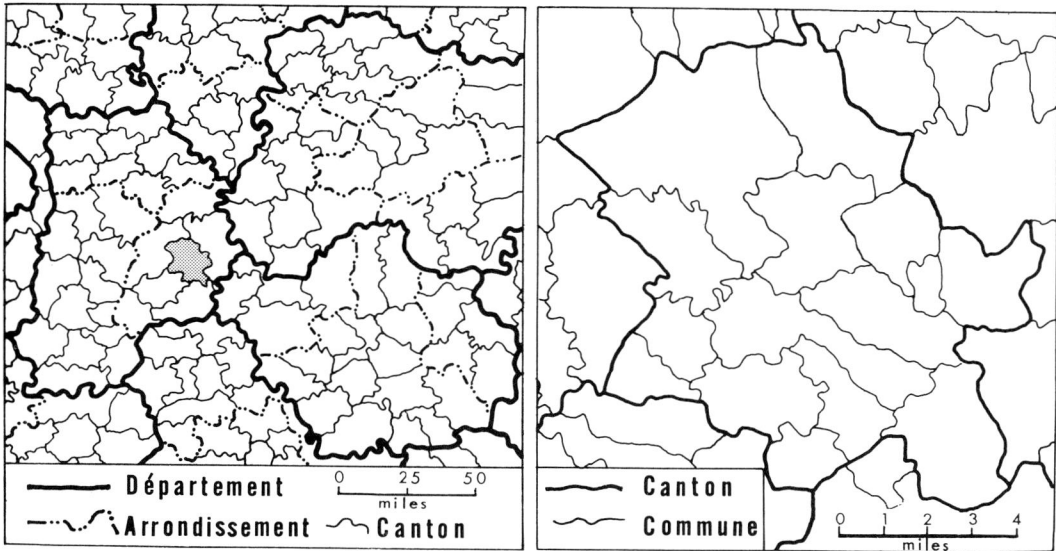

Exhibit 64 *Local government units in France.*

For each of the administrative areas described above there is an elected council, with wide powers, which may extend to certain quasi-legislative functions. The English practice has been for the state to delegate to local government all that can safely be delegated, subject only to review at the center. The differentiation of function between the three levels of local government is somewhat imprecise, but it is clear that the major functions and obligations rest with the administrations of the counties and county boroughs. These, for example, administer the educational system, maintain most of the roads, and assess and collect the local taxes. The county and county-borough boundaries are *strong* in so far as they break up into local units the major internal functions of government. Relatively, the boundaries separating urban and rural districts and municipal boroughs are *weak* because they divide up the operation of the less significant functions of government. The parish units, somewhat like the township units in the United States, are the least significant of all. Parish boundaries continue to be marked on topographical maps but no longer receive any recognition in the landscape.

All the local administrative areas are subject to change by act of the central government. There is a tendency for the number of urban and rural districts to diminish, and the boundaries of counties and county boroughs are not infrequently modified in the light of administrative convenience.

We discussed earlier the sense of loyalty which the different units of civil administration in the United States are able to evoke, and we noted that such emotions are minimal in the smallest civil divisions and small at all levels below that of the State. In Great Britain, with a longer history of civil administration, the changes in popular attitudes toward governmental divisions can be followed more closely. Formerly the parish was all-important. Its limits sometimes were forcibly impressed on the young by the custom of "beating the bounds," and parochial rivalries provided an outlet for ribald humor. This parish feeling has weakened but has by no means disappeared. The county has replaced the

Figure 34 *The marker which indicates the boundary between the* départements *of Moselle and of Meurthe et Moselle records also the line of the Franco-German boundary from 1871 until 1919.*   PHOTOGRAPH BY N. J. G. POUNDS

parish and, despite the recent manipulation of county boundaries, continues to attract a loyalty and affection that are unknown in this country. The British county has its iconography, mainly heraldic. Both sport and learned societies are organized on a county basis, and counties also formed the basis for the recruitment of the units of the British Army. The reorganization of the

army on a basis more in keeping with modern needs was widely regarded as an insult to the nation's deep-rooted feeling of belonging to a county.

France: The political geography of local administration in France differs sharply from that in Great Britain. Whereas local administration in Great Britain is the product of over a thousand years of development and change, that of France is the product of an arbitrary act by the French Constituent Assembly of 1790 (Exhibit 64). The former gives as much power as possible to the local unit; the latter centralized power in Paris. The former tries to perpetuate ancient regionalisms and territorial divisions; the latter, to obliterate them and to make France "one and indivisible." France was divided into eighty-three *départements;* their number has since been increased to ninety with changes in the boundaries of France itself. In an attempt to obliterate historical associations with the former French Provinces, the new *départements* were named for physical features, generally rivers, mountains, or hills.

Next below the *départements* are the *arrondissements,* and below the latter the *cantons,* and lastly the *communes.* The hierarchy of local government units in France may be represented in the following way:

State

Département   Département   Département

Arrondissement   Arrondissement   Arrondissement

Canton   Canton   Canton

Commune   Commune   Commune

In Metropolitan France, excluding Algeria, there were in 1960:
90 *départements;* average area, 2,366 sq miles

311 *arrondissements;* average area, 685 sq miles
3,081 *cantons;* average area, 70 sq miles
38,000 *communes;* average area, 6 sq miles

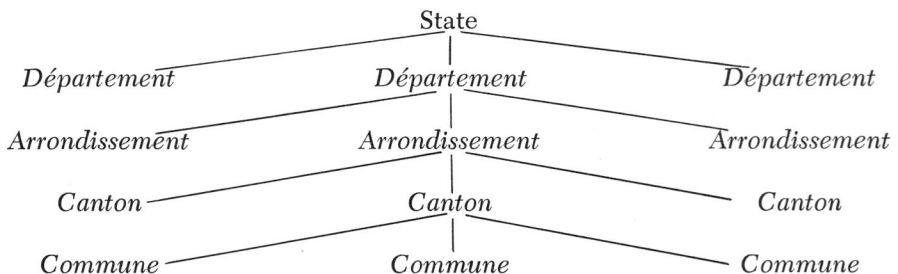

The only significant exception to this scheme consists of the city of Paris itself, which is made up of twenty *arrondissements,* divided into nine sectors, each with its own city government. Though very simple in its broad structure, the French hierarchy of administrative units has proved to have too many separate levels. *Arrondissement* and *canton* have little value, because there are few aspects of government that can be conveniently administered at this level, and they serve chiefly as units for election purposes. The burden of local government rests upon the *département* and the *commune,* each with its elected council and officials. The *préfet* (prefect) is the head of the government of the *département* and is the local representative of the state; the *maire* (mayor) is the elected official of the commune.

Changes in the boundaries between the local government areas of France have been of only minor significance since they were first established in the eighteenth century. This has been due in large measure to the extremely complex mechanism whereby such changes can be effected, but in part also to the smaller need for such changes in a country where there has been much less mobility of population than in either the United States or Great Britain.

The present structure of administrative units has failed to replace the ancient provinces in the minds and the affections of Frenchmen. It is not from Indre-et-Loire that a Frenchman would claim to come, but from Touraine. The iconography still belongs to the provinces, which today have no administrative function, not to the *départements,* least of all to the minor civil divisions of France.

Germany: The politico-geographical structure of German public administration has an outward resemblance to that of France, in that an orderly arrangement of units has been superimposed on an irregu-

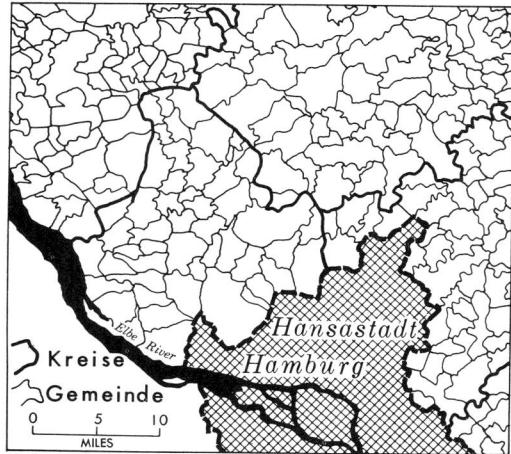

Exhibit 65   *Local government units in Germany.*

lar pattern of the historic States. The German system has, however, grown up over a period of almost a century and is not the result of a single governmental decision. West Germany is today a federal republic, in which the ten *Länder* form the autonomous units. The *Länder* are themselves divided into a comparatively small number of *Regierungsbezirke,* or administrative districts, and these into *Kreise,* or counties

Figure 35   *In Germany the boundaries of all levels of administrative areas are commonly marked by roadside signs. The Gemeinde of Meinholz, in the Kreis of Gifhorn, lies about seventy miles south of Hamburg.* PHOTOGRAPH BY N. J. G. POUNDS

(Exhibit 65). The *Kreise* are grouped into *Stadtkreise* (city–counties) and rural *Kreise.* At the lowest level are the *Gemeinden,* corresponding with the English parish and French *commune.* The smallest cities are ranked as *Gemeinden.* The cities of Hamburg and Bremen, which are constituted as separate *Länder,* have, like Paris, a city government distinct from the general administrative structure of the state. Each of the administrative levels has its elected councils and its own carefully formulated functions of government. The following illustrates the administrative hierarchy in the German Federal Republic:

ized, below the level of the state or federal unit, by areas at two levels of organization: a "county" level and a "*commune,*" "parish," or "township" level. Sometimes other units are interpolated either between the state and the county or between the county and the *commune,* but wherever these exist, their functions are somewhat limited and in a few instances their organization is an archaic survival. Table 15 on page 203 catalogues and attempts to equate these administrative districts in a number of states.

Although there is a considerable degree of variation within any one country

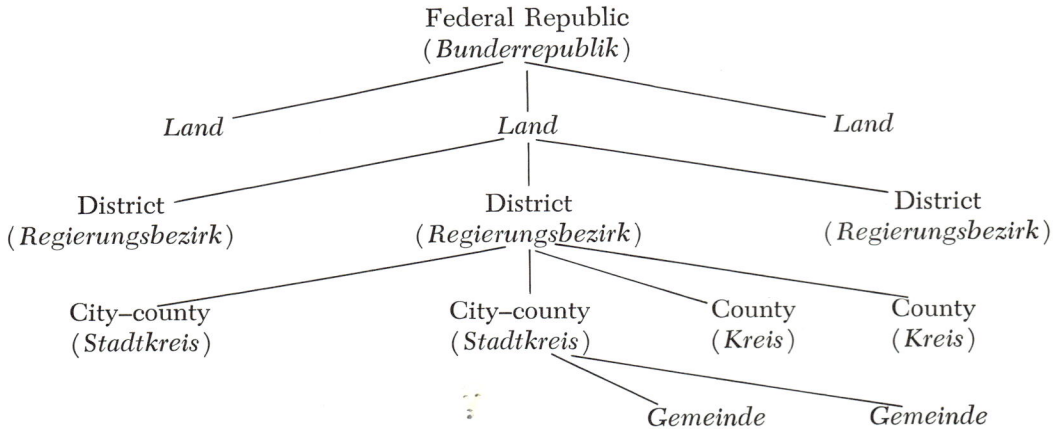

Federal Republic
(*Bunderrepublik*)

Land   *Land*   *Land*

District
(*Regierungsbezirk*)   District
(*Regierungsbezirk*)   District
(*Regierungsbezirk*)

City–county
(*Stadtkreis*)   City–county
(*Stadtkreis*)   County
(*Kreis*)   County
(*Kreis*)

Gemeinde   *Gemeinde*

10 *Lander*
33 *Regierungsbezirke*
139 *Stadtkreise*
425 *Land Kreise;* average area of *Kreise* about 500 sq miles
24,525 *Gemeinden;* average area, 10 sq miles

This examination of the number, size, and interrelationship of local government areas could be extended until all the sovereign states and colonial dependencies of the world had been covered. Such a task is clearly impossible, and a detailed consideration of the United States, Great Britain, France, and Germany must suffice.

Most such hierarchies are character-

in the size of the units at both the county and the *commune* levels, there is a certain similarity in the range of size of the corresponding units between the countries examined. Where there are striking departures from the average, these are in general explicable in geographical terms, for example, the large counties in the sparsely populated areas of Sweden and Finland,

TABLE 15 *Local Government Areas*

State	Regional level	County level	District level	Commune level
United States..........	State	County	. . .	Township
England and Wales.....	. . .	County and county borough	Urban and rural district	Parish
France...............	. . .	*Département*	*Arrondissement Canton*	*Commune*
Germany.............	*Land*	*Regierungsbezirk*	*Kreis* and *Stadtkreis*	*Gemeinde*
Italy.................	*Compartimenti*	Provinces	. . .	*Commune*
Poland...............	*Województwo*	. . .	*Powiat*	*Gmina*
Hungary.............	. . .	*Comitat*	. . .	
Denmark.............	. . .	*Amter*	. . .	
Finland.............	. . .	*Lanni*	. . .	*Pitaja*
Czechoslovakia........	. . .	*Kraj*	. . .	*Okres*
Thailand.............	. . .	*Changwat*	*Amphur*	*Tambon*

the large counties in the American West, and the large parishes in the moorland areas of the British Isles.

A final problem in this consideration of the size of local administrative units is the degree to which they reflect local loyalties and regionalisms. The *raison d'être* of each unit area is clearly to provide an area of suitable size and population to carry out the functions of government delegated to it. If the local government is to be successful, a certain degree of cohesion and homogeneity in the population is necessary. On the other hand, units at the county level were sometimes, as in France, made as arbitrary as possible in order to avoid encouraging too intense a feeling of local patriotism. There appears to be a direct relationship between the antiquity of the county as an administrative institution and the respect in which it is held. The English county attracts far greater loyalty than an American county, or a French *département*, or a German *Kreis*.

Social Consequences of Administrative Boundaries: Although the range of admin-

istration may be the same throughout all administrative units at the same level in a particular state, the interpretation or application of their functions may differ be-

Figure 36 *From 1919 until 1939 the path through the woods marked the boundary between Germany and Poland. It now divides the Polish provinces (Województwa) of Zielona Góra and Poznań.*
PHOTOGRAPH BY N. J. G. POUNDS

tween each. Administrative obligations, the maintenance of roads and schools, for example, may cost more in one township than in another, and the resulting problem may be solved by a higher tax rate in one than in its neighbors. This in turn may influence the location of homes or the establishment of industries. In this country, the range of difference at the township and county level is slight and probably has little measurable influence on settlement and land use. But as between the States themselves it is considerable. Differentials in gasoline, liquor, and sales taxes, in property taxes, in corporation laws, in the regulation of industry, and in the provision of public utilities all have a significant influence. Who has not seen the clustering of gas stations on one side of a state line, with written exhortations to fill up while gasoline is still cheap? Less apparent but no less real is the influence on industrial development through differentials in tax structure between neighboring administrative areas. In Great Britain the differentials at the county level are more conspicuous than here, especially in the levels of local taxation, and these are alleged to have had a considerable importance in attracting or deterring industry.

The question of differential tax rates between neighboring administrative areas raises at once the question of changing their boundaries. City government is more expensive than government in rural counties, and its tax levels are therefore higher. On the other hand, in most countries the cities are growing steadily in size, and around their periphery is often a residential area, inhabited mainly by people who work in the city center. The normal process of city growth carries the dormitory zone out beyond the geographical limits of the city, into the neighboring administrative units. Suburban dwellers benefit from the advantages of city life: shopping, entertainment, transportation facilities, sometimes even the public utilities developed to supply and serve the city and the latter's police and fire-protection services.

It is usually to the financial advantage of such suburban dwellers to remain outside the city limits. It is also in most cases to the advantage of the county or other unit in which they lie to retain them, as they often inhabit the areas with the highest taxable values. On the other hand, many suburban dwellers have moved out from downtown areas and have taken some industrial undertakings with them. Boston and many other American cities have lost heavily in tax income through this depreciation of land values near the center. Among the objectives of the much advertised "urban renewal" is the restoration of prosperity and higher tax values to such depressed areas of American cities. The basic problem is that the political unit, in this instance the city, has ceased to conform geographically with the urbanized area. The advantages of embracing the whole urbanized area within a single governmental unit are obvious. It avoids the duplication of the organs of government; it achieves economies that come with larger scale of operations, it facilitates the provision of public utilities, and it increases the tax income of the city. Yet the annexation by a city of any part of its surrounding territory is certain to be resisted. Undoubtedly many smaller peripheral communities have a strong corporate pride, which is intensified at the prospect of having the higher city taxes imposed on them. The decision in these cases is a political one. The evidence which should form the basis of the decision is overwhelmingly geographical; it is the question of the function and purpose of local administrative areas.

The larger American cities are often surrounded by a fringe of incorporated cities, many of them small, some lacking in the ordinary utilities and facilities which a city should offer, but all of them incorporated in order to resist annexation by the larger city which they envelop. The geographical expansion of most of the larger American cities is thus prevented by its encircling belt of small cities (Exhibit 66). Annexation is an issue only in those cities which are wholly or partially enclosed by territory that has never been incorporated, and this means, in general, the cities of small or medium size. Here the expansion of the urban limits is continuing, in the process of trying to make them accord with the boundary of the built-up and urbanized area ('Exhibit 67).

This problem is by no means confined to the United States. In Great Britain, the larger cities have been constituted as county boroughs, separate from the counties in which they lie. They are not subordinate to the counties and thus do not pay them taxes. The creation of a new county borough or the extension of the boundaries of an existing one diminishes the tax income of the surrounding county. In Germany, the problem is partially solved by the creation of *Stadtkreise*, or city counties which are large enough to satisfy the city's suburban needs at least for the time being. Two examples of the conflict of jurisdictions for the suburban areas should emphasize the main features of a controversy that is almost world-wide.

An example from Great Britain is provided by the city of Cambridge. It has a population of about 93,000 and is the seat of one of the leading universities in Great Britain. In all respects it deserves the status of county borough, such as its sister city of Oxford possesses. But the surrounding county is small (Exhibit 68) and predominantly agricultural. Apart from the city of Cambridge itself, the county of Cambridgeshire has no settlement of over 2,000 inhabitants. Its industries consist mainly of the processing of agricultural goods, and, de-

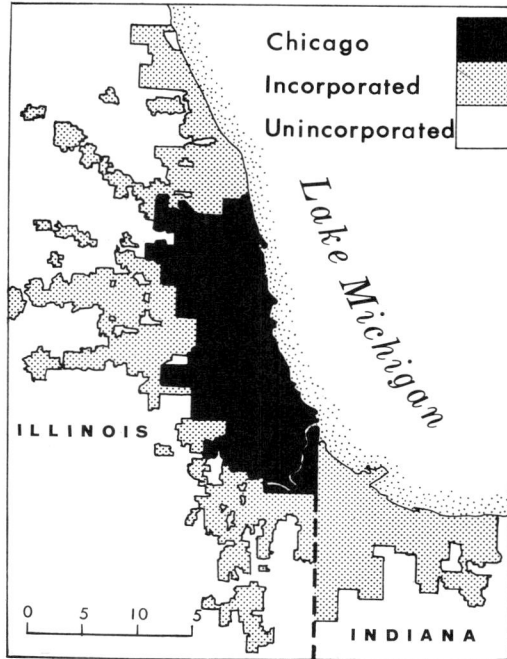

Exhibit 66 *Chicago and vicinity: incorporated cities.*

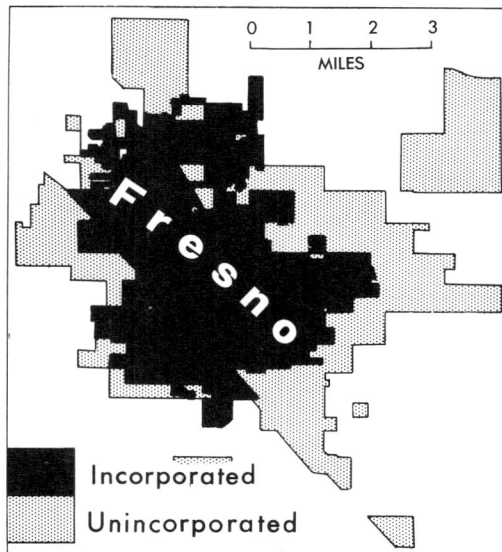

Exhibit 67 *City limits and urbanized area: Fresno.*

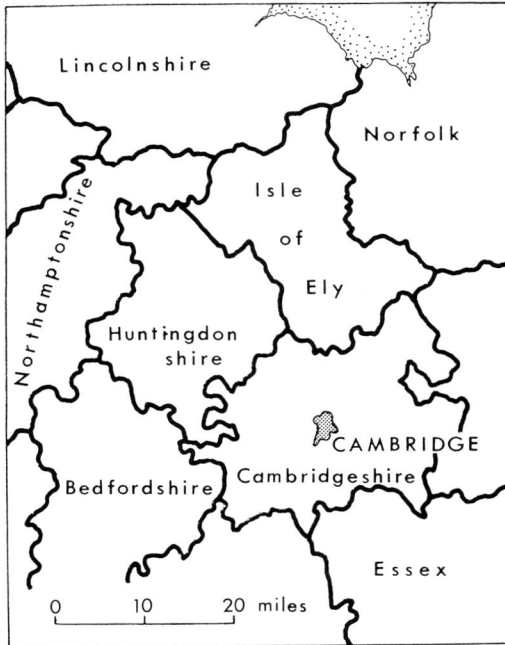

Exhibit 68 *Cambridgeshire and adjoining counties: city-county relationship.*

spite the generally high quality of its farm land, its tax income is relatively low. Taxes collected in the city of Cambridge constitute an important support for public services, including education, throughout the county. Cambridge's desire for the independent status of a county borough has hitherto been wrecked by the fact that this would do irreparable harm to the finances of the county. A solution would appear to be to merge two or more of the small counties which characterize this part of England, a remedy that would be highly offensive to the deep-seated county pride that is so prevalent in Great Britain.

SPECIAL DISTRICTS AND REGIONS

The problems of modern administration make it necessary to establish special-purpose administrative regions. Some of these are established by private agencies, such as telephone and utility companies, and are thus outside the sphere of public administration if not also of public supervision. Others are public, in so far as they have been established by the state or local government, and are in some way responsible to the elected representatives of the people. These include school districts and districts for the control of highways, for law enforcement, for the provision of public utilities and services, and for many other purposes. In general, where these districts overlap the normal units of civil administration, they cause a blurring of the latter. They create a zone of "areal compromise . . . between the ideal of no boundary and the restraint of a strong political line. It is a feature of the transition from one political division to another; the divisions tend either to merge or informally to create local boundaries to fit local circumstances."[3] In this country the role of the minor civil divisions, the town and township, which, in any case, exist over only about a third of the country, is of diminishing importance. Groups of neighboring townships tend increasingly to merge in order to carry on more effectively some of their functions. The tendency, in fact, is general for the administrative units at the lowest level to decline in significance, as they prove for many purposes to be uneconomically small.

Somewhat different from these districts, formed generally by the merging of civil divisions, are regional authorities and organizations which cut across existing administrative units. These are created usually for land and resource development, river control, the coordination of transportation and dock facilities, or other similar operations. All such organizations derive

[3] Edward Ullman, "The Eastern Rhode Island–Massachusetts Boundary Zone," *G.R.*, vol. 29, p. 302, 1939.

their authority ultimately from the state, and most of them must have, in order to operate, some powers to acquire land and to control land use. Some such authorities thus constitute a serious invasion of the rights and privileges of local government areas. They may also extend the prerogatives of the central government at the expense both of local government and of private enterprise. For these reasons the creation of such authorities commonly meets with a great deal of popular opposition.

Such special regional authorities may be grouped into: (1) planning authorities; (2) river- and flood-control authorities; (3) transportation authorities (including dock and harbor authorities); (4) authorities responsible for the supply of power and other public utilities. Obviously these functions overlap, and some of the more ambitious regional authorities, such as the Tennessee Valley Authority (TVA), may be said to belong in part to each category. Others, the Port of New York Authority, for example, are more restricted in their scope.

Planning Authorities: Planning authorities are the most widespread and numerous of the special regional authorities. Every city which has a zoning ordinance is planning the land use of its area. But we are concerned here with planning authorities which extend over two or more local government areas and to some extent *replace* the latter in the discharge of certain of the functions which may properly be said to be theirs. At their simplest, zoning laws require that industries should be located in areas of the city reserved for them and private housing and shops in other areas. Such laws are necessary if the value of property is to be maintained, congestion avoided, and the maximum use made of transportation facilities. In this country such plans have, with very few exceptions, been left to the governing authorities of the local units to formulate and implement, and regional planning has not been welcomed.

In Europe regional-planning authorities are more numerous and more important than here. For a time there was a planning authority for the whole Ruhr industrial area in West Germany (Exhibit 69). There is today an authority for the

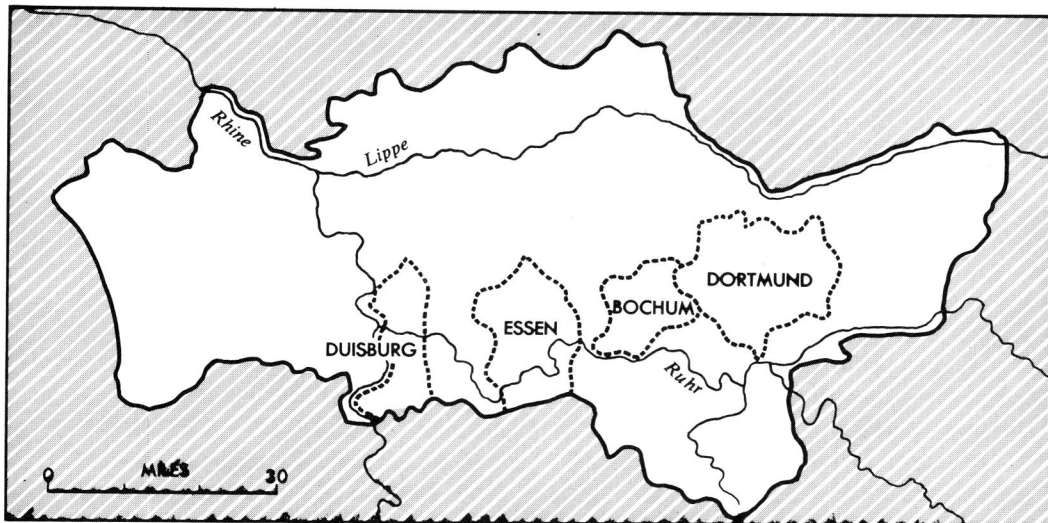

Exhibit 69 *Ruhr Planning Authority's Area. The Authority is no longer active.*

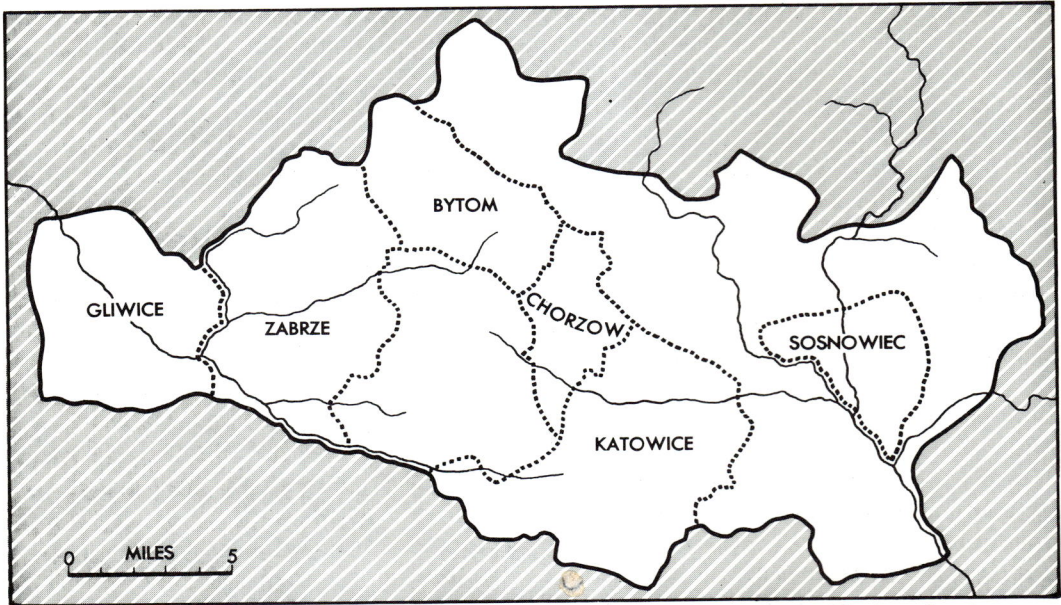

Exhibit 70   *Upper Silesian planning area.*

Upper Silesian industrial region of Poland (Exhibit 70), charged with responsibility for every form of land use and development within its area. It chooses the sites for factories and housing; it plans new roads and makes improvements in old roads; it controls the geographical pattern of railways, water supply, gas lines, and sewers, as well as public parks and recreational facilities. In Great Britain, where land is scarce and competition for it between conflicting forms of land use is acute, regional plans are especially numerous (Exhibit 71). All parts of Great Britain are subject to planning control, and the plans worked out for the industrial regions are extremely complex and detailed. One of the most ambitious of them is the Greater London Plan.

London has continued to grow, until with its factories, homes, shops, offices, and parks it covers an area of 721 square miles, and it threatens to grow yet larger. The London Plan of 1946 sought to check the outward expansion of the city. A so-called Green Belt was established around it within which industrial and urban development were not permitted. The expected growth of population and industry in the London region was to be accommodated in a number of new towns to be built beyond London's Green Belt (Exhibit 72). Other types of planning regions illustrated in Exhibit 71 are development areas and national parks. The former are essentially depressed areas to which the government is attempting to attract new industries by the offer of special concessions to industrialists. The latter, by contrast, are areas of great natural beauty which are to be preserved in their present mainly agricultural condition. New building is carefully controlled so that it does not detract from the amenities of the areas, but the current economic use of the park areas is in no way hindered. Great Britain cannot afford the space necessary

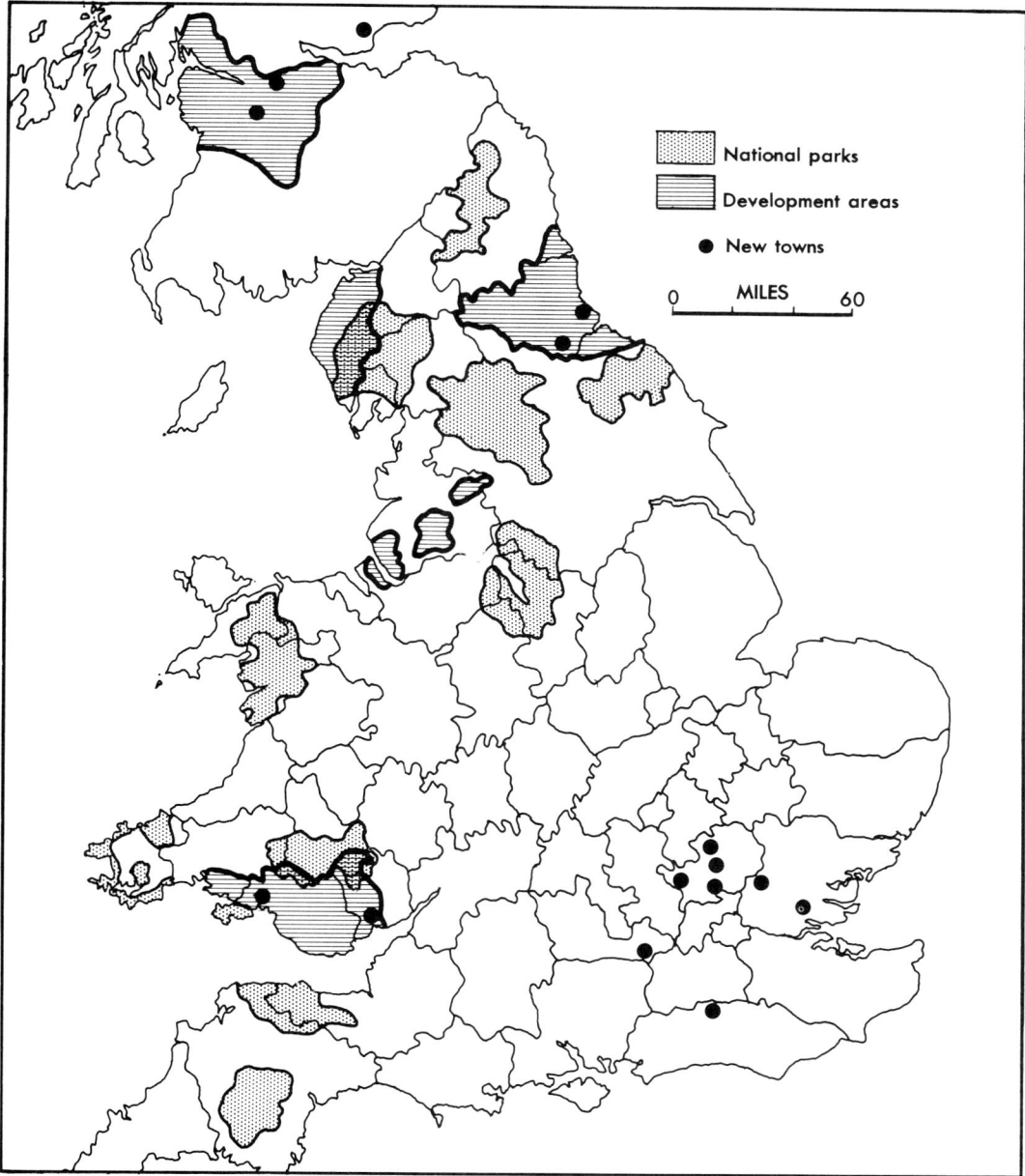

Exhibit 71 *Planning regions in Great Britain.*

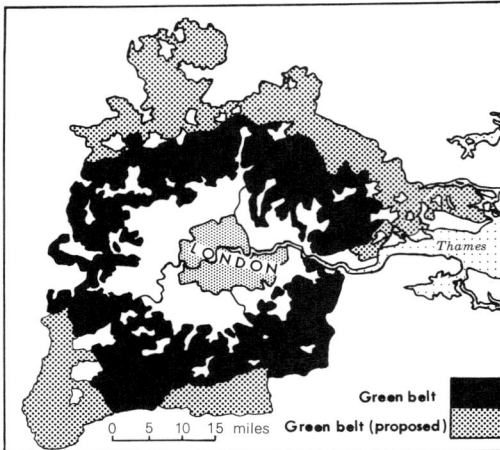

Exhibit 72   *London, the Green Belt and the New Towns.*

to establish the kind of national parks found in the United States, where they are essentially scenic and wildlife museums.

River- and Flood-control Authorities: These authorities are probably more numerous in the United States than regional planning authorities, because the need for them is more obvious. It is clear that no local government unit can alone control the floods that might occur along the course of a river that flows across its territory. Nor, in the last resort, is river control possible without some degree of authority over land use in the whole catchment area. The TVA (Exhibit 73), the most ambitious river-control program yet conceived and implemented, embraces both and adds to these control over navigation and power generation. But most such authorities are more limited in scope and aim to even out the discharge of the river, to construct preventive works along its banks, and thus to reduce the danger of floods. One of the best examples of an attempt to coordinate the work of controlling a river is probably that provided by the Missouri Basin Inter-Agency Committee. This body has super-

vision over an even larger area than the TVA but is differently constituted. Whereas the latter was imposed by the Federal government upon portions of no fewer than seven States, the latter operates on the basis of voluntary association between ten States which share the Missouri Basin and a number of federal agencies. The plans of the Missouri Valley Committee include the building of 138 dams and almost 40 local flood-protection projects, as well as the construction of levees along the river from Sioux City, Iowa, to its junction with the Mississippi. Many other rivers—the Ohio, Delaware, and Wisconsin among them—are subject to a single authority from source to mouth.

Transportation Authorities: Transportation, though usually subject to the jurisdiction of the State, is sometimes subject to an authority which spreads across two or more administrative units. Such an authority is the Port of New York Authority, a politically constituted body, empowered to supervise shipping, dock facilities and the railroads which connect with the docks in the two-state dock area (Exhibit 74). Similar in its constitution and powers is the Port of London Authority, with authority over "those areas of the Tidal Thames and its contiguous rivers and waterways, and dock systems where the each-way exchange between land and water transport can be observed; together with other inland installations which control this activity or are vitally dependent upon it." [4] The Interstate Commerce Commission and the Federal Aviation Agency, formerly the Civil Aeronautics Authority, in the United States have powers to regulate all matters pertaining to transportation that crosses state lines.

[4] Quoted by James Bird, *The Geography of the Port of London*, Hutchinson University Library, London, 1957, p. 184.

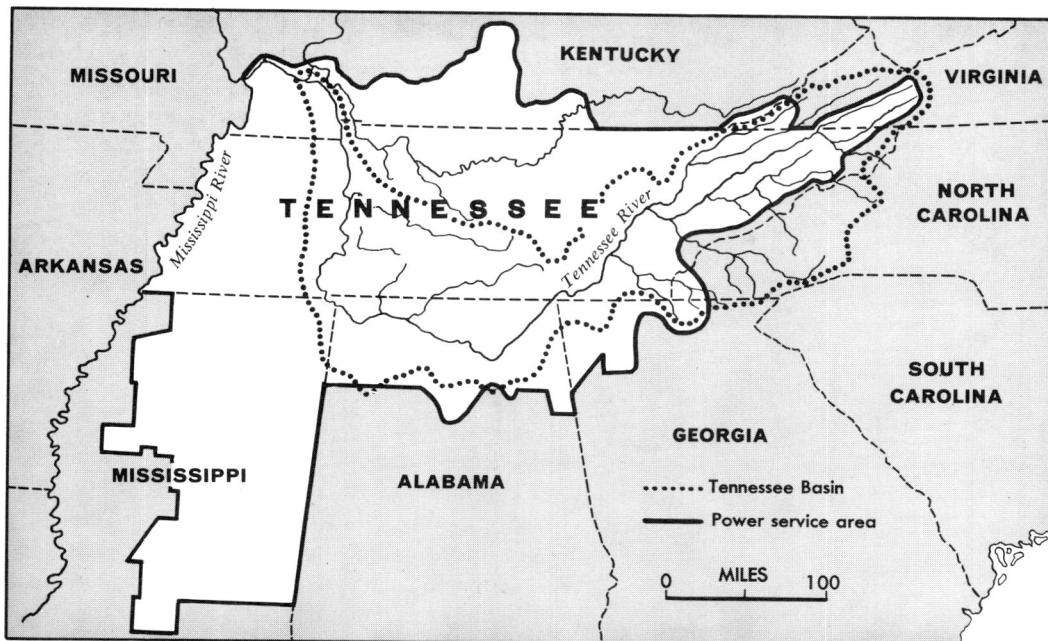

Exhibit 73   *The TVA area.*

Land transportation is less often subject to regional, as distinct from national, organization. In large cities, however, it is usually necessary to secure some coordination both between the types of transportation, bus, train, subway, streetcar, and between the city itself and its suburban, residential areas. The need for such a transportation authority is clearly greatest in the largest and most extensive urban areas of the world, greater New York and greater London. In London, the London Passenger Transport Board achieves this coordination over areas which embrace several local government units.

The provision of public services, such as electric power, water and gas, and recreational facilities, provides scope for·administrative fields which overlap local governmental units. In very few urban areas, indeed, is it possible to obtain a water supply from within the administrative limits of the city. Usually, water catchment and storage must be organized at a great distance and pipelines laid to the city. New York City, for example, has been obliged to construct ·reservoirs in the Catskill Mountains, about a hundred miles away. The desirability of securing the maximum advantages of size in power generation leads frequently to the erection of plant capable of serving the needs of several political units. In this country such services are commonly provided by private companies or corporations. These do not conform to the boundaries of the lesser civil divisions, nor, in some cases, to those of the State. In most States a public service commission, responsible to the State government, protects the interests of consumers and to some extent prevents overlapping and waste.

Most regional authorities pursue more than one of the functions listed above, be-

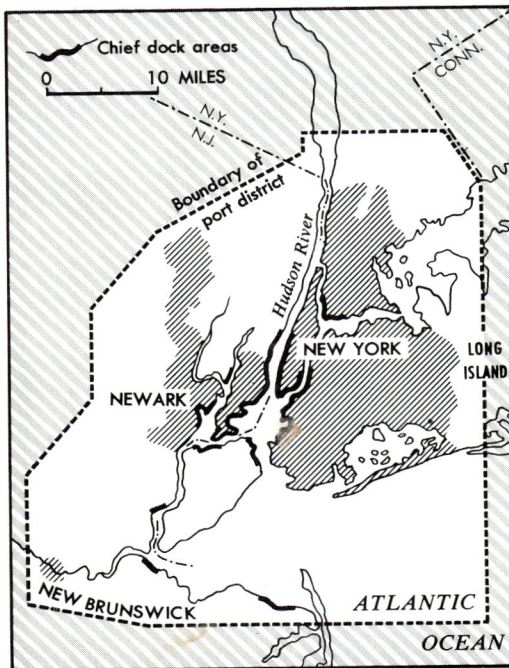

Exhibit 74   Area served by the Port of New York Authority.

authority (Exhibit 73). By 1959 the value of the authority's total investment in water control and power generation alone was about 2¼ billion dollars.

The creation of such powerful authorities represents an invasion of the sphere both of local government and of private enterprise by the national or Federal authorities. As such it is opposed by some conservative and business interests, as well as by some of those who wish to maintain effective and responsible organs of local government. On the other hand, it cannot be doubted that modern technology puts a premium upon large-scale operations in planning, flood control, and public services. Inevitably, the functions of the smallest administrative units are being eroded. Townships, for example, have almost wholly given up their function of road maintenance, in part because modern road equipment is larger and more costly than a single township can either purchase or fully use. Slowly and irregularly, it may be presumed, larger unit areas will be devised for different purposes, and it is only to be expected that these will rarely conform with one another and only occasionally with existing governmental divisions.

THE GEOGRAPHY OF POLITICAL CHOICE

Most important of all special geographical units are those set up for the conducting of elections and other acts whereby the public chooses between political objectives. In the United States the basic unit is the county. In all elections the numbers of the votes cast for all candidates are published for each county. For statewide offices, such as the governorship and the Senate, a plurality is required for the whole State, but for others, such as membership of the House or the State legislatures, a plurality is needed in only one

cause these are in many instances inseparable. None, however, is as all-embracing as the TVA. It was established by Congress in 1933 as a multipurpose Federal agency. Its object is the development of the economy and the improvement of the level of welfare of a vast area of about forty thousand square miles on the borders of the Old South. More specifically, it is charged with flood control, navigation, the generation and transmission of electric power, the manufacture of fertilizers and munitions, afforestation, housing, and social welfare. Its sphere of activity extends over 125 counties, divided among seven States, with a population totaling over three million. The TVA has constructed no fewer than eight large dams on the Tennessee River and its tributaries for the generation of power and has distributed power over a much larger area than that under its direct county or in a group of neighboring counties.

At a lower level is the precinct, the area within which all voters must go to a particular polling station in order to vote. The precinct must be clearly delimited, but it is a political division of convenience. The precinct as such is not represented in Congress or the legislature. It is merely a part of the mechanics of voting. Precincts in which the population is declining may be merged; those where it is increasing may be divided. The only criterion is that voting facilities should be sufficient for the number of persons who may be expected to vote.

The most important electoral unit below the State level is the congressional district, which elects a single member to the House. These districts consist of one or more counties. A State with, let us say, ninety counties may send twelve Representatives to Washington. The ninety counties are divided into twelve groups, approximately equal, not in *area*, but in *population*. But the population of a State changes. It is therefore required by the Constitution that the number of Representatives from each State should be revised after each decennial census, so that a State's total membership of the House is proportionate to its population. It is for the State officials to make whatever changes may be necessary within the State in the boundaries of congressional districts, by shifting a county from one district to another as may be required to maintain an approximate equality between them.

The problem arises in all countries where popular elections are conducted upon the basis of geographical areas, or constituencies. In most there is a periodic revision of the boundaries of electoral units, but always there is a time lag. The political geography never completely catches up with the economic and social, and in particular the urban areas always remain *under*represented.

The Gerrymander: Complete equality between congressional districts and between the corresponding units in other countries is unattainable. But this is not the only source of error or misrepresentation. "The gerrymander," wrote Prof. Carl O. Sauer, "is an American name for a political abuse, which, though by no means exclusively American, has been most widely practiced and generally tolerated in this country." [5] In essence, the gerrymander consists in drawing boundaries in such a way that significant groups form a permanent minority without means of political expression. Sauer argues that in this country distinct communities, especially in the less urbanized and industrialized areas, tend to correspond with distinctive physical regions. Boundaries of, let us say, congressional districts may be so drawn that they bring together into one unit voters with a common body of interests. They may be traditionally Democratic or Republican; they may be Negro, they may be factory workers, or they may belong predominantly to a particular religious group. On the other hand, the boundaries may be so drawn that they break up this sociogeographical unit, spreading it among several districts, in each of which it is consistently outvoted by other groups. Sauer quotes the example of the Missouri Ozarks, a region which is traditionally Republican in its sympathies but which was at the time broken up between no fewer than five congressional districts, in each of which the Ozark Republicans are outvoted by Democrats (Exhibit 75).

The term *gerrymander* stems from the action of Governor Elbridge Gerry of

[5] C. O. Sauer, "Geography and the Gerrymander," *American Political Science Review,* vol. 12, p. 403, 1918.

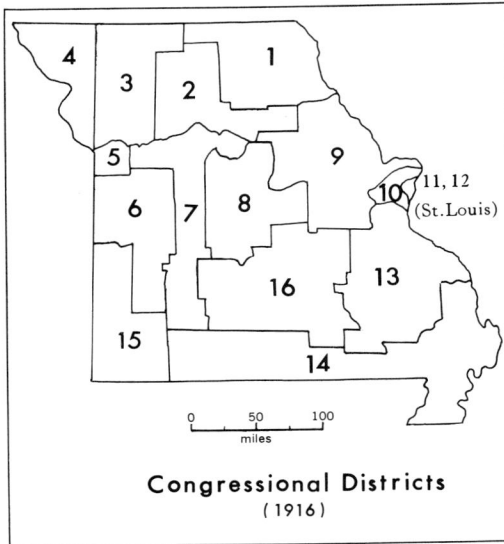

Exhibit 75 Congressional districts of Missouri.

Massachusetts, who in 1812 established an oddly shaped electoral district in order to favor his party (Exhibit 77). No less strange is the New York Twelfth District, in which a group of more or less isolated Republican districts in the predominantly Democratic Brooklyn were strung together by the Republican legislature in order to ensure at least one Republican congressman from this area. The Los Angeles Twenty-sixth and the Oklahoma First Districts (Exhibit 77) both owe their extraordinary appearance to the desire to pull together all parts of a like-minded minority in their particular parts of the State.[6]

Another example of a boundary change that savors strongly of gerrymandering was that made in 1946 to the urban district of Armagh, in Northern Ireland.[7] The map (Exhibit 78) shows the boundaries of the district before 1946,

[6] These instances were described in the *New York Times,* Nov. 27, 1960.

[7] Cited in J. R. V. Prescott, "The Function and Methods of Electoral Geography," *A.A.A.G.,* vol. 49, p. 301, 1959.

when it had an Irish Nationalist, or anti-government, majority, and after 1946, when the newly constituted district showed a Unionist, or progovernment, majority. Other examples, perhaps less glaring, could be selected from almost every country in which a party in power has the privilege of altering the boundaries of electoral districts, in order to make them conform more closely with a changed distribution of population. Such bodies would scarcely be human if they did not allow the scales to be tipped just a little in favor of maintaining themselves in power. The practice of weighting electoral districts in favor of the rural voter is one of the most persistent of gerrymander devices, and one most difficult to eradicate.

Voting Maps: It is a relatively easy matter to show on a map how people vote on a particular issue at election time. We do it regularly in the papers and magazines: one shading for counties or States which went Republican on a particular issue and another for those which went Democratic. But such maps have their limitations as well as their uses. In the first place, the map shows the *area* that chose a particular representative or course of action, not the number of *people* who made the choice. A large, thinly populated area that voted Republican in the presidential election of 1960, let us say Montana, will look on the map far more significant than a small, densely populated area, let us say Massachusetts, that voted Democratic. In fact, a mere inspection of the map shows that about two-thirds of the area of the United States voted Republican, but slightly less than half of the voters.

This objection to maps which show political choice can be overcome by using, instead of simple coloring or shading for the whole of each electoral division. some symbol which shows also the size of the voting public. In Exhibits 79, 80, and 81, an

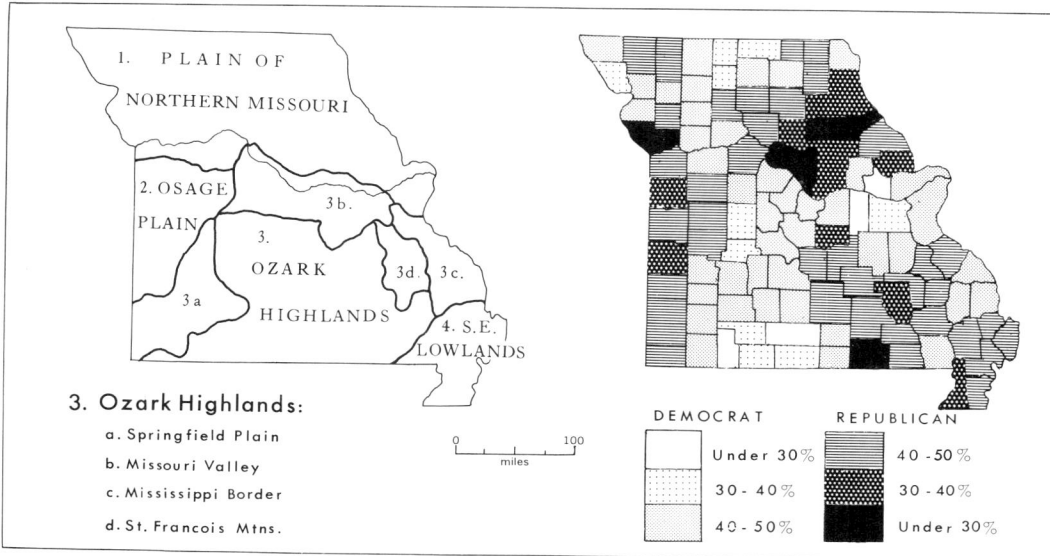

Exhibit 76　*The Missouri gerrymander: physical regions and election returns.*

attempt has been made to show the size of the electorate and also the way in which its votes were divided. This map is more accurate than those commonly published, but it is also more complex to draw and more difficult to interpret.

A second objection is that on most maps of voting behavior no attempt is made to show graphically the size of the plurality. A State which went Democratic, let us say, with 51 per cent of the votes, is shown in the same way as one with 75 per cent. It is possible to use types or gradations of shading to indicate the size of the plurality. Alternatively, the method of using circles to indicate the totality of voters and of dividing them proportionately according to how they voted can be used, though such maps usually require cartographic skills of a higher order than are usually to be found in a newspaper office.

A third feature of such maps is that they are best suited to the representation of simple issues: the election of a president, governor, or member of parliament,

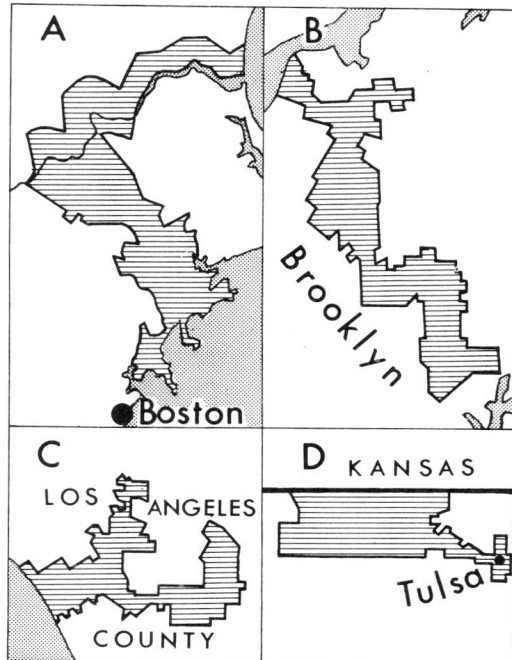

Exhibit 77　*Some gerrymanders: A, the original gerrymander; B, New York Twelfth District (1960); C, California Twenty-sixth District (1960); D, Oklahoma First District (1960).*

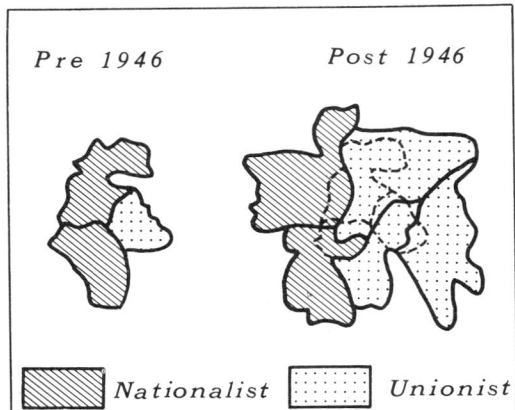

Exhibit 78 *Electoral divisions in the city of Armagh, Northern Ireland.* AFTER J. R. V. PRESCOTT

"As Your Representative, I Promise To Continue Our Fight Against Redistricting"

Figure 37 *Redistricting and the advantage which our present system of electoral divisions gives to the rural voter are frequent subjects for the cartoon artist.* COURTESY: HERBLOCK, WASHINGTON POST

or the choice, as in Italy, of whether to retain or abolish the monarchy. They are not really suited to showing political choice where there is a great variety of political parties. In such cases there is often a second ballot, restricted only to those candidates who received more than a certain number of votes in the first. The result of the voting often represents a temporary coalition of several minority groups, and its geographical significance is slight. In countries which have adopted the method of proportional representation the difficulties of showing cartographically the results of an election become very great indeed.

A final difficulty in the use of maps showing political choice is the arbitrary nature of most of the unit areas chosen. Political attitudes are usually grouped regionally. Commonly the so-called "natural" regions have a common way of life which is reflected in the political, social, and economic ideas which they have in common. The distinctiveness of such ideas is blurred whenever such regions are divided and incorporated with other and contrasted regions. This is, of course, the principle of the gerrymander, but in many areas where this abuse was never consciously practiced, boundaries nevertheless obscure rather than emphasize the regional contrasts in opinion. It is therefore desirable to use, in compiling such maps, the smallest possible unit areas, even those at the precinct level, when this is possible.

Carefully prepared maps showing political choice give a geographical representation of the data in a way that crude statistics cannot possibly do. A run of such maps serves to emphasize areas which are continuously of one party or the other and thus points up the existence of the strength of regional feeling. For example, Paullin's *Atlas of the Historical Geography of the United States* shows on a county basis the

Exhibit 79 *Mapping the presidential election, 1960: I.*

results of a series of presidential elections.[8] In all maps for the period 1868 to 1928 an area of eastern Tennessee and parts of neighboring North Carolina are shown as voting consistently Republican (or, in 1912, Progressive). This is essentially the region of the Cumberland Plateau, Appalachian Mountains, and southern Blue Ridge, a rugged area of poor soil, where the plantation agriculture of the Old South was never practicable. There is, of course, no necessary association between poor soil, back-

[8] Charles O. Paullin, *Atlas of the Historical Geography of the United States*, Carnegie Institution, Washington, D.C., 1932, pls. 102–111.

ward agriculture, and Republican sentiments: indeed, the predominantly Republican attitudes of Iowa, for example, demonstrate the contrary. But in Tennessee and North Carolina, as well as in parts of Georgia, Virginia, Kentucky, and Alabama, the hills were settled largely by people who filtered southward from Pennsylvania, bringing the political attitudes of the Northeastern States with them. Their separateness in their Southern habitat was emphasized by their distinct physical environment and by the restrictions which this imposed upon their economy. The Democratic sympathies of the surrounding areas

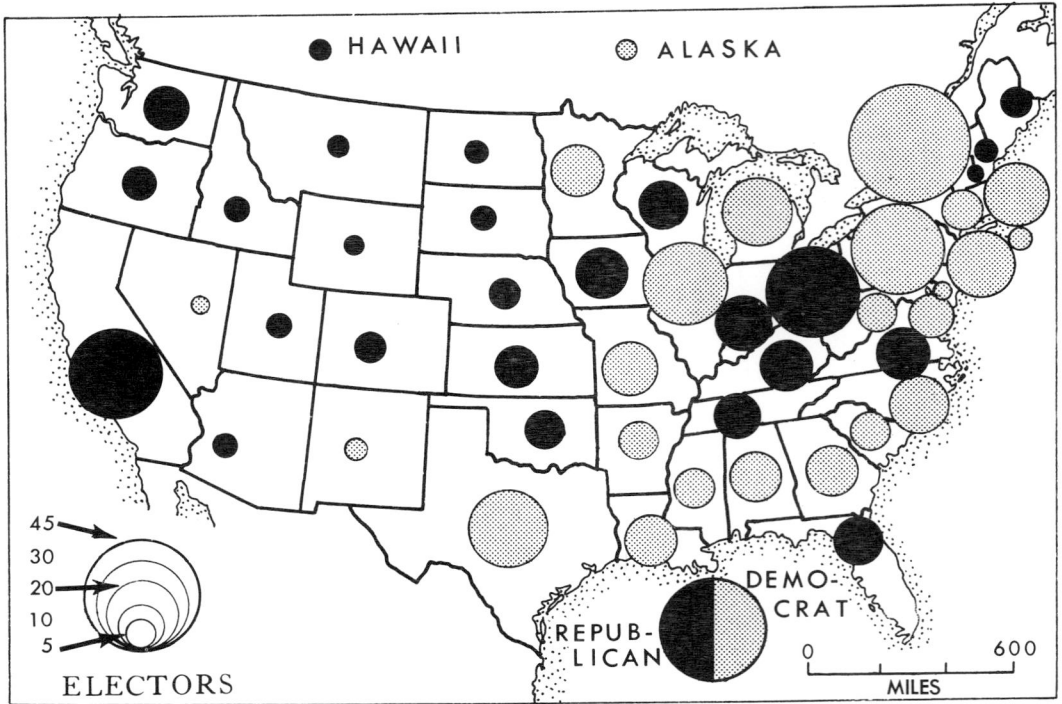

Exhibit 80   **Mapping the presidential election, 1960: II.**

have tended to reinforce the predominantly Republican outlook in these particular areas. The same phenomenon shows itself in the hills of western Kentucky and southern Illinois and in the Ozark Hills of Missouri (see page 213). Only a geographical analysis of voting patterns can bring out the continuity of the pattern of political behavior and show where, geographically considered, the significant lines of political and social cleavage occur.

Attempts are sometimes made to represent similarly the ways in which different parts of the nation regard such issues as tariff protection, prohibition, and woman suffrage. If these issues are placed directly before the electors and their choice is registered by the usual mechanism of voting, the compilation of a map presents no difficulties. If, on the other hand, the will of the people is expressed only indirectly, through

the vote in Congress of their senator or representative, the results can be suspect. There is no degree of certainty that when a member of Congress votes he expresses the will on that particular issue of the majority that elected him. Mapping the voting in the House as if this reflected the prevailing opinion in each of the representatives' districts leaves much to be desired, but it has frequently been done. On major issues the error may be small, but on those of less importance the House vote *may* be far from representative of opinions back home. Paullin's *Atlas*[9] gives a number of maps of voting in the House on major issues. It can be said only that these show a rough correlation with the regionalisms that manifest themselves more clearly at election time. A recent use of congressional voting

[9] *Ibid.*, pls. 112–131.

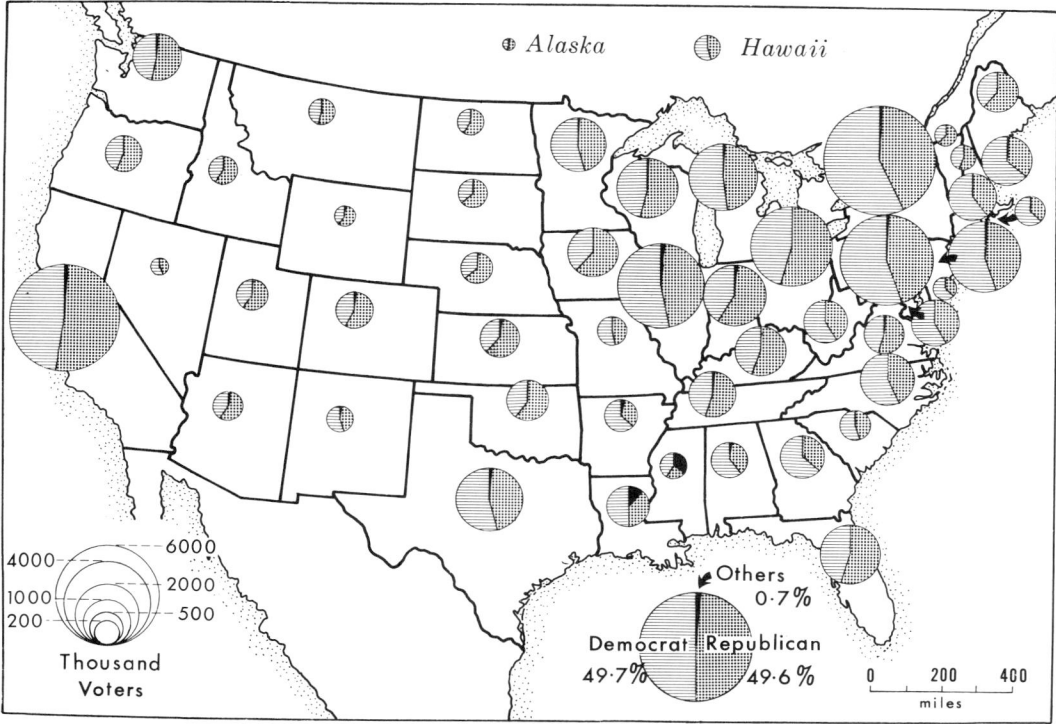

Exhibit 81 *Mapping the presidential election, 1960: III.*

to portray regional political choice has been made by Smith and Hart,[10] who studied nine House votes on the issue of tariff protection, beginning with the Smoot-Hawley Act of 1929. The maps that were prepared by these writers show very approximately the trends in regional feeling on these issues, but it has to be remembered that the representative votes as he sees fit, that, as has already been shown, the area which he represents may have been to some extent gerrymandered, and that rural interests may be represented more strongly than urban.

The subject of the geography of political choice has hitherto received little attention. This is surprising, because nothing

shows more clearly than the way in which people vote on significant issues the *political* differences between one region and another. One of the earliest such studies was that by Krehbiel of the British elections before 1916.[11] The writer, after studying the areas that usually voted Conservative and Liberal, respectively, found that "natural factors have contributed very materially" to the shaping of political opinion. Industrial and poor agricultural areas were mainly Liberal; the small cities and the better agricultural areas, predominantly Conservative. Now this has been changed, and Labor has, in general, inherited the former geographical strongholds of Liberalism.

Writing of the Italian elections of 1948,

[10] Howard R. Smith and J. F. Hart, "The American Tariff Map," *G.R.*, vol. 45, pp. 327–346, 1955.

[11] Edward Krehbiel, "Geographic Influences in British Elections," *G.R.*, vol. 2, pp. 419–432, 1916.

Kish noted "a striking correlation . . . between electoral results and elevation. Of the 339 minor civil divisions in Emilia, 96.5 per cent of those lying below 200 meters had a Left majority, while of those lying above 200 meters 93 per cent had a Center-Right majority."[12] The reason is that the hilly regions are inhabited by the small independent and rather conservative farmer and the plains by the tenant farmer, sharecropper, or laborer, who is more likely to be socialist.

A similar study of the pattern of voting in the Newfoundland referendum of 1948 on the question of whether Newfoundland and Labrador should become a Province of Canada also showed a sharp geographical division between areas which strongly favored and those which resisted incorporation. Continued independence was favored by a majority only on the Avalon Peninsula of southeastern Newfoundland. This area contains almost all the manufacturing industry, and it seems probable that the objection to union with Canada sprang from the desire for protection from the competition of Canadian industries.

Far too little work has been done on the geography of political choice. Among the many fields that are available for the writing of theses and term papers, few are as rewarding and as untouched as that of the geographical distribution of voting patterns.

BIBLIOGRAPHY

Anderson, William: *Units of Government in the United States*, Public Administration Service Publications 42, Chicago, 1934.
––– and Edward W. Weidner: *State and Local Government in the United States*, Henry Holt and Company, Inc., New York, 1951.

[12] George Kish, "Some Aspects of the Regional Political Geography of Italy," *A.A.A.G.*, vol. 43, p. 178, 1953.

Bird, James: *The Geography of the Port of London*, Hutchinson University Library, London, 1957.
Bowman, Isaiah: "An American Boundary Dispute: Decision of the Supreme Court of the United States with Respect to the Texas-Oklahoma Boundary," *G.R.*, vol. 13, pp. 161–189, 1923.
Brightman, George F.: "The Boundaries of Utah," *E.G.*, vol. 16, pp. 87–95, 1940.
Clapp, Gordon R.: *The TVA: An Approach to the Development of a Region*, University of Chicago Press, Chicago, 1955.
Congressional District Atlas of the United States, U.S. Department of Commerce, Bureau of the Census, 1960.
Crisler, Robert M.: "Republican Areas in Missouri," *Missouri Historical Review*, vol. 42, pp. 299–309, 1947–1948.
Cushing, Sumner W.: "The Boundaries of the New England States," *A.A.A.G.*, vol. 10, pp. 17–40, 1920.
Dean, Veva Kathern: "Geographical Aspects of the Newfoundland Referendum," *A.A.A.G.*, vol. 39, p. 70, 1949.
Freeman, T. W.: *Geography and Planning*, Hutchinson University Library, London, 1958.
Gilbert, E. W.: "Practical Regionalism in England and Wales," *G.J.*, vol. 94, pp. 29–44, 1939.
Governmental Units in the United States, 1942, U.S. Bureau of the Census, 1944.
Griswold, Erwin N.: "Hunting Boundaries with Car and Camera in the Northeastern United States," *G.R.*, vol. 29, pp. 353–382, 1939.
Harris, G. Montagu: *Comparative Local Government*, Hutchinson University Library, London, 1948.
Hoffmann, F.: "Die Verwaltungsgliederung der Staaten Europas ohne Sowjetunion," *Geographisches Taschenbuch, 1960–1961*, Franz Steiner Verlag GmbH., Wiesbaden, pp. 264–266, 1960.
Kish, George: "Some Aspects of the Regional Political Geography of Italy," *A.A.A.G.*, vol. 43, p. 178, 1953.
Kollmorgen, Walter: "Political Regionalism in the United States—Fact or Myth," *Social*

Forces, vol. 15, pp. 111–122, 1936–1937.

Krehbiel, Edward: "Geographic Influences in British Elections," *G.R.,* vol. 2, pp. 419–432, 1916.

Leuchtenburg, William Edward: *Flood Control Politics,* Harvard University Press, Cambridge, Mass., 1953.

Macdonald, Austin F.: *American City Government and Administration,* Thomas Y. Crowell Company, New York, 1942.

Martin, Lawrence: "The Michigan-Wisconsin Boundary Case in the Supreme Court of the United States," *A.A.A.G.,* vol. 20, pp. 105–163, 1930.

————: "The Second Wisconsin-Michigan Boundary Case in the Supreme Court of the United States, 1932–1936," *A.A.A.G.,* vol. 28, pp. 77–126, 1938.

Pattison, W. D.: *Beginnings of the American Rectangular Land Survey System, 1784–1800,* University of Chicago, Department of Geography, Research Paper 50.

Paullin, Charles O.: *Atlas of the Historical Geography of the United States,* Carnegie Institution, Washington, D.C., 1932.

Peake, H. J. E.: "Geographical Aspects of Administration Areas," *Geography,* vol. 15, pp. 531–546, 1929–1930.

Pounds, Norman J. G.: "Planning in the Upper Silesian Industrial Region," *Journal of Central European Affairs,* vol. XVIII, pp. 409–422, 1959.

Prescott, J. R. V.: "Nigeria's Regional Boundary Problems," *G.R.,* vol. 49, pp. 485–505, 1959.

Prescott, J. R. V.: "The Function and Methods of Electoral Geography," *A.A.A.G.,* vol. IL, pp. 269–304, 1959.

Sauer, Carl A.: "Geography and the Gerrymander," *American Political Science Review,* vol. 12, pp. 403–426, 1913.

Smith, Howard R., and J. F. Hart: "The American Tariff Map," *G.R.,* vol. 45, pp. 327–346, 1955.

Thomas, Benjamin E.: "Boundaries and Internal Problems of Idaho," *G.R.,* vol. IXL, pp. 99–109, 1949.

Turner, Frederick Jackson: "Geographical Influences in American Political History," *Bulletin of the American Geographical Society,* vol. 46, pp. 591–595, 1914.

Ullman, Edward: "The Eastern Rhode Island–Massachusetts Boundary Zone," *G.R.,* vol. 29, pp. 291–302, 1939.

Whittlesey, Derwent: "The Impress of Effective Central Authority upon the Landscape," *A.A.A.G.,* vol. 25, pp. 85–97, 1935.

Wright, John K.: "Sections and National Growth," *G.R.,* vol. 22, pp. 353–360, 1932.

————: "Voting Habits in the United States," *G.R.,* vol. 22, pp. 666–672, 1932.

Zink, Harold: *Government of Cities in the United States,* The Macmillan Company, New York, 1939.

9 GEOGRAPHICAL ASPECTS OF

RELATIONS BETWEEN STATES

Strife is the origin of all things . . . Peace is hence absurd or rather it is a pause in war.   BENITO MUSSOLINI

We dare not turn from the principle that morality and not expediency is the thing that must guide us.   WOODROW WILSON

IN THE SECOND CHAPTER WE GLANCED BRIEFLY AT THE THEORY THAT the state is an organism, the nature of which is to grow and expand. "A struggle for existence," wrote Charles Darwin, "inevitably follows from the high rate at which all organic beings tend to increase.[1] If states have a similar urge to expand, this is compatible only with a perennial condition of conflict between them for the control of that scarcest of all commodities, the land itself.

CONFLICT BETWEEN STATES

The inevitability of conflict was implicit in the political thought of many serious thinkers during the nineteenth and twentieth centuries and inspired the policies of the German National Socialists, the Italian Fascists, the Japanese imperialists, and the Russian Communists, though the philosophical basis in the case of the latter is different. It requires little imagination to see that there needs to be only one or two "social Darwinists" among the leaders of the major powers for a sense of conflict to spread among their neighbors. The protective rearmament in the countries of western Europe, which belatedly followed the demonstration of Germany's aggressive intentions in the 1930s, is only too clear an example. At the

[1] Charles Darwin, *Origin of Species.*

present time the heavy expenditure on arms and the deep interest in security of the United States in the face of Soviet threats exemplify the way in which the assumption of endemic conflict is imposed on a country which has not itself felt any urge to expand its territorial limits for half a century.

Whether one shares the view of Mussolini, quoted at the head of this chapter, or the conflicting outlook of Woodrow Wilson, one is obliged to regard conflict as something to be expected and to be guarded against. Thus it may be said that self-preservation is a minimal statement of the objective of every state's policy, though usually expressed with more subtlety and refinement. In President Truman's words, "One of the primary objectives of the foreign policy of the United States is the creation of the conditions in which we and other nations will be able to work out a way of life free from coercion."[2] The "Four Freedoms" of President Roosevelt is a further elaboration of the same theme.

The clarity with which decision-making authorities visualize the objective of their policy and the degree of dedication, efficiency, and ruthlessness with which they pursue it clearly vary from time to time and from one state to another. Whatever may sometimes be said about the disinterestedness or generosity of a state's policy, it is doubtful that it is ever inspired by any emotion more laudable than enlightened self-interest. To the social Darwinist, assistance to another state is treason, because each state is inevitably the enemy of all others. Alliances, friendships, and mutual assistance are acceptable or desirable only for the sake of the gains, immediate or long-term, that may accrue from them. Those furthest removed in their political viewpoint from social Darwinism can be almost

as cynical. Alexander Hamilton declared, as a general principle, "that the predominant motive of good offices from one nation to another, is the interest or advantage of the nation which performs them." To A. T. Mahan, "Self-interest is . . . a fundamental cause for foreign policy . . . it is vain to expect governments to act continuously on any other ground than national interest." "Policies," in the words of the Department of State, "are the courses of action taken by a nation in the interests of the welfare of its people. . . . It is the job of the Government, as the agent of the people, to promote these national interests."[3]

This chapter and those which follow are predicated on the assumptions that (1) conflict is never inevitable but always possible between states, (2) it is the function of government to assess the degree of possibility of conflict and, in the light of this assessment, to take whatever protective measures it judges necessary, (3) its decisions are motivated by national self-interest, however enlightened its judgment of these interests may be, and (4) its capacity to implement its policy is in rough proportion to the political power which it can command.

National Self-interest: It rarely happens that the nature of national self-interest is self-evident. If one considers, for example, the means by which Germany and Japan might have been defeated in the Second World War, one can criticize the choice actually made. The decision *not* to invade the Balkans, to allow the Soviet troops to occupy Czechoslovakia, and to allow West Berlin to become isolated in the Soviet-occupied zone seemed, in the light of what knowledge was available in 1944, the proper course to take. In retrospect these and other decisions seem suspect.

[2] President Truman, Message to Congress, Mar. 12, 1947.

[3] *Our Foreign Policy*, U.S. Department of State, Publication 4466, 1952.

The political objective has to be adjusted to the political power that is available to attain it, and policy will necessarily be conditioned by the prejudices and degrees of ignorance of the decision maker. Estimates of both policy and power are to some extent subjective and, thus, susceptible of more than usual error. The geographical factor is particularly important in the choice of both ends and means. This and the following chapter contain some examination of the geographical factor in foreign policy.

The Doctrine of Balance: The balance of power has been a mechanical policy for securing national safety since the fifteenth century, when the expression was first used. The assumption of the theory is that no state constitutes a threat to its neighbors unless its power is overwhelming. It was therefore incumbent on states to prevent such an accumulation of power in the hands of a single decision maker by a temporary combination of the states which felt themselves threatened by it. Modern European history can be interpreted as a series of shifting political patterns of states, each pattern brought into being to offset the allegedly excessive power held at the time by one state or a group of allied states. Through the nineteenth century, an uneasy peace was maintained in Europe by a pattern of alliances which changed as one state or another rose or declined in the scale of political power. At the beginning of the century, after the defeat of Napoleon, the pattern was aimed to neutralize France; at the end, it was aimed to counter the power of Germany. The balance broke down and war followed when Europe, divided into rival alliances, had no uncommitted states left who were both powerful enough and willing to redress the imbalance which developed. If it had been known in advance that the New World, in the form of the United States, would ultimately intervene to reestablish the balance of the

Old, the war of 1914 might never have broken out.

The participation by the United States in the First World War was followed by a withdrawal from the affairs of the Old World so complete that Germany was encouraged to believe that American intervention was not again probable. Yet once again American political power was able in 1942–1945 to redress a very serious imbalance. But this very victory gave such immense power to one of the victorious states that the balance has again become endangered.

The balance of power has been a means of maintaining peace and security only as long as there have been strong "neutralists" willing to lend their weight to one side or the other. At the present time, while two blocs face one another, the Western and the Communist, there is another group, the "uncommitted third," made up of India and many of the states in Southeast Asia and Africa. The important question is whether this group is collectively of sufficient political weight to influence the balance, if it were to add its political power to one scale or the other and, second, whether it would show enough cohesion to act with a sufficient degree of unity so that its action would be effective. The Belgrade Conference of uncommitted nations (September, 1961) suggested that they had neither the power nor, perhaps, the unanimity necessary for an effective balancer. It certainly appears doubtful at present that this third force is capable of playing this role effectively, not only because it is weak in those elements of power which have been discussed in earlier chapters, but also because the gulf between the "atomic" nations and those who do not possess this particular instrument of power is too wide to be easily bridged.

Neutral and Demilitarized Areas: The map shows, in addition to the third force, certain areas which are neutral. This at once raises the question of the nature of neutrality. These countries which are not committed to either bloc may be said to be neutral toward them. This neutrality may be only temporary and short-lived: the neutrality of the state which does not participate in a particular war and refrains from acts that favor one side or the other. On the other hand, neutrality may be formal, in which case the states have, as it were, contracted out of such conflicts before they could take place. Thus the Swiss Confederation, in 1815, declared itself to be neutral and refused to accept any political alliances or to take part in any wars lest it should itself be the victim of aggression. It was in accordance with this policy that Switzerland joined the League of Nations conditionally but has not become a member of the UN. Its neutrality has been respected in two world wars. In 1929, the Vatican City State, upon its establishment by treaty with the Italian government, also declared itself to be neutral. A condition of the peace treaty between the Allies of the Second World War and Austria (1955) was that the latter should also adopt a policy of neutrality.

In this instance, Austria did not consider that neutrality prevented her from joining both the UN and the EFTA (Chapter 12). Certain other states have at times avoided alliances and have conducted themselves as if neutrality were a deliberately chosen objective of policy. Sweden is such a state at present. On the other hand, the neutrality of Belgium and Luxembourg, guaranteed by their neighbors in the Treaty of London of 1831, was not respected by one of them, Germany, in 1914, and Belgium has since abandoned a policy of neutrality. It may be pointed out here that the exceptionally successful and prosperous neutrality of Switzerland seems to be a negation of the general thesis of social Darwinism, that growth is inevitable and conflict unavoidable.

It is possible for only a fragment of the territory of a state to be neutral. We have already (Chapter 3) discussed the function of neutral areas and zones as international boundaries. In these cases the states so divided have sovereignty over their respective parts of the neutral area, but this sovereignty is qualified [4] by the obligation on the neutral area to remain neutral, not, in other words, to take part in the implementation of policy directed toward the foreign state which it separates. The Moresnet territory, on the Belgian-German border, the neutral strip between Gibraltar and Spain, and the Finnish Aaland Islands appear to be all that remain of the formerly more numerous neutral areas of this category.

There are, however, other examples of neutral areas. In 1863, Great Britain gave the Ionian Islands, which her fleet had seized during the Napoleonic Wars, to Greece on condition that they become neutral. In the following year by an agreement between Great Britain and Greece, the neutrality was restricted to the islands of Corfu and Paxo.[5] The reason would appear to have been that Great Britain feared that the islands might one day be used militarily to threaten her seaborne communications through the Mediterranean Sea. A similar condition was imposed upon the Aaland Islands as part of the 1921 arbitration award that gave them to Finland. The Suez Canal was neutralized in 1888, though this status was presumably removed when, in 1956, the canal was taken over by the government of Egypt. In 1920 Norway undertook in a general treaty not to

---

[4] This, of course, raises the problem whether sovereignty so qualified ceases to be sovereignty.

[5] L. Oppenheim, *International Law*, Longmans, Green & Co., Inc., New York, 1943, vol. 2, p. 193.

erect any fortifications in Spitzbergen, nor to use the islands "for any warlike purposes."

The nature of the conditions thus imposed on these territories is not in every case clear. It would appear, however, that the governments of the states of which they are a part may not use these neutralized areas either in the prosecution of war or for static military defenses in time of peace. It is impossible to prevent the use of the population and resources which they contain from adding to the power potential of the state. The state merely renounces the use of those advantages which accrue from the geographical *location* of the neutralized areas. An interesting case in point is the renunciation by France in 1815 of the right to fortify the small Alsatian town of Huningue. This was in deference to the interests of the Swiss canton of Basel, which regarded itself as threatened by artillery mounted in Huningue. It is said that this "neutralization" of Huningue continued after the city had passed, with Alsace, to Germany in 1871.[6]

The political map shows two neutral zones of considerable size in the Middle East. The larger lies between Saudi Arabia and Kuwait. It arose, like the Moresnet area between Belgium and Germany, from the failure of two neighboring states to agree on a final line of division. They did, however, agree in 1922 to "share equal rights [i.e., in the neutral zone] until through the good offices of the government of Great Britain a further agreement is arrived at."[7] The good offices of Great Britain seem never to have been adequate to the task. In this area of about twenty-three hundred square miles, there are "no police, customs, fiscal or judicial administration."[8] Only the abundance of petroleum has existed to disturb this almost idyllic area. Both Kuwait and Saudi Arabia have each conceded its own half share of the resources to the petroleum companies, and two companies exploit the area with duplicated transportation and other fixtures, in fulfillment of the principle of joint sovereignty, but in defiance of every consideration of efficiency and common sense.

A similar neutral zone, untroubled so far by any mineral discoveries, was established in 1922 on the border of Saudi Arabia and Iraq. A small and rather vague neutral zone was also set up near the Buraimi oasis, in southeastern Arabia, to separate the warring sheiks. A neutral strip was also delimited to separate Israel from Jordan in the vicinity of Jerusalem. Lastly, a small area in the Middle East was temporarily declared neutral because it was the headquarters of the Mixed Armistice Commission. This minute area of El 'Auja had no regular inhabitants and apparently no resources of economic value.

A quasi neutrality exists along the southern shore of the Persian Gulf. This area is controlled by a small, though indeterminate, number of Arab sheiks whose intertribal wars in the nineteenth century threatened the safety of British trade in the area. For this reason, the British authorities secured an agreement with the sheiks by which the latter undertook not to conduct their wars into the gulf itself, while retaining complete freedom of action in other directions. It is from this agreement, or truce, that the Trucial Coast of Oman was named.[9]

If joint rule of a territory constitutes

[6] This case is discussed in J. L. Brierly, *The Law of Nations*, Oxford University Press, New York, 1955, pp. 169–170.

[7] Quoted in Alexander Melamid, "The Economic Geography of Neutral Territories," *G.R.*, vol. 45, pp. 359–374, 1955.

[8] *Ibid.*, p. 365.

[9] Alexander Melamid, "Political Geography of Trucial Oman and Qatar," *G.R.*, vol. 43, pp. 194–206, 1953.

neutrality, then three separate areas in Africa have at some time been neutral: the Sudan, formerly ruled jointly by Great Britain and Egypt, and Tangier and Melilla, both of which were in Morocco. Joint rule in the two latter examples appears to have been terminated by the grant of political independence to Morocco. The New Hebrides, an island group in the Southwest Pacific, has, since 1906, been ruled jointly by officials of France and Great Britain who exercise executive power alternately. This condominium has been described as "more decorative than useful," and as an administrative convenience it has not been conspicuously successful. A similar situation was created in the Canton and Enderbury Islands and in the Gilbert and Ellice group (Southwest Pacific Ocean) when in 1937–1938 both the United States and Great Britain claimed the islands and then agreed to administer them jointly. The problems of administration have been reduced immensely by the fact that the islands are uninhabited except for the personnel employed at an air station that has recently been established.

Lastly, the minute territory of Andorra in the mountain chain of the Pyrenees is jointly governed or administered by the President of the French Republic and the Bishop of the Spanish see of Urgel, an interesting survival of an almost medieval pattern of relationship.

The neutrality of a neutral state has in the past generally been respected, and the German invasion of Belgium in August, 1914, is the only conspicuous exception. At the present time the concept of neutrality, as distinct from neutralism, appears to be gaining in importance. Permanent neutrality was made a condition of peace for Austria; a neutral Laos is proposed. A neutral status, it is supposed, would effectively remove a state from both of the power blocs of this present age. Nazi Germany re-spected the neutrality of Switzerland; would, it may be asked, the Soviet Union do so? The Soviet Union differs from Switzerland, not merely politically, but in its social and economic structure. The two states are as different as communism and capitalism. There is an ideological reason why a member of the Communist bloc should not respect the neutrality of such a state as Switzerland for a longer period than suits its convenience. The very existence of communism is predicated upon the overthrow of capitalism, and the Communist creed requires that, in the end, the capitalist system, wherever found, should be overthrown. Neutrality and communism imply, therefore, a contradiction in terms. The status of neutrality may be a temporary convenience; it may provide a basis of compromise in particular disputes. It cannot from its nature provide a lasting solution to the problems of a state or group of states.

International Law: The relations between states are governed by a body of rules known as *international law*, which has grown since the Middle Ages from what was then called the *law of nature*. This was a body of precept and doctrine which any rational person would be expected to accept as morally correct, essentially reasonable, and binding upon himself and others. This law was continually being amended and modified as, in the light of new circumstances, new solutions to problems were reached. Such an opinion—and one that closely concerns us—was delivered by the early seventeenth-century Dutch jurist, Hugo Grotius, to the effect that no state may claim sovereignty over the high seas (see page 98). The freedom of the seas has been continuously recognized and asserted. Similarly, the right to use international rivers, that is, rivers that are shared by two or more countries, has become an important subject of international law, as has also the right to take water for irrigation and other purposes from such rivers. The right to sail a ship through straits and other inshore waters and to cross the territory of a neighboring state, whether by land or river, are both subject to the principles and decisions of international lawyers.

Because it may seem eminently reasonable for a state to be permitted to use a river or to have access to the sea, it does not necessarily follow that it will be able to do so. The denial by one state of a reasonable facility to another has been all too frequent. In 1921 the state of Lithuania closed its boundary with Poland and denied to the latter the right to export goods across Lithuania to the port of Memel. At the present time the state of Egypt denies to its neighbor, Israel, the right to send its ships through the Suez Canal and would also deny them access, through the Gulf of Aqaba, to the port of Elath if it were not for the UN military force that is stationed at Sharm el Sheik. In 1946, Albanian guns fired on British warships as they passed through the Corfu Channel; later, the Albanian authorities set mines in the channel. All these were breaches of international law. The first was settled when Poland presented an ultimatum to the Lithuanian government, demanding the immediate opening of the border. Egypt continues to defy the rules of international law, but the Corfu case was heard by the International Court of Justice, which gave judgment against Albania. The latter, despite a previous undertaking, refused to accept the verdict.

The basic weakness of international law is the absence, not of a court competent to hear the cases, but of a mechanism whereby cases may be brought compulsorily before it and its judgments enforced. The League of Nations and, after it, the UN sought to remedy this defect. The former applied "economic sanctions" against Italy in 1935–1936 for its invasion of Ethiopia, without, however, stopping the invasion or saving Ethiopia. The UN used more effective means to deter aggression and to restrict "brush-fire" wars—in Korea, in 1950; in the Middle East, in 1956; in the Congo, in 1960—by raising a military force of mixed nationality and using it effectively. But the UN, as a tribunal to hear international cases, suffers from the defect that its members, who judge the case, may also include both plaintiff and defendant. The UN has been effective in settling disputes that concern small states. It intervened in Korea against Red China only because Red China was not a member of the UN. It is very doubtful that the UN can take any effective action against the small number of Great Powers, armed both with atomic weapons and the power of the veto.

The Permanent Court of International Justice, which has performed great service in settling disputes between states, can act only in cases brought before it by the litigants, who agree in advance to accept the findings of the Court. The Court has no means at its disposal of enforcing its judgments. In the case of the territorial dispute between Sweden and Finland, for example, regarding jurisdiction over the Aaland (Ahvenanmaa) Islands, both states had agreed in advance to put the case before the Permanent Court of International Justice and to abide by its findings. As a result, the islands were placed under the sovereignty of Finland but were neutralized.

Treaties are the instruments by which sovereign states enter into contracts or agreements to perform certain acts or to accord certain facilities. They are negotiated by representatives of the states and subsequently are ratified by the governments, or by some other authority constitutionally appointed for the purpose. It is by means of a treaty that a state of war is formally terminated, that territory is transferred from one state to another, that agreements are reached to move minority peoples, and that trade agreements are made. Some of the rights and privileges confirmed by treaty may already be implicit in the rules of international law, but a treaty gives added confirmation that the right or privilege will be respected. Treaties usually run for a definite term of years; they sometimes make provision for their renunciation by one or more parties to the agreement. These loopholes do not, however, prevent a treaty, like any other form of contract, from being broken. Germany thus broke the terms of the Treaty of Versailles (1919) when her armies reoccupied the demilitarized Rhineland in 1936 and those of the Treaty of London (1831) when in 1914 they invaded Belgium and the Soviet Union those of her nonaggression pact with Poland by her invasion of 1939.

In this and following chapters we are concerned primarily with the ways in which claims to possess or to use specifically geographical objects, such as land and natural resources, are made and enforced. By what right does a state occupy the land on which it is established? What kind of evidence can be adduced in support of the claim for the territory of a neighboring state? How are conflicting claims brought by neighboring states to be evaluated?

CLAIMS TO TERRITORY

Undoubtedly most states would justify their occupation of most of their territory on grounds of *prescription*. In old English law the phrase "since the time whereof memory is not" was used to define an *immemorial* possession or right. So also in international law, "the acquisition of sovereignty over a territory through continuous and undisturbed exercise of sovereignty

Figure 38 *The political map of the world is strewn with territories that are in dispute. The slogan on this building in Szczecin, Poland, runs:* Byliśmy, jesteśmy, będziemy nad Bałtykiem, Odra i Nysa—"We were, are and will remain on the Baltic, Oder and Neisse." PHOTOGRAPH BY N. J. G. POUNDS

over it during such a period as is necessary to create under the influence of historical development the general conviction that the present condition of things is in conformity with international law is held to confer an incontrovertible right to it."[10] Thus a state undoubtedly embraces its core area, and usually a good deal more, by prescriptive right.

At the beginning of the ninteenth century the Spanish colonies in the New World revolted against their mother country and began to form the Latin-American republics of today. In 1810 they adopted the principle, which has come to be known as *uti possidetis juris*, that "the bounds of the newly created republics should be the frontiers of the Spanish provinces for which they were substituted."[11] Much of the area was still unoccupied, except perhaps by nomadic Indian tribes, but this claim to what was in effect a prescriptive right

[10] Oppenheim, *op. cit.*, vol. 1, p. 576.
[11] Arbitration decision of the Swiss Federal Council on the Colombia-Venezuela dispute, quoted in Norman Hill, *Claims to Territory in International Law and Relations*, Oxford University Press, New York, 1945, p. 154.

Figure 39 *A roadside sign in West Germany shows the map of Germany, as it was from 1919 to the Second World War, with the slogan "Divided into three? Never." This amounts to a promise by those responsible for the sign to restore the areas now occupied by Poland.* PHOTOGRAPH BY N. J. G. POUNDS

came to be recognized. This doctrine did not remove the causes of frontier disputes, which have been especially numerous between the Latin-American republics. It merely put them upon a kind of judicial basis and allowed them to be solved by appeal to the Spanish administrative boundaries. The issue thus became one of judicial interpretation of the ordinances of Spain.

A claim to territory based merely on the ground of a former possession of it is not likely, per se, to be accepted in international law, nor to be successful unless backed by the sanction of military power. The fact is, of course, that in some parts of the world, notably in Europe, territorial claims based on history are so conflicting that no equitable settlement could possibly be based on them.

Inheritance was an important basis for the claim to territory during the Middle Ages, for example, the claim of King Edward III of England to the throne of France. From the sixteenth to the eighteenth century inheritance remained an acceptable basis for a territorial claim. The wars of the Spanish Succession (1701–1713) and of the Austrian Succession (1740–1748) were fought to enforce territorial claims based on a hereditary title. But since the Revolutionary and Napoleonic Wars such legitimist claims have been less favored. The most recent that occurs to the author is that put forward by the King of Prussia in 1864 to the inheritance of the Danish duchies of Schleswig and Holstein. Since the territory of a state is no longer regarded as the personal possession of its ruler, it is difficult to believe that a territorial claim, based upon the descent and relationship of royal families, could today be given a moment's serious consideration.

Strategic Claims: A strategic claim is based on the assumption that the possession by a particular state of a certain area of land would give it a significantly greater military security. Under present conditions of war, it is doubtful whether the addition or subtraction of any small piece of territory could itself make much difference to the security of a state. Formerly, however, this was not so. An example was the delimitation of the boundary of France and Germany by the Treaty of Frankfurt (1871) in the vicinity of Belfort. France was allowed to retain enough territory to the east of the city to place it beyond the range of German guns. The boundary that was established by the same treaty across Lorraine was, it has been demonstrated,[12] guided primarily by the military-strategic needs of Germany (see Chapter 3).

[12] R. Hartshorne, "The Franco-German Boundary of 1871," *World Politics*, vol. 2, pp. 209–250, 1950.

Treaty settlements of the eighteenth century are full of references to fortresses and other works which had an exclusively military importance. The Treaty of Versailles demilitarized a belt of territory, several miles wide, to the east of the Rhine and allowed France and her allies to occupy temporarily the area west of the Rhine. The boundary of western Czechoslovakia, following the line of hills that enclose Bohemia, has a good historical justification but was adopted in part because it had a presumed military value. Some areas of Hungary were transferred to Czechoslovakia and Rumania, respectively, in order to assure non-Hungarian control of a railroad. One of the clearest examples of the cession by one country to another of segments of territory because they were thought to constitute a threat to the latter was the transfer of three salients of Bulgarian territory to Yugoslavia in 1919.

These small areas, with a total population of only about 68,000, were regarded as a threat, particularly to the north-south railroad line which followed the Vardar and Morava Valleys. The cession was much criticized and probably constitutes one of the last examples of the transfer of territory for this reason. The boundary between Italy and Austria was placed at the Brenner Pass, not, as language would have suggested, between Bozen and Trento, because of the supposed military advantages to Italy. In 1939, the Soviet Union demanded the cession of the Karelian isthmus from Finland because its close proximity was alleged to constitute a threat to the city of Leningrad.

Economic Claims: Transfers of territory for reasons of economic or resource development have become more important in recent years. The most recent examples are probably the several small areas transferred in 1948 from Germany to the Netherlands and Belgium, respectively. The

Figure 40 The Polish answer to the sign shown in Figure 39 is this map, photographed in Będzin, southern Poland, showing the present boundaries, with the claim that this area was Polish a thousand years ago. The inscription runs "A thousand years of the Polish State." PHOTOGRAPH BY N. J. G. POUNDS

areas transferred to the Netherlands together made up only about twenty-seven square miles and those to Belgium and Luxembourg about twenty-five square miles. The reason for the forced cession of each separate piece of land was either economic or technical: flood control, land drainage, railroad operation, and mining.

There have been relatively few transfers of territory since the end of the Second World War, in marked contrast to the very extensive cessions that followed the First World War, when the economic or resource motive was prominent. France took over the Saar coal mines, though the Saar territory was itself placed under the League of Nations; Belgium was assured the use of a railroad from Eupen to Malmédy, though between these two cities it actually ran through German territory. The cession to Czechoslovakia and Rumania of territory for the sake of the railroads they contained, the establishment of free zones in ports, the attempt to secure for Yugoslavia the port of Rijeka (Fiume), and the establishment of the Polish Corridor itself were all aimed at securing certain economic or technical privileges for particular states.

The map of Europe today does not differ greatly, except in the boundaries of Poland, the Baltic States, Finland, and Rumania, from that established after the First World War. The changes on the western border of Germany have already been noted. A very small area of Hungary, lying across the Danube from Bratislava, was then ceded for similar reasons to Czechoslovakia.

Two small areas in the French Alps have been ceded by Italy to France. All these and other minor changes have been prompted mainly by economic considerations. Similarly the nineteenth-century territorial changes in Latin America, resulting from the war between Chile, Peru, and Bolivia, and those between Bolivia and Paraguay and between Ecuador and Peru in the twentieth century must also be judged to have been primarily economic, as their purpose was to gain or retain access to a river or to the coast for purposes of trade or to acquire possession of mineral resources.

Ethnic Claims: Territorial changes due to economic claims have been numerous and important in the modern world, but the most important single ground for a claim to territory, and the one which today is most likely to gain acceptance, is based upon the ethnic composition of the population. It has to be a very strong economic claim indeed to stand against the desire of nations to be united under one government. The pattern of boundaries established at the end of the First World War both in Europe and the Middle East was said to have been based overwhelmingly on ethnic

considerations. British India was partitioned along communal lines as far as the broken communal boundaries permitted, even though this made nonsense of the irrigation works in parts of the Indus Basin. Jordan's occupation of the Judean hill country at the time when the British mandate for Palestine terminated and the state of Israel was created was also based upon the fact that the inhabitants of this poor and semiarid country were not Jews, but Arabs. At the Munich Settlement of September, 1938, German annexation of Czechoslovak territory was excused by the fact that the areas incorporated were German in language and culture.

The region at the head of the Adriatic Sea, where Italy and Yugoslavia meet, has been the scene of territorial claims and counterclaims, based both upon the ethnic composition of the population and economic needs of the two countries. At the end of the First World War Italy had possession of the port of Trieste together with its immediate hinterland, the peninsula of Istria. Fiume (Rijeka) was the subject of controversy because most of its population was Italian but was claimed as economically essential by Yugoslavia. It was seized by the Italian freebooter Gabriele D'Annunzio (1919) and after a short existence as a "free city" was incorporated into Italy. At the end of the Second World War, Fiume (Rijeka) was restored to Yugoslavia. The port of Trieste and its immediate hinterland were placed under allied military control and divided into two zones, of which zone A, made up of the city of Trieste and its immediate vicinity, has since been incorporated into Italy, while zone B has been incorporated into Yugoslavia. This solution was probably as equitable as any boundary could possibly be that was drawn through this region of mixed cultures.

Many other examples could be enumerated from Europe and southwestern and southeastern Asia, but enough have been presented to show that, in the present climate of opinion, the ethnic character of the people is more likely to be accepted as evidence for a change of boundary than any other reason.

Claims Based on Proximity: The possession of a given territory has commonly been regarded as giving a right to control any neighboring territory that had not already been settled and developed. The American nineteenth-century doctrine of manifest destiny was clearly an exemplification of this view. A claim of 1805 to the territory of Texas was based on the assumption that "when any European nation takes possession of any extensive sea coast, that possession is understood as extending into the interior country, to the sources of the rivers emptying within that coast, to all their branches, and the country they covered. . . ." [13] Most such claims did not limit themselves to the watershed but were conceived of as extending inland until territory subject to some conflicting claim was reached. It was on such a basis as this that claims to African territory by European colonial powers were largely made in the nineteenth century.

At the present time the doctrine of proximity is essentially the basis of the claim of Argentina to sovereignty over the Falkland Islands. Australia, New Zealand, Chile, and Argentina, the most southerly states on the globe, have based their claims to segments of Antarctica on grounds of proximity; and Chile and Argentina both claim the islands, known as the Falkland Islands Dependencies, which lie between their own continent and Antarctica, on the same basis. Unfortunately, the islands in question are as near to one country as to the other, and the conflicting claims have

not been resolved. Canada similarly claims sovereignty over islands lying north of Canada and between its coast and the pole.

Proximity has sometimes been conceived as giving to a state a kind of sphere of influence over some neighboring area. When, in 1823, President Monroe sent his famous message to Congress, that "We owe it . . . to candor and to the amicable relations existing between the United States and those Powers [of Europe] to declare that we should consider any attempt on their part to extend their system to any portion of this hemisphere as dangerous to our peace and safety . . . ," he was in fact establishing a very limited sphere of influence. "A sphere of influence involves no direct interference with administration of that sphere"; [14] the proclamation of such a sphere is merely a warning to other powers to limit their activities within it to those which could not in any degree impugn its independence and sovereignty. Great Britain has had since the sixteenth century a similar interest in the Low Countries, regarding them not so much a sphere of interest of her own as an area in which no other Great Power might be permitted to gain a preponderant interest. The United States has not yet gone to war in defense of the Monroe Doctrine—though she came quite near it in the dispute with Great Britain over Venezuela. Great Britain has, however, on several occasions found herself at war in defense of the integrity of the Low Countries. At the present time, the Soviet Union regards Finland as lying within its sphere of influence and, while it claims no sovereignty or direct control over Finland, does expect its advice to be sought and its counsel obeyed, at least in major foreign-policy decisions.

Such spheres of influence are com-

---

[13] Quoted by Albert K. Weinberg, *Manifest Destiny*, Baltimore, 1935, p. 51.

[14] Sir Thomas H. Holdich, *Political Frontiers and Boundary Making*, London, 1916, p. 96.

monly given a degree of recognition by other powers, though this may go no further than their refraining from making embarrassing demands. Occasionally this relationship is embodied in a treaty. In 1907 the United Kingdom and Russia actually delimited their spheres of interest in Persia (Iran). Such a clear definition of a state's subordinate position is unlikely to be openly expressed in the present climate of international opinion, though it may be tacitly recognized.

Geographical Claims: Claims to territory based on essentially geographical, as distinct from economic, considerations are in fact a reversion to a philosophical stand-point of the eighteenth century. The Irish Republic lays claim to the six counties of Northern Ireland because of the essential unity of the island of Ireland; Nehru once claimed a similar unity for the former territory of British India; Franco claimed that the Iberian peninsula also constituted such a unit, though in recent years he appears to have become somewhat more reticent on this point. The alleged unity of a river basin, such as that used by the United States as a basis for claiming Texas or in pressing the more extravagant claim which would have given her much of Canada, "The waters of the St. Lawrence and the Mississippi interlock in a number of

Figure 41 A Spanish frontier guard looks across at the Rock of Gibraltar, which the British have held since 1704. At intervals the Spanish government claims that it is Spanish territory and should be returned. COURTESY: PAUL POPPER

places . . . the great Disposer of Human Events intended these two rivers should belong to the same people," [15] is also essentially a geographical argument.

This kind of argument has in recent years been given a new significance. It is implicit in the early writers that they regarded the hilly or mountainous divides which lie between river basins as the operative force, holding the basins apart from one another. Today the technical problems of flood control and drainage, irrigation, and power generation are emphasizing the essential unity of river basins. Nasser's claim, on behalf of Egypt, to have a controlling voice in settling the destinies of the Sudan was not without a certain justification in technology. This aspect of geographical claims to territory is examined more fully in the next chapter.

Acquisition of Territory: A state can acquire territory in one of three ways. The first is by the cession of the territory of one state to another. Such a cession normally follows a war. Indeed there have been very few conflicts which have not been followed by a transfer of some territory. Each such transfer, at least in modern times, has been embodied in a formal treaty. Thus, Bolivia ceded territory to Chile after its defeat in the war of 1879; Finland, to the Soviet Union in 1940 and again in 1945; France, after its defeat at the hands of Prussia in 1870–1871; Germany, after its defeat in the First World War. There is nothing to prevent a state ceding the whole of itself to another, as Korea did to Japan in 1910.[16]

Sometimes such territory is purchased, as Alaska was in 1867 from Russia and the Virgin Islands from Denmark in 1916, or leased, as was the Canal Zone in 1903 from the Republic of Panama. Occasionally territory has passed as a marriage dowry, sometimes also as a pledge for the payment of a debt or fulfillment of an obligation. In each case the contractual obligation was formulated in a treaty.

The second method of acquiring territory is by occupation. Occupation is the act of taking over of territory in which there is no recognized sovereignty. Columbus, for instance, occupied parts of the New World; the European colonial powers occupied much of Africa, and the English colonists much of the Eastern seaboard of the United States, as well as Australia, New Zealand, and other territories. In none of these instances was the occupation on any kind of contractual basis, nor was it confirmed by a treaty. It was recognized by other states, and the European powers in question continued to occupy most of these territories until the latter gained independence. There have been only a few cases of disputed occupation. The most famous is that of eastern Greenland. This region of ice and bare rock, framed by an inhospitable coast, is almost uninhabitable and can be approached only with difficulty. Denmark claimed to have "occupied" this region, along with the rest of Greenland, early in the eighteenth century. During the present century Norway claimed sovereignty over the area, and the dispute was referred to the Permanent Court of International Justice. The Court ruled in 1931 that "occupation" consisted both in "the intention or will to act as sovereign, and some actual exercise or display of authority." Any display of authority in eastern Greenland was, from the nature of things, difficult. It was held by the Court, therefore, that "A slight exercise of authority will suffice when no state can show a superior claim." The recognition, tacit or overt, by several states of Denmark's sovereignty over eastern Greenland was cited, and the Court found that Denmark had shown its intention to

---

[15] Quoted in Weinberg, *op. cit.*, p. 53.

[16] Examples of this curious practice are discussed in Oppenheim, *op. cit.*, vol. 1, p. 549.

be sovereign and had taken adequate steps to display its authority.

Continuous settlement, however thinly scattered the settlers may be, is undoubtedly a display of authority. The South Polar continent, however, has never had permanent inhabitants, though the territory, or some part of it, is claimed by no fewer than seven states. A claim based on proximity, in order to become recognized, should be made good by occupation, and this has, in fact, not been done. The failure to make any regular or permanent display of authority, which from the nature of things would be difficult, is the fundamental reason for the continuation of the conflicting claims in this area.

The last method by which territory is acquired is by the work of nature, though nature may be assisted in this by man. Silt carried down the Mississippi River is borne by the current out through the distributaries of the delta and laid down upon the shallow sea floor beyond. By the continuous operation of this process the shore line progra, and the areal extent of the state is increased. The process may be assisted by man, as when, in the Netherlands, a wall is built to enclose a stretch of tidal land and the enclosed area is drained and made available for agriculture. Such extensions of territory create no political problem, and the territorial sea (see Chapter 4) of the state is measured from the new coast line.

Changes in rivers, by the operation of natural causes, may give rise to more serious problems. Rivers have often been chosen as boundaries because of their alleged permanence. But all rivers undergo a slow change. Not only are their beds slowly sunk or incised more deeply into the rock, but the rivers swing, or meander, as rock-forming material is worn from one bank and deposited on the other. Islands may form, and may also disappear, in the bed of the river. In time of flood, a river may even desert its original channel and form a new one. The quiet-flowing rivers of northwestern Europe were among the first to be used as boundaries, and the slowness with which they change was certainly an important factor in their success in this role. The Mississippi River was adopted throughout almost all its length as a boundary between States. The decision was made [17] by persons who probably had only a very slight acquaintance with the Mississipi, which is liable, especially in its lower reaches, to sudden and violent changes of course. As a result of such changes many square miles of land have been transferred from one bank to the other. The Rio Grande, adopted in 1848 as the boundary between the United States and Mexico, is liable to an even greater degree than the Mississippi to rapid changes in its course (see page 74). Other examples of such rivers, which serve also as boundaries, are the Murray in Australia, the lower course of the Danube, and the middle course of the Rhine. Many others could be listed merely by looking through a good atlas.

So far we have been examining ways in which territory may change hands in a wholly legal fashion, recognized by other states. Today, with the decay of international law, there may be transfers of territory or of sovereignty which are not recognized by law but which are nonetheless real. They involve interrupting the chain of responsibility or command within a state and its diversion in the direction of external sources of power. The government of a state may be controlled by that of another without even altering its legal forms or outwardly modifying its independence. This has been achieved within the Communist bloc. Permeating the countries of

[17] It was first adopted as a boundary in the Treaty of Paris, 1782, between the United States and Louisiana Territory. The treaty makers were certainly ignorant of the character of the river.

the bloc is the Communist Party, with its own means of communication and control. The Party in the Soviet Union can command the Party in Czechoslovakia or Rumania, and the latter controls the state. While Czechoslovakia and Rumania are legally independent and sovereign states, recognized as such in international law and by membership in the UN, this independence is in fact qualified by a high degree of extralegal control.

The governments of most of the satellites are effectively controlled by the Soviet Union and their foreign policies, as well as in large measure their domestic, directed by it. The Soviet Union and its East European allies vote together at the UN; they adopt the same line on current issues, and their diplomatic actions are so carefully synchronized that there can be no doubt that they are all dictated from Moscow. We can thus speak of a *neocolonialism*, by which a powerful state, like the Soviet Union, controls the destinies of a weaker by means that are not generally overt, like those of the old-style colonialism, but discreetly hidden in the mechanism of the Party. China's relations with North Korea and with North Vietnam belong also to this category of relationship.

We now turn to a discussion of three specific ways in which states, in pursuit of their own security and well-being, conflict with one another, namely, in their claims to the right of transit for persons and property across the territory of neighboring states, in their claims to some exclusive form of trade, and in their claims to use in whatever ways suit them the waters of rivers that they share with other states.

ACCESS TO THE SEA

No question raises with such clarity the conflict between so-called "rights" of states and the self-interest of their neighbors as that of access to the sea. It was

clearly stated in the United States in 1823 when the citizens of Franklin County, New York, presented to Congress a request that "the right might be secured to them of sending their exports . . . through the St. Lawrence to the Atlantic." [18] Congress favored this claim, and, on the instructions of John Quincy Adams, then Secretary of State, the matter was taken up by the United States Ambassador to the Court of St. James. The American claim was based upon the "general principles of the law of nations." "It was the duty of the government of the United States," wrote Adams, to secure to the inhabitants of its States and Territories bordering the Great Lakes and St. Lawrence River "the natural right of communicating with the ocean by the only outlet provided by nature. . . . " [19]

Adams argued that, whereas the rights enjoyed by Great Britain over the St. Lawrence River derived only from the "social compact"—an allusion to the liberal concept of the origin of the rights of sovereignty in a hypothetical social contract—the right to navigate the river was an overriding right because it was "a right of nature, preceding it in point of time." The British government received with some skepticism these arguments grounded upon natural law. Clay revived the claim three years later, again basing the American argument upon the premises of natural law. But the opening of the Erie Canal removed the immediate pretext for the claim, and the matter was allowed to rest for a while. In 1854, the Reciprocity Treaty guaranteed to American citizens "the right to navigate the River St. Lawrence, and the canals in Canada which were used as the means of communicating between the Great Lakes and the Atlantic Ocean."

This was not the first occasion when

[18] E. Schuyler, *American Diplomacy and the Furtherance of Commerce*, London, 1886, p. 282.
[19] Quoted by J. B. Moore, *A Digest of International Law*, 1906, vol. 1, p. 632.

the American government felt obliged to claim the right for its citizens to navigate the rivers which flowed from within its borders across the territory of adjoining states. Spaniards in Louisiana had obstructed American traders who had tried to sail down the Mississippi River to the Gulf. Jefferson protested. "The ocean," he wrote, "is free to all men, and their rivers to all their inhabitants. . . . When their rivers enter the limits of another society, if the right of the upper inhabitants to descend the stream is in any case obstructed, it is an act of force by a stronger society against a weaker, condemned by the judgment of mankind. . . ." [20] In 1795, the Treaty of San Lorenzo el Real gave to American citizens the right to sail across Spanish territory to the sea.

The argument that states have a "natural right" to an outlet to the sea and, conversely, that other nations have a right of access to them continued for many decades to be an overtone in American policy. It appears as a kind of corollary to the doctrine of the freedom of the seas. If the ocean is free to all mankind, it is reasonable to suppose that every people should have access to the shores of the ocean and the right to navigate all navigable rivers discharging into it since they are "only a natural prolongation of the free high seas." [21]

President Grant reiterated the old argument that the St. Lawrence was the "natural outlet to the ocean for eight states." A note to Brazil, in 1853, claimed the Amazon as a "great natural highway" up which American citizens should be allowed to sail in order to trade with the "back country" of Peru and Ecuador. "You are instructed," wrote Secretary of State Marcy to the Brazilian Ambassador, "to claim for our citizens the use of this natural avenue of trade. This right is not derived from treaty stipulations—it is a natural one—as much so as that to navigate the ocean. . . ." And again, in a note addressed to the American chargé d'affaires in Bolivia, he claimed "the free use of all the natural means of international communication, obviously designed by a wise Providence for the common benefit of all civilized nations." [22]

The Scheldt Question: The declaration of Jefferson, already mentioned, anticipated by a few months a similar but more widely known declaration of the French *Conseil Exécutif.* After the successful revolt of the Dutch in the sixteenth century, a boundary was drawn across the lower Scheldt, cutting the port of Antwerp off from the sea. By the Treaty of Münster, 1648, the lower Scheldt was closed to shipping from the upper river, and no ship was allowed by the Dutch to pass from Antwerp downstream to the sea. The Emperor Joseph II, who would not willingly see "his subjects deprived by policy of the advantages that nature had given them" demanded the opening of the Scheldt. The Dutch saw in this a threat to the prosperity of Amsterdam and strongly and successfully resisted the efforts of Joseph II. It remained for the armies of France to reopen the Scheldt in 1792 and for the French Executive Council to declare that "the obstacles and hindrances to trade which had hitherto existed . . . are directly contrary to the fundamental principles of natural law, . . . that the course of rivers is the common and inalienable property of all the countries through which they flow. . . . Nature no

---

[20] *American State Papers, Foreign Relations,* vol. 1, pp. 253–254; also G. Kaeckenbeeck, *International Rivers,* London, 1918, p. 206; *Jefferson's Works,* vol. 7, pp. 577–580.

[21] Barcelona Conference, *Verbatim Records and Texts Relating to the Convention on the Regime of Navigable Waterways,* League of Nations, Geneva, 1921, p. 26.

[22] Quoted by Moore, *op. cit.,* vol. 1, pp. 643–644.

more recognizes privileged peoples than privileged individuals."

At the end of the Napoleonic Wars, the Congress of Vienna, wishing to secure for the future the freedom to navigate the Scheldt, Rhine, and other rivers of international importance, codified the principles that had been established in the preceding years. It was these clauses which Secretary of State Adams invoked in support of his claim that American citizens should be free to navigate the St. Lawrence.

Thus, it came to be accepted in many quarters that a state has a right of access to the shores of the ocean and that such access is necessary for the development of commerce and industry and is sanctioned by natural law. Almost a century after Secretary Adams's claims, President Wilson, addressing the Senate in January, 1917, said that "So far as practicable . . . every great people now struggling towards a full development of its resources and of its powers should be assured a direct outlet to the highways of the sea. . . . With a right comity of arrangement no nation need be shut away from free access to the open paths of the world's commerce. . . ." Although he was at the time thinking primarily of the claims of Poland, he was careful to base the claim on something more fundamental than expediency. He made no reference to natural law, but there was probably little difference between his reasoning and that of Thomas Jefferson, John Quincy Adams, and Henry Clay.

Wilson admitted that annexation of territory was not always necessary to ensure access to the sea: "It can no doubt be done by the neutralization of direct rights of way under the general guarantee [i.e., the proposed League of Nations] which will assure the peace itself." In fact, access to the sea can be, and is, obtained in one of three distinct ways: (1) the right to use an "international" river, (2) the pos-

session of a "corridor" to the coast, and (3) transit rights across another country, with or without the rights of a free zone in a port of the latter.

The first of these, the right to use a navigable waterway to gain access to the sea across the territory of another state, is so important and is bound up so closely with questions of the use of the river for power and irrigation that the whole matter is deferred to the next chapter.

Corridors to the Sea: A corridor reaching to the seacoast implies a transfer of sovereignty over an area of land in order to give to the inland state an assured outlet to the ocean. It is implied that this consideration is alone responsible for determining the boundaries of the territory in question and that historical and ethnic factors are not important. It is probable, however, that no corridor has ever been established without at least paying lip service to other considerations, except in barren and uninhabited regions.

It is inevitable that a state would prefer to control a corridor rather than to have transit rights, or the freedom to use a river. While theoretically all should be equally protected in international law, in fact any attempt to close a corridor would be a violation of national sovereignty, while interference with the right of passage might be more easily condoned or excused.

Historically, the outstanding example of the acquisition of corridors to the sea is the expansion of Czarist Russia from the Moscow region toward the Baltic and Black Seas. Even a superficial reading of the events of the reign of Peter the Great demonstrates how vital he considered it to be to have a corridor to these seas. His conquest of Ingria in 1703 was followed by the foundation of St. Petersburg, which became, in the words of Pushkin, his "window on Europe." Peter the Great's occupation of Azov, at the mouth of the Donets River, was short-lived, but his successor, the Czarina Anne, obtained Azov permanently in 1739. To these should be added the annexation by Russia in 1860 of the Primorsk Province, leading to the establishment, a year later, of the port of Vladivostok.

Exclusive control over a corridor and over the commerce that would use it was in line with mercantilist economic thought in the eighteenth century. The advantages of such controlled outlets to the sea were apparent to certain individuals, such as Peter the Great, who pursued them with great vigor. But it is highly improbable that an "urge to the sea" ever constituted an underlying geographical compulsion running through the whole of Russian history.[23]

The Polish Corridor: The best-known and the most publicized of modern corridors is the Polish. In January, 1918, President Woodrow Wilson included in the Fourteen Points which he proposed as a basis of a world peace: "Thirteen. An independent Polish State should be erected . . . which should be assured a free and secure access to the sea. . . ." This idea had been slowly taking shape in Wilson's mind during the preceding year. He assumed that Poland should have an outlet to the sea, though this seems to have been based at first on the "natural" right of a state, rather than on ethnic considerations in the corridor area itself. Even at the Peace Conference, an American policy report stated that "if Poland does not thus secure access to the sea . . . Poles in Poland proper will probably have but a hampered and precarious commercial outlet, subject to alien . . . and hostile decision."[24]

Thus, the Americans were predisposed to the view that a state has a right to an outlet to the sea. Such a belief was in accord with opinions on international law that had been held in the United States for a century. The Poles themselves contributed most to putting the corridor issue on an ethnic basis by demonstrating that the so-called "Corridor" was predominantly Polish in language and sympathy. This double-barreled claim was successful, and as Haskins and Lord have pointed out, one barrel alone might not have carried the day:

> Poland needs an access to the sea, but it was not solely because she needed it that she obtained it. The Peace Conference probably would not have satisfied this desire if ethnical reasons had not authorized it to do so. The Conference did not invent the "Corridor": it existed already.[25]

During the interwar years the Poles were at great pains to emphasize that they had obtained their Corridor in virtue, not of the old doctrine of the right of access to the sea, but of the new Wilsonian doctrine of the rights of ethnic groups.

The Arctic Corridor: A less complex instance of the transfer of territory in order to give access to the sea is provided in Finland's Arctic Corridor. When Finland passed from Sweden to Russia in 1809 it retained many of its old institutions and became an archduchy, with the Russian Czar as its duke. In 1920, the independence of the Finnish Republic was recognized in the Treaty of Dorpat, and Finland retained the boundaries which it had possessed under the Czars except for the addition of the Corridor to the Arctic Ocean (Exhibit 82). The reason for the exception was clear. Though Finland has an extensive coast line on the Baltic Sea, most of it is icebound for

---

[23] This has been discussed by John A. Morrison, "Russia and Warm Water," *United States Naval Institute Proceedings,* vol. 78, pp. 1169–1179, 1952.

[24] Quoted in Louis L. Gerson, *Woodrow Wilson and the Rebirth of Poland,* Yale University Press, New Haven, Conn., 1953, p. 125.

[25] C. H. Haskins and R. H. Lord, *Some Problems of the Peace Conference,* Cambridge University Press, New York, 1920, p. 153.

a long period in winter, whereas the newly acquired strip of Arctic coast is ice-free throughout the year. It was the intention of Finland to establish a port at the end of the Corridor, but the port of Petsamo, twenty years afterward, had a population of only 2,000 and carried on a negligible foreign trade. In 1945 the Corridor and port reverted to the Soviet Union.

Three other regions of the world have been particularly productive both of corridors and of rights of transit to the sea: the Danubian and Balkan lands, the Middle East, and the Central Andean states. In each, the political fragmentation of the region, accompanied by the existence of geographical barriers to movement, has made access to the sea unusually difficult.

The Balkans: Prior to 1867 Hungary and Serbia had always been landlocked states. When Hungary was separated politically from Austria in 1867, its territory was made to include a corridor, which reached to the head of the Adriatic Sea and included the port of Fiume (Rijeka). It was also Serbia's political ambition to acquire some means of direct access to the sea (Exhibit 83).

Geographically the easiest route lay southward to the Aegean, but expansion in this direction would have met with opposition from both Greece and Bulgaria. Alternatively Serbia might reach out through the mountains of Turkish Albania to the shore of the Adriatic. This is what Serbia attempted to do in the First Balkan War (1912–1913). Had they been given to philosophizing, the Serbs would doubtless have proclaimed their right to the "natural" route which Providence had created for their use along the valley of the Drin and across Albania to the Adriatic Sea. Unfortunately for Serbia, the Great Powers intervened, denied her this corridor, and sealed up the outlet by creating the state of Albania.

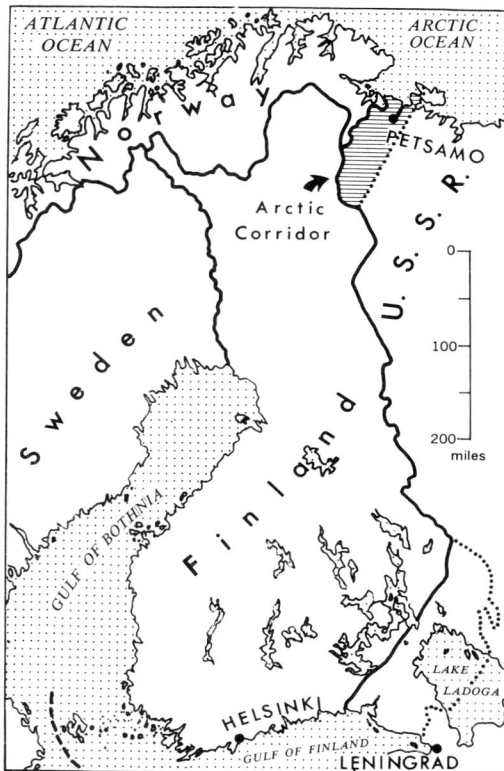

Exhibit 82   Access to the sea: Finland.

Serbia grew into Yugoslavia, but, despite the possession of a long coast line, the problem of access to the sea was not completely solved, because the Dinaric Mountains separated the populous and developed regions of Yugoslavia from the coast. For this reason, Yugoslavia claimed, and for a short time also held, the port of Rijeka (Fiume), but after 1924 had to be content with its small suburb of Šušak. In 1945, Yugoslavia again acquired possession not only of Rijeka but also of the whole of Istria, with only Trieste eluding her. This territory may perhaps be classed as a corridor in so far as Yugoslavia's ethnic claim, at least to some of the coastal cities, was not at first clear cut. It was later strengthened by the expulsion of much of the Italian population.

Exhibit 83   *Access to the sea: the Balkans.*

Bulgaria experienced a similar urge to reach the coast of the Aegean Sea. As a result of the First Balkan War of 1912–1913 she acquired a corridor across the non-Bulgarian territory of Thrace and, thus, gained access to the small ports of Kavalla and Dedeagats (Exhibit 84). The former was lost during the Second Balkan War, but Bulgaria retained the narrower corridor to Dedeagats until she was deprived of this, too, in 1919 by the Treaty of Neuilly. The Greek government did, however, undertake

Exhibit 84   *Access to the sea: Bulgaria.*

to afford to Bulgaria free access to an Aegean port, a privilege which the Bulgarians did not use.

The Middle East: The complex pattern of peoples and cultures has made access to the sea unusually difficult in the Middle East, but the Persian Gulf and Red Sea reach far into the land and considerably reduce the problem. Iraq and Jordan are essentially inland states. The former, in the boundary settlement of 1922, acquired a corridor reaching to the head of the Persian Gulf. It was a deltaic tract of land but included sovereignty over the Shatt-al-Arab, the river by which the Tigris and Euphrates reach the Persian Gulf.

The boundaries of both Palestine and Transjordan were made to converge on the head of the Gulf of Aqaba, so that each held a short stretch of about eight miles of this rocky coast. These were conceived of as corridors to the sea at the time when they were established, but neither was much used before the Second World War. Israel today retains her corridor to the Gulf of Aqaba, but the growth of the small settlement of Elath has been restricted by the Egyptian blockade of the gulf. The presence of a small UN force has, since the autumn of 1956, guaranteed the freedom of ingress to and egress from the port. All the precedents cited support the Israeli claim to the peaceful use of the Gulf of Aqaba and the narrow Strait of Tiran, by which it is entered.

About five miles to the east, the settlement of Aqaba has grown to be the most important commercial outlet of Jordan. Formerly, most of Transjordan's small trade had passed across Palestinian territory to the Mediterranean coast. An alternative route through Syria and Lebanon is long and costly, and so, with international assistance, port installations have been built at Aqaba and an all-weather road laid down from the gulf northward to meet the Amman-Mecca railroad.

The Andean States: A third region where the question of corridors to the sea has led to bitter feeling, and even to war, is in the Central Andean states of South America. The problem here is that the states of Bolivia and Paraguay are inland and have access to the ocean only across the territory of their neighbors (Exhibit 85). The problem of Paraguay is the simpler and is, in fact, partially covered by the internationalization of the Paraguay and Paraná Rivers. Bolivia raises a more delicate problem because she possessed until 1883 the now Chilean Province of Antofagasta. A treaty of 1904 assured to Bolivia an outlet to the Pacific Coast by the projected Arica–La Paz railroad, which was about to be built. This right was further defined in 1929. Bolivia might be able to use the tributaries of the Amazon and Paraguay Rivers, which rise within her borders, to gain access to the sea, though these are of doubtful economic value.

Reference has already been made to the opening of the Amazon to the commerce of the states which bordered its headwaters. This has brought with it competition between these states for access to the easily navigated tracts of the river. A dispute continued for over a century between Peru and Ecuador for control of the Oriente, a territory lying between the Marañon, or upper Amazon, and the Colombian border. Ecuador claimed an area which would have given her control of the Amazon River port of Iquitos, but she has had to remain content with the headwaters of the Napo and Putumayo Rivers. Recently, however, Ecuador has renewed her claim to a tract of land extending from the present boundary to the Marañon and Santiago Rivers and lying within Peruvian

Figure 42 **Israel possesses a corridor to the head of the Gulf of Aqaba.** *There the Israeli government is building the port of Elath, seen in this photograph.* COURTESY: ISRAELI OFFICE OF INFORMATION

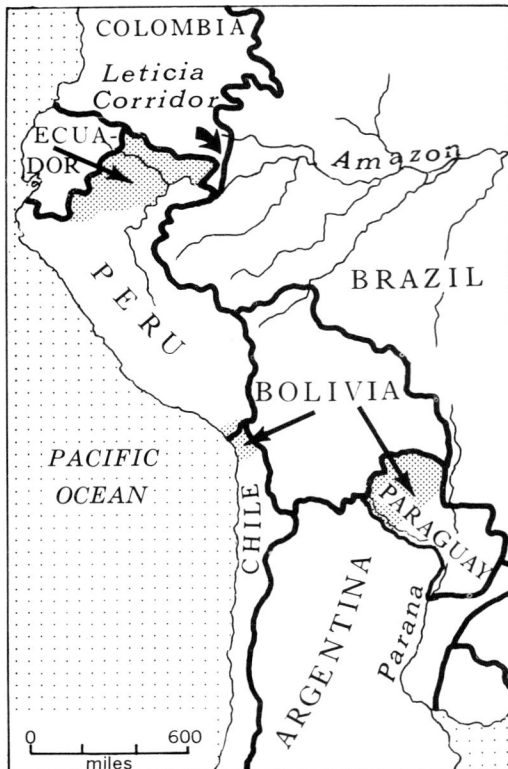

Exhibit 85   *Access to the sea: the Andean states.*

later were modified in 1927 to give the Belgian Congo this narrow strip of territory.

A final example of territorial corridors are the boundaries of the States of Alabama and Mississippi. Following the purchase of Florida from Spain in 1819, the long panhandle of West Florida was partitioned, and sections were allocated to the newly created States of Mississippi and Alabama, thus giving them corridors to the Gulf Coast. Though there soon ceased to be any necessity for these outlets, some excuse for them can be found in the military history of the previous years. The port of Mobile grew up on Alabama's corridor, but Mississippi, well equipped with ports along the Mississippi River, has shown no comparable development.

Right of Transit: It has, in fact, come to be accepted that an inland state has the right "to have the same facilities for access to the sea . . . as if the journey had taken place on the territory of a single state." [26] The issues involved were clarified at the Barcelona Conference on Freedom of Transit, and about forty nations signed the Convention on Freedom of Transit that was adopted in 1921, and thirty-two of them have since ratified the Convention. [27] The signatories undertook to assist the movement of goods across their territories, to levy

territory. It cannot be said. that the volume of her commerce has apparently suffered by her failure to reach the navigable Amazon.

In 1922 Colombia obtained from Peru the narrow but conspicuous Leticia Corridor, thus giving her a frontage of about seventy-five miles on the Amazon. At present both Colombia and Peru have access to the more easily navigated part of the Amazon, and Peru now controls the "ocean" port of Iquitos. Ecuador has access only to the almost unnavigable headwaters of the Amazon.

The Congo Republic has a narrow corridor linking it with the shore of the Atlantic Ocean. These boundaries, first defined at the Berlin Conference of 1885,

[26] Osborne Mance, *International Road Transport, Postal Electricity and Miscellaneous Questions,* Oxford University Press, Oxford, 1947, p. 174.

[27] The Barcelona Convention was ratified by Albania, Belgium, the British Empire (colonial dependencies only; New Zealand and India ratified separately), Bulgaria, Chile, Czechoslovakia, the Free City of Danzig (through Poland as intermediary), Denmark, Estonia, Finland, France (also on behalf of Syria and Lebanon), Germany, Greece, Hungary, Iran, Iraq, Italy, Japan, Latvia, Luxembourg, the Netherlands (with its dependencies, including the Netherlands Indies), Norway, Poland, Rumania, Spain, Sweden, Switzerland, Thailand, Turkey, and Yugoslavia. Information supplied by the UN.

Figure 43 *Pipelines are used increasingly for long-distance transportation of fluids like oil. International pipelines can be constructed only after an agreement between the countries involved has prepared the way for them. This photograph, taken near Banias, Syria, shows the oil pipeline from the Kirkuk oil field, Iraq, to the Mediterranean coast of Syria. It is 556 miles long and is made up of six 30-inch pipes.* COURTESY: SHELL PHOTOGRAPHIC UNIT

no discriminatory tolls or taxes, and to fix freight charges which, "having regard to the conditions of the traffic and to considerations of commercial competition between routes, are reasonable as regards both their rates and the method of their application."

Legally, then, such countries as Hungary and Czechoslovakia had the right to export and import goods through any convenient port across the territory of their neighbors, as these had all acceded to the Barcelona Convention. Some states which did not sign the international convention nevertheless entered into bilateral agreements with their neighbors permitting them the right of access to the sea. The movement of Canadian goods across northern Maine to the Maritime Provinces and the

port of Halifax was governed by an Anglo-American convention of 1871. Portugal made similar agreements regarding access to the sea across her African territories from the (Belgian) Congo, Transvaal, and Rhodesia. Bolivia has similar rights across northern Chile, in addition to her rights in regard to the navigation of international rivers. Before 1935 there were arrangements by which the inland state of Abyssinia had access to Red Sea and Gulf of Aden ports, and Iraq obtained a right of transit to the Mediterranean coast across both Transjordan and Palestine.

Closely akin to these rights was that claimed by the Czarist government over the Chinese Eastern Railway across Manchuria, which shortened by over five hundred miles

Figure 44 *The importance of the right of transit across the territory of another state has never been so great as along the routes that lead to West Berlin. Here the road from West Berlin is seen beginning its hundred-mile course across the East Zone to Helmstedt, on the border of West Germany.* PHOTOGRAPH BY N. J. G. POUNDS

the journey to Vladivostok. Until 1905, Russia also had operating rights over the South Manchurian Railway, which linked its east-west lines with the Dairen Peninsula and Port Arthur. In fact, there is only one clear case of a coastal state in modern times regularly refusing to allow an inland state to have access to its coast: the Lithuanian refusal from 1920 to 1939 to allow movement across her borders from Poland.

While there has been no change in the legal status of transit rights during the past twenty years, the actual practice of nations has undoubtedly deteriorated. This has happened in two distinct ways. In the first place, states have used their ability to interfere with the right of transit of goods across their territory as an instrument of national policy. The clearest examples of this have occurred in the Middle East: Egypt's interference with the rights of Israel; the obstruction and even destruction of pipelines by other Middle Eastern states; and interference by Soviet and East German authorities with the rights of access to West Berlin.

Elsewhere the threat or even the fear that transit rights would be denied has prevented some countries from making use of rights which were legally theirs. Though there has been no overt interference with the movement of goods, the fear of such interference has not always been absent from India and Pakistan and from Turkey and Syria, and suggestions have again been heard in Canada that a corridor across the Alaskan Panhandle would be more advantageous to British Columbia than the existing transit rights. The use that is now being made of the Israeli and Jordan corridors to the Gulf of Aqaba demonstrates that corridors can be effective in cases where a right of transit would in all probability have been denied. It may thus be said that, with a weakening of the efficacy of legal restraints on states, territorial corridors are seen to have greater value than simple rights of transit.

The freedom of movement, established between the two world wars by international agreements, has been prejudiced, second, by the division of the greater part of the world into two hostile camps. The existence of the Iron Curtain has not in itself restricted the right of transit across it. Czechoslovak exports are currently being shipped through the port of Hamburg, and Hungarian goods pass through the ports of Rijeka and Trieste. The case of the freedom of access from the German Federal Republic to West Berlin is, in fact, a different matter, but the 1948 blockade of Berlin and more recent threats to its communications suggest that the countries bordering the Iron Curtain may not indefinitely honor the transit rights of others. The fear that a privilege may be denied restrains nations and states from planning to make regular use of it. Goods do not pass, for example, from the main body of Communist Europe to its outlying member, Albania, across intervening Yugoslavia, despite the fact that Yugoslavia and all the "satellites" are signatories of the Barcelona Convention.

The late nineteenth century and first two decades of the present century were probably the period when the concept of a "free and secure access to the sea," as manifested in territorial corridors, enjoyed its widest acceptance. During the interwar years there was a tendency, politically motivated in part, to deprecate the need for corridors and to stress the adequacy of guaranteed rights of transit. Since the end of the Second World War, with a weakening of the rule of law, the tendency has been in the opposite direction, stress being laid once again on the value of acquiring corridors in order to maintain a secure access to the sea.

BIBLIOGRAPHY

Alexander, Lewis M.: "Recent Changes in the Benelux-German Boundary," *G.R.*, vol. 43, pp. 69–76, 1953.

Bindoff, S. T.: *The Scheldt Question*, George Allen & Unwin, Ltd., London, 1945.

Bloomfield, L. M.: *Egypt, Israel and the Gulf of Aqaba*, The Carswell Company, Ltd., Toronto, Canada, 1957.

Bonjour, E.: *Swiss Neutrality*, George Allen & Unwin, Ltd., London, 1946.

Brierly, J. L.: *The Law of Nations*, Oxford University Press, New York, 1955.

Deutschland und der Korridor, Wilhelm von Kries (ed.), Volkand Reich Verlag, Berlin, 1933.

Freeman, T. W., and Mary M. Macdonald: "The Arctic Corridor of Finland," *S.G.M.*, vol. 54, pp. 219–230, 1938.

Hartshorne, R.: "The Polish Corridor," *J. of G.*, vol. 36, pp. 161–176, 1937.

Haskins, C. H., and R. H. Lord: *Some Problems of the Peace Conference*, Cambridge University Press, New York, 1920.

Hill, Norman: *Claims to Territory in International Law and Relations*, Oxford University Press, New York, 1945.

Hoffman, George W.: "The Netherlands Demands on Germany: A Post-war Problem in Political Geography," *A.A.A.G.*, vol. 42, pp. 129–152, 1952.

Kain, R. S.: "Bolivia's Claustrophobia," *Foreign Affairs*, vol. 16, pp. 704–713, 1938.

Kerner, Robert J.: *The Urge to the Sea: The Course of Russian History*, University of California Press, Berkeley, Calif., 1942.

McGovern, W. M.: *From Luther to Hitler*, Houghton Mifflin Company, Boston, 1946.

Mance, Osborne: *Frontiers, Peace Treaties International Organization*, Oxford University Press, Oxford, 1946.

———: *International Road Transport, Postal, Electricity and Miscellaneous Questions*, Oxford University Press, Oxford, 1947.

Melamid, Alexander: "The Political Geography of the Gulf of Aqaba," *A.A.A.G.*, vol. 37, pp. 231–240, 1947.

———: *Political Geography of Trucial Oman and Qatar*, *G.R.*, vol. 43, pp. 194–206, 1953.

———: "The Economic Geography of Neutral Territories," *G.R.*, vol. 45, pp. 359–374, 1955.

Morrison, John A.: "Russia and Warm Water," *United States Naval Institute Proceedings*, vol. 78, pp. 1169–1179, 1952.

Newbigin, M. I.: *Geographical Aspects of the Balkan Problems*, G. P. Putnam's Sons, New York, 1915.

Oppenheim, L.: *International Law*, vol. 1, *Peace*, vol. 11, *Disputes, War and Neutrality*, Longmans, Green & Co., Inc., New York, 1955.

Platt, Robert S.: "Conflicting Territorial Claims in the Upper Amazon," *Geographical Aspects of International Relations*, University of Chicago Press, Chicago, 1938, pp. 243–276.

Pounds, N. J. G.: "A Free and Secure Access to the Sea," *A.A.A.G.*, vol. IL, pp. 256–268, 1959.

———: *Divided Germany and Berlin*, Searchlight Series, no. 1, D. Van Nostrand Co., Princeton, N.J., 1962.

Smogorzewski, Casimir: *Poland, Germany and the Corridor*, Williams & Norgate, Ltd., London, 1930.

Thoman, Richard S.: *Free Ports and Foreign-trade Zones*, Cornell Maritime Press, Cambridge, Md., 1956.

Treaties: The chief collections of international treaties are *League of Nations Treaty Series*, United Nations, New York; Edward Hertslet, *Map of Europe by Treaty*, 4 vols., Butterworth & Co. (Publishers), Ltd., London, 1875–1891; Edward Herts-

let, *Map of Africa by Treaty*, 3 vols., H.M. Stationery Office, London, 1909; *United Nations Treaty Series*, United Nations, New York.

Wayper, L. C.: *Political Thought*, English Universities Press, London, 1954.

Wright, L. A.: "A Study of the Conflict between the Republics of Peru and Ecuador," *G.J.*, vol. 98, pp. 253–272, 1941.

10 THE POLITICAL GEOGRAPHY

OF FOREIGN TRADE

. . . The removal so far as possible of all economic barriers and the establishment of an equality of trade conditions among all the nations. . . .   WOODROW WILSON, FOURTEEN POINTS

THE CONTROL OF FOREIGN TRADE BECAME AN INSTRUMENT OF POLICY during the Middle Ages in Europe and during the earlier centuries of modern times was developed, in effect, into a powerful political weapon. The commercial theory of the time, known as *mercantilism,* was based upon a false economic theory, namely, that wealth consists in gold and silver and that it is of advantage to a state to accumulate bullion and to hold it in its vaults. Export was encouraged only if it led to a net import of bullion. National self-sufficiency was held to be the ideal. Nothing should be imported if it could possibly be produced at home; colonies were valued if they could supply the deficiencies of the home countries. Great Britain thus valued the Southern Colonies in North America, which could produce sugar, rice, and tobacco, above New England, which, for climatic reasons, produced much the same articles as Great Britain herself. For a time, Great Britain even preferred acquiring the West Indian islands of Martinique and Guadeloupe to Canada, because the former could supply tropical goods, which the latter could not.

CONTROL OF TRADE

The first serious and successful attack on the commercial doctrines of mercantilism was made by Adam Smith when, in 1776, he published his *Wealth of Nations*. In one compelling paragraph he demonstrated the advantages of specialization and trade:

> The natural advantages which one country has over another in producing particular commodities are sometimes so great that it is acknowledged by all the world to be in vain to struggle with them. By means of glasshouse, hot-beds and hot-walls, very good grapes can be raised in Scotland, and very good wine can be made of them at about thirty times the expense for which at least equally good can be brought from foreign countries. Would it be a reasonable law to prohibit the importation of all foreign wines merely to encourage the manufacture of claret and burgundy in Scotland? But if there would be a manifest absurdity in turning towards employment thirty times more of the capital and industry of the country than would be necessary to purchase from foreign countries an equal quantity of the commodities wanted, there must be an absurdity, though not altogether so glaring, yet exactly of the same kind, in turning towards any such employment a thirtieth, or even a three-hundredth part more of either.[1]

The simple argument that it would be better for all if goods were produced and crops grown in the areas best suited to them gained some acceptance. During the nineteenth century it led to a widespread liberalizing of trade. It came gradually to be assumed that the function of government in this respect was not to attempt to control the nature and volume of trade, but the reverse. Government should stand apart; its only positive role should be to remove obstacles to the freedom to trade. This was the golden age of *laissez faire*, when the direction of trade was left to the merchant and what was good for the merchant was, in general, considered to be good for the country.

[1] Adam Smith, *Wealth of Nations*, chap. 1.

Previously governments had controlled trade by (1) direct prohibitions of the export or import of goods, (2) a kind of quota system, by which specific quantities of specified goods were permitted to enter into trade, and (3) the imposition of tariffs, usually on imports, but occasionally also on exports. In no state during the nineteenth century was there complete freedom of trade. No state could afford to forgo the revenue which it derived from duties, nor could most governments long restrain themselves from using commerce as an instrument of policy, shaping its nature and direction to suit their political ends. Great Britain pursued the policy of free trade most consistently in the nineteenth century because she had the most to gain from it. Her industrial development was, at least to begin with, so far ahead of that of other countries and her production so much cheaper that she had no real need to protect her industries. Rather it was a question of other countries, which desired to industrialize, needing protection from British competition. Germany, for example, instituted a thorough enquiry in 1878 into the position of her iron and steel industry, which led to the conclusion that, if this industry was to be expanded it must be protected from outside competition, at least until it had got properly started. Very soon afterward German import duties were raised on a wide range of manufactured goods.

The Protection of Industry and Agriculture: In Chapter 6 we examined the resource base of the state, the extent to which its natural endowment and the degree of utilization of this endowment are a source of strength or weakness. It is clear that no developed state is completely self-sufficient, or free from dependence on others for materials. In many instances, as, for example, that cited by Adam Smith, a country is capable of producing some commodity at a high cost but could import it more cheaply. Common sense suggests that the commodity should be imported. But to rely heavily on trade with other countries to supply goods which are scarce or expensive to produce raises two definite problems.

The first is the vulnerable position in which the state is thereby placed. For example, no country is more dependent on imported foodstuffs than is Great Britain, and this excessive dependence was very nearly fatal in both world wars. The instrument of tariff protection is used to modify this dependence by placing import duties on certain foodstuffs and by making monetary grants to farmers for the production of specific crops. Thus, a subsidy may make it profitable to grow sugar beets and therefore reduce to about a half the dependence upon imported cane sugar. It makes little difference how the government implements its policy, whether by tariff protection, thus raising prices, or by subsidy to the producer, thus raising taxes. The result is to limit the volume of imports. Numerous examples could be cited from all the developed countries of attempts to protect those branches of agriculture and of industry which are considered strategically important.

The second problem is the obligation to pay for the goods imported. This can be done in three ways: (1) by means of exports, (2) by means of services performed by the importing country, and (3) by means of payments in gold, securities, or some other internationally acceptable medium. Clearly, this last means cannot be employed except in an emergency, and only a few countries are able to perform services on a large enough scale to influence greatly their ability to purchase abroad. Great Britain is such a country, with its merchant fleet, its banking and insurance services, and its international commodity markets.

The United States is another, as are also Switzerland, Greece, Japan, and a few others.

A state which is heavily dependent upon imports to feed its population and supply its industries is thus obligated to obtain, by exports and services, the means whereby to pay for these imports. Its policy is necessarily directed toward acquiring and retaining markets. Most states have a two-way obligation: to import a variety of goods which they cannot produce or produce only in limited quantities and, second, to export goods with which to pay for them. The search for markets is as necessary for survival as the search for materials, and generally much more difficult.

In this context it is convenient to divide states into primary producers and industrialized states. The former export almost exclusively or mainly the crude products of field, forest or mine, with only the most rudimentary refinement; the latter are able to export processed, refined, or manufactured goods. The price that is earned by the export of primary goods is liable to wide fluctuations—wider than the variations in price of manufactured goods. Thus, in time of trade depression, the price received for primary products is lowered far more than the price of the manufactured goods that have to be bought. Under such circumstances, primary producers may combine in an attempt to prevent prices from sagging too low. They may begin to develop industries of their own, in order to avoid so dangerous a dependence on exports of raw materials. They may make agreements with industrially developed countries for the sale of some agreed part of their crop, often in return for concessions to the latter. What course a state takes is a matter of political decision, and many a country has bartered political concession for some market advantage for its products. This, then, is a general statement of the problem; let us turn to a more detailed examination of particular examples.

Preemptive Buying and Barter Agreements: In February, 1960, the Soviet government negotiated a commercial agreement with Cuba, undertaking to purchase a considerable part of the Cuban sugar crop over a period of five years. The price was agreed upon and was announced; what secret conditions there were is unknown, but Cuba was heavily dependent upon selling its sugar crop and by no means certain of being able to sell it elsewhere. Cuba may well have been willing to pay high in political concessions for so favorable an economic opportunity.

In the 1930s, the German government negotiated a series of agreements with the countries of southeastern Europe by which it undertook to buy a large part of the agricultural surplus of these countries. The time was that of the Depression. The inefficient agriculture of southeastern Europe could not find markets and was in the dilemma outlined above. Germany rescued these countries, paying them nominally a good price, though in so-called "blocked" marks that could be spent only in Germany. In the words of a commentator on Germany's economic foreign policy:

Germany's main object in her trade expansion in South Eastern Europe was not to obtain cheap imports for her current requirements, but to secure an area of economic dependence in the event of war. With that object in view it was sound policy to forego some immediate economic gain in favor of the economic as well as strategic advantages to be derived later from complete political and economic domination. The policy itself, and the extent to which it was successful, received striking illustration even before the outbreak of war in the German trade agreement with Rumania of March 1939, which went far beyond the scope of a normal trade agreement in laying down a comprehensive plan for the reorganization of the whole Rumanian economy to fit in with Germany's import needs.[2]

These two examples illustrate the ways in which the precarious position of the primary producers can be exploited for political ends by any state unscrupulous enough to do so. There can be no doubt that the United Kingdom and the United States have on occasion used this method.

Preemptive buying, in short, is the buying up of all or most of an available product in order to prevent anyone else from doing so. This may be done, as was shown on page 159, in order to prevent a strategic material from falling into the hands of an enemy. It may also be done, as was the case in the two examples just quoted, to place the seller in a dependent position politically. As we review the countries of the world, especially those uncommitted to either the Western or the Communist blocs, we find numerous examples of this use of commercial policy for political ends, as each bloc attempts to bring the uncommitted third into some kind of dependence upon itself.

Preferential Tariffs: As, during the later nineteenth century and early twentieth, many states gradually raised the level of their tariffs, they began to grant preferential rates to those which they particularly desired to favor. Sometimes a state conferred various degrees of preference, corresponding in some way with the political valuation set upon the friendship of each state. The most far-reaching preferential trade agreements ever made were those negotiated at Ottawa in 1933 by the members of the British Commonwealth. The commerce of the former British Empire had, to some extent, been based upon the export by Great Britain of manufac-

[2] H. W. Arndt, *The Economic Lessons of the Nineteen-thirties*, Oxford University Press, Oxford, 1944, pp. 194–195.

tured goods to her Colonies, in return for the import of raw materials and foodstuffs. The most important part of the Empire was now made up of self-governing Dominions, intent themselves on building up manufacturing industries. Nevertheless, they were all importers of manufactured goods and were dependent to some extent on the export of raw materials. In a sense, the Ottawa Agreements constituted a reversion to the earlier function of the Empire:

> During the post-war decade, the Dominion raw-material producers . . . found increasing difficulty in marketing their large surpluses and keeping up the prices of their products. . . . As far as Great Britain was concerned, the main motive for the adoption of Imperial preference was probably political, the desire to strengthen the political unity of the Empire. . . .[3]

We should not, however, underestimate the United Kingdom's desire for a protected market for her factory products. As far as New Zealand, let us say, was concerned, the chief motive was securing a share of the British market for her butter, cheese, and frozen meat, in competition with Denmark, the Netherlands, and Latin America. Of course, many other examples from without the Commonwealth could be cited, for example, the preference granted by the United States to Philippine sugar and the substantial quota formerly allowed to the sugar growers of Cuba.

Thus we see the mechanism of tariffs and the system of quotas being manipulated in order to weld political partners more closely together, to establish a political dependence or, conversely, to terminate the dependence of one state on another that might become hostile. Trade, in each such instance, is being used as a weapon in conflict. If peace is to be assured, it is surely as necessary to remove the causes of economic warfare as it is those of military.

[3] *Ibid.*, p. 105.

THE LIBERALIZING OF TRADE

Complete freedom of trade remains an ideal whose realization must be judged highly improbable, if not impossible. Nevertheless, some easing of the restraints on trade is both possible and desirable.

The Open Door: Spain controlled so closely the trade of her Latin-American colonies that it was, in fact, impossible to do any business with the Spanish settlers or to trade with the Indians of the Spanish Empire—at least legally—without the consent of the authorities in Madrid. As a special concession (the *Asiento*) Great Britain was permitted by the Treaty of 1714 to send one ship, loaded with general merchandise, once a year to the Spanish-American colonies, and a war[4] resulted when this restriction was exceeded. This is an extreme example of the exercise of a trade monopoly over a major part of the earth's land surface.

A century and a half later a dispute arose in Central Africa. The territory at issue was the huge basin of the Congo River, which lies across the equator and was thought at the time to contain untold wealth. Africa was being carved up (see Chapter 14) by European nations, which competed with one another for the land and the resources it contained. The Congo Basin, or at least much of it, had been opened up by a private company, of which the King of the Belgians was chairman. Such a state of affairs did not recommend itself to other European powers, which saw the possibility of their exclusion from the supposedly lucrative trade of this area. In 1885 they[5] combined to regulate the

[4] Known as the *War of Jenkins' Ear*, from Captain Jenkins, who claimed to have lost an ear at the hands of the Spaniards when he took an additional merchant ship to Spanish America.

[5] The treaties were signed by the leading European states, including Belgium, and by the United States, which did not ratify.

situation by means of the so-called Congo Basin Treaty. This treaty:

. . . dealt with important issues of equality, without respect of nation, in the exploitation of African resources, both in matters of industrial development and of individual settlement. It included declarations relating to the abolition of the slave trade, and the neutrality of these African territories in the event of war. It provided for the free navigation of the Niger and the Congo. . . . The original treaty provided for completely free trade within the area to which it applied.[6]

This area was very much wider than the basin of the river Congo itself. It included all East Africa (Kenya, Uganda, and Tanganyika), Nyasaland, and parts of Northern Rhodesia and of what was then called French Equatorial Africa, as well as of Portuguese Angola and Mozambique. Within these broad areas the established commercial policy was that of the Open Door. All comers could be and, indeed, had to be served, provided that there were goods left for sale, and all comers were free to sell to the territories involved. There were to be no discriminatory or preferential tariffs. Tariffs were not forbidden, but they had to be the same for all.

Preferential tariffs were ruled out in some parts of West Africa also as a result of agreements between the British and French. It would have been desirable to extend this system more widely, but clearly no state would have readily opened its commercial doors in this way and thus deny itself the use of the commercial weapon in the pursuit of its policies unless it had been certain that other states would follow its example. In 1919 the opportunity arose of offering the Open Door to the colonial territories taken from Germany during the First World War. These were in Africa and

the Southwest Pacific, in all about ten separate territories. They were entrusted, as mandates (see Chapter 14) to other powers (France, Great Britain, Belgium, Japan, South Africa, Australia, and New Zealand). The mandatory powers in each case were obliged to:

. . . guarantee freedom of conscience and religion . . . [and to secure] the prohibition of abuses such as the slave trade, the arms traffic and the liquor traffic, and the prevention of the establishment of fortifications or military and naval bases and of military training of the natives . . . and [to] secure equal opportunities for the trade and commerce of other Members of the League.[7]

The door was open, though not wide open. The freedom to trade with the mandated territories was limited to League members; the United States was never a member, and Japan, Italy, and Germany left the League. Furthermore, South Africa has never fully honored its obligations toward South-West Africa.

Most-favored-nation Clause: One of the methods used in the nineteenth century to secure more liberal trade was to write into commercial agreements a "most-favored-nation" clause. By this clause in a treaty "all favours which either contracting party has granted in the past, or will grant in the future, to any third State must be granted to the other party." [8] The general effect of this clause was gradually to reduce the tariff levels of all countries to the level enjoyed by the most-favored trading partner of each. It therefore tended to make general the *lowest* tariff rates. In spite of this practice, however, tariffs were tending to increase irregularly in the 1920s. To some extent this was because markets

[6] Lord Hailey, *An African Survey,* Oxford University Press, Oxford, 1938, p. 1341.

[7] *Covenant of the League of Nations,* art. 22, sec. 5.

[8] L. Oppenheim, *International Law,* Longmans, Green & Co., Ltd., London, 1955, vol. 1, pp. 971–972.

were changing rapidly; exporters were obliged to find new outlets for their goods as old markets declined. The "new" countries were engaged in building up industries, some of them uneconomic and justified only by the strategic advantages to be gained from them. Such industries had, of necessity, to be highly protected. Germany and Japan became exporters of consumers' goods on an increasing scale in the later years of the nineteenth century and early years of the twentieth. A memorandum on tariffs, written in 1927, declared that:

Europe remains today with its tariffs higher and more complicated, less stable and more numerous than in 1913. Moreover, Europe has failed to restore its former system of commercial treaties, and the habit has developed of putting tariffs designed for purposes of negotiation into force before these negotiations take place. If, as has often happened, these tariffs have failed to result in agreement, the obstruction remains higher than before . . .[9]

Conferences designed to bring about a general lowering of tariffs met with little success, and the tensions which resulted from this commercial conflict played a part, though certainly not an essential part, in generating the frictions which culminated in the Second World War.

The road to every war has been paved with good intentions. From the First World War came proposals for liberalizing trade and for preventing control over trade and resources from being used as an instrument of political policy. That these proposals were largely ineffective has been made clear. Out of the Second World War came the Havana Conference of 1946, the Havana Charter, and the General Agreement on Tariffs and Trade (GATT).

[9] Quoted in *Commercial Policy in the Interwar Period: International Proposals and National Policies*, League of Nations, Geneva, 1942, p. 37.

The General Agreement on Tariffs and Trade: The Havana Charter, designed to secure a far-reaching liberalization of trade, failed to gain sufficient ratification to become effective. Thus did the good resolutions engendered by the war evaporate during the peace which followed. Nevertheless, a compromise agreement was reached at Geneva, in 1947, and was embodied in the agreement commonly known as GATT. About half the states of the world have now ratified this agreement, and these states are responsible for about 80 per cent of the world's trade. The agreement lays down rules for the conduct of international trade and provides a mechanism for a wider extension of the most-favored-nation clause and for the lowering of tariffs, easing of quota restrictions, and prevention of the practice of dumping. The agreement also seeks to regulate and simplify the rules governing goods in transit and the mechanics of customs examination and valuation. Its operation nevertheless remains sufficiently elastic to give some protection to the underdeveloped countries, which are trying to protect their young industries, as well as to some other countries caught in balance-of-payments difficulties, and obliged to limit imports.

The agreement has had a considerable measure of success in reducing the artificial obstacles to trade. States are able to buy and sell more widely than before, and given the fact that they normally buy in the cheapest market, this has encouraged the production of goods in areas best suited to produce them. This in the words of GATT, leads to the "raising of standards of living, ensuring full employment and a large and steadily growing volume of real income and effective demand, developing the full use of the resources of the world and expanding the production and exchange of goods."

TECHNICAL ASPECTS OF TRADE

This discussion of freedom and restriction in trade has been based upon the assumption that trade is conducted by merchants, acting for themselves or on behalf of exporters and importers, within a framework prescribed by their own governments. Within the Communist bloc there are no merchants; at least, there are none above the level of the petty village trader. In each state within the bloc trade is a government monopoly. It is conducted by agreements between the governments, which provide, in general, for the exchange of given quantities of one group of commodities for given quantities of another. The price mechanism generally is not used to adjust the size of the groups of commodities. A stronger member of the bloc can exploit a weaker, and has frequently done so, because the volume of this barter trade has not been clearly measured against a world standard of prices.

Over and above the clear instances of exploitation of one state by another that have occurred in this way are the political implications of this kind of trade. Czechoslovakia, for example, obtains a large part of her iron ore from the Soviet Union, in exchange for specified products of her engineering industries. Means of transportation have been built, extended, or improved specifically for this traffic, and a pattern of trade, created by commercial treaty, is, as it were, frozen by the technical means created to carry it on. Czechoslovakia is made dependent upon a continued flow of trade along the same routes from the same source. Economic hostages are given for future political behavior. Poland, which in recent years tried to break clear of such a regimented pattern of trade, found that the web in which she had become entangled was too strong for more than a small degree of freedom of trade to be possible.

Foreign trade between states is conducted by ship, by railroad, by truck, and, to a very limited extent, by air. International trade by ship may be conducted entirely over inland waterways: across the Great Lakes to Canada, or by Rhine river steamer between Switzerland, France, Germany, and the Netherlands. International trade may be entirely by means of land transport: out of one country and into the next by railroad or road transport, or sometimes across the territory of one or more intervening states. Some international trade makes use of both land transport across the territory of neighboring states and water transport upon the high seas and on nationally controlled rivers and canals. But by far the greatest part of international trade is by ocean-going ship.

A cargo from the Middle West, for example, may be taken by rail to Chicago and there transferred to an ocean-going freighter which carries it through the Great Lakes and down the St. Lawrence Seaway, that is, through Canadian territory, to the high seas. In the Dutch port of Rotterdam it might be transferred to a Rhine river barge and thus conveyed *through* Germany to the Swiss port of Basel. In the river port of Basel it might again be put on a freight train to end its journey in Austria. Such a journey would be complex, but not unusual. The freight, destined from the American Middle West to Austria, would thus pass across the territory of four intermediate states and be handled in the ports of two of them. The fact that a cargo can make such a journey, without undue delay and without being burdened by duties and tolls other than the necessary charges for transport and handling, is itself a tribute to the good will and cooperation of the states involved in this particular transaction.

In this section we are concerned with some of the mechanical or technical problems involved in facilitating the smooth flow of trade. The most significant of these, the right of one state, in the course of its trade with a second, to ship goods *across* the territory of a third, has been examined already (pages 244 to 247). This raises the question whether states have, in fact, a legal right to "diplomatic, commercial, postal, telegraphic intercourse, of intercourse by railway," and whether there exists "a right for foreigners to travel and reside on the territory of every State." There is, it is said, in law, "no such fundamental right of intercourse." [10] Privileges and facilities of this nature are dependent upon treaties and agreements, and the attempts of the League of Nations, UN and other bodies and organizations to generalize them and to give them a universal application have not been wholly successful.

Maritime Trade: Maritime trade is, as is quite obvious, conducted by means of ships, which are loaded and unloaded in ports. The right of acesss to ports is clearly of fundamental importance. In 1923 a convention, similar in its nature to that defining and accepting the principle of the right of transit, was prepared by a committee of the League of Nations and accepted at the Second General Conference on Communications and Transit, held in the same years at Geneva. Up to the outbreak of the Second World War the Convention had been ratified by twenty-three states together, in most instances, with their colonies. The second article of the Convention defined the conditions which the committee regarded as basic for intercourse between states:

Subject to the principle of reciprocity, every contracting state undertakes to grant to the vessels of every other contracting state equality of treatment with its own vessels, or those of any other state whatsoever, in its maritime ports as regards freedom of access to the port, the use of the port, and the full enjoyment of the benefits as regards navigation and commercial operations which it affords to vessels, their cargoes and passengers. The equality of treatment thus established is to cover facilities of all kinds such as allocation of berths, loading and unloading facilities, as well as dues and charges of all kinds levied in the name of, or for the account of, the Government, public authorities, concessionaries, or undertakings of any kind. [11]

The right to sail the high seas is, as has been pointed out in Chapter 4, an absolute right guaranteed in international law. The territorial waters, over which a state claims sovereignty, are also regarded as "open to merchantmen of all nations for inoffensive navigation. . . . And it is the common conviction that every State has by customary International Law the *right* to demand that in time of peace its merchantmen may inoffensively pass through the territorial maritime belt of every other state." [12]

Straits: A strait is a waterway joining two branches of the ocean and separating two (or more) areas of land. [13] The Strait of Gibraltar, at the western entrance to the Mediterranean Sea, the Straits of Bab-el-Mandeb, at the southern entrance to the Red Sea, and the Straits of Malacca, between Sumatra and Malaya, are examples of straits through which sails a significant part of the world's shipping. Straits may

[10] Oppenheim, *op. cit.*, vol. 1, p. 321.

[11] As paraphrased in Sir Osborne Mance, *International Sea Transport*, Oxford University Press, Oxford, 1945, pp. 22–23.

[12] Oppenheim, *op. cit.*, vol. 1, p. 493. Not all jurists, however, are as emphatic as this.

[13] See Erik Bruel, *International Straits: A Treatise on International Law*, Copenhagen, 1947, vol. 1, pp. 17–25.

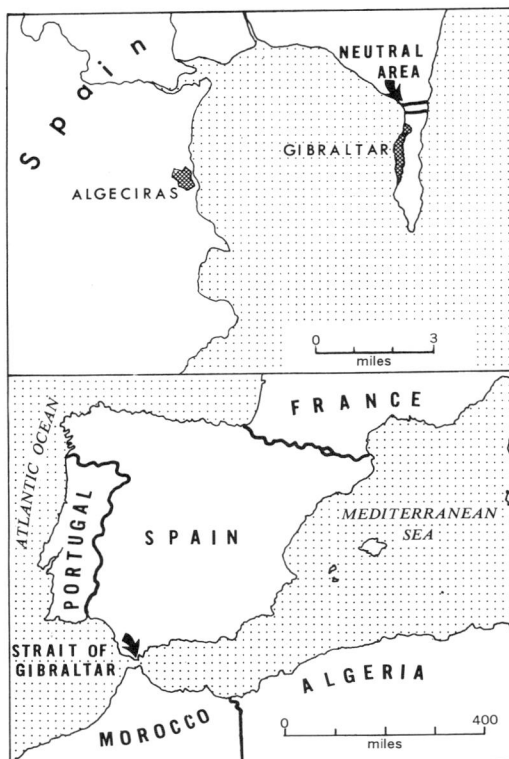

Exhibit 86   Strait of Gibraltar.

be as narrow as a few hundred yards, as are the Turkish Straits near Istanbul, or as wide as 20 miles, such as the Straits of Dover, between Great Britain and France, or the Bering Strait between the Soviet Union and Alaska. In general, the same rules apply to control over the waters of straits as over the territorial sea. If the strait is wider than 6 miles, on the assumption that the territorial sea is not more than 3 miles, there is a belt of water lying through its midst which must be regarded as part of the high seas; if the strait is less than 6 miles, then the whole of the waterway belongs territorially to the states which border it. If two states border a strait on opposite sides, then their sovereignty over it, if it is a narrow one, is divided by a line running through the middle of the strait.

But, by definition, straits are ways through or between land masses. They serve to shorten a voyage, and most straits have been at some time or other centers of international trade, even if now they do not all serve this function. Few ships now sail through the Straits of Magellan or Torres Strait, and even fewer through the Bering Strait, but the Danish Straits and the Straits of Gibraltar, of Bab-el-Mandeb, of Hormuz, of Dover, and of Malacca remain of very great commercial importance. This significance, both in trade and in naval strategy, which attaches to certain straits is reflected in the efforts made by certain powers to prevent them from falling completely, or even partly, into the hands of an enemy or rival, while seeing that the waterway remains open for their own use. Great Britain has been particularly adroit in gaining control of several of the straits through which passes much of the world's commerce: Gibraltar, Aden, Singapore, and the Falkland Islands are only the most important of a large group of places, strategically placed to command and control these significant waterways. It was not enough that the law of nations confirms the right of innocent passage through straits, whatever their width. National security seemed to require that steps be taken to safeguard this right under all conditions. This is not to excuse the occupation of overseas military bases, merely to show that the powerful state could in this way use its power to make itself even stronger. Following is an examination of the political geography of four significant straits.

The Strait of Gibraltar: The waterway which separates the south of Spain from the shores of Northwest Africa is, at its narrowest, 8.6 miles wide (Exhibit 86). It is thus clear that an area of the high seas links the Atlantic Ocean with the Mediterranean Sea through the midst of the strait. The Rock of Gibraltar lies on the Spanish side, at the inner, or eastern, end of the strait, in a position that allows it to control the passage. The most southerly point of Spain, the headland of Tarifa, is better placed than Gibraltar to command the strait but has no harbor and is not so easily defended as the rock itself. Gibraltar was seized in 1704 from Spain and has since been garrisoned by Great Britain, despite repeated claims to the small territory by Spain. It does not serve as a significant commercial port and, in fact, has negligible economic importance.

The southern shore of the strait is part of Morocco. A diplomatic struggle was conducted in the early years of the present century for control of this area between Germany, France, Spain, and Great Britain. The last-named was anxious chiefly to exclude German influence and, if she could not control Morocco herself, at least to see to it that it was in the friendly hands of France or in the innocuous possession of Spain. While Morocco passed under French protection, the south shore of the strait was occupied by Spain and the city of Tangier was effectively neutralized by being placed under an international regime (page 227). This continued until 1956, when the French protectorate ended and Tangier and the Spanish zone were reabsorbed into Morocco. There has never been any question of the complete freedom of navigation through the strait. The objectives of political control of the shores of the strait has been to keep the strait either open in wartime or open only for the ships of specific countries.

The Turkish Straits: The Turkish Straits are more complex than the Strait of Gibraltar. They join the Black Sea with the Mediterranean Sea, not directly, but by means of two straits, the Bosporus and the Dardanelles, and a small intervening sea, the Sea of Marmara (Exhibit 87). The straits are narrow. The Dardanelles, which

Exhibit 87   The Turkish Straits.

are 41 miles long, vary in width from under 1 mile to over 4 miles. The Bosporus is in each respect smaller; its length is about 18.6 miles, and its width varies from 600 yards to 2 miles. There is no question, then, that the whole waterway lies within the territorial limits of Turkey. Its importance, however, in the commerce of the Black Sea countries, which include, of course, the Soviet Union, is so great that, unlike the Strait of Gibraltar, it has been kept open for trade by international guarantee.

From the time, in 1453, when the Turks captured Constantinople and thus gained possession of both sides of the waterway, the straits were closed for over three centuries to all vessels that were not either Turkish or sailing in the service of Turkey. This period of arbitrary closure of the straits was ended by the Treaty of Kutchuk Kainardji (1774). By this date Czarist Russia had become established on the north shore of the Black Sea, which had hitherto been mainly under Turkish control. First, Russian ships sailed on the Black Sea, in defiance of Turkish authority; then, by the Treaty of 1774, they gained the right to sail through the straits and into the Mediterranean Sea. This concession was limited to ships of restricted size, which were further subject to any administrative orders which the Turks might issue. On one occasion vessels passing through the straits were subjected to search by the Turkish authorities, in order to prevent certain goods from reaching Russia. The narrowness of the Bosporus and the mounting of Turkish guns on its banks made it virtually impossible to evade these restrictions. By 1800 Turkey had extended to most of the more important commercial powers this limited right to navigate the straits, and during the first half of the nineteenth century this privilege was extended to all states likely to make use of it.

Thus, the right of free navigation for merchant ships was established, but this did not extend to warships. In 1798, a short-lived alliance between Turkey and Russia, which had become, and were to remain, traditional enemies, allowed Russian warships to sail through the Bosporus and excluded from the Black Sea the ships of every other nation. This agreement was terminated a few years later by the fresh outbreak of war between Turkey and Russia. By this time, however, western European powers, in particular Great Britain, had become apprehensive about the possible consequences of allowing Russian warships free passage through the straits and into the Mediterranean Sea. An international agreement of 1841 declared the straits to be open to merchant shipping but closed to warships, except those of Turkey. The Turks, nevertheless, did all in their power to make the navigation of the straits difficult and burdensome for the merchant vessels of other states by insisting

that the voyage be made during the hours of daylight and that a written permit be first obtained and then shown at the forts along the waterway, under penalty of being fired upon.

Such, in fact, was the status of the straits at the time of the First World War, which Turkey entered on the side of Germany and Austria. The disastrous failure of the British to force a way through the straits in the Gallipoli campaign of 1915, and thus to bring supplies to their Russian allies, pointed up the enormous strategic as well as commercial advantage possessed by Turkey in virtue of its command of the straits. When the war was over, the victors were determined that the straits should be open for all shipping. The British, in particular, still smarting from their costly defeat in 1915, were determined that the straits should not again be fortified. The Treaty of Sèvres (1920) provided for the complete demilitarization of the straits together with the Sea of Marmara and the islands which command the southern approaches to the straits. The Treaty of Sèvres was, in fact, superseded by the Treaty of Lausanne (1923) between the wartime allies and the Republic of Turkey, and a fresh Convention of the Straits was prepared and accepted. Complete freedom of navigation in time of peace for merchant ships of whatever nationality, without formalities or charges, was proclaimed and also guaranteed by the states which signed the treaty. There was also to be freedom to send warships through the straits, though in this case there was a restriction on the total military tonnage that could be in the Black Sea at one time. This freedom was restricted in Turkey's favor in the event of war.

The Lausanne Treaty reflected the thinking that was general at the end of the First World War. It was liberal, in maintaining the greatest possible degree of free-

Figure 45 *The Turkish Straits provide a water communication between the* **Black Sea and the Mediterranean.** *This photograph shows the Bosporus and one of the Turkish castles, now ruined, on the European side of the strait.* COURTESY: TURKISH INFORMATION OFFICE

dom of navigation. It was easy, at this time, to proclaim the freedom of both merchant and military craft to use the straits. The Soviet Union had a fleet of negligible importance, and there had ceased to be any need to fortify the straits against a Soviet Union that could not possibly have continued the aggressive policy of the Czars toward the Mediterranean Sea. By the 1930s this situation had changed. The Soviet Union was now an industrialized power, with a fleet which could have enabled it to revive the earlier Russian policy of expansion toward the south. Furthermore, it was increasingly doubtfu that the signatories of the Lausanne Treaty had either the willingness or the ability to enforce their guarantee of the freedom of navigation. In these circumstances, Turkey requested permission to refortify the straits, and in this both the Soviet Union and Great Britain concurred, the former in order to exclude the warships of other powers from the Black Sea, the latter in the hope of preventing Soviet warships from issuing into the Mediterranean Sea and there becoming a threat to the safety of commercial shipping. The complete freedom of commercial navigation was reiterated, but more severe restrictions were placed on the movement of warships,

Exhibit 88   *The Danish Straits and Kiel Canal.*

and the implementation of the terms of the treaty was left to Turkey itself.

This Convention, concluded at Montreux in 1936, continues to govern the regime of the Turkish Straits. The Soviet Union has on several occasions claimed the right to share in the direct administration of the straits, in other words, to establish Soviet bases on the shores of the straits. This has been resisted by Turkey, and in this matter Turkey has had the support of the Western world.

The Danish Straits: In their commercial and political importance the Danish Straits resemble the Turkish. They give access from the main shipping lanes of the world to an important enclosed sea, the Baltic, which, like the Black Sea, is bor-

dered in part by the territory of the Soviet Union. Geographically, the Danish Straits are more complex than the Turkish (Exhibit 88). They consist of no fewer than three parallel waterways:

1. The Little Belt, between the Danish peninsula of Jylland (Jutland) and the island of Fyn, which is narrow, twisting, difficult to navigate and very little used

2. The Great Belt, between the islands of Fyn and Sjaelland, which is wider, deeper, and more easily navigated

3. The Sound, between Sjaelland and the Swedish mainland, in all respects the most easily navigated and most important passage

From the earliest years of the Danish state until the middle of the seventeenth century, Denmark had held both sides of all three waterways. Not until 1658 did Sweden occupy the eastern shore of the sound which has since separated the two countries. During the Middle Ages, the Danish control of the straits, which was as vigorous as that exercised by Turkey over the Turkish Straits, led to conflict with the league of trading cities known as the Hanseatic League. The following centuries witnessed Denmark's emergence as a leading European power, in large measure by virtue of her control of the straits and her ability to restrict the important commerce which passed through them from the Baltic Sea into the North Sea.

The sound is, at its narrowest, less than 3 miles wide. There can be no question that, in the modern concept of territorial limits, it is made up of territorial waters. The King of Denmark claimed sovereignty over it and, from early in the fifteenth century, began to charge a toll on each ship passing through "territory" which he owned. Even after the opposite shore had been ceded to Sweden, Denmark claimed that only the land, with no part whatever of the waterway, had been ceded and continued to levy the sound "dues." There were protests against this interference with the freedom to navigate the sound, but little overt action was taken before the nineteenth century, when the volume of shipping between the North and Baltic Seas increased sharply. In 1848 the United States protested vigorously, claiming that "Under the public law of nations, it cannot be pretended that Denmark has any right to levy duties on vessels passing through the Sound from the North Sea to the Baltic. Under that law, the navigation of the two seas connected by this strait is free to all nations; and therefore the navigation of the channel by which they are connected ought also to be free. . . ." The United States rejected emphatically the argument that, because the Danish government for four hundred years had exacted tolls, it had acquired thereby a right to continue to do so. It was the American claim that led ultimately to the Conference of Copenhagen (1857), by which the freedom of navigation of the sound was established and all hindrances, obstructions, and tolls were abolished, subject to the payment to Denmark by the states whose ships used the sound of a lump sum as indemnity for the loss of revenue.

The Strait of Magellan: The Strait of Magellan, between the mainland of South America and the island of Tierra del Fuego, also became subject to international agreement. The strait is 357 miles long, very

Figure 46 The Sound is the most easily navigated water communication between the Baltic and the North Sea, but it is under three miles wide, and the Danish government formerly demanded a toll of passing ships. This is the Renaissance castle of Helsingör—Shakespeare's Elsinore—at which the levy was formerly made. PHOTOGRAPH BY N. J. G. POUNDS

Figure 47   *The Strait of Magellan is bleak, inhospitable, and difficult to navigate, but it provided a safer passage than the voyage around Cape Horn. By treaty, the strait was in 1881 thrown open to all shipping.*   COURTESY: EWING GALLOWAY

winding, and, in places, extremely narrow. Furthermore, it is not an essential strait, like those already discussed, in the sense that it cannot be avoided. Ships can sail round Cape Horn and thus avoid it completely, but the route through the Strait of Magellan is somewhat shorter and much safer than the route around "the Horn." The eastern (Atlantic) approaches to the strait lie in Argentina's territorial waters, but as a whole the strait is Chilean. The channel was used increasingly during the nineteenth century, and not even the opening of the Panama Canal in 1914 had an appreciable influence on the volume of traffic passing through it. A few years ago about two thousand passages of the strait were made each year.

The republics of Chile and Argentina had each been in existence for many years before either laid claim to the territory in which the Strait of Magellan lay. It was not until 1855 that they agreed that the principle of *uti possidetis* (see page 229) should apply here; the only difficulty was to discover how the former Spanish government had divided the administration of this area. Meanwhile, states outside Latin America were deeply interested in the situation. A British report declared the Strait of Magellan to be "one of the chief ocean highways of the world," and the British were somewhat alarmed at the possibility of interference with shipping by one of the South American Republics. The government of the United States was as forthright in its statement of policy regarding the Magellan Strait as it had been earlier regarding the Danish. "The Government of the United States will not tolerate exclusive claims by any nation whatsoever to the Straits of Magellan, and will hold responsible any Government that undertakes, no matter on what pretext, to lay any impost or check on United States commerce through those Straits." [14] In 1881, agreement was reached between Chile and Argentina largely through the mediation of the U.S. Department of State. The treaty delimited the boundary shown on the map (Exhibit 89). The strait itself was neutralized; no fortifications or military works might be erected on its banks, and the channel was to be open to the shipping of all nations.

[14] J. B. Moore, *A Digest of International Law,* vol. 1, p. 664.

Exhibit 89 *Strait of Magellan.*

These four are the only straits that have been subject to international regulation, and in each instance it has been agreed that they should be open to all peaceful navigation. The rule, thus established and applied, may be said to apply to all other straits. It is impossible to list all of them here. The sea passages between the islands of the West and East Indies

TABLE 16. *International Straits*

Strait	States separated	Minimum width, miles
Strait of Dover	Great Britain, France	21
Strait of Messina	Italy	2
Strait of Otranto	Italy, Albania	45
Skagerrak	Denmark, Norway	70
Kattegat	Denmark, Sweden	38
North Channel	United Kingdom	12
Sicilian Straits	Italy, Tunis	90
Strait of Bab-el-Mandeb	Ethiopia-Yemen	20
Strait of Hormuz	Trucial Oman, Iran	40
Strait of Malacca	Malaya, Indonesia	25
Palk Strait	India, Ceylon	25
Formosa Strait	Formosa, China	90
Tsushima Strait	Japan, Korea	95
Torres Strait	Australia, New Guinea	90
Bass Strait	Australia	130

must run to hundreds. Most have little commercial importance, owing either to navigational hazards or to their position *off* the main shipping lanes. Table 16 lists the straits most used by the world's commerce, together with the minimum width of the waterway. From the latter it can be judged whether the strait is made up entirely of territorial waters, though reference should be made to the territorial limits claimed by the states which border it.

INTERNATIONAL CANALS

Canals which have been cut from sea to sea, and are large enough to be used by seagoing ships, are analogous to straits. They can be regarded almost as artificial straits of extreme narrowness. They may be, like the Suez and Corinth Canals, cut at sea level so that the salt sea water extends right through them, or they may,

like the Panama Canal, be carried over higher land with the aid of locks, fed with fresh water from streams and rivers. Most canals have been cut to supplement rivers; they join one point of land to another and can be navigated only by barges built for the purpose. Such canals are discussed in the next chapter. Here we are concerned only with canals which have been cut to join two seas, and thus to shorten a sea voyage, and which are normally used only by seagoing vessels.

Such canals are not numerous. Indeed only four can be listed, and one of these is of only minor importance: the Suez, Panama, Kiel, and Corinth Canals. To these is sometimes added the Soviet Baltic–White Sea Canal, but this is an essentially domestic concern of the Soviet Union and has never been open to international commerce. A small canal was once cut across part of the Khalkidhiki peninsula, in north-

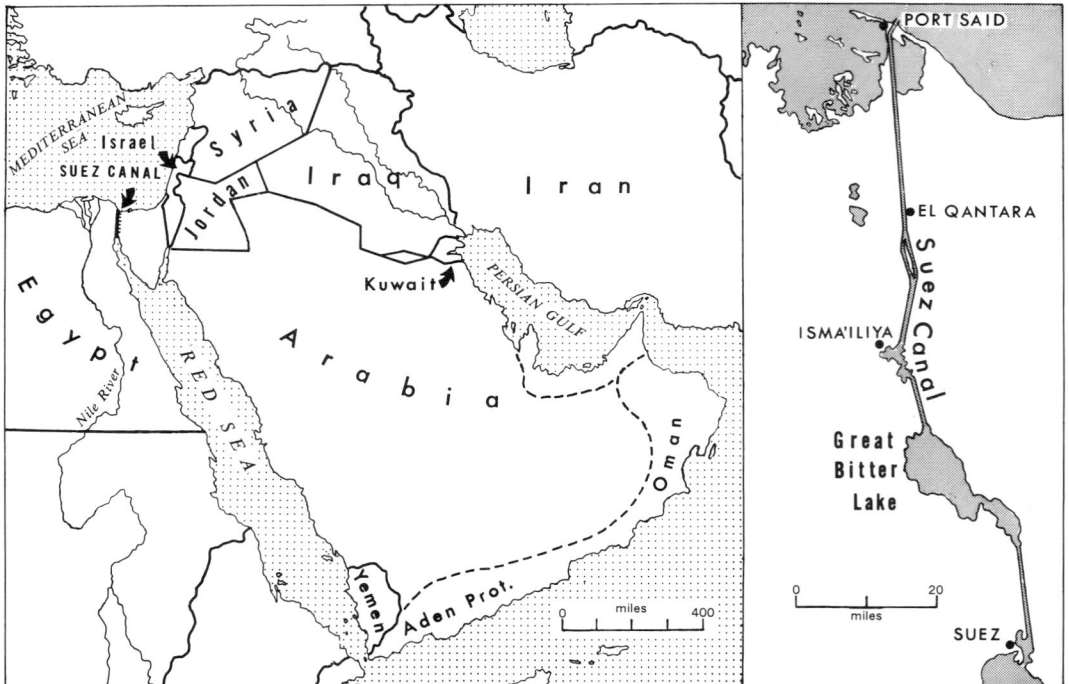

Exhibit 90 *Suez Canal.*

Figure 48 *The Suez Canal is the most important of all international canals. It is fully used and is in fact not adequate to all present-day needs. The ship in the foreground is tied up while the approaching ship passes. This photograph shows the low-lying and level nature of the desert across which the canal has been cut.* COURTESY: EWING GALLOWAY

ern Greece, but this has long ago been abandoned. There is also a long-standing proposal to construct a canal across the narrow Isthmus of Kra, on the borders of Malaya and Thailand.

Suez Canal: The oldest of these and the most important in terms of the tonnage using it is the Suez Canal (Exhibit 90). The present canal was opened in 1869, but it is merely the last of several which have, in some way or other, joined the Red Sea with the Mediterranean Sea. It

is a sea-level canal and requires no locks; only its entrances are protected by jetties from silt carried by the sea current. Its length is 101 miles, inclusive of two lakes, Timsah and Great Bitter Lake, through which it passes. The minimum width of the deep channel is 197 feet, sufficient for large ships to pass.

The opening of the canal reduced the distance from northwestern European ports to India by about five thousand miles, shortened to a lesser extent the voyage to the Far East, and greatly reduced the importance of the older route around the Cape of Good Hope. In 1955, the year preceding the Suez crisis and the blocking of the canal, 14,666 vessels passed through, with a total tonnage of 115,756,398. The largest share of the shipping (about 20 per cent) using the canal is British, followed by Norwegian (16 per cent), Italian (8 per cent), and French (7 per cent). Ships flying the "flags of convenience" of Liberia and Panama together make up 20 per cent of the total. There can be no question that the Suez Canal is one of the major focal points of world trade. The world tanker fleet has been built on the assumption that tankers will be able to reach the Persian Gulf by the short route through the canal, and in many other respects the closing of the canal, with the consequent lengthening of the voyage, would put a severe strain on the existing shipping capacity.

The canal was cut by a company—the Suez Canal Company—much of whose capital was originally French. The British share—about 44 per cent—was acquired when, in 1875, the Prime Minister, Disraeli, purchased the shares which had been allotted to the Khedive of Egypt. This dramatic purchase underlined the fact that Great Britain was already the biggest user of the canal and had the most to lose should the canal fall into the hands of a power hostile to herself.

Actually, the Canal Company had a lease of the canal for a period of ninety-nine years from the date of the opening of the canal. At the end of this period, that is, in 1968, it would revert to Egyptian ownership, and the affairs of the company would presumably be closed. Great Britain was not the only state for whose economy the canal had become vital; all European countries were interested in it. At Constantinople, in 1888, nine states joined to sign the Suez Canal Convention, which declared, "The Suez Maritime Canal shall always be free and open, in time of war as in time of peace, to every vessel of commerce or of war, without distinction of flag. Consequently, the High Contracting Parties agree not in any way to interfere with the free use of the Canal, in time of war as in time of peace. . . ." [15] This undertaking did not prevent Great Britain from occupying Egypt and, after this occupation had terminated, from continuing to maintain forces on the canal itself, until these were withdrawn in 1954.

In July, 1956, the Egyptian government nationalized the canal. It was the fear that the Convention of 1888 would not be fully honored, rather than the fact of nationalization itself, that provoked the Suez crisis a few months later. The effect of the short-lived war and of the consequent damage to the canal was to demonstrate to western European states, faced with an immediate gasoline and oil shortage, the immense importance of the canal to their economy. Fears that Egypt would be unable to cope with the technical problems of the operation have proved to be unfounded. Since it was cleared of obstacles in the spring of 1957, the canal has been operated smoothly and the Egyptian government has adhered to the letter of the 1888 Convention, except in one respect. Israeli ships, and ships sailing to or from an Israeli port, have not been allowed to pass through the canal. The reason given is that Egypt is in a state of war with Israel and has been since the truce of 1949. [16]

Panama Canal: The Panama Canal was cut, like the Suez, in order to avoid a long, costly, and even hazardous voyage around the southern tip of South America.

[15] *Suez Canal Convention*, Oct. 29, 1888, Art. 1.

[16] This is not to excuse or condone Egypt's action. The state of war was terminated by the truce of Feb. 24, 1949, and, legally considered, Egypt thereby lost the right to treat Israel as a belligerent.

Figure 49 *The Panama Canal was cut across much more difficult terrain than the Suez. The photograph shows the Gaillard (Culebra) cut in the distance and the Pedro Miguel Lock in the foreground.* COURTESY: EWING GALLOWAY

The construction of the canal was technically a more difficult problem than that of cutting the Suez Canal; maintenance is more expensive, and canal tolls are higher. This has been the chief reason why the Panama Canal has not completely replaced the Magellan Straits–Cape Horn route (see 264). Nevertheless, the volume of shipping using the canal is increasing at the present time. In 1958 a total of 9,187 passages of the canal were made, and the cargo carried through it amounted to over 48 million tons. Twenty-two per cent of the shipping in 1958 was of United States registration, 13 per cent British, and the remainder divided between 39 nationalities.

The canal was constructed by the United States Government on land leased in 1903 in perpetuity from the Republic of Panama (Exhibit 91). The Canal Zone is a strip of territory about ten miles wide, over which the United States exercises an effective sovereignty. The canal itself is open to the commerce of all nations, and a clause of the Hay-Pauncefote Treaty (1902), by which the United States leased the Canal Zone, is reminiscent of the 1888 Suez Canal Convention: "The canal shall be free and open to the vessels of commerce and of war of all nations . . . on terms of entire equality, so that there shall be no discrimination against any such nation, or its citizens or subjects, in respect of the conditions or charges of traffic or otherwise. . . ." Even before the canal had been opened, fears were expressed regarding its vulnerability, and the building of an alternative canal was advocated. In 1914, by the Bryan-Chamorro Treaty, the United

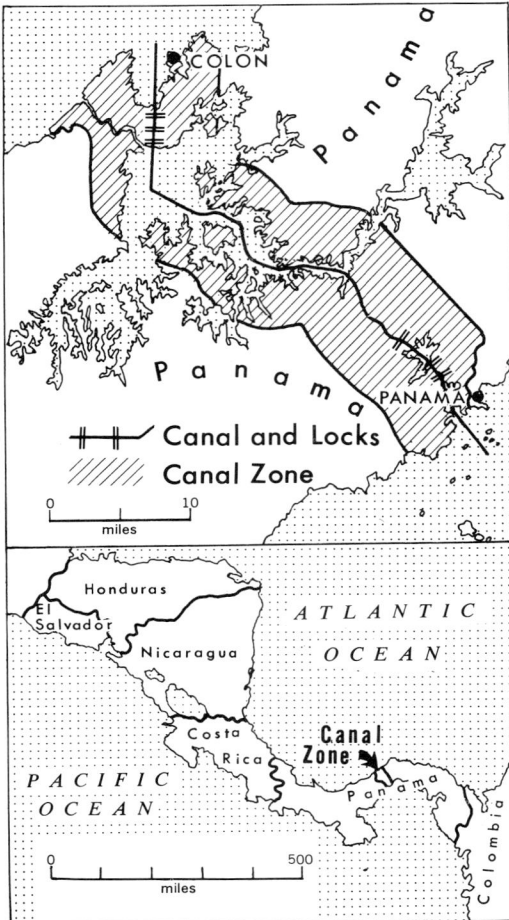

Exhibit 91   *Panama Canal.*

States obtained from the Republic of Nicaragua "the exclusive right in perpetuity to
construct a canal across Nicaragua." [17] This
right, acquired as a kind of insurance,
has never been exercised.

Kiel Canal: The Kiel Canal was cut
by the German government across the
base of the Danish peninsula and was
opened for shipping in 1914 (Exhibit 88).
It lay entirely within German territory and
was designed to shorten the voyage from
German Baltic seaports to the North Sea
by eliminating the voyage through the

sound and around the north of Denmark.
Its purpose was as much strategic as commercial. No international agreement regulated either its construction or its use, and
until 1919 it was entirely at the disposition
of the German government. The Treaty of
Versailles declared the canal to be open
to the peaceful commerce of all nations,
and a subsequent decision of the Permanent Court of International Justice declared, ". . . it has become an international
waterway intended to provide under Treaty
guarantee easier access to the Baltic for
the benefit of all the nations of the world
. . . the Kiel Canal must be open, on a
footing of equality, to all vessels, without
making any distinction between war vessels and vessels of commerce." [18]

In 1936 the German government denounced those clauses of the Versailles
Treaty which relate to the Kiel Canal, fortified it, and allowed passage only to vessels of states which it regarded as friendly
to itself. Since the end of the Second World
War, the canal has again been open on
conditions of equality, though this new
freedom has not been guaranteed so far
by treaty.

Corinth Canal: The Corinth Canal,
which cuts the Peloponnese off from the
rest of Greece, is open to navigation under
similar conditions. It is much used; 7,806
vessels passed through in 1938, but they
were mainly small coasting craft for which
the voyage around the south of Greece
might be difficult or even dangerous. Thus,
it can be assumed that all canals which are
suitable for ocean-going vessels and whose
function it is to join sea to sea are open
as freely to the shipping of the world as
straits, but the examples cited show that
this freedom was not achieved without
great difficulty and in the face of the vested
interests and exclusive privileges of many
states.

[17] Mance, *op. cit.*, p. 19.

[18] Quoted in Mance, *op. cit.*, p. 16.

Figure 50 The Baltic–North Sea Canal, formerly known as the Kiel Canal, was cut for strategic and military rather than economic purposes. It is now, however, open to all shipping that desires to avoid the voyage around the north of Denmark. COURTESY: EWING GALLOWAY

FREE PORTS AND FREE ZONES

The freedom which a state has to send its ships to any part of the world and, in peacetime, to the ports of any other, is not without restrictions of a somewhat technical order. Let us assume that an exporter in the Dominican Republic desires to ship a small cargo—less, that is, than the normal load of a small freighter—to Denmark. The volume of trade between these states is small; there may be no regular sailings between them, and the chances of a tramp steamer calling at a port of the Dominican Republic and then sailing on to Denmark are slight. One the other hand, cargo vessels sail regularly and frequently from New York to Hamburg. It is not difficult

to consign the goods from the Dominican Republic to New York, and Hamburg has frequent sailings to the ports of Denmark. So this is the way the cargo travels, and it is transshipped in the ports of both New York and Hamburg. The mere fact of being unloaded from one vessel, taken, perhaps, to a different dock, and then reloaded exposes the cargo to the import duties of both the United States and of West Germany, and with some cargoes this could add greatly to the price of the goods when they reached Denmark. On the other hand, this type of handling is normally lucrative and adds appreciably to the total turnover of the ports, which thus try to encourage it. The best way of doing so obviously is to

Figure 51 *The Corinth Canal is less important and is less used than the Baltic–North Sea Canal. It was cut across the Isthmus of Corinth and separates the Peloponnesus from the rest of Greece.* COURTESY: AEROFILMS

eliminate customs examination and payment of duties on the goods which are in transit and are lying in the port only during the short pause between unloading and loading.

For this reason the United States government in 1936 established a free zone on a small section of Staten Island, in the Port of New York. Free zones have since been established in New Orleans, San Francisco, Los Angeles, and Seattle, and a zone is now proposed at Mayaguez, in Puerto Rico.

The modern free port is an area of a port separated from the customs area of a nation by a stockade. Ships may enter such a port, discharge, load and depart without customs formalities. The goods may be stored, repacked, manufactured, and re-exported without customs formalities. Only when the goods pass the barrier to reach the consuming public of the country do they undergo customs revision and pay the necessary duty.[19]

The free zone is just a convenience, designed to allow goods from several countries to be gathered together at major shipping points, or entrepôts, from which they can be more conveniently shipped to distant parts of the world. Some ports of the world have so little trade of their own—that is, trade in goods which are produced or consumed in the state in question—that they are overwhelmingly entrepôt ports. Hong Kong is a well-known example. A free zone such as that on Staten Island would be quite inadequate to meet the needs of Hong Kong, which is entirely a "free port," to which the commerce of Formosa and the Chinese mainland, of the Philippines, Vietnam, and Cambodia, and of other countries of Southeast Asia is brought for transshipment and export to Europe, America, or other distant parts of the earth. Singapore and Tangier fulfill a similar function. Gibraltar is also a free port, though its importance, compared with that of the others named, is quite small.

It is technically difficult to institute a free port in a country which itself levies high tariffs, owing to the ease with which smuggling could be carried on. Free ports are found in countries which are territorially very small and which have, in any case, very low tariffs, such as those mentioned. Other free ports are Aden, the Canary Islands and other Spanish colonial dependencies, Colon, on the Panama Canal, and Port Said, on the Suez Canal.

More often only a section of a port, the free zone, is thus free of customs. Free zones are found in many parts of the world but are most common in Europe. Those of

[19] Roy S. MacElwee, *Port Development*, New York, 1926, p. 381.

the United States were set up without any intention of providing a convenience for one country in particular. Similarly those of Germany and of the Scandinavian countries serve the needs of all countries. That of Hamburg, which is one of the largest free zones both in the area which it covers and the tonnage of goods handled, consists of a group of docks on the south bank of the river Elbe. These are separated from the city and from the rest of the dock area by a wall, at which the customs examination of goods entering Germany from the free zone is made. Other free zones in German ports are at Emden, Bremen, Bremerhaven, Cuxhaven, and Kiel, and such zones are also found at Copenhagen (Denmark) and Göteborg, Malmo, and Stockholm (Sweden).

Other free zones in European ports are more limited in scope and are a means of giving to an inland state its own access to the sea. For example, the Republic of Czechoslovakia was given by the Treaty of Versailles a ninety-nine year lease of free zones in the German ports of Hamburg and Stettin (now Szczecin). It chose only to accept that in Hamburg. This Czechoslovak free zone was separate and distinct from the free zone already mentioned and was used only for goods in transit through Germany to and from Czechoslovakia. Goods entered the Czechoslovak zone from the seagoing vessel and were then sent on by rail or by river barge direct to Czechoslovakia, and vice versa, without becoming subject to German customs examination. Czechoslovakia in 1921 obtained by treaty with Italy the use of another free zone in the port of Trieste. The relevant clauses of this agreement run as follows:

2. . . . Shed No. 55 shall be used in suitable proportion for the loading of goods destined for immediate export by sea and for the unloading of goods arriving by sea. . . .

5. The Czechoslovak government or its

authorized representative shall cause the shed to be opened and closed by its own officials, and shall keep the keys thereof, assuming entire and sole responsibility for the goods deposited therein. . . .

13. A Czechoslovak Customs Office . . . shall be established in Shed 55, and this Office, through its own officials, shall be entitled to carry out all the transactions connected with the Customs service . . .[20]

The free zone in the port of Szczecin, which had been declined by Czechoslovakia at the end of the First World War, was accepted at the end of the Second, after the city had passed into the possession of Poland. It was used for a number of years but has now been given back to Poland. It seems that the facilities of Hamburg are not only sufficient for Czechoslovakia's needs but are also better located.

Hungary, under a similar geographical disability to that of Czechoslovakia, negotiated for the use of free zones in Trieste and Fiume (Rijeka). France similarly used Belgian ports, and Yugoslavia obtained a free zone in the Greek port of Thessaloníki. Similar arrangements existed for the handling of Polish commerce in the port of Danzig (Gdańsk) up to 1939. Palestine offered to Iraq the use of a free zone in the port of Haifa, but the Iraqi government did not find it necessary to accept this offer. Less formal arrangements exist for the handling of Germany's exported coal and imported iron ore in the Dutch port of Rotterdam and of Sweden's iron-ore export in the Norwegian port of Narvik. Until 1939, Russia had such rights in the Latvian port of Riga. There are free zones in the ports of Beirut and Tripoli (Lebanon), designed to serve the needs of the Middle Eastern states in their hinterland,

[20] "Convention . . . Regarding Concessions and Facilities . . . in the Port of Trieste, March 23, 1921," *League of Nations Treaty Series*, vol. 32, p. 242.

and in the port of Arica, in northern Chile, which, in a similar fashion serves the needs of Peru and Bolivia.

The Free City: The free city is an extension of the meaning and purpose of the free zone and free port. Though there were numerous self-governing commercial cities in medieval Europe, there have been few recent examples. The foremost example in the twentieth century was the Free City of Danzig (Gdańsk). The reasons for its establishment were clear. Its population was overwhelmingly German; yet, as a port, its chief function was to serve the commerce of Poland. There was reason to believe that Polish interests would not be well served if the port were part of Germany, yet to allow it to be incorporated in Poland would be to violate the political aspirations of most of its citizens. So Danzig was made a free city, responsible to the League of Nations, which appointed a High Commissioner to administer it. The Free City of Danzig was in a customs union with Poland, though politically separate. The experiment might ultimately have been successful if Hitler and the Nazis had not been determined to use it as a pretext for war with Poland.

A similar situation arose at Fiume (Rijeka), a city mainly Italian in population, which served as outlet for a hinterland that had become mainly Yugoslav. Allotted first to Yugoslavia, then seized by D'Annunzio, Fiume was established as a free city in 1920 and ultimately incorporated into Italy. Since 1945 Fiume (Rijeka) has again become a part of Yugoslavia. Yugoslavia also claimed the city and port of Trieste, which, with the surrounding areas, were occupied by British and American troops as the Free Territory of Trieste. In 1954 an agreement was reached between the occupying powers and the governments of Italy and Yugoslavia whereby the territory was divided between them. Italy took over the Free City of Trieste, undertaking to maintain it as a free port. Although these conditions have not been formally embodied in a treaty, the arrangement has received the *de facto* approval of the UN and has today an air of permanence.

PIPELINES

Petroleum has in recent years been increasingly important in international trade. It can be transported in specially built and equipped vessels, but obviously some other means of transportation is necessary from the oil wells to the port. The simplest and, provided that the volume of oil is sufficient to justify it, the cheapest way is by pipeline. The United States is traversed by a system of pipelines which distribute the oil from its points of origin in Texas or Oklahoma and elsewhere to most parts of the continent. The fact that a similar network of pipelines has not been established, radiating from other oil-producing areas, is to be attributed principally to the obstacles presented by various political boundaries.

The construction of an international pipeline raises problems of transit more complex than those considered so far. The right of transit, both for persons and for goods, which has been the subject of numerous agreements, guarantees merely the right to use existing facilities. It does not include the right to improve or extend existing roads or railroads. An international pipeline requires the construction of a new transportation facility, and one, furthermore, that may be of no direct value to the state whose territory is merely crossed by it. And the pipeline further requires pumping stations at intervals along it, as well as terminal or port facilities.

The first international agreement to construct a pipeline was made between Great Britain and France and related to the Middle Eastern lands for which they held the mandate. It was not, however, until 1932–1934 that pipelines were completed from the Iraqi oil fields to the Syrian port of Tripoli and the Palestinian port of Haifa.

During the Second World War, pipelines were built in order to satisfy wartime needs: from the Great Bear Lake region of northern Canada to Skagway in the Alaskan Panhandle; from England, under the Channel, to France and then on to northwest Germany; and from India to the interior of China. These pipelines were not conceived of as having commercial value, and only the Skagway line remains in use.

From 1928 onward, the Republic of Bolivia entered into agreements with Brazil, Paraguay, and Argentina, in which each agreed to assist in laying down pipelines across their territories for the purpose of distributing Bolivian oil. Oil production, however, remains negligible, and the pipelines have not yet been constructed. In 1944, the United States government entered into agreements for the construction of a pipeline from the newly opened east Arabian oil field to the coast of the Mediterranean Sea.

The pipeline constructed by the French from their Saharan oil field to the Mediterranean coast of Algeria is not an international pipeline, but an international pipeline has more recently been laid down from eastern Algeria to a Tunisian port on the Gulf of Gabes. Extensive international pipelines are at present being planned or are under construction in both western and eastern Europe. A 2,500-mile pipeline is being built from near Kuibyshev in the U.S.S.R., across Byelorussia to the Polish border, where it will fork, the northern line running across Poland to East Germany, the southern to Czechoslovakia and Hungary. In western Europe, a pipeline is planned to extend from the French Mediterranean port of Marseilles, northward up the Rhône Valley, and thence to the Rhine, which it will follow as far as Cologne. Pipelines will run from here to both the Netherlands port of Rotterdam and to a German North Sea port. It will thus be possible to pump oil into the pipeline system from any one of three widely separated ports and to supply a wide area of western Europe. A pipeline is also planned to extend inland from the Italian port of Genoa and to run *under* the Great St. Bernard Pass, by a tunnel that is yet to be built, to a refinery in Switzerland.

Such pipelines can be built only as a result of international agreement by the countries directly concerned. A pipeline is the cheapest means of conveying oil overland, but it is also the one that is most vulnerable. For a state to draw a considerable part of its oil supply by pipeline across the territory of a neighbor implies a considerable degree of trust. The only instances, however, of an interruption of the transit traffic in oil—and these were very serious ones—have been the closure by Jordan of the Iraq-Haifa pipeline and, more recently (1956), the pipeline from Iraq through Syria to the coast of Lebanon.

INTERNATIONAL AIR TRANSPORT

The airplane can fly over any part of the earth. Its movements are, however, far more circumscribed than any form of movement on the earth's surface. In most countries a traveler can go wherever the technical conditions exist for him to travel. Airplanes usually have to keep to specific corridors and fly at specific altitudes. It is a principle of international law that a state possesses sovereignty over its own air space, as fully as it does over what lies in the rocks beneath its surface. There has been

some question whether this sovereignty extends indefinitely outward into space, and the most widely held opinions are that it does, at least as far out as powered aircraft can fly (see page 113).

As early as 1919 a body of principles was formulated, in an attempt to regulate the growing volume of air traffic. A Convention for the Regulation of Aerial Navigation was drawn up at the Paris Conference. It asserted that "every state has complete and exclusive sovereignty in the air space above its territory and territorial waters." At the same time, however, signatories to the Convention undertook to accord to all other signatories the "right of innocent passage," while reserving the right to restrict and to limit this right for reasons of safety or strategy. In 1947 a new Convention on International Civil Aviation came into effect. It followed the lines of the older Convention and asserted the right of innocent passage and also the right to make emergency landings in the territory of other states. This Convention has been ratified by about half the states of the world, but the omission from the list of signatories of the whole of the Communist bloc deprives the Convention of the importance which it might otherwise have. Every country today restricts flights across its territory by the airplanes of other countries, usually allowing them to use only certain specified corridors. The three corridors from West Germany across East Germany to Berlin are a familiar example. Other countries have refused to authorize ordinary commercial flights across their territory. Iran, for example, does not allow flights between Europe and India along its southern coast, and flights between Central Europe and Turkey may not cross Bulgaria.

The airplane may, theoretically at least, take the shortest, that is, the great-circle route, between points on the earth's surface. This freedom is, however, restricted by the obligation to avoid flying over prohibited areas and to keep to certain air corridors. Long-distance flights, such as those from northwestern Europe to South Africa, to Japan, and to Australia or from New York to the more southerly states of Latin America, must necessarily be diverted somewhat fro the direct route to their objective to take advantage of available airfields for refueling. Now that jet planes are becoming important in long-distance flights, the availability of airfields presents yet more serious difficulties, owing to the length of runway required by these airplanes. Thus the technical requirements of aircraft and the restrictions of the states over which they fly combine to hamper a mode of transportation that should be the freest of all.

BIBLIOGRAPHY

Arndt, H. W.: *Economic Lessons of the Nineteen-thirties*, Oxford University Press, Oxford, 1944.

Bastable, C. F.: *The Commerce of Nations*, Methuen & Co., Ltd., London, 1927.

Brown, A. J.: *Industrialization and Trade*, Royal Institute of International Affairs, London, 1943.

Commercial Policy in the Interwar Period: International Proposals and National Policies, League of Nations, Geneva, 1942.

Hodgson, R. A.: *Introduction to International Trade and Tariffs*, Sir Isaac Pitman & Sons, Ltd., London, 1932.

Industrialization and Foreign Trade, League of Nations, Geneva, 1945.

Mance, Sir Osborne: *International Sea Transport*, Oxford University Press, Oxford, 1945.

Morgan, F. W.: *Ports and Harbours*, Hutchinson University Library, London, 1952.

Mountjoy, Alan B.: "The Suez Canal, 1935–55," *Geography*, vol. 52, pp. 186–190, 1957.

Oppenheim, L.: *International Law*, vol. 1, Longmans, Green & Co., Ltd., London, 1955.

Patterson, E. M.: *An Introduction to World Economics*, The Macmillan Company, New York, 1947.

Pounds, Norman J. G.: "A Free and Secure Access to the Sea," *A.A.A.G.*, vol. 49, pp. 256–268, 1959.

Raw Material Problems and Policies, League of Nations, Geneva, 1946.

Sargent, A. J.: *Seaports and Hinterlands*, A. and C. Black, Ltd., London, 1938.

Sealy, Kenneth R.: *The Geography of Air Transport*, Hutchinson University Library, London, 1957.

Thoman, Richard S.: *Free Ports and Foreign-trade Zones*, Cornell Maritime Press, Cambridge, Md., 1956.

Van Cleef, E.: *Trade Centers and Trade Routes*, D. Appleton-Century Company, Inc., New York, 1937.

11 THE POLITICAL GEOGRAPHY

OF RIVERS

The TVA idea, of the planned development of natural regions such as river valleys, has already found its way into the world's general thinking.　JULIAN HUXLEY

Contracting States shall accord free exercise of navigation to the vessels flying the flag of any one of the other Contracting States on those parts of navigable waterways under its sovereignty or authority.　STATUTE ON THE REGIME OF NAVIGABLE WATERWAYS, 1921

RIVERS HAVE ALWAYS INFLUENCED DEEPLY THE IMAGINATION OF MAN. Always changing yet permanent, they seemed, with mountains, to be the most enduring features of the earth's surface. The dangers and the devastation brought about by floods contrast with the rich silt which they deposit and the irrigation water which they provide for crops. Rivers furnished the earliest and today still furnish one of the more important means of long-distance travel. The earliest civilizations grew up on the banks of rivers and, if we may believe one of the more illustrious interpreters of human history, owed their rise to the stimulus provided by the alternating floodtime and low water. The first maps showed only two features with a fair degree of accuracy, the coast line and the rivers, and when some physical feature had to be chosen as a boundary, what was more obvious than to select the permanent, unchanging, and unmistakable course of a river? Most early boundaries, especially in Europe, were river boundaries, because, it was thought, there could be no disagreement about them. In contrast, and sometimes also in conflict, with the idea that the river formed a boundary so clear-cut that there could be no dispute was the view of the unity of the river basin. Long before the TVA was conceived, the view was popularly held that the network of tributaries of a river provided a bond of union for the area they served, that the waterways, like the arteries of the human body, provided a means of life to the whole. The idea is not so fanciful as it seems. The complete dependence of Egypt, the Sudan, and the Punjab, both East and West, upon irrigation from rivers completes the analogy. Considerably more than two thousand years ago Herodotus described Egypt as "the gift of the Nile," and Egypt's continuing life is dependent upon the river's annual floods.

Among the innumerable ways in which man makes use of the rivers that flow through his lands, four seem to have particular importance in a discussion of their political-geographical importance. Rivers, first, serve as boundaries, for which purpose, as we have seen, they are not always as permanent and as unchanging as one could wish boundaries to be. This aspect of the use of rivers has already been examined in Chapter 3. Rivers, second, have been used in certain parts of the world as a source of water for irrigation and human consumption from time immemorial. To these has been added in recent years the use of river water in industrial processes, especially for the cooling of electrical generators. Much of the water that is abstracted for industrial purposes is subsequently returned, though often contaminated by the chemicals with which it has been in contact. These latter pass back into the stream and travel with the current toward the river's mouth, sometimes poisoning the water, killing the fish, and

making it unsuitable for other usual functions.

Navigation is the third way in which man makes use of a river. In many instances the river, in its primitive condition, is already suitable for navigation. But often the increasing size of river craft, the need to continue navigation at all seasons of the year, and the necessity of maintaining a sufficient depth of water lead to the regulation of the stream and to the building of locks and lateral canals.

The river basin, lastly, constitutes a functional unit, not in the somewhat mystical sense conceived by earlier writers, but simply because water flows from all points in the basin toward its lowest point, which is usually where it enters the sea. Floods begin, most often, high up the tributaries, but they normally do the most damage in the plains that lie along the lower course of a river. Silt is washed from the hills, but the river deposits this material in its plain tract, where it may choke the channel and intensify the danger of floods. The control of rivers, as has been learned from the experience of the United States, should begin in their upper reaches.

If the problem of regulating and using a river were entirely a national one, we should not be giving much space to it here. In many instances, and those frequently the most critical, it is an international one, because the river basin is shared by two or more states. Agreements between states regarding the navigation of a river which they share are the easiest to achieve, perhaps because the use of a river for this purpose detracts nothing from it. Agreements to share the water itself for irrigation or some other purpose are incomparably more difficult to attain, and there is so far no instance of an international agreement to regulate and develop the whole drainage basin of a river as a physical unit.

NAVIGATION OF INTER-NATIONAL RIVERS

From the earliest periods of human history rivers have been used for navigation and for the transport of bulky commodities. In the United States the rivers that flowed westward from the Appalachian Mountains were among the chief means by which the early settlers reached the Mississippi. Rivers were vital channels in the penetration of South America and of Russia. In Europe rivers were formerly used for navigation on a scale that now seems almost unbelievable. The smallest rivers were regularly used by the smallest possible boats. Rivers whose current was too swift for the upstream movement were used in the downstream direction only. Small, roughly built boats were made in the hills and navigated to some point near the mouth, where the cargo was unloaded and the boat itself was broken up and sold as lumber for building or burning. But few river routes, in Europe at least, escaped without the imposition of tolls. For the mere privilege of navigating a boat up- or downstream a toll became payable to numerous persons whose only right to the toll was that they owned some section of the bank and were able to enforce their demands, just as the King of Denmark was able to exact a toll on ships passing through the sound (see page 262). Even more vexatious was the obligation to unload the cargo of each passing boat at certain cities and to expose it for sale for a certain period before reloading what remained and resuming the voyage. Inevitably, the plethora of tolls and exactions killed the traffic on many rivers, forcing merchandise to use slower and more costly means of land travel. On the river Rhine alone, between Switzerland and the sea, there were at one time over thirty toll stations, and the amount of toll levied was, in many in-

stances, far greater than the value of the cargo.

The Scheldt Question: The river Scheldt was the first international river to be thrown open to the shipping of all the countries that bordered it. We have already seen (pp. 238 and 239) that the lower course of the river was closed in the seventeenth century by the Dutch and the port of Antwerp, lying at the head of the estuary, barred to seaborne traffic. In 1792, the river was "freed" by the French Revolutionary armies, and, with a magnificent gesture, the Executive Council of the Republic declared the Scheldt to be "the common, inalienable property of all the countries which it bounds or traverses." [1]

Navigation of the Rhine: The advance of the boundary of France to the river Rhine ended for good the onerous restrictions that had been placed on the navigation of the river. Tolls were not wholly abolished, because it was found to be necessary to raise money to pay for services, such as pilotage, setting buoys, and marking the channel. It was not until 1868, however, that the Convention of Mannheim swept away the last of the serious restrictions, and the Rhine "stepped forth from the middle ages." [2]

The Congress of Vienna: The conference which met at Vienna in 1814 for the purpose of restoring peace to Europe after the Napoleonic Wars first attempted to define in a general way the freedom of navigation on international rivers. The Final Act of the Congress of Vienna declared:

Art. 108: The Powers whose territories are separated or traversed by the same navigable river engage to regulate, by common consent, everything regarding its navigation. For this

[1] Quoted in G. Kaeckenbeeck, *International Rivers,* Grotius Society Publications 1, London, 1918, p. 32.
[2] E. J. Clapp, *The Navigable Rhine,* London, 1911, p. 13.

Figure 52 **The Rhine is now the most used river in Europe, but at one time the traffic was burdened by heavy tolls.** *This photograph shows the castle of Kaub, built to serve as a toll station, and now used as a signal station to control the movement of shipping on the river.* COURTESY: SHELL PHOTOGRAPHIC UNIT

purpose, they will name commissioners who shall assemble at latest six months after the termination of the Congress, and who shall adopt, as the bases of their procedings, the following principles.

Art. 109: The navigation of the rivers referred to in the preceding article, along their whole course from the point where each of them becomes navigable, to its mouth shall be entirely free, and shall not, as far as commerce is concerned, be prohibited to anyone; due regard being had, however, to the regulations for the policing of navigation; which

regulations shall be alike for all and as favourable as possible to the commerce of all nations.

These provisions were made to apply only to the rivers Scheldt, Meuse, and Rhine and to their navigable tributaries. The matter was not taken up for the Danube until 1856, for the Central African rivers until in 1885, and not until after the First World War for most other rivers.

Navigation of the Danube: The Treaty of Paris of 1856, which ended the Crimean

War, provided for the freedom of navigation on the Danube in accordance with the principles previously decided upon at the Congress of Vienna. A commission was established for the river Danube to regulate the conditions of navigation and to secure for the riparian states that freedom which the earlier treaties had established only in very general terms.

The Congo Treaty: When in 1885 the nominal basin of the Congo River was thrown open to the trade of all states (see page 254), its navigable rivers were opened to their shipping. The area covered by the Congo Act included not only the basin of the river Congo and its tributaries but also the Niger River. The middle courses of both these rivers are separated from the lower by rapids which are difficult or impossible to navigate. In subsequent agreements these interior stretches of river, as well as the lakes of Central Africa, were opened, without restriction, to international commerce.

There are other examples of agreements reached by states during the nineteenth century to share the right of navigation on specific rivers. The claims of the upstate New Yorkers to use the St. Lawrence River as a means of reaching the sea have already been mentioned (see page 237). This particular claim was not, however, fully recognized and embodied in a treaty between the governments of the United States and Great Britain, which acted for Canada, until 1871. This freedom was then extended to the whole of the Great Lakes system of waterways, and subsequently to the canals built to supplement the navigational facilities of the river and lakes.

In 1847, both Iran (Persia) and the Turkish Empire, which then included the territory of Iraq, agreed on the common use of the Shatt-el-Arab, the river formed by the junction of the Tigris and Euphrates.

A year later, the United States and Mexico agreed similarly to permit the mutual use of the Rio Grande and Colorado River, and in 1851 Brazil agreed to allow Peruvian vessels to navigate the Amazon River as a means of reaching Peru from the Atlantic Ocean. At this the United States protested, claiming the right for the ships of all states at peace with Brazil to navigate the Amazon.

This raised an important question: Was the right to use an international river for navigation limited to the ships of the riparian states, or was it open to any vessels trading with the riparian states? The latter had been the interpretation given to the freedom of navigation on the Rhine and Danube. A few years later Brazil and Peru conceded that the Amazon and certain of its tributaries should be open to the ships of all nations, whether riverine or not.

During the nineteenth century, so many of the important international rivers of the world were opened to the navigation of ships of all states that it became almost the rule that any river which is shared by two or more states is by right open to the peaceful shipping of all.

There has been some ambiguity in the use of the term *international* in this context. A *national* river is clearly one which lies wholly within the boundaries of a single state. An *international* river is one whose drainage basin is shared by two or more states. Oppenheim uses the term *non-national* to describe such rivers, reserving the expression international only for rivers which have become subject, in respect of their navigation, to an international jurisdiction. There are few navigable rivers that have not, theoretically at least, become subject to international control of some kind, so that nonnational is almost synonymous with international. The term international is used here of all rivers that belong to two or more states and is not limited to those on which the freedom of navigation is guaranteed by treaty. This appears to be the sense in which it is used by both Mance and the Convention on the International Regime of Navigable Waterways.

Treaty of Versailles and Barcelona Convention: For a general statement of these rights to navigate international rivers it was necessary to wait until after the First World War. The Treaty of Versailles (1919) contained certain regulations of a general nature touching international rivers and added three more rivers to the accepted list: the Elbe, Oder (Odra), and upper, or "fluvial," Danube. For each a mixed commission was established to regulate and supervise navigation. Other treaties of peace, signed in 1919–1920 declared the Niemen, Vistula, Morava (Czechoslovakia), Tisza, and Pruth to be international rivers on which the shipping of all nations was to be permitted on terms of complete equality.

The Peace Conference at Paris (1919–1920) also appointed a commission to examine the whole question of the freedom of navigation on international rivers. The Commission met at Barcelona in 1921 and drew up the Convention which contains the basic principles of navigation on international rivers. The Convention was limited only to international rivers naturally navigable and to lateral canals (such as the St. Lawrence Seaway) constructed to remedy the shortcomings of the natural waterway. Tolls payable for the use of such waterways must be for services performed, such as pilotage, setting buoys, and improving the navigable channel.

The Convention was binding on only the states which ratified it. Some states had no navigable international rivers—the United Kingdom and Italy, for example; others, such as the United States, had made agreements with each of their neighbors

governing the use of the navigable rivers which they shared. Germany and the other states defeated in the First World War had been obliged to accept in advance the conditions drawn up by the Barcelona Conference. The only international river of the Soviet Union that was already significant for navigation—the Amur—was covered by other agreements, as was also the Prut, at that time Rumanian. The Convention thus became binding on little more than thirty states, which did, however, include most of the larger and more important. This number was reduced in 1936, when Germany denounced the navigational clauses of the Treaty of Versailles and refused to abide by them.

Thus a liberal regime was established during the years between the First and the Second World Wars by which almost all *international* rivers capable of being used by commercial vessels became open to the ships of all nations without discrimination. Only two exceptions appeared: Venezuela retained for her own nationals the right to navigate both the Orinoco River above the river port of Ciudad Bolivar and the Gulf of Maracaibo inland from the port of that name,[3] and Lithuania closed the river Niemen to navigation as a result of her territorial dispute with Poland.

Practice differs considerably from principle. By law the river Amur, which separates the Soviet Union from the Chinese Province of Manchuria, is an international river on which freedom of navigation was guaranteed by treaty in 1934. In fact, however, the navigation commission provided for in the treaty has never been set up, and freedom of navigation certainly does not exist on this river, any more than it does

[3] Speech of Venezuelan delegate, Barcelona Conference, *Verbatim Records and Texts Relating to the Convention on the Regime of Navigable Waterways*, League of Nations, Geneva, 1921, p. 31.

on other Soviet or Chinese rivers which have been thrown open to the shipping of other nations by international agreement.

There are many ways of nullifying a legal freedom of navigation without actually refusing admission of vessels to the river. Tolls, compulsory pilotage, restrictions on navigation by night, the keeping of swing bridges closed against shipping, and failure to mark correctly and clearly the navigable channel have all been used. There are degrees of freedom, and these are sometimes difficult to discover, and impossible to represent on maps, because they are continually changing with the changes in political objective and policy.

Canal Navigation: The right to navigate inland canals presents peculiar problems. The signatories to the Barcelona Convention accepted the obligation to extend to all nations the right to navigate canals which merely supplement navigable rivers or which are constructed merely to avoid obstacles in the river. This, of course, covered, for example, the lateral canal which borders the Rhine above Strasbourg. It would cover also the Welland Canal and the St. Lawrence Seaway, as it would also the lateral canals which have been replaced by the latter, if the freedom of navigation of these waterways had not already been guaranteed by agreement between the United States and Canada. Most other canals, however, are not international. They begin and end within the territory of a single state. The German Mittelland Canal links the Rhine with Berlin and the Oder (Odra). It has been given a kind of international status by the division of Germany into a West and an East German Republic but does not formally rank as an international canal. The movement of goods from West Germany along the canal to Berlin is governed by agreement between the Western Powers and the Soviet Union, though neither the spirit nor the letter of this

agreement has always been honored by the Soviet side.

By the Treaty of Versailles, Germany was required to open the projected ship canal across southern Germany from the Rhine to the Danube to the shipping of all nations.[4] This was somewhat unusual. An analogous canal in the United States would be that which connects Lake Michigan at Chicago with the Des Plaines River and so with the Mississippi. Non-American ships cannot claim to use this waterway as of right, though it is unlikely that they would, under ordinary conditions, be denied the privilege of using it.

In Europe a network of large-scale canals has been planned and, in part, constructed, to link the great rivers of the Continent: the Rhine, Rhône, Danube, Elbe, Oder, Vistula, Niemen, Prut, Dniepr, and Volga. "Thus," in the words of Mance, "but for the war [i.e., of 1939–1945], it might have been possible within a decade to navigate large barges from the North Sea to the Caspian and from the Baltic to the Black Sea."[5] Little has yet been done east of the Oder to link up the great navigable rivers of the European plain. Such connections between the Dniepr and the Vistula, and the Vistula and the Oder, have been proposed by the Communist governments of Poland and the Soviet Union, and it is possible that their construction may be begun in the near future. At its western end this system would be linked by way of the Rhine, Meuse, and Scheldt with the waterways of the Low Countries, by the Rhine-Marne Canal with the Paris area, and by the Rhine-Saône Canal with the Rhône. The operation of such a complex system of natural, regulated, and artificial waterways would appear to call for

---

[4] This canal has still not been completed.
[5] Sir Osborne Mance, *International River and Canal Transport*, Oxford University Press, Oxford, 1944, p. 75.

the extension to it of the freedom of navigation which the Barcelona Convention guaranteed to certain rivers. In particular, agreement on the size of locks and minimum width and depth of the canal must be reached. At present it would be a very small barge that could navigate *all* the existing waterways and use all the locks. Then, too, many states reserve such internal navigation—other than that on international rivers—for the ships of their own nationals. In Mance's words:

If each country on the Continent reserved its own domestic trade for its own vessels, the general cost of waterway transport would rise. For example, a Dutch motor barge may carry a cargo from Rotterdam to the Ruhr; at the Ruhr she picks up a cargo for Dijon in France; in Paris a cargo is waiting for her to take back to Antwerp. Under the French regime, this barge would be prohibited from taking a load from Dijon for Paris and would have to make the voyage empty. The free movement of these tramp vessels would assist in meeting seasonal tonnage requirements in different parts of the Continent. A more satisfactory arrangement might be found by way of general or regional conventions providing for free circulation of tramp barges, including cabotage over the various waterways on the basis of reciprocity, while still leaving the different countries free, if they so desired, to reserve to their own flag regular local services on national waterways. . . .[6]

This freedom of movement has, in effect, been achieved within the countries of the European Community (Chapter 12).

The Low Countries: The use of inland waterways is more developed in Europe than in any other continent, and in no parts of Europe are canals so important as in Belgium and the Netherlands and in neighboring parts of France and Germany. The general flatness of the terrain, the availability of water, and the existence here

of several large, navigable rivers have encouraged the building of a complex network of interconnecting canals. This region, furthermore, serves as the maritime outlet for the industrial regions of Belgium, northwest Germany, and parts of northern France. It contains three of the most important ports of the Continent, the Dutch ports of Amsterdam and Rotterdam and the Belgian port of Antwerp. Farther away, to west and east, respectively, are the French port of Dunkirk and the German ports of Emden, Bremerhafen, Bremen, and Hamburg. These ports are all in competition for the seaborne commerce of northwest Europe, and in this competition the opening or closing, the improvement or neglect of a waterway of international significance can play a vital role.

The rivalry of Belgian and Dutch ports is long-standing. The river Scheldt was opened to commerce by the French at the end of the eighteenth century, and since that date the competition between Antwerp and Rotterdam, the ports best suited to handling the traffic from the Belgian industrial region and the transit traffic from northwest Germany, has been intense. The map (Exhibit 92) shows that the river Rhine provides a direct water route from the industrial Ruhr to the port of Rotterdam. The Meuse (Maas) similarly carries traffic northward from the Belgian industrial region to the network of natural and improved waterways near Rotterdam. The hinterland of Antwerp for water-borne traffic is the basin of the Scheldt, and even this is encroached upon by the canal from Ghent northward to the western Scheldt at Terneuzen. We are here concerned with (1) the attempts of the port of Rotterdam to maintain its grip on the seaborne trade of the German Rhineland and part of the Belgian industrial region and (2) the attempts of Antwerp to attract to itself part of the Rhine traffic and most of that of the

[6] *Ibid.,* p. 25.

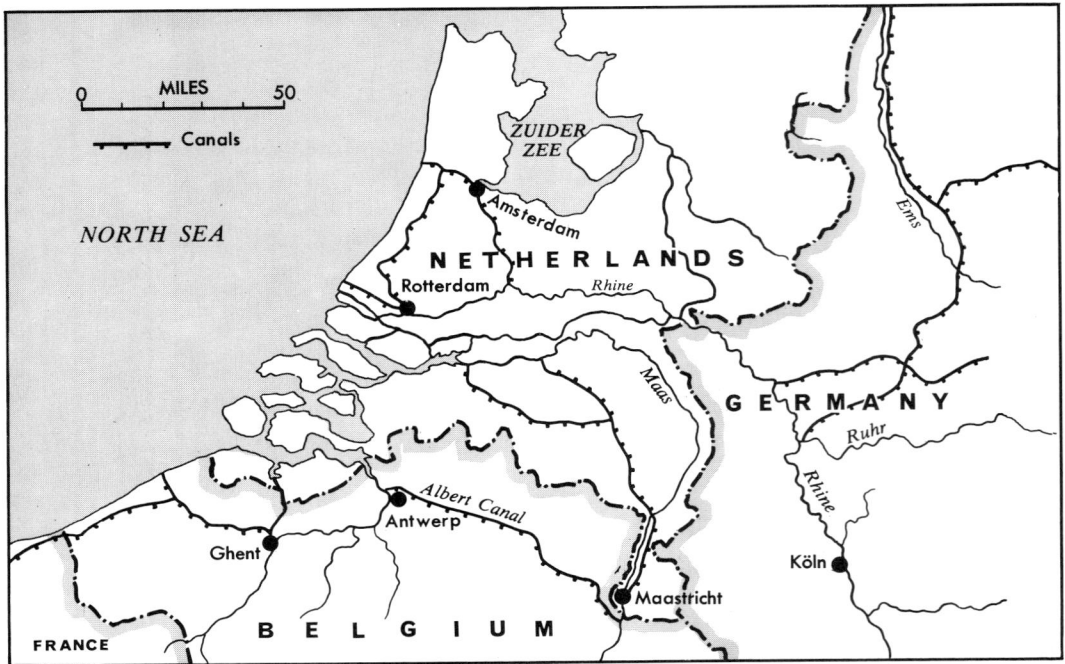

Exhibit 92   *Waterways near the Rhine mouth.*

Belgian industrial region. This was something more than the competition of two great ports, each anxious above all to keep their port facilities fully occupied. It took on the aspects of an international rivalry in which each contestant was backed by the force of public opinion and supported by the power of its own state.

The Dutch improved the Rhine as a waterway, constructed elaborate docks, in which goods were transshipped from ocean-going freighter to Rhine barge, and cut the New Waterway to join the port of Rotterdam with the sea at Hoek van Holland. But Rhine barges could, with only a relatively short extension of their journey, pass down the Waal to the Hollandsch Diep and thence, between the Dutch islands, to the Scheldt and the port of Antwerp. From the navigational standpoint this is a difficult journey for river barges. The Hollandsch Diep is notoriously hazardous, and

some of the passages require careful marking. Lastly, the vessels have to cross either Walcherne or Zuid Beveland, once islands and now, as the result of land reclamation, peninsulas of the mainland. Canals were cut across them, and vessels bound for Antwerp acquired by treaty the right to use them. The Dutch were obliged to maintain, though not to widen, deepen, or otherwise improve, these waterways, which were of service chiefly to their rival, the port of Antwerp. To Belgian proposals that an entirely new canal should be cut from Antwerp to the Hollandsch Diep or the river Waal the Dutch proved obdurate.

By the Treaty of Versailles (1919) Germany was required, if asked to do so, to assist in the building of a canal directly from Antwerp eastward to the Rhine near Ruhrort. Such a canal would at once shorten the journey by water from the Ruhr to Antwerp and possibly make it more economical than the voyage down the Rhine to Rotterdam. It proved impracticable, however, to construct such a canal without crossing the narrow southward extension of the Netherlands called South Limburg, and this the Dutch firmly refused to allow.

The port of Ghent, which in size and installations is much smaller than either Antwerp or Rotterdam, is linked directly to the western Scheldt by a ship canal which is part Belgian, part Dutch. The size of vessels that may use the port of Ghent is directly related to the condition in which the Dutch maintain their section of the Terneuzen Canal.

In 1925, however, the Belgian and Dutch governments reached an agreement that would have satisfied the Belgians on many of these points. Among other things, the Netherlands government agreed to allow the construction of international canals from near Antwerp north to the Hollandsch Diep and eastward to the Rhine. Other concessions to the Belgian point of view included an agreement to improve certain Dutch waterways regularly used by vessels sailing to Antwerp. But the treaty proved to be too generous from the Netherlands point of view; it was not ratified and never came into operation. Its failure brought about a worsening of relations between the two countries and led to a period of competitive canal building in an attempt by both Rotterdam and Antwerp to capture the seaborne trade of the Belgian industrial region. Old and rather small canals linked the Liège area with Antwerp. The Dutch then constructed the Juliana Canal, which bordered and supplemented the river Maas (Meuse), from Maastricht northward for about twenty-five miles until the river itself became sufficiently wide and navigable to be used regularly by large barges. The Belgians retaliated by cutting the Albert Canal, from the Meuse (Maas) below Liège across the Campine to Antwerp.

The formulation of these competitive plans led to a wrangle between the two states regarding the supply of water to the two canals. All canals are heavy consumers of water. Each time a ship passes through a lock, a lockful of water is sent downstream. A busy canal could conceivably require the use of more water, especially in a dry season, than the river Meuse could supply, and now two canals were drawing from the river in the vicinity of Liège and Maastricht. The complaint of each country against the other was taken before the Permanent Court of International Justice, which rejected both pleas.

Belgium and the Netherlands have since this date moved closer together politically, and the acrimony has been removed from their relations with one another. In recent years there have been no major disputes regarding the operation of the waterways that link the two countries. But no amount of political agreement can prevent Antwerp and Rotterdam from being commercial rivals competing for the privilege of handling a limited volume of commerce. It should be emphasized that the disputes in this area did not hinge upon the legal right of the vessels to use these waters. Though they were not all international waterways in the strict sense, they were in fact open to all peaceful shipping that was able to use them. The issues involved were the improvement and extension of facilities which would benefit primarily other countries and, in particular, a rival port.

THE USE OF WATER FROM INTERNATIONAL RIVERS

Some reference has already been made to the problem that is presented when too much water is taken from a river. Belgium and the Netherlands each accused the other of doing just this in order to supply their respective canals. Similarly Canada has protested that Chicago takes so much water from Lake Michigan, and thus from the Great Lakes–St. Lawrence waterway system, and sends it down to the Mississippi that the level of the Great Lakes is lowered.

Every state has the right to do what it likes with the water of rivers which are exclusively its own. Law on this matter varies from one state to another. It differs from the Mediterranean countries, where, in general, Roman law prevails, to common-law countries, which in general disapprove more strongly than the former of any interference with a river's natural flow. The Roman-law opinion is, broadly speaking, what we should expect in a region which depends heavily on irrigation for agriculture. The common-law opinion is in keeping with physical conditions in northern Europe, where irrigation is, in general, not practiced and rivers are used primarily for navigation and the generation of power.

International law holds, like common law, that a state "is not only forbidden to stop or divert the flow of a river which runs from its own to a neighboring state, but likewise to make such use of the water of the river as either causes danger to the neighboring state or prevents it from making proper use of the flow of the. river on its part." If, therefore, it could have been demonstrated that Belgium, the Netherlands, or the city of Chicago had, by their respective actions, seriously diminished the flow of the Maas or the St. Lawrence, they would have been guilty of an infringement of this law.

The problem posed by the state which dips too deeply into the waters of a river which only flows *through* its territory has only recently become important but is likely to grow in significance in the future. The world's population is growing rapidly and the world's rainfall is not. Crops do not grow and food cannot be produced without water. As knowledge of health and hygiene spreads, the personal use of water increases and modern factory industry, which is slowly spreading to the underdeveloped countries, also makes increasing demands on water supply. The amount of water being discharged by the world's rivers into the seas and oceans is diminishing, and it is probably true to say that that which does make its way to the sea is increasingly polluted.

American cities are facing increasingly acute problems of water supply. Los Angeles reaches out to the Colorado River; New York City pipes water down from the Catskill Mountains; others draw water from lakes and rivers and face not only the problem of the adequacy of the supply but also of its suitability for human consumption.

The water of the Rio Grande is fully committed. The water of its upper reaches is divided, by an agreement of 1939, between the riparian States: Colorado, New Mexico and Texas:

This compact defines the rights of each State to the waters and accounts for stream flow and water use by each State in accordance with those rights. Definite schedules, which vary with the annual water yield, are established for delivery of annual volumes of water at key points in the Rio Grande Basin, and divergence from those schedules is accounted for as "debits" or "credits." Debits arise from failure to deliver the scheduled supply of water by any State and impose certain restrictions on that State's use of water. Credits for any State are created by delivery of water at key points in excess of that required by schedules and confer on that State further rights for use of water.[7]

The division of the waters of the middle Rio Grande between Texas and Mexico

[7] *Ten Rivers in America's Future*, Report of the President's Water Resources Policy Commission, vol. 2, p. 293, 1950.

was governed by a treaty of 1906. "The United States agreed to deliver to Mexic 60,000 acre-feet annually, except in the case of extraordinary drought or serious accident to the irrigation system in the United States." [8] A dam built across the river near El Paso, Texas, controls the supply of water to Mexico. The discharge of the river builds up again near its mouth, but, except at floodtime, very little water in the middle course of the river goes unused.

The waters of the Colorado River are similarly used (Exhibit 93). The States which share its drainage basin agreed in the Colorado River Compact of 1922 on an allocation of the water between themselves, after agreeing to allow a certain amount to enter Mexico. California has since exceeded the amount agreed upon, and Arizona, with ambitious plans for the development of irrigated agriculture in the central parts of the State, appealed to the Supreme Court for a judgment to restrain the extended use by California of the water of the Colorado River. The opinion prepared by the "master" appointed by the Court favors Arizona. Half the water in the Colorado River above Lees Ferry, near the Utah-Arizona line, may be used in the up-river States. The 7.5 million acre-feet which may normally be expected to pass this point, after allowing for a certain minimum flow into Mexico, are to be divided as follows:

	Acre-feet
California	4,400,000
Arizona	2,800,000 (1,000,000 from the Gila River)
Nevada	300,000

This opinion—it is not yet a judgment —has been a severe blow to California's plans to develop the southern parts of the

[8] *Loc. cit.*

Exhibit 93 *The Colorado river system.*

State, and California is now planning to bring water from the north to the extreme south. In the following pages three examples of the international division of the waters of a single river or river system are discussed. They are more important than

Exhibit 94 *The Columbia River system.*

Exhibit 95   The Nile.

the United States and Canada. The treaty provides for the building of dams on both the Columbia and the Kootenay for the purpose of generating power as well as regulating their discharge and preventing floods. Among the proposed dams will be the Libby Dam on the Kootenay River, which will back up water for a very considerable distance into Canada.

The Waters of the Nile: It is impossible to exaggerate the importance of the river Nile in human history. On its banks was formed one of the earliest political societies. The alluvium deposited along its lower course provided a rich soil, which the annual floods watered with the greatest regularity, while deserts to west and east gave to early Egypt a physical protection that allowed its civilization to develop almost unhindered and unmolested. The source of the floods which have come down the river late each summer throughout the whole span of human history was a mystery until, in the middle nineteenth century, the source of the river was discovered.

The Nile, in fact, has two sources (Exhibit 95). The main river, known as the White Nile, rises in Lake Victoria, which lies on the equator. It receives tributaries from Uganda and the Congo and then flows northward into the Sudan. It is fed by the equatorial rains which fall at all seasons, but on its course northward toward the Mediterranean Sea it flows across first a region of light summer rain and then the desert, where there is practically no rain at all.

Here, however, the White Nile is joined by rivers, the Blue Nile and Atbara in particular, which come down from the highlands of Ethiopia. This region receives heavy summer rains but is dry for the rest of the year. About June, the Blue Nile and other Ethiopian rivers begin to flood. The flood wave moves downstream through the Sudan and reaches lower (that is, north-

the cases of the Rio Grande, Colorado, or Columbia, because on them have hung not only the lives of far greater numbers of human beings but also the issues of peace and war in the Middle East and India.

In January, 1961, the Columbia River and its tributary, the Kootenay, which rise in the Canadian Province of British Columbia and join to flow across the State of Washington to the sea (Exhibit 94), became the subject of an agreement between ern) Egypt in August. After the flood wave has passed, the level of the Ethiopian rivers falls very low, and the Atbara commonly dries out in winter. Thus, we have a steady flow from the equatorial region which varies little in the course of a year and a short period of violent flood in late summer brought down from the Ethiopian mountains.

The flow of the Nile and its tributaries has been measured with great care. The volume of water passing any point along the river varies somewhat from one year to another, just as the weather in Ethiopia or Uganda varies. The figures given here are averages. About 21 billion cubic meters leaves Lake Victoria each year and is joined by about 7 billion more from tributaries that flow from the Congo and the southern parts of the Sudan. This flow of about 28 billion is then reduced by evaporation in the Sudd region to a half of its original content but is again raised to 27 billion by the Sobat, the first of the tributaries to join the White Nile from Ethiopia. The river continues to suffer minor losses through evaporation but at Khartoum is joined by the Blue Nile, with an average discharge of 50 billion cubic meters, most of which comes during the summer flood season. The Atbara delivers only about 10 billion, almost all of it in the summer.

After making allowances for evaporation, about 85 billion cubic meters is on the average available for use by Egypt and the Sudan. At present this water is used in the following manner:

	Millions of cu m
Used for irrigation in Sudan	4,000
Used for irrigation in Egypt	48,000
Loss by evaporation	3,000
Enters Mediterranean Sea	30,000
Total	85,000

Egypt is almost rainless, and most of its population of 25,365,000 (1959) prac-

Figure 53 *An ingenious cartoon expresses the geographical realities in the competition between Egypt and the Sudan for the water of the Nile.*
COURTESY: LONG, MINNEAPOLIS TRIBUNE

tice agriculture by means of irrigation. Furthermore, this population is at present increasing at the rate of about 400,000 per year. The extension of agriculture in Egypt is limited, not so much by lack of cultivable land as by lack of water. It is, therefore, a major objective of government policy to increase Egypt's share of the total water brought down by the Nile. This can be done best by preventing the loss of the water which at present makes its way to the sea. The loss occurs chiefly in summer, when more water comes down the flooded river than the Egyptians are able to use. The storage for later use of this summer surplus is the primary objective of the high dam now being built at Aswan.

A second aspect of Egyptian policy may be described as preventive, to prevent upstream states from increasing their share of the total water of the Nile system.

Figure 54 *More of the Nile's water will be used in the future for irrigation, as a result of* (a) *the building of the Aswan High Dam and* (b) *the agreement on water use reached between Egypt and the Sudan. Here is seen an irrigation canal under construction in the Cezira district, near Khartoum.* COURTESY: INTERNATIONAL BANK FOR RECONSTRUCTION AND DEVELOPMENT

Sudan's needs are less than those of Egypt. The population is smaller—about 11,459,000—and a substantial number are pastoralists and thus do not use the river waters for irrigation. Furthermore, south of Khartoum there is a small, but regular, rainfall, which increases as the equator is approached. On the other hand, the land between the Blue and White Nile—the Gezira, as it is called—is good cotton-growing country, and there is a great temptation to extend the area under cotton cultivation by dipping more deeply into the water brought down by the rivers. Such a prospect has been frightening to the Egyptian authorities. Even more threatening was the

announced plan of the Italians, when they occupied Ethiopia (after 1935), of diverting the Blue Nile from its northward course to the Sudan and of making it flow eastward to irrigate the dry lands of Eritrea. Egypt's recent attempts to bring about political union with the Sudan were motivated, in part, by the urgent need to have some control over what happens to the waters of the Nile before they flow into Egypt.

The Nile Basin is shared by five states: Uganda, Congo, Ethiopia, Sudan, and Egypt. The supply from the Congo is too small to influence greatly Egypt's political relations with that state. Uganda is not likely to use the river, except for the generation of hydroelectric power, and this should not greatly influence its discharge, but both Ethiopia and the Sudan could greatly diminish the flow of the river by increasing their own use of its water for irrigation. The problem is basically one of so regulating the flow of the river that losses both to the sea and by evaporation are reduced to a minimum. Egypt's plan for a high dam at Aswan is certainly not the best, but it is the only one that would leave the impounded waters under Egyptian control. The ideal scheme would undoubtedly be a system of storage reservoirs in the Ethiopian Mountains, where they could be built more easily and where they would result in a smaller loss through evaporation owing to the cooler temperature at the greater altitude. Such a solution to the problem would, however, be highly improbable under present political conditions.

In 1959 the governments of Egypt and the Sudan reached agreement on the utilization of the Nile waters within the sectors of the river which they control. On the assumption that the average discharge of the river is 85 billion cubic meters,[9] the water will be apportioned as follows:

	Billions of cu m
Used in Sudan	18.5
Used in Egypt	55
Lost by evaporation, chiefly from the Aswan Lake, and by discharge to the sea	11.5
Total	85

This clearly makes better use of the waters, and the heavy loss through evaporation has been diminished through the better siting of dams. The completion of the Aswan high dam will form a lake reaching

back upstream for 400 miles,[10] which will in turn inundate considerable areas of the Sudan. Egypt will compensate the Sudan for the damage which results. "There is no region in Africa," in the words of W. Fitzgerald, "where geography suggests more clearly than in the Nile basin the need for economic and political cooperation between states." [11]

The Indus River System: The Indus River rises inside Tibet and flows across Kashmir, between the parallel ranges of the Karakorum and Himalayan Mountains, before breaking through the latter range and entering the plains of the Punjab. From here to the sea its course lies in Pakistan. Its left bank, or eastern, tributaries are the so-called Five Rivers of the Punjab, the Jhelum, Chenab, Ravi, Beas, and Sutlej. The first two rise in Kashmir and except for their headwaters are Pakistani rivers. The Ravi draws from both Kashmir and India and for a distance actually forms the boundary of India and Pakistan. The Beas and Sutlej rise in India and, after their junction, form for a distance the boundary between India and Pakistan, before entering Pakistan to join the Indus River (Exhibit 96).

The Indus and the five Punjab rivers are important chiefly as a source of irrigation water. Canals divert the water from the rivers, as these leave the hills, and distribute it over the *doabs*, or areas of higher land that separate the rivers. The system of canals was expanded during the nineteenth century but bore no simple relationship to the religious or communal groups of the Punjab. Very approximately, Muslims predominated in the west, Hindus in the east, and Sikhs (closely affiliated with the Hindus) in the central area through

[9] The *New York Times* cites the average as 84 billion; in point of fact, in extreme years it may be either under 50 or over 110 billion.

[10] Published estimates vary; one figure is 227 miles, or only 100 miles into Soudanese territory.

[11] Walter Fitzgerald, *Africa*, London, 1943, p. 429.

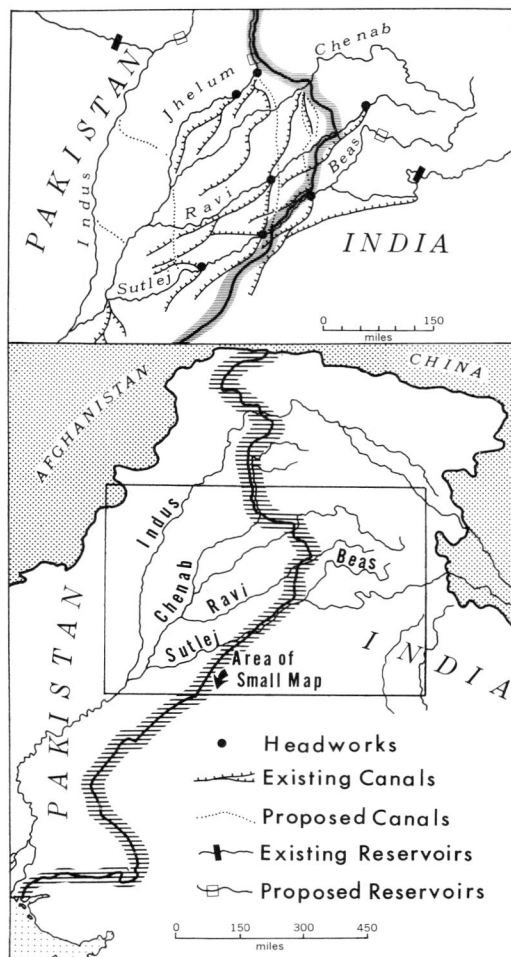

Exhibit 96　*The Indus system.*

which the boundary of India and Pakistan was drawn. The boundary line of the new states was delimited by a boundary commission, whose terms of reference delegated to it the obligation "to demarcate [*sic*] the boundaries of the two parts of the Punjab, on the basis of ascertaining the contiguous majority areas of Muslims and non-Muslims. In doing so, it will take into account other factors." [12]

[12] As quoted in O. H. K. Spate, "The Partition of the Punjab and of Bengal," *G.J.*, vol. 110, p. 205, 1947.

The other factors were primarily economic in nature. When the boundary commission made its enquiries, passions were high and it is understandable (if not also excusable) that the communal or religious differences chiefly influenced the course of the boundary. "Meanwhile the most serious 'other factor'—the desirability or necessity of avoiding so far as possible any disruption of the canal systems on which the prosperity of all communities depended—was largely lost sight of or at most received formal lip-service." [13] The irrigation area chiefly affected by the partition was that lying between the Ravi and the Sutlej Rivers. Here canals, originating in territory that was to become Indian, delivered water to fields that were to become Pakistani. Fully as serious a problem as the division of the irrigated area was the fact that all the rivers of the Punjab had their sources in Kashmir or India. Since the partition of the Punjab in 1947, there has been a prolonged dispute between India and Pakistan regarding the division of the waters. Pakistan's need is greater, but India is in a position to control the larger part of the water. Whatever solution might be adopted, a heavy capital investment would certainly be needed both for extensions to the canal system and for the building of dams and other works. For this reason, the International Bank for Reconstruction and Development, a source of part of this capital, has been active in trying to arrange a settlement of the dispute. In 1960 an agreement was reached whereby India was permitted to draw an increased volume of water from the more easterly rivers, the Ravi, Beas, and Sutlej, which would be used to irrigate areas lying to the south of the last river. Pakistan, for her part, would be recouped by receiving more water from the Jhelum and Chenab, which rise in India

[13] Spate, *op. cit.*, pp. 201–222.

Figure 55 Despite the lack of an international agreement on the use of the water of the river Jordan, Israel is rushing ahead with the building of works to regulate the flow of the river. Here a dam is seen under construction on the Jordan near Lake Huleh. COURTESY: ISRAELI OFFICE OF INFORMATION

or in Indian-held parts of Kashmir. The construction of the costly dams, canals, and other works is to be financed by a loan from the World Bank. This complex and costly arrangement may be said to be due to the simple fact that the Punjab was partitioned with more regard to communal feelings than to hydraulic engineering.

The Jordan River: The Jordan and its few small tributaries make up a river system that is minute beside the Nile and the Indus. But the political problems which it raises are no less acute and have proved to be even more intractable. The Jordan rises near Mount Hermon, in the Republic of Lebanon, and flows southward through a deep and narrow rift valley to enter the Dead Sea, less than 120 miles from its source. Its total discharge, derived mainly from the mountains in Lebanon and from the hills of northern Israel, is small, and the river flows into a small, landlocked sea, useless for navigation and too salty for irrigation. In its course (Exhibit 97) it flows through two small lakes, of which the larger is the familiar Sea of Galilee. Until 1948, the boundary of Palestine and Transjordan followed the river very closely; since then, the incorporation of the Judean hill country in the Kingdom of Jordan has made the relationship of the boundary to the river much more complex. The Jordan now flows from Lebanon to Israel, passing a very small Syrian bridgehead. The Sea of Galilee is wholly Israeli, but for some twenty miles to the south of the Sea of

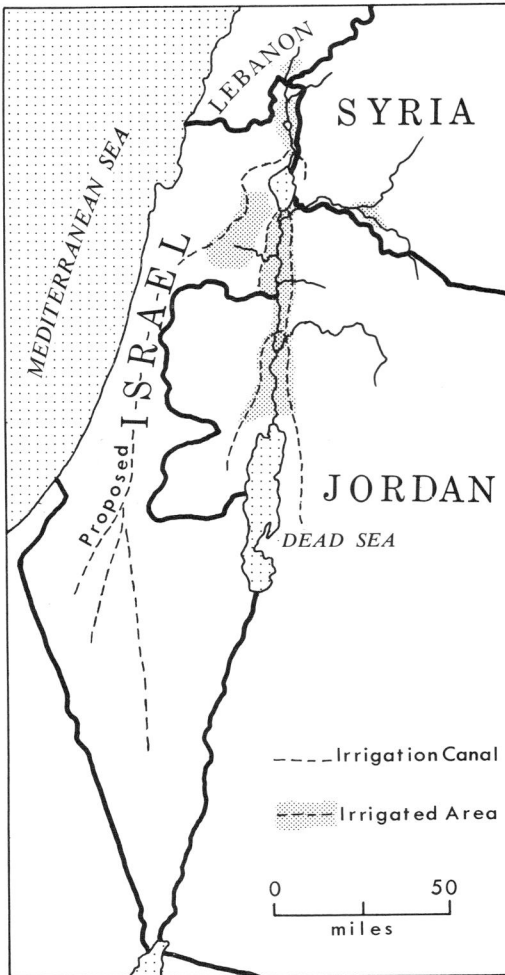

Exhibit 97   *River Jordan.*

plain into full production, and relieving the present heavy dependence on food imports. . . . In the mountainous northern sector, there is a slight surplus of water because the amount of cultivable land is limited. But in the south, potentially fertile lands lie idle without sufficient water to irrigate this semi-desert region. . . . To be reasonably self-sufficient, Israel must expand her irrigated area by at least a half million acres. . . .[14]

Jordan's plight is no less serious:

She has had to absorb a half million Palestinian Arabs and the amount of her cultivated land is not even enough to support the Kingdom's own population of 1,000,000. Even by full utilization of the Yarmuk River [a major tributary of the Jordan running between Jordan and Syria] and of her share of the Jordan River waters, the Kingdom of Jordan would still lack sufficient irrigable land for her present swollen population.[15]

Needs as great as these might have been expected to lead to a rational scheme for the fullest possible utilization of the waters of the Jordan. Instead, mutual jealousies and suspicions and the continual threat of Syrian attack if work is continued on the diversion canal near Lake Huleh have halted all work.

In 1955, a special representative of the United States government examined the problem, made proposals, and offered the financial aid of his government in implementing them. His plan called for the division of the estimated average flow of the river as follows:

	Cu m	
To Lebanon.	35,000,000	⎫
To Syria.	132,000,000	⎬ 62 per cent
To Jordan.	477,000,000	⎭
To Israel.	400,000,000,	38 per cent

The Syrian share would be derived largely from the Yarmuk River. This scheme was

[14] *New York Times,* May 6, 1956.
[15] *Ibid.*

Galilee the Jordan forms the Israeli-Jordanian boundary. Then the river becomes and remains Jordanian.

The whole region is dry, and in Israel and Jordan the shortage of water is serious. The immigration of Central European Jews has brought the Israeli population up to 2,061,000 (1959), and the continued arrival of fresh immigrants makes the extension of cropland an urgent necessity:

For Israel, tapping the Jordan offers the only possible means of bringing the southern accepted by all the states involved except Syria, and on this obstacle it broke down.

At present the Israelis are able to carry on only some small-scale irrigation along the western bank of the upper Jordan. Israeli plans call for a canal from the Jordan, north of the Sea of Galilee, which will supply water to an irrigated region near Nazareth and will then deliver water by a pipeline to the Negev, in the south of Israel. It appears from press reports that work has begun on this pipeline. The Arab states of Syria and Lebanon, which stand to lose nothing from this undertaking, now threaten to stop the flow of the Hasbani and Banyas Rivers, which are, respectively, the Lebanese and Syrian headwaters of the Jordan.

The Unity of River Basins: The political problems of three river basins have been examined in some detail. They serve, along with the North American instances that were cited earlier, to show that river basins constitute physical units. If they are to be used for irrigation or navigation, if the lands bordering them are to be reclaimed or drained, reafforested or preserved from soil erosion the river basin must be treated as a single unit. Most rivers of the world present some technical or economic problem, though most are national rivers and the problems are, therefore, of no significance in international politics. The TVA makes an administrative unit out of a river basin, and the establishment and operation of the Authority has not been without its political difficulties although the whole of it is comprehended within the limits of a single State. These have been national, not international, disputes. An international body has never yet been created to control or supervise the discharge and the use of the waters of an international river as a whole. The navigation commissions of the Rhine, Danube, and other rivers have had no jurisdiction

Figure 56   The Israeli government plans to divert water from the Jordan to the dry southern regions of Israel. Here the water pipeline is seen under construction. COURTESY: ISRAELI OFFICE OF INFORMATION

outside the sphere of navigation. The St. Lawrence Seaway Authority has wider powers, but these fall far short of those which the TVA has been given to control the basin of the Tennessee River. Many rivers—not least among those just examined —would be immeasurably benefited if they could be entrusted to a body similar to the TVA. Such a plan has been urged upon the states which border the river Danube. Here a river system flows through, or borders, no fewer than nine separate states. The river is a commercial highway on which the physical conditions of navigation need improvement. Along its banks, especially in Hungary and Yugoslavia, is good agricultural land that awaits drainage. From the mountains that enclose it descend tributaries, carrying not only floodwaters but also silt and shingle, which are spread out over the plains along the river's course. Yet formal agreement between the Danubian states has been limited to navigational matters, and the accord here has not extended much beyond the political question of the right to sail a ship up and down the river and its major tributaries.

The eighteenth-century writers who argued that the boundaries between states should follow the lines of the hills which separate river basins had, in fact, a better case than even they supposed, in the functional unity of the river basins. It is impossible to improve upon the way in which David Lilienthal has made this point:

I write of the Tennessee Valley, but all this could have happened in almost any of a thousand other valleys where rivers run from the hills to the sea. For the valleys of the earth have these things in common: the waters, the air, the land, the minerals, the forests. In Missouri and in Arkansas, in Brazil and in the Argentine, in China and in India there are just such rivers, rivers flowing through mountain canyons, through canebrake and palmetto, through barren wastes—rivers that in the violence of flood menace the land and the people, then sulk in idleness and drought—rivers all over the world waiting to be controled by men—the Yangtze, the Ganges, the Ob, the Parana, the Amazon, the Nile. In a thousand valleys in America and the world over there are fields that need to be made strong and productive, land steep and rugged, land flat as a man's hand; on the slopes, forests—and in the hills, minerals—that can be made to yield a better living for people.[16]

BIBLIOGRAPHY

Al-Khashab, Wifiq Hussain: *The Water Budget of the Tigris and Euphrates Basin*, University of Chicago, Department of Geography, Research Paper 54, 1958.

Bindoff, S. T.: *The Scheldt Question*, George Allen & Unwin, Ltd., London, 1945.

Bloomfield, L. M., and Gerald F. Fitzgerald: *Boundary Waters Problems of Canada*

[16] David E. Lilienthal, *TVA*, Overseas Editions, Inc., New York, 1944.

and the United States, The Caswell Company Ltd., Toronto, Canada, 1958.

Curti, G. Philip: "The Colorado River: Its Utilization by Southern California," *Geography*, vol. 42, pp. 230–238, 1956–1957.

Development of Water Resources in the Lower Mekong Basin, Economic Commission for Asia and the Far East, Flood Control Series 12, Bangkok, 1957.

East, W. G.: "The Danube Routeway," in *An Historical Geography of Europe*, Methuen & Co., Ltd., New York, 1935, pp. 368–391.

Finer, Herman: *The TVA: Lessons for International Application*, International Labor Organization, Montreal, 1944.

Hajnal, H.: *The Danube, Its Historical, Political and Economic Importance*, M. Nijhoff, The Hague, 1920.

Hartley, Joseph R.: *The Effects of the St. Lawrence Seaway on Grain Movements*, Indiana Business Report 24, Bloomington, Ind., 1957.

Hurst, C. K.: "Water in International Affairs," *Behind the Headlines*, vol. 16, no. 3, September, 1956.

Hurst, H. E.: *The Nile*, Constable & Co., Ltd., London, 1957.

Ionides, M. G.: "The Disputed Waters of the Jordan," *Middle East Journal*, vol. 7, pp. 153–164, 1953.

Kaeckenbeeck, G.: *International Rivers*, Grotius Society Publications, 1, London, 1918.

Karan, Pradyumna P.: "Dividing the Water: A Problem in Political Geography," *P.G.*, vol. 12, no. 1, pp. 6–10, 1961.

Khalaf, Jassim M.: *The Water Resources of the Lower Colorado River Basin*, University of Chicago, Department of Geography, Research Paper 22, 1951.

Lilienthal, David E.: *TVA*, Overseas Editions, Inc., New York, 1944.

MacMichael, Harold: "Egyptian-Sudanese Relations," *Middle Eastern Affairs*, vol. 10, pp. 102–108, 1959.

Oppenheim, L.: *International Law*, Longmans, Green & Co., Ltd., London, 1955, vol. 1.

Pounds, N. J. G.: "Patterns of Trade in the Rhineland," in *Science, Medicine and History*, Oxford University Press, New York, 1953, vol. 2, pp. 419–434.

Spate, O. H. K.: "The Partition of the Punjab and of Bengal," *G.J.*, vol. 110, pp. 201–222, 1947.

Stevens, G. G.: "The Jordan River Valley," *International Conciliation*, January, 1956.

Ten Rivers in America's Future, Report of the President's Water Resources Policy Commission, vol. 2, 1950.

Timm, Charles A.: *The International Boundary Commission, United States and Mexico*, University of Texas Press, Austin, Tex., 1941.

12 THE POLITICAL GEOGRAPHY

OF INTERNATIONAL ORGANIZATIONS

Members of the League undertake to respect and preserve as against external aggression the territorial integrity and existing political independence of all members of the League. COVENANT OF THE LEAGUE OF NATIONS

There exists a degree of culture where national antagonism vanishes altogether, and where one stands, so to speak, above nations, and feels the weal or woe of a neighboring people as if it had happened to one's own. GOETHE, GESPRÄCHE MIT ECKERMANN

IN THE LAST THREE CHAPTERS WE HAVE BEEN CONCERNED PRIMARILY with conflict between states. Conflict was seen to be not continuous but interrupted by agreements grudgingly arrived at and by alliances to be broken when the opportunity served. The only conclusion to be derived from such a picture is that conflict is inevitable between the members of that group of quasi organisms know as states. The social Darwinist predicates his belief that conflict is necessary and the "survival of the fittest" desirable on the assumption that a state is an "organic" entity and must thus obey the "laws" which define the growth of organisms. We have seen earlier (Chapter 1) that the organic theory of the state has neither empirical nor logical foundation. Nevertheless, the decision makers in states, despite their countless protestations to the contrary in preambles to treaties and in their public utterances, act as if they had accepted the social Darwinist's view of the state.

It is refreshing, then, to come to the study of international agreements, organizations, and instruments that are based on the opposite view, that survival depends, not on a conflict from which the fittest to survive will emerge victorious, but on cooperation and collaboration between nations. The extremes, international conflict and international cooperation, are in fact so mixed that it is sometimes difficult to tell which of the two predominates in particular decisions. The Organization for European Economic Co-operation (OEEC), for example, has been a major factor in the economic recovery of western Europe since 1949. It is an instance of collaboration to develop resources and to share the economic aid made available by the United States. It sprang from the proposal made in 1947 by Gen. George Marshall, then Secretary of State, and this offer was itself motivated, at least in part, by a sense of conflict. It was an American move in the cold war to capture the friendship and loyalty of west European countries and, because a prosperous friend is a greater source of strength than an impoverished one, to rebuild their economies. It is not the purpose of this chapter to separate the idealism from the chauvinism. It is rather to examine the geographical factors that have been significant in the formation of these groupings of states, however broad their idealism or narrow their self-interest.

WORLD ORGANIZATIONS

The most idealistic and general organizations of states—and for that reason the least geographical—have been the League of Nations and its successor, the UN. Geography is concerned with "areal differentiation," and membership of one or other of these organizations has been almost worldwide. It follows that the lack of variation from one part of the world to another in membership of, or attitude to, these bodies almost precludes their study from the field of political geography—almost, but not quite, for not all states were members of the League of Nations. The United States Senate never ratified the Treaty of Versailles (1919), in which was incorporated the Covenant of the League of Nations. The Soviet Union was not admitted to membership until 1934, and in 1933 Germany resigned from it, followed by several other states within a few years. Furthermore, most of the microstates did not join the League. The absences from the League of Nations have an explanation that is partially geographical. American absention is partly explicable in terms of the "isolationist" feeling in the United States, itself a geographical phenomenon. The absence from the membership lists of many of the very small states was in part a function of their neutrality, in part of their small resources, the explanation of which is again largely geographical. Germany, Italy, and Japan left the League because their territorial ambitions could not be realized without war, and thus conflict between these countries and the League itself was inevitable.

The UN, with a membership of 110 in October, 1962, still is short of encompassing the world by some twenty states. Of these the largest and most important is Red China. Next in importance are the Federal (West) and Democratic (East) Republics of Germany, the two Koreas, and the two Vietnams. The exclusion of Red China is purely political. The division of Germany, Korea, and Vietnam places these states in a somewhat equivocal position; Switzerland and the Vatican City State are neutral, and the small states of Andorra, Bhutan, Liechtenstein, Monaco, and San Marino have never sought membership and probably would not have the financial resources with which to become members.

Thus the list of members and nonmembers of the UN has nothing essentially geographical about it. The same is true of the membership list of the Specialized Agencies of the United Nations, such as the International Labor Organization, World Health Organization, and the Food and Agriculture Organization. Several states which are not members of the UN have joined certain of the Specialized Agencies, in whose work they have reason to be particularly interested. Thus the Vatican City State is a member of the Universal Postal Union and of the International Telecommunication Union. The German Federal Republic has been admitted to all the Specialized Agencies and South Vietnam to most of them. On the other hand, the member states do not necessarily participate in the activities of each of the Specialized Agencies. The Communist countries are not represented in either the International Monetary Fund or the International Bank for Reconstruction and Development, and most of them are absent from the Food and Agriculture Organization.

Only in the most general way can this pattern of participation in the UN and its Specialized Agencies be described as geographically significant. Other international organizations are, however, regional in scope. The nature of the alliance, pact, or agreement clearly separates the "ins" from the "outs." The member states of each such alliance form a regional group which is generally compact and clearly definable in geographical terms. The study of such groupings of states belongs much more clearly to political geography; their geographical extent can be examined and explained, their strategic and economic strengths and weaknesses measured, and the degree to which their internal harmony is motivated by external conflict assessed.

About a dozen such international groupings deserve consideration. Some are mainly economic in function; some are wholly political, and others have marked cultural or religious overtones.

ECONOMIC GROUPINGS OF STATES

There are no economic groupings of states that are not also to some degree political. The years of the Second World War, when the governments of several European countries found themselves in exile in London or elsewhere, saw many proposals for the closer union of states. Most of these aspirations evaporated in the stormy days of peace that followed. The projected federation of Poland and Czechoslovakia came to nothing. No attempt was ever made to implement the proposed union of Yugoslavia and Greece. Out of all these proposals only one was ever implemented, the Benelux Union of Belgium, the Netherlands, and Luxembourg. The foundations of the Union were laid in 1922, when a customs union was established between Belgium and Luxembourg. Customs barriers and even frontier checks were abolished along the boundary separating the two states. Their currencies became freely exchangeable, and a common market within the two states was established. In 1947 this union was extended by the incorporation of the Netherlands. The customs union of the three states was realized gradually. Duties were not abolished immediately on goods moving from Belgium-Luxembourg into the Netherlands, and vice versa; they were reduced by degrees, and agriculture and industry in each of the two areas adjusted themselves slowly over the years to the other.

The Low Countries had, of course, a long history of political union and collaboration, which was interrupted by the wars of the sixteenth century, when the Spaniards asserted their control over the more southerly provinces. After this date, the closure of the Scheldt and the long wrangle over navigation rights and facilities embittered relations between the Belgians and the Dutch. The two states drifted apart and the Union has had the difficult task of bridging this antipathy.

The Netherlands is more an agricultural than an industrial state. Belgium is the reverse. One might have expected the economies of the two to adjust to one another without serious difficulty. This, however, did not happen. Belgium's agriculture was a high-cost business and had been protected by tariffs. It was necessary at first to give the Belgian produce growers some protection against the cheaper Dutch goods. As a result of competition between the brewing industries, in which the Netherlands held a decided advantage, and in coal mining, steel production, and a wide range of factory industries, in most of which the advantage lay with Belgium, the creation of the Union was fraught with difficulties. It was, however, an object lesson in the problems inherent in the creation of an economic union.

Amid the difficulties and frustrations of the early days of the Benelux Union, it was not easy to envisage the advantages that could accrue from it. Benelux, acting together in commercial and other negotiations, is no longer a small power. This was demonstrated very clearly when Benelux acted jointly in the negotiations that accompanied the establishment of the OEEC. But this strength through union is not the only advantage. An early report on the Union gave

. . . reason to expect that the expansion of the home market which the economic union will bring about, will lead to a more rational geographical and technical distribution of labor, to a higher level of production and to lower costs. This and a greater abundance of commodities suitable for exchange purposes will serve to promote exports. . . . All this may naturally be accompanied by an increase in imports. In this way, the union will mean

not less but more trade with foreign countries.[1]

These hopes have been realized, and the success of Benelux has had a great influence on the decision to carry into effect a wider and more ambitious plan, the Common Market.

The European Coal and Steel Community: Like Benelux, the ECSC was a political union for limited economic objects. The geographical area which it covered was larger; the fields of human activity, more limited. In 1950 the French Foreign Affairs Minister, Robert Schuman, proposed a common market for western Europe in coal, iron, and steel and the raw materials from which the latter are made. The background of this proposal is to be found in the events of the previous years: the growing rift between the Western Powers and the Soviet bloc; the need for closer union among the latter; the question of the Saarland, an area German in language and sympathy, but with coal and steel industries that were tied economically to France; the failure of attempts to internationalize the Ruhr coal-field and industrial area; and France's urgent need for an assured supply of good-quality coking coal for her iron-smelting industry, which only West Germany could supply (Exhibit 98). Hovering above these considerations, which were internal to Europe, there was the specter to the industry of western Europe that lay in the competition and loss of markets, as a result of the plans for the industrialization of the underdeveloped countries of the world. Western Europe had long been an important exporter of steel and steel goods. A report of the Economic Commission for Europe (ECE) of the UN had in the previous year drawn the attention of European politicians to the fact that this market might contract disastrously unless European

[1] *Rotterdamsche Bank,* 1947, no. 4, p. 41.

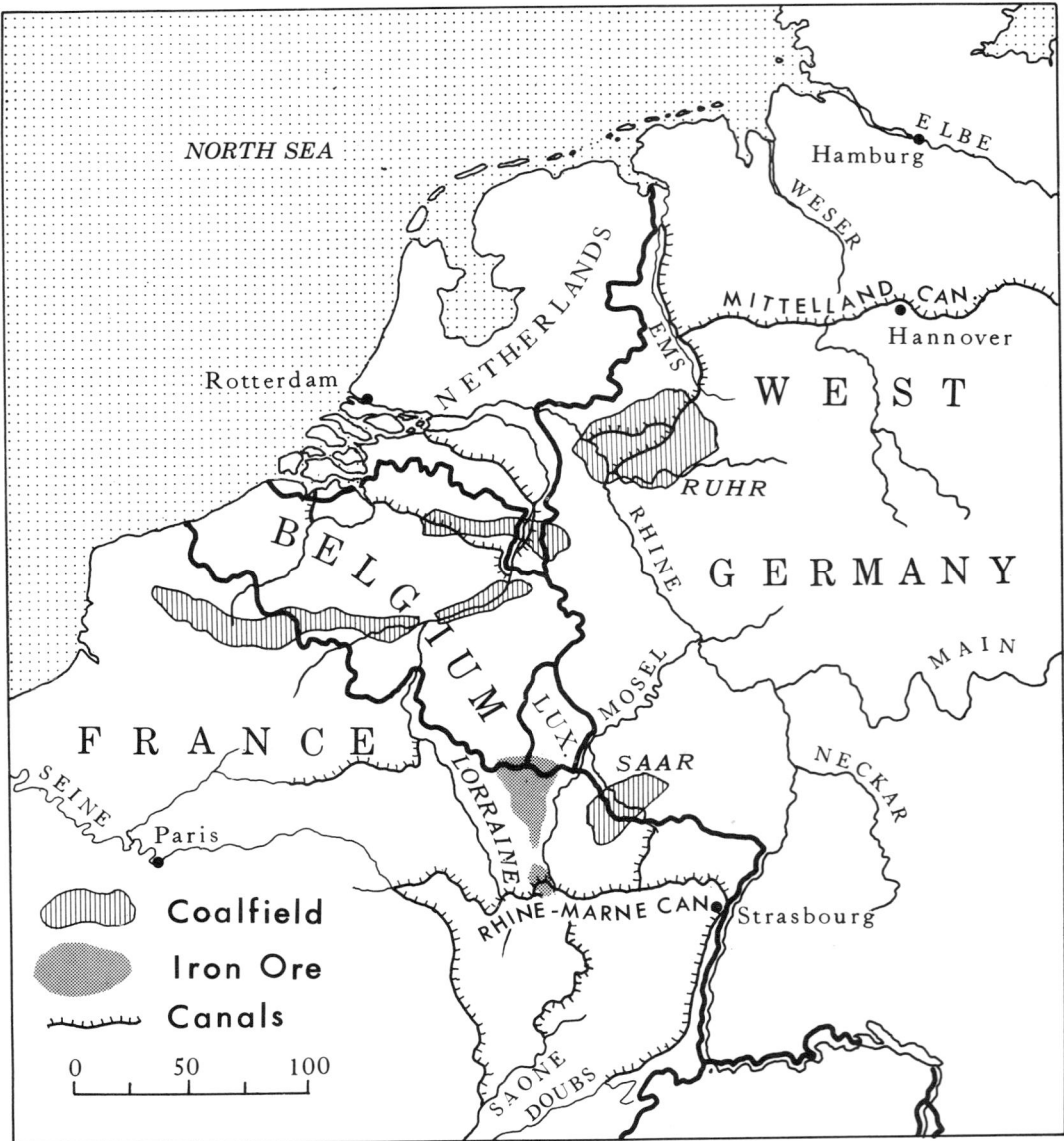

Exhibit 98   *Coal fields, iron ore, and waterways in northwestern Europe.*

industrialists could rationalize their plant and produce more cheaply. The Schuman proposal was an attempt to secure greater economies in production and thus to maintain or to widen the overseas market.

Schuman's proposal was well received, and later, in the same year, six countries, France, West Germany, the Benelux group, and Italy, sent representatives to draw up the terms of an agreement. Great Britain showed interest in the movement but declined to join it. In 1952 the treaty establishing the ECSC was signed and subsequently ratified by each of the six states.

It came into effect soon afterward and has continued until 1959, when the organization was merged with the Common Market.

The object of the ECSC was to diminish the costs of production. Professor Parker has described its operation in the coal industry of the member states:

The Schuman Plan's ideal for the European coal industry can be pictured by reference to a map of Europe, showing coal deposits, existing mines and coking installations, and the location of the market for the different commercial grades and sizes of coal and coke. According to the supposed economic ideal then, fuel should be supplied where demand is most intense from the sources whose exploitation involves minimum total physical costs of mining, processing and transport. If the Ruhr area, for example, yielded all sizes and grades of coal so abundantly and easily that every part of the entire market could be supplied by it at a lower delivered cost than by any other area, then mining should be concentrated in this exceedingly productive region. But transport charges are so great, and the market so extensive, relative even to the Ruhr's resources, that the other deposits will in fact be mined. The French, Saar, Belgian and Dutch mining industries each has a market area of its own, protected by the costs of transporting coal from other regions into it, by the rise in mining costs elsewhere as other regions increase their output, and the special characteristics of the coals found in different beds. This latter fact means also that the different mining districts penetrate with their special grades of coal into the market areas of one another.

The market areas of the different mining regions are at present supposed to be artificially distorted from their ideal limits. One group of mines may have cost advantages over others from other than purely physical reasons. Consumers in one industry or region may enjoy lower delivered prices than other consumers similarly situated. In the former case, a region with artificially low costs is producing and selling coal which embodies a higher physical cost than coal from another region; in terms of physical resources coal is costing more than necessary to produce. In the latter case, coal is not going to those consumers who would pay most for it; it is being sold to satisfy less intense demands while more intense demands are not filled. The ideal of the Schuman Plan is to eliminate all artificial cost and price differentials and enable the market to operate freely, adjusting rates of production and consumption by means of market price movements and permitting labour and investment funds to enter the regions of highest prospective yields, as envisaged in traditional economic theory.[2]

The same argument applies no less to the mining of iron ore and the supply of pig iron and scrap metal to steelworks, of iron to foundries, and of half-finished steel goods to engineering works and construction projects. The coal-mining and iron and steel industries of most countries had formerly enjoyed some kind of protection, not only because goods from outside paid a duty on entering, but also because they were assisted by preferential rail rates, insurance schemes, and other disguised subsidies. The treaty establishing the Community requires the abolition of all such aids, which might serve to cover up the disadvantages of a particular works or location. Nothing should be allowed to protect the weak branch of the industry or detract from the strong.

Clearly, the same circumstances would arise here as had already made the early years of Benelux difficult. Protection of industry, whatever its form, was to be stripped away gradually until, in the end, every works was left in its nakedness to face the cold breath of international competition. This stage has been achieved with a rapidity that varied from one industry to

[2] N. J. G. Pounds and W. N. Parker, *Coal and Steel in Western Europe*, Indiana University Press, Bloomington, Ind., 1957, pp. 356–357.

another. In a few instances legal decisions became necessary, as no state, despite the good will shown, had any desire to give away one iota more than it had contracted to do.

The Community is changing the map of the coal-mining and iron and steel industries in western Europe. The Ruhr is the largest and most efficient producer of coal. Belgium and northern France are relatively inefficient producers, owing in part to the age of the mines, in part to the very contorted and disturbed nature of the coal seams worked. Many mines in this area cannot face the competition of the German mines, or even that of the newer mines in the Netherlands and the Campine coal field of northern Belgium. Government assistance to them has now run out; the less well placed have been closed and the miners moved to other mines or absorbed into other sources of employment. The result of this process in Belgium, France, and elsewhere is the lowering of the average price of coal.

Cheaper fuel brings about naturally a lowering of production costs in other branches of industry, including the manufacture of iron and steel. The low-cost producers are extending their activities; the high-cost producers are going out of business. The steel capacity in the Ruhr and Lorraine is being increased; electric steel production in northern Italy and in the French Alps, where hydroelectric power is available, is also increasing, whereas at some of the older centers of production in France and in central and southern Germany it is declining in importance. Further shifts in industrial location may be expected. New plants will be established at whatever sites, within the area of the six states of the Community, appear to be the most advantageous. At present, coastal locations which can receive imported iron ore and also fuel brought by river or canal

barge from the Ruhr are gaining in importance.

This development must necessarily in some degree alter the power balance between states. The mere fact, for example, that some parts of the Belgian coal-mining industry are being deliberately reduced must be to the advantage of the German and the Dutch mines, where employment and production may be expected to increase. Any weakening that Belgium might suffer through this change might be expected to be offset by the lower price of coal that is made available to her and by the consequent advantage of this to all branches of her industry. It is impossible, however, to avoid some degree of structural unemployment as a result of these changes. All economic growth and industrial change are necessarily accompanied by unemployment, as demand and hence production are switched from one branch of industry to another. Unemployment breeds political discontent. But the Community has been careful, by continuing protection longer than might otherwise have been thought desirable, to reduce to a minimum the distress caused by changes in the location of production.

The Common Market: Those who negotiated the treaty of the ECSC anticipated that it would be extended to a wider field of economic activity and also to a larger area of Europe. Discussions of this wider economic union were spread over several years. Seventeen countries of western Europe participated. Disagreements were quick to show themselves. The six states which had participated so successfully in the ECSC wanted to create in the shortest possible time a common market for all articles of commerce. Other European countries were unwilling to go so far. The United Kingdom made much of her commercial ties with the Commonwealth, which, it was held, would conflict with her obligations as a member of the proposed Common Market. France, on the other hand, wanted a market made up of the member states which would have common tariff barriers against the rest of the world and none between themselves. This would tend to create a functional unity of the states which joined it, and this functional unity might lead ultimately, it was supposed, to some form of political union.

The other parties to the discussions desired only a free-trade area. The member states would reduce or abolish the tariffs between themselves but would retain their own varied tariffs against all other states. This would clearly have raised considerable administrative difficulties. Goods from elsewhere might, for example, have entered France, a high-tariff country, by way of the Netherlands, which has traditionally imposed low tariffs. Such a possibility would clearly make it necessary for goods entering one member state from another to carry some kind of certificate of origin, showing that they originated within the Common Market.

In the end, the six states, France, the Benelux group, West Germany, and Italy, which were already pledged to the closest economic cooperation, signed the Rome Treaty of 1958, which created the *European Economic Community* (EEC), otherwise known as the *Common Market* (Exhibit 99). The tariffs which surrounded the Community were to be near the average of the previous tariffs of the six states. Internal tariffs were to be progressively lowered, until complete freedom of trade within the Community was achieved. The Rome Treaty came into effect in January, 1959, when the first reductions were made in the internal tariffs of the Community, a process that is due to be completed by January, 1966.

But what of the eleven other states which had declined to go along with so far-reaching a proposal? In November, 1959, seven of these, Great Britain, Denmark, Norway, Sweden, Austria, Switzerland, and Portugal, came together to form the *European Free Trade Association* (EFTA). Its purpose is more limited than that of the EEC. It aims over a period of ten years to reduce tariffs on trade between its members in *industrial goods*. The exclusion of agricultural goods was an attempt to maintain some protection for the agricultural industries of these countries. Nor is a common tariff around the group as a whole envisaged. Each will keep its present tariffs, along with preferential agreements and other trading arrangements with states outside the group.

But the European Free Trade Association has not been particularly successful. The United Kingdom found membership of the EFTA no compensation for exclusion from the Common Market. In the summer of 1961 the British government applied for membership of the latter and was followed by some of its fellow members of EFTA. The matter is yet, as of September, 1962, far from being settled, and it remains possible to speak of Europe as still "at sixes and sevens."

Thus thirteen of the seventeen states of "free" Europe find themselves in different camps, in two different leagues, each of which has its own rules. Trade between the United Kingdom and Denmark or between France and Germany will be facilitated by the removal of all obstacles in its way. That between the United Kingdom—a member of the "Seven"—and France—one of the "Six"—will not. Trade *within* each of the groups is likely to be encouraged, perhaps at the expense of trade between members of the two groups. Table 17 shows the direction of trade carried on by the seven members of the EFTA in 1958, that is, just before its formation.

It is remarkable how little trade the

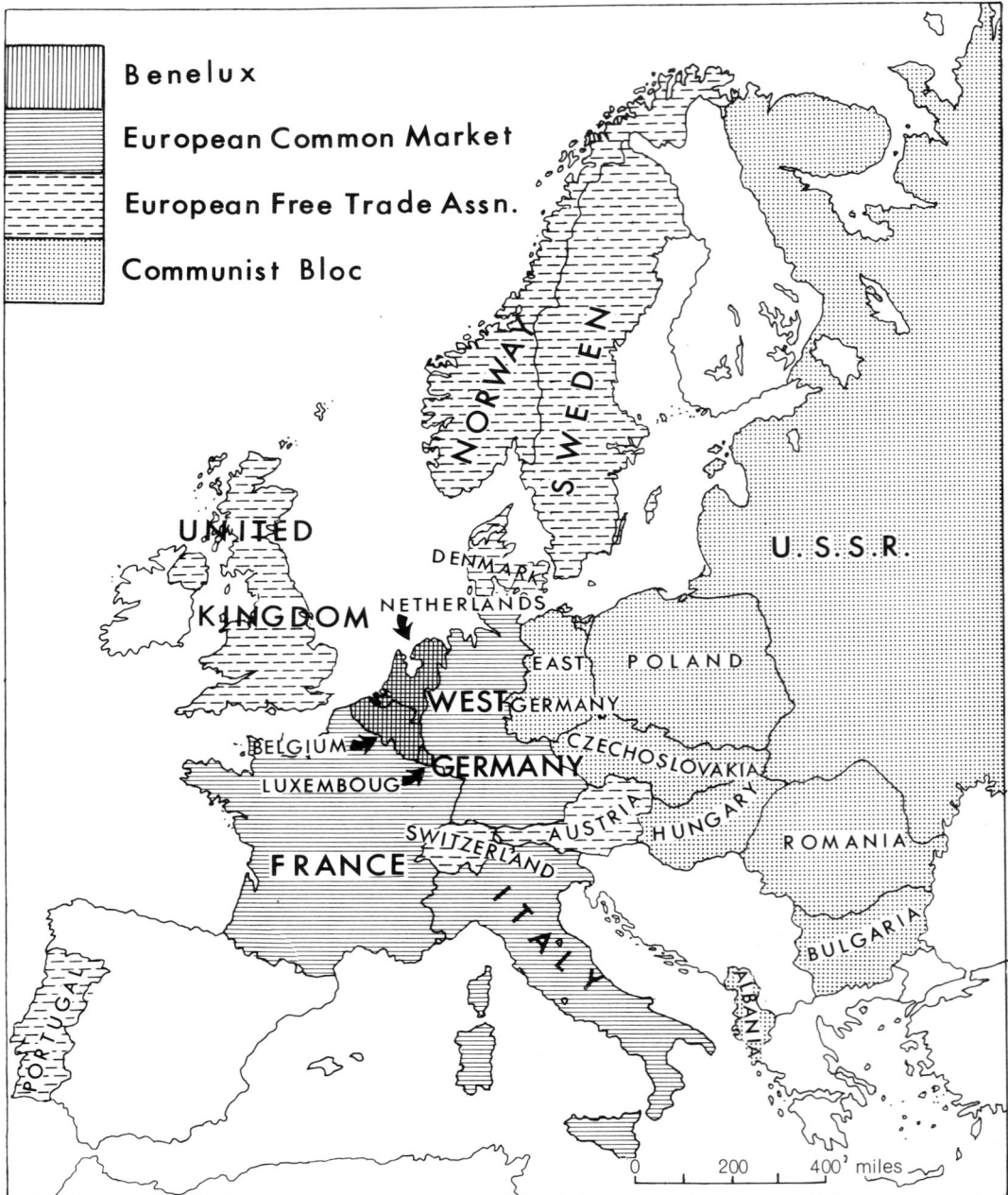

Exhibit 99   *Common Market and Outer Seven.*

TABLE 17 *Where European Free Trade Association Countries Get Their Imports, 1958*

Exporter-Importer	Austria	Den-mark	Norway	Portugal	Sweden	Switzer-land	United Kingdom	All EFTA
Austria............	. . .	3	2	1	6	13	8	33
Denmark..........	3	. . .	21	1	34	6	116	180
Norway...........	2	17	. . .	2	28	3	56	107
Portugal..........	1	2	1	. . .	3	1	15	22
Sweden...........	4	48	74	5	. . .	9	135	275
Switzerland.......	16	10	7	6	18	. . .	36	94
United Kingdom....	17	109	72	22	118	35	. . .	373
EFTA.............	43	189	177	37	207	66	366	1,085
EEC..............	208	173	165	67	353	359	535	1,859
OEEC.............	256	363	344	105	563	428	1,027	3,086
Rest of the world...	127	115	124	66	281	183	2,753	3,649
World............	383	478	467	171	844	611	3,780	6,735

members of the EFTA carried on with one another and how large was their trade with members of the rival group, the EEC The Seven are, with the exception of the United Kingdom, "small" countries, in which agriculture is relatively important. As their physical environments are not dissimilar. one would not expect a great deal of trade with one another in agricultural products, and agricultural goods, furthermore, are not included in the EFTA agreement. The United Kingdom, on the other hand, carries on a volume of trade that is a good deal larger than that of the rest of the Seven together. Though British trade within the EFTA makes up only a small percentage of its own total trade, it is in reality much larger in quantity than the intra-Association trade of the rest of the group. Most of the Seven, however, carry on more trade with the Six than they do with one another. One might expect this share to diminish, at least relatively, as trade within the Seven increases. There is at least a danger that Europe may become divided into two competing trade groups, between which a "trade war" might develop.

The Organization for Economic Co-operation and Development: In the summer of 1947 Europe was still suffering from the results of the Second World War. There were serious shortages; vital articles of food were rationed; many of the cities lay, partially at least, in ruins; and industrial production was recovering only very slowly. Behind the specter of hunger and want there stalked that of communism, and there was a very real danger that it would attempt to take over the states of central and western Europe. The United States was distant from all this, yet felt its impact in two ways—economically, in the diminished trade that resulted from European impoverishment, and politically, in the mounting danger of communism. It was at this time that the Secretary of State, George C. Marshall, made a speech at Harvard in which he offered American aid in the recovery of the devastated continent. "Our policy," he said, "should be the revival of an organic economy in the world so as to permit the emergence of political and social conditions in which free institutions can exist." The objective of this policy was a political one, the survival of free institutions in general, and of those of the United States in particular.

It would [he went on] be neither fitting nor efficacious for the American Government to undertake to draw up unilaterally a program designed to place Europe on its feet economically. That is the business of the Europeans. The initiative, I think, must come from Europe. The role of this country should consist of friendly aid in drafting of the European Program, of friendly support of such a program, so far as it may be practical for us to do so. The program should be a joint one, agreed to by a number of, if not all, the European nations.

No country of Europe, not even the Soviet Union, was excluded from General Marshall's offer. The British and French Foreign Ministers reacted immediately and favorably. Within a few weeks they had called a conference to discuss means of implementing it. Within five weeks of General Marshall's speech, the representatives of sixteen European nations met in Paris. They acted quickly and established a committee, which, in time, produced a report on Europe's needs and a program for the economic recovery of the Continent.

The sixteen nations, in addition to the United Kingdom and France, which had taken the lead in organizing the conference, were Portugal, Italy, Belgium, Luxembourg, the Netherlands, Denmark, Switzerland, Norway, Sweden, Finland, Iceland, the Irish Republic, Greece, Turkey, and Austria. The Soviet Union and Spain were not invited, and the invitation was declined by the Soviet satellites of eastern Europe. The states which accepted the offer then constituted the *Organization for European Economic Co-operation* (OEEC), which

was in 1949 joined by the German Federal Republic (West Germany). Spain and Yugoslavia have since participated in the work of the Organization, without formally becoming members.

The increase of agricultural and industrial production within the resulting "Seventeen," and the achievement of financial stability, were the primary objectives of all in joining the Organization. These objectives could be realized only by (1) accepting General Marshall's generous offer of American aid and (2) cooperation between themselves in sharing this help and in using their own more modest resources. It is impossible to trace here the expansion of the activities of OEEC or to describe the high degree of success which they achieved. American supplies allowed, first, for a higher level of production and then helped to keep inflation within bounds. Capital goods were used in the reequipment of European industry. The Organization has worked to establish a more liberal trade and tariff regime in Europe. In 1958 it established the *European Monetary Agreement*, the object of which was to improve yet more the convertibility of European currencies. The Organization has tried to influence the investment policy of its member nations, with the object of preventing overlapping and of achieving the maximum results from investments made. Technical committees were constituted, to report and advise on means of improving the efficiency of agriculture, industry, and transportation. In the context of cooperation in the field of industry and technology an agreement was reached in 1958 to establish a *European Nuclear Energy Agency* (Euratom), to further the development of atomic power for industrial purposes. Already a start has been made in constructing atomic-energy stations to be jointly owned and operated by the member states.

In 1960 the OEEC changed both its title and its function. It became the *Organization for Economic Co-operation and Development* (OECD). While fostering economic cooperation between the states of Europe, OECD gives greater emphasis to the relations between Europe and the underdeveloped nations of the world and to the encouragement of multilateral trade on a world basis.

The organizations that have been described are predominantly economic in nature. They are international organizations aiming to liberalize trade and to make the most of the resources for industry and agriculture that they possess. Their objectives are not without political overtones, but their immediate aim is increased production and a higher level of welfare. They constitute the first significant breach in the views, tacitly held if not overtly expressed, of the social Darwinists. Unfortunately, however, this growing functional unity among the groups of states which make up these several associations is paralleled by a rift, which has grown deeper during the past ten to fifteen years, between these groups on the one hand and the Soviet bloc on the other. Far from being liberalized, trade between these two groups of states is smaller in volume than before the Second World War and is very much more tightly controlled by their governments. If zones of conflict have become fewer, they have, nevertheless, become more intense.

The Colombo Plan: The Plan for Co-operative Economic Development in South and South-East Asia was prepared in 1950. Its object is to pursue in Southeast Asia the same kind of objectives that OEEC pursued in Europe. The problems facing the representatives of the countries of Southeast Asia, who met at Colombo (Ceylon) in 1950, were, however, rather different from those which were faced at a similar meeting in Paris three years earlier. The states represented at Paris were developed industrial countries whose productive capacity had been devastated and dislocated by six years of war. The problems which confronted the Colombo Conference were those of low standards of living, inadequate capital, insufficient mechanical and scientific skills, and a population that was growing faster than agricultural production. The situation in Southeast Asia was summarized in a report on the Colombo Plan:

There are over 570 [3] million people living in the area—for the most part hard-working men and women of simple dignity and faith. Many of them are skilled in craftsmanship and in fashioning lovely things with their hands. They have inherited ancient cultures and philosophies, and their forefathers were creating beautiful works of art at a time when many Western countries were peopled only by primitive savages. But no man can give of his best or enjoy life to the full when his stomach is empty and his body weakened by disease, and that is the condition of millions in South and South-East Asia today.

The great majority live in villages and depend for a livelihood on the land. But not enough land is being cultivated to support so many millions, and those who work it are not trained and equipped to get the best out of the soil. As a result food is scarce and lacking in variety. The ordinary diet of most of the people in the area is mainly cereals, pulses and other starchy foods which do not provide the fats and proteins for proper nutrition. A man may get as little as 12 ounces of cereals a day; this is in fact the present ration in many Indian towns. Average food consumption over the area as a whole works out at well under 2,000 calories a day, compared with about 3,000 in Britain.

[3] The population of the member states, excluding Japan, is now about 675 million.

The peoples of South and South-East Asia have to live hard and many must die young. The proportion of babies who die during their first year is more than four times as high as in Britain, and average expectation of life at birth is less than half as long. Some eight people out of every ten are unable to read or write. Acute overcrowding exists in towns and villages alike, with a one- or two-roomed hut of mud or bamboo often serving the needs of a whole family—and sometimes of their animals as well.

All over the area the populations are growing rapidly—growing by about 20,000 every day. One child in every three born into the world today is a child of South and South-East Asia. At this rate the present population of 570 million will have increased to 720 million by 1970. That will mean an extra 150 million people to feed in less than twenty years, the equivalent of the whole population of the United States.

One reason for this startling increase is the lowering of the death-rate through improvements in public health. But in the long run experience suggests that a general improvement in living standards exercises a steadying influence on the rise in population. In some countries in the area the birth-rate of the middle classes is already declining; for instance, it has been found in East Bengal that the size of families tends to be smaller on holdings of ten acres than on those of five.

It is clear that a great expansion of agricultural and industrial production will be needed to provide for the increase in population, even without any improvement in the standard of living. There is evidence to show that output per head has actually declined over the past ten years; this trend must be reversed.[4]

The Colombo Plan seeks to remedy this situation by raising the output of both agriculture and industry, by extending the area of agricultural land, by improving the technical level of agriculture, and by in-

dustrial development. Such undertakings necessitate a very heavy capital investment in irrigation works, in cement and fertilizer plants, and in other forms of industry. Table 18 shows how backward in these respects were the Colombo Plan nations in 1949 by comparison with the United States and United Kingdom. It shows how far the countries of Southeast Asia had to go before they could even approach the European or American level of industrial development and production. The original members of the Colombo group of nations were British Borneo, Cambodia, Ceylon, India, Laos, Malaya, Pakistan, Singapore, and Vietnam.[5] Burma and Nepal joined in 1952, Indonesia in 1953, and Japan, the Philippines, and Thailand in 1954. The plan included also states outside the geographical area of Southeast Asia, but interested in it, and able to provide capital and technical assistance: the United States, Canada, the United Kingdom, Australia, and New Zealand. Assistance and cooperation between this group of twenty nations are aimed to ensure that the wisest use is made of available capital and resources in raising the level of welfare of as many people as possible.

Investment capital is supplied in part by the member states lying outside the area and in part by the International Bank (see Chapter 14). To a small extent, the Asiatic members of the Plan are able to supply technical assistance to one another, but much of the expert advice and guidance is supplied by the United States and United Kingdom. Investment in the member countries of Southeast Asia has been on a mounting scale. In a five-year period (1954–1959) a sum of 17,726 million dollars was invested in the fourteen member states within Southeast Asia, a total of about $26 per head of population. Thanks to the Plan,

---

[4] *New Horizons in the East*, H.M. Stationery Office, London, 1950, pp. 6–11.

[5] Now South Vietnam only.

TABLE 18 *Indices of Economic Development in the Colombo Plan Nations*

Unit per thousand population	India	Pakistan	Ceylon	Malaya	United Kingdom	U.S.A.
Electricity production (thousand), kwhr.........	13	1.9	9.6	117	1,033	2,296
Coal consumption, tons......	80	18	28	85	3,884	3,473
Steel consumption, tons.....	3.8	1.3	6	16	194	364
Cement consumption, tons...	7.2	3.6	19	25	148	229
Carrying capacity of railroad wagons, tons.............	10	8.8	4.5	13	276	556
All-weather roads, miles.....	0.32	0.1	0.9	0.9	3.7	2.2

the Colombo states appear jointly to be holding the balance even between population and food production, but it may be questioned how much longer the level may be maintained, in the face of a population which continues to expand rapidly.

The Colombo Plan is primarily economic, like the OEEC and its successor, the OEDC, but it, too, has political overtones. Higher productivity and welfare are conceived of as means of achieving greater political stability. Overtly, the Colombo Plan is not drawn up in terms of the East-West conflict. Indeed, some of its members, notably Burma, Indonesia, Nepal, and perhaps India, are neutralist in their political outlook. It is generally supposed, however, that the ability of the Communists to create trouble in Southeast Asia varies inversely with the trend in the level of human welfare in that area, and the Plan aims to raise this level. The Colombo Plan is also paralleled by an international organization which is openly political in its aims, the South-East Asia Collective Defence Treaty (see below). Its eight members are also members of the Colombo Plan, and three other members of the latter (British Borneo, Malaya, and Singapore) are members of the Commonwealth.

Council of Economic Mutual Assistance: In 1949 the Soviet Union issued an invitation to all countries of Europe to "participate in broad economic co-operation" with itself. This was the Soviet Union's reply to the Marshall Plan. The invitation was, of course, accepted by the Communist countries of eastern Europe. Yugoslavia also accepted but was refused membership. Details of the progress of economic collaboration between these states have not fully been made public, but we know that agreements were reached between Poland and Czechoslovakia for the use of one another's ports and for the "coordination . . . of their programs of production in order to apportion the fabrication of determined products." Unquestionably, considerable progress has been made in fitting the economic plans of these two countries together so that they complement one another and also in adjusting them to the plans of other countries within the bloc. But the economic cooperation between the Council of Economic Mutual Assistance (CEMA) countries differed fundamentally from that created in the European Common Market and the EFTA. The latter is based on private enterprise and guarantees to the producer freedom to sell his products anywhere within the area where he can find a market and, with certain limitations, freedom to establish his works wherever he finds it most profitable. The CEMA is an agreement between governments which themselves control all industrial undertakings and all trade within their respective states. Through the mechanism established by CEMA some degree of integration has been secured between the development plans of each of the member states. Trade has continued, however, to be based mainly on bilateral barter agreements negotiated between them. It appears, nevertheless, that these trade agreements, as well as investment plans and other forms of economic development, are first cleared through CEMA.

The basis of the planned development in the Communist countries remains national. Each country draws up its own economic plans and carries them out. Although there is, as we have seen, a considerable measure of cooperation between them, this partnership is based upon international treaty. It is more formal and less flexible than the collaboration achieved in, let us say, the Common Market, through the mechanism of private enterprise.

POLITICAL GROUPINGS OF STATES

It is very difficult—impossible, in fact—to distinguish between international organizations which are primarily economic and those which are first and foremost political. Every economic organization of the kind examined so far is to some extent political. It has been created by political action, and its purpose is, in some measure, to serve political ends. Some of the organizations discussed are paralleled by other organizations which are avowedly political in their purpose. The economic organizations are generally broader than the political

and include states whose neutralist leanings would prevent them joining a political group. The OECD is thus broader than the political group, NATO, which it may be said to parallel (Table 19). The Colombo Plan is similarly broader than SEATO.

The following international organizations seem to be the most important of those whose objects are mainly political (Exhibit 100).

Council of Europe: By 1948 the cold war had become a reality, and many of the states of western Europe began to group themselves, as if in self-defense. In 1948 the representatives of five of them met at Brussels and signed a treaty by which they all undertook to collaborate "in economic, social and cultural matters and for *collective self-defence*." The German Federal Republic and Italy subsequently joined the organization. Although the plans for the unification of the military forces of the member states broke down, the seven member states nevertheless agreed in 1955 to establish the *Western European Union*, the objective of which was to provide the mechanism of consultation and cooperation, by which the original objectives of the Brussels Treaty might be fulfilled.

The Brussels powers also agreed in 1949 to establish a *Council of Europe.* "The aim of the Council of Europe is to achieve a greater unity between its members for the purpose of safeguarding and realizing the ideals and principles which are their common heritage, and facilitating their economic and social progress." [6] Its objective is political; the means which it employs are consultation and discussion. Its organs are a Council of Ministers and a Consultative Assembly, in both of which all the member states are represented. As the name of the Assembly suggests, the body as a whole exists to discuss problems, to initiate ideas,

---

[6] *Statute of the Council of Europe*, art. 1.

TABLE 19 *Membership of European Political and Economic Organizations*

Political		Economic
Council of Europe	*NATO*	*OEEC*
Austria	Belgium	Austria
Belgium	Canada	Belgium
Denmark	Denmark	Denmark
France	France	France
German Federal Republic	German Federal Republic	German Federal Republic
Greece	Greece	Greece
Iceland	Iceland	Iceland
Irish Republic	Italy	Irish Republic
Italy	Luxembourg	Italy
Luxembourg	Netherlands	Luxembourg
Netherlands	Norway	Netherlands
Norway	Portugal	Norway
Sweden	Turkey	Portugal
Turkey	United Kingdom	Spain
United Kingdom	United States	Sweden
		Switzerland
		Turkey
		United Kingdom
		Yugoslavia

TABLE 20 *Membership of Asiatic Political and Economic Organizations*

SEATO	*Colombo plan*
Australia	Australia
France	Canada
New Zealand	Burma [1]
Pakistan	Cambodia [1]
Philippines	Ceylon [1]
Thailand	India [1]
United Kingdom (with dependencies)	Indonesia [1]
United States	Laos [1]
	Malaya [1]
	Nepal [1]
	New Zealand
	Pakistan
	Philippines
	Thailand
	United Kingdom (with dependencies)
	Vietnam [1]

[1] Not in SEATO.

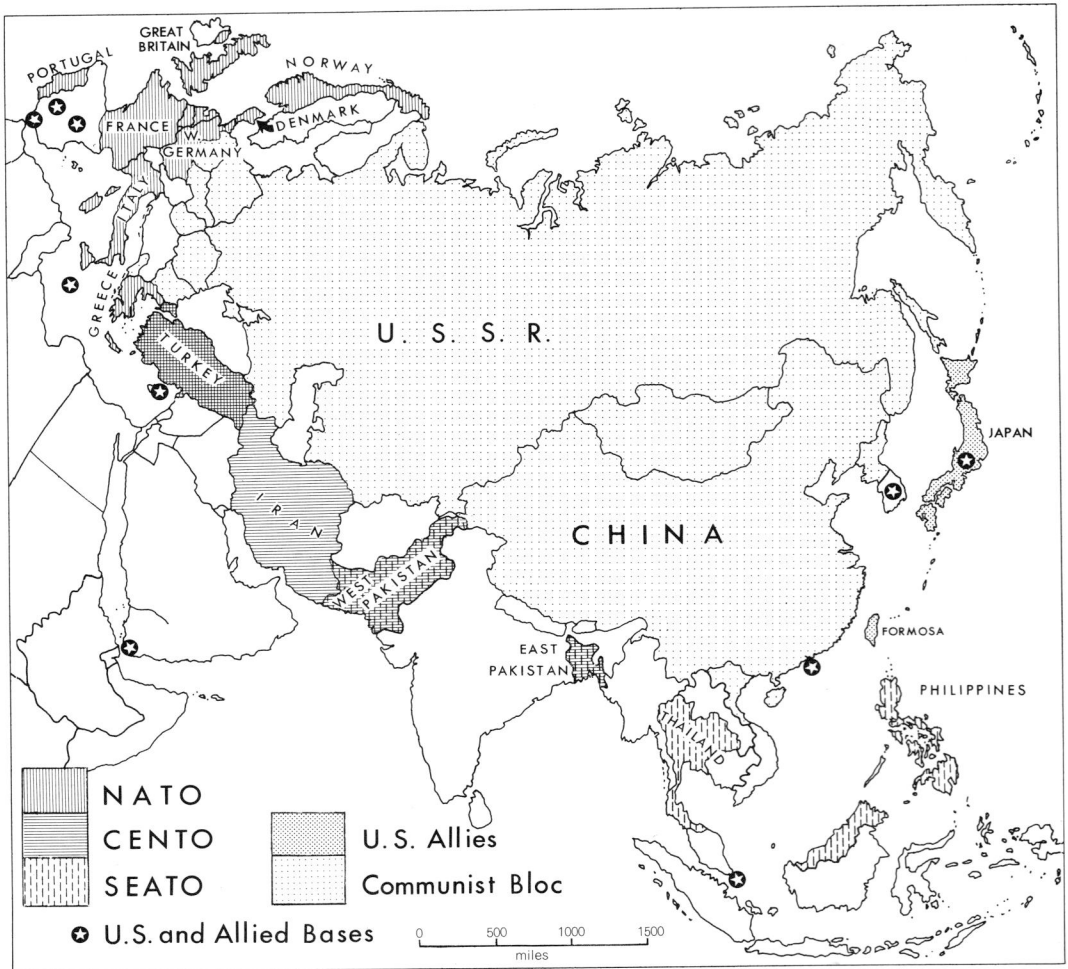

Exhibit 100   *Free-world alliances in the Old World.*

and to give advice, not to make political decisions, and the fact that its headquarters are in Strasbourg, and not in one of the political capitals, tends to remove it from the arena of practical politics. It has no real political power and perhaps little practical importance, but it is the germ from which a "parliament of Europe" might one day emerge. It is less "political" and more idealistic than the North Atlantic Treaty Organization (NATO), a fact which is reflected in the circumstance that the neutral state of Austria is a member. It is just a little more political than OECD, and this is

shown by the fact that Switzerland is a member of the latter, but not of the Council of Europe.

North Atlantic Treaty Organization: This Organization is in the highest degree political, as the treaty itself makes clear:

The parties to this treaty . . . are determined to safeguard the freedom, common heritage, and civilization of their peoples, founded on the principles of democracy, individual liberty, and the rule of law. They seek to promote stability and well-being in the North Atlantic area. They are resolved to unite their efforts for collective defence for the preservation of peace and security. They therefore agree to this North Atlantic Treaty.[7]

The North Atlantic Treaty was signed in Washington, D.C., in April, 1949, by Belgium, Canada, Denmark, France, Iceland, Italy, Luxembourg, the Netherlands, Norway, Portugal, the United Kingdom, and the United States. Greece, Turkey, and the German Federal Republic were subsequently admitted to membership. The member states pledged themselves to develop their power, both individual and collective, and to resist aggression, and they also agreed "that an armed attack against one or more of them in Europe or North America shall be considered an attack against them all," and thus they undertook to assist the victim of such aggression. The treaty is not concerned with economic cooperation; that is taken care of by other bodies. It has political objectives only—the security and well-being of the states which belong to it—which it pursues with the aid of the combined power of its fourteen members.

The Central Treaty Organization: In 1955, representatives of Turkey and Iraq met in Baghdad and signed a pact in which the two states pledged assistance to one another in the defense of their territory. Later in the same year, the pact was signed by Pakistan and Iran as well as by two outside powers with interests in the Middle East, the United States and United Kingdom. In 1949, Iraq withdrew from the pact, and its headquarters, which had hitherto been in Baghdad, were transferred to Ankara (Turkey). By the terms of the pact, its members undertook to "co-operate for their security and defence," [8] and the details of this cooperation were worked out in a number of subordinate agreements.

The pact was political. The Soviet Union had long presented a threat to the territorial integrity of Turkey and Iran, which it bordered, and, less directly, to Iraq and Pakistan, from which the Soviet territory was separated by that of other states. The pact was a statement of the resolve of these states, with the support of the United States and United Kingdom, to resist this threat to their integrity.

South-East Asia Collective Defence Treaty: By a treaty signed at Manila (Philippines) in 1954, three states of Southeast Asia, Pakistan, Thailand, and the Philippines, together with Australia and New Zealand, and three other states with interests in the area, the United States, United Kingdom, and France, established a defense system for Southeast Asia (Table 20). The parties to the treaty each recognized "that aggression . . . in the treaty area against any of the parties . . . would endanger its own peace and safety . . ." [9] and agreed that they would take joint action. The United States added the condition that its obligations were limited to resisting Communist aggression. The treaty further defined the area within which it would act. "As used in this treaty, the treaty area is the general area of South-East Asia including also the entire territories of the Asian parties and the general area of the South-West Pacific not including the Pacific area north of 21°30′ North latitude." [10] The parallel of latitude which defines the northern limit of what might be called the area of interest of the treaty powers was so chosen that it just excludes the island of Taiwan (Formosa). The powers are thus, in effect, saying that they would view with alarm, and would take appropriate action, in the event of the aggression of Communist China against, say, Laos or Burma, but not against Nationalist China.

We have just examined briefly four organizations, in each of which states are

---

[7] *North Atlantic Treaty,* preamble.
[8] *Baghdad Pact,* 1955, art. 1.

[9] *South-East Asia Collective Defence Treaty,* art. 4 (1).
[10] *Ibid.,* art. 8.

grouped for political purposes. The treaties which established three of them have military clauses, and each of them requires that its members assist one another in case of aggression. Of course, there are several sources from which aggression might come, but from only one of these is aggression sufficiently likely to warrant such protective measures, namely, the Communist bloc.

The map (Exhibit 100) shows how those three military groups are distributed. They form a kind of semicircle, almost continuous from Norway, through Denmark, West Germany, France, Italy, and Greece to Turkey. In Turkey the NATO group overlaps the Central Treaty Organization (CENTO) group, and this in turn overlaps the South-East Asia Treaty Organization (SEATO) group in Pakistan. The line is less continuous in southern Asia, where neutralist opinion is stronger, but it is extended to the northeast by the agreement between the United States and Nationalist China, by the United Kingdom's uncertain foothold on the Chinese mainland at Hong Kong, and by the United States occupation of the Ryukyu and Bonin Islands and by her alliance with Japan. In the extreme northeast, at the end of this chain, over twelve thousand miles from Norway, is Alaska. Behind this "front line" of defense lie the rearward bases: Iceland, the United Kingdom, Spain, Malta, and Cyprus, British East Indian possessions, Australia, and New Zealand. This makes up a curious geographical pattern, to which we shall return in the last chapter.

CULTURAL-POLITICAL ORGANIZATIONS

The motivation of the international organizations that have just been discussed lies largely in the fear of Communist aggression, and if this fear could by some miracle be made to disappear, it is probable that the treaty organizations themselves would wither away. We now have to consider briefly some organizations the mainsprings of which are as much cultural as political.

Organization of American States: This union of the republics of the New World was established in 1948, but the idea which it embodies is very much older. In the early days of their independence, several of the republics supported a movement, led by Simon Bolivar, which aimed at their association in a political and cultural organization. The Latin-American republics derived, with the exception of Brazil, from the provinces of the former Spanish Empire. Their language, except in Brazil, was Spanish, and the Portuguese language and culture of Brazil had basic affinities with that spoken and practiced in the rest of Latin America. The cultural ties between the Latin-American republics were strong, but their territorial disputes were also vigorous. Conferences of the Latin-American states were called in the middle years of the nineteenth century. The chief business at these meetings was the discussion of alleged threats from the United States and France. "These conferences showed," in the words of J. B. Trend, "if nothing else, that the new republics considered themselves a single family of nations." [11] Little came of these early conferences. Then the United States took the lead. A motive for this action was the American interest in developing trade with the countries of Latin America and, with this end in view, a desire to maintain peace between the Latin-American republics themselves. In 1890 most of these were represented at a conference held in Washington, D.C. The more positive proposals, such as that for a customs union, failed to gain acceptance. Neverthe-

[11] J. B. Trend, *South America*, Oxford University Press, New York, 1941, p. 104.

less, it was from this conference that the *Pan-American Union* grew. One of its first acts was to create an *International Union of the American Republics*, with a central office to handle its affairs.

This Union was not created by outside pressures, as have been the political organizations, already discussed, in the Old World. The republics had very little to fear from without, though some exaggerated the United States into a bogey of dangerous proportions. It must be admitted that United States actions in Panama and Nicaragua and the invasion of Mexico, during the war with Pancho Villa, may have given some slight pretext for these fears. The achievements of the successive conferences of the American states lay rather in the field of improving their relations with one another, of settling their own internal disputes, and of improving conditions for trade. There was some antagonism toward the United States at the conferences held earlier in the twentieth century. The Montevideo Conference of 1933 first showed a change in this attitude. The economic depression, the surpluses in the Latin-American countries of coffee, cocoa, sugar, and meat, and, above all, the failure of attempts at disarmament and the worsening international position—all encouraged the republics to drop their slightly hostile attitude to the United States. For its part, the United States renounced the truculent methods it had sometimes adopted, and President Roosevelt demonstrated, by his acts as well as his words, that he wanted the United States to be the "good neighbor" of the republics which lay to the south.

The solidarity of the American republics, including the United States, was greatly strengthened after the Montevideo Conference. The extent of Nazi (German) and Fascist (Italian) intrigues in South America became a matter of alarm, and it was apparent that, if Germany and Italy succeeded in controlling the European continent, the broad Atlantic was not really broad enough to give complete protection to the New World.

After the outbreak of the Second World War, in September, 1939, the American states attempted to establish a "safety belt" around their shores, an area of sea 300 miles wide within which they tried, though entirely unsuccessfully, to maintain neutrality. A year later, at the Havana Conference (1940) the American states decided that they would not recognize the transfer of any nonindependent territory in the New World from the possession of one European power to that of another. In other words, French and British possessions would not be allowed to pass into German or Italian control. Thus, a vaguely sensed threat from Europe against the independence of the American republics had succeeded in welding them into a tighter union than they had ever known before.

This closer union was expressed in 1948 in the formation at the Bogotá Conference of the *Organization of American States*. All twenty-one American republics are members:

Argentina	Dominican Republic	Nicaragua
Bolivia	Ecuador	Panama
Brazil	El Salvador	Paraguay
Chile	Guatemala	Peru
Colombia	Haiti	United States
Costa Rica	Honduras	Uruguay
Cuba	Mexico	Venezuela

Canada is the only independent American state that does not belong to it. No colonial territories are represented. The Organization continues to hold periodic conferences, but a Council, with headquarters in Washington, is in permanent session. A Secretariat, with departments given over to economic and social matters, to legal and cultural affairs, and to technical cooperation and assistance, intensifies the collaboration, which has been growing now for a century, between the republics of the New World.

Arab League: The Arab League was formed in 1945 and from the first bore a certain resemblance to the Organization of American States. It was formed by a group of states which had a cultural bond, not one that was threatened by outside pressures. The Arab peoples were distinguished by both their Arab language and their religion of Islam. It does not follow that every Muslim in the Middle East or North Africa speaks Arabic, nor that every speaker of Arabic is a Muslim. To a large extent, however, these two aspects of culture coincided. Most of the Arabs had been subjects of the Turkish Sultan, until the collapse of the Turkish Empire at the end of the First World War. The Turks of Turkey were for the greater part Muslims, but were not Arabs, and Arabic was not a language of Turkey. The lands inhabited by Arabs were divided up into several political units, one of which, Syria (with Lebanon), was placed under French mandate (Chapter 13) and three, Iraq, Transjordan, and Palestine, under British. Saudi Arabia. along with Yemen and the sheikdoms of the Persian Gulf area, remained independent. Egypt, which is mainly an Arab state, remained for a few years longer under restricted British control, and Libya, also an Arab state, remained an Italian colony until the end of the Second World War.

Between the First and Second World Wars the sense of unity between the Arab peoples deepened. It was strengthened by their struggle for complete political independence. After this had been achieved, with the expulsion of the French from Syria, Arab opposition to the creation of a Jewish state in the British-held territory of Palestine served further to hold the Arabs together. But Arab unity always presented great difficulties. Loyalty to tribal leaders is still strong among the Arabs, and rivalry

between these leaders, especially between the Saud family of Saudi Arabia and the Hashemite family of Jordan and, until 1958, of Iraq, served to deepen the divisions.

In 1944, the representatives of the independent Arab states met at Alexandria to discuss a proposed closer union between them. Frictions between them prevented the establishment of a unitary state, or even of a federal state. The best they could achieve was a league of states, which undertook, when necessary, to cooperate in common political action. The signatories of the Alexandria Protocol of 1945 were:

Egypt	Jordan
Iraq	Saudi Arabia
Syria	Yemen
Lebanon	

Since that date, Libya, the Sudan, Tunisia, Morocco, Kuwait, and Algeria have joined the League (Exhibit 101).

The role of the Arab League in unifying the countries of the Middle East has not been prominent. Apart from language and religion, the only force tending to hold them together has been their common hostility to the state of Israel. The forces dividing them are the jealousies that exist between the leaders of the Arab peoples.

Islam has not become an effective bond of union between the countries of the Middle East. It is the religion of too large and diverse an area of the world, reaching from West Africa to Turkestan and from Morocco to Indonesia. It embraces peoples as diverse as the Kazakhs and the Malays, the Fula of Northern Nigeria, and the Bosnians of Yugoslavia. Perhaps, too, the adoption of religion as a unifying factor among a group of states is contrary to the current secular trend. Gone, one hopes, are the days of a jihad, or holy war, fought primarily to extend the area of a religious faith. Many of the outward symbols of Islam have been compulsorily removed

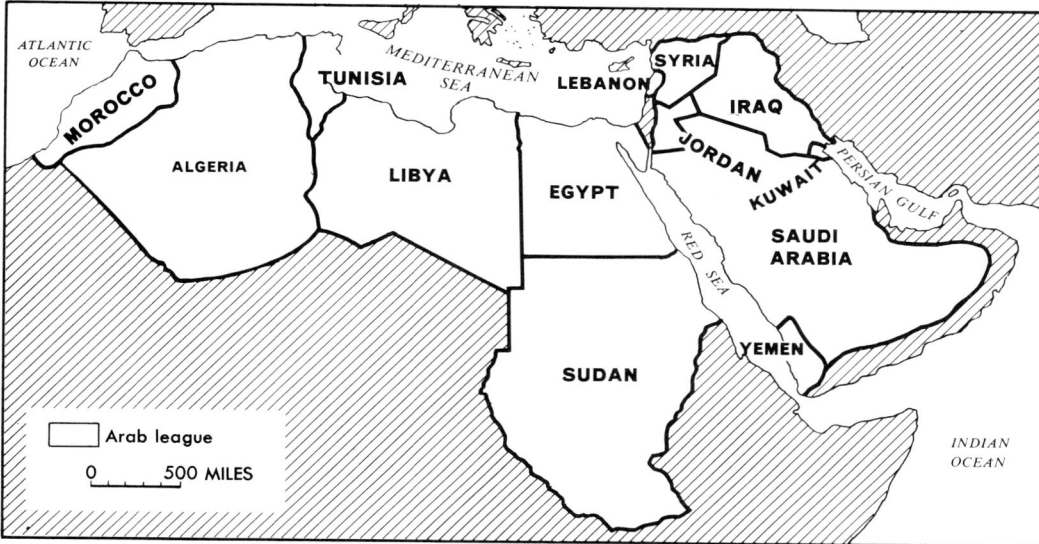

Exhibit 101   *Arab League.*

from Muslim Turkey. The partition of India and the creation of the Muslim state of Pakistan have been the most recent major political events that were made to hinge on religious affiliation; perhaps they will prove to be the last.

The distribution of the Arabic language is far from conforming with that of Islam. It is the language of Syria, Iraq, Jordan, and the Arabian states. It is the normal language of Egypt, Libya, and the Sudan; it is spoken in Tunisia, Algeria, Morocco, and West Africa, but its importance is challenged throughout these areas by local, non-Arabic languages as well as by English and French. It would appear that the Arab-Muslim world is too indefinite and too diffuse to form a close and lasting political organization, unless such a union is forced upon it by external pressures. So far, such pressures have not been strong enough to achieve this result.

British Commonwealth: This is the least formal and most successful of such groupings of states. It originated in the territories occupied, and in part colonized,

by the British peoples from the sixteenth to the twentieth century. Some of these territories broke away from the Empire and its successor, the Commonwealth, at various times during the past two centuries, such as the United States, Burma, and the Irish Republic. But in the remaining territories increasing degrees of political freedom and independence were permitted, until the greater part of the former Empire consisted of politically independent sovereign states.

Canada became, in effect, a self-governing state in 1867, Australia in 1901, New Zealand in 1907, and the Union of South Africa in 1910. These were at first known as *Dominions.* Their changed status was clearly defined for the first time at the Imperial Conference held in 1926: they were then defined as "autonomous communities within the British Empire, equal in status, in no way subordinate to one another in any aspect of their domestic or foreign affairs, though united by a common allegiance to the Crown, and freely associated as members of the British Commonwealth of Nations." The shreds of political and juridical control which the government of the United Kingdom had continued until this time to exercise over the Dominions were gradually relinquished.

After the Second Warld War, the independence of the Dominions was more strongly emphasized. The term Dominion was dropped, and the former Empire came to be called the Commonwealth. As more Colonies were granted statehood and political independence, some ceased to be members of the Commonwealth. India and Pakistan, Ghana and Malaya have remained within the Commonwealth; the Irish Republic, Burma, the Sudan, and the Union of South Africa have left.

Membership in the Commonwealth has nothing to do with the acceptance of the British monarch as king or queen. The declaration of 1926 had spoken cf "common allegiance to the crown." India and Pakistan have renounced this allegiance, without in any way prejudicing their membership in the Commonwealth. They are republics but accept the Queen of England as "the symbol of the free association of its independent member nations, and as such the Head of the Commonwealth." It is likely that other members of the Commonwealth will also adopt a republican constitution in the near future. The fact is that the monarch has ceased to be significant as a bond of union within the Commonwealth; the ties of loyalty and self-interest are sufficient.

The Commonwealth is made up of four groups of territories (Exhibit 102):

1. The self-governing states, which are voluntarily associated in the Common wealth:

United Kingdom	Ceylon	Tanganyika
Canada	Ghana	Jamaica
Australia	Malaya	Trinidad and
New Zealand	Nigeria	Tobago
India	Sierra Leone	Western Samoa
Pakistan	Cyprus	

To this list others will be added in the very near future: Kenya, Uganda, British Guiana, Rhodesia and Nyasaland, and the rest of the British West Indies, and in the not too distant future perhaps also North Borneo and Sarawak, Mauritius, and other small and fragmented territories.

2. The Federation of Rhodesia and Nyasaland. Southern Rhodesia is a self-governing territory; Northern Rhodesia and Nyasaland are British protectorates (Chapter 13). Together they enjoy a high degree of political independence but are not technically or legally independent.

3. The Colonies and protectorates. These are very numerous and, with the exception of British East Africa, are generally small in area. Although dependent upon the Colonial Office, a department of the British government in London, the local peoples are in fact associated to varying degrees in the government of the territories themselves. The next chapter, on colonialism, deals more fully with the status of these territories.

4. The territories under trusteeship (see Chapter 13). These are limited in area and resources. While some are directly under the government of the United Kingdom, others are administered by South Africa, Australia, or New Zealand.

What, it may fairly be asked, are the function and purpose of the Commonwealth, and why do its self-governing members remain in it? The non-self-governing, of course, are not yet free to leave. It is clear that the Commonwealth was not formed, like NATO or SEATO, as an organization for self-defense, nor, like the Common Market, did it originate in a realization on the part of its members of the advantages to be derived from economic cooperation. It is true, however, that the Commonwealth has come to be, in some respects, both a defense community and an economic community. But it originated

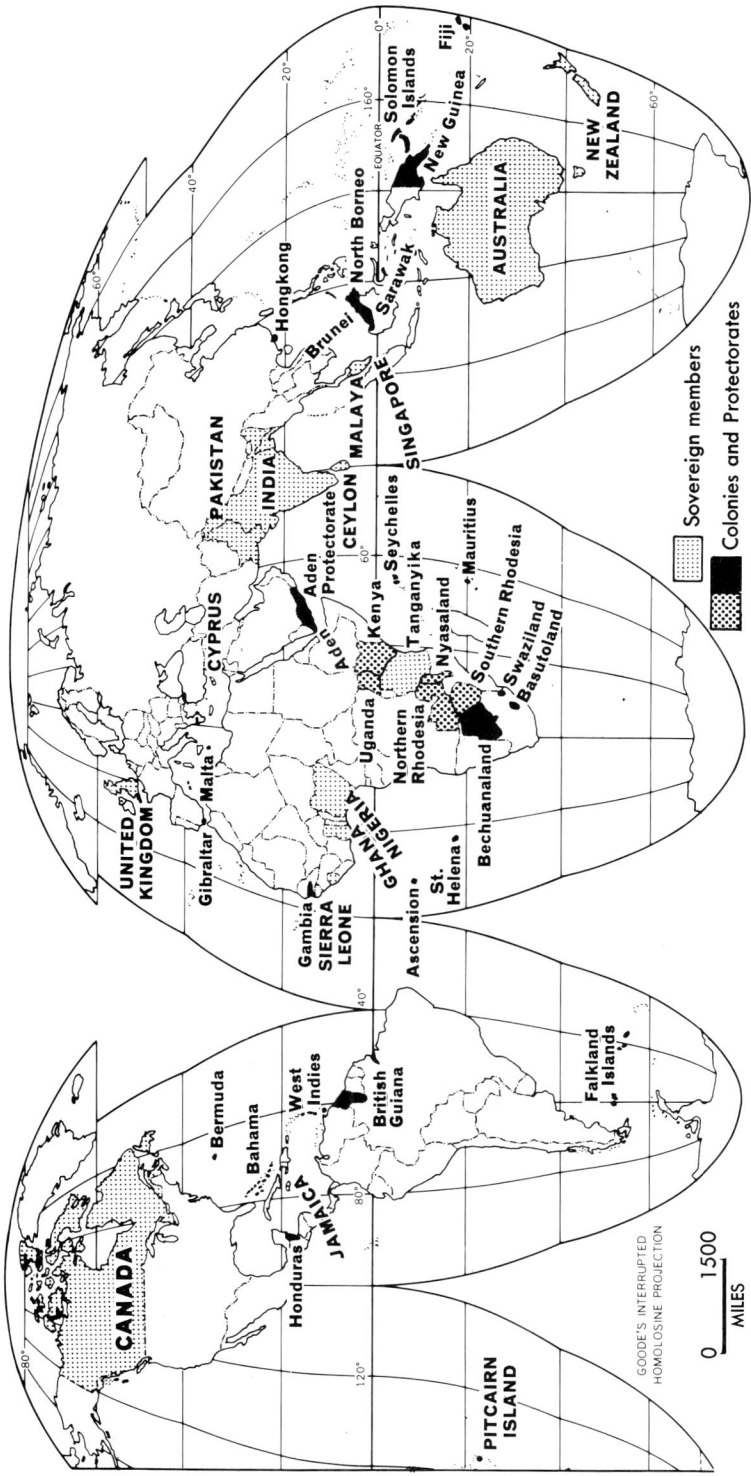

Exhibit 102   *The Commonwealth.*

323

as neither of these. The Commonwealth is a kind of club, though a highly informal one. Members are free to leave, but in fact very few have done so. Membership in the club carries with it very few obligations, and indeed the benefits seem so considerable that membership may be accounted a privilege A conspicuous feature of this club is the loyalty which its members feel for one another. They are under no obligation to fly to one another's aid if one of them should be attacked, but they are unlikely to remain neutral in such an event. This moral support —for it is little more than that—is of considerable value to a state, such as Australia or New Zealand, which lies remote from its allies and exposed, at least until the end of the Second World War, to the armed aggression of the Japanese. Who can say that the risk of attack from Southeast Asia may not again arise? In the case of these two states, geographical isolation is an important factor in strengthening the bonds of the Commonwealth.

Common forms of government, methods of administration, and codes of law also provide a strengthening to the fabric of the Commonwealth. The threats that have developed during the twentieth century to democratic forms of government have had the effect of increasing the coherence between at least the independent members. The unity of thought on political matters within the Commonwealth must not be exaggerated. As the British Prime Minister said at Cape Town in February, 1961, in the course of a very outspoken criticism of South Africa's racial policy:

The independent members of the Commonwealth do not always agree on every subject. It is not a condition of their association that they should do so. On the contrary the strength of our Commonwealth lies largely in the fact that it is a free association of independent sovereign states, each responsible for ordering its own affairs but cooperating in the pursuit of common aims and purposes in world affairs.

The racial policy of South Africa, for example, found little support in other parts of the Commonwealth, and on this account South Africa left it. Some members object strongly also to Australia's policy of excluding Asiatic and other nonwhite peoples. The overt and formal criticism of South Africa's policy of *Apartheid* (Chapter 14) has led (May, 1961) to South Africa withdrawing from the Commonwealth.

The Commonwealth, lastly, has forged an important economic bond of union. From the earliest days of the Empire a large proportion of the trade of the Colonies had been with the United Kingdom. In the early 1930s the Colonies and Dominions, like all primarily agricultural regions, were finding increasing difficulty in marketing their products. At the same time, industrial countries were finding that their markets were contracting. At an imperial conference held at Ottawa in 1932, the members of the Commonwealth agreed to reduce import duties on all goods imported from one another. Thus New Zealand butter gained in the British market at the expense of Danish and Dutch. Coffee from Kenya was cheaper than coffee from Brazil. Conversely, British automobiles, chemicals, and machinery became cheaper in the markets of the Commonwealth than similar products made in Germany, France, or the United States.

The Ottawa Tariff Agreements have been severely criticized. Naturally those countries which saw their goods being cut out of the British market by the lower-priced—because lower-taxed—imperial product were indignant. Even within the Commonwealth there were critics:

[While] Nyasaland wanted a sheltered market for her tobacco, Mauritius and the West Indies wanted a sheltered market for their sugar, Palestine [Israel] clamoured for an alteration in the terms of the Mandate so that the preferential tariff could be extended to Palestinian oranges. The greater part of the Colonial Empire agreed with the Dominions that price increases on a limited range of their imports were well worth the great boon of a sheltered market for their exports. . . .[12]

But there were many producers within the Commonwealth—the cocoa growers of Ghana, tin miners of Malaya, palm-oil producers of Nigeria—who depended heavily on the market outside the Commonwealth. In fact their nonimperial market was more important to them than their imperial. In 1933, only 32.5 per cent of the exports of the United Kingdom's Colonies actually went to the United Kingdom, and only 24.4 per cent of their imports came from the United Kingdom. The lowering of United States tariffs would have interested them far more than the lowering of British.[13] The fact was that the Commonwealth was not, and could never become, a self-sufficient economic unit. A large part of the trade of its members was necessarily with countries outside the Commonwealth. In the amusing words of W. K. Hancock, the arguments for the Ottawa Agreements "were true in abstract theory and false in statistical application. They were just as right and just as wrong as a cook would be if she set out to make a pudding with all the wrong quantities of all the right ingredients." [14]

The advantages of the Ottawa Agreements—at least for those members of the Commonwealth which actually did benefit from them—are now beginning to wear off. The general level of tariffs is being lowered (see page 255), and the advantages conferred on imperial trade are reduced now to small proportions. Nevertheless it is prob-

ably true to say that the Ottawa Agreements gave an impression—probably an exaggerated one—of the economic cohesion of the Commonwealth.

Other empires, including the "empire" of France, now called the French Community, have recently changed from groups of dependent territories into groups of associated states. They are becoming, like the Commonwealth, a rather exclusive type of club. But in spite of this change, discussion of these empires is postponed to the next chapter, on Colonies and Colonialism.

BIBLIOGRAPHY

Antonius, G.: *The Arab Awakening*, H. Hamilton, London, 1938.

Atiyah, E.: *The Arabs*, Penguin Books, London, 1955.

Benoit, Emile: *Europe at Sixes and Sevens*, Columbia University Press, New York, 1961

Colombo Plan for Co-operative Economic Development in South and South-East Asia, Annual Reports.

Deutsch, Karl, et al.: *Political Community and the North Atlantic Area*, Princeton University Press, Princeton, N.J., 1957.

Diebold, W.: *The Schuman Plan: A Study in Economic Co-operation*, Praeger, New York, 1959.

Economic Survey of Europe, United Nations, New York, published annually.

European Coal and Steel Community: *General Report on the Activities of the Community*, Luxembourg, published annually.

European Integration, C. Grove Haines (ed.), Johns Hopkins Press, Baltimore, 1957.

Everyman's United Nations, United Nations Office of Public Information, New York, 1959.

Goormaghtigh, John: "European Coal and Steel Community," *International Conciliation*, no. 503, May, 1955.

Hancock, W. K.: *Argument of Empire*, Penguin Books, London, 1943.

Herring, Hubert: *Good Neighbors: Argentina,*

---

[12] W. K. Hancock, *Argument of Empire,* Penguin Books, London, 1943, p. 91.

[13] *Ibid.*, p. 94.

[14] The American tariffs had recently (1930) been raised by the Smoot-Hawley Act.

Brazil, Chile and Seventeen Other Countries, Yale University Press, New Haven, Conn., 1948.

Lindsay, K.. *Towards a European Parliament*, Secretariat of the Council of Europe. Strasbourg, 1958.

Mayne, Richard: *The Community of Europe*, Victor Gollancz, Ltd., London, 1962.

New Horizons in the East, H.M. Stationery Office, London, 1950.

The North Atlantic Treaty Organization: the NATO Handbook, Paris, 1959.

Nuseibeh, H. Z.: *The Ideas of Arab Nationalism*, Cornell University Press, Ithaca, N.Y., 1956.

Pounds, N. J. G., and W. N. Parker: *Coal and Steel in Western Europe*, Indiana University Press, Bloomington, Ind., 1957.

Smith, C. G.: "Arab Nationalism, A Study in Political Geography," *Geography*, vol. 43, pp. 229–242, 1958.

Spulber, N.: *The Economics of Communist Eastern Europe*, The Technology Press of Massachusetts Institute of Technology and John Wiley & Sons, Inc., New York, 1957.

Stateman's Yearbook, St. Martin's Press, Inc., New York, published annually.

Western Co-operation in Brief, H.M. Stationery Office, London, 1960.

Western Union, published for the United Nations Association by Hutchinson and Co., London, 1948.

Wheare, K. C.: *The Statute of Westminster and Dominion Status*, Oxford University Press, Oxford, 1953.

Yearbook of the United Nations, United Nations, New York, published annually.

13 COLONIES AND COLONIALISM

Whereas various real and powerful motives of pride, prestige and pugnacity, together with the more altruistic professions of a civilising mission, figured as causes of imperial expansion, the dominant motive was the demand for markets. . . . J. A. HOBSON, IMPERIALISM

National possession of a dependency does not mean that commodities are obtainable from it for nothing. NORMAN ANGELL, THE GREAT ILLUSION

FEW WORDS HAVE BEEN MISUSED AS MUCH AS COLONY AND COLONIALISM. To some they conjure up a picture of oppression and exploitation. Others have regarded them as an essential ingredient of political power, as an important source of national wealth, or as an expression of man's humanitarian instincts and of the desire of the more advanced peoples to assume the "white man's burden" of assisting the less advanced. Yet others regard colonialism as essentially evil and colonialists as exploiters of the weakness and backwardness of fellow men. All these views are mistaken. Modern colonialism has not been oppressive or exploitative, if only because such methods would in the long run defeat their own ends. Nor do colonies add greatly to national wealth. Goods obtained from colonies have to be paid for. The cost of administering colonies is generally high, and the obligations incurred are considerable, though it would be a gross exaggeration to say that these have been deliberately incurred for the sake of suffering humanity.

J. A. Seeley remarked that Britain's empire was acquired "in a fit of absence of mind." In so far as its establishment was not planned in advance and the acquisition of each fragment of it was contingent upon events at the time, this is true. Indeed, the building up of all empires, except perhaps the former empires of Germany and Japan, was accidental rather than premeditated, explained and excused after the event, rather than prepared for in advance in the formulation of public policy.

According to the Charter of the UN:

Members of the United Nations which have or assume responsibilities for the administration of territories whose peoples have not yet attained a full measure of self-government, recognize the principle that the interests of the inhabitants of these territories are paramount, and accept as a sacred trust the obligation to promote to the utmost, within the system of international peace and security established by the present Charter, the well-being of the inhabitants of these territories. . . .[1]

The members of the UN undertook:

. . . [to respect] the culture of the peoples concerned [and to ensure] their political, economic, social and educational advancement, their just treatment, and their protection against abuses; to develop self-government, to take due account of the political aspirations of the peoples, and to assist them in the progressive development of their free political institutions, according to the particular circumstances of each territory, their peoples, and their varying stages of advancement.

The conscientious fulfillment of these obligations would leave little room for profit. Why, then, are there colonies?

THE COLONIAL EMPIRES

There are today eight powers which may be said to have formal colonies; that is to say, they control in some degree the political, and thereby the social and cultural, destinies of other lands and other peoples which are internationally recognized as dependent. These powers are:

[1] *Charter of the United Nations*, art. 73.

Denmark	Spain
France	United Kingdom
Netherlands	United States
Portugal	Norway

A similar group of states has ceased in recent years to be colonial powers, through the loss in one way or another, of their dependent territories:

Germany	Japan
Italy	Sweden

A further group, made up of Belgium, Australia, and New Zealand—the last two members of the Commonwealth—may be considered colonial in so far as they still hold certain underdeveloped territories in trust for the UN. Thus at the present time no fewer than eleven states are, in the formal sense, colonial powers. To this list some would add South Africa, in virtue of its occupation of South-West Africa, in origin a mandated territory.

It is difficult, however, to arrive at a satisfactory definition of colony. It is obvious that a colony does not possess sovereignty and that to some degree its policies are determined, and its administration controlled, from without. It is commonly assumed that a colony lies remote from the state which controls it and that it must be overseas. In general this is the case. The United Kingdom and France, for example, occupied and settled areas in other parts of the world that were different physically and culturally from themselves. But Czarist Russia during the nineteenth century extended its political authority into Central Asia and across Siberia to the Pacific Ocean. It also occupied areas that were physically different from the core area of European Russia, in which the Russian state originated, and it controlled peoples who were ethnically and culturally distinct from the Russians themselves. It is true that many of these peoples, the Kazakhs, Turkmen, Tadzhiks, and Uzbeks, for example, have, at least theoretically, autonomy within their particular Soviet Socialist Republics and participate, in theory at least, in decision making at the highest level through their elected representatives. Most of the Soviet Union is thus superficially removed from the scope of the term colony, though the reality of Soviet colonialism cannot be doubted. At the same time, however, there are a number of areas, known variously as Autonomous Soviet Socialist Republics, autonomous regions, and national areas, in which autonomy is restricted even by the terms of the Russian constitution. In the case of the national area, the political rights of the local peoples are minimal, and their destinies are in fact controlled from Moscow

Not all the lesser ethnic groups have even the façade of self-government, and there was in fact remarkably little difference between European conquest and colonization in Africa and that of Russia in Central Asia. Chinese imperialism is even more thinly disguised. It is true that the constitution of the Chinese People's Republic provides for autonomy in distinctive cultural and ethnic areas and that certain autonomous regions have been established. It remains true, nevertheless, that the Chinese People's Republic conquered and annexed Tibet and Sinkiang and that to neither of these territories has it accorded any significant degree of autonomy. It is thus unrealistic to restrict the opprobrious terms of colony and colonialism to the overseas activities of the group of formally colonial powers.

Nor is this question limited to the Soviet Union and China. The underdeveloped and sparsely populated areas of the Amazon forest in northwestern Brazil, the Canadian Arctic, the Northern Territory of Australia, and the Territories of India have restricted political rights. They are governed and taxed without complete political

representation, and their status is legally analogous to that of the national areas of the Soviet Union. Should they also be regarded as colonies? It seems unquestionable that, if the sea had separated, for example, northern Australia from the rest of Australia, as it does New Guinea, northern Australia would now be regarded as a colony. As it is, northern Australia is treated as an integral part of Australia; its affairs are internal affairs and thus excluded from the supervision and control of the UN. Australia may be morally bound by the injunctions contained in Article 73 of the UN Charter, but any breach of these obligations could not be considered by the UN, because it would be a matter internal to a sovereign state.

Some of the new countries, only recently freed from old-style colonialism, seem today to be developing a neocolonialism of their own, witness Morocco's ambitions to expand and to incorporate much of Mauritania and part of Algeria, Indonesia's desire to include western New Guinea, Iraq's designs on Kuwait, and Afghanistan's hope for a greater Pushtu-speaking state.

The area of the world that can be considered colonial in the old, formal sense has been steadily diminishing for the past century. The total area that is deprived of democratic means of expression or even of the elementary freedoms has not. Table 21 shows the gradual disappearance of the earlier pattern of imperialism, in which a certain territory was internationally recognized as a colony of another and no one pretended that it was otherwise. This table cannot show the rise of neocolonialism, which differs from the older colonialism in the façade of independence, autonomy, and self-determination that has been drawn across it. In the past it was possible to prepare a map of dependent territories because their status was formally recog-

TABLE 21   *Areas Administered by the Formally Imperial Powers, 1900–1960*

Imperial power	Area, sq miles [4]				
	1900	*1920*	*1945*	*1958*	*End of 1960*
Australia............	....	183,557 [2]	183,557 [2]	183,557 [2]	183,557 (est.)
Belgium............	905,144	926,054 [2]	926,054 [2]	926,054 [2]	20,910 [2]
Denmark...........	879,672	839,782	839,782	839,782	839,782
France.............	4,587,085	4,662,895 [2]	4,587,085 [2]	4,586,889 [2]	3,722,249
Germany...........	1,231,513				
Italy..............	245,882	926,084	926,084	198,018 [1]	
Japan.............	....	86,074 [1]	86,074 [1]		
Netherlands........	2,048,626	2,048,626	2,048,626	215,027	215,027
New Zealand.......	....	1,125 [2]	1,125 [2]	1,125 [2]	1,125 [2]
Norway............	....	23,951	21,216	24,216	24,216
Portugal...........	808,253	808,253	808,253	806,735	806,735
South Africa........	....	318,016 [3]	318,016 [3]	318,016 [3]	318,016 [3]
Spain..............	132,425	132,425	132,425	114,164	114,164
United Kingdom....	8,964,571	5,322,614 [2]	3,970,618 [2]	2,882,951 [2]	2,509,689 [2]
United States.......	342,203	116,538	968	1,797 [2]	1,797 [2]
Total	20,145,373	16,372,043	14,828,667	11,074,115	8,732,676
Percentage of land area.............	36	30	26	19	16

[1] Trusteeship territories.

[2] Includes trusteeship territory.

[3] Mandated territory under the League of Nations; South Africa has not accepted the trusteeship.

[4] Antarctica is excluded from this table, but Greenland is included.

nized, and for the same reason one could calculate their area and population. But for the new colonialism this is no longer possible. There are autonomous areas in the Soviet Union and China whose autonomy has never got beyond the statute book or constitution. There are legally sovereign states, like Hungary, which are in all major aspects of policy dependent; there are autonomous regions in the Soviet Union that have never known self-government. It is always difficult to estimate how far removed the reality is from the theoretical relationship between such territories and governments. For this reason it is virtually impossible to map the new colonialism

with the fineness and precision used in studying the old, and quite impossible to tabulate areas and populations subjected to it. One may legitimately speak of the neocolonial empires of China and the Soviet Union; one may perhaps speak of the neocolonial pretensions of Morocco, Ethiopia, Indonesia, Egypt, and other "new" countries, which have got rid of European imperialism only to start a fresh imperialism of their own.

The methods adopted by the new colonial powers are varied. Their chief concern appears to be to disguise the fact that their association with their colonies is not a voluntary one. The relationship is disguised: it is represented as the free expression of the will of the subordinate peoples; the "colony" may have a constitutional autonomy which is contradicted in practice; the decision makers in the dependent territory may receive instructions through the Communist Party or, indeed, through some other political, ideological, or cultural association; and, lastly, the new instrument of the new imperialism may have the tanks and aircraft of its foreign friend and protector stationed near its borders, or even established at camps within its territory.

THE END OF THE OLD IMPERIALISM

Much of the area covered by Table 21 is poor in resources, both agricultural and mineral, and is sparsely populated. The larger part of what remains of the Spanish Empire is made up of desert. After the cession of the Virgin Islands to the United States in 1917 and the establishment of Iceland as a sovereign state a year later, the Danish Empire has consisted only of the almost uninhabited waste of Greenland. The Norwegian possessions consist of Svalbard (Spitzbergen) and a few uninhabited islands. It might almost be said that today (1961) only parts of West Africa and a few minute dependencies, like Hong Kong, Macau, and Singapore, among colonial dependencies, have a population that could possibly be described as even moderately dense.

Today fewer than fifty million people, under 2 per cent of the total population of the world, live in non-self-governing territories. The proportion has been dropping even more sharply than the ratio of the area of dependent territories to the land surface of the globe, as the more densely populated have been the first to

Figure 57 *Relics of empire: The harbor of Hong Kong, with the Chinese mainland in the distance. The area shown is part of the British Crown Colony of Hong Kong.* COURTESY: SHELL PHOTOGRAPHIC UNIT

gain independence. In the very near future, the non-self-governing peoples will amount to less than 1 per cent of the world's population. So many new states have been created out of the existing empires that very little of the latter may be expected to remain after a few years.

The British West Indies and the Rhodesian Federation and East Africa are likely to follow Ghana, Nigeria, and Sierra Leone into both independence and the UN. The Belgian Congo has gained independence and may be followed by the mandated territories of Ruanda-Urundi and Tanganyika. There is likely to remain, after another decade or two, just a hard core of colonial territory, lacking the resources, the population, and, perhaps, even the will for independence. This is likely to include the ice-covered island of Greenland, desert areas in Africa and, perhaps, in southern Arabia, small, bleak islands in the stormy South Atlantic, and perhaps a few small territories, like Gibraltar, Aden, and the Panama Canal Zone, whose importance is strategic, and whose employment and welfare are dependent upon this function.

REASONS FOR COLONIALISM

Colonialism is "the process by which peoples or nations conquer, subdue and then permanently dominate . . . other peoples or nations." [2] Colonialism differs from military occupation or temporary conquest in so far as it is based upon international recognition and implies some degree of permanence. Hitler declared that his "protectorate" of Bohemia and Moravia and his "Government-General" of Poland would last a thousand years; in fact, they lasted, respectively, six and five years and were not generally recognized. The Japanese conquest of parts of China lasted somewhat longer than this but never achieved an air of permanence. None of these examples of occupation is regarded as colonialism.

The motives for colonization, as for all human activities, are mixed. Modern colonialism may perhaps be said to have begun in the fifteenth century with the occupation by the Portuguese of bases on the African coast, followed by the establishment of trading posts in India. Before the century was over, Spaniards had reached and had claimed certain parts of the West Indies and Central America, and the Pope had proposed a line of division between the colonial territories acquired and yet to be acquired by Spain and Portugal.

The Moral Obligation: The motives of both Spaniards and Portuguese were a strange amalgam of piety and greed. The *Chronicle of Guinea* describes how Prince Henry the Navigator of Portugal, after a Portuguese slave raid on the coast of West Africa, derived satisfaction when "he reflected with great pleasure upon the salvation of those souls [that is, the slaves'] that were lost." [3] The chronicler does not tell us what pecuniary advantage he also derived, though this was probably not inconsiderable. This missionary motif continued to infuse and excuse colonial enterprise until the present time. The missionary enterprise of Las Casas in the sixteenth century and the activities of eighteenth-century Spanish missionaries in California and New Mexico went some way to redeem the greed and the spoliation of which other Spaniards were guilty.

The activities of missionaries were broadened in the nineteenth century, the period of the most rapid colonial development, to embrace also medical care and education. Nor was this attention to welfare left only to the private enterprise of missionary groups. The colonial powers themselves engaged in at least its nonreligious aspects. Their motives were as mixed in this as they had been when the original colonies were acquired. Hospitals, doctors, and schools all made for a better life for colonial peoples; they also made for increased agricultural and industrial production.

During the nineteenth century the colonial powers came gradually to the belief that colonialism was not destined to last forever, that colonies might be expected to gain in political maturity and ultimately to achieve political independence. This trend may, perhaps, be said to have stemmed from the Durham Report of 1838, which called for the initiation in Canada of a system of responsible government. It was several years before this was, in fact, introduced, but before the end of

[2] John Strachey, *The End of Empire*, Victor Gallancz, Ltd., London, 1960.

[3] Quoted in Edgar Prestage, *The Portuguese Pioneers*, London, 1933, p. 72.

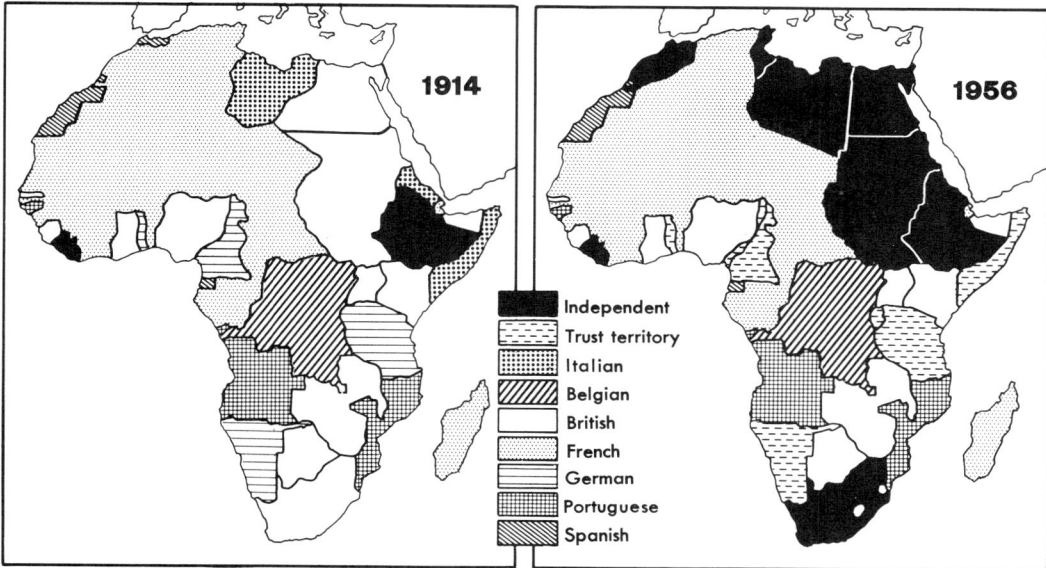

Exhibit 103   *Colonialism in Africa: 1914 and 1956.*

the century Canada had made great progress along the road that led to independence and statehood. Australia, New Zealand, and South Africa, among the territories of the British Empire, followed in the wake of Canada. This was easy, because these areas had been settled mainly by people from Great Britain. The settlers had brought with them the common law and some knowledge of and respect for the parliamentary and judicial systems that had grown up in England. It seemed only right to allow to these expatriates the same political rights that they would have enjoyed if they had remained in Great Britain. Thus it was that the colonies in temperate latitudes, suited by their climate to white settlement, were the first to rise from colonialism to statehood.

Political maturity, as judged by the standards of Europeans, clearly came more slowly in tropical colonies (Exhibits 103 and 104). Here Europeans made up only a small proportion of the total population, because, in general, they could not settle and work, as they could in more temperate latitudes. They tended to form a professional and administrative elite. Sometimes they mixed on equal—or nearly equal—terms with the local peoples. More often they held themselves aloof and allowed their lives to center in their clubs.

Most colonial powers had accepted an obligation in respect of the allegedly backward areas. The Congo Act of 1885 declared that:

All the Powers exercising sovereign rights or influence in the aforesaid territories [see page 253] bind themselves to watch over the preservation of the native tribes, and to care for the improvement of the conditions of their moral and material well-being. . . . They shall . . . protect and favor all religious, scientific or charitable institutions and undertakings created and organized for the above ends, or which aim at instructing the natives and bringing home to them the blessings of civilization.[4]

The Congo Act stressed the paramount importance of welfare, without, however, mentioning the desirability of developing

[4] *General Act of the Conference of Berlin,* 1885, art. 6.

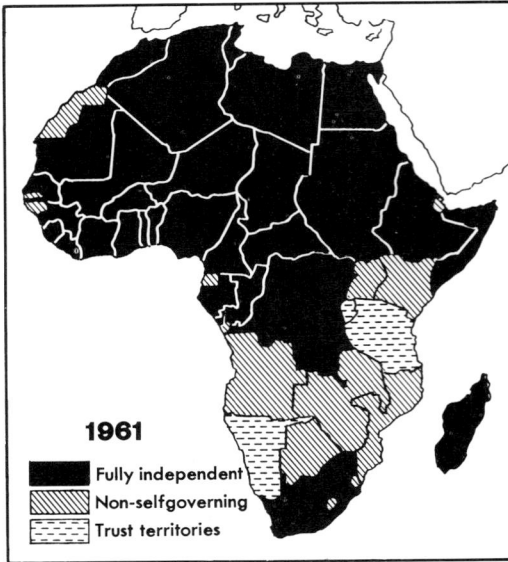

1961
- ■ Fully independent
- ▨ Non-selfgoverning
- ▦ Trust territories

Exhibit 104   *Colonialism in Africa: 1961.*

institutions of political self-government. Indeed, the authors of the treaty probably regarded self-government in the Congo Basin as neither desirable nor practicable. The Covenant of the League of Nations (1919) marked a great advance. In the articles related to the mandates system it clearly envisaged self-government as the ultimate objective:

1. To those colonies and territories which as a result of the late war [i.e., the war of 1914–1918] have ceased to be under the sovereignty of the states which formerly governed them and which are inhabited by peoples *not yet able to stand by themselves* under the strenuous conditions of the modern world, there should be applied the principle that the well-being and development of such peoples form a sacred trust of civilization. . . .

2. The best method of giving practical effect to this principle is that the tutelage of such peoples should be entrusted to advanced nations who, by reason of their resources, their experience or their geographical position, can best undertake this responsibility. . . .[5]

[5] *Covenant of the League of Nations*, art. 22. Italics supplied.

The Covenant went on to specify that the kind of administration to be established in these areas was to be adjusted to the degree of advancement reached by their native peoples. Though this declaration related specifically only to the former German colonies and to the Middle Eastern territories taken from the Turkish Empire, it had been drawn up by colonial powers (France, Italy, the United Kingdom).[6]

Some twenty-five years later, the Charter of the UN was drawn up. It stated in no uncertain terms the obligations of colonial powers toward their colonies. It asserted "the principle of equal rights and self-determination of peoples"[7] and in a strongly worded clause declared that:

Members of the United Nations which have or assume responsibilities for the administration of territories whose peoples have not yet attained a full measure of self-government, recognize the principle that the interests of the inhabitants of these territories are paramount, and accept as a sacred trust the obligation to promote to the utmost . . the well-being of the inhabitants of these territories, and, to this end. . . .

. . . To develop self-government, to take due account of the political aspirations of the peoples, and to assist them in the progressive development of their free political institutions, according to the particular circumstances of each territory and its peoples and their varying stages of advancement.[8]

The Charter of the UN clearly looks forward to the time when colonies cease to exist and the land surface of the globe is divided only into autonomous political units. Then the moral obligation of the imperial powers will have been discharged, and the white man may lay aside his burden. This burden has unquestionably be-

[6] The United States, which also participated, was a quasi-colonial power at this time.
[7] *Charter of the United Nations*, chap. IX, art. 55.
[8] *Ibid.*, chap. XI, art. 73.

come a heavy one. In the early years of colonialism, colonies were, in one way or another, a considerable source of profit, and the white man was so well paid for supporting his burden that he could afford to take on additional moral obligations. The profit has long since gone out of the practice of colonialism, and the moral obligations have increased as the international conscience of the world has grown more sensitive.

The Economic Motive: The economic motive has never been absent from colonialism. The Portuguese wanted first slaves, ivory, and other products of tropical Africa and later the silks and spices of the Orient, which they retailed at a handsome profit in the markets of northwestern Europe. The Spanish conquistadors also sought first the bullion and later whatever wealth from the New World they were able to substitute for it. The gold and silver which they discharged upon the European market effected a price revolution. The Dutch similarly sought the spices of the East Indies and displayed a complete lack of scruple in achieving their ends. The British followed them, and built an empire in India, only because the Dutch succeeded in excluding them from the East Indies France followed Great Britain, and for a long period the two were rivals for the control of India.

It was in keeping with the mercantilist thought of the age that those colonies were most desired which could contribute most to the economy of the home country. Possessions in India were worth fighting for because they yielded silk, cotton, spices, bullion, and gem stones, unobtainable in Europe. The simple fact that the British Empire in India was built up by a private company, the East India Company, is itself evidence of the fact that profit was to be had—and had abundantly—from the possession of colonies. The United Kingdom valued most, amongst her American Colonies, those which could produce sugar, cotton, and tobacco, commodities that could not be grown in her own damp, cool islands. She even placed a couple of islands in the West Indies ahead of Canada for a time in the mid-eighteenth century for the same reason.

During the seventeenth and eighteenth centuries colonies were thought of as providing an exclusive source of certain scarce commodities. The colonial powers exercised a jealous control over their dependencies, excluding competition, thus keeping down the prices they had to pay for goods, and gaining for themselves the whole of the profit to be had by retailing these articles in Europe. Only under strong pressure did Spain consent in the early eighteenth century to the visit of a single British vessel each year to the Spanish American colonies for trade. French, British, Dutch, and Portuguese rivalry in South and Southeast Asia was also a desperate business, and the victor's prize was exclusive control of the trade of the area in question.

In the nineteenth century the emphasis on trade tended to give place to a concentration on development, the establishment of plantations, the opening of mines, and, as a necessary adjunct of these, the building of roads and railroads. In extreme cases there was a grievous exploitation of the native peoples. The Congo "atrocities," alleged to have been perpetrated by the servants of King Leopold II of the Belgians, stirred the feelings of a European public that was not easily moved. The "culture system" of the Netherlands East Indies was an undisguised levy on the production of the native peoples. There were few colonial empires in which forced labor was not practiced, and in some areas it was almost the rule. Tropical produce—foodstuffs and raw materials, such as cotton, oils, and lumber—was demanded in increasing quantities by the growing industrial centers of Europe, and the advantages to an industrializing country of having its private source of supply of at least some of the desired materials were great. At the same time, however, attempts were being made to liberalize trade with colonial territories, so that the exclusiveness which had previously stamped the policy of the imperial powers came to be somewhat attenuated. The first important move in this direction was the establishment of the titular Congo Basin as an area within which tariff discrimination in favor of or against any nation was excluded (see pages 253–254). The second was the extension of the same principle to the territories subject to the Mandates Commission of the League of Nations.

Only a small part of the total area of colonial territories was ever actually made subject to the Open Door policy, but a change in the direction of trade was increasing greatly the commercial importance of the colonies in temperate latitudes. During the nineteenth century, with the rapid expansion of population in Europe, the luxury goods of commerce, the silks and spices which had previously dominated the colonial trade, declined sharply in relative importance. Their place was taken by wheat and preserved or frozen meat, by wool, cotton, oilseeds, and lumber. The chief sources of most of these commodities were the temperate lands, such as Canada and Australia, where Europeans had formed colonies which were now burgeoning into statehood. There was never any question of reserving the trade in these commodities for the home country. Production was increasing, and the need to sell was paramount, whoever the purchaser might be. Thus it may be said that by the end of the nineteenth century any purchaser of colonial products was free to obtain them wherever he wished. The possession of colonies conferred no advantages or privileges in this respect.

The relative decline of colonies as

sources of raw materials and foodstuffs is abundantly demonstrated by a report of the League of Nations of 1937. In it the statement was made that "the total present production of all commercially important raw materials in all colonial territories is no more than about 3 per cent of world production." [9]

The argument of the previous paragraphs has been that the possession of colonies has ceased to confer any particular advantage in obtaining raw materials and foodstuffs and that these have come to be obtainable equally well in the open market. Why then, it may be asked, did Germany, Italy, and Japan complain so bitterly of their lack of colonies? To some extent their complaints were a political weapon and were used to justify rearmament and an aggressive foreign policy. To some extent, perhaps, the lack of colonies was thought to be a stigma, which reflected adversely on the vigor and vitality of the state. A more substantial reason for seeking colonies was given by the German Minister of Finance:

The colonial problem of Germany cannot be got rid of with the argument that a sufficient supply of raw material can be assured to her by the policy of the Open Door. Only the possibility of buying a sufficient quantity in our currency can produce a proper balance . . . for Germany.[10]

In other words, Germany did not possess the required foreign exchange to buy in the open market, but if she had possessed colonies capable of supplying her needs, she could have paid in her own German marks. These, in turn, would in all probability have been useful to the colonies only

[9] League of Nations, document A27, 1937, 11B.

[10] Speech of Count von Krosigk in 1936, quoted in *Germany's Claim to Colonies*, Royal Institute of International Affairs, New York, 1938, p. 30.

Figure 58 *The island and port of Malta were formerly important links in the British control of the sea route from Europe to the Orient. In the foreground are seen some of the island's earlier fortifications, now converted into walks and parks.* COURTESY: EWING GALLOWAY

for spending *in* Germany *on* German products, irrespective of whether or not these were what the colonies really desired. The only way out of this dilemma would be to make all currencies concerned freely convertible into one another. This has not been achieved completely. The United Kingdom continues to purchase tobacco from Rhodesia or East Africa, where she can pay for it in sterling, rather than from the United States, where she would be required to pay in a harder dollar currency. Many similar examples could be quoted, but their total significance is probably smaller today than it was in the 1930s, when this currency argument was used by Germany.

The Strategic Motive: When, about the year 1500, the Portuguese established their colonies in India and Southeast Asia, they were careful at the same time to set up bases on the African coast, which might serve for refitting and supplying their ships with food and water. The Dutch similarly established themselves at Cape Town, and eventually the British also acquired bases on the African coast. It became necessary not only to provision ships but also to give them protection. The early bases were generally fortified, and some were chosen largely because of the ease with which they could, if necessary, be defended. Strategic bases, thus acquired, served not merely to protect the shipping lanes but also to strengthen the power of one imperial power in its struggles with others. The United Kingdom, for example, seized Gibraltar in 1704 and succeeded in holding it. It has no economic value whatever, except in so far as it serves to protect the shipping lanes which pass near it. The island of Minorca, in the Balearic group, was also taken in 1708 but was lost again in 1756.

> The British. . . after the long French wars, retained St. Lucia [in the West Indies] for the sake of its harbour, and Ceylon mainly for its naval base of Trincomalee; they kept Malta and, for a time, Corfu to secure their Mediterranean route to the East, and the Cape [i.e., the Cape of Good Hope] and Mauritius, to guard the long ocean route thither. Presently they founded Singapore to hold the straits that open upon the Far East. Similarly, nineteenth century France took Tahiti, New Caledonia, Obok, and Mayotte, that "little Gibraltar" in the Mozambique channel at least as much for naval as for commercial or cultural ends. . . .[11]

In the late nineteenth century Germany openly sought to acquire control of strategic areas, such as Samoa, and strategic considerations were not insignificant when the United States acquired Hawaii and Puerto Rico. The acquisition of the Panama Canal Zone, and the opening of the canal across it in 1914, necessitated also the establishment of bases that would guarantee to the United States the continued freedom to use it. Puerto Rico, the Virgin Islands, purchased from Denmark in 1917, the base of Guantanamo, in Cuba, and the bases leased from the United Kingdom in 1940 formed a widely spread screen to protect the Atlantic approaches to the canal. In the same way, the United Kingdom, with its control of Gibraltar, Malta, and Cyprus and, for a time also, of the Palestinian Mandate, could control the Mediterranean approaches to the Suez

[11] E. A. Walker, *Colonies*, Cambridge University Press, New York, 1944, p. 32.

Canal, while Aden commanded the approach from the Indian Ocean.

It is difficult to separate strategic from commercial colonies and dependencies. A colony that is strategically located, such as Singapore, is likely to have great commercial potentialities as well. Most colonial powers have to some extent used their colonial territories for recruiting armies, though only France has done this on a large scale. After her defeat at the hands of Germany, in the war of 1870–1871, France set out to redress the balance by extending her colonial empire and by adding to her military strength by means of armies recruited in the colonies. Most important were the Senegalese units from West Africa and the Spahis and others from North Africa. Great Britain regularly maintained units recruited in India, though the most famous regiments of the Indian Army, the Gurkhas, were in fact recruited from the independent state of Nepal by an arrangement between its king and the British government.

Colonies and Migration: Most European countries have at some time or other regarded themselves as overpopulated, and those which possessed colonies looked upon them as places wherein this surplus might be settled. At the end of the sixteenth century, the English regarded themselves as too numerous for their resources, and this belief contributed to the settlement of the North American Colonies. Up to the time of the American Revolution, there was a steady flow of British immigrants to North America, along with very much smaller numbers of French to Quebec and yet smaller numbers of Dutch, Germans, Swedes, and others. For a time in the late eighteenth and early nineteenth centuries Great Britain restricted the migration of skilled workmen and then, with the fear of overpopulation ever present, allowed almost unrestricted migration. In

Figure 59 **The function of the British Crown Colony of Gibraltar is wholly strategic.** *There is almost no flat land on the Rock of Gibraltar, and its role continues to be to guard the passage between the Mediterranean Sea and the Atlantic Ocean.* COURTESY: BRITISH INFORMATION SERVICES

the period from 1846 to 1932, over fifty million persons migrated from Europe to the Americas or to the "new lands" of the Old World. The chief sources of this migration and the approximate numbers of the emigrants were as follows:

Source of migration	Approximate number of emigrants
British Isles	18,020,000
Italy	10,092,000
Austria-Hungary	5,196,000
Germany	4,889,000
Spain	4,653,000
Russia	2,253,000

The numbers who left Europe before 1846 probably did not exceed twelve million, most of whom went to North and South America. Spain and Portugal both excluded others than their own nationals from settling in their colonies, though the Portuguese colonies adopted a more liberal policy after they had achieved independence.

There was no restriction on immigration into North America until the late nineteenth century or into Australia and New Zealand until about 1900. In each of these areas the first restrictions on immigration were caused by the arrival of large numbers of Asiatics, and subsequent immigration policy was in large measure colored by the fear of the arrival of even greater numbers of orientals.

Almost 40 per cent of the total migration from Europe was actually from the British Isles, including, of course, Ireland. This went largely to territories under British control: to the thirteen Colonies before 1776 and to Canada, Australia, New Zealand, the United States, and British-controlled parts of Africa after this date. A very small fraction of this migration consisted of criminals, who were sent first to the State of Georgia and later to Australia. The rest was made up of voluntary emigrants from the British Isles who supposed the opportunities available in the Colonies to be greater than those at home. In large measure the British colonies may be said at this time to have provided an outlet for a population that was certainly surplus in Ireland and probably so in the rest of the British Isles.

The French Empire came to be almost as extensive as the British, but, unlike the British, it was not extensively settled by the French themselves. Despite occasional fears to the contrary, France never really felt herself to be overpopulated. Beginning in the 1830s, the French conquered and settled northern Algeria, but the number of Frenchmen who crossed the Mediterranean was small. The French have always shown themselves reluctant to leave France, and the number who have settled in the French colonies has been very small. The total French emigration between 1846 and 1932 was only about half a million. Migration to the surviving colonies of Spain and Portugal, during the nineteenth century, was even less, and the Germans made no serious attempt to settle the colonial possessions which they acquired late in the century. Apart from Great Britain, the states which in the nineteenth and twentieth centuries possessed colonies neither used them nor needed them to settle surplus population. The countries which really had surplus population, the eastern European and Balkan states, Italy, and the countries of South and East Asia, had no colonies.

One particular aspect of British colonization deserves mention. Many parts of the British Empire were already densely settled by the native peoples, such as India and some of the African colonies. To these areas there came swarms of British civil servants, administrators, and soldiers, to work there for a term of years and then to return to Britain, to enjoy their pensions and reminisce about the greatness of the Empire they served. It was with very good reason that J. R. Seeley characterized the British Empire as "a vast system of outdoor relief for the upper classes." It was a very subtle way of solving at least one of the problems of population pressure—the demand of the upper classes for jobs consistent with what they consideerd to be the dignity of themselves and their families.

COLONIAL EMPIRES AND COLONIAL POLICIES

In the following pages an account is given of the empires of the major colonial powers and of the policies of the latter toward them. The Dutch Empire has been reduced to very small proportions; the Belgian has been liquidated, apart from a small trusteeship territory. The German colonial empire, interesting for the ruthless efficiency with which the Germans pursued their objectives, disappeared formally in 1919—it had been conquered by British and French some years earlier. The Italian Empire was lost at the end of the Second World War. The Danish Empire is limited to Greenland, that of Norway to Svalbard (Spitzbergen), and that of the United States—excluding the Commonwealth of Puerto Rico—is restricted to a few small islands in the West Indies and the Pacific Ocean. We are left with the British, French, Spanish, and Portuguese Empires, the only empires which continue to cover any considerable area.

THE BRITISH EMPIRE

In the words of E. A. Walker, "the British Colonial Empire is not so easy to define, since it is the rearward portion of an empire which resembles a procession, a large part of which has long since crossed the flood that divides dependence from autonomy, and part is crossing now." [12] At its greatest extent the Empire covered 27.4 [13] per cent of the land surface of the earth, but long before it had achieved its maximum extension in Africa and the Middle East, it had begun to contract in Canada, with the grant of dominion status and virtual independence. As of 1961, over three-quarters of this vast area is made up of independent sovereign states, most of them members of the Commonwealth. The rest is made up of territories still in some degree dependent upon the government of the United Kingdom. The territories which together make up the British Commonwealth and Empire are listed, with their areas and populations, in Appendix III.

The existing colonial dependencies of the United Kingdom form an extraordinarily varied group, both constitutionally and geographically. They range from the self-governing territories of Southern Rhodesia and Singapore to Aden and British Borneo, in each of which popular participation in government is minimal. Geographically they range from the densely peopled and intensively cultivated West Indian islands to the thinly peopled and economically almost valueless Falkland Islands. They include the protectorates of Zanzibar, Uganda, Nyasaland, Bechuanaland, and the Maldive Islands, to cite only four of a particularly heterogeneous group, and possessions like Gibraltar, whose importance is wholly strategic.

The United Kingdom cannot be said to have had a consistent policy toward its dependencies. It has never, like France, attempted to streamline their organization. British policy has been empirical, and in so far as it has been successful, this is probably because it has never generalized, but has

faced each people and each problem separately. In so far as there is a feature common to all British colonial policies, it has probably lain in the acceptance of the principle, embodied in the Durham Report of 1838, that popular government should be encouraged. But whether this popular government should follow the pattern of British parliamentary democracy or whether it should be based upon native institutions was a question on which the British were never prepared to be dogmatic.

In general, they tended to support native institutions and to "protect" native rulers where this was practicable. An extreme case was the perpetuation in India of the rule of the "princes"—over three hundred of them, each of whom had made his own contract with the British government. It took the Republics of India and Pakistan to sweep away this illogical and outmoded system, after they had gained independence.

Indirect Rule: This policy of "indirect rule" received its clearest and perhaps most successful administration in Nigeria. There, under the very enlightened administration of Lord Lugard, who became High Commissioner in 1900, the practice was adopted of using the native institutions of chieftain and tribe as the channels through which the Europeans governed the country. In the words of Lord Hailey, indirect rule is "the system by which the tutelary power recognizes existing African societies and assists them to adapt themselves to the functions of local government." [14] The reasons for adopting a system of indirect rule are clear. The transition from an African or an Asiatic society to a European cannot be made abruptly, if, indeed, it can be made at all. The problems of Africans who had lost their respect for their own tribal ethics and institutions, without acquiring a respect

[12] *Ibid.,* p. 6.
[13] Grover Clark, *The Balance Sheets of Imperialism,* Columbia University Press, New York, 1936, p. 23.

[14] Lord Hailey, *An African Survey,* Oxford University Press, New York, 1938, p. 413.

for any other, were becoming acute. The native societies and systems of government were far from perfect, but at least they provided some framework within which the individual might live:

> Even an imperfect and tyrannical native African administration, if its extreme excesses were controlled by European supervision, would be, in the early stages, productive of far less discomfort to its subjects than well-intentioned but ill-directed efforts of European magistrates, often young and headstrong, and not invariably gifted with sympathy and introspective powers. If the welfare of the native races is to be considered, if dangerous revolts are to be obviated, the general policy of ruling on African principles through native rulers must be followed for the present.[15]

The basic principles worked out in Nigeria were extended to the British Cameroun, Tanganyika, Uganda, and other parts of British Africa. They were applied, however, only imperfectly and locally in Kenya, and scarcely at all in Southern Rhodesia and the Union of South Africa. The basic reason for the difference was geographical. Indirect rule could become a political objective only where the tribal structure had remained relatively intact, and this structure had survived only in areas, such as West Africa, where European settlement was negligible, and the reasons for the failure of Europeans to establish themselves here were basically climatic. The highlands of Kenya and the uplands of Southern Rhodesia and of the Union of South Africa all attracted white settlers, and in the societies that resulted there was no room for an essentially African social and political structure. The experience of the territories within which indirect rule has been practiced has been happier than in those where it has not. A valid criticism of indirect rule, however, is that, by perpetuat-

ing—almost fossilizing—a tribal unity, it slowed down the emergence of a genuine feeling of nationhood and concept of statehood.

But in many dependent territories, indirect rule could not have been pursued. Native institutions were too immature, native peoples too mixed or too recently arrived within the areas. The British West Indies form an example. This fact was recognized in the Covenant of the League of Nations when it allowed Class C mandates to be "administered under the laws of the Mandatory as integral portions of its territory."[16] In each of these the policy has been pursued of associating the local peoples in the mechanism of government gradually, as they appeared able to assume the burden. The usual mechanism was a parliament made up partly of elected, partly of nominated members, with the former gradually assuming a more important and the latter taking on a less important role.

The United Kingdom can certainly be accused of undue caution in recognizing the capacity of the native peoples to rule themselves, but during the present century she has not failed to hold out the hope that all dependent territories may attain to self-government and statehood. The greatest reluctance to hand over the reins of power has been manifested in those dependencies where peoples of contrasted cultures have lived side by side without adjusting to one another. On the island of Cyprus, the clash between the Greeks and the Turks, differing from one another in almost every aspect of culture, had postponed the independence of the island until 1960, when agreement was at last reached between the two groups. The clash of Chinese and Malayan in Malaya, of European

---

[15] Sir George Goldie, quoted in *ibid.*, p. 417.

[16] *Covenant of the League of Nations*, art. 22, sec. 6.

and African in Kenya, the Rhodesias, and Nyasaland may long postpone complete independence. The government of the United Kingdom is wise to be cautious. The communal riots in India and Pakistan, the Mau Mau terrorism in Kenya, and race riots in Nyasaland and in the Rhodesian Copper Belt are evidence of the intense hatred that can develop between racial groups (see page 364).

The Protectorates: A large part of the dependent empire is made up of protectorates. In theory these are territories in which native institutions and rulers have been preserved and guaranteed against interference from without. Thus the native princes of India were "protected"; they continued to administer their States' internal affairs, but in effect had no foreign policy, because none was needed, the British government carrying on all foreign relations on their behalf.

In some instances, the protecting power, in this instance the United Kingdom, limited itself to its primary duties. In others, it interfered in the internal affairs of the protectorate, which it reduced to complete dependency. The native princes of India, and such "protected" rulers as the Sultans of Johore (in the Malay Peninsula) and of Zanzibar (in East Africa) and the King of Buganda (in Uganda) remained the ultimate powers in the internal affairs of their respective States; in others, the protected area became assimilated to the nonprotected and essentially colonial area, and the distinction for practical purposes disappeared. Some individual territories are in fact composites of colony and protectorate. Kenya, for example, is both; the coastal region is a protectorate; the interior, a colony. The colony of Aden, consisting of the minute area surrounding the city and port of that name, has as its hinterland the vast Aden Protectorate. Nigeria (until its independ-

ence in 1960) and the Central African Federation of Rhodesia and Nyasaland are made up partly of colony, partly of protectorate. The distinction derives, of course, from the conditions under which the territory was acquired by the British Empire. It is sometimes based on contrasted geographical conditions: the Aden Protectorate, for example, is a desert area with only a small, seminomadic population that is notoriously resentful of outside interference or control. The Bechuanaland Protectorate in South Africa is similarly a semiarid and thinly peopled region over which close supervision by the colonial power might be difficult and costly. But no essentially geographical conditions could explain the division of Sierra Leona (West Africa) into 256 square miles of colony and 27,669 square miles of protectorate or the fact that in the Uganda Protectorate, so called, the protectorate covers only the Province of Buganda and that the Eastern, Northern, and Western Provinces of Uganda are administered under indirect rule.

The trusteeship territories, for the administration of which the United Kingdom is responsible to the UN, have been touched upon earlier and will be referred to again. The Federation of Rhodesia and Nyasaland enjoys a high degree of self-government. but it is not yet technically a sovereign state. The rest of this untidy empire is made up of Crown Colonies. Their administration is ultimately the responsibility of the Colonial Office, which, through its head, the Minister of State for Colonial Affairs, is responsible to the British Parliament. They are administered each by an appointed governor and nominated officials. There is always some degree of local participation in government, though in some instances this is very small. This is the rear end of the procession that is slowly and unevenly moving toward the still-distant objective of independence.

THE FRENCH COMMUNITY

The administrative system of the colonial empires reflects the national character of the colonizing powers. The empire of the United Kingdom, in the words of a former colonial minister, has "no cut and dried pattern." It has "adopted and adapted existing systems, changing them readily as the need arose and experience taught." [17] This pragmatic approach has produced that untidy, but effective, organization which we have briefly reviewed. It appears to justify Seeley's remark that the British Empire was "acquired in a fit of absence of mind." At least, it was acquired without forethought, and administered with a minimum of preconceived ideas about the nature and purpose of colonies.

Not so the empire of France. The French mind is logical, orderly, and rigid, and anything as chaotic as the organization of the Commonwealth would be distasteful to it. In E. A. Walker's words:

Whether as a monarchy, an empire or a republic, she has aimed at a centralized and uniformly governed empire. Her colonial policy today reflects at once her devotion to the Revolutionary doctrine of the Rights of Man, with the emphasis on equality and fraternity rather than on liberty, and the resolve that the empire must make France strong so that she may continue to be *la grande nation*.[18]

In the seventeenth and eighteenth centuries France was the rival of Britain in the quest for colonies, and for much the same reason. Defeated in the wars of the eighteenth century, France lost most of her overseas possessions. Only a few, notably the West Indian islands of Guadeloupe and Martinique, have carried over from the first colonial empire of France to the

second, which was built up in the nineteenth century. France created her second empire in a period of two generations in the nineteenth century. It began with the occupation of Algeria in 1830 and was continued, after the military defeat at the hands of Prussia in 1870–1871, in Southeast Asia, in West, North, and Central Africa, and in Madagascar. It culminated in the assumption in 1919 of the mandate for Syria (with Lebanon) and for part of Togoland and most of the Cameroun.

The motives of the French were, of course, mixed, but, being a logical and clear-thinking people, they analyzed their motives with greater clarity (though perhaps with less honesty) than the British. They needed the resources of colonies in order to redress the balance of Europe, now tipped against France by the unification and industrial and military growth of Germany. France used the material resources and, above all, the manpower of her colonies to this end. When, in 1923, she used Senegalese troops to occupy part of the German industrial region of the Ruhr, she was demonstrating to the world her manpower resources and at the same moment she was administering to Germany what most Germans regarded as an intolerable insult.

Assimilation and Association: "Liberty, equality, fraternity" had been the slogan of the French Revolution, and the ideas which it expressed continued through the nineteenth century to permeate French policy and institutions. The equality of man was loudly—even raucously—asserted by the French, as, for instance, when they billeted Senegalese troops on race-conscious Germans. There was no segregation in any part of the French Empire. Race and color were never made a criterion for the possession of voting rights or for the attainment of political office or administrative position. This would have been one of the more positive

---

[17] Lord Cranborne, in 1942, quoted in *Towards Self-government in the British Colonies*, British Information Services, New York, 1950, p. 6.

[18] Walker, *op. cit.*, pp. 100–101.

and valuable contributions of French colonialism, if it had not been coupled with a cultural arrogance. The greatest boon which France could possibly impart to her colonial territories was, in her opinion, to give them French culture and civilization. The French policy thus became one of *assimilation*. All colonial peoples who showed the will and ability to become French in language and custom were welcomed as partners in the task of civilization. Those who spurned this were treated as peoples who had seen the light and had rejected it. They had no part in the French scheme of things. All over the French Empire cities were made to look as much like French provincial cities as possible, and along their streets the French colonials would sit drinking their *apéritifs* as if they were on the sidewalks of Paris, where most of them would certainly have preferred to be.

It is doubtful that a policy of assimilation could have been made to work in any part of the colonial world. All non-European peoples have a culture for which they have some respect. France was a little unfortunate in having among her colonial peoples many with a strong and assertive culture who despised the French as much as they were themselves despised by the French. Foremost among these were the Muslims of North Africa, of parts of West Africa, and of Syria. These peoples had a system of religious belief, a code of law that was in part derived from it, and a social organization that were at least as coherent as those of the French who settled among them. Very few Arabs ever succumbed to the attractions of becoming French, except in a technical and legal sense. Similarly, the peoples of Cambodia and Cochin China, of Annam and Laos, all in Southeast Asia, had their own religion, mainly Buddhist, and their cultures, which were older than those of France. They were unas-

similable. Only in West and Central Africa, where the religious aspect of culture at least was less coherently developed, did the French have some success. In Martinique and Guadeloupe, also, there was no effective indigenous culture—the Negroes were immigrants like the French themselves —to compete with that which the French brought.

Assimilation, then, failed in most of the French colonial empire. It was replaced by the idea of *association*, which began to inspire French colonial policy after the First World War. The practice of association recognizes that many—perhaps most— of the colonial peoples cannot be assimilated but that an elite among them can. It aims at "transforming a native *élite* into Frenchmen and leaves the masses to learn enough French for workaday purposes and, if all goes well, to earn a better living than they have done hitherto." [19] It uses native institutions if it serves the purposes of the French to do so; it makes no attempt to preserve or protect them. The policy of association has postponed the fulfillment of the ultimate end, assimilation; it has not denied its validity.

French Union and French Community: The empire of France (Exhibit 105) was always highly centralized. The French conceived of France and the empire forming a political and economic unit. They looked "to a future in which the advance of civilization of the subject peoples will be recognized not by the creation of local representative institutions but by fuller representation in the central government." [20] This was merely the political expression of the doctrine of assimilation. The older French colonies, in most of which assimilation has made some progress, are organized as *départements* (counties) of France and are

[19] *Ibid.*, p. 10.
[20] Hailey, *op. cit.*, p. 138.

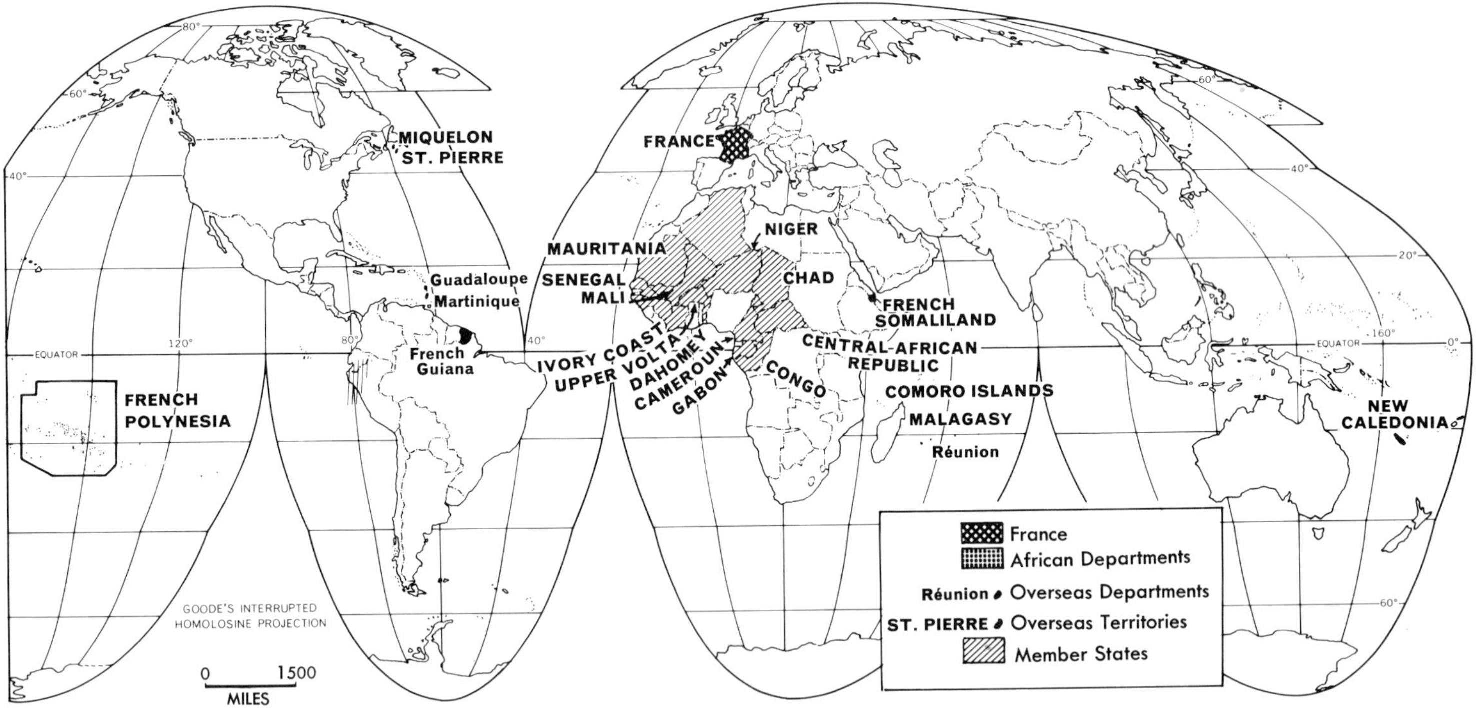

Exhibit 105 *The French Community.*

represented in the French National Assembly, meeting in Paris. They are:

Départements	
Sahara	2
Martinique	1
Guadeloupe	1
Réunion	1
French Guiana	1

Until the summer of 1962 the twelve *départements* of Algeria would have been included in this list. When the French occupied Algeria in the 1830s, they forced back the native Berbers (Arabs) into the hills of the interior—*refoulement,* they called it—where they lived, sullen and resentful, divided by religion, race, and culture from the French, and awaiting a chance to regain the land for themselves. This opportunity came in the summer of 1962 when the long Algerian war ended and France recognized the independence of the Republic of Algeria.

In 1946 the French, pursuing their ideal of a "centralized and uniformly governed empire," established the French Union—*L'Union Française.* This consisted, on the one hand, of Metropolitan France and its overseas *départements* and, on the other, of the associated territories and states. The President of France was the head of the Union, whose administrative organs were a High Council, with delegates from France and each of the associated states, and an Assembly of elected representatives.

The French Union was highly centralized, and it collapsed against the resistance of the Algerians in what the French had persuaded themselves was one of the most thoroughly assimilated parts of their empire. The war in Algeria and the debacle in French Indo-China thoroughly discredited the Fourth Republic, and General de Gaulle became chief of state. A new constitution was devised and, in October, 1958,

was offered to the French people both at home and overseas. It was accepted, and the French Community—*La Communauté Française*—replaced the French Union (see Appendix IV). It also proved to be a streamlined organization, but it had the merit of being less centralized than the Union. To some extent it was a movement in the direction of the Commonwealth, but without the capacity of the latter to adapt itself to every shade of local circumstance.

It is too early to say whether or not the French Community will be more stable and more successful than the French Union. It is in closer accord with the revolutionary spirit of the mid-twentieth century than the organizations that have preceded it. But, even so, here is a very much higher degree of centralization than the Commonwealth has retained. The Community has an Executive Council, presided over by the President of the French Republic, which provides for a unity of policy unknown in the British Commonwealth. This bond may prove too close, and the republics may in turn leave the Community and become sovereign and independent.

OTHER COLONIAL EMPIRES

The remaining colonial empires are small in extent and relatively unimportant. The largest of them territorially, that of Belgium, has largely been liquidated with the independence of the Belgian Congo. The Dutch Empire was reduced to small proportions when Indonesia gained independence, and the empires of Spain and Portugal, though still quite extensive, are sparsely peopled and relatively undeveloped. There remain only the rather anomalous empires of Denmark, and Norway, and the United States.

The Belgian Empire: Until the summer of 1960 the empire of Belgium was made up of the huge area of the Congo and the small trusteeship territory of Ruanda-Urundi.

	Area, sq miles	Population, 1959
Congo............	904,757	13,124,000
Ruanda-Urundi....	20,455	4,568,000

It was not until 1908 that Belgium took over the administration of the Congo. The region had been explored thirty years earlier by H. M. Stanley, and his glowing reports of its resources led to the formation of a private international group, the Congo Association, with King Leopold II of Belgium at its head, to exploit these riches. Counterclaims to possession of the Congo led to the Berlin Conference of 1885 (see pages 253–254), at which the Congo Free State was established, with Leopold as its head. The Congo Free State was virtually the private possession of Leopold and his associates. Their exploitation of it caused a scandal and created an embarrassing situation for the Belgian government, which, however, had no control over the private actions of its king.

On the death of Leopold II the Belgian government somewhat reluctantly assumed responsibility for the Congo, which came to be called the Belgian Congo. The Belgian administration had to live down the reputation which the servants of Leopold II had acquired. Its mechanism was somewhat similar to that of France. It was highly centralized, and little scope was allowed for the political self-expression of the Africans. On the other hand, the Belgian Congo included vast areas of primeval forest, where democracy, as understood in Brussels, could certainly not be made to work, and primitive tribes, including the pygmies, who could not have understood it anyway. The mineral wealth, especially of the rich Katanga region in the south, was great, and the physical conditions of parts of the basin favored the establishment of plantations of oil palm and rubber. To some extent the Belgian administration initiated the French policy of association and tended to encourage an African elite which it associated with itself in governing the country.

The costs of developing this huge country have been high, and the Belgians have in part financed it by the profits made from mining and agriculture. An efficient and honest, but autocratic and patriarchal government is not sufficient, as the Belgians discovered, to prevent political unrest. The more mature and vocal sections of the African population have demanded first autonomy and then independence. The Belgian government has reluctantly agreed, and an independent Republic of the Congo came into being in the summer of 1960. The Congo was manifestly unprepared for independence: under the paternal Belgian regime, its people had not learned even the rudiments of self-government. The Congo Republic at once dissolved into anarchy, and King Leopold's shoddy empire ended, as it had begun, with atrocity and murder. It seems, however, that from its ruins may emerge a loosely federated state, in which the federal units, like those of Nigeria (page 42), will be based upon tribal groups.

Ruanda and Urundi had been part of the former German colony of Tanganyika but after the First World War were mandated to Belgium. These territories differ sharply from most of the Congo. They lie at a greater altitude, they are grassland or savanna country, and among their peoples are the tall, strong Watussi tribes. The tribes of Ruanda and Urundi have been used to provide labor for the Belgian Congo, in which there has always been a shortage of workers for plantation and mines. Ruanda and Urundi are not being included within an independent Congo.

Indeed, the geographical and ethnic contrasts had obliged the Belgians to separate them administratively more and more from the Congo. Independence for the trusteeship territory has been postponed owing to the tribal warfare that has taken place there between the Watussi and the Bahutu in recent years, but this also seems likely to be granted in the near future.

The Dutch Empire: The empire of the Netherlands was founded about 1600, when the ships of the Dutch East India Company sailed to Southeast Asia to trade in spices and other exotic goods. They made for the Spice Islands, drove out the Portuguese, who had got there first, and successfully excluded the British, who tried to break in later. The Dutch then got possession of islands and bases, including the Cape of Good Hope and Ceylon, that would guarantee their control of the sea route to the East Indies. In the seventeenth century they also developed trade with the tropical areas of the New World and occupied Surinam (Dutch Guiana) and half-a-dozen islands, including Curaçao and Aruba, lying off the coast of Venezuela.

For a couple of centuries the Dutch policy was one of unrestricted exploitation In the East Indies, the Dutch employed what was termed the *culture system*, by which they forced the native peoples to cultivate certain areas with specific crops exclusively for the use of the Dutch. In the second half of the last century the culture system was gradually abandoned, as new ideas of the rights and obligations of colonial powers gained acceptance. At the beginning of the present century the so-called "ethical" policy was adopted, and the Dutch government devoted an increasing proportion of its attention and its resources to furthering the welfare and to supporting the native institutions of the peoples of the East Indies. It seemed at one time that the economic development of

the East Indies was overwhelmingly in favor of Europeans and was concentrated excessively on export crops. This imbalance seems to have been corrected, though Indonesians complained that too much of their more densely peopled islands was in white-owned plantations.

The Dutch encouraged native Indonesian institutions at the local level and ruled "indirectly" through the self-governing village community, but at a higher level of government their policy was autocratic and based upon a large measure of direct control from the Netherlands. The Dutch did little to encourage a belief in future independence, and, despite their very considerable achieving in the fields of economic development and welfare, they aroused little affection for themselves. The islands of Indonesia were occupied by the Japanese during the Second World War. Immediately after the Japanese defeat, an independent Republic of Indonesia was proclaimed, and, after four years of rather desultory fighting, the Dutch themselves recognized the Republic.

Indonesia had been the most extensive and the richest part of the empire of the Netherlands. Its loss, followed by the confiscation of all Dutch assets in Indonesia, was a blow both to the prestige and to the economy of the Netherlands and led the Dutch to look more carefully to the well-being of their remaining colonial territories. These are as shown in Table 22. By a statute of 1954 each of the three territories of Surinam, the Netherlands Antilles, and Netherlands New Guinea became an autonomous unit within the Kingdom of the Netherlands, though they continued to be grouped together for mutual assistance and protection. These territories are widely contrasted in their population and their degrees of development. The Netherlands Antilles, or at least the two islands first named in the table, are densely peopled

TABLE 22   *The Dutch Empire*

	Area, sq miles	Population, 1959
Surinam (Dutch Guiana)......	55,105	255,000
Netherlands Antilles (Curaçao, Aruba, Bonaire, St. Maarten, St. Eustatius, Saba).........	382	195,000
Netherlands New Guinea......	160,576	700,000

and industrialized, with an economy based on the refining of Venezuelan petroleum. At the opposite extreme, Dutch New Guinea is a region of tropical jungle, still in part unexplored though known to contain extensive deposits of minerals. The Dutch administered the area as part of their dependency of the Netherlands East Indies. When the latter gained independence as the Republic of Indonesia, the Dutch retained West New Guinea in their own hands. Its cession has been angrily demanded by the government of Indonesia, and Dutch occupation of the area is likely to terminate within a few years.

The Spanish Empire: The Spanish Empire of today is the poor remnant of a great empire on which, according to the proud boast of its king, the sun never set. The British and Dutch had nibbled away at it in the seventeenth and eighteenth centu-

TABLE 23   *The Spanish Empire*

	Area, sq miles	Population, 1959
Ifni........................	741	53,000
Spanish Sahara..............	105,388	25,000
Spanish Guinea (continental Guinea and the island of Fernando Po).............	10,852	216,000
Spanish Moroccan possessions..	82	145,000

ries. Early in the nineteenth, the Latin-American colonies revolted, and at the close of the nineteenth, the Philippines, Puerto Rico, and a number of less important islands were lost as a result of the Spanish-American War. Lastly, the Spanish-held protectorate of Northern Morocco, which had been subdued only with great difficulty by Spanish arms, was in 1956 reincorporated into the independent state of Morocco, with the exception only of five fragments of territory on the Mediterranean coast of Morocco, the so-called Plazas de Soberanía. Spain retains the areas shown in Table 23.

Most of the Spanish possessions are sparsely peopled desert. "With the possible exception of Fernando Po, they have had very little attention from their home government, and there is little evidence of any effort to improve either the political or social status of the native people, or to introduce modern systems of administration. There is nothing which points to the establishment of self-governing institutions." [21] In 1950, the Spanish government prohibited the establishment of any foreign enterprise on the territory of Spain's African colonies. The Spanish Empire must be the only one in which not only political freedom but also economic progress is forbidden.

The Portuguese Empire: Like the Spanish Empire, the Portuguese is also all that remains of a formerly more extensive area. The Portuguese were driven from many of their possessions in Southeast Asia and Africa by the Dutch and the British, and their most extensive possession, Brazil, broke away in 1822. What remains, however, is more extensive, more valuable, and slightly better administered than the shabby empire of Spain (Table 24).

[21] Lord Hailey, *The Future of Colonial Peoples,* Oxford University Press, New York, 1943, pp. 35–36.

TABLE 24   *The Portuguese Empire*

	Area, sq miles	Population, 1959
Cape Verde Islands.........	1,556	195,000
Portuguese Guinea..........	13,944	565,000
São Tomé and Principe Islands.................	370	64,000
Angola....................	481,226	4,550,000
Mozambique..............	297,654	6,310,000
Portuguese possessions in India (Goa, Damão, and Diu, each with dependent areas [1]).................	1,537	649,000
Macau....................	6	215,000
Portuguese Timor..........	7,330	496,000

[1] Some of the dependencies, forming enclaves within India, have ceased to be *de facto* parts of the Portuguese Empire.

The Portuguese claim to pursue a policy of assimilation, similar to that of France, but their pretensions have never been matched by serious attempts to educate the people, and their policy has been much less successful. The Portuguese possessions are undoubtedly lagging in the movement from colonial dependency to statehood, but, until 1961, there was no serious political unrest under the easy going rule of Portugal. The shock of the Congo war has had a tonic effect in neighboring Angola, where native unrest, coupled with the disfavor with which Portuguese imperialism was viewed by the rest of the world, has led to the granting of a limited autonomy. Portugal has tended to monopolize the trade of her colonies by giving their products a considerable preference in the Portuguese market.

The Danish and Norwegian Empires: The Faroe Islands, in the North Atlantic Ocean, are considered an integral part of Denmark. Greenland was until 1953 entirely non-self-governing, but since then it has been accorded the same degree of local self-government as the rest of Denmark. Greenland covers an area of 839,782 square miles, of which over 80 per cent is covered by ice. The population of Greenland is about twenty-seven thousand, of whom fewer than two thousand are Europeans. The state of Norway formally incorporated the arctic island group of Svalbard in 1920, and since that date has added the uninhabited Jan Mayen and some other small, unvalued arctic islands.

The Empire of the United States: The American system of government has provided since its earliest years for the inclusion of non-self-governing territories. The territorial status, through which all States in the Union, except the original thirteen, have passed, is a dependent one, though in each instance there was the expectation that it would last for only a restricted period. No State has had a territorial status for more than sixty years [22] and few for more than twenty-five. Alaska was purchased from Russia in 1867 and was governed directly by the United States until it achieved territorial status in 1912. In the meanwhile, the Spanish-American War had brought a crop of dependent territories. By the Treaty of Paris of 1898, Spain ceded Puerto Rico, Guam, and the Philippine Islands to the United States. In the same year the Hawaiian Islands were annexed by the United States at the request of their inhabitants. In 1899, part of the island group of Samoa was acquired by the United States with the agreement of Germany and the United Kingdom. In 1903, the Panama Canal Zone was leased by the United States from the Republic of Panama. Theoretically sovereignty over the zone is still vested in the Panamanian government, but the lease is in perpetuity and the United States exer-

[22] The State of Hawaii became a Territory in 1900 and the fiftieth State in 1960.

cises effective sovereignty. In 1917, the United States purchased from Denmark the Danish portion of the Virgin Islands in order to protect the easterly approaches to the canal.

In 1940, a number of small areas in the British West Indies were leased for the purpose of constructing military bases to protect the approaches to the Panama Canal. Most of these have been returned to the West Indies, but the United States continues to control a military base at Guantanamo, in Cuba, and by treaty arrangement with its allies holds a considerable though fluctuating number of bases in Europe, Morocco,[23] Taiwan, and Japan.

In 1919 the mandate for certain of the former German possessions in the Pacific Ocean was entrusted to Japan. In 1947, the trusteeship for these territories, known as the Marshall, Caroline, and Mariana groups, was transferred to the United States. In 1952 the United States established a curious control over the Ryukyu Islands, which lie between Japan and Taiwan, and also over the Bonin and Kazan groups. By the terms of the peace treaty with Japan, the United States assumed "the right to exercise all and any powers of administration, legislation and jurisdiction" over these islands, while a residual sovereignty remained with Japan. A year later the American government handed back the most northerly islands in the Ryukyu group but continues to occupy the remainder.

In 1935 the Philippines became autonomous under the name of the Commonwealth of the Philippines. This status was to last for a period of ten years, at the end of which the islands were to gain complete independence. This probationary period was interrupted by the Japanese invasion, and it was not until 1946 that the Republic of the Philippines came into exist-

[23] Restored to Morocco, 1958.

TABLE 25 *Overseas Territories and Possessions of the United States*

Territory	Area, sq miles	Population, 1959
Virgin Islands................	15	24,000
Panama Canal Zone (sovereignty vested with the Republic of Panama).........	648	56,000
Guam.......................	206	60,000
American Samoa.............	76	20,000
Marshall, Caroline, and Mariana groups (trust territories).	687	67,000
Ryukyu, Bonin, and Kazan groups (sovereignty vested with Japan)...............	899	823,000
Midway and Wake..........	5	0

ence. Puerto Rico attained the status of a Territory in 1917 and in 1952 became the autonomous Commonwealth of Puerto Rico. A year later the President of the United States informed the UN that, if at any time the responsible body in Puerto Rico "adopts a resolution in favor of more complete or even absolute independence," the United States government would concur in this desire. Puerto Rico thus stands to the United States as Canada or Australia does to the United Kingdom. It is free to sever its connection but has been too wise to do so. The territorial possessions of the United States today are mainly small and of strategic value only. With an area of only 2,531 square miles, the dependent empire of the United States must surely rank as one of the smallest the world has known.

CONCLUSION

This review will have shown how confusing and continually changing has been the pattern of colonies in the modern world. Only the French have striven for simplicity of organization. Only the Americans have acquired and retained dependencies for a specific purpose, namely, strategy. All other colonial empires have just grown, and as the needs and desires of the colonial powers have changed through the centuries, so have the nature and the organization of the dependent territories. At the beginning of this chapter were listed and discussed the most important reasons—other than military protection—for acquiring colonies. No state has ever openly justified its possession of dependencies on any of these grounds. No doubt colonies were acquired in the high hope of economic advantage, of the exclusive control of scarce materials, of gaining an outlet for surplus population, but in no instance were these hopes justified for long. The cost of colonies, at least of the old-style *colonies d'exploitation,* soon came to outweigh the material advantages to be gained from them.

The three main arguments for possessing colonies turn out to be three great fallacies— and they are seen to be dangerous as well as costly fallacies when account is taken of the results of the struggle for colonies not only or even primarily in cash but in lives lost, in wars caused, and in the pyramided hatreds which so gravely threaten new wars.[24]

The old colonial powers have taken decades, even centuries, to learn this lesson, and it seems that the former colonies may take almost as long to forget the experience and the hatreds that it nurtured. Must we assume that the exponents of the new imperialism will take equally long to learn that the control and exploitation of one people by another does not work, and, in the long run, does not pay?

[24] Grover Clark, *The Balance Sheet of Imperialism,* Columbia University Press, New York, 1936, p. 5.

APPENDIX III

The British Empire and Commonwealth

A. Independent and self-governing states within the Commonwealth	Date of independence or dominion status	Area, sq miles	Population, 1957
Canada (with Newfoundland)....	1867	3,549,960	16,589,000
Australia....................	1901	2,974,581	9,643,000
New Zealand.................	1907	103,740	2,229,000
India.......................	1947	1,138,814	392,440,000
Pakistan....................	1947	364,737	84,450,000
Ceylon.....................	1948	25,332	9,165,000
Ghana......................	1957	91,843	4,763,000
Malaya.....................	1957	50,690	6,279,000
Nigeria.....................	1960	373,250	32,433,000
Cyprus.....................	1960	3,571	536,000
Sierra Leone................	1961	27,908	2,120,000
Tanganyika.................	1961	361,682	8,760,000
Western Samoa.............	1962	1,129	104,000
Jamaica....................	1962	4,409	1,671,000
Trinidad and Tobago.........	1962	1,979	817,000

B. Territories not wholly self-governing and independent	Area, 1960, sq miles	Population, 1957, thousands
Africa:		
Gambia	3,991	290
Kenya	224,884	6,254
Mauritius	720	587
Rhodesia and Nyasaland	483,697	7,450
St. Helena and dependencies	47	5
Seychelles	154	41
Zanzibar and Pemba	1,019	285
High-commission territories		
Basutoland	11,711	651
Bechuanaland	274,832	331
Swaziland	6,678	260
Asia:		
Aden, Colony and protectorate	111,940	790
Brunei	2,000	73
Hong Kong	386	2,583
North Borneo	29,375	397
Sarawak	47,478	640
Singapore	224	1,460
America:		
Bahamas	4,400	123
Bermudas	20	42
British Honduras	8,864	84
British West Indies	1,613	854
British Guiana	83,000	549
Europe:		
Gibraltar	2	25
Malta	116	319
Oceania:		
Solomon Islands	11,103	104
Fiji	7,064	354
Gilbert and Ellice Islands	347	40
Pitcairn	2	0
Tonga	270	57
Canton and Enderby Islands [1]	20	0
New Hebrides [2]	5,713	52
	1,824,146	45,661

[1] Condominium with the United States.
[2] Condominium with France.

C. Territories which have voluntarily left the Empire or Commonwealth	Date of independence	Date of leaving the Commonwealth	Area, sq miles
Irish Republic....	1921	1949	26,600; formerly part of United Kingdom
Egypt...........	1923	1923	386,198; under temporary British administration, 1882–1923
Burma..........	1948	1948	261,789; formerly part of British India
Israel..........	1948	1948	20,700; formerly the mandated territory of Palestine
Sudan..........	1956	1956	967,500; formerly a condominium, jointly ruled by the United Kingdom and Egypt
Jordan..........	1946	1946	96,500; formerly the mandated territory of Trans-jordan
Iraq............	1932	1932	444,442; formerly a mandated territory
South Africa......	1910	1961	472,359; formerly a Dominion
Somaliland.......	1960	1960	67,936; formerly a British protectorate

APPENDIX IV

The French Community

1. France.
2. The overseas *départements*, which are legally and administratively a part of France.
3. The overseas territories, which do not have complete independence but are administratively dependent on the government of France. The reasons for their lower status are their generally sparse population or their generally underdeveloped nature. They are:
   a. French Polynesian islands, of which the Society and Marquezas Islands are the most important
   b. New Caledonia and its dependencies
   c. French Somaliland
   d. Comoro Islands
   e. Saint-Pierre and Miquelon
   f. Wallis and Fortuna Islands (West Pacific) and southern and antarctic islands.
4. Other members of the Community. These are the former administrative divisions of French West Africa, Central Africa, and Malagasy, organized as so many "republics." Each has a form of government based on the French model; each is a coequal member of the Community. The analogy with the independent dominions of the British Commonwealth is obvious. The separate republics are sovereign. Guinea, which rejected the constitution, was assumed to have withdrawn from the Community and is now an independent sovereign state. Two of the republics, Senegal and Sudan, in 1959 joined to form the Federal Republic of Mali but in the following year separated again. The original republics were thirteen in number:

Senegal	Niger
Mali	Gabon
Mauritania	Congo
Upper Volta	Tchad
Dahomey	Central Africa
Ivory Coast	Madagascar
Cameroun	

5. The condominium of the New Hebrides, in which the rule of the island group is shared by two commissioners, one French, the other British.

BIBLIOGRAPHY

Cambridge History of the British Empire, 8 vols., Cambridge University Press, Cambridge, 1929–(in progress).

Carrington, C. E.: *An Exposition of Empire*, Cambridge University Press, New York, 1947.

Church, R. J. Harrison: *Modern Colonialism*, Hutchinson University Library, London, 1951.

Clark, Grover: *The Balance Sheet of Imperialism*, Columbia University Press, New York, 1936.

The French Colonial Empire, Royal Institute of International Affairs, London, 1940.

Germany's Claim to Colonies, Royal Institute of International Affairs, London, 1938.

Hailey, Lord: *An African Survey*, Oxford University Press, New York, 1938.

———: *The Future of Colonial Peoples*, Oxford University Press, New York, 1943.

Hancock, W. K.: *The Argument of Empire*, Penguin Books, London, 1943.

Hobson, J. A.: *Imperialism*, G. Allen and Unwin, Ltd., London, 1938.

Kimble, George H. T.: *Tropical Africa*, 2 vols., The Twentieth Century Fund, Inc., New York, 1960.

Lugard, Lord: *The Dual Mandate in British Tropical Africa*, W. Blackwood & Sons, Ltd., Edinburgh, 1922.

Macmillan, W. M.: *The Road to Self-rule*, Faber & Faber, Ltd., London, 1959.

The Mandates System: Origin—Principles—Application, League of Nations, Geneva, 1945.

Political and Strategic Interests of the United Kingdom, Oxford University Press, New York, 1939.

Robinson, G. W. S.: "Ceuta and Melilla: Spain's Plazas de Soberanía," *Geography*, vol. 43, pp. 266–269, 1958.

Strachey, John: *The End of Empire*, Victor Gallancz, Ltd., London, 1960.

Walker, E. A.: *Colonies*, Cambridge University Press, New York, 1944.

Ward, Barbara: *The International Share-out*, Thomas Nelson & Sons, Ltd., London, 1938.

Wheare, K. C.: *The Constitutional Structure of the Commonwealth*, Oxford University Press, Oxford, 1960.

Wiens, Harold J.: *Pacific Island Bastions of the United States*, Searchlight Series, no. 4, D. Van Nostrand & Co., Princeton, N.J., 1962.

Williamson, J. A.: *Short History of British Expansion*, 2 vols., Macmillan & Co., Ltd., London, 1945.

14 THE UNDERDEVELOPED WORLD

I believe we should make available to peace-loving peoples the benefits of our store of technical knowledge in order to help them realize their aspirations for a better life. PRESIDENT HARRY S. TRUMAN, JANUARY 20, 1949

If the color of the skin is to determine mastery, the future will be too horrible to contemplate. THE NEW YORK TIMES, APRIL 11, 1960

WE HAVE SEEN IN THE PREVIOUS CHAPTER THAT THE PROPORTION OF the earth's surface that is under colonial rule has been shrinking for many years. In a relatively short period of time colonial empires, in the old sense of that term, will have disappeared. Their place will be taken by independent states, linked, sometimes on a voluntary basis, in associations, which will be the ghostlike survivors of the former dependent empires. Yet this vanishing imperialism is leaving behind it a legacy of problems, stemming in part from the unbalanced economic development which it brought about, in part from the mixing of peoples which resulted, in part also from the prejudices and hostilities which it generated.

The distinction has already been made between the colonies established in temperate latitudes, where peoples of European origin can live normal lives and perform the kind of work which they did in their European homeland, and those founded in the tropics, where none of these conditions apply. This distinction is fundamental. In the former, settlers of European stock lived European lives and acquired a European type of government and, lastly, independence. In the latter they settled in very small numbers, served as a self-conscious elite, and always sighed for the green fields and cool climate of home. They did not constitute an important body of permanent settlers because, rightly or wrongly, they were convinced that their type of life was impossible in the tropics. As a general rule they looked upon frequent leaves of absence in a cooler climate and early retirement as essential.

Between these extremes are lands which partake in some way of the character of both. They are areas within the tropics where, owing to the local circumstances of relief and climate, conditions are obtained which are generally suitable to European settlement. Such areas include the highlands of Central America and the Andean states, the Brazilian Plateau, the highlands of Kenya and of other parts of East Africa, the plateaus of Rhodesia and of the Union of South Africa, the hills and mountains of India, and the northern parts of Australia. To these it might not be inappropriate to add some parts of the American South. It is in these marginal areas, which, to put it crudely, are neither exclusively black man's nor exclusively white man's land, that the aftermath of colonialism has been most burdensome.

COLONIES AND INDEPENDENCE

The colonial peoples have, without exception, desired and demanded political independence. In a very imprecise fashion they seemed to identify this independence with a freedom from alleged exploitation and with an accession of wealth. In short, this lack of freedom was thought of as the chief cause of the differences between themselves and the powers which once controlled their destinies. This is demonstrably not the case. The Republic of Guinea voted against De Gaulle's new constitution in 1958 and thus acquired political independence. At the same time its inexperienced government discovered with a shock that, with the ending of the paternal French control, there disappeared also markets and economic aid. An East African native leader wrote that, when Africa has

won its fight against foreign control, "the continent will be free to concentrate on its battle for the consolidation of its freedom, the achievement of economic, political and moral equality before the whole world." [1] The achievement of this equality is not automatic, because economic progress does not necessarily accompany political independence. Many of the new states emerging may be disillusioned, and the rosy dawn of statehood has, in not a few former colonies, ushered in a very stormy day.

The fact is that, with a few exceptions, the new states are economically weak and politically unstable and immature. This is a political fact of great importance. Economic weakness, as manifested in the lack of balance in the development and use of resources, the lack of markets, and the difficulty of obtaining capital to finance development projects, is serious, not merely to the countries concerned but to the rest of the free world. Economic depression breeds unrest, weakens the fledgling governments of the new states, and creates the openings through which the economic and political influence of the Communist bloc may insinuate itself. In the following pages certain features of the political geography of the former colonial empires and of some underdeveloped, but nevertheless independent, nations are examined.

The Raisons d'Être of the New States: In an earlier chapter we sought for the *raison d'être* of states, the cohesive force that holds them together, and in most instances we found it in a deep sense of belonging together, itself the product of historical and cultural factors. Most of the established states (including all that have once been imperial powers) have grown slowly. To a large degree they assumed their geographical shape *before* this present age of nationalism, and their problems

[1] *New York Times*, Mar. 27, 1960.

of unity have in the main long since been laid to rest. The states now emerging from colonial status have not been formed in this way. It is true that in some instances the imperial power by its judicious handling of the local peoples was able to weld them together, thereby creating a sense of unity. This has happened in India, which the British found, in the seventeenth and eighteenth centuries, a maze of little states, often feuding with one another, and which they left with some sense of unity, though not enough to prevent it from splitting along communal lines into the Republics of Pakistan and India. This success was not achieved in all dependencies, least of all in the African. The number of straight-line boundaries in Africa is itself evidence of their artificiality. Most African colonies began as bases on the coast. Their boundaries with one another reflected, not so much conditions in Africa, as the power balance between the imperial states themselves. They were the product of bartering around a conference table in London, Paris, or Berlin. The boundaries severed tribal areas, separating friendly tribes and throwing hostile tribes together. It would have required a sympathetic and understanding colonial government to maintain peace and harmony between the disparate elements of many colonial territories. Not only was this often absent, but the colonial administrators themselves, in some instances, contributed deliberately to the mutual distrust between tribal and other groups within their colonial dependencies, with the object of minimizing the threat to their own authority.

Before surrendering its authority in Nigeria the British government appointed a commission whose terms of reference required it "to ascertain the facts about the fears of the minorities in any part of Nigeria and to propose means of allaying those fears whether well or ill founded." The re-

sulting report [2] made it clear that the minorities were numerous and their fears genuine. "In each of the three Regions of Nigeria," it declared, "we found either a minority or a group of minorities who described fears and grievances which they felt would become more intense when the present restraints were removed and who suggested as a remedy a separate state or states." [3] The latter course was clearly impossible, if only because of the number and complexity of the minorities. The commission therefore urged the maintenance of the unity of the state and recommended the building up of a sense of cohesion.

In state after state, the celebration of independence day has been marred by communal disturbances between tribes and groups, each fearful that the other may gain power. In no African state have these disturbances been worse than in the Congo and the French trusteeship territory of the Cameroun. "Cameroon's trouble springs from the fact that she has no ethnic, religious, or geographic unity. Her densely populated north is dominated by a powerful Moslem ruling class that treats the pagan masses as virtual slaves. The north is fifty years behind the rest of the country in social and educational development." [4] Even among the more developed Bamileke peoples of southern Cameroun there are strong economic and social differences that have led to violence.

The Republic of Mauritania, within the French Community, has a sparse and semi-nomadic population, two-thirds of it Moorish and Muslim, the remaining third Negro and related far more closely to the Negroes of Senegal than to the Moors.

[2] *Nigeria: Report of the Commission Appointed to Enquire into the Fears of the Minorities and the Means of Allaying Them,* H.M. Stationery Office, London, 1958.

[3] *Ibid.,* p. 87.

[4] *New York Times,* Jan. 3, 1960.

Forces are active in fomenting the differences between the Moorish and Negro population of Mauritania and in inciting the Negro element to seek union with the Senegal or Mali. The little colony of Gambia, almost surrounded by Senegal, is threatened with absorption by the latter when it gains independence from the United Kingdom. Attempts by some of the local people to create the concept of a "Gambian nation" seem foredoomed to failure. Time is running out, and a sense of cohesion, of belonging to a nation rather than to a tribe, cannot be created overnight.

The future of the Congo raises in an acute form the question of maintaining as independent states the territorial units that were created by colonialism. The Belgians had tended to discourage rather than to promote the idea of Congo unity. The ethnic diversity is matched by the variety of physical environment. The southern province of the Congo, known as Katanga, is a plateau region, clothed with savanna and containing rich deposits of copper. Superficially it resembles Northern Rhodesia more closely than it does the rest of the Congo. Suggestions that it might merge with Northern Rhodesia have been angrily rejected, but such an outcome to the present situation is not impossible. For the rest, the only rational solution to the Congo problem appears to be the creation of a rather loose confederation, but this would raise even greater problems than the Nigerian Federation because of the greater size and variety in the Congo Republic.

The boundaries of the new states of Africa are at present irrational, in so far as they do not clearly respond to either economic or human conditions, and they may for a long period remain fluid.

The *raisons d'être* of many of the new states lie entirely in the fact that that is how the imperial powers of the nineteenth century shaped them. Their territorial limits are like old bottles into which the strong, new wine of African nationalism has been poured. It has burst some of the bottles and threatens to do so to others. Peoples, broken up by the boundaries drawn in the nineteenth century, may be reunited; Ethiopia's federation with Eritrea, the temporary union of Senegal and Sudan to form the short-lived Mali Federation, Morocco's absorption of the Spanish Zone of northern Morocco and the city of Tangier, Rhodesia's threat to the Katanga province of the Congo, and the possibility of Ruanda-Urundi and Nyasaland going their separate ways are only symptoms of a radical reorganization of territory, as Africa passes from colonialism to statehood.

Plural Societies: In a great many of the colonial and former colonial territories peoples live on sharply differing economic and cultural planes. A recent writer on Gambia observed that "Bathurst [the capital] has a veneer of sophistication. But go a few miles into the protectorate and life is nearly as primitive as in the heart of the Congo." [5] Throughout Africa one finds tribal and detribalized Africans, Africans who have been assimilated to European society and those who know neither agriculture nor any social organization larger or more complex than the family group. Nor are these contrasts among the native peoples confined to Africa. They exist in India, Indonesia, and other countries of Southeast Asia, and they are present in Central and South America.

Europeans have not always been as solicitous as they might have been for the welfare of the more backward peoples of their empires. There is no reason to suppose that the more advanced among the native peoples, upon whom power has now devolved, will be any kinder toward their less advanced fellow-citizens. In fact, the

[5] *New York Times*, Mar. 21, 1960.

imperial governments had to some extent restrained the exploitation or the oppression of the more backward by the more advanced societies. The almost feudal domination in parts of West Africa of the Muslim tribes over the Negroid is likely to deteriorate before it gets better. In Ruanda-Urundi there have been bloody attacks by the Watussi tribes on their former serfs, the Bahutu, while the Belgians still retained control over the area. These attacks are not likely to be diminished by independence. Such acts are to be deplored on humanitarian grounds. They are a source of weakness to the new states, they facilitate intrigue and encourage interference from without, and they hinder the development of natural resources for the benefit of all.

WHITE MEN IN THE TROPICS

So far we have considered only the conflicts which arise between peoples, contrasting in culture, who are nevertheless all native to the area. The conflicts between native peoples and immigrants, generally of European origin, are not less important and receive usually far greater publicity. The following classification of territories occupied and, to some extent, settled by peoples of European origin is offered only because it is a means of analyzing the factors in present racial conflicts:

1. Areas where peoples of European origin have completely or almost completely assimilated the native peoples. At the time of the first English settlements on the Eastern seaboard, here were no more than 2 million native Americans. The number of fullbloods is now minute. About 350,000 persons are now classed as Indians; some live on reservations, but most live in all respects like their fellow-citizens of European origin and may in fact be indistinguishable from them.

A somewhat analogous relationship has been achieved in parts of Canada and of Latin America. In some respects, especially in the latter, the European way of life has been modified by contact with that of the Latin-American Indian. But at least European settlers of predominantly Spanish origin and the native Indian peoples have grown together, so that such differences as still remain have little political significance in at least some of the Latin-American republics.

2. Areas where part of the native peoples have become assimilated to the Europeans, leaving, however, some tribes resentful and hostile to both. Two contrasting examples of this partial assimilation are Algeria, which has been discussed on page 347, and the Philippines. Other examples are the overseas *départements* of France in the New World, those parts of Latin America where the native Indian peoples still practice their traditional way of life, and the Portuguese Empire, in which, however, only a minute proportion of the native population has in fact become assimilated.[6]

3. Areas where European peoples have neither assimilated nor been assimilated by the native peoples to any significant degree. The two live their separate lives side by side, the former in their clubs, the latter in their villages. They have different cultures, different values, and radically different standards of living. Such areas must, however, be divided into those where the Europeans have come to do a job—as civil servant, doctor, teacher, or technician—to earn a pension, and then to go home, and those where the European has come, settled, and made his home. In the former case, the Europeans may sometimes regard their function as one of preparing the native peo-

[6] It has been estimated that less than 1 per cent of the population of Angola has been assimilated: *World Today*, vol. 17, p. 286, 1961.

ples for independence. They can pull out without inconvenience; or they may stay on for a while after independence. Their presence does not really constitute a serious political problem, only because it can be terminated at short notice. Such has been the case in the former British colonies in West Africa, Uganda, British Honduras, British Guiana, in former French Equatorial and West Africa and Sudan, and, above all, in British India, Burma, and Ceylon. A few Dutch settled in the former Dutch East Indies, but most of the Dutch employed by the Dutch government and by commercial undertakings active in the area had their homes in Europe, and it was there that they hoped to retire.

The basic reason for the lack of permanent European settlement in areas of this kind is climatic. The continuous heat and humidity make a European pattern of life difficult. Such a life is hard on families, and especially on children, who have usually to be sent to school in Europe. Generalizations must not, however, be too sweeping; there are many exceptions. Europeans have succeeded in making permanent homes in Singapore and Hong Kong and in most of the West Indian islands; and Sarawak, on the island of Borneo, was actually ruled until recently by its "white rajahs," descendants of a buccaneering Englishman who settled there early in the nineteenth century.

In other territories, peoples of European descent have been able to settle, make homes, and cultivate the soil. They have neither hope nor expectation of returning to the land of their ancestors. Latin America, South Africa, Rhodesia, or Kenya has become their home, and here they intend to live side by side with the African or Latin-American Indian. The conditions which permit such a dual society to develop are mainly geographical. These areas lie within or close to the tropics, but the land rises into a plateau, up to six thousand feet above the sea level in places. This is high enough to reduce the temperature and humidity to levels at which Europeans can live in comfort for most of the year.

Republic of South Africa: The earliest European settlements were established on the coast and were conceived of more as staging points on the sea route to India and the Far East than as points of departure for the conquest and settlement of the hinterland. Nevertheless, the occupation of the interior followed early in the nineteenth century. Among the settlers near the Cape of Good Hope were farmers of Dutch ancestry. Their outlook was narrow and intolerant, and they regarded themselves almost in the light of a chosen people, whose privilege it was to oppress and exploit all whose skin color was darker than their own. They had resolved the problems presented by the juxtaposition of European and African by enslaving the latter and using them as labor on their farms. In 1806 the United Kingdom annexed South Africa. The British government had already abolished trade in slaves, and in 1832 it abolished the institution of slavery itself, paying a monetary compensation to those who thus lost their source of unpaid labor. The relations between the Dutch settlers and the British had long been strained, because the British government had for many years tried to mitigate the abuses of slavery. The Dutch, Calvinist and fundamentalist, regarded their way of life as thoroughly consistent with the Scriptures. They resented the British interference with their practices, and after they had found that the British were not to be dissuaded from their policy, the Dutch "Boers" migrated.

This was the Great Trek, "the central event in South Africa's history." [7] (See Fig-

7 *Cambridge History of the British Empire,* vol. 8, *South Africa,* p. 318.

ure 2, page 10.) The Dutch farmers loaded their possessions onto their wagons and, driving their stock before them, trekked northward across the dry, dusty Karroos and on to the High Veld, a rolling plateau which stretched north into Central Africa. Here grass grew, and the Boers could graze their animals, grow crops, and live the isolated and self-sufficient life that they wanted. British rule tried to catch up with them, and throughout the remainder of the nineteenth century they struggled to be free of control from this quarter. At the same time they had to defend themselves from the Bantu peoples, Negroid African people who during the nineteenth century pressed southward toward the Cape.

On the Veld, the Boers established two republics, the Orange Free State and the Transvaal. These two states were born of the struggle against both the British and the Bantu, and the heroic—almost legendary—events of their early years continue to dominate their politics and their political relations. So often today the Boer farmer thinks of himself still as fighting to preserve his culture against both the African and other Europeans, just as his ancestors did a century and more ago. In the Boer War of 1899–1902, the British defeated the Boers and brought the two Boer republics again under British rule. In 1910, the Union of South Africa was established, consisting of two Boer states, the Orange Free State and the Transvaal, in which the dominant language was Afrikaans, and two mainly English-speaking states, Cape of Good Hope and Natal. The government of the Union has certain features which are reminiscent of a federal system, but it is in fact unitary. The Boers outnumber the Europeans of British origin [8] and dominate the country politically.

[8] There are small numbers of settlers of French and other origin.

The total population of the Union of South Africa is estimated (1958) to be about 14.4 million, made up of:

White................. 3,011,000 (Boers approximately 1,700,000)
African............... 9,606,000
Colored.............. 1,360,000
Asiatic............... 441,000

The "colored" population is half-caste, part European, part African. Its status had been somewhat higher than that of the African, but the present policy of the Afrikaans majority tends to equate it with the native African. The Asiatics are mainly Indians whose ancestors came to Natal, a century ago, to work on the sugar plantations.

The domestic policy of the Afrikaans-speaking majority can be understood only in the light of the history of their settlement in the Union. It is one of *Apartheid,* or "separateness," of white and African peoples. What is advocated is an extreme form of racial segregation. There has never been any pretense that the facilities offered to the African are "separate *but equal.*" They are just separate. In the near future, the Africans will cease to be represented in Parliament; the representation of the colored is both biased and inadequate, and the Asiatics have none. Every effort is made to restrict the movements of Africans, to prevent them from going to places of higher education and from taking skilled jobs. Nowhere in the world is the doctrine of white supremacy pursued so ruthlessly and with such violence as in South Africa.

Apartheid is the policy of the South African Nationalists, and the Nationalists are mainly Boer. They outnumber the non-Boer Europeans and are thus able to impose their policy by parliamentary action. But it must not be supposed that the English-speaking South Africans are entirely opposed to *Apartheid.* Many of them approve this policy of separateness of the races, though they would not, in general, carry their policy to the extremes advocated by the Nationalists. The tensions in South Africa have led to rioting and violence. The trend in Africa and the rest of the world is away from such a policy of segregation based upon ideas of racial superiority. How long it can be maintained in South Africa, in the face of condemnation by the public opinion of much of the world, is uncertain. Here is an almost unique example of a state which has chosen deliberately to exacerbate its communal conflicts, to prevent assimilation of subnational groups, and thus to weaken its international power potential. It has chosen to alienate its neighbors and to antagonize its friends. Its government cannot be said to enjoy confidence or respect, it cannot exert its proper influence in international affairs, and it presumably supposes that world events will pass it by. In the nineteenth century South Africa might have lived on in isolation, but today isolation, as a policy, is impossible even for the most isolated state—and South Africa is not so remote as that.

The Highlands of Central Africa: Racial tension between native colored peoples and white immigrants is most intense in the Union of South Africa. But it is potentially as serious in the "highlands" of Rhodesia, Nyasaland, and Kenya. The geographical conditions invite European settlers. Here is plateau country, high, dry, and cool enough for peoples of Anglo-Saxon stock to establish and operate farms and plantations, especially if they have Africans to do the rougher work. The territories in question are all under British rule, though the Federation of Rhodesia and Nyasaland is autonomous, but not yet fully independent. The population of these areas is shown in Table 26. Over the region as a whole Europeans make up 1.3 per cent of the total population, a much smaller percentage than in the Union, and other non-African peoples 1.2 per cent.

Rhodesia grew from the ambitious plans of Cecil Rhodes, an eccentric imperialist whose ambition it was to create a vast empire under the British crown in Central Africa. For a time Rhodesia was an appendage of the British government at

TABLE 26 *Population of East and Central Africa*

	Total population (1959 estimates)	Europeans (estimates)	Others (estimates)
Federation of Rhodesia and Nyasaland:			
Southern Rhodesia.....	3,000,000	200,000	14,200
Northern Rhodesia.....	2,360,000	64,800	6,950
Nyasaland............	2,770,000	6,700	9,710
British East Africa:			
Kenya...............	6,450,000	64,700	206,200
Tanganyika [1]........	9,076,000	20,598	76,536
Uganda Protectorate...	6,517,000	3,450	36,700

[1] Trusteeship territory; independence gained in December, 1961.

the Cape. But it then moved slowly away from dependence on the Union and toward self-government. An important reason for this lay in the nature of its white population. This was predominantly of British stock. Very few Boers penetrated this far north, and there was a desire to keep free of the Union, in which the Boer element was threatening to become dominant. Furthermore, the building of railroads from Southern Rhodesia to Portuguese ports in Angola and Mozambique diminished Rhodesia's commercial dependence on the Union. Europeans settled mainly in Southern Rhodesia, partly because its climate is more suitable, partly because of its greater ease of access, and here the white population amounts to nearly a tenth of the whole. It feels its position to be less precarious and its security less threatened than in Northern Rhodesia and Nyasaland.

A deliberate policy of segregation has never been pursued in Rhodesia. While the African has not been exactly welcomed into the white society that has intruded into his, he has been given the vote and has been allowed to participate in local politics provided that he can demonstrate what the white man considers a sufficient level of education. He is not excluded by law from any trade or profession, though white-controlled unions have sometimes made it difficult for him to enter.

Southern Rhodesia is in a peculiar federal union with Northern Rhodesia and Nyasaland. In each of these the European element is smaller, both relatively and absolutely, and, because it has felt its security to be more threatened, has tended to adopt a more repressive policy toward the African. Very broadly the white settlers in Northern Rhodesia and Nyasaland favor federation because it tends to give them the protection of the strongly placed white minority in Southern Rhodesia. The Africans in these two areas in general oppose federation be-

cause they think of it as preventing their independence as African states.

In Ghana, Guinea, Liberia, and a growing list of other African states, the Africans govern themselves. In the Union of South Africa, they are governed without their own consent. In Rhodesia they may qualify for the privilege of voting and of helping to rule themselves if they can demonstrate an adequate level of education. The reasons for this difference in status are to a large extent geographical. Although there are other factors, it may broadly be said that political freedom for Africans varies inversely with the suitability of their climate for Europeans.

The "White" Highlands of Kenya: The highlands of Kenya are one of the highest and coolest regions of intertropical Africa. Large areas lie at over seven thousand feet above sea level, and though much is fit only for grazing land, there are extensive areas of good volcanic soil. The immigration of Europeans—mainly British—followed the building in 1901 of the railroad from the port of Mombasa inland to the

Figure 60 White farmers have large estates in the highlands of Kenya, which they cultivate with African labor. Sometimes they may lend a hand in field work, but clearly do not dress for such a part.
COURTESY: BRITISH INFORMATION SERVICES

Protectorate of Uganda. Much of the plateau looked empty, deceptively empty. The agricultural Kikuyu people had only recently been driven out of the fertile plateau area by the nomadic, pastoral Masai. The latter demanded, even if they did not need, extensive areas for their stock, and the Kikuyu themselves hoped to be able eventually to return to their former settlement areas.

However, the railroad was in debt and needed a paying freight. This could best be provided by developing plantation agriculture in the highlands. Between 1903 and 1938, about eleven thousand square miles was alienated by the government to European farmers, and provision was made to alienate a further fifty-seven hundred square miles. On the other hand about fifty thousand square miles—not all of it good land—has been set aside as reserves for the African. The allocation of land to Europeans has been generous:

> The average European farm is one of 600 first-class acres, whilst that of the Kikuyu averages eight acres—one-quarter of which is too poor to cultivate. Thus, whilst most of the European areas are unused, there is great land hunger and population pressure in the African reserves which average 250 per square mile, and in parts of North Kavirondo, Embu and Kiambu reach up to 1,500 per square mile. . . . Sometimes up to 70 per cent of the adult able-bodied males are absent from the reserves and this, and the over-grazing and soil erosion due to general overcrowding, leads to even poorer farming and poverty, thus forcing the African away from his own tiny plots and from his family into being a landless laborer.[9]

This is the background of the African secret society, the Mau Mau, and its re-

[9] R. J. Harrison Church, *Modern Colonization*, Hutchinson University Library, London, 1951, p. 57.

cent acts of terrorism against the white settlers in the Kenya Highlands.

The same plateau that makes up much of Kenya extends also through Uganda and Tanganyika, but these territories have been protected against a development similar to that of Kenya and Southern Rhodesia by their legal status. Uganda is a protectorate in part of which an African king continues to rule; Tanganyika, after ceasing to be a German colony, became a mandate and is now a trusteeship territory under the UN. Only in Algeria and to a small degree in Morocco and Tunis has a problem arisen in any way similar to that of the territories just discussed (see page 345). In French Africa (outside Algeria) white settlement was on a very small scale. On the eve of the creation of the French Community there were fewer than two hundred thousand Europeans in "French" Africa, considerably less than 1 per cent of the total population. The majority of these probably expected to educate their children and spend their last years, not in Africa, but in France. The proportions of Europeans in the empires of Spain and Portugal is even less.

The basic problem in Rhodesia, Nyasaland, and Kenya, as well as in Algeria, has been the alienation of land by the government to European settlers. In most instances the government's title to the land was a poor one, based on a misunderstanding of native law and custom. The consequences of this have been summarized by Church:

> Wherever colonists backed by political power and superior technical and financial resources have established themselves . . . they have ultimately secured the most fertile, healthiest and most accessible lands and tended to segregate the indigenous peoples into the poorer, less hospitable and least accessible lands. The settlers, having acquired

the best lands and in proportions far greater per head than those left to the native peoples, have then buttressed their position with special commercial, financial and other privileges. . . . Pressure of population among the natives leads to soil impoverishment and erosion and the insufficiency of land, whilst the poverty and remoteness of native reservations cause the adult able-bodied males to migrate, which further impoverishes local farming. The effects of white settlement in semi-tropical and tropical lands where there was or is considerable local population have been almost wholly adverse on soil fertility of native lands.[10]

White settlements were established—and later abandoned—by the Italians when they held Libya. Dutch settlement in the hilly islands of Indonesia was terminated by the ending of Dutch rule and the evacuation of the Dutch settlers. European population in the colonial West Indies is negligible, and in the territories of Southeast Asia it was never large and is now virtually withdrawn. In Africa alone is the clash of white and colored politically significant today.[11]

In Latin America the immigration and settlement of peoples of European origin, primarily Spanish and Portuguese, among a widely scattered native Indian population have led to every degree of fusion and of separation. There are countries, like Argentina and Uruguay, which are almost wholly European in their population. There are parts of others—the highlands of Ecuador, Peru, and Bolivia, for example—which are almost exclusively Indian. On the other hand, Paraguay and some parts of most of the other Latin-American republics are

almost wholly mestizo, with scarcely a trace either of pure Indian or of pure European. Latin America is far from being free of the kind of communal problem that has been discussed in the foregoing pages, but this problem has been greatly reduced by (1) the readiness of the immigrants as a whole to mix and intermarry with the native Indian peoples and (2) the geographical separation of the more strongly contrasted communities.

Of what value to the colonial powers has been this white settlement of certain tropical areas? Except in the Republic of South Africa migration has been on too small a scale to provide any solution to population problems at home. In all probability, the total number of European settlers in Africa, inclusive of both Algeria and South Africa, does not greatly exceed 4.5 million and makes up only about 1 per cent of the continent's population. The white-settled areas of Africa cannot be said to have strategic value, though there have been rumors that the British proposed to develop a military base in Kenya to replace those in Egypt, Iraq, and Jordan which have been lost in the Middle East. It is doubtful that the United Kingdom has derived significant economic advantage from those areas. In general they are relatively high-cost producers of tropical goods, which sell well in the British market only because of the imperial preferential tariff.

4. Areas where non-European peoples remain unassimilated to one another. Migration into colonial dependencies has not been limited to peoples of European origin. Many others have been attracted by opportunities for work, and not a few have been taken there involuntarily to provide slave labor. The Negro peoples of African origin in the United States, the Caribbean, and at least the northern coastlands of South America are descended from such

---

[10] *Ibid.*, p. 60.

[11] Discussion of segregation in the United States has been deliberately omitted. Its legal basis is crumbling; the land problem is different in nature and less significant in the United States, and the Negroes are strictly no more native than are the whites.

unwilling immigrants to the New World. Arabs spread along the east coast of Africa, where they were long prominent in the slave trade. More recently Indians have been attracted to this area. They came to Natal to work on the sugar plantations, and throughout East Africa they came as laborers on plantation and railroad and have since become important as petty traders. Indians have spread also to Malaya and Burma, and to Indonesia, where they have imparted a Hindu character to the culture of Bali. They grow sugar in Mauritius and in the British West Indies, where almost half the total population of Trinidad is of "East" Indian origin.

Another non-European people which has become remarkably adept at settling in a wide variety of environment is the Chinese. They went to Malaya to work on the plantations; they have come to dominate the tin industry, and they now make up almost 40 per cent of the population of the Federation. The city of Singapore has become, in the main, a Chinese city. The Chinese have spread to East Africa and Ceylon, to Indonesia and the Philippines, and, like the Indians, they have settled in the British West Indies and British Guiana. They also came to Hawaii and California during the second half of the nineteenth century and thence have moved to all parts of the United States. The Chinese are probably the most ubiquitous of all non-European peoples.

The Negroes, Chinese, and Indians are the most important of non-European migrants, followed by the Arabs and Armenians. Their settlement in other areas than their homeland creates political problems no less than the settlement of Europeans. In some areas, notably Hawaii and the Caribbean region, the non-European immigrants have become assimilated to the local non-European peoples. In others, they remain a separate and distinct people, with their own traditions and observances, their own economic pursuits, and sometimes even their own particular settlement areas. With the exception of the Chinese in Malaya and Singapore, the non-European immigrants have shown no disposition to take over the reins of government. The rivalry between themselves and the local peoples is economic rather than political in nature. It hinges on the African's dislike of the Indian trader, so often more sharp-witted than himself, and the similar distrust of the Indonesian and the Filipino for the Chinese who run plantations and serve as commercial middlemen.

In Malaya, however, the Chinese have immigrated and settled in such numbers that they constitute a political as well as economic threat to the more easygoing Malays. In the Federation of Malaya, the Malays are just outnumbered (census of 1957) by non-Malays, among whom the Chinese predominate. In the Crown Colony of Singapore, the Chinese immigrants greatly outnumber all other peoples, as evidenced in the table.

	Malays	*Chinese*	*Indians*	*Others*	*Total*
Federation of Malaya.....	3,126,706	2,332,936	695,985	123,136	6,278,863
Singapore.....	197,557	1,092,514	124,094	34,382	1,448,547

SOURCE: Census of Malaya, 1957; Singapore estimates, 1959.

Figure 61 *Singapore is now for all practical purposes an independent state, though the British continue to hold a military base here. It is well placed to command shipping passing from the Indian Ocean to the Pacific.* COURTESY: SHELL PHOTOGRAPHIC UNIT

Politics have tended to take on an ethnic character and to resolve themselves into a contest between Malay and Chinese. The presumed threat to the well-being of the Malays—very much the less aggressive people—was a factor which increased the reluctance of the British to hand over power to the local peoples, and it is a reason for the continued separate position of Singapore. The inclusion of Singapore within the Malayan Federation would give the Chinese an over-all majority; as it is, they are left with political control of Singapore alone. This rather unsatisfactory compromise may be upset in the near future by the creation of a broader federation to include not only Malaya itself but also Singapore and the present British possessions in Borneo.

The Case of Israel: The state of Israel present a special problem. The Jews are a mainly European people who claim that in migrating to Israel they are returning to their ancestral home. The Diaspora, or scattering of the Jews over the face of the earth, coupled with the persecutions which they suffered, led to a desire to return to their Promised Land. The modern Zionist movement was founded at the end of the nineteenth century by Theodor Herzl, but it did not become politically significant until 1917. In that year Arthur Balfour, the British Foreign Secretary, sent a note to Chaim Weizmann, leader of the Jewish Zionist Organization, undertaking on behalf of the British government to exert himself at the end of the First World War to establish in Palestine "a national home for the Jewish people." In 1920 the United Kingdom was entrusted by the League of Nations with the mandate for Palestine, on the condition that it fulfill the terms of the Balfour Note. This the British did, but with characteristic slowness and caution.

At the time when the mandate was given to the United Kingdom, Palestine was a dry, infertile, neglected country, inhabited mainly by Arabs, and suffering from centuries of neglect by the Turkish government. The population then numbered about 750,000. Undoubtedly the land was capable of supporting more, but there could be a large Jewish immigration only at the expense of changes both in the way of life of the Arabs and in the capital investment in agriculture. The British attempted, therefore, to restrict and control Jewish immigration and to prevent it from running ahead of the development of resources. The British were too cautious; the Jews and their supporters, too optimistic. Up to the outbreak of the Second World War, about 300,000 had migrated to Palestine. The British authorities were thinking in terms of partitioning the area into Jewish and Arab states and were careful always to reserve enough land for the Arabs. Partition plans broke down. When the war was over, there was a flood of Jews seeking to leave Europe for their Promised Land. A three-cornered struggle developed between the Jews, whose object was to make Palestine a Jewish state, the Arabs, trying to maintain their position in a country that was as much their home as it was that of

the Jews, and the British authorities, trying to maintain a balance between Jew and Arab and to moderate the ardor of both.

Under these conditions British rule ended in 1948; much of the hill country of Judea was annexed by Transjordan, which then assumed its present name of Jordan, and the Gaza "Strip" was occupied by Egypt. Almost 1 million Arab refugees fled from Israel into Jordan, Egypt, and other Arab states of the Middle East. The state of Israel was established and in 1950, by legislative enactment, ruled that "every Jew shall be entitled to come to Israel as an immigrant." Since the end of the Second World War considerably over 1 million Jews have come to Israel, most of them from central and eastern Europe. About 216,000 non-Jews, most of them Arabs, have remained, making up (in 1958) about 10 per cent of the total population.

The conflict of Jew and Arab was for a long period an internal problem of Palestine. The Jews are now so firmly in control that this has ceased to be the case. The problem has become an external one. The fierce hostility toward Israel of her Arab neighbors, Jordan, the United Arab Republic, and, though to a lesser degree, Lebanon, is the central fact in Middle Eastern politics. And this bitterness is exacerbated, on the one side by a million unassimilated Arab refugees, on the other by the unwillingness of the United Arab Republic to negotiate a treaty of peace with Israel. The Israeli problem, like that of the Chinese in Malaya, and the Indians in East Africa and Natal, is basically that of an immigrant people unable to be assimilated by the local population.

The Poor White: In most instances the non-European peoples, whose migration and settlement we have just considered, came to their new homes because there was a labor shortage there. The immigrants possessed skills or aptitudes not found locally. They were employed on railroads and plantations and in mines. They came from densely populated countries, where land was valuable and wages were low. In their new homes they still, in general, constituted cheap labor. We have briefly surveyed the political and economic conflicts that have arisen from the competition of these immigrants with the local peoples. No less significant is their conflict with immigrant European peoples. Most of the immigrant non-Europeans perform unskilled or semiskilled work. It is sometimes assumed that most Europeans serve in a technical or managerial capacity. This is, in fact, not the case. All European societies contain a proportion of people whose occupation can at best be only semiskilled. In South, Central, and East Africa the lowest social fringe of the white population is in direct competition with non-European. The living standards and wage rates of the latter are low and thus carry down with them the corresponding levels of the whites. To some extent this has happened in the American South, though here the standards of the Negroes have been raised far more than those of the whites have been depressed. This has not been the case in South and Central Africa, or in parts of the Portuguese and Spanish Empires, or in parts of Latin America.

The "poor whites" are the white peoples who, in the conditions of these plural societies, are obliged to compete for their livelihood with the colored, and not infrequently to compete unsuccessfully owing to their poorer physiological adaptation to the climate of the tropics.

The poor white is a social rather than a political problem. He is, irrationally though perhaps naturally, opposed to all ideas of racial equality. He usually supports racial segregation and white supremacy.

The mainsprings of his racial feelings, however they may be disguised or explained, are basically economic. The solution to the poor-white problem is to remove the plural structure of society and to assimilate the colored to the level of the white.

The White-Australia Policy: When Europeans discovered it, Australia was a vast and almost empty continent, with a small native population, quite unable to satisfy the exacting demands of white farmers and plantation owners. Northern Australia is intertropical, and its climate, especially in Queensland, is hot, humid, and suited to the growth of sugar cane, rice, and cotton, but not always to the health of peoples of European origin. As settlers, mainly of British extraction, spread over the grasslands of New South Wales and Victoria, attempts were made to supply them with sugar and other tropical products from the coastlands of Queensland. These became successful when, in the 1860s, Kanakas, or South Sea Islanders, were brought in to do the heavy manual labor.

Figure 62 *The only thing that is unique in this scene in the sugar fields is that all the workers are white. The photograph was taken in the Bundaberg district of southern Queensland.* COURTESY: AUSTRALIAN NEWS AND INFORMATION BUREAU

Most of the Kanakas were indentured laborers, and some were slaves in all except name. They spread from the sugar fields, where they had no competitors, to sheep and cattle farms, where they competed with whites, and opposition to their immigration grew. Australian self-respect revolted "against a thinly veneered slave-trading; political democracy feared the effect on free institutions of a race incapable of an equal franchise; the working classes to a man fought against the menace of lower wages and restricted employment." [12] But northern Queensland, it was claimed, could be developed only with colored labor. Whenever the movement gained strength for banning the use of Kanaka labor, a secession movement made headway in northern Queensland. The circumstances were remarkably similar to those which existed in the United States a few decades earlier. In 1890 the further importation of Kanakas was declared to be illegal. At once the secession movement in northern Queensland gained momentum. But the British government was unsympathetic to it, and the Australian government claimed that it could develop tropical Queensland with white labor. Opposition to Kanaka labor increased, and the old-style Queensland sugar plantations, reminiscent of the cotton plantations of the Old South, gradually disappeared.

The white-Australia policy was gradually formulated. After its formation in 1901 the Commonwealth government made available funds for the repatriation of the Kanakas, and the Colonial Sugar Refining Company undertook to work its plantations with white labor. The Kanakas had been brought to Australia by the Australians themselves. A graver threat to white supremacy was the possibility of the immigration of Indians and Chinese. In fact,

[12] *Cambridge History of the British Empire*, vol. 7, pt. i, *Australia*, p. 309.

one of the factors favoring federation was the knowledge that only a federal law would be likely to be successful in excluding Asiatics. In the words of Deakin, later Federal Prime Minister, the people demanded that "we should be one people, and remain one people, without the admixture of other races." An immigration law was enacted for the purpose of restricting the right of entry to peoples of European background. All would-be immigrants were subjected to a literacy test. At first the law required that this should be in English, but this was later amended to "any prescribed language." It was not difficult to select a language which an unwanted immigrant would not possibly be able to understand.

The white-Australia policy has been successful in its immediate objective. In 1933, the total population of non-European origin, excluding the Australian aborigines, was under twenty-three thousand, of whom about a half were Chinese. A rather smaller number was made up of half-castes. Thus only one person in more than two hundred had even a trace of non-European ancestry. Yet this result has been achieved at a price, of which the high cost of sugar in Australia is only a symptom. Agricultural development in northern Australia is with white labor, and white labor in Australia is highly paid. Not only is the domestic sugar highly protected and very expensive; so also are other tropical products from the Queensland coastlands. The north of Australia is underpopulated and underdeveloped. Resources are lying unused, while to the north and northwest lie the overcrowded lands of India and China. It is irrelevant to say that, if Australia were to open her doors to Asiatics, she could not take enough of them to make an appreciable difference to the population pressure in South and East Asia. These countries have long cast longing eyes on the empty lands of Australia, and if the fortunes of war had gone differently between 1942 and 1945, Chinese farmers might now be growing rice along the shores of the Gulf of Carpentaria.

THE UNDERDEVELOPED NATIONS

The confused ethnic patterns and the rivalries and conflicts between ethnic groups that have been brought together mainly as a result of European imperialism are only one of the problems that confront the new states that are emerging from colonialism. Another is their lack of capital for economic development. This is not to say that colonial powers deliberately neglected the economic development of their colonies, merely that this development was one-sided. Most colonial powers for a long period looked upon their colonies as sources of primary commodities, notably of foodstuffs, of industrial raw materials o` vegetable origin, and of minerals. Factories were established and transportation networks constructed, but the object of these was primarily the preparation and marketing of raw materials. In general manufacturing industries were not actively discouraged, but capital was not readily made available for their establishment. The tendency was implicit among colonial powers for them to look on colonies as markets for their manufactured goods and sources of their raw materials.

Colonies are far from being the only territories that have been starved of capital for economic development. Many countries which never in fact constituted colonial dependencies nonetheless remained poor and underdeveloped. Most of the countries of eastern Europe, southern Europe with the exception of Italy, Turkey, Iran, Afghanistan, and Thailand in Asia,

Figure 63 *This mural, on a building in the University of Mexico City, represents the ideal of all plural societies. It depicts the European Spanish (right) and Mexican Indian (left) peoples merged to form the Mexican people (center). The realization of this ideal still lies far in the future.* PHOTOGRAPH BY N. J. G. POUNDS

Ethiopia and Liberia in Africa, and most of Latin America[13] belong to this category.

During the nineteenth century such territories as these attracted investment capital for the building of docks and railroads, for geological prospecting and the equipment of mines, but not, as a general rule, for the building up of industry, except for the necessary processing of domestic raw materials. Though these were sovereign states, their economic status was more closely analogous to that of colonial dependencies. The industrial development of

[13] Latin America remained colonial until the early years of the nineteenth century, but its republics have been independent long enough to be included in a category different from that of the new states of Africa.

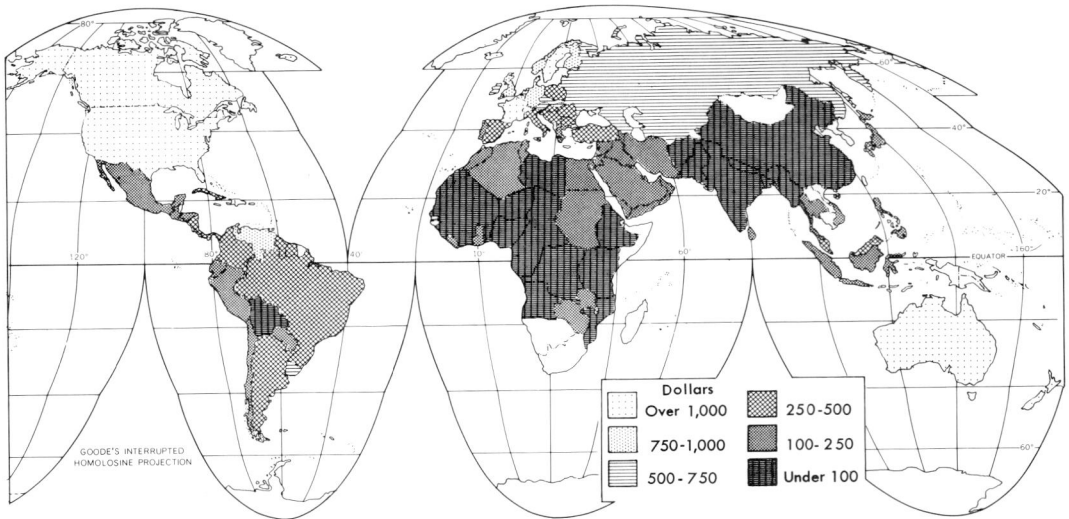

Dollars

Over 1,000   250-500

750-1,000   100-250

500-750   Under 100

GOODE'S INTERRUPTED
HOMOLOSINE PROJECTION

Exhibit 106   *World map of national income statistics.*

Latin America presents an interesting case study. The stimulus to industrial development was, in the words of Lloyd J. Hughlett:

. . . external in nature and was founded on a pressing world need for Latin-American raw materials, rather than stemming from a home market and domestic manufacturing. New industries and plants sprang up following the First World War. However, the impetus in the years immediately following 1918 proved inadequate for converting sufficient capital and business from the traditional outlets of agriculture and mining into the manufacturing facilities that had taken root in many of the countries.[14]

The slight extent and the one-sided nature of industrial development both in Latin America and in other underdeveloped countries spring mainly from the lack of investment capital. And foreign capital has not been made available in Latin America, as, for instance, it has in Australia or Canada, because a market of sufficient size was

[14] Lloyd J. Hughlett (ed.), *Industrialization of Latin America*, McGraw-Hill Book Company, Inc., New York, 1946, p. 4.

not foreseen for the products of industry. This smallness of the local market is directly connected with the poverty and the low technical level of most of the predominantly agricultural populations in underdeveloped countries.

The Measurement of Underdevelopment: It is very difficult indeed to form any estimate of the degree of underdevelopment in the more backward countries of the world. Economic advance is a function of resources, capital, education and skill, initiative, and other factors, none of which is susceptible of precise measurement. The map of national income statistics (Exhibit 106) affords the most readily available measure, but it is only a very rough one. Its statistical basis is highly unreliable for the poorest countries and ignores the fact that these areas are very much less dependent upon a money economy than the more advanced. Services which earn no monetary reward, such as the labor of the peasant farmer and the mutual assistance afforded by members of the village community to one another, are most difficult to evaluate. Table 27 shows the lower half of the map

TABLE 27 *National Income of Certain Underdeveloped Countries*

State or area	National income per head, local currency	National income per head, United States dollars
United States	$2,110	2,110
United Kingdom	£342	958
Puerto Rico	$473	473
Ireland	£163	456
Cyprus	£142	398
Cuba	362 pesos	362
Union of South Africa		342
Costa Rica	1,713 colones	302
Spain	13,010 pesetas	282
Panama	262 balboas	262
Mexico	2,927 pesos	236
Portugal	5,662 escudos	198
Philippines	387 pesos	194
Turkey	1,076 Turkish pounds	188
Iraq	62 dinars	173
Honduras	331 lempiras	165
Guatemala	162 quetzales	162
Colombia	914 pesos	150
Ecuador	2,502 sucres	144
Vietnam	4,837 piasters	138
Rhodesia and Nyasaland	£44	123
Ceylon	553 Ceylon rupees	116
Peru	2,223 soles	111
Cambodia	2,767 riel	79
Congo	3,689 francs	74
Nigeria	£24	67
India	289 Indian rupees	61
Pakistan	247 Pakistani rupees	52
Burma	227 kyat	48

SOURCE: *National Income Statistics, 1958*, United Nations, New York.

of national incomes, though not all the underdeveloped countries are included. All countries listed here may be regarded as in some degree underdeveloped, and the United States and United Kingdom are added for purposes of comparison.

The significance of this table in the context of this book lies in the fact that people in these countries are poor. A century or more ago this fact might not have had much political significance, because the people would not have had standards by which to judge their poverty. Today they have, and, furthermore, they are convinced that the condition in which they find themselves can be remedied. In the words of a report recently presented to a Senate committee:

One of the greatest social consequences of the technological revolution is the idea that starvation and poverty are no longer inevitable. For most of men's history the welfare of the masses depended on the harvest. . . . Not their efforts but the will of the gods determined men's lot on earth. The technological revolution has forever banished this passive response to material welfare. Thinking people in all lands start from the assumption that if poverty exists, it is not because of the gods but because of men's ignorance or lack of will. Since it is believed to be within the competence of man to change man's fate, the task of changing it has become one of the deepest obligations of the political and intellectual leaders of every underdeveloped country.[15]

Today citizens of the underdeveloped countries look upon all Americans as wealthy and upon most Europeans as only a degree poorer than the Americans. They want aid—technical and financial—from the more advanced countries and in recent years have come to assume that they will receive it. They expect living standards to be leveled upwards; they hope that they too may come to enjoy that "freedom from want" which they have assumed to be the birthright of the more advanced nations, and some of them suspect that their own poverty is a consequence of some ill-defined exploitation by the more advanced states.

The underdeveloped countries are not powerful in the sense that they are able to formulate policy and implement it irrespective of the desires and interests of other states. But they do have political importance. Most have a vote in the UN. Some are strategically located and could thus constitute a valuable ally to one or other of the Great Power blocs. Economic and technical aid to underdeveloped countries undoubtedly springs in part from the

humanitarian desire to improve the level of human welfare, but undoubtedly it is strongly influenced by the desire to enlist their sympathies and win their friendship. But friendship is difficult to buy, and allies can be easily lost as soon as a monetary value is placed upon cooperation. The United States has been by far the largest dispenser of aid to underdeveloped countries, but she has not always acquired friends in return for her material assistance. In many instances she has at best closed a door to a potential enemy. This issue has been clearly put by Buchanan and Ellis:

The United States cannot stand idly by and witness the recruitment of the populous countries of Asia and perhaps even of Africa and Latin America to Communism. Not that the United States can purchase friendship or political allies by its loans, grants, or technical aid; for the gratitude of the recipient countries may be strongly tinged with injured pride or suspicion, and at best will be only transitory. Rather, the guiding fact is that a country of satisfactory material well-being is rarely, if ever, a voluntary convert to the ranks of Communism. Even if the level of living is painfully low, if there is a reasonable chance of betterment, if the way to economic progress seems to lie open, if, in short, there is hope of satisfying national and personal feelings of worth and dignity, it is unlikely that these cravings will impel a country to sacrifice its independence to a foreign monster.[16]

More succinctly, the Maxwell Graduate School's report on *United States Foreign Policy* declared that:

If the non-Communist nations fail to achieve adequate rates of economic growth, more and more people will be persuaded by the arguments of the Communists and more and more of the world will fall prey to Communist political systems. It is clear where the

[15] *United States Foreign Policy: A Study Prepared at the Request of the Committee on Foreign Relations, U.S. Senate, by Maxwell Graduate School,* Government Printing Office, 1959, p. 15.

[16] Norman S. Buchanan and Howard S. Ellis, *Approaches to Economic Development,* The Twentieth Century Fund, Inc., New York, 1955, p. 429.

obligations of all freemen lie; it is to do every-thing in their power to help the underdevel-oped countries abolish their poverty so that they can choose freedom without having to pay the price of hunger.[17]

The Direction of American Aid: The improvement of the level of human welfare has been the guiding idea in American over-seas investment in recent years. To a lesser extent it has influenced British, French, German, and other capital-exporting coun-tries. The political power that can be made to result—it might be added—has un-doubtedly been the only important factor influencing the direction of Soviet overseas investment and also that of the satellites of the Soviet Union.

Humanitarian feelings would lead the United States to give aid to *all* underde-veloped areas. Shortage of resources leads to the limitation of this aid to those areas where it will be politically—as distinct from economically and socially—most ef-fective. Unquestionably, Paraguay, for ex-ample, is a poor and backward country which could benefit greatly from American technical aid. The countries of western Europe are economically and technically more advanced and, even after six years of war, possessed a higher standard of living than Paraguay; yet it was the former, and not the humble Latin-American re-public, that received American aid on a massive scale. This can be explained in terms of close American ties of sentiment and friendship with Europe and of Amer-ica's desire to rebuild the economy of an important trading partner. But the funda-mental reason is political and strategic, the desire to attach the countries of western Europe firmly and indissolubly to the Amer-ican cause and to prevent their great re-sources and industries from falling into the hands of the opposite camp. Paraguay was

[17] *United States Foreign Policy*, 1959, p. 16.

thought to be less threatened by commu-nism, perhaps because it is geographically more remote from the Soviet Union.

Most of the American capital invest-ment in and technical aid to underdevel-oped countries is handled by governmental agencies. These have assumed many forms since the end of the Second World War. Some aid was canalized through the United Nations Relief and Rehabilitation Admin-istration (UNRRA), which operated in the years immediately following the Second World War; some by the Interim Aid Pro-gram and the Greece-Turkey Aid Program. Aid to Europe consequent upon the ac-ceptance of the Marshall Plan by the western European nations was adminis-tered by the European Recovery Program. Other administrative machinery was set up to give aid to China and Korea. The Technical Cooperation Program, known also as the Point Four Program, was author-ized in 1950 "to help raise standards of living in less developed areas through the extension of technical knowledge and skills." In 1952 these and other programs were combined by the Mutual Security Act into a single program. Its purpose was declared in the terms of the act to be:

. . . to maintain the security and promote the foreign policy of the United States by autho-rizing military, economic and technical assist-ance to friendly countries to strengthen the mutual security and individual and collective defenses of the free world, to develop their resources in the interest of their security and independence and the national interest of the United States and to facilitate the effective participation of these countries in the United Nations system for collective security.

Nowhere has the subordination of eco-nomic aid to political ends been expressed more clearly and succinctly.

Published figures shown in the table divide the aid provided into military and nonmilitary assistance, with the latter accounting for slightly over half the total.

	1948–1954	Total to 1959
Military assistance..........	18,588	25,994
Nonmilitary assistance......	18,227	26,488

SOURCE: *U.S. Statistical Abstract, 1959, 1960*, in millions of dollars.

Nonmilitary aid consists in part of outright grants of food and materials to relieve present suffering, but much of it can be regarded as technical aid or capital investment. The greater part has been allocated to specific countries, so that a fairly precise picture of the geographical distribution of American aid is possible. By major regions, nonmilitary aid in the period 1948–1958 has been distributed as follows:

	In thousands of dollars
Far East...............	4,812,360
Near East	2,491,680
South Asia.............	955,513
Africa.................	184,855
Europe.................	14,894,792
Latin America..........	325,380

SOURCE: Based on *U.S. Statistical Abstract, 1959.*

In addition to these sums which have been allocated to specific areas, a considerable sum has been allocated to what is termed "interregional" projects. These include programs as varied as malaria eradication, aid to Hungarian refugees and other escapees from Communist eastern Europe, and the sending of Christmas packages. Such interregional expenditures during the same period amounted to over five hundred million dollars.

The map (Exhibit 107) shows the distribution of aid under the Mutual Security Program and its predecessors during the period 1948–1958. A comparison of this map with that of military alliances (NATO, CENTO, SEATO, etc.) (Exhibit 100) shows their basic similarity. The bulk of nonmilitary aid has gone to those states which at the time were common members with the United States of mutual defense pacts. This is only the implementation of the expressed aims of the program of maintaining simultaneously military preparedness and conditions of prosperity in those countries which were thought to be potential allies of the United States and at the same time vulnerable to communism. The criterion was, in the main, geographical. Turkey and Greece were clearly in the right place at the right time to receive liberal technical aid; the republics of Latin America were not. That semicircle of states which almost encircles the Russian heartland received, for reasons that are obvious, the greater part of the aid under this program. But recent events in Africa and in Latin America may lead to a reevaluation of their relative importance in the geography of strategy.

The United Kingdom has similarly given assistance to underdeveloped countries, especially those which belong to the Commonwealth. The scale has been very much smaller and the political motivation somewhat less conspicuous.

The Communist countries have also given such aid to underdeveloped countries (Exhibit 108):

Soviet bloc economic activity has taken the form of an increase in trade and in credits to the underdeveloped countries. The overall magnitudes are not large compared with those of the Western World. For example, total Soviet bloc non-military loan commitments made to all underdeveloped countries amounted by the end of 1958 to about $1.6 billion, of which only about $400 million had actually been disbursed by that date.[18]

[18] *Ibid.*, p. 23.

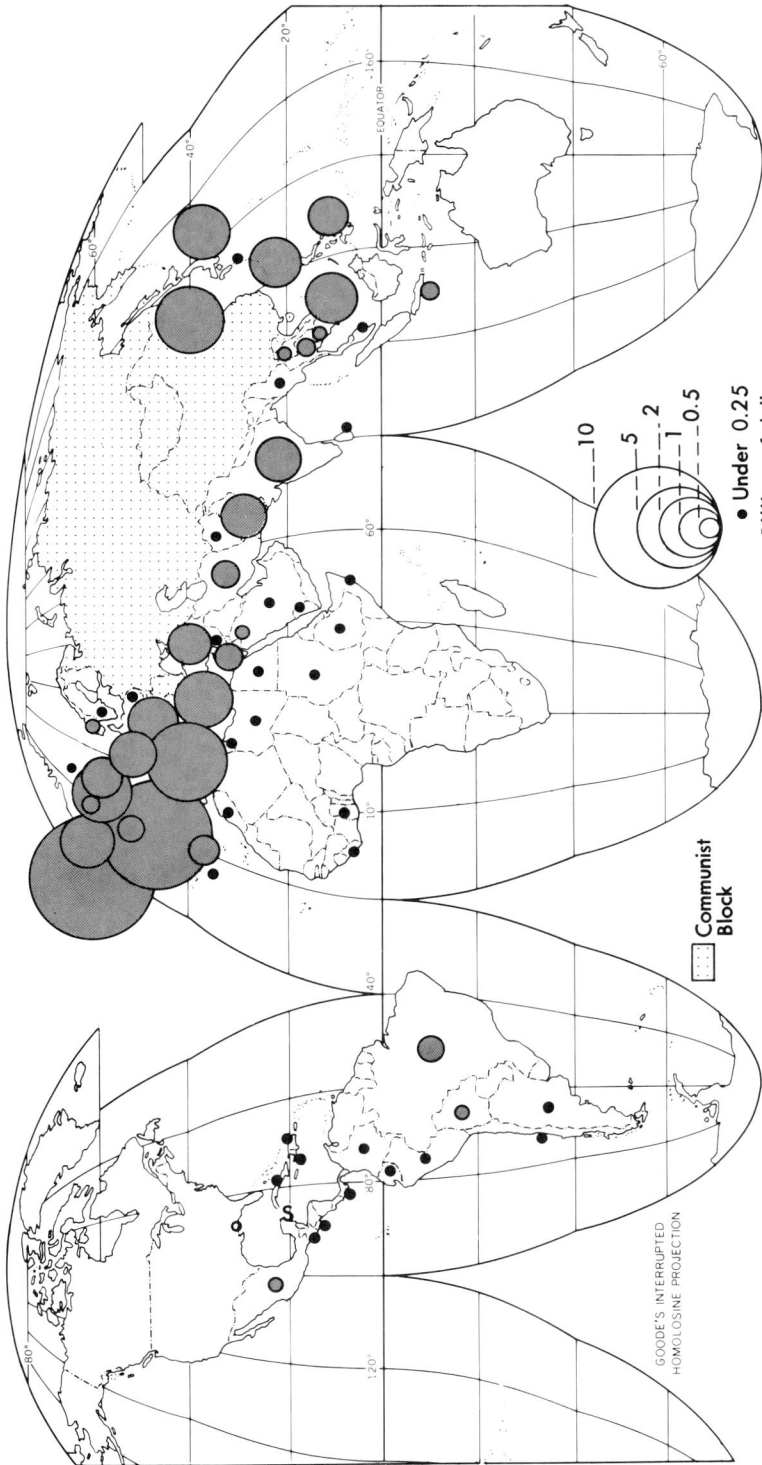

Exhibit 107 *World map: distribution of United States nonmilitary foreign aid.*

Communist
Block

10
5
2
1
0.5

• Under 0.25

Billions of dollars.

GOODE'S INTERRUPTED
HOMOLOSINE PROJECTION

EQUATOR

379

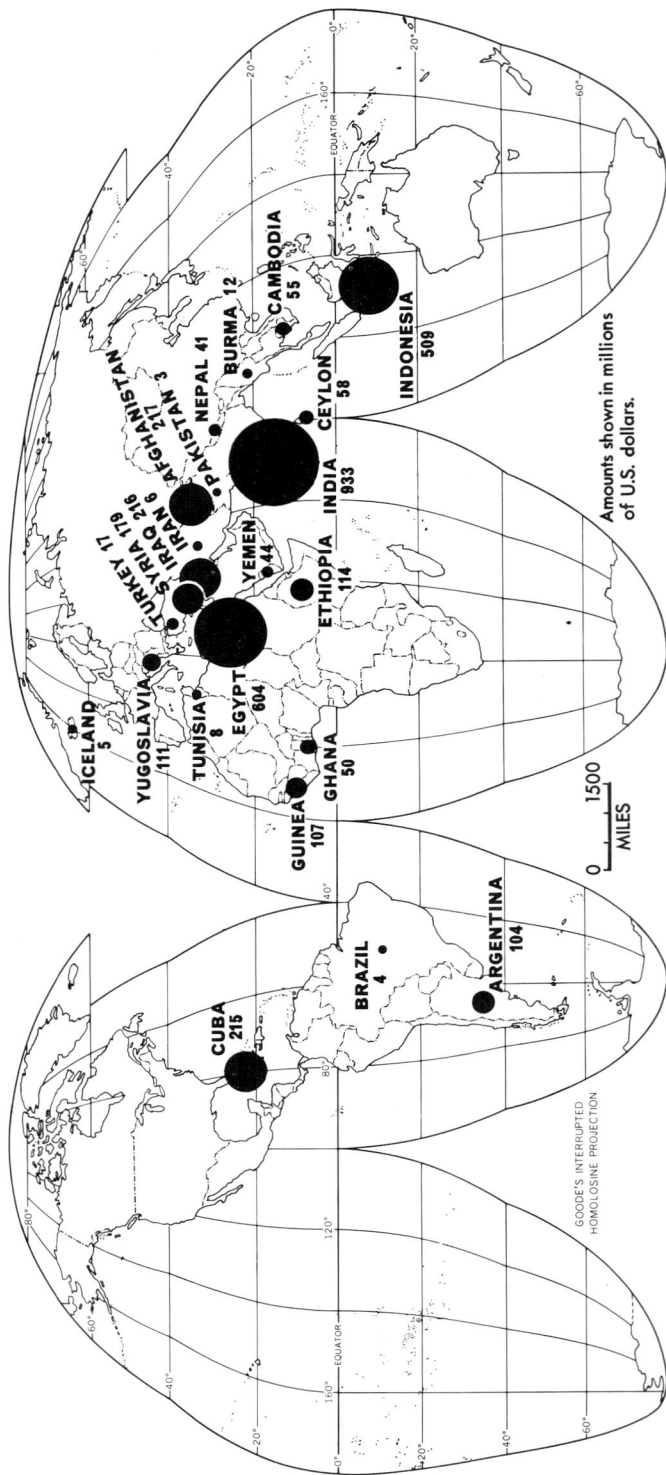

Exhibit 108 *World map: distribution of U.S.S.R. foreign aid.*

Amounts shown in millions
of U.S. dollars.

ICELAND 5
YUGOSLAVIA 111
TURKEY 17
SYRIA 179
IRAQ 216
IRAN 8
AFGHANISTAN 277
PAKISTAN 3
NEPAL 41
BURMA 12
CAMBODIA 55
INDONESIA 509
CEYLON 58
INDIA 933
YEMEN 44
EGYPT 604
TUNISIA 8
ETHIOPIA 114
GHANA 50
GUINEA 107

CUBA 215
BRAZIL 4
ARGENTINA 104

0   1500
MILES

GOODE'S INTERRUPTED
HOMOLOSINE PROJECTION

Figure 64 *The World Bank invests in capital development projects which may be expected to yield a return within a very few years. This is a road being built in Japan with the help of a loan from the Bank.* COURTESY: INTERNATIONAL BANK FOR RECONSTRUCTION AND DEVELOPMENT

There is, of course, a danger that a country that comes to depend on Soviet economic aid will in time be obliged to subordinate its policy to that of the Soviet Union. It should be remembered, however, that such a price has been demanded by the Soviet Union on only one occasion and that then the recipient of Soviet aid, namely, Yugoslavia, rebelled against Soviet political domination. If capital investment in an underdeveloped country tends ultimately to raise the living standards, it should be welcomed. "We must," in the words of the Maxwell Graduate School's report, "have sufficient confidence in our own policies to welcome Soviet trade and loans when they do contribute to the economic welfare of other countries, and draw attention to their shortcomings when they do not." [19] The former should be regarded as contributing to stability and, thus to peace.

[19] *Ibid.*, p. 24.

World Bank: It would be unfortunate if aid to underdeveloped countries were conditional only upon political exigencies. Aid and investment, as part of governmental policy, cannot be divorced from the political situation, but poverty is as acute and suffering as great in countries of little strategic value as in those close to the Iron Curtain. The most important organization for international investment without political overtones and conditions is the *International Bank for Reconstruction and Development*. It was created in 1944 and began to operate two years later. Its object is to increase production and improve living standards. It operates as one of the Specialized Agencies of the United Nations with capital subscribed by member nations. Its criteria for investment are the worthwhileness of a project in terms of the fund's objectives, not its political desirability to one country or another. In the first twelve

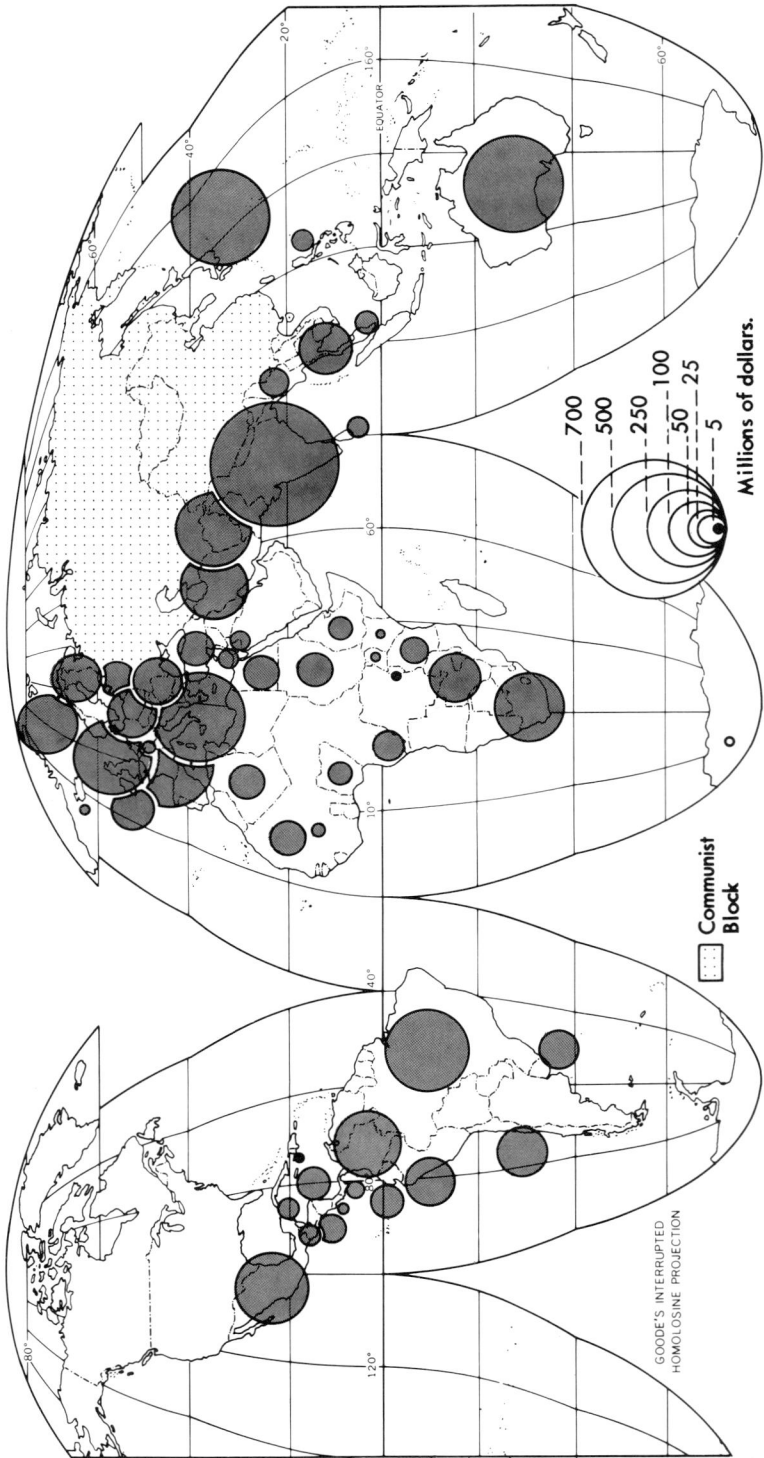

Exhibit 109 *World map: distribution of World Bank investment.*

Millions of dollars.

700
500
250
100
50
25
5

Communist
Block

GOODE'S INTERRUPTED
HOMOLOSINE PROJECTION

years of its existence, the Bank made 219 separate loans, distributed over no fewer than 49 countries. All projects financed by the Bank were of the nature of capital investment and included transportation and dock facilities, electric power generators, and factory and irrigation development. To receive support from the World Bank projects must be technically feasible and show evidence of being financially profitable. Loans by the Bank bear an interest for the duration of the loan and must be repaid at the end. A map of the World Bank's operations (Exhibit 109) differs sharply from that of the activities of the American Mutual Security Agency, because the distribution of investment projects has not been influenced significantly by political considerations.

Land Reform: Economic growth and the attainment of higher levels of welfare are wholly dependent upon technical aid and capital investment. In most underdeveloped countries there are other elements in their relative backwardness. The methods by which land is held are almost as important as the means by which it is cultivated, and land reform has commonly been a necessary prelude to the improvement of agriculture and the increase of crop yields. Private ownership of land or, at least, the assurance of continued tenancy is conducive to initiative on the part of the farmer. The consolidation of farm holdings into large lots and the creation of farms of economic size are also necessary if farm incomes in the underdeveloped countries are to be increased. Such land reform does not usually go unopposed, however apparent may be its advantages to the economy as a whole. Resistance comes from the greater landowners and the richer peasants, whose security is threatened by the dismemberment of their estates; it comes, also, from the conservatism, prejudice, and superstition of the peasant, to whom the ways

of his ancestors are good enough for him. Not unrelated to the problem of land reform is that of the prevention of soil erosion. There are few parts of the world where soil erosion is not an imminent danger, and the technical reforms in agriculture—the creation of larger fields and perhaps the greater use of mechanical equipment—will increase the danger of losing the topsoil through the action of wind or rainwash.

The overcoming of such resistance to change is a political matter. In no country has a land reform of any kind gone unopposed, both by those who stood ultimately to gain and by those who might expect to lose. Such internal reforms—or the lack of them—are a matter of concern to other states in so far as they affect internal stability and welfare, and thus political policy and power. It is no accident that in Spain, before the Franco revolution, anarchism and other extremist ideologies were most active in those parts in which the greater part of the land was held in great estates by absentee landlords.[20]

Land reform programs often induce changes that are both economically important and politically popular; their consistent support in many places would help identify the United States as promoting progress rather than defending the status quo. . . . The United States might well plan to commit a sizable sum each year to help reorganize land use in the world's less developed areas, and entrust to the United Nations (through the Food and Agricultural Organization and the U.N.'s regional economic commissions) the working out of detailed plans for the application of these funds.[21]

Internal reform in most underdeveloped countries should supplement external aid. In not a few instances—the loans of the

[20] Gerald Brennan, *Spanish Labyrinth,* Cambridge University Press, New York, 1943.

[21] *United States Foreign Policy,* 1959, p. 35.

Figure 65 *The Kariba Dam, on the Zambezi River in Southern Rhodesia, has been financed by the World Bank and is one of the most ambitious development projects in Africa.* COURTESY: UNITED NATIONS

World Bank for irrigation development in the Punjab, for example—aid has been made conditional on an improvement in the social and political conditions in the area.

The Underdeveloped Nations and Neutralism: With an almost monotonous regularity the newly appointed prime ministers of the new nations proclaim, first, that they intend to develop their countries and, second, that they will accept aid from any source that may offer it. This has occasionally been the prelude to a tussle between the states already "developed," for the privilege of helping the more backward. Occasionally, a new state has been, as it were, captured by the West or the East, as Pakistan, Thailand, and Lebanon have by the West and Cuba and Afghanistan by the East. Other states, perhaps wiser and more wary than these, have trodden a middle path, avoiding an exclusive dependence on either side, and accepting aid from both, with appropriate gestures of good will all round. India and the uncommitted nations of Africa belong to this group. By their policy of neutralism they perhaps avoid the attachment of political strings to the economic aid which they receive. Perhaps, by playing one side against the other, as Afghanistan and Egypt seemed for a time to do, they think they can obtain more aid.

There has been relatively little co-operation and collaboration between these underdeveloped and uncommitted nations. A group of them met at Bandung, in Indonesia, in 1955, to discuss policy. More recently a group of uncommitted states held a conference at Casablanca, in Morocco. In September, 1961, another group of such neutralist countries was represented at a meeting at Belgrade, Yugoslavia. No kind of permanent organization, or even coherent policy, has emerged from any of these meetings. Although it became clear that the neutralist states could be useful to the Western and Eastern blocs, it became clear also that collectively they are too weak to influence significantly the policy of the two major power blocs. The list of states which were represented at Belgrade constitutes a kind of nucleus of a possible uncommitted bloc:

Afghanistan	Ethiopia
Burma	Ghana
Cambodia	Guinea
Congo (Léopoldville)	India
Cyprus	Indonesia
Egypt	Yugoslavia

Even if this group could agree among itself on policy and methods and, further, be reinforced by other neutral-minded states, it still would not have the power to influence significantly the political acts of the major blocs. The neutralists will continue to be wooed by both sides, to accept help from both West and East, and to hope that in time they may acquire the power and the standing to be a major voice in the councils of the nations.

Conclusion: The improvement of the level of human welfare is a matter of deep concern, not merely to those peoples whose standards are low, but also to those with the highest. All parts of the world and all peoples are so closely interknit that the privileged and the unprivileged cannot live side by side without danger to the former. The highest national incomes per capita are based upon factory production, which is most successful when it is carried out on a massive scale. The developed countries need markets, which the peoples of the underdeveloped world could supply if their purchasing power were increased. The imperialisms of the nineteenth century were to some degree attempts to use the purchasing power of the dependent territories in the service of the industries of the imperial powers. But the imperialists' policy of using the purchasing power of colonies to absorb their own industrial surpluses tended, in general, to stereotype a pattern of industrial countries on the one hand and of agricultural and primary producers on the other. Such an international division of functions and responsibilities is dangerous. In times of slump or depression, the prices of agricultural and primary goods drop more sharply than those of manufactured goods, with social consequences that may be serious in the extreme. Partly for this reason some countries, some of the South American republics, Australia, and New Zealand among them, have attempted to diversify their economies by building up manufacturing industries. But in most underdeveloped countries the possession of industries, especially heavy industries, is a prestige symbol, conferring a sense of well-being and a feeling of equality with the more developed countries. Unquestionably the broadening of the economic base of such countries is desirable in itself. But the establishment of branches of industry for which the country has few or none of the raw materials and in which it is likely to become a relatively high-cost producer solves no problems. Very few of the less developed countries, for example, have the geographical capacity to operate successfully an iron and steelworks; yet the prestige and the sense of power which such an industry is thought to confer appear to be leading a number of underdeveloped countries to consider building one.

There is a danger that development in some of the underdeveloped countries will be influenced by the illusion of power and prestige to assume forms that in the long run are unwise. The danger is no less great that the direction of overseas investment by the developed powers will be influenced unduly by political considerations. Given the "revolution of rising expectations" which has characterized the last generation, there are now no areas and no peoples without hopes of improved conditions. To disappoint these expectations anywhere is to take a political risk, because communism may be encouraged to perform what the non-Communist world has failed to do.

BIBLIOGRAPHY

Bowles, Chester: *Ideas, People and Peace,* Harper & Brothers, New York, 1958.

Buchanan, Norman S., and Howard S. Ellis: *Approaches to Economic Development,* The Twentieth Century Fund, Inc., New York, 1955.

Church, R. J. Harrison: *Modern Colonization,* Hutchinson University Library, London, 1951.

Emerson, Rupert: *From Empire to Nation,* Harvard University Press, Cambridge, Mass., 1960.

Foreign Aid Program: Compilation of Studies and Surveys Prepared under the Direction of the Special Committee to Study the Foreign Aid Program, U.S. Senate, 1957.

Galbraith, John Kenneth: *Economic Development in Perspective,* Harvard University Press, Cambridge, Mass., 1962.

Ginsburg, Norton: *Atlas of Economic Development,* University of Chicago Press, Chicago, 1961.

Ginsburg, Norton (ed.): *Essays on Geography and Economic Development,* University of Chicago, Department of Geography, Research Paper 62, 1960.

Hirschman, Albert O.: *The Strategy of Economic Development,* Yale University Press, New Haven, Conn., 1958.

Hoffmann, Paul G.: *One Hundred Countries— One and One Quarter Billion People,* Committee for International Economic Growth, Washington, D.C., 1960.

Hughlett, Lloyd J. (ed.): *Industrialization of Latin America,* McGraw-Hill Book Company, Inc., New York, 1946.

Kimble, George H. T.: *Tropical Africa,* The Twentieth Century Fund, Inc., New York, 1960.

Murdock, G. P.: *Africa: its Peoples and their Culture History,* McGraw-Hill Book Co., Inc., New York, 1959.

Myrdal, Gunnar: *Rich Lands and Poor: The Road to World Prosperity,* Harper & Brothers, New York, 1957.

National Income Statistics, United Nations, New York.

Nigeria: Report of the Commission Appointed to Enquire into the Fears of the Minorities and the Means of Allaying Them, Cmnd. 505, H. M. Stationery Office, London, 1956.

Rostow, Walter W.: *The Stages of Economic Growth,* Cambridge University Press, Cambridge, 1960.

Theobald, Robert: *The Rich and the Poor,* Mentor Books, New York, 1961.

United States Foreign Policy: A Study Prepared at the Request of the Committee on Foreign Relations, U.S. Senate, by Maxwell Graduate School, Syracuse University, U.S. Government Printing Office, 1959.

15 THE POLITICAL PATTERN OF

THE WORLD

It appears to me . . . that in the present decade we are for the first time in a position to attempt, with some degree of completeness, a correlation between the larger geographical and the larger historical generalizations.   H. J. MACKINDER

One intellectual excitement has . . . been denied me. Men wiser and more learned than I have discerned in history a plot, a rhythm, a predetermined pattern. These harmonies are concealed from me. I see only one emergency following upon another as wave follows upon wave, only one great fact with respect to which, since it is unique, there can be no generalizations, only one safe rule for the historian: that he should recognize in the development of human destinies the play of the contingent and the unforeseen.   H. A. L. FISHER

IN THE LAST CHAPTER WE INTRODUCED A GEOGRAPHICAL PATTERN INTO the interplay of national policies. We saw a vast, semicircular land area, all of it under Communist control, surrounded by a circle of states, all of them committed in varying degrees to the opposite political creed. This pattern has a simplicity and boldness which suggest that it is not merely the product of local or temporary circumstance and that the opposition of forces presented here results not merely from errors of political judgment. It has an air of permanence and inevitability that seems to put it beyond the range of influence of mere political decision.

387

VIEWS OF THE POLITICAL WORLD

Such a view is not new. In some form or other this apposition of an area, which approximates that which now comprises the Communist bloc and the encircling ring of states, had been foreshadowed in the analyses of Mackinder, Spykman, and others. Nor have these authors been the only ones to discern a geographical pattern in the changing fortunes of political societies and to see in the course of human history the unfolding of a plan as simple and as harmonious as it is inevitable. Such explanations are as old as the writing of history itself. To condense such views within the compass of a single chapter and to show their influence upon political thought and action are far too big a subject. There is space here to summarize in only the briefest terms a few of the more salient of such views of the political world and, furthermore, to limit this discussion only to those which relate political action to physical environment.

The Greek View of the Political World:
The Greek state, at least in the classical period, was small in area and its citizens so few that they could be gathered together in a single town meeting. The physical setting of the typical Greek city-state was described in Homer's Odyssey:

Along the shore of the gray sea there are soft water-meadows, where the vine would never wither; and there is plenty of land level enough for the plough, where they could count on cutting a deep crop at every harvest time, for the soil below the surface is exceedingly rich. Also it has a safe harbour, in which there is no occasion to tie up at all. You need neither cast anchor nor make fast with hausers. . . . Finally, at the head of the harbour there is a stream of fresh water, running out of a cave in a grove of poplar-trees.[1]

[1] Homer, *The Odyssey*, book IX, E. V. Rieu's translation, Penguin Classics, pp. 144–145.

There the Greeks could establish a small, self-sufficient city-state, and only in such a setting could those political virtues which the Greeks esteemed be cultivated. The Greeks detested and despised the despotisms of the Middle East, with which they were familiar. The reason for these contrasting political systems they found in the physical environments themselves. Hippocrates considered:

. . . the problem why the Asiatics are of a less warlike and a more tame disposition than the Europeans. The deficiency of spirit and courage observable in the human inhabitants of Asia has for its principal cause the low margin of seasonal variability in the temperature of that continent, which is approximately stable throughout the year. Such a climate does not produce those mental shocks and violent bodily dislocations which would naturally render the temperament ferocious and introduce a stronger current of irrationality and passion than would be the case under stable conditions. . . . Inhabitants of mountainous, rocky, well-watered country at a high altitude, where the margin of seasonal climatic variation is wide, will tend to have large-built bodies constitutionally adapted for courage and endurance. . . . Inhabitants of sultry hollows covered with water-meadows, who are more commonly exposed to warm winds than to cold . . . will—in contrast—not be large-built or slim, but thick-set, fleshy and dark-haired. . . . Courage and endurance will not be innate in their characters to the same degree.[2]

It is implicit in the classical writers that the free institutions of Greece could be supported and maintained only by a people of energy, spirit, and courage. Such institutions, therefore, should not be expected in the tropical lands of Asia.

[2] Hippocrates, *Influences of Atmosphere, Water and Situation*, book 16, as quoted by A. J. Toynbee, *Greek Historical Thought from Homer to the Age of Heraclius*, pp. 165–166.

The Determinist View: The Greek view of the state was highly determinist. The Greeks conceived of political institutions and political behavior as influenced or even controlled by their physical setting. Yet their view was highly general and naïve. Two aspects of the environment were thought of as dominant, climate and relief. A soft climate bred soft men, willing to submit to tyrants and lacking in the resolution to defend their liberties and privileges. A rugged terrain, thin-soiled and poor, bred a tough race, hardened by the daily struggle for survival. For over two thousand years political thought has borne, in some measure, the stamp which the Greeks gave it, and overtones of Greek thinking are with us still. It was only a few years ago that Carlo Sforza, the Italian Foreign Minister, explaining why he thought his country would never turn to communism, declared: "Communism is a creed of the plains; my country is mountainous." Geographical determinism assumes many shapes. There are those, like the Greeks, who regard relief and climate as the main determinants of political change. Man is held to respond involuntarily to the stimulus of his environment. He does not act consciously, and there is no place for perception and judgment in his response, any more than there is when we pick up a cold or acquire a sinus infection. Such views need little discussion. It may suffice to say that President Truman wisely did not trust to the rugged terrain of Greece and Turkey to prevent a Communist seizure of power in these countries. It is perhaps true that a mountainous terrain, with, in all probability, a low population density and relatively difficult communications, is a difficult area in which to organize political revolution and to maintain a strict governmental control. But there is nothing inherent in the nature of mountainous territory which makes it less vulnerable to commu-

nism than the plains. The romantic image of the freedom-loving mountaineer is so deeply etched in our minds that it is difficult to realize that it has little historical justification. Schiller's description of the Alps as

Das Haus der Freiheit [3]

or Wordsworth's lines:

> Two voices are there; one is of the sea,
> One of the mountains; each a mighty Voice:
> In both from age to age thou didst rejoice,
> They were thy chosen music, Liberty. [4]

present an appealing and romantic, though thoroughly fallacious, view. One must beware of allowing such illusions to influence political action and of assuming that the mountain state is inherently less likely to succumb to a totalitarian regime than one of deeper soil and more gentle relief.

Other writers have picked out yet other elements of the physical environment as the chief determinants of political change. Some have seen the political unification of France as a consequence of the direction of its river systems [5] and the convergence of rivers upon the Paris area. The lack of political unity in Germany before the last century has also been attributed to the physical diversity of the terrain. At best, such explanations emphasize a necessary—though not sufficient—element or factor in change; at worst, they attribute a causal function to phenomena which, in all probability, have no relevance whatever.

In part, at least, the Greeks had seen the mechanism of causation as something automatic. Physical environment influenced the human organism and thereby inclined it to this or that course of action. When Herodo-

[3] W. Schiller, *Wilhelm Tell*, Act I, Scene 3, line 388.
[4] William Wordsworth, *Thoughts of a Briton on the Subjugation of Switzerland*, 1807.
[5] James Fairgrieve, *Geography and World Power*, London, 1921, pp. 153–160.

tus wrote that "Soft countries . . . invariably breed soft men, and it is impossible for one and the same country to produce splendid crops and good soldiers. The Persians . . . elected to live as an imperial people in a rough country rather than to cultivate the lowlands as some other nation's slaves," [6] he regarded this as an inevitable and unvarying condition, which man could not escape. More recent extensions and refinements of the determinist line of thought have treated the physical influence as something less than automatic. A given combination of physical conditions is held to incline man so strongly to a particular course of political action that he is unlikely to deviate from it. It might be said that, according to this version of determinism, historical change and political action can, with a high degree of probability, be judged from the physical environment. Thus, when certain writers emphasized the unifying role of the rivers in France, they were demonstrating that the political unification of France, on the basis of its drainage systems, was, if not an inevitable, at least a highly probable, development. Again, to take another example from France, the alleged "natural boundaries," consisting of the Pyrenees and Alps, the river Rhine, and the sea, were held by some to be so obviously the best boundaries for France that it would have been the height of political blindness and stupidity not to use them as such. Perhaps the clearest example of this *necessity*, or *imperative*, which is thought of as having been imposed on political policy by physical environment, is Russia's alleged "urge to the sea." Russia's policy from early modern times is conceived as the consistent pursuit of a single objective: the coast and an ocean port to

west, south, and east. [7] We have already seen (page 239) that this interpretation of Russian history does not bear careful examination.

All these "necessities," which, it is claimed, have been imposed on the course of history by its physical setting, have gained credence in some quarters, and all, it is suggested here, have little or no historical validity. It is, perhaps, of little significance if a body of historians hold to a fallacious opinion as long as the matter remains one of academic controversy only. If, on the other hand, an erroneous opinion on an alleged geographical necessity is allowed to influence policy, the matter is of much deeper significance. It can be argued that the striving for natural boundaries—itself a misinterpretation of French history [8]—was allowed to influence French attempts to expand eastward to the Rhine in 1919. It could even be argued that France's allies were prepared to condone this expansion because of its supposed quality of inevitability. John Morrison has demonstrated [9] with even greater clarity that the attribution to Russia of a consistent policy of expansion to the sea, and the assumption that such a policy was reasonable and in the nature of things, led to the surrender to Stalin in 1945 of even more than he had dared to ask for.

There is a very grave danger that an *idée fixe* may arise regarding the relationship of the state and of national policy to the facts of physical geography, that a fixity of policy may be attributed to the other

[6] Herodotus, *History*, book IX, chap. 22, as quoted in Arnold J. Toynbee, *Greek Historical Thought from Homer to the Age of Heraclius*, London, 1924, pp. 164–165.

[7] This view of Russian history has been propounded by Robert J. Kerner, *The Urge to the Sea: The Course of Russian History*, University of California, Berkeley, Calif., 1942.

[8] This misinterpretation of French history has been discussed on p. 60.

[9] John A. Morrison, "Russia and Warm Water," *United States Naval Institute Proceedings*, vol. 78, pp. 1169–1179, 1952.

side, and that one's own interests may be misconstrued. "Unconscious captivity to a prevailing body of ideas," wrote James C. Malin, "is a condition most difficult to combat. It might be easier to persuade people to accept into their system ideas toward which they were actively hostile." [10] The dangers that could arise from allowing policy to be influenced by preconceived—though erroneous—ideas of what policy, one's own and also that of one's opponents, should be are all too obvious to go into at length.

Climatic Determinism: One aspect of determinist ideas deserves special consideration: the view that climate and climatic change are the chief determinants of the rise and decline of political power. There are many variants of the climatic interpretation of history. The oldest and simplest—that inherited from the Greeks—regards both climate and man as static. Climates favorable to civilization, such as that of Greece, will probably continue to be so; those unfavorable, such as that of equatorial regions, are likely to remain hostile. The Greeks foresaw no change in either climate or the human organism, nor could they anticipate changes in their relationship as a result of technological development. More recent theories recognize that climate is changing and that technological developments allow man to adapt to an increasing range of climate.

Foremost among such theories that relate historical change to climate is that associated with Ellsworth Huntington. His basic assumption was that certain conditions of temperature and atmospheric pressure, primarily those associated with the passage of cold fronts, are especially conducive to human effort. He regarded civili-

zation as the product, in the main, of a gradual increment in human energy and considered that civilization, in consequence, is dependent upon the frequency of fronts or, as Huntington expressed it, upon storminess. The following passage illustrates the argument:

Physical vigor is one of the main factors in the growth of civilization. From this we go on to see that mankind as a whole has a definite level of optimum temperature at which health and vigor are best. . . . Thus, if all other influences were eliminated, we should expect civilization to advance most rapidly in climates which have few or no months with temperatures above the optimum and many below, but none far below, the optimum. . . . Cyclonic storms encourage progress by presenting a challenge which is great enough to be highly stimulating, but not great enough to be permanently discouraging. . . . The passive Egyptian peasant knows nothing of any such stimulus. . . . The Dark Ages and the Revival of Learning [i.e., the Renaissance] occurred at opposite phases of a long climatic cycle. Storminess apparently reached a low ebb in the Dark Ages but was abundant and violent in the fourteenth century. . . . The Dark Ages were characterized by widespread depression of mental activity, whereas the Revival of Learning ushered in a period of alertness and hope. . . . At their stages of highest development ancient Greece and Egypt appear to have been distinctly more stormy than now. . . .[11]

It is difficult to substantiate the view that climate, and in particular frontal activity, does in fact have as marked an influence on human energy as Huntington supposed. Historians would probably object to the thesis that human energy is the chief factor in creativity. The historical evidence for past climates is scanty, and there can be no doubt that Huntington took

[10] James C. Malin, "The Contriving Brain as the Pivot of History," *Issues and Conflicts*, University of Kansas Press, Lawrence, Kans., p. 340, 1959.

[11] Ellsworth Huntington, *Mainsprings of Civilization*, New York, 1945, pp. 275, 335–336, 343, 375.

unwarranted liberties with it. Many of his assertions regarding past climates are unverifiable, and his strictures on the Dark Ages and other "depressed" periods are merely value judgments. Huntington, lastly, made no clear distinction between power and civilization. He tended to assume that a civilized people was also a politically powerful people and, conversely, that any state that was politically dominant had also a cultural level above the average. There is no reason whatever for equating great political power with a high cultural level. Even if Huntington's arguments were more acceptable than in fact they are, they would have little relevance to political geography because they contain no model which permits the future movements of the foci of political power to be predicted, because they make no attempt to show the direction of future climatic change.

In a more recent work on climate and power, Markham argues that power depends, not on the enjoyment of optimum climatic conditions, but on the capacity of man to adapt, by technological means, to climates that depart widely from the optimum.[12] The civilization of ancient Egypt developed under optimum climatic conditions. A civilization of comparable level could develop in succession in Crete, Greece, and Italy, countries of alleged increasing climatic severity, only when man had developed the means of creating and maintaining an artificial climate. This he was able to do, the author claims, by building homes that could be both heated and insulated. The Roman hypocaust[13] was allegedly the chief factor in the dispersion of Roman civilization and power. The Indus-

trial Revolution and the increasing use of coal were the chief factors in the development during the past two centuries of political power in northwestern Europe. Central heating and air conditioning are, of course, the most recent developments in the creation of artificial climates, and they are supposed by this author to be among the reasons for the great political power of the United States.

Unfortunately, one can draw little consolation from the fact that the Russians have few amenities such as air conditioning and central heating. The evidence which Markham adduces in support of his thesis is strained. There is, for example, no reason to suppose that there were hypocausts in more than a small proportion of the homes in the Roman Empire or that our own overheated interiors are conducive to efficiency, inventiveness, and enterprise. This is just another glib attempt to see some order or pattern in the sequence of historical events. It is an amusing academic exercise, innocuous as long as it is divorced from political decision. But any suggestion that power is a function of "climatic control," in this present age, not only is academic foolishness but also could lead to political disaster.

The School of Natural Law: Two more lines of thought, both of them referred to in Chapter 1, deserve restatement here. The natural-law thesis holds that the physical universe is orderly and meaningful. The components of the universe have meaning and purpose; as man was thought of as the end to which all other aspects of the universe were subordinated, their meaning must be found in their capacity to serve him. The earth in particular was held to have been created by a supreme being to serve as the home of man. To say that the earth is not preeminently suited to this end is to deny either the omnipotence or the benevolence of God. To do

[12] S. F. Markham, *Climate and the Energies of Nations*, Oxford University Press, New York, 1942, pp. 24ff.

[13] A room heated by the passage of hot gas from a fireplace through channels built beneath the floor.

this, it is claimed, would be wrong. It follows, therefore, that physical nature was designed to serve man's best interests, and man's duty is to choose the course of action that harmonizes best with the dictates of nature. In 1792 the French National Convention was debating the annexation of Savoie (Savoy). One of the representatives, the Abbé Grégoire, called upon the assembly to consult nature itself and ascertain what it prescribed in this regard. "All relations, physical, moral and political require this union," he said; "ceaselessly the Alps have been forcing it [i.e., Savoie] into the realm of France, and the natural order would be violated if France and Savoie were not united." [14] Again, there was thought to be a proper size for the state (see page 29), and there were *natural* boundaries and obstacles which seemed to have been designed by nature to serve this purpose. The fallacy—apart from the teleological assumption on which the theory was founded—lay in the assumption that man is rational enough to look dispassionately at the physical environment and to judge what best suits—or constitutes the best compromise between—the needs of himself and of his neighbors. The French found during the Revolutionary period that nature always allowed them to do exactly what they wanted to.

The Organic View of the State: The views summarized so far of the relationship between the state and political power on the one hand and the environment on the other have this in common: with the exception of the static view of the Greeks, they embody no general theory which could be used as the basis for prediction. We can know neither the climate nor the

technology of the future. [15] Therefore, even if we could assume that any of the theories discussed were logically sound, there could be no basis for applying them. This is not true of the organic theory of the state. The idea that the state is an organism, that, like all organisms, it grows, matures, decays, and dies, has already been discussed (pages 28–29), and its importance cannot be overemphasized. According to this view, the state is engaged in a continuous struggle with all other states for survival. The virile state expands, and since the area of the inhabitable world is finite, this can be only at the expense of states less vigorous than itself. Constant military preparedness is essential, and aggression is a means of satisfying the alleged necessity for growth. The careers of Adolf Hitler and Benito Mussolini illustrate the disastrous consequences of the conscious acceptance of the view that the state is committed to a policy of expansion for survival.

The organic view permits of prediction only if one can accept the view that all states must expand territorially if they are to survive as separate states. Any such policy as that of coexistence must be ruled out; biological species do not undertake to refrain from their struggle for survival, it is claimed; states should not do so either. Any government that accepted the organic theory of the state, as that of Nazi Germany appears to have done, must necessarily pursue a policy of aggression. The glib assertion of Neville Chamberlain, after the Munich Settlement had surrendered a major part of Czechoslovakia to Germany, that this meant "peace in our time" should have been recognized for the foolishness that it was. There could be no lasting peace with a state which believed that expansion

[14] Quoted in Norman J. G. Pounds, "France and 'Les Limites Naturelles' from the Seventeenth to the Twentieth Centuries," *A.A.A.G.,* vol. 44, p. 54, 1954.

[15] See Karl R. Popper, *The Poverty of Historicism,* Routledge and Kegan Paul, Ltd., London, 1957, for the application of this argument.

and aggression were a condition of existence.

Yet the organic theory of the state is fallacious. "Geographical space and the society that occupies it necessarily attains some element of organization, but in no proper sense does it take on the character of organism." [16] It has no life or will other than that of the aggregate of its citizens, and its future is what their descendants make it. The idea that a state must grow if it is to live and that there is virtue in mere size is not only erroneous but also dangerous.

GLOBAL STRATEGIC VIEWS

The ideas discussed so far have been attempts to introduce order into and offer explanations of the course of human history. Any clarification which they may have afforded of the present political pattern has been entirely coincidental. Yet they were thought to deserve mention in this chapter because either they saw the determinant of change in some aspect of the physical environment or they have at some time influenced political ideas and political action. We turn now to a rather more detailed discussion of two contrasted bodies of writings which seek to find order and reason in the geographical distribution of states. This geographical pattern is liable to sudden changes as territory is transferred from one state to another and as new states are created from the ruins of old. Any explanation of the political pattern must take these changes into account if it is to carry conviction. It must offer an explanation of the changing geographical pattern and some prediction for the future. These writings in some measure fulfill these conditions. They are more *political* than the ideas previously discussed, because they examine

[16] Malin, *op. cit.*, p. 350.

existing conditions and suggest policy. Their importance lies to a large degree in the fact that they *may* have influenced policy.

Mahan and Sea Power: The older of these two bodies of ideas, and the more limited in scope, is that associated with the name of A. T. Mahan. Captain Mahan was a sailor: to him, in his own words, the sea is "a great highway; or better, perhaps, . . . a wide common, over which men may pass in all directions, but on which some well-worn paths show that controlling reasons have led them to choose certain lines of travel rather than others." [17] Trade is normal for all states, and seaborne trade especially so for those states which border the sea:

Foreign necessaries or luxuries must be brought to its ports, either in its own or in foreign ships, which will return, bearing in exchange the products of the country, whether they be fruits of the earth or the work of men's hands; and it is the wish of every nation that this shipping business should be done by its own vessels. The ships that thus sail to and fro must have secure ports to which to return, and must, as far as possible, be followed by the protection of their country throughout the voyage. . . . In these three things—production, with the necessity of exchanging products; shipping, whereby the exchange is carried on, and colonies, which facilitate and enlarge the operations of shipping and tend to protect it by multiplying points of safety—is to be found the key to much of the history, as well as of the policy, of nations bordering the sea. [18]

Mahan found six conditions affecting the sea power of nations. These were:

1. The geographical location of the state, whether it fronts upon more than one sea, and whether there is an easy com-

[17] A. T. Mahan, *The Influence of Sea Power upon History 1660–1783*, 1949 ed., Boston, p. 25.
[18] *Ibid.*, pp. 26–28.

munication by water between these seas; whether it has exposed land boundaries; whether it can command important trade routes, control strategic bases, and threaten the territory of a potential enemy with its ships.

2. The "physical conformation of the state," by which Mahan meant the configuration of its coast line:

The seaboard of a country is one of its frontiers; and the easier the access offered by the frontier to the region beyond, in this case the sea, the greater will be the tendency of a people toward intercourse with the rest of the world by it. If a country be imagined having a long seaboard, but entirely without a harbor, such a country can have no sea trade of its own, no shipping, no navy. . . . Numerous and deep harbors are a source of strength and wealth, and doubly so if they are the outlets of navigable streams, which facilitate the concentration in them of a country's internal trade; but by their very accessibility they become a source of weakness in war, if not properly defended.[19]

3. Next Mahan listed extent of territory, by which he meant the length of the coast line and the relative ease or difficulty of protecting it.

4. The size of the population is also important because to it is related the ability of a state to build and man its ships.

5. National character, in particular, an "aptitude for commercial pursuits," for sea power is "really based upon a peaceful and extensive commerce," [20] is also important.

6. The character and policy of the government will determine whether the best of natural advantages and the richest human resources will actually materialize in sea power.

Mahan's discussion was cast in general terms, but repeatedly he came back to the example of the United States. An ac-

tive seaborne trade, he argued, is desirable, and needs, furthermore, the protection of a navy and of strategic bases. The vulnerability of a long coast line, the frontage on two oceans, the difficulty of access from one to the other (the Panama Canal had not been cut when Mahan wrote), and the wide, empty oceans to west and east, across which enemy ships might move almost unnoticed—all these factors he saw as limiting the security of the United States and increasing the need for sea power:

. . . The distance which separates her from other great powers, in one way a protection, is also a snare, encouraging a sense of isolation and security. . . . It may safely be said that it is essential to the welfare of the whole country that the conditions of trade and commerce should remain, as far as possible, unaffected by an external war. In order to do this, the enemy must be kept not only out of our ports, but far away from our coasts.[21]

Mahan did not openly advocate the acquisition of colonies, but he pointed clearly to the immense strategic advantages which Great Britain derived from having overseas possessions. He helped to shape a climate of opinion that saw virtue in the the possession of strategic bases and danger from beyond the wide expanse of the ocean.

Of course, Mahan's argument is dated. He thought in terms of ships propelled by steam power, and he took his examples mostly from the days of sail. But his lesson was learned in time, and a line of naval bases was drawn from the Aleutians, through Hawaii, Panama, and the West Indies, to Newfoundland. Even so, the events at Pearl Harbor in December, 1941, showed that the enemy could not always "be kept not only out of our ports, but away from our coasts."

Mahan's examination of the past and recommendations for the future were well

[19] *Ibid.*, p. 35.
[20] *Ibid.*, p. 50.

[21] *Ibid.*, pp. 87–88.

grounded in the geography and technology of his age. The technology of transportation has changed a great deal in the seventy years that have passed since he wrote. Air power has in large measure replaced sea power, and the air envelops the whole earth, the sea only part of it. In the days of sea power alone, danger threatened only the coast line; now danger may threaten from any point of the compass. In the past, the possession of a few island bases was thought to be enough; now nothing less than a complete circuit of airfields, launching sites, and radar posts may be sufficient. Bases in Thule, Iceland, and on the mainland of western Europe supplement the naval bases in Guantanamo and Pearl Harbor.

This view of Mahan, that a state with a significant coast line should aim also to possess sea power and that sea power needs to be supported by the possession of overseas military and strategic bases, clearly leads to a competition between sea powers for the possession of such bases. Much of his book, from which the foregoing quotations have been made, is devoted to the history of the struggle between France, Spain, and Great Britain for the occupation and control of just such possessions. In the period of history examined by Mahan there were few sea powers; their number has since increased, and during the present century there has been a very acute struggle for possession of strategic bases. The entry of Germany, Italy, and Japan into the contest for them sharpened international tension and diminished the stability of the political map. Until the end of the Second World War, sea powers aimed at the control of bases upon which their power was in part based. British seapower in Southeast Asia was based upon Singapore and Hong Kong. Gibraltar, Malta, and Aden were bases on a sea route, of vital significance to Great Britain, which passed through the Suez Canal. The Suez crisis of 1956 was in part a struggle on the part of Great Britain and France to prolong their control of the Suez Canal. But the contest between imperial powers for the possession of bases has been replaced by a conflict between these powers and the indigenous, colonial peoples for retention of the bases. Great Britain no longer rules Cyprus but has succeeded in retaining control of certain military bases on the island. The Maltese are restless; Castro announces the imminent end of the United States base at Guantanamo; Ceylon has terminated the Trincomalee naval base; the French no longer have Dakar, and their hold on Bizerte is uncertain; the Italians have lost Rhodes and Tripoli. In every overseas strategic base there are local interests that seek to terminate its occupation by an outside power. It needs no great perspicacity to see that, in the near future, a curtain of naval bases, as Mahan conceived it, will cease to be politically practicable.

Mackinder and the Heartland: Of much greater significance than Mahan's study of sea power was the paper which Halford J. Mackinder read to the Royal Geographical Society of London in 1904.[22] Few papers presented to a learned society have been more significant than this one. It has aroused controversy and discussion for over half a century and continues to be a part of the basic reading in political geography. It is claimed that it inspired both the Swede Kjellen and the German Haushofer in their studies of Geopolitics. Indirectly it may have influenced the German strategy of conquest in the 1940s. Here, clearly, we have a paper that contains both analysis of the political pattern of the world and prediction based upon this analysis. Yet it is not a good paper. Its boldness and

[22] Halford J. Mackinder, "The Geographical Pivot of History," *G.J.*, vol. 23, pp. 421–437, 1904.

simplicity have been achieved at the expense of inaccuracies and inattention to historical and geographical detail. "It would be difficult," wrote James C. Malin, "to find an essay of comparable length and reputation that is more indefensible in terminology and ideas than Mackinder's. . . ."[23] This is difficult to deny.

Mackinder's argument, briefly summarized, is this: "European civilization is . . . the outcome of the secular struggle against Asiatic invasion." This generalization he attempts to substantiate by appeal to historical detail:

Through the steppe . . . there came from the unknown recesses of Asia, by the gateway between the Ural mountains and the Caspian sea, in all the centuries from the fifth to the sixteenth, a remarkable succession of Turanian nomadic peoples—Huns, Avars, Bulgarians, Magyars, Khazars, Patzinaks, Cumans, Mongols, Kalmuks. Under Attila the Huns established themselves in the midst of the Pusstas [sic], in the uttermost Danubian outlier of the steppes, and thence dealt blows northward, westward, and southward against the settled peoples of Europe. A large part of modern history might be written as a commentary upon the changes directly or indirectly ensuing from these raids. The Angles and Saxons, it is quite possible, were then driven to cross the seas to found England in Britain. The Franks, the Goths, and the Roman provincials were compelled, for the first time, to stand shoulder to shoulder on the battlefield of Châlons, making common cause against the Asiatics, who were unconsciously welding together modern France. Venice was founded from the destruction of Aquileia and Padua; and even the Papacy owed a decisive prestige to the successful mediation of Pope Leo with Attila at Milan. Such was the harvest of results produced by a cloud of ruthless and idealess horsemen sweeping over the unimpeded plain—a blow, as it were, from the great Asiatic hammer striking freely through the vacant space. . . .

[23] Malin, op. cit., pp. 339–363.

Nor was the impact of the peoples from Central Asia, he continued, felt only in Europe: "All the settled margins of the Old World sooner or later felt the expansive force of mobile power originating in the steppe. Russia, Persia, India, and China were either made tributary, or received Mongol dynasties. . . ."

The region from which these invaders came, in the center of Asia, "is on the whole a steppe-land supplying a wide-spread if often scanty pasture." Mobility—what Mackinder called a "horse and camel mobility" —was relatively easy over the steppe, and we are invited to believe that the "ruthless and idealess horsemen" could turn in any direction they wished from their pivot area. Thus he conceived of their pressure as exercising as profound an influence on the course of history in the Middle East and South and East Asia as he supposed that it had in Europe.

This pivot area (Exhibit 110) "is characterized by a very remarkable distribution of river drainage. Throughout an immense portion of the centre and north, the rivers have been practically useless for purposes of human communication with the outer world. The Volga, the Oxus, and the Jaxartes drain into salt lakes; the Obi, the Yenisei, and the Lena into the frozen ocean of the north. . . . Thus the core of Euro-Asia . . . is wholly unpenetrated by waterways from the ocean." The "geographical pivot of history" was that vast area of Eurasia, drained either to inland lakes or to a frozen northern ocean, and thus inaccessible to ships and to sea power.

A map (Exhibit 110) which accompanied the paper showed, enclosing the pivot area on the west, south, and east, the inner, or marginal, crescent, consisting of those areas of Eurasia, from Scandinavia to Manchuria, which are drained to the ocean and are, presumably, accessible to sea power. Outside this again, and sepa-

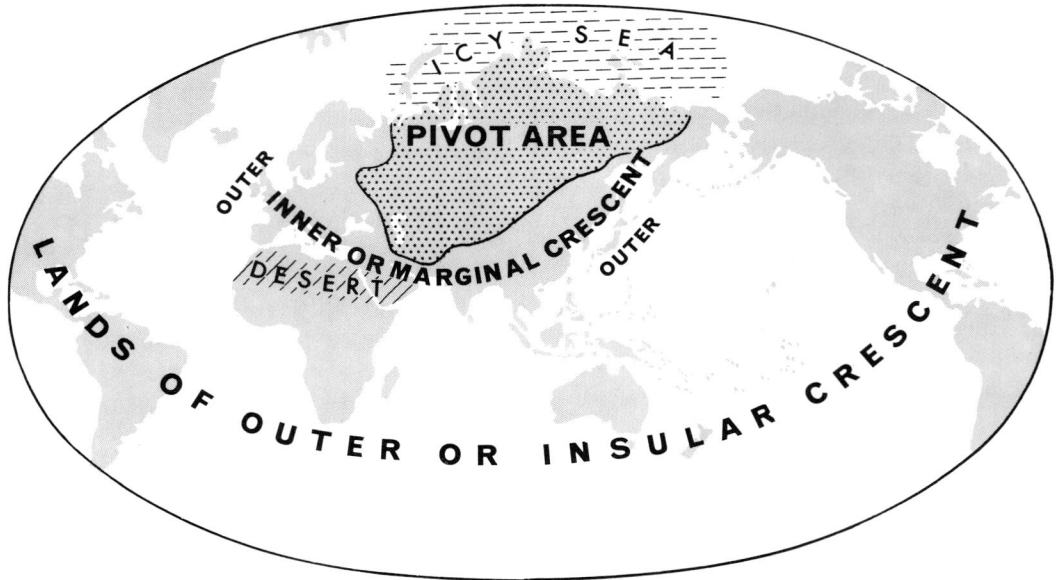

Exhibit 110   *Mackinder's pivot area, based on his map of 1904.*

rated from it by seas of varying width, are the *lands of the outer*, or *insular, crescent.* Sea power gave a kind of unity, especially after the opening of the Suez Canal, to the lands of the inner crescent. Ships, whether those of western Europe or of Japan, could sail up the rivers, as they did those of China, and dominate and control the lands of the inner crescent.

When he examined the relationship of the pivot area and the inner crescent, Mackinder found "a certain persistence of geographical relationship." This relationship—one of continuing outward pressure from the pivot area—he expected to continue and to be intensified. "Is not the pivot region of the world's politics that vast area of Euro-Asia which is inaccessible to ships, but in antiquity lay open to the horse-riding nomads . . .?" and "Is it not today about to be covered with a network of railways?" This was Mackinder's prediction: if Turkic and Tartar nomads, equipped only with the horse and camel, could so shape the course of history in the peripheral lands

of the inner crescent, what might not a modern power, its mobility enhanced by the railroad, achieve in this respect? "This might happen if Germany were to ally herself with Russia." It could also happen "were the Chinese . . . , organized by the Japanese, to overthrow the Russian Empire and conquer its territory." In such an event "France, Italy, Egypt, India, and Korea would become so many bridgeheads where the outside navies would support armies" in order to prevent the powers of the pivot area from expanding down to the sea.

"Formal statements of philosophies of history," wrote J. C. Malin, "may come after the event and when such limited validity as they possess has already become largely if not altogether obsolete." [24] This is abundantly true of Mackinder's thesis. He wrote at the end of the railway age, not at its beginning. The pivot area had dominated the course of human history in the age of horse and camel mobility; how much

[24] *Ibid.*, p. 339.

more would it dominate if the pivot area were to become, as Mackinder confidently expected, crisscrossed by railroad lines? This railroad network has still, after the lapse of half a century, not been built. Instead, the aircraft, whose existence in 1904 Mackinder had barely acknowledged, has come in many respects to replace the railroad. Mackinder presented his analysis at a time when the railroad had for some sixty years dominated transportation. Well might he have anticipated further increase in its importance. He also belonged to a nation that cherished the notion that it was made up of sailors and that its prosperity was founded upon sea power. He visualized the naval powers of the inner and outer crescents, notably France, Italy, Japan, and Great Britain itself, as patrolling the seaways and influencing, if not controlling, the powers that encircled the pivot area. He conceived the range of power of the maritime powers as extending over the basins of all rivers discharging to the ocean, except, of course, those which flowed to the frozen Arctic and were thus inaccessible. But to assume that, because a river flows to the ocean, its basin can therefore be dominated by a maritime power is naïve in the extreme. Even if the rivers were navigable to their sources—which, of course, none of them are—recent experience of maritime powers in sending warships up the Chinese rivers would demonstrate the contrary.[25]

Mackinder's paper was presented at the beginning of the air age and yet failed to take account of this new form of mobility. His map, which is in fact a Mercator projection of the world enclosed within an ellipse, is misleading. It exaggerates the extent of the Arctic Ocean and creates the illusion that beyond the northern coast of Siberia is only ice and yet more ice, when,

in reality, only twelve hundred miles from Cape Chelyuskin lies the most northerly point of Greenland.

Fifteen years after the reading of Mackinder's paper, he published a small book, *Democratic Ideals and Reality.*[26] This was a somewhat labored expansion of the earlier thesis, but it incorporated certain new ideas and certain modifications of his original analysis. In the book he emphasized the relative ease of movement through the south Russian steppe from the pivot area, here for the first time called the *heartland,* into eastern Europe. This he contrasted with the greater difficulty of movement from the heartland into the peripheral regions of South and East Asia:

There was no impediment to prevent the horsemen from riding westward into regions drained by such wholly European rivers as the Dnieper and Danube. In sharp contrast to this open passage from the Heartland into Europe is the system of mighty barriers [i.e., the Himalaya and related ranges] which separate the Heartland along its eastern and southeastern border from the Indies. . . . The conclusion to which this discussion leads is that the connection between the Heartland, and especially its more open western regions of Iran, Turkestan, and Siberia, is much more intimate with Europe and Arabia than it is with China and India.[27]

The heartland of 1919 was not quite the same as the pivot area of 1904. "The Heartland, for the purposes of strategical thinking, includes the Baltic Sea, the navigable Middle and Lower Danube, the Black Sea, Asia Minor, Armenia, Persia, Tibet, and Mongolia. . . . The Heartland is the region to which, under modern conditions, sea-power can be refused access, though the western part of it lies without

[25] The cases of the "Panay" and "Amethyst" come to mind.

[26] Halford J. Mackinder, *Democratic Ideals and Reality,* Constable & Co., Ltd., London, 1919; Pelican Books, Ltd., London, 1944.

[27] *Ibid.,* pp. 78, 82.

the region of Arctic and Continental drainage." [28] When Mackinder wrote the second time, the events of the First World War were fresh in his mind. The navies of Great Britain and her empire had failed to force an entry through the Turkish Straits into the Black Sea, and German mines had excluded them from the Baltic Sea. Sea power was evidently capable of dominating a much less extensive area than Mackinder had at first supposed.

Lastly, Mackinder no longer regarded the heartland as completely invulnerable to powers of the inner marginal crescent. Indeed, the heartland had its Achilles' heel, that region of the south Russian steppe through which the German armies had advanced in 1917. He no longer contemplated the possibility of the Japanese controlling the heartland and using it as a springboard for control of the Old World. Instead, if any power outside the heartland itself could do this, it would be from the west, by way of the steppe corridor that joins the heartland with eastern Europe. At no point does Mackinder appear to have envisaged the possibility that the Russians themselves might organize and develop their own vast spaces and great resources. The heartland had lost none of its focal importance, but this importance would be realized most probably by any power that succeeded in approaching it by way of eastern Europe and the steppe.

Mackinder attributed to the Germany of Kaiser Wilhelm II the intention of dominating eastern, or Slav, Europe and from this vantage point of aiming at control of the heartland. This geographical fact was the reality of which democracy was warned to beware. The events of the First World War, he emphasized, "were the result of a fundamental antagonism between the Germans, who wished to be Masters in East

Europe, and the Slavs, who refused to submit to them." [29] Addressing himself to the statesmen of Great Britain and her allies, he wrote:

Unless you would lay up trouble for the future, you cannot now accept any outcome of the War which does not finally dispose of the issue between German and Slav in East Europe. You must have a balance as between German and Slav, and true independence of each. You cannot afford to leave such a condition of affairs in East Europe and the Heartland, as would offer scope for ambition in the future, for you have escaped too narrowly from the recent danger. . . . When our Statesmen are in conversation with the defeated enemy, some airy cherub should whisper to them from time to time this saying:

Who rules East Europe commands the Heartland:
Who rules the Heartland commands the World-Island:
Who rules the World-Island commands the World. [30]

The events of two world wars have given some slight measure of support to this conclusion of Mackinder. Twice [31] the German armies, from their bases in eastern Europe, invaded Russia and on the first occasion dictated peace terms to the defeated Russian government. Mackinder would have us believe that these invasions were made possible only by the open nature of the terrain in European Russia. It is more than possible that the determining factor was not the physical geography of the area but the contrasting technical levels of the opposing forces. Yet on both occasions the German armies failed to penetrate

---

[28] *Ibid.*, pp. 86–87.

[29] *Ibid.*, p. 113.
[30] *Ibid.*
[31] The first occasion was 1917, when the Germans overran the Ukraine and imposed the Treaty of Brest Litovsk (March, 1918) on the Russians. The second was in 1941–1943, when the German armies reached Stalingrad.

deeply—if at all—into the pivot area, as Mackinder originally conceived it. The same could be said of Napoleon's invasion of Russia in 1811–1812. Are we justified in assuming, as Mackinder had argued, that the heartland is immune to attack from the maritime states? Sea power has nothing to do with the question: of course, no ship could be navigated from the ocean into the heartland, but the sea powers of the marginal crescents are all in some degree land powers. Some, in fact, have placed far more stress upon their armies than upon their navies, all are amphibious, and the dichotomy between land and sea power is, in the final analysis, a false one. On several occasions, in the past two or three centuries, armies from states of the marginal crescent have invaded Russia and have failed either to reach or to establish themselves in the heartland. It would be wrong to assume that the heartland must, of geographical necessity, always remain inviolate. These invasions took place in the course of wars *between* states of the marginal crescent. Each invader had to contend with a second front farther west, and it was this threat in each instance which prevented a deeper and perhaps more lasting penetration of the heartland. Conclusions drawn from a comparison of historical events, each of which is unique, are rarely profitable, and to allow such conclusions to influence policy is the height of political folly.

In 1943, Mackinder offered yet another modification of his own theory,[32] which was too strongly influenced by contemporary events to have great value. The heartland is still, he wrote, the greatest natural fortress on earth. For the first time in history it is manned by a garrison sufficient

[32] Halford J. Mackinder, "The Round World and the Winning of the Peace," *Foreign Affairs*, July, 1943, pp. 595–605.

both in number and in quality. But this time he cast his net wider. He separated off from the heartland that part of the Soviet Union lying east of the Yenisei River, "a rugged country of mountains, plateaus and valleys, covered from end to end with coniferous forests." This he called Lenaland. In opposition to "heartland Russia" he established the "Midland Basin," consisting of the North Atlantic Ocean, the Eastern United States, and western Europe. East Central Europe, very broadly the former German realm, thus separated the midland basin from the Russian heartland, and these two areas he described as enveloped and insulated by a girdle of desert: Saharan, Arabian, Iranian, Tibetan, and Mongolian. This belt of empty lands he extended, through his newly created Lenaland, to Alaska, the Canadian Arctic, and the deserts of the American West. In this desert belt he saw "a practically continuous landspace covering some twelve million square miles. . . . [For a] long time to come it will break social continuity between major communities of mankind on the globe." Within this girdle of desert and tundra, he foresaw the midland basin and the Russian heartland acting together in amity to eliminate the danger that sprang from the militant Germany that lay between.

Comment on this, third of Mackinder's analyses, is made superfluous by the subsequent course of events; China has entered the Communist sphere, and the barrier constituted by the Saharan and Arabian deserts has not prevented the spread of cold-war rivalries to Central Africa. In no respect have this analysis and the forecasts based upon it held up. The fundamental error in this as in Mackinder's earlier papers was his inability to make allowances for technological advance. At a time when bombers were reducing many of Europe's cities to ruins and nullifying the effectiveness of capital ships, Mackinder could nevertheless

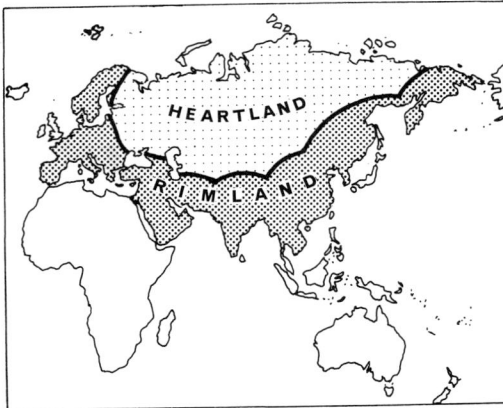

Exhibit 111   *Spykman's Rimland.*

write that air power was capable of "effecting few permanent changes in the strategical conditions."

Spykman and the Rimland: It is impossible to reject Mackinder's original thesis out of hand, equally impossible to accept all its implications. It is not surprising, then, that numerous attempts have been made to reshape the heartland thesis and to bring it into closer accord either with historical and geographical fact or with existing political realities. One of the earliest restatements of his thesis, other than those which he made himself, was that of N. J. Spykman.[33] Spykman accepted the "opposition between Russian land power and British sea power," but he emphasized more than Mackinder had done the role of the tier of states which encircled the heartland. To this tier he gave the name of *rimland*, making it correspond approximately with Mackinder's inner, or marginal, crescent (Exhibit 111). With somewhat greater insight than Mackinder had shown, Spykman demonstrated that "there has never really been a simple land-power—sea-power opposition. The historical alignment has always been in

[33] N. J. Spykman, *The Geography of the Peace*, Harcourt, Brace and Company, Inc., New York, 1944.

terms of some members of the rimland with Russia, or Great Britain and Russia together against a dominating rimland power." Despite the variety of political combinations that could be, and have been, created between Russia, the rimland states, and the sea states, Spykman sees the fundamental issue in the contest between Russia and the enveloping sea power (primarily Great Britain at this time) for control of the rimland states. He urged that American policy should be directed to the control of the rimland states or, at least, to the prevention of their control by the Soviet Union. Truman's policy of aid to Greece and Turkey in 1947 was in line with this policy; so also was the policy of "containment" advocated by George F. Kennan.[34]

Continental and Maritime Rimlands: A further variant of the heartland thesis, and one that has a greater regard for the complex history of its peripheral lands, has been advanced by Donald W. Meinig.[35] "Our definitions of heartland and rimland," he wrote, "must . . . be rooted in cultural, or, I should like to term them, functional criteria. . . . Our criteria, therefore, must rest primarily upon the actual functional orientation of the people or state, not upon simple position in relation to land and sea." Mackinder's heartland, in each of its variant forms, had been defined in terms of physical geography. But, according to Meinig:

A more stable yet functional heartland may be defined as that portion of the great Eurasian steppe and desert belt bounded on the west by the Volga basin and the Caspian Sea, on the north by the southern margin of the great northern forest, on the east by the highlands forming the inner margin of the historic Chinese culture arena, and on the south

[34] See Stephen B. Jones, "Global Strategic Views," *G.R.*, vol. 45, pp. 492–508, 1955.
[35] Donald W. Meinig, "Heartland and Rimland in Eurasian History," *Western Political Quarterly*, vol. 9, pp. 553–569, 1956.

by the nearly continuous mountainous zone from Sikang, through the Himalayas, Hindu Kush, and Kopet Dagh to the southern end of the Caspian.

The characteristics of this area he defined as similarity in physical features and cultural development, interior location, "centrality with respect to all the remaining mainland," and the fact that it includes "the nexus of all the historic land routes interconnecting the several rimland areas of China, India, the Levant and Europe."

Meinig's heartland is smaller than any of those conceived by Mackinder and is surrounded by a broad rimland. It is with the orientation of this rimland that he is primarily concerned. Mackinder, and Spykman after him, had regarded this enclosing belt as, by and large, the realm of sea power. In this point Meinig differs most significantly from his predecessors. He divides this area into (1) continental rimland and (2) maritime rimland. The difference between the two is not geographical, but functional. It depends on the orientation of the states, and this orientation itself has changed for most parts in the course of time.

The case of China is particularly clear and, at this present time, relevant. A seaward orientation has alternated with a landward:

In her early history only a very shallow fringe of the southern coast was of maritime orientation. The basic cultural pattern developed in the northern interior near the contact zone with the heartland. Land-based northerners have dominated Chinese culture throughout most of her history and whenever they have been in political control, as under the Han, T'ang, Mongol, and Manchu dynasties, China has been oriented primarily inwardly as a landed, peasant society with her strategic frontier resting upon the steppe zone of the heartland region. On the other hand, when control was exercised by South China

groups, as under the Southern Sungs, the Mings, and the recent Nationalist government, a strong maritime outlook was emphasized.

The replacement of Nationalist by Communist control represented the reversion from the outward, maritime orientation to an inward orientation toward the Soviet Union.

So also can the changes in orientation of India and Southeast Asia, of the Middle Eastern countries, and of Europe be analyzed. Western Europe has generally looked outward to the oceans; Central Europe has fluctuated. Germany's alliances with Czarist Russia and with its successor, the Soviet Union, belong to its inward-looking phase (Exhibit 112). Today the so-called Iron Curtain marks with greater precision than ever before the boundary between continental and maritime rimland. This boundary is not fixed, because it is not grounded exclusively in the facts of geography. It fluctuates; Yugoslavia within the span of only a few years has found itself on each side, and, translated into these terms, the American policy of containment has been to prevent any part of the maritime rimland from transforming itself into part of the continental rimland.

It was implicit in Mackinder's thesis that the islands and island groups which lie beyond the coast of Eurasia are necessarily maritime in their interests. Nothing could be further from the truth. An island people is not necessarily a seafaring people. Great Britain, in virtue of its navy, its merchant marine, its fishing fleet, and its overseas possessions, must rank as a maritime power, but it has not always been so. It was not nature or instinct that drew the British to the sea and beyond the sea, but the difficulty of supplying their needs from within their own islands. The Irish, on the other hand, have remained obstinately averse to seafaring activities. The Japanese, occupy-

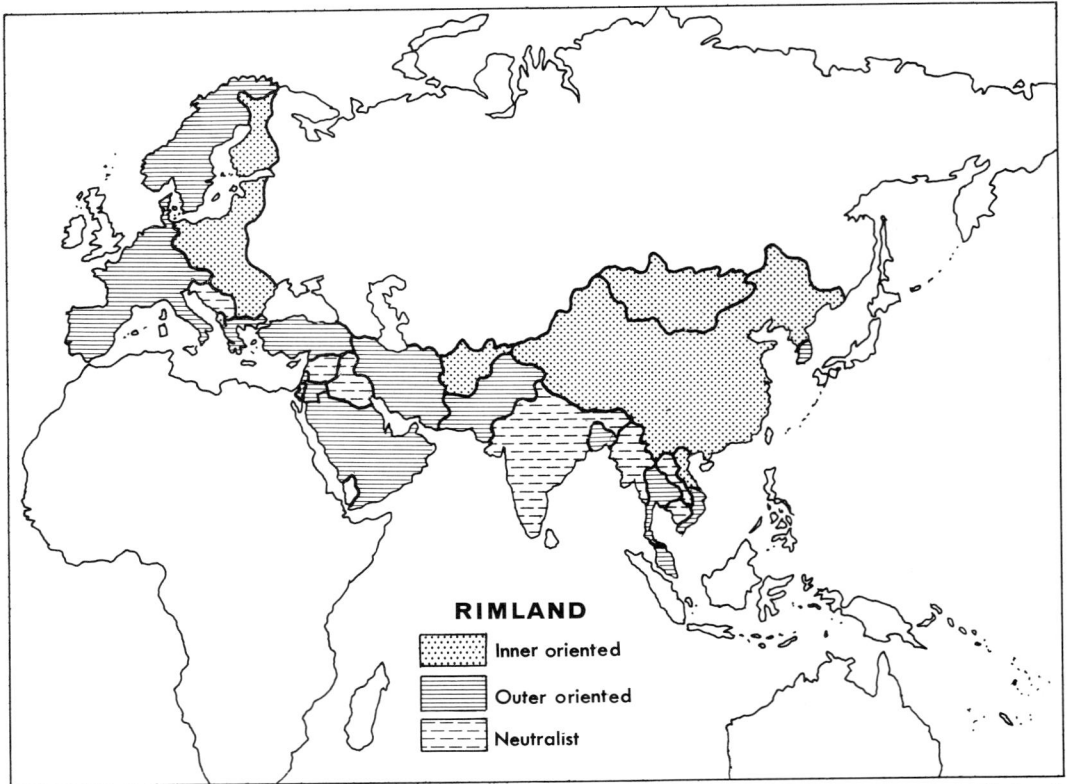

Exhibit 112   *Inner- and Outer-oriented Rimland.*

ing a somewhat similar location off the coast of the Euro-Asiatic land mass, had a period of maritime activity during their early history; then, in the seventh century, they cut themselves off from outside contacts. In this condition they remained until, in 1853, Commodore Perry demonstrated how much the rest of the world had changed since the Japanese had begun to seclude themselves and, in 1867, the Tokugawa period of isolation ended. Few island groups can demonstrate such complete changes of outlook, in turn *extrainsular* and *intrainsular,* to use the terminology of Meinig, but most, if not all, have, in some degree, shown such alterations.

Thus, in place of the outward-looking marginal crescents of Mackinder, we have a rimland and neighboring island groups, in part and at times inward-looking toward the heartland, and sometimes and to some extent outward-looking to the oceans. It is difficult to detect any rhythm in these changes of orientation, and thus no prediction is possible. One cannot say, in Mackinder's words, that whoever controls the heartland rules the rimland—only that whatever political power controls the heartland is likely, under certain conditions, to dominate some part of the rimland and may aim at controlling it all. Mackinder's thesis had been too rigid; it ignored too many situations which contradicted it, and, despite its many disclaimers, it was too fatalistic. Meinig leaves scope for the play of personality and policy; he merely sketches an analytical framework within which the interplay of heartland and rimland can be studied.

THE CONTEMPORARY ROLE OF THE HEARTLAND

Mackinder has been criticized for leaving the advance of technology out of his synthesis, for thinking in terms of past rather than of future methods of transportation and war. Do the modifications and extensions of Mackinder's thesis that have been reviewed make the same kind of error, that of planning the next war's strategy in terms of the last war's weapons and logistics? Only one major conflict can possibly be envisaged, that of the so-called free world versus the Communist world. All lesser conflicts must take their color from this. If we equate the Communist world with the Soviet Union, China, and their satellites, we are presented with a compact area, encircled—or almost so—by members of the free world. The geographical arrangement of the territorial bases of both the major contestants suggests that the struggle is likely to take the shape of an outward pressure by the members of the Communist bloc and of attempts by the encircling tier of states to restrain this pressure. If this is so, then the analyses presented by Mackinder, Spykman, and others have a very considerable element of truth and may be said to give us a framework within which to analyze the international situation now, in the year 1962. We are being confronted with a series of outward jabs from the bloc countries, directed toward now Berlin and Germany, now Turkey, Iran, or Afghanistan, now Laos, Vietnam, the offshore islands and Formosa, or Korea. The pressure is not always long sustained, and it is not in every instance military, though it is generally backed by the armed strength of the Soviet Union. These events are suggestive

of that "persistence of geographical relationship" to which Mackinder referred, and they appear to justify some kind of policy of containment.

But although history goes on repeating itself, because, perhaps, of its common features, which are geography and human nature, it always does so with a difference. Technology and ideology change in the meanwhile. The continued reliance on a sort of modified Mackinder thesis, which is the essence of the containment thesis, emphasizes the unchanging geographical factors and the continuation into the present of the old power lusts of the Russian Czars. It fails to take into consideration the advance in technology and the power of ideological forces.

The technological advances of the greatest significance in this regard have been the development of weapons of hitherto inconceivable explosive power and, at the same time, the perfecting of the mechanisms—manned aircraft, rockets, and perhaps satellites—for delivering these more powerful weapons to their targets. In the past, wars have been won by the movement of armies over the ground and by surface engagements on land and sea. The use of aircraft and rockets during the Second World War was subordinate and, some would argue, not of fundamental importance until, on August 6, 1945, an atomic bomb was dropped on Hiroshima. Wars had hitherto been won by "push of pike." The brush-fire wars of recent years have also been fought with traditional technology. We are led to suppose, however, that in any major war in the future very heavy reliance would be placed on nuclear weapons.

If this latter assumption is correct, expansion from the Soviet heartland will not necessarily be against the enclosing and "containing" ring of states. Given a rocket with a range of about ten thousand miles, direct attack could be launched from somewhere within the Soviet Union against any point on the earth's surface. The policy of containment was predicated upon the assumption that Soviet aggression would be by land armies moving outward from the Soviet Union over the land surface. A wall or rampart of free nations ceases to be a sufficient protection against the aggression of an enemy that can attack directly at any point behind it.

We dare not assume that the old-style containment thesis has outlived its usefulness. Expansion from the Soviet-controlled area by traditional means of aggression or attack is easier, cheaper, and less likely to provoke violent retaliation than the use of the newest rocket-propelled nuclear warheads. Any weakening of the ability of the West to bring traditional kinds of military aid to the containing nations, such as Turkey, Iran, Pakistan, or South Korea, would invite attack on these countries with traditional weapons. Any loss of momentum in the build-up of nuclear weapons would invite a kind of atomic blackmail by the Soviet Union. There are two alternative patterns of strategy, the traditional and the nuclear, and one of the strongest weapons in the Communist armory is its apparent ability to dictate the technological pattern of a future war and to prepare for it. The free world has to plan for the possibility of war at two levels, localized, brush-fire wars, roughly conforming to the geographical pattern prescribed by Mackinder, and also global and nuclear war. Containment is no longer enough.

As well as changing technology, the Mackinder thesis and the modifications of it failed to take changing ideology into account. At no point have they allowed for the fact that, over parts of the globe remote from the heartland itself, social and political conditions might predispose people to favor a sociopolitical system similar to that of the Soviet Union and to welcome Soviet or Chinese aggression that might bring such a system nearer reality. Granted that such an attitude would be strongly influenced by propaganda and that it would not be based upon accurate knowledge of economic, social, and political conditions within the Soviet bloc, nevertheless the African or Latin American who is revolted by the poverty and ignorance around him *may* turn to Marxism or to communism for a solution to his problems. There may be enough like-minded persons to form the nucleus of a party or even to seize political power. There are no geographical limits to this kind of attack on the institutions of the free world. It constitutes a kind of "fifth column," operating everywhere behind the containing tier of states that, as we saw in Chapter 12, is linked unevenly together in NATO, CENTO, and SEATO. It operates in Cuba and Ghana, in the Congo and the Middle East, in Bolivia and Indonesia. The only defense against it is the elimination of poverty and want. There will in all probability be Communist intellectuals for a very long period of time; the mounting human misery in many—if not also in most—of the underdeveloped nations makes their work easier for them and plays into their hands.

On balance, it seems likely that Soviet and Chinese aggression will knock at the doors in turn of the enclosing and containing tier of states. This was *the* weapon of the Russian Czars and even of their predecessors, the undisciplined Mongol tribes. It continues to be *a* weapon of the Soviets, supplemented and reinforced by the threat of nuclear attack in depth and by the opportunities, wherever and whenever they arise, of revolution far behind the lines. A threefold policy, containment, the nuclear deterrent, and economic aid, is necessary to withstand this three-pronged Communist strategy.

GEOPOLITICS

In the preceding pages we have reviewed a few of the many attempts that have been made to analyze the political-geographical pattern of the world and to predict the future trend of events. It is not always clear whether the authors of these views saw in the physical environment a force which compels man, through influencing his character and health or through some other physiological mechanism, to act in a certain way or whether it merely "advises us . . . given our preferences."[36] Nor is it apparent how the German school of geopoliticians regarded this relationship between geography and policy. Geopolitics, according to the German journal that was its formal mouthpiece:

. . is the science which deals with the dependence of political events upon the soil [i.e., the physical setting]. It is based upon the broad foundations of geography, especially political geography. . . . Geopolitics aims to furnish the weapons for political action, and the principles for guidance in political life. . . . Geopolitics must become the geographical conscience of the State.[37]

In other words, so it appears, the study of geopolitics should suggest the future course of political action and, like the still, small voice of conscience, keep reminding politicians of what they should do in the best interests of their country. Yet geopolitics was something more than strategy, because it helped to formulate the objective of policy as well as being the means by which that objective might ultimately be reached.

One cannot appreciate the objectives and influence of German geopolitics without understanding something of the career of Karl Haushofer, who gave it the form and substance which we know. Karl Haushofer was a career officer in the German Army. In 1908 he was sent on a military mission to Japan. His voyage there, with stops at numerous military and naval bases, most of them British, gave him time to contemplate Britain's world power. The prospect did not please him, and it became one of his objectives to help Germany to break through this supposed ring of British power, which girdled the Old World. He was impressed with what he saw in Japan; he liked the political unity which he found, and the subordination of person and party to the collectivist concepts of the state, and would have been happy if such a monolithic political system could have been established in Germany.[38]

Haushofer was at this juncture provided with ammunition from an unexpected source. He read Mackinder's paper of 1904 on the geographical pivot of history. Here were both analysis and prescription. The pivot area (later called the heartland) can dominate the Old World: therefore Germany must ally herself with the ruler of the heartland, Russia, and with her break the fetters which Haushofer believed Great Britain had cast around the world island. The German government did not take the advice of its rather junior officer. Germany was defeated, and that officer contributed his own explanation of the defeat: Germany's leaders had stumbled into the war completely unaware of its world-political connotations. While they had worked out their military strategy down to the last detail, their political strategy betrayed

---

[36] Ladis K. D. Kristof, "The Origins and Evolution of Geopolitics," *Journal of Conflict Resolution*, vol. 4, p. 19, 1960.

[37] Quoted from *Zeitschrift für Geopolitik*, in Hans W. Weigert, *Generals and Geographers*, Oxford University Press, New York, 1942, p. 14.

[38] Andreas Dorpalen, *The World of General Haushofer*, Farrar & Rinehart, Inc., New York, 1942, p. 4. Most would claim that Haushofer's Germany fell little short of Japan in these respects.

their lack of understanding of the real issues at stake.[39]

Haushofer had learned another lesson during his stay in Japan, namely, that space (*Raum*) is also a factor in power. He listened to the claim of the Japanese propagandists that their people required more space and that the mere fact that the population was growing fast in itself justified them in taking it. Confronted by the more numerous Chinese, Russians, and Americans, Japan could find security only in a larger population and, of course, in the possession of land to support this increase. Planned conquest in Korea and China was to satisfy at once the political, territorial, and economic needs of Japan.[40]

A final element was introduced into Haushofer's thought from the geographical writings of his own fellow-countrymen, reinforced by those of a Swede, Rudolf Kjellen. This was the concept of the state as an organism for which growth is a rule of life. From these elements, location, space, and growth, Haushofer forged the terrible weapon of German *Geopolitik*. Perhaps its most concise definition comes, not from Haushofer himself, but from his disciple, the geographer Otto Maull:

> Geopolitik concerns itself with the state, not as a static concept, but as a living being. Geopolitik investigates the state primarily in relation to its environment—its space—and attempts to solve all problems resulting from spatial relationships. . . . Geopolitik is concerned with the spatial *requirements* of a state while political geography examines only its space *conditions*. In putting geography at the service of space-conscious politics, Geopolitik devotes itself to questions of the future. Are the space needs of a state met? If not, how can they be brought into accord with geograph-

ical conditions? In what direction should any change be made? The extent to which these questions are answered determines a state's national and economic structure and influences its foreign relations. . . . Geopolitik . . . is a discipline that weighs and evaluates a given situation and by its conclusions seeks to guide practical politics.[41]

Haushofer and his followers repeatedly described their "science" as dynamic. They never recognized that a political condition could long remain stable, if only because the "laws" of the state organism prescribed growth and the growth of one such entity could be only at the expense of others. "Every nation," wrote Haushofer, "is primarily concerned with the task of maintaining itself in a hostile environment, and since its very existence depends on the possession of an adequate space, the preservation and protection of that space must determine all its policies. *If the space has grown too small, it has to be expanded* [italics supplied]." [42] Haushofer presented no criteria by which the adequacy of a nation's "space" might be measured, other than the mathematical ratio of people to land. Presumably each state is the judge of its own needs. He did, however, claim that two nations in particular, the German and the Japanese, stood in dire need of greater space. Expansion he regarded as a categorical imperative, in the Kantian sense, for all nations. It should be "the guiding principle of small and handicapped countries who want to attain or to regain a place in world politics." The futility and the hypocrisy of this advice is apparent from another passage in Haushofer's voluminous

---

[39] *Ibid.*, p. 14.
[40] Charles A. Fisher, "The Expansion of Japan: A Study in Oriental Geopolitics," *G.J.*, vol. 115, pp. 1–19, 179–193, 1950.

[41] Otto Maull, *Das Wesen der Geopolitik*, Leipzig, 1936, p. 31, as quoted in Dorpalen, *op. cit.*, pp. 24–25.
[42] Karl Haushofer, "Geographische Grundzuge auswartiger Politik," *Suddeutsche Monatshefte*, vol. 24, pp. 258ff., 1926–1927, as quoted in Dorpalen, *op. cit.*, pp. 38–39.

writings: "Great powers, unencumbered in their movements, can set themselves important long-range objectives—small countries, on the other hand, find obstacles in their way wherever they turn."[43] Geopolitics had the power to satisfy the urge of great powers to expand at the expense of the weak. The power politics of the *Grossmachte* were thus held to derive their sanction from a kind of natural law. The concept of "living space," or *Lebensraum*, became the core of Haushofer's *Geopolitik*, in particular the *Lebensraum* of Germany itself. This, he argued repeatedly, was inadequate for Germany's needs, and it could be extended only at the expense of the Slav countries to the east. Alliance with Russia would not only permit this ambition to be realized but would also establish German influence in that pivot area in which, following Mackinder, he placed the fulcrum of world power. Haushofer made his points with the aid of maps, which were simple, striking, and misleading. Arrows were used to suggest action, expansion, or attack; shading was used to suggest the associations which Haushofer desired to convey, and his maps were drawn, not upon the projection which gave the least distortion, but upon that which emphasized the relationships which he wished to exaggerate. He was a master of cartography as a tool of propaganda used for nationalistic purposes.

Geopolitics was described by an American geographer as "the application of geographical principles . . . in the game of power lusts"[44] and by an English geographer as "political geography charged with emotion, and thus containing implicitly . . . or explicitly, a call to action."[45] It was never more than a rationalization of the cruder ambitions of the German Reich, for whose fulfillment it prescribed a course of expansion and aggression. It was a justification in terms of geographical influences and an allegedly natural urge to expand, of those aggressive intentions which in turn it helped to shape. The question immediately comes to mind whether this insidious teaching had any practical influence. Previously in this book we have come across false geographical ideas which have misdirected policy; did *Geopolitik* do the same? The answer to this question has been much debated. Much of the propaganda and of the foreign policy of Nazi Germany was in keeping with the teachings of Haushofer, but it is far from certain that Haushofer did, in fact, help to give it this orientation. As Carl Troll has said, "Karl Haushofer's political influence was greatly overestimated during the war."[46] His relations with the National Socialist party were not particularly close. He had met Hitler but seems to have had no real influence over him, and the only high-ranking Nazi who openly shared Haushofer's views was Rudolf Hess.[47] The objectives of policy which led to the series of crises from 1934 to 1939 were fully in line with Haushofer's views. He would have approved heartily of the agreement with the Soviet Union, the Ribbentrop-Molotov Pact of August, 1939, for, as we have seen earlier, he visualized German military power as being di-

---

[43] Karl Haushofer, *Weltpolitik von Heute*, Berlin, 1936, pp. 22ff., quoted in Dorpalen, *op. cit.*, pp. 95–97.

[44] Weigert, *op. cit.*, Oxford University Press, New York, 1942, p. 213.

[45] Eva G. R. Taylor, *Geography of an Air Age*, Royal Institute of International Affairs, London, 1945, p. 37.

[46] Carl Troll, "Geographical Science in Germany during the Period 1933–1945," *A.A.A.G.*, vol. 39, p. 133, 1949.

[47] ". . . It was he who introduced Hitler to the geopolitical ideas of General Karl Haushofer." William L. Shirer, *The Rise and Fall of the Third Reich*, New York, 1960, p. 48.

rected from the heartland. But this does not mean that he contributed to the Pact. He would equally strongly have disapproved of the breach between Germany and the Soviet Union and of Hitler's attack on the latter in June, 1941. Whether Haushofer's "science," had it been allowed fuller scope, would have been less disastrous for the world at large than the intuitions of that mad genius, Adolf Hitler, is unknowable. At most, it may be said that Haushofer contributed to that climate of opinions which regarded aggression and conquest as a natural and proper role for a powerful state.

Geopolitics and Political Geography: The term geopolitics has acquired a sinister connotation. It implies a distortion and misuse of the facts of geography in the interests of aggressive national policy. This is unfortunate, for it is a good word, and we need a term to cover the geographically oriented study of politics. Ladis Kristof has attempted to rehabilitate the term.[48] "Geopolitics," he wrote, "should cover all the field parallel to and intermediate between political science and political geography." Its study should embrace "the investigation of the objective impact of 'natural' environment on . . . politics."[49] Many of the writers discussed earlier, the Greeks, Bodin, Montesquieu, Rousseau, Mahan, Ellsworth Huntington, were geopoliticians. The German school of Haushofer merely diverged from the narrow path of scientific inquiry, distorting evidence and twisting conclusions to serve the narrow ends of policy. Real geopolitics resembles political geography. Indeed, according to Kristof, it is difficult to distinguish between them:

[48] Ladis K. D. Kristof, "The Origins and Evolution of Geopolitics," *Journal of Conflict Resolution,* vol. 4, pp. 15–51, 1960.

[49] *Ibid.,* pp. 35–36.

The only real difference between political geography and geopolitics is in emphasis—in the focus of attention. *Political Geography* tends to focus . . . on the geographical phenomena; it gives a political interpretation and studies the political aspects of geographic phenomena. *Geopolitics* . . . tends to focus on the political phenomena and attempts to give a geographical interpretation and study the geographical aspects of these phenomena.

Whether this book is geopolitics or political geography, the reader who uses it can best judge. Kristof's revival of the term geopolitics is probably premature and may remain so as long as most people associate the term with the inhuman policies of Hitler's Third Reich.

BIBLIOGRAPHY

Bowman, Isaiah: "Geography vs. Geopolitics," *G.R.,* vol. 32, pp. 646–658, 1942.

Dorpalen, Andreas: *The World of General Haushofer,* Farrar & Rinehart, Inc., New York, 1942.

Fawcett, C. B.: "Marginal and Interior Lands of the Old World," *Geography,* vol. 32, pp. 1–12, 1947.

Fisher, Charles A.: "The Expansion of Japan: A Study in Oriental Geopolitics," *G.J.,* vol. 115, pp. 1–19, 179–193, 1950.

Foundations of National Power, H. H. Sprout and M. Sprout (eds.), Princeton University Press, Princeton, N.J., 1945.

Gyorgy, Andrew: *Geopolitics: The New German Science,* University of California Press, Berkeley, Calif., 1944.

Jones, Stephen B.: "Global Strategic Views," *G.R.,* vol. 45, pp. 492–508, 1955.

———: "Views of the Political World," *G.R.,* vol. 45, pp. 309–326, 1955.

Kiss, George: "Political Geography into Geopolitics: Recent Trends in Germany," *G.R.,* vol. 32, pp. 632–645, 1942.

Kristof, Ladis K. D.: "The Origins and Evolution of Geopolitics," *Journal of Conflict Resolution,* vol. 4, pp. 632–645, 1960.

Mackinder, Halford J.: "The Geographical Pivot of History," *G.J.*, vol. 23, pp. 421–437, 1904.

———: *Democratic Ideals and Reality*, Constable & Co., Ltd., London, 1919; Penguin Books, Ltd., London, 1944.

———: "The Round World and the Winning of the Peace," *Foreign Affairs*, July, 1943, pp. 595–605.

Malin, James C.: "The Contriving Brain as the Pivot of History," *Issues and Conflicts*, University of Kansas Press, Lawrence, Kans., pp. 339–363, 1959.

Meinig, Donald W.: "Cultural Blocs and Political Blocs: Emergent Patterns in World Affairs," *Western Humanities Quarterly*, vol. 10, pp. 203–222, 1956.

———: "Heartland and Rimland in Eurasian History," *Western Political Quarterly*, vol. 9, pp. 553–569, 1956.

Popper, Karl R.: *The Poverty of Historicism*, Routledge and Kegan Paul, Ltd., London, 1957.

Spykman, N. J.: *The Geography of the Peace*, Harcourt, Brace and Company, Inc., New York, 1944.

Strausz-Hupé, Robert: *Geopolitics*, G. P. Putnam's Sons, New York, 1942.

Troll, Carl: "Geographical Science in Germany during the Period 1933–1945," *A.A.A.G.*, vol. 39, pp. 99–137, 1949.

Weigert, Hans W.: *Generals and Geographers*, Oxford University Press, New York, 1942.

Whittlesey, Derwent: *German Strategy of World Conquest*, Farrar & Rinehart, Inc., New York, 1942.

INDEX